13

The
Six Sigma
Handbook

The
Six Sigma
Handbook

A Complete Guide
for Greenbelts, Blackbelts,
and Managers at All Levels

THOMAS PYZDEK

McGraw-Hill
New York San Francisco Washington, D.C.
Auckland Bogota Caracas Lisbon London
Madrid Mexico City Milan Montreal New Delhi
San Juan Singapore Sydney Tokyo Toronto

Quality Publishing
Tucson

McGraw-Hill

A Division of The McGraw-Hill Companies

 Quality Publishing

This book was published under the title *The Complete Guide to Six Sigma* by Quality Publishing, 1999, isbn: 0–930011–60–0.

2 3 4 5 6 7 8 9 0   BKM/BKM   0 6 5 4 3 2 1 0

ISBN 0–07–137233–4

The sponsoring editor for this book was Richard Narramore, the editing supervisor was Ruth W. Mannino, and the production supervisor was Charles Annis.

Printed and bound by Bookmart.

McGraw-Hill books are available at special quantity discounts to use as premiums and sales promotions, or for use in corporate training programs. For more information, please write to the Director of Special Sales, Professional Publishing, McGraw-Hill, Two Penn Plaza, New York, NY 10121-2298. Or contact your local bookstore.

This book is printed on acid-free paper.

Contents

Preface	*xi*
Introduction	*xiii*
Chapter 1 Six Sigma leadership	1
Leadership case studies	1
Six Sigma at Motorola, Inc.	1
Six Sigma at General Electric	3
Creativity and Six Sigma	6
Learning models	8
Six Sigma's technical component	21
Qualifications	23
Information systems requirements	24
Integrating Six Sigma with other information systems technologies	24
OLAP, data mining, and Six Sigma	30
Six Sigma readiness evaluation	31
Assessing organizational culture on quality	31
Surveys and focus groups	32
Change agents and their effects on organizations	49
Managing change	49
Roles	51
The job of change agent	52

Six Sigma teams   59
   Process improvement teams   60
   Work groups   61
   Other self-managed teams   62
   Facilitation techniques   64
   Member roles and responsibilities   74
   Performance evaluation   77
   Team recognition and reward   79
Chapter 2   Six Sigma training and education   83
   Importance of top-down support and strategic planning
      for quality training   86
   Training subgroups and topics   87
      Management training—general quality principles   87
      Employee training—implementation of quality plans   93
      Facilitator training   95
   Training needs analysis   97
   Post-training evaluation and reinforcement   99
   Tools   104
      Lectures, workbooks, case studies, on-the-job-training   105
      Use of technology in training   128
Chapter 3   Principles of Six Sigma   133
   Elements of customer-driven organizations   133
      Becoming a customer-and market-driven enterprise   135
      Elements of the transformed organization   137
   Six Sigma versus Three Sigma   140
   Kano model of customer expectations   143
      Customer expectations, priorities, needs, and "voice"   143
      Garden variety Six Sigma only addresses half of the Kano
         customer satisfaction model   144
      QFD to relate customer requirements to internal
         specifications   145
      Data collection and review of customer expectations,
         needs, requirements, and specifications   150

Chapter 4   Six Sigma organizational performance goals and metrics   151
Attributes of good metrics   151
Financial analysis   155
    Time value of money   155
    Cost of quality   163
    Calculating the value of retention of customers   180

Chapter 5   Managing Six Sigma projects   185
Planning   188
    Integrated quality initiatives   189
    Short- and long-term quality plans and objectives   191
    Feedback loops   193
    Performance measures   195
    Relevant stakeholders   215
    Benchmarking   216
    Budgeting   223
    Benefit-cost analysis   226
Project management implementation   230
    Management support and organizational roadblocks   230
    Short-term (tactical) plans   236
    Cross-functional collaboration   237
    Continuous review and enhancement of quality process 239
    Documentation and procedures   240

Chapter 6   Principles of measurements and data   243
Measurement   243
    Scales of measurement   243
    Reliability and validity of data   246
    Repeatability and reproducibility studies   252

Chapter 7   Basic Six Sigma methods   269
Problem solving tools   269
    Process mapping   269
    Flow charts   272
    Check sheets   274

Pareto analysis	277
Cause and effect diagrams	280
Scatter plots	284
7M tools	290
Affinity diagrams	290
Tree diagrams	293
Process decision program charts	294
Matrix diagrams	295
Interrelationship diagraphs	296
Prioritization matrices	297
Activity network diagram	300
Other continuous improvement tools	301
Knowledge discovery tools	304
Run charts	305
Descriptive statistics	312
Histograms	316
Exploratory data analysis	323
Chapter 8 Intermediate Six Sigma methods	**331**
Enumerative versus analytic statistical methods	331
Enumerative statistical methods	335
Basic probability concepts	337
Theoretical expected value	342
Assumptions and robustness of tests	346
Distributions	347
Statistical inference	369
Tolerance and confidence levels, significance level	372
Hypothesis testing/Type I and Type II errors	373
Analytic statistical methods	377
Basic control charts	377
Pre-Control	434
EWMA charts	438
Process capability analysis	452
Process control for short and small runs	464

Chapter 9   Advanced Six Sigma methods   499
   DOE   499
      Terminology   500
      Power and sample size   502
      Design characteristics   503
      Types of design   504
   Examples of applying common DOE methods using software   511
      Two way ANOVA with no replicates   511
      Two way ANOVA with replicates   513
   Empirical model building and sequential learning   520
      Phase 0: Getting your bearings   522
      Phase I: The screening experiment   523
      Phase II: Steepest ascent (descent)   529
      Phase III: The factorial experiment   532
      Phase IV: The composite design   535
      Phase V: Robust product and process design   540
   Data mining, artificial neural networks, and virtual process
      mapping   546
   Regression and correlation analysis   552
      Linear models   552
      Least-squares fit   560
      Correlation analysis   656
   Chi-square contingency tables   568
   Reliability analysis   569
      Basic reliability terms and principles   569
      Assessing design reliability   576
      Monte Carlo simulation   577
   Risk assessment tools   595
   Safety analysis   600
   Process simulation   603
      Simulation tools   604
      Model development   607
      Management constraints   610

Backlog 611

The simulation 612

Statistical tolerancing 620

Appendix

Table 1—Glossary of basic statistical terms 627

Table 2—Area under the standard normal curve 635

Table 3—Critical values of the *t*-distribution 638

Table 4—Chi-square distribution 640

Table 5—*F* distribution (α=1%) 643

Table 6—*F* distribution (α=5%) 645

Table 7—Poisson probability sums 647

Table 8—Tolerance interval factors 651

Table 9—Durbin-Watson test bounds 655

Table 10—*y* factors for computing AOQL 659

Table 11—Control chart constants 660

Table 12—Control chart equations 662

Table 13—Table of d_2^* values 664

Table 14—Power functions for ANOVA 666

Table 15—Factors for short run control charts for individuals,
X-bar and R charts 675

Table 16—Significant number of consecutive highest or lowest
values from one stream of a multiple-stream process 677

Table 17—Sample customer survey 678

Table 18—Process σ levels and equivalent PPM quality levels 682

References 683

Index 695

♦ ♦ ♦

Preface

In 1988 Bob Galvin, accepting the first *Malcolm Baldrige National Quality Award* for Motorola, briefly described something he called Six Sigma. The attendees included a contingent of Baldrige Judges and Examiners and many of us confidently assumed that we knew precisely what Mr. Galvin was talking about. As one of the attendees, I believed that he was speaking of statistical process control, process capability, meeting requirements, the sort of thing that quality engineers had been advocating for years. There was a consensus among quality engineers and statisticians that "process capability" was, roughly, 'plus or minus three sigma.' A process controlled at this level would produce a small percentage of defective items due to occasional problems, but that was thought to be acceptable. In the 1980s American automotive companies had tightened up the definition to mean plus or minus four sigma; which brought the defect rate down to a few parts per thousand. Mr. Galvin's reference to Six Sigma seemed to me to be a minor modification of a tried-and-true statistical approach.

I was wrong.

Speaking only for myself, the linkage of Motorola's program to the classical process control approach served mainly to obscure the fact that Bob Galvin was describing something entirely new. Six Sigma, as applied and developed by Motorola, is such a drastic extension of the old idea of statistical control of manufacturing processes as to qualify as an entirely different subject. The statistical difference between the two is staggering. A six-sigma process will produce failures at a parts-per-million (PPM) or even parts-per-billion (PPB) level. This contrasts with the old three sigma process which produces parts-per-thousand failures. This difference of three to six orders of magnitude is profound. In science a difference in scale of this magnitude qualifies a subject as a new science, as when one goes from the study of neurons to the study of human psychology.

In short, Six Sigma was not just a modification of the old idea of three sigma quality levels, it was an entirely new thing. Motorola's senior executives saw that achieving such high levels of quality enabled their company to use quality as a strategic weapon, rather than as simply a cost-control device. However, to make that happen they had to extend the idea far beyond manufacturing. Six Sigma had to become a way of doing things throughout the entire organization. This task is far more difficult than simply improving the control of a machine or assembly process. It requires nothing short of a transformation in the way an organization perceives its environment and its role in that environment. The organization that embraces Six Sigma is, at a fundamental level, different than a traditional organization. It responds differently to the same stimulus, becomes concerned about things that other organizations ignore, and ignores things that other organizations become concerned with.

Six Sigma is, in essence, a new way to manage the enterprise. Although Six Sigma has a strong technical component, it is not primarily a technical program. It is a *management* program. Any organization that fails to keep this foremost in mind is doomed to fail in their efforts to become a world-class organization.

♦ ♦ ♦

Introduction

The goal of this book is to provide you with the guidance and direction necessary to realize Six Sigma's promise, while avoiding traps and pitfalls commonly encountered. In this book you will find a complete overview of the management and organization of Six Sigma, the philosophy which underlies Six Sigma, and those problem solving techniques and statistical tools most often used in Six Sigma.

The book begins with a discussion of leadership issues in Chapter 1. Unfortunately, this book cannot provide the leadership of a Bob Galvin or a Jack Welsh. Nor is it a substitute for the years of study and experience required to reach the technical proficiency of a Black Belt or Master Black Belt. However, with top management's commitment and the efforts of the right people, the information in this book can help your organization achieve its goal of becoming a world-class operation.

In leading Six Sigma, it is important to understand that it is primarily a new approach to management, not a technical program. The goals of Six Sigma are so ambitious—a 100X quality improvement every two to three years—as to constitute a completely different way of running the business. True, there is a significant technical component involved. But all the technical expertise in the world will fail to produce results unless the working environment is receptive to the ideas and changes that Six Sigma recommends.

Six Sigma can also be viewed as a creativity program. The activities undertaken by Six Sigma teams are designed to discover new and better ways to do things. Often, the biggest obstacles faced by an organization is dealing with the destructive nature of creativity. It is difficult to abandon a comfortable routine or an investment in existing technology just because a better way has been discovered. However, this is precisely what Six Sigma demands. Understanding what it takes to allow "creative destruction" to flourish is a primary responsibility of Six Sigma leaders.

Chapter 1 describes the "Six Sigma Organizational Paradox" which faces leaders, namely the need to encourage variation, slack, and redundancy within the organization while simultaneously working to eliminate these same things in processes. Also covered are the various levels of technical proficiency required for Six Sigma, along with criteria for selecting personnel for Six Sigma training. The interrelationship between Six Sigma and information systems is discussed.

Chapter 2 presents material needed to develop a comprehensive approach to training people for Six Sigma.

Chapter 3 describes the basic principles of customer-centered organizations. Six Sigma requires customer-focus that is rigorous and data based; mere platitudes will not suffice. The statistical meaning of the term "Six Sigma" is contrasted with the old three sigma quality levels as it concerns customer satisfaction. This is followed by a discussion of determining customer requirements and translating these requirements into internal specifications. Chapter 3 concludes with an overview of the sequential nature of business processes and the need for virtually perfect process performance to assure that customers experience Six Sigma quality levels.

Chapter 4 examines principles of good metrics and how these metrics are applied in Six Sigma. Particular emphasis is placed on financial metrics.

Chapter 5 discusses management of Six Sigma projects. The project is the basic unit of activity within Six Sigma. It is the vehicle by which leadership's vision becomes reality. Every aspect of project management is covered in depth.

Chapter 6 provides an overview of the fundamental principles of good measurement. Both "hard" and "soft" measurements are covered, reflecting the recognition that Six Sigma performance levels require quantifying such things as customer satisfaction and aesthetics as well as physical properties of products and processes.

The discussion proceeds in Chapter 7 to a presentation of the problem solving tools most often used in Six Sigma. These include check sheets, Pareto analysis, cause and effect diagrams, scatter plots, process flow charts and maps, and many others. The emphasis of Chapter 7 is on descriptive methods of analysis. The goal of descriptive methods is orientation of the individual or team. At this stage of analysis and problem solving it is vital to get an overall idea of the nature and scope of the opportunity. The discussion moves on to exploratory data analysis (EDA). While descriptive methods are typically applied to raw data, EDA allows the re-expression of this data through numerous transformations, as well as providing simple, graphical methods of summarizing the data with minimal loss of information. Information can often be more easily obtained from the summary than from the raw data.

Chapter 8 covers the use of intermediate level statistical tools. The chapter opens with a discussion of enumerative and analytic statistical approaches. Next, the chapter describes such enumerative statistical methods as hypothesis testing, confidence intervals, tests for the mean, variance and standard deviation, etc. The chapter concludes with a presentation of the analytic statistical tools of control charts, including attributes and variables control charts as well as exponentially weighted moving average (EWMA) charts and control of short and small run processes.

Chapter 9 covers more advanced topics in Six Sigma, including design of experiments (DOE), response surface methods (RSM), chi-square contingency table and cross-tab analysis. One decision I struggled with in writing this book was where to draw the line on the discussion of these advanced topics. The subject matter is broad and deep enough to easily fill an entire bookshelf. My compromise was to provide minimal details on the mathematics of commonly used procedures, opting instead to provide examples using computer programs easily accessible to readers (such as Microsoft™ Excel) and other specialized software. In this day and age I view it as unlikely that a serious user of advanced Six Sigma techniques will not have access to statistical software. The use of neural networks for modeling systems is briefly described and its use in conjunction with design of experiments is discussed.

Chapter 9 also includes an overview of reliability engineering relevant to Six Sigma, including reliability calculation for series systems using the exponential distribution, reliability apportionment, and computer simulation of systems. The use of risk assessment tools is described, including FMEA and fault tree analysis. Product safety issues are discussed and safety calculations described. Finally, the issue of statistical tolerancing is discussed.

It is important to remember that not all personnel require all of the material in this book. Leadership should be familiar with the materials in Chapters 1, 2, 3, 4, and the measurement portion of Chapter 5. In addition to this material, Six Sigma champions should understand the materials in Chapter 5. Six Sigma team members should be familiar with Chapter 5 and the problem solving tools in Chapter 6. "Green belts" should know all of the materials in Chapters 5 and 6. "Black Belts" should be familiar with all of the material and know how to apply all of the statistical methods to common problems using computers. "Master Black Belts" should understand the mathematical theory on which the statistical methods are based and be able to assist Black Belts in applying the methods correctly in unusual situations. Whenever possible, statistical training should be conducted only by Master Black Belts. Otherwise the familiar "propagation of error" phenomenon will occur; i.e., Black Belts pass on errors to green belts, who pass on greater errors to team members. If it becomes necessary for Black Belts and Green Belts to provide training, they should do so only under the guidance of Master Black Belts. For example, Black Belts may be asked to provide assistance to the Master during in-class discussions and projects. Because of the nature of the Master's duties, communications and teaching skills should be judged as important as technical competence in selecting candidates. Persons with advanced statistical and computing skills but lacking communications skills can still play an important role, but they should not be considered Masters unless they can pass these skills along to others.

1

Six Sigma
Leadership

LEADERSHIP CASE STUDIES
Six Sigma at Motorola, Inc.[*]

Motorola learned about quality the hard way: by being consistently beaten in the competitive marketplace. When a Japanese firm took over a Motorola factory that manufactured television sets in the United States, they promptly set about making drastic changes in the way the factory operated. Under Japanese management, the factory was soon producing TV sets with 1/20th the number of defects they had produced under Motorola management. In the late 1970s and early 1980s the company responded to the competitive pressure by engaging in a publicity campaign decrying "unfair" competition and calling for political protection solutions. Finally, even Motorola's own executives had to admit "our quality stinks," (Main, 1994) and Motorola decided to take quality seriously. Motorola's CEO at the time, Bob Galvin, started the company on the quality path and became a business icon largely as a result of what he accomplished in quality at Motorola.

---

[*]Some material in this section is from *Malcolm Baldrige National Quality Award 1988 Winner Motorola Inc.*, National Institute for Standards and Technology, 1988.

Today, Motorola is known worldwide as a quality leader. To accomplish its quality and total customer satisfaction goals, Motorola concentrates on several key operational initiatives. At the top of the list is "Six Sigma Quality," a statistical measure of variation from a desired result. In concrete terms, Six Sigma translates into a target of no more than 3.4 defects per million products, customer services included. At the manufacturing end, this requires "robust designs" that accommodate reasonable variation in component parts while providing consistently uniform final products. Motorola employees record the defects found in every function of the business, and statistical technologies are made a part of each and every employee's job.

Reducing the "total cycle time"—the time from when a Motorola customer places an order until it is delivered—is another vital part of the company's quality initiatives. In fact, in the case of new products, Motorola's cycle-time reduction is even more ambitious; the clock starts ticking the moment the product is conceived. This calls for an examination of the total system, including design, manufacturing, marketing, and administration.

Motorola management demonstrates its quality leadership in a variety of ways, including top-level meetings to review quality programs with results passed on through the organization. But all levels of the company are involved. Non-executive employees contribute directly through Motorola's Participative Management Program (PMP). Composed of employees who work in the same area or are assigned to achieve a specific aim, PMP teams meet often to assess progress toward meeting quality goals, to identify new initiatives, and to work on problems. To reward high-quality work, savings that stem from team recommendations are shared.

To ensure that employees have the skills necessary to achieve company objectives, Motorola spent in excess of $170 million on worker education between 1983 and 1987. About 40 percent of the worker training provided by the company is devoted to quality matters, ranging from general principles of quality improvement to designing for manufacturability.

Motorola knows what levels of quality its products must achieve to top its competitors. Each of the firm's six major groups and sectors has benchmarking programs that analyze all aspects of a competitor's products to assess their manufacturability, reliability, manufacturing cost, and performance. Motorola has measured the products of some 125 companies against its own standards, verifying that many Motorola products rank as best in their class.

Motorola acknowledges that they made many mistakes. One of the most serious was to start the training for quality at the bottom of the company. Many workers were unable to understand statistical process controls and other techniques without remedial education, and they couldn't turn to their untrained bosses for help. Even those who understood the concepts completely were not able to apply them in the unreceptive workplace. Motorola's director of training and education estimates that Motorola wasted $7 million trying to train from the bottom up. Recognizing their mistake, the company established "Motorola University" and put thousands of Motorola executives through executive training. Bob Galvin himself spent time in the classroom. By 1992 the company was spending $110 million per year on instruction.

As a result of these efforts, Motorola can now perform such feats as building pagers and cell phones in lots ranging from one unit to 100,000. Through mass customization the factory can fill a precise order within minutes of receiving it. Thanks in large part to its six sigma activities, the company dominates such key high-tech industries as pagers, cell phones, and mobile communications, and is a significant force in many others.

Six Sigma at General Electric

GE enjoys the distinction of having the highest market capitalization of any public company, $321 billion. CEO Jack Welch attributes part of this success to the company's Six Sigma program. GE expects to reap $5–$10 billion in cost reductions alone from their investment in Six Sigma. Financial analysts list quality at the top of the list of themes being pursued by GE. Accrediting this focus as one reason for its success, Standard and Poor states:

Quality involves a company-wide initiative to boost quality and lower costs. The company believes that this should boost margins.*

The GE annual report prominently states "...Our six sigma quality initiative is changing the way we do everything." Success stories abound. Manufacturing examples include the following:

- At a color lab in the GE Plastics plant in Singapore a Six Sigma team reduced the lead time for matching colors of GE resins to customer requirements by 85%, a distinct competitive advantage in the fast-paced global market for plastics.
- Using Six Sigma tools and methodology, a team from GE Medical Systems and the GE Research and Development Center developed the new Performix™ 630 tube with key attributes that customers want. This new generation in tube technology offers dramatically longer tube life, faster patient exams and improved image quality.
- A Black Belt led a Six Sigma team that improved on-time delivery, increased productivity and saved $4 million for GE Appliances by changing the test and repair process for refrigerators. The team replaced a continuous test loop, from which refrigerators were pulled off the line for repairs and then returned, with eight test cells in which dedicated operators test refrigerators for possible mechanical problems and make any necessary adjustments before the electrical test is done.

The approach is used in non-manufacturing areas as well. For example:

- As part of the Loan Workout Consistency Team at GE Capital Mortgage Insurance, a Black Belt and Master Black Belt applied Six Sigma to the process of working with delinquent borrowers to find alternatives to foreclosure. By cutting defects in the workout process by 96%, GE Capital was able to offer borrowers quicker solutions while reducing claims payments by $8 million.

---

*Standard and Poor's Stock Report, GE, February 6, 1999.

- An administrative associate for GE Aircraft Engines in Canada used her Six Sigma training as a Green Belt on a project to make the paperwork perfect every time GE Canada imports a marine and industrial engine, parts or tooling for a Canadian customer. In addition to cutting customs costs, her project has reduced border delays by at least 50%.

Jack Welch asks each GE employee to become a "quality lunatic." The company is investing hundreds of millions of dollars to train its employees to become Master Black Belts, Black Belts, and Green Belts. These technical leaders work with teams throughout the company to pursue quality and process improvements.

According to *Business Week*, three years after starting its push for Six Sigma GE was running at a Sigma level of three to four. The gap between that and the Six Sigma level is costing the company between $8 billion and $12 billion a year in inefficiencies and lost productivity.

It was no small decision to launch a quality initiative because it called for massive investment in training tens of thousands of employees in a disciplined methodology heavily laden with statistics. To make the ideas take hold throughout General Electric required the training of so-called master black belts, black belts, and green belts to impose the quality techniques on the organization.

Welch launched the effort in late 1995 with 200 projects and intensive training programs, moved to 3,000 projects and more training in 1996, and undertook 6,000 projects and still *more training in 1997*. According to *Business Week*, the initiative has been a stunning success, delivering far more benefits than first envisioned by Welch. In 1997, Six Sigma delivered $320 million in productivity gains and profits, more than *double Welch's* original goal of $150 million. "Six Sigma has spread like wildfire across the company, and it is transforming everything we do," boasts Welch (Byrne, 1998).

CREATIVITY AND SIX SIGMA*

Paleontologist and evolutionary biologist Stephen Jay Gould was intrigued by the invitation to visit Japan. It seems that he and a Japanese counterpart each were to deliver a lecture on a common topic: creativity. Demonstrating considerable originality, if not creativity, of his own, Gould's lecture probably surprised the fastidious Japanese. According to Gould the watchwords of natural creativity are the following: sloppiness, poor fit, quirky design, and above all else, redundancy (Gould, 1993).

Gould proceeds to make his case using examples from natural evolution. Consider the bacteria, says Gould. In one sense bacteria represent nature's greatest success story. Evidence indicates that bacteria have been around on Earth almost as long as rocks, which is to say, a *very* long time. Bacteria are extremely efficient. A bacterium consists of a single cell with an internal genetic program devoid of junk and slop. It has single copies of essential genes. But bacteria have remained bacteria for 3.5 billion years, and they will probably still be bacteria when the sun explodes. Gould observes:

> If each gene does one, and only one, essential thing superbly, how can a new or added function ever arise? Creativity in this sense demands slop and redundancy.

In nature, redundancy such as being able to breathe through the nose as well as the mouth means that nature can experiment here without causing suffocation. Thus noses become anteater snouts and elephant trunks. Slop creates variation in each generation, so the slightly more successful trait can be discovered and passed along to future generations.

Slop? Redundancy? Poor fit? Quirky design? Propose this approach in a traditional firm and people will likely wonder if you've taken leave of your senses. These are the very things managers and engineers spend their professional

---

*From *The End of Management*, Copyright © 1999 by Thomas Pyzdek. Reprinted by permission.

lives tracking down and killing. To suggest that they be *deliberately* incorporated into the design of the organization is blasphemy. I have a pen from the Statistics Division of the American Society for Quality which says: all work is process, processes vary, reduce variation. Each time you click the pen, these slogans are shown in turn. This is given as a formula for quality. If a firm becomes obsessive about eliminating variation, it is also a formula for disaster. Creativity *requires* variation.

Gould's principles of natural creativity are precisely those needed for creativity in human organizations as well. Consider the 3M "15% rule." This informal rule provides that certain 3M employees can use up to 15% of their time to pursue projects of their own choosing. 3M gives a lot of credit for their well known creativity to the existence of this rule. Inventions that have resulted from it include Post-It Notes.™ This is an example of building slack into the organization. The practice wouldn't be possible in a highly efficient organization. If there were no redundancy or slack, the loss of an individual for 6 hours per week would be too disruptive to tolerate.

Excessive efficiency is the enemy of creativity.

Successful Six Sigma organizations are naturally more creative because they incorporate the very things that traditional management works to prevent, such as the following:

- There are multiple employees performing the same jobs—redundancy. This redundancy is essential if people are to have time to work on process improvement teams and other Six Sigma activities.
- The same jobs are done differently by different employees: variation. This built-in variability is a natural source of ideas for process improvement. Why does employee A get a higher yield than employee B? Why is process X so much better than the supposedly identical process Y? Major payoffs come from applying powerful statistical techniques to data to discover variation and use it to plan future improvements.

- The constant experimenting by people trying to find ways to improve leads to many failures and much waste: inefficiency. Six Sigma experiments, even those conducted under the guidance of Black Belts, often produce unacceptable results. This is how people learn. The organization committed to eliminating waste at any cost will sacrifice future improvement to short-term efficiency.

At Nucor Steel people have a saying: "If it's worth doing, it's worth doing poorly." In other words, don't study an idea to death with experts and committees. Get on with it and see if it works (Iverson, 1998). Nucor estimates that about half of the new ideas their employees attempt fail. But the other half succeed! People who aren't experts produce an abundance of quirky designs, designs that sometimes work better than the experts believed possible. And, like natural complex adaptive systems, the Six Sigma enterprise rewards the successful, leading to adaptation and higher payoffs for everyone.

Learning models
PDCA (PLAN-DO-CHECK-ACT)

The PDCA cycle, which Deming refers to as the PDSA cycle (Deming, 1993, p. 134), is a flow chart for learning and process improvement. The basic idea began with Shewhart's attempt to understand the nature of knowledge. Shewhart believed that knowledge begins and ends in experimental data but that it does not end in the data in which it begins. He felt there were three important components of knowledge (Shewhart, 1939, 1986): a) the data of experience in which the process of knowing *begins*, b) the prediction in terms of data that one would expect to get if one were to perform certain experiments in the *future*, and c) the degree of belief in the prediction based on the original data or some summary thereof as evidence. Shewhart arranged these three components schematically as shown in Figure 1.1.

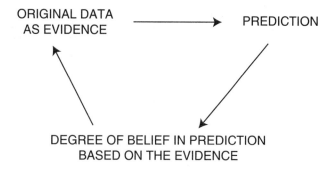

Figure 1.1. The three components of knowledge.

Since knowledge begins with the original data and ends in new data, these future data constitute the operationally verifiable meaning of the original data. However, since inferences or predictions based upon experimental data can never be certain, the knowledge based upon the original data can inhere in these data only to the extent of some degree of rational belief. In other words, according to Shewhart, knowledge can only be *probable*. Also, the data are not "facts" in and of themselves, they are merely measurements that allow us to draw inferences about something. In other words, *we can not have facts without some theory*.

Shewhart applied these principles in many practical ways. For example, he identified the three steps of quality control in manufacturing as specification, production, and judgment of quality (inspection). He noted that, in practice, specifications could not be set without first having some information from inspection to help establish process capability; furthermore, this information could not be obtained until some units had been produced. In short, Shewhart modified the sequence of specification-production-inspection as shown in Figure 1.2. He also observed that the specification-production-inspection sequence corresponded respectively to making a hypothesis, carrying out an experiment, and testing the hypothesis. Together the three steps constitute a dynamic scientific process of acquiring knowledge.

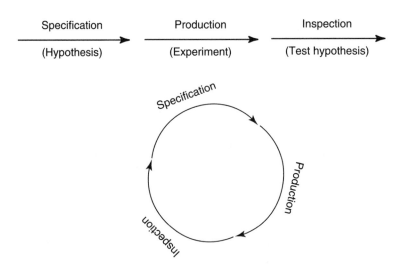

Figure 1.2. Scientific process of acquiring knowledge.

Note that Shewhart's model of knowledge forms a circle. Shewhart followed the teachings of philosopher C.I. Lewis (1929), who believed that all good logics are circular. The essence of this view is to see knowledge as dynamic. It changes as new evidence comes in. As Shewhart put it (Shewhart, 1939, 1986 p. 104):

> Knowing in this sense is somewhat a continuing process, or method, and differs fundamentally in this respect from what it would be if it were possible to attain certainty in the making of predictions.

Shewhart and Deming revised the above model for application to the improvement of products and processes. The new model was first called the PDCA cycle, later revised by Deming to the Plan-Do-Study-Act, or PDSA cycle (Deming, 1993, p. 134). The Shewhart-Deming PDSA cycle is shown in Figure 1.3.

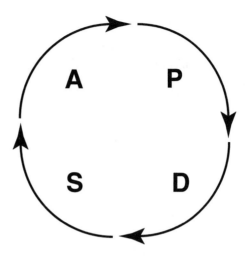

Figure 1.3. The Shewhart-Deming PDSA cycle for learning and improvement.

Plan a change or a test, aimed at improvement. This is the foundation for the entire PDCA-PDSA cycle. The term "plan" need not be limited to large-scale planning on an organization-wide scale; it may simply refer to a small process change one is interested in exploring.

Do. Carry out the change or the test (preferably on a small scale). It is important that the DO step carefully follow the plan, otherwise learning will not be possible.

Study the results. What was learned? What went wrong?

Act. Adopt the change, or abandon it, or run through the cycle again.

The PDCA approach is essentially a management-oriented version of the original Shewhart cycle, which focused on engineering and production. A number of other variations have been developed; two of Deming's variations are shown in Figure 1.4.

Deming's lectures to Japanese Executives in 1950

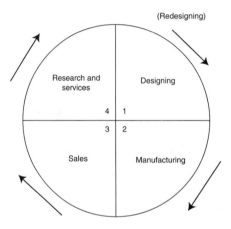

Deming's Lectures to Japanese Engineers in 1950

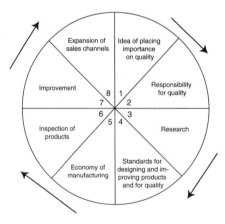

Figure 1.4. Some variations of the PDCA-PDSA cycle.

Juran depicts quality as a "spiral," as shown in Figure 1.5.

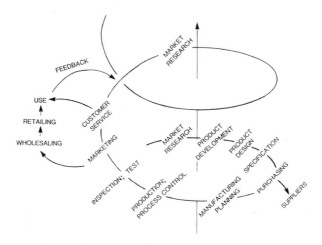

Figure 1.5. Juran's spiral of progress in quality.

Because of their historical origins and logical appeal, circular diagrams are ubiquitous in the quality field. In quality management, the circle represents continuous improvement of quality by continuous acquisition of knowledge.

DYNAMIC MODELS OF LEARNING AND ADAPTATION

The PDSA cycle describes planning and learning in an environment at or near a stable equilibrium. The PDSA loop indicates that plans are continuously improved by studying the results obtained when the plans are implemented, and then modifying the plans. However, the PDSA model fails to account for the activities of other agents, which is a characteristic of complex adaptive systems, such as a market economy. For this situation I propose a new model, the Select-Experiment-Adapt (SEA) model depicted in Figure 1.6.

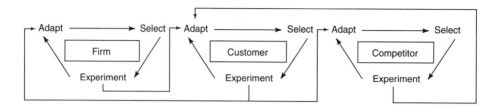

Figure 1.6. The Select-Experiment-Adapt (SEA) model
for non-linear systems.

In real life, experimentation goes on constantly. Experimenting involves executing a performance rule activated by a message received from the environment. We observe something, or induce something based on thinking about past observations, and decide which course of action would be most beneficial. The action taken in response to the environmental messages is called a *performance rule*. Adaptation occurs by adjusting the strength of the performance rule based on the payoff we actually received from it. Repeated iterations of the SEA cycle mimics what computer scientist John Holland calls the *bucket brigade algorithm* (Holland, 1996) which strengthens rules that belong to chains of action terminating in rewards. The process amounts to a progressive confirmation of hypotheses concerned with stage setting and sub-goals.

SEA versus PDSA

In the PDSA cycle, the plan documents the theory being tested. Deming believed that a statement which conveys knowledge must predict future outcomes, with risk of being wrong, and that it fits without failure observations of the past. Rational prediction, according to Deming, requires theory and builds knowledge through systematic revision and extension of theory based on comparison of prediction with observation. Without theory there is nothing to revise, so experience has no meaning (Deming, 1993).

The SEA model, unlike the PDSA cycle, contains positive feedback loops, making this a dynamic, nonlinear system. These systems act like both common and special causes in the Shewhart-Deming model. Virtually undetectable minor differences (common causes) are greatly amplified by positive feedback and produce unpredictably large effects (special causes). Because of positive feedback the behavior of even simple systems like the one shown in Figure 1.6 is unpredictable, even in principle. Of course, this illustration grossly oversimplifies reality. In the real world there are many competitors, competitors for our customers, many customers, regulation, many employees changing things in our firm, and so on. But the conclusion is the same: long-term forecasting is impossible, and therefore long-term planning is invalid. The "P" (plan) in the PDSA cycle cannot be used for other than short-term planning or systems in a state of "control" in the Shewhart-Deming sense.

The "S" (study) element is also suspect. What exactly are we studying? The effect of the action we took in the "A" (act) step? This won't work because the observed effects are also influenced, even overwhelmed, by actions taken by other agents. Thus, we may falsely conclude that our actions had an effect when in fact they did not, leading to superstitious learning. For example, a special promotion is run and sales increase, leading to the conclusion that the promotion was a success. But in fact the special promotion just happened to coincide with a customer promotion that created a temporary increase in demand for the product.

Or the conclusion might be reached that these actions did not have an effect when in fact their effect was masked by activities by other agents. For example, perhaps the new marketing program would have worked except that a competitor had a short term sale and the customer was under pressure to hold costs down due to a temporary cash flow problem.

Learning and the SEA model

In the SEA model, there is no "learning" per se. There is merely strategic adaptation. Computers can be programmed to modify performance rules based on payoffs, but the computer doesn't learn anything. It merely "discovers" new performance rules through successful adaptations based on repeated trial and error, i.e., through iterations of the SEA loop. Learning in the human sense involves discovering *principles* that explain the reasons for the increased or decreased payoffs obtained by applying the performance rules. This is a different thing entirely than simply discovering that a particular performance rule gives a somewhat higher payoff. Learning makes it possible to skip one or more generations of adaptation.

One model that incorporates learning in a dynamic environment, the Select-Experiment-Learn (SEL) model, is shown in Figure 1.7.

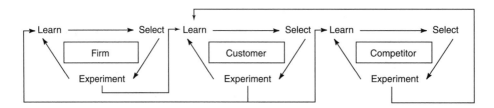

Figure 1.7. The Select-Experiment-Learn (SEL) model for dynamic systems.

SEL also differs from PDSA. Shewhart realized the value of discovering scientific principles; he also understood that progress was possible even without this knowledge. However, Shewhart believed that it was possible to apply natural laws to achieve "control within limits," i.e., statistical certainty. What Shewhart called a state of statistical control, I will call statistical equilibrium. A system exhibits statistical equilibrium when its future performance is predictable within limits which can be determined using linear, negative feedback models. Chaos theory and complexity theory show that in dynamic environments, i.e., environments influenced by positive feedback, even this level of control is impossible to achieve.

The SEL model is designed for a dynamic environment; it does not attempt to develop long-range strategic plans based on super-human knowledge and foresight. Instead, SEL seeks principles that are useful for making predictions, recognizing that positive feedback and the actions of other agents make it difficult to identify the effects of these principles. Furthermore, other agents may also acquire this knowledge and modify their behavior, thereby negating the principle. For example, cooperation and reciprocity may appear to be principles that applies to all human cultures. However, since the principle applies to agents, future behavior can not be predicted with even statistical certainty. If others realize that you are applying this principle, they can take advantage of your predictability. Of course, until new breakthrough principles are learned, gradual continuous improvement can still be obtained by using the SEA model. The cumulative improvement from SEA can be significant (e.g., natural evolution).

Essentially, when environments are dynamic the SEA and SEL models replace the equilibrium environment PDSA learning model with dynamic adaptation (SEA) and agent-based learning (SEL). Centralized control schemes (plans) are replaced by self-control or at least local control by meta-agents. Six Sigma activities should employ all three strategies for improvement. Here are some general guidelines for determining when to apply a given approach:

- SEA applies unless formal, controlled experiments are underway. Follow a mini-max strategy: minimize central planning and control to the maximum extent possible. Allow individual employees maximum freedom to experiment and change their work environment and processes to seek better ways to do things.
- When processes are influenced by positive feedback from other agents, apply the SEA and SEL models. Eliminate long-term strategic planning and strive to cultivate an environment with maximum ability to adapt to change.
- When processes are at or near equilibrium and not influenced by positive feedback loops, PDSA applies. Since PDSA is planning based, the use of formal teams is justified. Rigorously apply the tools of process control, formal design of experiments, etc.

Illustration of PDSA, SEA and SEL

The chart below shows the percentage change in the S and P 500 index of stocks over a period of 100 months. The data reflect the buying and selling activities of millions of investors. The data reflect statistical control, i.e., equilibrium behavior, for the entire period; PDSA functioned quite well for investors during the period. Using control charts the predicted return for the next month is between -11.2% and +12.6%.

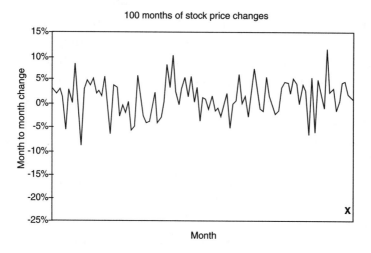

100 months of stock price changes

But this process proved to be distinctly non-linear. In the month #101, investors (agents) reacted to a price drop by selling, which caused the price to drop further, which caused still more selling. In other words, this dynamic process encountered a positive feedback loop. The result of this SEA behavior: a drop of nearly 22% (indicated by an "X" on the chart), a far greater drop than predicted by linear statistical models.

Some investors were not influenced by the positive feedback. Using SEL logic, they examined macro and micro factors and found no reason for the plunge. Rather than selling, they either held on to their shares or bought more. For a while, it appeared that this strategy would backfire: the market dropped another 9% the next month. But it eventually recovered, regained all of the lost ground, and moved back into positive territory.

THE SIX SIGMA MANAGEMENT PARADOX

The Six Sigma Management Paradox can be stated simply:

> To attain Six Sigma performance we must minimize process variability, slack and redundancy by building variability, slack and redundancy into our organizations.

Six Sigma involves an intense effort to reduce process variation to a minimum, so that processes consistently meet or exceed customer expectations and requirements. However, revolutionary rates of improvement and levels of quality can be achieved only by breakthroughs in thinking. These creative breakthroughs can be obtained only if the organization allows teams and individuals the freedom to try many new things. By definition, introducing something new also increases variation. Whenever something new is tried, there is a risk of failure, which in the short term increases waste. There must be slack available—i.e., extra resources—to allow the organization to function effectively despite this waste. Finally, creative activities will attract the best minds in the organization like a light attracts a moth. The organization must possess sufficient operational redundancy to assure that critical functions continue despite the absence of these key personnel.

Leaders must be constantly vigilant to assure that the paradox is understood. A fundamental principle of Six Sigma is reduction of variability. When one learns a new principle there is a tendency, especially in the beginning, to go overboard in applying it. The tendency is to apply this principle to *everything*. Advocates examine every process with an eye toward bringing it under control; i.e., making it efficient, capable and predictable. In the early stages the payoffs from these activities are often huge because the organization is awash in wasted resources and non-productive or counter-productive activity (i.e., redundancy and slack). However, as progress continues there is less and less unplanned slack in the organization. If care isn't taken, the end result of Six Sigma can be an organization which is unable to grow and adapt to a changing environment.

The common form of modern organizations is what I call "hard-wired." The organization chart is the blueprint for this machine and the policy and procedure manuals are the operating instructions. The idea is, like a circuit board, certain outputs (products, services, profits) will be produced when certain inputs (money, people, ideas) are provided. Such organizations can become highly efficient; resources are carefully managed to avoid waste. However, they can also be very inflexible and difficult to change. These organizations tend to rely heavily on formal mechanisms, such as chartered teams, to create change. Senior management forces the various functions to provide resources to the teams (people, facilities, etc.), in effect tapping into the main resource circuits to draw off energy for change. Maintaining the momentum for change in these organizations requires perpetual vigilance by top management because the "true" resource owners—the managers of the functions whose resources are being appropriated—are constantly trying to stop the energy drain from their areas. Such organizations are constantly fighting "resistance to change." In the 1980s firms like IBM and General Motors offered good examples of such organizations. Six Sigma tends to work poorly in hard-wired organizations. It is difficult to get the required resources and the necessary permissions to conduct experiments and make process changes. Furthermore, transferring the lessons from successful Six Sigma projects to other parts of the organization tends to be extremely difficult.

A second type of organization is the "soft-wired" organization. In a soft-wired organization there are floating resources that are not fully under the control of a particular function. Like the RAM of a computer, these resources can be easily reconfigured to perform a variety of different activities. A computer can be an accounting machine one minute, an engineering machine the next, and a game machine after that. 3M's tradition of allowing certain technical people to claim 15% of their time to pursue projects of their own choosing is an example of soft-wiring. The Brazilian company Semco has freelance engineers who report to no one and receive a share of the proceeds from any successful ideas and innovations they dream up. There are many other examples of soft-wiring, and they produce amazing results. The soft-wired organizational form is well suited to the rapid but directed change required for Six Sigma.*

SIX SIGMA'S TECHNICAL COMPONENT

Although it is primarily a new approach to management, Six Sigma has a strong technical component. Six Sigma technical leaders include people with a background in advanced statistical analysis using computers, as well as various subject matter experts who serve on teams. There are multiple levels of expertise, ranging from the ability to use basic methods to in-depth understanding of mathematical theory. Persons possessing various levels of expertise are sometimes called by names borrowed from the martial arts, e.g., those with advanced backgrounds are "Black Belts", those with intermediate levels of training "Green Belts," etc. We will use the term "technical leader" to describe persons with advanced training in all aspects of Six Sigma, including Six Sigma philosophy, statistical analysis, information systems, applications, and project management. The subject matter that each level of technical leader needs to master is described in the introduction to this book.

---

*The third type of organization is the emergent organization, which I call the Spontaneous Enterprise and write about extensively in my book, *The End of Management*. Scientists call these organizations "complex adaptive systems." Complex adaptive systems are all around us, from the rainforest, to the brain, to the free market. These systems are vastly more complex than any business firm, and also very orderly. Until recently we could only marvel that these amazing systems could exist and function so beautifully without a leader or a plan. Scientists have begun to discover the rules that govern such systems. This new knowledge allows a deeper understanding of how these systems function. With our new understanding we can see how more effective human organizations might be designed, e.g., organizations that depend on self-organization for order, rather than on a costly and ineffective system of rules and hierarchy. At this time there are only a few organizations of this type, such as the credit card behemoth Visa®. However, as we learn from these pioneers we should see more Spontaneous Enterprise organizations. Since Six Sigma is a management program, it would need to be radically modified to work in a Spontaneous Enterprise. A possibility is that Six Sigma technical leaders would play important supporting roles to leaders in the Spontaneous Enterprise, providing them with information to help them maintain a competitive edge. In any event, this is an issue for some future date rather than current Six Sigma activities.

Technical leaders are catalysts who can effectively train and lead people and teams. Although they receive broad management direction and require the support of senior leaders, they are able to function effectively with a bare minimum of guidance. These people work with and advise management on the formulation and implementation of project plans. They also work with teams to actually carry out the projects.

An important role of the technical leader is to stimulate management thinking by presenting new ways of thinking and doing things. They are, in a sense, "translators" who understand the language of management (finance, organization, governance) as well as that of the project team (technical metrics, problem solving, statistics). They often act as information conduits, bringing significant policy issues to the attention of senior leaders by demonstrating the concrete impact of policy decisions on operational effectiveness.

According to ASQ and the Six Sigma Academy, technical leaders (Black Belts) perform the following tasks:

Mentoring—Cultivating a network of experts in the factory or site.

Teaching—Providing formal training to local personnel in new strategies and tools.

Coaching—Providing one-on-one support to local personnel.

Transferring—Passing on new strategies and tools in the form of training, workshops, case studies, local symposia, etc.

Discovering—Finding application opportunities for Breakthrough Strategies and tools, both internal and external (e.g., suppliers and customers).

Identifying—Surfacing business opportunities through partnerships with other organizations.

Influencing—Selling the organization on the use of Breakthrough Strategies and tools.

Qualifications

In addition to mastery of the subject matter, the highest levels of technical leadership require additional background. Perhaps the most stringent requirements are for Black Belt Instructors, i.e., for the people who provide instruction to Six Sigma Black Belts. ASQ lists the following requirements for this position:

> A Six Sigma Black Belt Instructor shall have demonstrated growth and accomplishment as a manager or consultant in operations and quality and shall meet the following general qualifications:
> - ASQ Senior Member or Fellow
> - Ten or more years of operations/quality experience as a manager or consultant
> - Experience in teaching advanced statistics and design of experiments
> - Experience in working with senior management
> - Graduate degree desirable
> - Certified Six Sigma Black Belt desirable

Of course, these are only ASQ's requirements. It is likely that the requirements for an organization will differ. However, in selecting instructors it is important to look for expertise in the three major areas addressed by the ASQ criteria: broad experience, proven instructional ability, and technical depth.

Candidates for technical leader (Black Belt) status are technically oriented individuals held in high regard by their peers. They should be actively involved in the process or organizational change and development. Candidates may come from a wide range of disciplines and need not be formally trained statisticians or engineers. However, because they are expected to master a wide variety of technical tools in a relatively short period of time, technical leader candidates will probably possess a background in college-level mathematics. Coursework in statistical methods should be considered a strong plus. Successful candidates will also be comfortable with computers. At a minimum, they should understand one or more operating systems, spreadsheets, database managers, presentation programs, and word processors. As part of their training they will be required to become proficient in the use of one or more advanced statistical analysis software packages. The software will make it possible to perform easily the advanced analyses described in this book.

INFORMATION SYSTEMS REQUIREMENTS

Six Sigma technical leaders work to extract actionable knowledge from an organization's information warehouse. To assure access to the needed information, Six Sigma activities should be closely integrated with the information systems (IS) of the organization. Obviously, the skills and training of Six Sigma technical leaders must be supplemented by an investment in software and hardware. It makes little sense to hamstring these experts by saving a few dollars on computers or software. Six Sigma often requires the analysis of huge amounts of data using highly sophisticated algorithms. The amount of time required to perform the analysis can be considerable, even with today's advanced processing equipment. Without state-of-the-art tools, the situation is often hopeless.

Integrating Six Sigma with other information systems technologies

There are three information systems topics that are closely related to Six Sigma activities:

- Data warehousing
- On Line Analytic Processing (OLAP)
- Data mining

The first topic relates to what data is retained by the organization, and therefore available for use in Six Sigma activities. It also impacts how the data is stored, which impacts on ease of access for Six Sigma analyses. OLAP enables the analysis of large databases by persons who may not have the technical background of a Six Sigma technical leader. Data mining involves retrospective analysis of data using advanced tools and techniques. Each of these subjects will be discussed in turn.

DATA WAREHOUSING

Data warehousing has progressed rapidly. Virtually non-existent in 1990, now every large corporation has at least one data warehouse and some have several. Hundreds of vendors offer data warehousing solutions, from software to hardware to complete systems. Few standards exist and there are as many data warehousing implementations as there are data warehouses. However, the multitiered approach to data warehousing is a model that appears to be gaining favor; recent advances in technology and decreases in prices have made this option more appealing to corporate users.

Multitiered data warehousing architecture focuses on how the data are used in the organization. While access and storage considerations may require summarization of data into multiple departmental warehouses, it is better for Six Sigma analysis if the warehouse keeps all of the detail in the data for historical analysis. The major components of this architecture are (Berry and Linoff, 1997):

- *Source systems* are where the data comes from.
- *Data transport and cleansing* move data between different data stores.
- The *central repository* is the main store for the data warehouse.
- The *metadata* describes what is available and where.
- *Data marts* provide fast, specialized access for end users and applications.
- *Operational feedback* integrates decision support back into the operational systems.
- *End users* are the reason for developing the warehouse in the first place.

Figure 1.8 illustrates the multitiered approach.

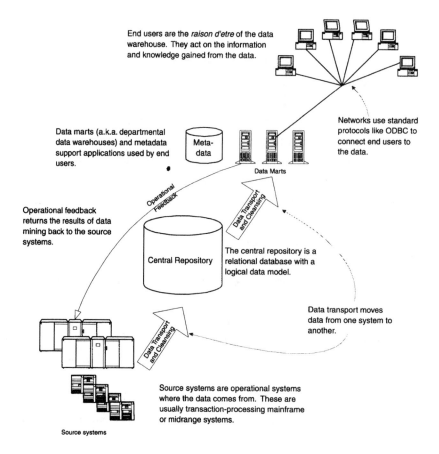

End users are the *raison d'etre* of the data warehouse. They act on the information and knowledge gained from the data.

Networks use standard protocols like ODBC to connect end users to the data.

Data marts (a.k.a. departmental data warehouses) and metadata support applications used by end users.

Meta-data

Data Marts

Operational Feedback

Data Transport and Cleansing

Operational feedback returns the results of data mining back to the source systems.

Central Repository

The central repository is a relational database with a logical data model.

Data transport moves data from one system to another.

Data Transport and Cleansing

Source systems are operational systems where the data comes from. These are usually transaction-processing mainframe or midrange systems.

Source systems

Figure 1.8. The multitiered approach to data warehousing.

From *Data Mining Techniques for Marketing, Sales, and Customer Support,* by Michael J.A. Berry and Gordon Linoff, New York, John Wiley and Sons, 1997. Used by permission of the publisher.

Every data warehouse includes at least one of these building blocks. The data originates in the source systems and flows to the end users through the various components. The components can be characterized as hardware, software, and networks. The purpose is to deliver information, which is in turn used to create new knowledge, which is then acted on to improve business performance. In other words, the data warehouse is ultimately a component in a decision-support system.

OLAP

On-line analytic processing, or OLAP, is a collection of tools designed to provide ordinary users a means of extracting useful information from large databases. These databases may or may not reside in a data warehouse. If they do, then the user obtains the benefit of knowing the data has already been cleansed, and access is likely to be more efficient. OLAP consists of client-server tools that have an advanced graphical interface to access data arranged in "cubes." The cube is ideally suited for queries that allow users to slice-and-dice the data in any way they see fit. OLAP tools have very fast response times compared to SQL queries on standard relational databases.

The basic unit of OLAP is the *cube*. An OLAP cube consists of subcubes that summarize data from one or more databases. Each cube is composed of multiple dimensions which represent different fields in a database. For example, an OLAP cube might consist of warranty claims arranged by months, products, and region, as shown in Figure 1.9.

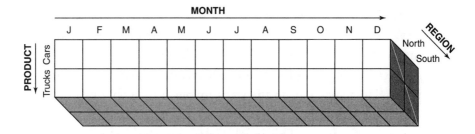

Figure 1.9. An OLAP cube.

DATA MINING

Data mining is the exploration and analysis by automatic or semi-automatic means of large quantities of data in order to uncover useful patterns. These patterns are studied in order to develop performance rules, i.e., new and better ways of doing things. Data mining, as used in Six Sigma, is directed toward improving customer satisfaction, lowering costs, reducing cycle times, and increasing quality.

Data mining is a grab-bag of techniques borrowed from various disciplines. Like Six Sigma, data mining alternates between generating questions via knowledge discovery, and testing hypotheses via designed experiments. Six Sigma and data mining both look for the same things in evaluating data, namely *classification, estimation, prediction, affinity grouping, clustering* and *description*. However, data mining tends to use a different set of tools than traditional Six Sigma tools; therefore it offers another way to look for improvement opportunities. Also, where Six Sigma tends to focus on internal business processes, data mining looks primarily at marketing, sales, and customer support. Since the object of Six Sigma is, ultimately, to improve customer satisfaction, the external focus of data mining provides both feed forward data to the Six Sigma program and feed back data on its success.

Data Mining is a process for retrospectively exploring business data. There is growing agreement on the steps involved in such a process and any differences relate only to the detailed tasks within each stage.[*]

Goal definition—This involves defining the goal or objective for the data mining project. This should be a business goal or objective which normally relates to a business event such as arrears in mortgage repayment, customer attrition (churn), energy consumption in a process, etc. This stage also involves the design of how the discovered patterns will result in action that leads to business improvement.

Data selection—This is the process of identifying the data needed for the data mining project and the sources of this data.

[*]http://www.attar.com/tutor/deploy.htm.

Data preparation—This involves cleansing the data, joining/merging data sources and the derivation of new columns (fields) in the data through aggregation, calculations or text manipulation of existing data fields. The end result is normally a flat table ready for the application of the data mining itself (i.e. the discovery algorithms to generate patterns). Such a table is normally split into two data sets: one set for pattern discovery and one set for pattern verification.

Data exploration—This involves the exploration of the prepared data to get a better feel prior to pattern discovery and also to validate the results of the data preparation. Typically, this involves examining descriptive statistics (minimum, maximum, average, etc.) and the frequency distribution of individual data fields. It also involves field versus field scatter plots to understand the dependency between fields.

Pattern discovery—This is the stage of applying the pattern discovery algorithm to generate patterns. The process of pattern discovery is most effective when applied as an exploration process assisted by the discovery algorithm. This allows business users to interact with and to impart their business knowledge to the discovery process. For example, if creating a classification tree, users can at any point in the tree construction examine/explore the data filtering to that path, examine the recommendation of the algorithm regarding the next data field to use for the next branch, then use their business judgement to decide on the data field for branching. The pattern discovery stage also involves analyzing the ability to predict occurrences of the event in data other than that used to build the model.

Pattern deployment—This stage involves the application of the discovered patterns to solve the business goal of the data mining project. This can take many forms:

Patterns presentation—The description of the patterns (or the graphical tree display) and their associated data statistics are included in a document or presentation.

Business intelligence—The discovered patterns are used as queries against a data base to derive business intelligence reports.

Data scoring and labeling—The discovered patterns are used to score and/or label each data record in the database with the propensity and the label of the pattern it belongs to.

Decision support systems—The discovered patterns are used to make components of a decision support system.

Alarm monitoring—The discovered patterns are used as norms for a business process. Monitoring these patterns will enable deviations from normal conditions to be detected at the earliest possible time. This can be achieved by embedding the data mining tool as a monitoring component, or through the use of a classical approach, such as control charts.

Pattern validity monitoring—As a business process changes over time, the validity of patterns discovered from historic data will deteriorate. It is therefore important to detect these changes at the earliest possible time by monitoring patterns with new data. Significant changes to the patterns will point to the need to discover new patterns from more recent data.

OLAP, data mining, and Six Sigma

OLAP is not a substitute for data mining. OLAP tools are a powerful means for reporting on data, while data mining focuses on finding hidden patterns in data. OLAP helps users by quickly presenting data to confirm or disconfirm ad hoc hypotheses, obviously a valuable knowledge discovery tool for Six Sigma teams. It is, essentially, a semi-automated means of analysis. OLAP and data mining are complementary, and both approaches complement the standard arsenal of tools and techniques used in Six Sigma. Both OLAP and data mining are used for *retrospective studies*, that is, they are used to generate hypotheses by examining past data. Designed experiments help users design *prospective studies*, that is, they test the hypotheses generated by OLAP and data mining. Used together, Six Sigma, data mining and OLAP comprise a powerful collection of business improvement tools.

SIX SIGMA READINESS EVALUATION
Assessing organization culture on quality

Juran and Gryna (1993) define the company quality culture as the opinions, beliefs, traditions, and practices concerning quality. While sometimes difficult to quantify, an organization's culture has a profound effect on the quality produced by that organization. Without an understanding of the cultural aspects of quality, significant and lasting improvements in quality levels are unlikely.

Two of the most common means of assessing organization culture is the focus group and the written questionnaire. These two techniques are discussed in greater detail below. The areas addressed generally cover attitudes, perceptions, and activities within the organization that impact quality. Because of the sensitive nature of cultural assessment, anonymity is usually necessary. The author believes that it is necessary for each organization to develop its own set of questions. The process of obtaining the questions is an education in itself. One method that has produced favorable results in the past is known as the critical-incident technique. This involves selecting a small representative sample ($n \approx 20$) from the group to be surveyed and asking open-ended questions, such as:

> "Which of our organization's beliefs, traditions and practices have a beneficial impact on quality?"

> "Which of our organization's beliefs, traditions and practices have a detrimental impact on quality?"

The questions are asked by interviewers who are unbiased and the respondents are guaranteed anonymity. Although usually conducted in person or by phone, written responses are sometimes obtained. The order in which the questions are asked (beneficial/detrimental) is randomized to avoid bias in the answer. Interviewers are instructed not to prompt the respondent in any way.

It is important that the responses be recorded verbatim, using the respondent's own words. Participants are urged to provide as many responses as they can; a group of 20 participants will typically produce 80–100 responses.

The responses themselves are of great interest and always provide a great deal of information. In addition, the responses can be grouped into categories and the categories examined to glean additional insight into the dimensions of the organization's quality culture. The responses and categories can be used to develop valid survey items and to prepare focus-group questions. The follow-up activity is the reason so few people are needed at this stage—statistical validity is obtained during the survey stage.

Surveys and focus groups

There are any number of reasons why a firm may wish to communicate with its customers. A primary reason is the evaluation of the customer's perception of the firm's product and service quality and its impact on customer satisfaction. The purpose may be to obtain an idea of the general condition of quality and satisfaction, or a comparison of the current levels with the firm's goals. A firm might wish to conduct employee surveys and focus groups to assess the organization's quality structure.

STRATEGIES FOR COMMUNICATING WITH CUSTOMERS AND EMPLOYEES

There are four primary strategies commonly used to obtain information from or about customers and employees:

- sample surveys
- case studies
- field experiments
- available data

With sample surveys, data are collected from a sample of a universe to esti-mate the characteristics of the universe, such as their range or dispersion, the frequency of occurrence of events, or the expected values of important uni-verse parameters. The reader should note that these terms are consistent with the definition of enumerative statistical studies described in Chapter 8. This is the traditional approach to such surveys. However, if survey results are col-lected at regular intervals, the results can be analyzed using the quality control tools described in Chapter 8 to obtain information on the underlying process. The quality manager should not be reticent in recommending that survey budgets be allocated to conducting small, routine, periodic surveys rather than infrequent "big studies." Without the information available from time-ordered series of data, it will not be possible to learn about processes which produce changes in customer satisfaction or perceptions of quality.

A case study is an analytic description of the properties, processes, condi-tions, or variable relationships of either single or multiple units under study. Sample surveys and case studies are usually used to answer descriptive ques-tions ("How do things look?") and normative questions ("How well do things compare with our requirements?"). A field experiment seeks the answer to a cause-and-effect question ("Did the change result in the desired outcome?"). Use of available data as a strategy refers to the analysis of data previously col-lected or available from other sources. Depending on the situation, available data strategies can be used to answer all three types of questions: descriptive, normative, and cause-and-effect. Original data collection strategies such as mail questionnaires are often used in sample surveys, but they may also be used in case studies and field experiments.

SURVEYS

Survey development consists of the following major tasks (GAO, 1986, 15):

1. initial planning of the questionnaire
2. developing the measures
3. designing the sample
4. developing and testing the questionnaire
5. producing the questionnaire
6. preparing and distributing mailing materials
7. collecting data
8. reducing the data to forms that can be analyzed
9. analyzing the data

Figure 1.10 shows a typical timetable for the completion of these tasks.

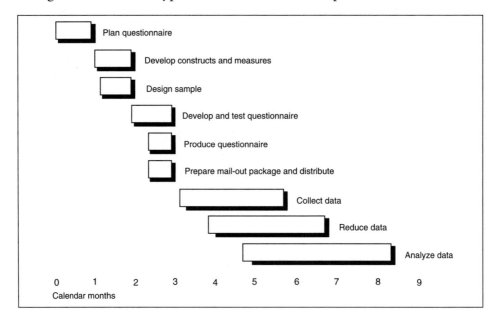

Figure 1.10. Typical completion times for major questionnaire tasks.

From *Developing and Using Questionnaires*, Transfer Paper 7, p. 15, Washington, DC: GAO Program Evaluation and Methodology Division.

GUIDELINES FOR DEVELOPING QUESTIONS

The axiom underlying the guidelines shown below is that the question-writer(s) must be thoroughly familiar with the respondent group and must understand the subject matter from the perspective of the respondent group. This is often problematic for the quality professional when the respondent group is the customer; methods for dealing with this situation are discussed below. There are eight basic guidelines for writing good questions:

1. Ask questions in a format that is appropriate to the questions' purpose and the information required.
2. Make sure the questions are relevant, proper, and qualified as needed.
3. Write clear, concise questions at the respondent's language level.
4. Give the respondent a chance to answer by providing a comprehensive list of relevant, mutually exclusive responses from which to choose.
5. Ask unbiased questions by using appropriate formats and item constructions and by presenting all important factors in the proper sequence.
6. Get unbiased answers by anticipating and accounting for various respondent tendencies.
7. Quantify the response measures where possible.
8. Provide a logical and unbiased line of inquiry to keep the reader's attention and make the response task easier.

The above guidelines apply to the *form* of the question. Using the critical incident technique to develop good question *content* is described below.

RESPONSE TYPES

There are several commonly used types of survey responses.

- **Open-ended questions**—These are questions that allow the respondents to frame their own response without any restrictions placed on the response. The primary advantage is that such questions are easy to form and ask, using natural language, even if the question writer has little knowledge of the subject matter. Unfortunately, there are many problems with analyzing the answers received to this type of question. This type of question is most useful in determining the scope and content of the survey, not in producing results for analysis or process improvement.

- **Fill-in-the-blank questions**—Here the respondent is provided with directions that specify the units in which the respondent is to answer. The instructions should be explicit and should specify the answer units. This type of question should be reserved for very specific requests; e.g., "What is your age on your last birthday? ____ (age in years)."

- **Yes/No questions**—Unfortunately, yes/no questions are very popular. Although they have some advantages, they have many problems and few uses. Yes/no questions are ideal for dichotomous variables, such as defective or not defective. However, too often this format is used when the measure spans a range of values and conditions, e.g., "Were you satisfied with the quality of your new car (yes/no)?" A yes/no response to such questions contains little useful information.

- **Ranking questions**—The ranking format is used to rank options according to some criterion, e.g., importance. Ranking formats are difficult to write and difficult to answer. They give very little real information and are very prone to errors that can invalidate all the responses. They should be avoided whenever possible in favor of more powerful formats and formats less prone to error, such as rating. When used, the number of ranking categories should not exceed five.

- **Rating questions**—With this type of response, a rating is assigned on the basis of the score's absolute position within a range of possible values. Rating scales are easy to write, easy to answer, and provide a level of quantification that is adequate for most purposes. They tend to produce reasonably valid measures. Here is an example of a rating format:

> *For the following statement, check the appropriate box:*
> *The workmanship standards provided by the purchaser are*
> ☐ *Clear*
> ☐ *Marginally adequate*
> ☐ *Unclear*

- **Guttman format**—In the Guttman format, the alternatives increase in comprehensiveness; that is, the higher-valued alternatives include the lower-valued alternatives. For example:

  Regarding the benefit received from training in quality improvement:
  ☐ *No benefit identified*
  ☐ *Identified benefit*
  ☐ *Measured benefit*
  ☐ *Assessed benefit value in dollar terms*
  ☐ *Performed cost/benefit analysis*

- **Likert and other intensity scale formats**—These formats are usually used to measure the strength of an attitude or an opinion. For example:

  Please check the appropriate box in response to the following statement:
  "The quality auditor was knowledgeable."
  ☐ *Strongly disagree*
  ☐ *Disagree*
  ☐ *Neutral*
  ☐ *Agree*
  ☐ *Strongly agree*

Intensity scales are very easy to construct. They are best used when respondents can agree or disagree with a statement. A problem is that statements must be worded to present a single side of an argument. We know that the respondent agrees, but we must infer what he believes. To compensate for the natural tendency of people to agree, statements are usually presented using the converse as well, e.g., "The quality auditor was not knowledgeable."

When using intensity scales, use an odd-numbered scale, preferably with five categories. If there is a possibility of bias, order the scale in a way that favors the hypothesis you want to disprove and handicaps the hypothesis you want to confirm. This way you will confirm the hypothesis with the bias against you—a stronger result. If there is no bias, put the most undesirable choices first.

- **Semantic differential format**—In this format, the values that span the range of possible choices are not completely identified; only the end points are labeled. For example:

Indicate the number of times you initiated communication with your customer in the past month.

few   *many*
(2 or less)   □   □   □   □   □   □   □   *(20 or more)*

The respondent must infer that the range is divided into equal intervals. The range seems to work better with seven categories rather than the usual five.

Semantic differentials are very useful when we do not have enough information to anchor the intervals between the poles. However, they are very difficult to write well and if not written well the results are ambiguous.

SURVEY DEVELOPMENT CASE STUDY[*]

> This actual case study involves the development of a mail survey at a community hospital. The same process has been used by the author to develop customer surveys for clientele in a variety of industries.
>
> The study of service quality and patient satisfaction was performed at a 213 bed community hospital in the southwestern United States. The hospital is a non-profit, publicly funded institution providing services to the adult community; pediatric services are not provided. The purpose of the study was to:
>
> 1. Identify the determinants of patient quality judgments.

[*]The survey referenced by this case study is located at Appendix 17.

2. Identify internal service delivery processes that impacted patient quality judgments.

3. Determine the linkage between patient quality judgments and intent-to-patronize the hospital in the future or to recommend the hospital to others.

To conduct the study, the author worked closely with a core team of hospital employees, and with several ad hoc teams of hospital employees. The core team included the Nursing Administrator, the head of the Quality Management Department, and the head of Nutrition Services.*

The team decided to develop their criteria independently. It was agreed that the best method of getting information was directly from the target group, in-patients. Due to the nature of hospital care services, focus groups were not deemed feasible for this study. Frequently, patients must spend a considerable period of time convalescing after being released from a hospital, making it impossible for them to participate in a focus group soon after discharge. While the patients are in the hospital, they are usually too sick to participate. Some patients have communicable diseases, which makes their participation in focus groups inadvisable.

Since memories of events tend to fade quickly (Flanagan, 1954, p. 331), the team decided that patients should be interviewed within 72 hours of discharge. The target patient population was, therefore, all adults treated as in-patients and discharged to their homes. The following groups were not part of the study: families of patients who died while in the hospital, patients discharged to nursing homes, patients admitted for psychiatric care.**

The team used the Critical Incident Technique (CIT) to obtain patient comments. The CIT was first used to study procedures for selection and classification of pilot candidates in World War II (Flanagan, 1954). A bibliography assembled in 1980 listed over

---

*The nutrition services manager was very concerned that she get sufficient detail on her particular service. Thus, the critical incident interview instrument she used included special questions relating to food service.

**The team was unable to obtain a Spanish-speaking interviewer, which meant that some patients that were candidates were not able to participate in the survey.

seven hundred studies about or using the CIT (Fivars, 1980). Given its popularity, it is not surprising that the CIT has also been used to evaluate service quality.

CIT consists of a set of specifically defined procedures for collecting observations of human behavior in such a way as to make them useful in addressing practical problems. Its strength lies in carefully structured data collection and data classification procedures that produce detailed information not available through other research methods. The technique, using either direct observation or recalled information collected via interviews, enables researchers to gather firsthand patient-perspective information. This kind of self-report preserves the richness of detail and the authenticity of personal experience of those closest to the activity being studied. Researchers have concluded that the CIT produces information that is both reliable and valid.

This study attempted to follow closely the five steps described by Flanagan as crucial to the CIT: 1) establishment of the general aim of the activity studied; 2) development of a plan for observers or interviewers; 3) collection of data; 4) analysis (classification) of data; and 5) interpretation of data.

Establishment of the general aim of the activity studied

The general aim is the purpose of the activity. In this case the activity involves the whole range of services provided to in-patients in the hospital. This includes every service activity between admission and discharge.* From the service provider's perspective the general aim is to create and manage service delivery processes in such a way as to produce a willingness by the patient to utilize the provider's services in the future. To do this the service provider must know which particular aspects of the service are remembered by the patient.

Our general aim was to provide the service provider with information on what patients remembered about their hospital stay, both pleasant and unpleasant. This information was to be used to construct a new patient survey instrument that would be sent to recently discharged patients on a periodic basis. The information obtained

---

*Billing was not covered in the CIT phase of the study because patients had not received their bills within 72 hours.

would be used by the managers of the various service processes as feedback on their performance, from the patient's perspective.

Interview plan

Interviewers were provided with a list of patients discharged within the past 3 days. The discharge list included all patients. Non-psychiatric patients who were discharged to "home" were candidates for the interview. Home was defined as any location other than the morgue or a nursing home. Interviewers were instructed to read a set of predetermined statements. Patients to be called were selected at random from the discharge list. If a patient could not be reached, the interviewer would try again later in the day. One interview form was prepared per patient. To avoid bias, 50% of the interview forms asked the patient to recall unpleasant incidents first and 50% asked for pleasant incidents first. Interviewers were instructed to record the patient responses using the patient's own words.

Collection of data

Four interviewers participated in the data collection activity, all were management level employees of the hospital. Three of the interviewers were female, one was male. The interviews were conducted when time permitted during the interviewer's normal busy work day. The interviews took place during the September 1993 time period. Interviewers were given the instructions recommended by Hayes (1992, pp. 14–15) for generating critical incidents.

A total of 36 telephone attempts were made and 23 patients were reached. Of those reached, three spoke only Spanish. In the case of one of the Spanish-speaking patients a family member was interviewed. Thus, 21 interviews were conducted, which is slightly greater than the 10 to 20 interviews recommended by Hayes (1992, p.14). The 21 interviews produced 93 critical incidents.

Classification of data

The Incident Classification System required by CIT is a rigorous, carefully designed procedure with the end goal being to make the data useful to the problem at hand while sacrificing as little detail as possible (Flanagan, 1954, p. 344). There are three issues in doing so: 1) identification of a general framework of reference that will account for all incidents; 2) inductive development of major area and subarea categories that will be useful in sorting the incidents; and 3) selection of the most appropriate level of specificity for reporting the data.

The critical incidents were classified as follows:

1. Each critical incident was written on a 3x5 card, using the patient's own words.
2. The cards were thoroughly shuffled.
3. Ten percent of the cards (10 cards) were selected at random, removed from the deck and set aside.
4. Two of the four team members left the room while the other two grouped the remaining 83 cards and named the categories.
5. The ten cards originally set aside were placed into the categories found in step 4.
6. Finally, the two members not involved in the initial classification were told the names of the categories. They then took the reshuffled 93 cards and placed them into the previously determined categories.

The above process produced the following dimensions of critical incidents:

• Accommodations (5 critical incidents)
• Quality of physician (14 critical incidents)
• Care provided by staff (20 critical incidents)
• Food (26 critical incidents)
• Discharge process (1 critical incident)
• Attitude of staff (16 critical incidents)
• General (11 critical incidents)

Interpretation of data

Interjudge agreement, the percentage of critical incidents placed in the same category by both groups of judges, was 93.5%. This is well above the 80% cutoff value recommended by experts. The setting aside of a random sample and trying to place it in established categories is designed to test the comprehensiveness of the categories. If any of the withheld items were not classifiable it would be an indication that the categories do not adequately span the patient satisfaction space. However, the team experienced no problem in placing the withheld critical incidents into the categories.

Ideally, a critical incident has two characteristics: 1) it is *specific* and 2) it describes the service provider in *behavioral terms* or the service product with *specific adjectives* (Hayes, 1992, p. 13). Upon reviewing the critical incidents in the General category, the team determined that these items failed to have one or both of these characteristics. Thus, the 11 critical incidents in the General category were dropped. The team also decided to merge the two categories "Care provided by staff" and "Attitude of staff" into the single category "Quality of staff care." Thus, the final result was a five dimension model of patient satisfaction judgments: Food, Quality of physician, Quality of staff care, Accommodations, and Discharge process.

A rather obvious omission in the above list is billing because the patients had not yet received their bill within the 72 hour time frame. However, the patient's bill was explained to the patient prior to discharge. This item is included in the Discharge process dimension. The team discussed the billing issue and it was determined that billing complaints do arise after the bills are sent, suggesting that billing probably is a satisfaction dimension. However, the team decided not to include billing as a survey dimension for these reasons: 1) the long time lag until bills had been received would significantly reduce the patient's recall of the details of the hospitalization; 2) the team feared that the patient's judgments would be overwhelmed by the recent receipt of the bill; and 3) a system already existed for identifying patient billing issues and adjusting the billing process accordingly.

Survey item development

As stated earlier, the general aim was to provide the service provider with information on what patients remembered about their hospital stay, both pleasant and unpleasant. This information was then to be used to construct a new patient survey instrument that would be sent to recently discharged patients on a periodic basis. The information obtained would be used by the managers of the various service processes as feedback on their performance, from the patient's perspective.

The core team believed that accomplishing these goals required that the managers of key service processes be actively involved in the creation of the survey instrument. Thus, ad hoc teams were formed to develop survey items for each of the dimensions determined by the critical incident study. The teams were given brief instruction by the author in the characteristics of good survey items. Teams were required to develop items that, in the opinion of the core team, met five criteria: 1) relevant to the dimension being measured; 2) concise; 3) unambiguous; 4) one thought per item; and 5) no double negatives. Teams were also shown the specific patient comments that were used as the basis for the categories and informed that these comments could be used as the basis for developing survey items.

Writing items for the questionnaire can be difficult. The process of developing the survey items involved an average of three meetings per dimension, with each meeting lasting approximately two hours. Ad hoc teams ranged in size from four to eleven members. The process was often quite tedious, with considerable debate over the precise wording of each item.

The core team discussed the scale to be used with each ad hoc team. The core team's recommended response format was a five point Likert-type scale. The consensus was to use a five point *agree-disagree* continuum as the response format. Item wording was done in such a way that agreement represented better performance from the hospital's perspective.

In addition to the response items, it was felt that patients should have an opportunity to respond to open-ended questions. Thus, the survey also included general questions that invited patients to comment in their own words. The benefits of having such questions is well known. In addition, it was felt that these questions might generate additional critical incidents that would be useful in expanding the scope of the survey.

The resulting survey instrument contained 50 items and three open-ended questions and is included in the Appendix.

Survey administration and pilot study

The survey was to be tested on a small sample. It was decided to use the total design method (TDM) to administer the survey (Dillman, 1983). Although the total design method is exacting and tedious, Dillman indicated that its use would assure a high rate of response. Survey administration would be handled by the Nursing Department.

TDM involves rather onerous administrative processing. Each survey form is accompanied by a cover letter, which must be hand-signed in blue ink. Follow up mailings are done 1, 3 and 7 weeks after the initial mailing. The 3 and 7 week follow-ups are accompanied by another survey and another cover letter. No "bulk processing" is allowed, such as the use of computer-generated letters or mailing labels. Dillman's research emphasizes the importance of viewing the TDM as a completely integrated approach (Dillman, 1983, p. 361).

Because the hospital in the study was small, the author was interested in obtaining maximum response rates. In addition to following the TDM guidelines, he recommended that a $1 incentive be included with each survey. However, the hospital administrator was not convinced that the additional $1 per survey was worthwhile. It was finally agreed that to test the effect of the incentive on the return rate $1 would be included in 50% of the mailings, randomly selected.

The hospital decided to perform a pilot study of 100 patients. The patients selected were the first 100 patients discharged to home starting April 1, 1994. The return information is shown in the table below.

Table 1.1. Pilot patient survey return information.

A. NUMBERS
Surveys mailed: 100
Surveys delivered: 92
Surveys returned as undeliverable: 8
Survey returned, needed Spanish version: 1

Total surveys returned: 45
Percentage of surveys delivered returned: 49%

Number delivered that had $1 incentive: 47
Number returned that had $1 incentive: 26
Percentage returned that had $1 incentive: 55%
Number delivered that had no $1 incentive: 45
Number returned that had no $1 incentive: 19
Percentage returned that had no $1 incentive: 42%

B. SURVEY RESPONSES BY MAILING
Number of surveys returned after:

Initial mailing: 12
One week follow up: 16
Three week follow up: 8
Seven week follow up: 9

Although the overall return rate of 49% is excellent for normal mail-survey procedures, it is substantially below the 77% average and the 60% "minimum" reported by
Dillman. As possible explanations, the author conjectures that there may be a large
Spanish-speaking constituency for this hospital. As mentioned above, the hospital is
planning a Spanish version of the survey for the future.

The survey respondent demographics were analyzed and compared to the demographics of the non-respondents to assure that the sample group was representative. A
sophisticated statistical analysis was performed on the responses to evaluate the reliability and validity of each item. Items with low reliability coefficients or questionable
validity were reworded or dropped.

FOCUS GROUPS

The focus group is a special type of group in terms of purpose, size, composition, and procedures. A focus group is typically composed of seven to ten
participants who are unfamiliar with each other. These participants are selected because they have certain characteristic(s) in common that relate to the
topic of the focus group.

The researcher creates a permissive environment in the focus group that
nurtures different perceptions and points of view, without pressuring participants to vote, plan, or reach consensus. The group discussion is conducted
several times with similar types of participants to identify trends and patterns
in perceptions. Careful and systematic analysis of the discussions provides
clues and insights as to how a product, service, or opportunity is perceived.

A focus group can thus be defined as a carefully planned discussion
designed to obtain perceptions on a defined area of interest in a permissive,
non-threatening environment. The discussion is relaxed, comfortable, and
often enjoyable for participants as they share their ideas and perceptions.
Group members influence each other by responding to ideas and comments
in the discussion.

In quality management, focus groups are useful in a variety of situations:

• prior to starting the strategic planning process

- generating information for survey questionnaires
- assessing needs, e.g., training needs
- testing new program ideas
- determining customer decision criteria
- recruiting new customers

FOCUS GROUP ADVANTAGES

The focus group is a socially oriented research procedure. The advantage of this approach is that members stimulate one another, which may produce a greater number of comments than would individual interviews. If necessary, the researcher can probe for additional information or clarification. Focus groups produce results that have high face validity; i.e., the results are in the participant's own words rather than in statistical jargon. The information is obtained at a relatively low cost very quickly.

FOCUS GROUP DISADVANTAGES

There is less control in a group setting than with individual interviews. When group members interact, it is often difficult to analyze the resulting dialogue. The quality of focus group research is highly dependent on the qualifications of the interviewer. Trained and skilled interviewers are hard to find. Group-to-group variation can be considerable, further complicating the analysis. Finally, focus groups are often difficult to schedule.

OTHER CUSTOMER INFORMATION SYSTEMS

- Complaint and suggestion systems typically provide all customers with an easy-to-use method of providing favorable or unfavorable feedback to management. Due to selection bias, these methods do not provide statistically valid information. However, because they are a census rather than a sample, they provide opportunities for individual customers to have their say. These are moments of truth that can be used to increase customer loyalty. They also provide anecdotes that have high face validity and are often a source of ideas for improvement.
- Customer panels are composed of a representative group of customers

who agree to communicate their attitudes periodically via phone calls or mail questionnaires. These panels are more representative of the range of customer attitudes than customer complaint and suggestion systems. To be effective, the identity of customers on the panel must be withheld from the employees serving them.

• Mystery shoppers are employees who interact with the system as do real customers. The identity of the mystery shopper is withheld from employees.

Once customer feedback has been obtained, it must be used to improve process and product quality. A system for utilizing customer feedback is shown in Figure 1.11.

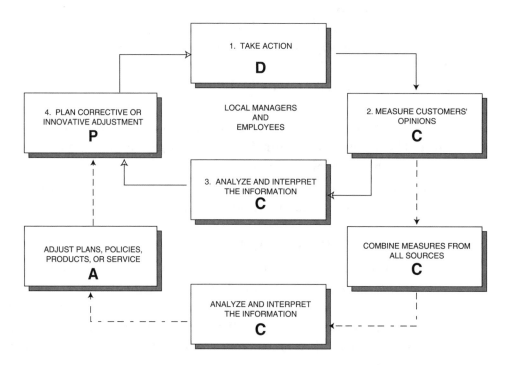

Figure 1.11. System for utilizing customer feedback.
From Daltas, A.J. (1977). "Protecting service markets with consumer feedback,"
Cornell Hotel and Restaurant Administration Quarterly, May, pp. 73–77.

1. *Take action*: Local managers and employees serve customers' needs on a daily basis, using locally modified procedures along with general corporate policies and procedures.
2. *Measure customers' opinions*: By means of a standardized and locally sensitive questionnaire, determine the needs and attitudes of customers on a regular basis.
3. *Analyze and interpret the information*: Comparing financial data, expectations, and past attitude information, determine strengths and weaknesses and their probable causes.
4. *Plan corrective innovative adjustment*: Determine where and how effort should be applied to correct weaknesses and preserve strengths. Repeat the process by taking action—step 1—and maintain it to attain a steady state or to evolve in terms of customer changes.

A similar process can take place at higher levels, using aggregated data from the field and existing policy flows of the organization. Although this system was developed by marketing specialists, note that it incorporates a variation of the classical Shewhart quality improvement PDCA cycle.

CHANGE AGENTS AND THEIR EFFECTS ON ORGANIZATIONS
Managing change

Experts agree: change is difficult, disruptive, expensive, and a major cause of error. Given these problems, it's reasonable to ask: Why change? Here are the most common reasons organizations choose to face the difficulties involved with change:

- **Leadership**—Some organizations choose to maintain product or service leadership as a matter of policy. Change is a routine.
- **Competition**—When competitors improve their products or services to provide greater value, a company is forced to change. Refusal to do so will result in the loss of customers and revenues and can even lead to complete failure.

- **Technological advances**—Effectively and quickly integrating new technology into an organization can improve quality and efficiency and provide a competitive advantage. Of course, doing so involves changing management systems.
- **Training requirements**—Many companies adopt training programs without realizing that many such programs implicitly involve change. For example, a company that provides employees with SPC training should be prepared to implement a process control system. Failure to do so leads to morale problems and wastes training dollars.
- **Rules and regulations**—Change can be forced on an organization from internal regulators via policy changes and changes in operating procedures. Government and other external regulators and rule-makers (e.g., ISO for manufacturing, JCAHO for hospitals) can also mandate change.
- **Customer demands**—Customers, large and small, have the annoying habit of refusing to be bound by policies. The nice customers will demand that policy and procedures be changed. The really nasty customers don't say anything at all, they simply go somewhere else to do business.

Johnson (1993a, p. 233) gives the following summary of change management:

1. Change will meet resistance for many different reasons.
2. Change is a balance between the stable environment and the need to implement TQM. Change can be painful while it provides many improvements.
3. There are four times change can most readily be made by the leader: when the leader is new on the job, receives new training, has new technology, or when outside pressures demand change.

4. Leaders must learn to implement change they deem necessary, change suggested from above their level, and change demanded from above their level.

5. There are all kinds of reaction to change. Some individuals will resist, some will accept, and others will have mixed reactions.

6. There is a standard process that supports the implementation of change. Some of the key requirements for change are leadership, empathy, and solid communications.

7. It is important that each leader become a change leader. This requires self-analysis and the will to change those things requiring change.

Roles

Change requires new behaviors from everyone involved. However, four specific roles commonly appear during most successful change processes (Hutton 1994, pp. 2–4):

- Official change agent. An officially designated person who has primary responsibility for helping management plan and manage the change process.
- Sponsors. Sponsors are senior leaders with the formal authority to legitimize the change. The sponsor makes the change a goal for the organization and ensures that resources are assigned to accomplish it. No major change is possible without committed and suitably placed sponsors.
- Advocate. An advocate for change is someone who sees a need for change and sets out to initiate the process by convincing suitable sponsors. This is a selling role. Advocates often provide the sponsor with guidance and advice. Advocates may or may not hold powerful positions in the organization.

- Informal change agent. Persons other than the official change agent who voluntarily help plan and manage the change process. While the contribution of these people is extremely important, it is generally not sufficient to cause truly significant, organization-wide change.

The position of these roles within a typical organizational hierarchy is illustrated graphically in Figure 1.12.

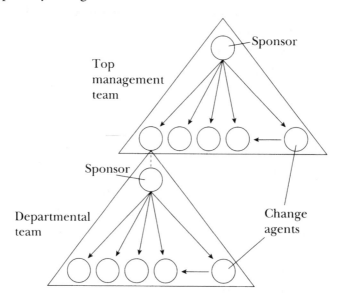

Figure 1.12. Cascading of sponsorship.

From Hutton, D.W. (1994). *The Change Agent's Handbook: A Survival Guide for Quality Improvement Champions.* Copyright © 1994 by David W. Hutton. Reprinted with permission.

The job of change agent
GOALS

There are three goals of change:

1. Change the way people in the organization think. Helping people change the way they think is a primary activity of the change agent. All change begins with the individual, at a personal level. Unless the individual is willing to change his behavior, no real change is possible.

Changing behavior requires a change in thinking. In an organization where people are expected to use their minds, people's actions are guided by their thoughts and conclusions. The change agent's job starts here.

2. Change the norms. Norms consist of standards, models, or patterns which guide behavior in a group. All organizations have norms or expectations of their members. Change cannot occur until the organization's norms change.

3. Changing the organization's systems or processes. This is the "meat" of the change. Ultimately, all work is a process and quality improvement requires change at the process and system level. However, this cannot occur on a sustained basis until individuals change their behavior and organizational norms are changed.

MECHANISMS USED BY CHANGE AGENTS

The change agents help accomplish the above goals in a variety of ways. Education and training are important means of changing individual perceptions and behaviors. In this discussion, a distinction is made between training and education. Training refers to instruction and practice designed to teach a person how to perform some task. Training focuses on concretes that need to be done. Education refers to instruction in how to think. Education focuses on integrating abstract concepts into one's knowledge of the world. An educated person will view the world differently after being educated than before. This is an essential part of the process of change.

Change agents help organize an assessment of the organization to identify its strengths and weaknesses. Change is usually undertaken to either reduce areas of weakness, or exploit areas of strength. The assessment is part of the education process. Knowing specific strengths and weaknesses is useful in mapping the process for change.

Change agents play an important role in quality improvement (remember, "improvement" implies change). As shown in Figure 1.12, change agents are in strategic positions throughout the organization. This makes it possible for them to assist in the coordination of the development and implementation of quality improvement plans. Quality improvement of any significance nearly always involves multiple departments and levels in the organization.

In the final analysis, all we humans really have to spend is our time. Change agents see to it that senior management spends sufficient time on the transformation process. Senior managers' time is in great demand from a large number of people inside and outside of the organization. It is all too easy to schedule a weekly meeting to discuss "TQM" for an hour, then think you've done your part. In fact, transforming an organization, large or small, requires a prodigious commitment of the time of senior leadership. At times the executive will not understand what he or she is contributing by, say, attending team meetings. The change agent must constantly assure the leader that time spent on transformation activities is time well spent.

One way of maximizing the value of an executive's time investment is for the executive to understand the tremendous power of certain symbolic events. Some events generate stories that capture the essence of management's commitment (or lack of it) to the change being undertaken. People repeat stories and remember them far better than proclamations and statements. For example, the following story is told by employees of a large U.S. automotive firm:

> In the early 1980s the company was just starting their quality improvement effort. At a meeting between upper management and a famous quality consultant, someone casually mentioned that quality levels were seasonal—quality was worse in the summer months. The consultant asked why this should be so. Were different designs used? Were the machines different? How about the suppliers of raw materials? The answer to each of these questions was "No." An investigation revealed that the problem was vacations. When a worker went on vacation, someone else did that job, but not quite as well. And that "someone" also vacated a job, which was done by a replacement, etc. It turned out that the one person going on vacation led to six people doing jobs they did not do routinely. The solution was to have a vacation shutdown of two weeks. This greatly reduced the number of people on new jobs and

brought summer quality levels up to the quality levels experienced the rest of the year.

This worked fine for a couple of years since there was a recession in the auto industry and there was plenty of excess capacity. However, one summer the senior executives were asked by the finance department to reconsider their shutdown policy. Demand had picked up and the company could sell every car it could produce. The accountants pointed out that the shutdown would cost $100 million per day in lost sales.

The vice president of the truck division asked if anything had been done to address the cause of the quality slippage in the summer. No, nothing had been done. The president asked the staff "If we go back to the old policy, would quality levels fall like they did before?" Yes, he was told, they would. "Then we stay with our current policy and shut down the plants for vacations," the president announced.

The President was challenged by the vice president of finance. "I know we're committed to quality, but are you sure you want to lose $1.4 billion in sales just to demonstrate our commitment?" The President replied, "Frank, I'm not doing this to 'demonstrate' anything. We almost lost our company a few years back because our quality levels didn't match our overseas competition. Looking at this as a $1.4 billion loss is just the kind of short-term thinking that got us in trouble back then. I'm making this decision to *save* money."

This story had tremendous impact on the managers who heard it, and it spread like wildfire throughout the organization. It demonstrated many things simultaneously: senior leadership's commitment to quality, political parity between operations and finance, the devastating effects of seemingly harmless policies, the damage caused by past short-term things, and the result of long-term thinking in a specific instance, etc. It is a story worth 100 speeches and mission statements.

LEADERSHIP SUPPORT ACTIVITIES

The change agent provides technical guidance to the leadership team: presenting management with alternative strategies for pursuing the transformation, educating on methods that can be used to implement the strategies, and selecting key personnel for key transformation jobs.

Change agents help to monitor the status of quality teams and quality projects relating to the transformation (see Chapter 5 for a complete discussion of project management). In addition to being a vehicle for local quality improvement, projects can be used as one of the mechanisms for actually implementing the transformation. If used in this way, it is important that projects be properly chartered to align the project activities with the goals of the transformation. All teams, chartered or not, must avoid projects and methods that conflict with the goals of the transformation. Project team membership must be planned carefully to assure that both task and group maintenance roles are properly filled. Project charters must identify clearly the scope of the project to prevent the confusion between teams that results from overlapping charters.

Change agents also serve as coaches to senior leaders. Culture involves innumerable subtle characteristics and behaviors that become unconsciously "absorbed" into one's being. At times, it is nearly impossible for the individual executive to see how his or her behavior or relationships are interpreted by others. The change agent must quietly advise leadership on these issues.

The press of day-to-day business, combined with the inherent difficulties of change, make it easy to let time slip by without significant progress. Keeping operations going is a full-time job, and current problems present themselves with an urgency that meeting a future goal can't match. Without the constant reminders from change agents that goals aren't being met, the leadership can simply forget about the transformation. It is the change agent's job to become the "conscience" of the leadership and to challenge them when progress falls short of goals.

CHANGE NETWORKS

Change agents should work to develop an internal support network. The network provides resources to support the change process by disseminating education and guidance. The network's tasks will eventually be subsumed by normal operations, but in the early stages of the transformation it is vital that the network exist since the control of resources is determined by the existing infrastructure and may be difficult to divert to the change process. Usually, the members of the network are formal and informal change agents in various areas of the organization.

Once the network has been established, it is the change agent's job to assure that the activities in the network are consistent with and in support of the organization's vision. For example, if a hospital has a vision where physicians obtain real-time clinical information and decision support at the patient's bedside, then a financially based and centralized information system is inconsistent with that vision. The change agent, especially the formal change agent, provides leadership and moral support to network members, who may otherwise feel isolated and vulnerable. Change agents ensure that members of the network receive the education and guidance they need. Finally, the change agent acts as a conduit and a stimulant to maintain regular communication in the network. This may take the form of setting up an e-mail list, scheduling lunches for network members, etc.

TRANSFORMING STAFF FUNCTIONS

Table 1.2 illustrates the contrast between the way that staff functions used to operate under the traditional system of management, and the way they can operate more effectively.

Table 1.2. How staff functions are changing.

From Hutton, D.W. (1994). *The Change Agent's Handbook: A Survival Guide for Quality Improvement Champions.* Page 220. Copyright © 1994 by David W. Hutton. Reprinted with permission.

	FROM	TO
Role	Customer—for information, evidence, and reports from others	Supplier—of information, expertise, and other services
Strategy	Control—by imposition of policies and procedures, and by audit and inspection	Support—by gearing efforts to the needs of others Self-control by client
Goal	Departmental achievement of departmental objectives	Collective achievement of the organization's objectives
Style of working with others	Competitive, adversarial	Integrating, collaborative
Focus of attention	Some aspects of outcomes; for example, product quality, financial results Some pieces of the process; for example, adherence to policy and procedure	The relationship between the entire underlying process and the achievement of all the desired outcomes
Image	Regulator, inspector, policeman	Educator, helper, guide

There are several ways in which change agents can assist staff functions in transforming their roles:

- Collaborate with staff functions.
- Encourage staff functions to take a proactive approach to change.
- Make support functions partners in the support network.
- Encourage staff members to become role models.

- Help staff functions develop transition plans that are aligned and integrated with the overall transformation plan.
- Encourage staff members to share their concerns.

SIX SIGMA TEAMS

Perhaps the most important thing management can do for a group is to give it time to become effective. This requires, among other things, that management work to maintain consistent group membership. Group members must not be moved out of the group without very good reason. Nor should there be a constant stream of new people temporarily assigned to the group. If a group is to progress through the four stages described later in this chapter, to the crucial performing stage, it will require a great deal of discipline from both the group and management. Another area where management must help is creating an atmosphere within the company where groups can be effective. The methods for accomplishing this are discussed throughout this book.

The structure of modern organizations is based on the principle of division of labor. Most organizations today consist of a number of departments, each devoted to their own specialty. A fundamental problem is that the separate functional departments tend to optimize their own operations, often to the detriment of the organization as a whole.

Traditional organizations, in effect, create barriers between departments. Departmental managers are often forced to compete for shares of limited budgets; in other words, they are playing a "zero sum game" where another manager's gain is viewed as their department's loss. Behavioral research has shown engaging in zero sum games, i.e., thinking in terms of win-lose, leads to self-destructive, cut-throat behavior. Overcoming this tendency requires improved communication and cooperation between departments.

Interdepartmental teams are groups of people with the skills needed to deliver the value desired. Processes are designed by the team to create the value in an effective and efficient manner. Management must see to it that the needed skills exist in the organization. It is also management's job to see that they remove barriers to cooperation.

There are two ways to make quality improvements: improve performance given the current system, or improve the system itself. Much of the time improving performance given the current system can be accomplished by individuals working alone. For example, an operator might make certain adjustments to the machine. Studies indicate that this sort of action will be responsible for about 5%–15% of the improvements. The remaining 85%–95% of all improvements will require changing the system itself. This is seldom accomplished by individuals working alone. It requires group action. Thus, the vast majority of quality improvement activity will take place in a group setting. As with nearly everything, the group process can be made more effective by acquiring a better understanding of the way it works.

Process improvement teams

Management of cross-functional projects is discussed in Chapter 5. This section will focus on the team aspect of process improvement activity.

Process improvement teams focus on improving one or more important characteristics of a process, e.g., quality, cost, cycle time, etc. The focus is on an entire process, rather than on a particular aspect of the process. A process is an integrated chain of activities that add value. A process can be identified by its beginning and ending states, e.g., manufacturing's beginning state is procurement; its ending state is shipment. Methods of analyzing and characterizing processes are discussed throughout this book. Usually several departments are involved in any given value-added process.

Process improvement teams work on both incremental improvement (KAIZEN) and radical change (reengineering). The team is composed of members who work with the process on a routine basis. Team members typically report to different bosses, and their positions can be on different levels of the organization's hierarchy.

Process improvement projects must be approved by the process owner, usually a senior leader in the organization. Process improvement teams must be chartered and authorized to pursue process improvement. All of this falls in the area of project management which is discussed in Chapter 5.

Work groups

Work groups focus on improvement within a particular work area. The work area is usually contained within a single department or unit. The process owner is usually the department manager. Team members are usually at the same level within the organization's hierarchy and usually report to one boss.

Work group members are trained in the use of quality control techniques and supported by management. The idea is that all workers have an important contribution to make to the quality effort and the work group is one mechanism for allowing them the opportunity to make their contribution.

QUALITY CIRCLES

An example of a work group is the quality circle. Quality circles originated in Japan and Japanese companies continue to use quality circles on a massive scale. Quality circles were tried on a massive scale in America, with only limited success. However, the quality circle is the historical forerunner of the modern quality improvement work team; a study of them reveals a great deal about the success factors needed for successful use of other types of work groups.

Quality circles are local groups of employees who work to continuously improve those processes under their direct control. Here are some necessary steps that must be completed before circles can succeed:

- Management from the top level to the supervisory level must have a clear idea of their organization's purpose. Everyone in the organization must be committed to helping the organization achieve its purpose.

- Senior leadership must have an effective organization for dealing with company wide issues such as quality, cost, cycle time, etc. (e.g., the cross functional form discussed earlier).
- Attention must be focused on processes rather than on internal politics and reporting relationships.
- Personnel involved must be trained in cooperation skills (e.g., team work, group dynamics, communication and presentation skills). This applies to area supervisors and managers, not just circle members.
- Personnel involved must be trained in problem-solving skills (e.g., the traditional QC tools, the 7M tools, brainstorming, etc.)
- Circle participation must be encouraged by local management.

However, this author believes that circles have an important place and that they can succeed anywhere providing the proper corporate environment exists. This environment did not exist in Western business organizations in the 1970s, and for the most part they still do not exist. Merely grafting quality circles onto a traditional command-and-control hierarchy won't work. There were many reasons why quality circles failed in America; they are the same reasons why work groups fail to this day.

1. The quality circle in an American firm was isolated, not part of a companywide quality control effort. As a result, circles were usually unable to deal successfully with problems involving other areas of the company. There were no resources in other areas to draw upon.
2. Key management personnel moved about too frequently and circles were not provided with consistent leadership and management support.
3. Employees transferred in and out of circle work areas too frequently. Without stability in the membership, circles never developed into effective groups. Building effective teams takes time.

Other self-managed teams

In addition to process-improvement teams and work groups, there are many other types of teams and groups involved to some extent in Six Sigma. Self-managed teams are a way to reintegrate work and flatten the management hierarchy. If properly implemented and managed, the result can be improved quality and productivity. If poorly implemented and managed, the result can be additional problems.

Self-managed teams are often given some of the responsibilities that, in traditional organizations, are reserved to management. This includes the authority to plan and schedule work, hiring, performance assessment, etc. This is essentially a reversal of over 90 years of scientific management. While difficult to implement successfully, the result is a leaner, more efficient organization, higher employee morale, and better quality. Several preconditions are necessary to assure success:

1. **Communicate and listen**—Encourage two-way, honest, open, frequent communication. The more informed employees are, the more secure and motivated they will be.

2. **Train employees**—An empowering culture is built on the bedrock of continuing education in every form imaginable. If an employee doesn't know what to do, how to do it right, or most important, why it is done a certain way and what difference it makes, don't expect him to feel or act empowered.

3. **Team employees**—No one has found a technological alternative to cooperation when it comes to building a positive work climate. Teams make it possible for people to participate in decision-making and implementation that directly affects them.

4. **Trust employees**—Support team decisions even if they aren't the outcomes you had in mind. Trust teams with information and allow them to fail.

5. **Provide feedback**—Find people doing things right. Recognize efforts as well as results by finding ways to frequently and creatively say thank you. Share the glory in every way possible. Give frequent specific performance feedback (good news as well as bad).

Facilitation techniques

WHEN TO USE AN OUTSIDE FACILITATOR

It is not always necessary to have an outside party facilitate a group or team. While facilitators can often be of benefit, they may also add cost; the use of facilitators should, therefore, be carefully considered. The following guidelines can be used to determine if outside facilitation is needed (Schuman, 1996):

1. **Distrust or bias**—In situations where distrust or bias is apparent or suspected, groups should make use of an unbiased outsider to facilitate (and perhaps convene) the group.

2. **Intimidation**—The presence of an outside facilitator can encourage the participation of individuals who might otherwise feel intimidated.

3. **Rivalry**—Rivalries between individuals and organizations can be mitigated by the presence of an outside facilitator.

4. **Problem definition**—If the problem is poorly defined, or is defined differently by multiple parties, an unbiased listener and analyst can help construct an integrated, shared understanding of the problem.

5. **Human limits**—Bringing in a facilitator to lead the group process lets members focus on the problem at hand, which can lead to better results.

6. **Complexity or novelty**—In a complex or novel situation, a process expert can help the group do a better job of working together intellectually to solve the problem.

7. **Timelines**—If a timely decision is required, as in a crisis situation, the use of a facilitator can speed the group's work.

8. **Cost**—A facilitator can help the group reduce the cost of meeting—a significant barrier to collaboration.

SELECTING A FACILITATOR

Facilitators should possess four basic capabilities (Schuman, 1996):

1. Ability to anticipate the complete problem-solving and decision-making process.
2. Use of procedures that support both the group's social and cognitive processes.
3. Neutrality regarding content issues and values.
4. Respect for the group's need to understand and learn from the problem-solving process.

Facilitation works best when the facilitator:

- Takes a strategic and comprehensive view of the problem-solving and decision-making processes and selects, from a broad array, the specific methods that match the group's needs and the tasks at hand.
- Supports the group's social and cognitive processes, freeing the group members to focus their attention on substantive issues.
- Is trusted by all group members as a neutral party who has no biases or vested interest in the outcome.
- Helps the group understand the techniques being used and helps the group improve its own problem-solving processes.

PRINCIPLES OF TEAM LEADERSHIP AND FACILITATION

Human beings are social by nature. People tend to seek out the company of other people. This is a great strength of our species, one that enabled us to rise above and dominate beasts much larger and stronger than ourselves. It is this ability that allowed men to control herds of livestock, to hunt swift antelope, and to protect themselves against predators. However, as natural as it is to belong to a group, there are certain behaviors that can make the group function more (or less) effectively than their members acting as individuals.

A group will be defined as a collection of individuals who share one or more common characteristics. The characteristic shared may be simple geography, i.e., the individuals are gathered together in the same place at the same time. Perhaps the group shares a common ancestry, like a family. Modern society consists of many different types of groups. The first group we join is, of course, our family. We also belong to groups of friends, sporting teams, churches, PTAs, and so on. The groups differ in many ways. They have different purposes, different time frames, and involve varying numbers of people. However, all effective groups share certain common features. In their work, *Joining Together*, Johnson and Johnson (1999) list the following characteristics of an effective group:

- Group goals must be clearly understood, be relevant to the needs of group members, and evoke from every member a high level of commitment to their accomplishment.

- Group members must communicate their ideas and feelings accurately and clearly. Effective, two-way communication is the basis of all group functioning and interaction among group members.

- Participation and leadership must be distributed among members. All should participate, and all should be listened to. As leadership needs arise, members should all feel responsibility for meeting them. The equalization of participation and leadership makes certain that all members will be involved in the group's work, committed to implementing the group's decisions, and satisfied with their membership. It also assures that the resources of every member will be fully utilized, and increases the cohesiveness of the group.

- Appropriate decision-making procedures must be used flexibly if they are to be matched with the needs of the situation. There must be a balance between the availability of time and resources (such as member's skills) and the method of decision-making used for making the decision. The most effective way of making a decision is usually by consensus (see below). Consensus promotes distributed participation, the equalization of power, productive controversy, cohesion, involvement, and commitment.

- Power and influence need to be approximately equal throughout the group. They should be based on expertise, ability, and access to information, not on authority. Coalitions that help fulfill personal goals should be formed among group members on the basis of mutual influence and interdependence.

- Conflicts arising from opposing ideas and opinions (controversy) are to be *encouraged*. Controversies promote involvement in the group's work, quality, creativity in decision-making, and commitment to implementing the group's decisions. Minority opinions should be accepted and used. Conflicts prompted by incompatible needs or goals, by the scarcity of a resource (money, power), and by competitiveness must be negotiated in a manner that is mutually satisfying and does not weaken the cooperative interdependence of group members.

- Group cohesion needs to be high. Cohesion is based on members liking each other, the desire of each member to continue as part of the group, the satisfaction of members with their group membership, and the level of acceptance, support, and trust among the members. Group norms supporting psychological safety, individuality, creativeness, conflicts of ideas, growth, and change need to be encouraged.

- Problem-solving adequacy should be high. Problems must be resolved with minimal energy and in a way that eliminates them permanently. Procedures should exist for sensing the existence of problems, inventing and implementing solutions, and evaluating the effectiveness of the solutions. When problems are dealt with adequately, the problem-solving ability of the group is increased, innovation is encouraged, and group effectiveness is improved.

- The interpersonal effectiveness of members needs to be high. Interpersonal effectiveness is a measure of how well the consequences of behavior match intentions.

These attributes of effective groups apply regardless of the activity in which the group is engaged. It really doesn't matter if the group is involved in a study of air defense, or planning a prom dance. The common element is that there is a group of human beings engaged in pursuit of group goals.

FACILITATING THE GROUP TASK PROCESS

Team activities can be divided into two subjects: task-related and maintenance-related. Task activities involve the reason the team was formed, its charter, and its explicit goals.

The facilitator should be selected before the team is formed and he or she should assist in identifying potential team members and leaders, and in developing the team's charter. The subject of team formation and chartering is discussed in detail in Chapter 5.

The facilitator also plays an important role in helping the team develop specific goals based on their charter. Goal-setting is an art and it is not unusual to find that team goals bear little relationship to what management actually had in mind when the team was formed. Common problems include goals that are too ambitious, goals that are too limited and goals that assume a cause and effect relationship without proof. An example of the latter would be a team chartered to reduce scrap assuming that Part X had the highest scrap loss (perhaps based on a week's worth of data) and setting as its goal the reduction of scrap for that part. The facilitator can provide a channel of communication between the team and management.

Facilitators can assist the team leader in creating a realistic schedule for the team to accomplish its goals. The issue of scheduling projects is covered in Chapter 5.

Facilitators should assure that adequate records are kept on the team's projects. Records should provide information on the current status of the project and should be designed to make it easy to prepare periodic status reports for management. The facilitator should arrange for clerical support with such tasks as designing forms, scheduling meetings, obtaining meeting rooms, securing audio visual equipment and office supplies, etc.

There are other activities where the facilitator's assistance is needed:

Meeting management—Schedule the meeting well ahead of time. Be sure that key people are invited and that they plan to attend. Prepare an agenda and stick to it! Start on time. State the purpose of the meeting clearly at the outset. Take minutes. Summarize from time-to-time. Actively solicit input from those less talkative. Curtail the overly talkative members. Manage conflicts. Make assignments and responsibilities explicit and specific. End on time.

Communication—The idea that "the quality department" can "assure" or "control" quality is now recognized as an impossibility. To achieve quality the facilitator must enlist the support and cooperation of a large number of people outside of the team. The facilitator can relay written and verbal communication between the team and others in the organization. Verbal communication is valuable even in the era of instantaneous electronic communication. A five minute phone call can provide an opportunity to ask questions and receive answers that would take a week exchanging e-mail and faxes. Also, the team meeting is just one communication forum; the facilitator can assist team members in communicating with one another between meetings by arranging one-on-one meetings, acting as a go-between, etc.

FACILITATING THE GROUP MAINTENANCE PROCESS

Study the group process. The facilitator is in a unique position to stand back and observe the group at work. Are some members dominating the group? Do facial expressions and body language suggest unspoken disagreement with the team's direction? Are quiet members being excluded from the discussion?

When these problems are observed, the facilitator should provide feedback and guidance to the team. Ask the quiet members for their ideas and input. Ask if anyone has a problem with the team's direction. Play devil's advocate to draw out those with unspoken concerns.

TEAM DYNAMICS MANAGEMENT, INCLUDING CONFLICT RESOLUTION

Conflict management is a duty shared by the facilitator and the team leader. The facilitator can assist the leader by assuring that creative conflict is not repressed, but encouraged. Explore the underlying reasons for the conflict. If "personality disputes" are involved that threaten to disrupt the team meeting, arrange one-on-one meetings between the parties and attend the meetings to help mediate.

The first step in establishing an effective group is to create a consensus decision rule for the group, namely:

> No judgment may be incorporated into the group decision until it meets at least tacit approval of every member of the group.

This minimum condition for group movement can be facilitated by adopting the following behaviors:

- *Avoid arguing for your own position.* Present it as lucidly and logically as possible, but be sensitive to and consider seriously the reactions of the group in any subsequent presentations of the same point.
- *Avoid "win-lose" stalemates in the discussion of opinions.* Discard the notion that someone must win and someone must lose in the discussion; when impasses occur, look for the next most acceptable alternative for all the parties involved.
- *Avoid changing your mind only to avoid conflict and to reach agreement and harmony.* Withstand pressures to yield which have no objective or logically sound foundation. Strive for enlightened flexibility; but avoid outright capitulation.
- *Avoid conflict-reducing techniques such as the majority vote, averaging, bargaining, coin-flipping, trading out, and the like.* Treat differences of opinion as indicative of an incomplete sharing of relevant information on someone's part, either about task issues, emotional data, or gut level intuitions.

- *View differences of opinion as both natural and helpful rather than as a hindrance in decision-making.* Generally, the more ideas expressed, the greater the likelihood of conflict will be; but the richer the array of resources will be as well.
- *View initial agreement as suspect.* Explore the reasons underlying apparent agreements; make sure people have arrived at the same conclusions for either the same basic reasons or for complementary reasons before incorporating such opinions into the group decision.
- *Avoid subtle forms of influence and decision modification.* E.g., when a dissenting member finally agrees, don't feel that he must be rewarded by having his own way on some subsequent point.
- *Be willing to entertain the possibility that your group can achieve all the foregoing and actually excel at its task.* Avoid doomsaying and negative predictions for group potential.

Collectively, the above steps are sometimes known as the "consensus technique." In tests it was found that 75% of the groups who were instructed in this approach significantly outperformed their best individual resources.

STAGES IN GROUP DEVELOPMENT

Groups of many different types tend to evolve in similar ways. It often helps to know that the process of building an effective group is proceeding normally. Bruce W. Tuckman (1965) identified four stages in the development of a group: forming, storming, norming, and performing.

During the *forming* stage a group tends to emphasize procedural matters. Group interaction is very tentative and polite. The leader dominates the decision-making process and plays a very important role in moving the group forward.

The *storming* stage follows forming. Conflict between members, and between members and the leader, are characteristic of this stage. Members question authority as it relates to the group objectives, structure, or procedures. It is common for the group to resist the attempts of its leader to move them toward independence. Members are trying to define their role in the group.

It is important that the leader deal with the conflict constructively. There are several ways in which this may be done:

- Do not tighten control or try to force members to conform to the procedures or rules established during the forming stage. If disputes over procedures arise, guide the group toward new procedures based on a group consensus.
- Probe for the true reasons behind the conflict and negotiate a more acceptable solution.
- Serve as a mediator between group members.
- Directly confront counterproductive behavior.
- Continue moving the group toward independence from its leader.

During the *norming* stage the group begins taking responsibility, or ownership, of its goals, procedures, and behavior. The focus is on working together efficiently. Group norms are enforced on the group by the group itself.

The final stage is *performing*. Members have developed a sense of pride in the group, its accomplishments, and their role in the group. Members are confident in their ability to contribute to the group and feel free to ask for or give assistance.

COMMON PROBLEMS

Table 1.3 lists some common problems with teams, along with recommended remedial action (Scholtes, 1988).

Table 1.3. Common team problems and remedial action.

PROBLEM	ACTION
Floundering	• Review the plan • Develop a plan for movement
The expert	• Talk to offending party in private • Let the data do the talking • Insist on consensus decisions
Dominating participants	• Structure participation • Balance participation • Act as gate-keeper
Reluctant participants	• Structure participation • Balance participation • Act as gate-keeper
Using opinions instead of facts	• Insist on data • Use scientific method
Rushing things	• Provide constructive feedback • Insist on data • Use scientific method
Attribution (i.e., attributing motives to people with whom we disagree)	• Don't guess at motives • Use scientific method • Provide constructive feedback
Ignoring some comments	• Listen actively • Train team in listening techniques • Speak to offending party in private
Wanderlust	• Follow a written agenda • Restate the topic being discussed
Feuds	• Talk to offending parties in private • Develop or restate ground rules

Member roles and responsibilities
PRODUCTIVE GROUP ROLES

There are two basic types of roles assumed by members of a group: task roles and group maintenance roles. Group task roles are those functions concerned with facilitating and coordinating the group's efforts to select, define, and solve a particular problem. The group task roles shown in Table 1.4 are generally recognized:

Table 1.4. Group task roles.

ROLE I.D.	DESCRIPTION
Initiator	Proposes new ideas, tasks, or goals; suggests procedures or ideas for solving a problem or for organizing the group.
Information seeker	Asks for relevant facts related to the problem being discussed.
Opinion seeker	Seeks clarification of values related to problem or suggestion.
Information giver	Provides useful information about subject under discussion.
Opinion giver	Offers his/her opinion of suggestions made. Emphasis is on values rather than facts.
Elaborator	Gives examples.
Coordinator	Shows relationship among suggestions; points out issues and alternatives.
Orientor	Relates direction of group to agreed-upon goals.
Evaluator	Questions logic behind ideas, usefulness of ideas, or suggestions.
Energizer	Attempts to keep the group moving toward an action.
Procedure technician	Keeps group from becoming distracted by performing such tasks as distributing materials, checking seating, etc.
Recorder	Serves as the group memory.

Group maintenance roles are another type of role played in small groups. Group maintenance roles are aimed at building group cohesiveness and group-centered behavior. Included are those behaviors shown in Table 1.5.

Table 1.5. Group maintenance roles.

ROLE I.D.	DESCRIPTION
Encourager	Offers praise to other members; accepts the contributions of others.
Harmonizer	Reduces tension by providing humor or by promoting reconciliation; gets people to explore their differences in a manner that benefits the entire group.
Compromiser	Assumed when a group member's idea is challenged; admits errors, offers to modify his/her position.
Gate-keeper	Encourages participation, suggests procedures for keeping communication channels open.
Standard setter	Expresses standards for group to achieve, evaluates group progress in terms of these standards.
Observer/commentator	Records aspects of group process; helps group evaluate its functioning.
Follower	Passively accepts ideas of others; serves as audience in group discussions.

The development of task and maintenance roles is a vital part of the team-building process. Team building is defined as the process by which a group learns to function as a unit, rather than as a collection of individuals.

COUNTER-PRODUCTIVE GROUP ROLES

In addition to developing productive group-oriented behavior, it is also important to recognize and deal with individual roles which may block the building of a cohesive and effective team. These roles are shown in Table 1.6.

Table 1.6. Counterproductive group roles.

ROLE I.D.	DESCRIPTION
Aggressor	Expresses disapproval by attacking the values, ideas, or feelings of other. Shows jealousy or envy.
Blocker	Prevents progress by persisting on issues that have been resolved; resists attempts at consensus; opposes without reason.
Recognition-seeker	Calls attention to himself/herself by boasting, relating personal achievements, etc.
Confessor	Uses group setting as a forum to air personal ideologies that have little to do with group values or goals.
Playboy	Displays lack of commitment to group's work by cynicism, horseplay, etc.
Dominator	Asserts authority by interrupting others, using flattery to manipulate, claiming superior status.
Help-seeker	Attempts to evoke sympathy and/or assistance from other members through "poor me" attitude.
Special-interest pleader	Asserts the interests of a particular group. This group's interest matches his/her self-interest.

The leader's role includes that of process observer. In this capacity, the leader monitors the atmosphere during group meetings and the behavior of individuals. The purpose is to identify counterproductive behavior. Of course, once identified, the leader must tactfully and diplomatically provide feedback to the group and its members. The success of SPC is, to a great extent, dependent on the performance of groups.

MANAGEMENT'S ROLE

Perhaps the most important thing management can do for a group is to give it time to become effective. This requires, among other things, that management work to maintain consistent group membership. Group members must not be moved out of the group without very good reason. Nor should there be a constant stream of new people temporarily assigned to the group. If a group is to progress through the four stages described earlier in this chapter, to the crucial performing stage, it will require a great deal of discipline from both the group and management.

Another area where management must help is creating an atmosphere within the company where groups can be effective.

Performance evaluation

Evaluating team performance involves the same principles as evaluating performance in general. Before one can determine how well the team's task has been done, a baseline must be established and goals must be identified. Setting goals using benchmarking and other means is discussed elsewhere in this book (see Chapter 5). Records of progress should be kept as the team pursues its goals.

Performance measures generally focus on group tasks, rather than on internal group issues. Typically, financial performance measures show a payback ratio of between 2:1 and 8:1 on team projects. Some examples of tangible performance measures are:

- productivity
- quality
- cycle time
- grievances
- medical usage (e.g., sick days)
- absenteeism
- service
- turnover
- dismissals
- counseling usage

Many intangibles can also be measured. Some examples of intangibles effected by teams are the following:

- employee attitudes
- customer attitudes
- customer compliments
- customer complaints

The performance of the team process should also be measured. Project failure rates should be carefully monitored. A p chart can be used to evaluate the causes of variation in the proportion of team projects that succeed. Failure analysis should be rigorously conducted. The continuous improvement strategies described in Chapter 1 should be utilized, as should the continuous improvement tools discussed in Chapters 7 thru 9.

Aubrey and Felkins (1988) list the effectiveness measures shown below:

- leaders trained
- number of potential volunteers
- number of actual volunteers
- percent volunteering
- projects started
- projects dropped
- projects completed/approved
- projects completed/rejected
- improved productivity
- improved work environment
- number of teams
- inactive teams
- improved work quality
- improved service
- net annual savings

Team recognition and reward

Recognition is a form of employee motivation in which the company identifies and thanks employees who have made positive contributions to the company's success. In an ideal company, motivation flows from the employees' pride of workmanship. When management enables employees to do their jobs and produce a product or service of excellent quality, there will be motivation.

The reason recognition systems are important is not that they improve work by providing incentives for achievement; rather, they make a statement about what is important to the company. Analyzing a company's employee recognition system provides a powerful insight into the company's values in action. These are the values that are actually driving employee behavior. They are not necessarily the same as management's stated values. For example, a company that claims to value customer satisfaction but recognizes only sales achievements probably does not have customer satisfaction as one of its values in action.

Public recognition is often better for two reasons:

1. Some (but not all) people enjoy being recognized in front of their colleagues.
2. Public recognition communicates a message to all employees about the priorities and function of the organization.

The form of recognition can range from a pat on the back to a small gift to a substantial amount of cash. When substantial cash awards become an established pattern, however, it signals two potential problems:

1. It suggests that several top priorities are competing for the employee's attention, so that a large cash award is required to control the employee's choice.
2. Regular, large cash awards tend to be viewed by the recipients as part of the compensation structure, rather than as a mechanism for recognizing support of key corporate values.

Carder and Clark (1992) list the following guidelines and observations regarding recognition:

Recognition is not a method by which management can manipulate employees. If workers are not performing certain kinds of tasks, establishing a recognition program to raise the priority of those tasks might be inappropriate. Recognition should not be used to get workers to do something they are not currently doing because of conflicting messages from management. A more effective approach is for management to first examine the current system of priorities. Only by working on the system can management help resolve the conflict.

Recognition is not compensation. In this case, the award must represent a significant portion of the employee's regular compensation to have significant impact. Recognition and compensation differ in a variety of ways:

- Compensation levels should be based on long-term considerations such as the employee's tenure of service, education, skills, and level of responsibility. Recognition is based on the specific accomplishments of individuals or groups.
- Recognition is flexible. It is virtually impossible to reduce pay levels once they are set, and it is difficult and expensive to change compensation plans.
- Recognition is more immediate. It can be given in timely fashion and therefore relate to specific accomplishments.
- Recognition is personal. It represents a direct and personal contact between employee and manager.

Recognition should be personal. Recognition should not be carried out in such a manner that implies that people of more importance (managers) are giving something to people of less importance (workers).

Positive reinforcement is not always a good model for recognition. Just because the manager is using a certain behavioral criterion for providing recognition, it doesn't mean that the recipient will perceive the same relationship between behavior and recognition.

Employees should not believe that recognition is based primarily on luck. An early sign of this is cynicism. Employees believe that management says one thing but does another.

Recognition meets a basic human need. Recognition, especially public recognition, meets the needs for belonging and self-esteem. In this way, recognition can play an important function in the workplace. According to Maslow's theory, until these needs for belonging and self-esteem are satisfied, self-actualizing needs such as pride in work, feelings of accomplishment, personal growth, and learning new skills will not come into play.

Recognition programs should not create winners and losers. Recognition programs should not recognize one group of individuals time after time while never recognizing another group. This creates a static ranking system, with all of the problems discussed earlier.

Recognition should be given for efforts, not just for goal attainment. According to Imai (1986), a manager who understands that a wide variety of behaviors are essential to the company will be interested in criteria of discipline, time management, skill development, participation, morale, and communication, as well as direct revenue production. To be able to effectively use recognition to achieve business goals, managers must develop the ability to measure and recognize such process accomplishments.

Employee involvement is essential in planning and executing a recognition program. It is essential to engage in extensive planning before instituting a recognition program or before changing a bad one. The perceptions and expectations of employees must be surveyed.

PRINCIPLES OF EFFECTIVE REWARD SYSTEMS

Kohn (1993) believes that nearly all existing reward systems share the following characteristics:

1. They punish the recipients.
2. They rupture relationships.
3. They ignore reasons for behavior.
4. They discourage risk-taking.

Most existing reward systems (including many compensation systems) are an attempt by management to manipulate the behaviors of employees. Kohn convincingly demonstrates, through solid academic research into the effects of rewards, that people who receive the rewards as well as those who hand them out suffer a *loss* of incentive—hardly the goal of the exercise!

Rather than provide cookbook solutions to the problem of rewards and incentives, Kohn offers some simple guidelines to consider when designing reward systems.

1. *Abolish incentive pay* (something Deming advocated as well). Hertzberg's hygiene theory tells us that money is not a motivator, but it can be a *de*motivator. Pay people generously and equitably, then do everything in your power to put money out of the employee's mind.

2. *Reevaluate evaluation.* Review performance appraisals and alternatives. (Benneyan, 1994)

3. *Create conditions for authentic motivation.* Money is no substitute for the real thing—interesting work. Here are some principles to use to make work more interesting:

   a. *Design interesting jobs.* Give teams projects that are intrinsically motivating, e.g., meaningful, challenging, achievable.

   b. *Collaborative.* Help employees work together, then provide the support needed to make it possible for the teams to accomplish their goals.

   c. *Freedom.* Trust people to make the right choices. Encourage them when they make mistakes.

2

Six Sigma
Training and Education

Although the terms are loosely synonymous, a distinction can be made between *training* and *education*. The dictionary defines the two terms as follows:

Educate

1. To develop the innate capacities of, especially by schooling or instruction.
2. To stimulate or develop the mental or moral growth of.

Train

1. To coach in or accustom to a mode of behavior or performance.
2. To make proficient with specialized instruction and practice.

Education is seen to be more general and more focused on mental processes. In other words, education teaches people how to *think*. It enhances the mind's ability to deal with reality. Education is more theoretical and conceptual in nature. The *essentials* of past knowledge are taught for the purpose of teaching students how to appraise new events and situations. Education equips students to acquire new knowledge. Generally, people bring a certain *educational background* to their job with them. Employers typically fund ongoing education of employees, but they do not usually provide it for the employees. Education is more likely the responsibility of the individual employee, possibly because education is more generally applicable and more "portable" than is training. Thus, the employee's education is readily transferable to new employers.

Training focuses more on *doing*. Training is more job-focused than education. The emphasis is on maintaining or improving skills needed to perform the current job, or on acquiring new job skills. Training is usually paid for, and often provided, by the employer. Often, training is employer-specific and the skills acquired may not always transfer readily to another employer.

Quality improvement requires change, and change starts with people. People change when they understand why they must change and how they must change to meet their own personal goals. People join organizations because doing so helps them meet certain of their own goals. Conversely, organizations hire people to help achieve the organization's goals. When organizations set new goals they are, in effect, asking their employees to think differently, to perform new tasks, and to engage in new behaviors. Organizations must be prepared to help employees acquire the knowledge, skills, and abilities (KSAs) required by these new expectations. Training and education are the means by which these new KSAs are acquired.

Like all work, training and education is a process. The sequence of steps in this process follows (Johnson, 1993b, pp. 239–240):

1. Consider the training objectives.
2. Develop a training plan.
   a. The training plan must dovetail with other company plans such as strategic quality, business, and market plans, and it must be supported by the budget.
   b. It must match the organization's training objectives.
   c. It must be planned around available assets.
   d. It must meet organizational goals.
   e. Individual lesson plans must be developed as required.
3. Select the training team. The trainer must:
   a. Be interested in training.
   b. Be committed to quality.
   c. Enjoy people.
   d. Have patience.

   e. Want the training assignment.
   f. Be empathetic.
   g. Be willing to train to the audience's level.
   h. Be respected by colleagues.
   i. Have time for training and training preparation.
4. Prepare the trainers.
   a. Provide training for the trainer:
      1. In-house
      2. Outside sources—seminars, Toastmasters
   b. Provide training methods:
      1. Lecture or presentation
      2. On-the-job
      3. Demonstration
      4. Self-study
      5. Role playing
      6. Case studies
      7. Discussion
   c. Practice actual training exercises.
   d. Critique trainer and training material.
5. Prepare trainees.
   a. Emphasize the benefit to the employee.
   b. Make clear how it will improve the organization and its quality.
   c. Make clear any requirements that will transpire as result of the training.
6. Train.
7. Evaluate the training.
   a. Did training meet the objectives?
   b. Trainees can be surveyed about training.
   c. Work processes and quality can be reviewed for improvement.
   d. Trainees can be tested on training.
   e. Results can be tabulated to improve on future training.

IMPORTANCE OF TOP-DOWN SUPPORT AND STRATEGIC PLANNING FOR QUALITY TRAINING

In the traditional organization, the training department is another "silo," with its own budget and special interests to protect. In this system the training plans are often not tied to strategic plans. Instead, these plans tend to serve the needs of the trainers and others in the training department, rather than serving the needs of the organization as a whole. The effect on the organization's performance is the same when any organizational unit pursues its own best interest rather than the organization's interests: negative return on investment, damaged morale, etc.

Six Sigma organizations take a different approach entirely. The training plans of these organizations are tied directly to the current and future needs of external customers. These needs are, in turn, the driver behind the organization's strategic plan. The people who develop the strategic plan also develop the strategic training plan. The strategic training plan provides the means of developing the knowledge, skills, and abilities that will be needed by employees in the organization in the future. Of course, training is also provided for the maintenance of skills used on a daily basis. Training executives in the modern organizations report directly to senior leadership, reflecting the greater degree of importance placed on human resource development in modern organizations.

The chief deliverable of the planning process is the annual training plan. The annual training plan is a step in the implementation of the longer-term strategic training plan. The plan's focus is neither internal nor external, rather it spans the entire process. The plan makes provision for training of suppliers, employees, and customers. New product training is also included.

The annual training plan includes a budget which lists those resources that are required to provide the training. The training budget traditionally includes a brief cost/benefit analysis. Cost/benefit analysis for training, as for all expenditures for intangibles, is challenging. Estimating cost is usually simple enough. Examples of training costs include:

- trainer salaries
- consulting fees
- classroom space and materials
- lost time from the job
- staff salaries
- office space of training staff

Estimating *benefits* with the same degree of precision is problematic. It is usually counterproductive to attempt to get high precision in such estimates. Instead, most organizations settle for rough figures on the value of the trainee to the company. Some examples of training benefit include:

- improved efficiency
- improved quality
- increased customer satisfaction
- improved employee morale
- lower employee turnover
- increased supplier loyalty

Training budgets are tangible evidence of management support for the goals expressed in the training plan. In addition, management support is demonstrated by participating in the development of the strategic training plan. In most cases, senior management delegates the development of annual training plans and budgets to the training department staff.

TRAINING SUBGROUPS AND TOPICS
Management training—general quality principles

In an organization truly committed to quality, every manager is, in a sense, a "quality manager." Quality management includes the elements shown in Figure 2.1

I. QUALITY STANDARDS
  A. Total Quality Management (TQM)
  B. Continuous Process Improvement
  C. Cycle-Time Reduction
  D. Supplier Management
  E. Customer Service
  F. Quality Award/Quality Standards Criteria (for example, Baldrige Award, ISO-9000)

II. ORGANIZATIONS AND THEIR FUNCTIONS
  A. Organizational Assessment
  B. Organizational Structures (for example, matrix, hierarchical)
  C. Quality Functions within the Organization
  D. Communication within the Organization
  E. Change Agents and Their Effects on Organizations
  F. Management Styles (for example, by facts and data, by coaching/other leadership styles)
  G. Business Functions

III. QUALITY NEEDS AND OVERALL STRATEGIC PLANS
  A. Linkage between Quality Function Needs and Overall Strategic Plan
  B. Linkage between Strategic Plan and Quality Plan
  C. Theory of Variation (common and special causes)
  D. Quality Function Mission
  E. Priority of Quality Function within the Organization
  F. Metrics and Goals that Drive Organizational Performance
  G. Formulation of Quality Principles and Policies
  H. Resource Requirements to Manage the Quality Function

IV. CUSTOMER SATISFACTION AND FOCUS
  A. Types of Customers (for example, internal, external, end-user)
  B. Elements of Customer-Driven Organizations
  C. Customer Expectations, Priorities, Needs, and "Voice"
  D. Customer Relationship Management and Commitment (for example, complaints, feedback, guarantees, corrective actions)
  E. Customer Identification and Segmentation
  F. Partnership and Alliances Between Customers and Suppliers

Figure 2.1—*Continued on next page . . .*

Figure 2.1—*Continued* . . .

    G. Communication Techniques (for example, surveys, focus groups, satisfaction/complaint cards)

    H. Multiple-Customer Management and Conflict Resolution

    I. Customer Retention/Loyalty

V. PROJECT MANAGEMENT

    A. Planning

    B. Implementation

VI. CONTINUOUS IMPROVEMENT

    A. Tools

    B. Cost of Quality

    C. Process Improvement

    D. Trend Analysis

    E. Measurement Issues

    F. Concurrent Engineering and Process Mapping

VII. HUMAN RESOURCE MANAGEMENT

    A. Leadership Roles and Responsibilities

    B. Quality Staffing Issues

    C. Quality Responsibilities in Job/Position Descriptions

    D. Post-Training Evaluation and Reinforcement

    E. Team Formation and Evolution

    F. Team Management

VIII. TRAINING AND EDUCATION

    A. Importance of Top-Down Support and Strategic Planning for Quality Training

    B. Training Subgroups and Topics

    C. Training-Needs Analysis

    D. Post-training Evaluation and Reinforcement

    E. Tools

Figure 2.1. Elements of quality management.

LEADERSHIP TRAINING

Leaders should receive guidance in the art of "visioning." Visioning involves the ability to develop a mental image of the organization at a future time. The future organization will more closely approximate the ideal organization, where "ideal" is defined as that organization which completely achieves the organization's values. How will such an organization "look?" What will its employees do? Who will be its customers? How will it behave towards its customers, employees, and suppliers? Developing a lucid image of this organization will help the leader see how to proceed with the primary duty of transforming the present organization. Without such an image in mind, the executive will lead the organization through a maze with a thousand dead-ends. Conversely, with a vision as a guide, the transformation process will proceed on course. This is not to say that the transformation is ever "easy." But when there is a leader with a vision, it's as if the organization is following an expert scout through hostile territory. The path is clear, but the journey is still difficult.

Leaders need to be masters of communication. Fortunately, most leaders already possess outstanding communication skills; few rise to the top without them. However, training in effective communication is still wise, even if it is only refresher training for some. Also, when large organizations are involved, communications training should include mass communication media, such as video, radio broadcasts, print media, etc. Communicating with customers, investors, and suppliers differs from communicating with employees and colleagues, and special training is often required. Communication principles are discussed in the previous chapter.

When an individual has a vision of where he wants to go, he can pursue this vision directly. However, when dealing with an organization, simply having a clear vision is not enough. The leader must *communicate* the vision to the other members of the organization. Communicating a vision is a much different task than communicating instructions or concrete ideas. Visions of organizations that embody abstract values are necessarily abstract in nature. To effectively convey the vision to others, the leader must convert the abstractions to concretes. One way to do this is by living the vision. The leader demonstrates these values in every action taken, every decision made, the meetings attended or ignored, and behavior at meetings whether paying rapt attention or doodling absentmindedly on a notepad. Employees who are trying to understand the leader's vision will pay close attention to the behavior of the leader.

Another way to communicate abstract ideas is to tell stories. In organizations there is a constant flow of events. Customers encounter the organization through employees and systems; suppliers meet with engineers; literally thousands of events take place every day. From time-to-time an event occurs that captures the essence of the leader's vision. A clerk provides exceptional customer service; an engineer takes a risk and makes a mistake; a supplier keeps the line running through a mighty effort. These are concrete examples of what the leader wants the future organization to become. These stories should be repeated to others and the people publicly recognized who made the stories. The leader should also create stories, even if it requires staging an event. There is nothing dishonest about creating a situation with powerful symbolic meaning and using it to communicate a vision. For example, Nordstrom has a story about a sales clerk who accepted a customer return of a defective tire. This story has tremendous symbolic meaning because Nordstrom doesn't sell tires! The story illustrates Nordstrom's policy of allowing employees to use their own best judgment in all situations, even if they make "mistakes," and of going the extra mile to satisfy customers. However, it is doubtful that the event ever occurred. This is irrelevant. When employees hear this story during their orientation training, the message is clear. The story serves its purpose of clearly communicating an otherwise confusing abstraction.

Leaders need training in conflict resolution. In their role as process owner in a traditional organization, leaders preside over a report-based hierarchy trying to deliver value through processes that cut across several functional areas.

The inevitable result is competition for limited resources, which creates conflict. Of course, the ideal solution is to resolve the conflict by designing organizations where there is no such destructive competition. Until then, the leader can expect to find a brisk demand for conflict-resolution services.

Finally, leaders should demonstrate strict adherence to ethical principles. Leadership involves trust, and trust isn't granted to one who violates a moral code that allows people to live and work together. Honesty, integrity, and other moral virtues should be second-nature to the leader.

MANAGEMENT TRAINING

Leadership involves taking the organization to a future where the organization's members behave differently than they do today. Management involves operating existing systems to deliver value to customers, and improving these systems to provide better value. The skills involved in management are different than those needed to lead the organization. This is why, at times, effective managers make poor leaders and vice-versa.

Managers design processes. Processes combine material and human resources in a particular way to add value. Effectively performing this task requires a background in organization theory and development, theory of motivation, job design, and performance evaluation. While background in these areas is typically part of the requirement for employment as a manager, managers should receive continuous training in all of these areas to maintain and enhance their skills.

In addition to the traditional skills, managers in modern quality-focused organizations also need excellent interpersonal skills. These skills are employed in a variety of roles, such as:

Coaching—A coach doesn't simply tell the players what to do, he or she helps them do it. A baseball pitching coach studies the theory of pitching and the individual pitcher and provides guidance on how to hold the ball, the windup, the delivery, etc. The coach is constantly trying to find ways to help the pitcher do a better job.

Mentoring—The manager-mentor understands the organization to such a degree that he has acquired wisdom regarding the way it works. This allows him to see relationships that are not apparent to the employee. The mentor helps the employee avoid organizational obstacles and to negotiate the barriers.

Negotiation—Managers must negotiate with others in the organization, as well as with suppliers and customers, to acquire the resources necessary to accomplish the department's goals. Obtaining these resources without engendering ill-will requires negotiating skill.

Conflict resolution—Like the leader, the manager is responsible for the work of many people. When these people cannot resolve their own differences, the manager must provide guidance.

Managers should also receive training in the fundamentals of accounting and finance. This information is essential to such activities as cost-benefit analysis, budgeting, and quality costs.

Finally, managers should possess certain technical skills that are crucial to their ability to carry out quality improvement projects. This includes the quality control and quality management tools described in Chapter 7. Managers must understand enough about measurement issues in the social sciences to be able to monitor the effectiveness of their employee and customer initiatives (see Chapter 4). Deming lists an understanding of theory of variation as one of the cornerstones of his system of profound knowledge. This requires rudimentary statistical skills. Managers without this training will misdiagnose problems, see trends where none exist, overreact to random variation, and in general make poor decisions.

Employee training—implementation of quality plans

Training should be driven by the organization's needs, which are well understood by the senior leadership. The best way to do this, from a training perspective, is to have the senior leaders conduct the training personally. The primary purpose of training by senior leaders is to communicate the relationship of the training to the organization's mission. Effective leaders will have developed a clear vision of the way the organization will look at some future date, a plan to get there, and a commitment to the plan. This should all be communicated through training conducted by the leaders themselves.

Train-the-trainer programs are quite popular as a way of "leveraging" limited training talent. With more trainers, more people can be trained in a shorter time. However, as Deming pointed out, something is lost when the master trains the trainer who trains the student, etc. Deming's funnel experiments show that the result is to move further and further away from the correct message (off to the "milky way"). Training should be conducted by training masters. Technology such as videotape, CD ROM, cable systems, etc., can provide a means for reaching large numbers of people. It is possible to have interactive training conducted electronically.

Many companies, for example, Ford Motor Company, believe that technology is easily transferred from one organization to the next, while the knowledge and experience of employees is much more difficult to transfer. This gives the organization an edge over its competitors that cannot be quickly overcome.

When quality improvement plans are implemented, the nature of the work being done changes. People involved in or impacted by the new approach must receive two different types of training: conceptual and task-based.

Conceptual training involves explanation of the TQM principles driving the change and a shift from an internal, product-based perspective to a customer and process-based focus. Rather than viewing their jobs in isolation, employees must be taught to see all work as a process, connected to other processes in a system. Rather than a goal of "control," where activities are done the same way indefinitely, employees learn that continuous improvement is to be the norm, with processes constantly being changed for the better. The PDCA cycle discussed in Chapter 1 is helpful here. Such ideas are radically different and difficult to assimilate. Patient repetition and "walking the talk" are essential elements of such training.

Conceptual training also involves teaching employees the basics of problem-solving. Data-driven process improvement demands an understanding of the fundamentals of data collection and analysis. The quality control tools discussed in Chapter 8 and the quality management tools discussed in Chapter

7 must be understood by all employees involved in implementing the new approach.

When jobs are reintegrated, the duties expected of each employee change, often radically. Task-based training is necessary to help employees acquire and maintain new skills and proficiencies. Employees are given new responsibilities for self-control of process quality. To effectively handle these new responsibilities employees must learn to use information in ways they never did before. Often employees are asked to help design new information systems, enter data, use computer terminals to access information, read computer output, make management presentations, etc. These skills must be acquired through training and experience. Quality plans that do not include adequate employee training are commonplace, and a primary cause of the high rate of failure of quality plans.

Facilitator training

The duties of the facilitator are described in Chapter 1. These techniques require that the facilitator possess certain unique skills. It is unlikely that an individual who is not a facilitator will already possess the needed skills. Thus, it is likely that facilitator training will be needed.

A good part of the facilitator's job involves communicating with people who are working on teams. This role involves the following skills:

Communication skills—Quite simply, the facilitator who cannot communicate well is of little use to the modern organization.

Meeting management skills—Schedule the meeting well ahead of time. Be sure that key people are invited and that they plan to attend. Prepare an agenda and stick to it! Start on time. State the purpose of the meeting clearly at the outset. Take minutes. Summarize from time-to-time. Actively solicit input from those less talkative. Curtail the overly talkative members. Manage conflicts. Make assignments and responsibilities explicit and specific. End on time.

Presentation skills—Know the reason for speaking to this audience (inform/educate or convince/persuade); perform the task; solicit the desired audience response.

Presentation preparation—Prepare a list of every topic to be covered. Cull the list to those select few ideas that are most important. Number the points. Analyze each major point. Summarize.

Use of visual aids—A visual aid in a speech is a pictorial used by a speaker to convey an idea. Well-designed visual aids add power to a presentation by showing the idea more clearly and easily than words alone. Whereas only 10% of presented material is retained from a verbal presentation after 3 days, 65% is retained when the verbal presentation is accompanied by a visual aid. However, if the visual aids are not properly designed, they can be distracting and even counterproductive. ASQ reports that poor visuals generate more negative comment from conference attendees than any other item.

Facilitators must be sensitive to non-verbal communication. There is much more to communication than mere words. Facilitators should carefully observe posture and body movements, facial expressions, tone of voice, fidgeting, etc. If the facilitator sees these non-verbal signals he should use them to determine whether or not to intervene. For example, a participant who shakes his head when hearing a particular message should be asked to verbalize the reasons why he disagrees with the speaker. A person whose voice tone indicates sarcasm should be asked to explain his attitude. A wallflower who is squirming during a presentation should be asked to tell the group her thoughts.

Facilitators should be active listeners. Active listening involves certain key behaviors:

- Look at the speaker.
- Concentrate on what the speaker is saying, not on how you will respond to it.
- Wait until the speaker is finished before responding.
- Focus on the main idea, rather than on insignificant details.
- Keep emotional reactions under control.

Because all of the work of facilitators involves groups, facilitators should have an in-depth understanding of group dynamics and the team process (see Chapter 1). Also, because the groups and teams involved are usually working on quality improvement projects, the facilitator should be well versed in project management principles and techniques (see Chapter 5).

TRAINING NEEDS ANALYSIS

The first step in the development of the strategic training plan is a training needs assessment. The training needs assessment provides the background necessary for designing the training program and preparing the training plan. The assessment proceeds by performing a task-by-task audit to determine what the organization is doing, and comparing it to what the organization should be doing. The assessment process focuses on three major areas:

Process audit—As stated numerous times, all work is a process. Processes are designed to add values to inputs and deliver values to customers as outputs. Are they operating as designed? Are they operated consistently? Are they measured at key control points? If so, do the measurements show statistical control? The answers to these questions, along with detailed observations of how the process is operated, are input to the development of the training plan.

Assessment of knowledge, skills and abilities—In all probability, there will be deficiencies (opportunities for improvement) observed during the process audits. Some of these deficiencies will involve employee knowledge, skills, or abilities (KSAs). The first principle of self-control is that employees must know what they are doing. Management's job doesn't end by simply giving an employee responsibility for a particular process or task; management must also provide the employee with the opportunity to acquire the KSAs necessary to successfully perform their new duties. This means that if the employee is asked to assume new duties as a member of a quality improvement team, they are given training in team skills; if they are to keep a control chart, they receive training in the maintenance and interpretation of the charts, etc. Since employees are expected to contribute to the implementation of the organization's strategic plan, they should be told what the plan is, and how their job contributes to the plan.

Assessment of employee attitudes—Attitudes are emotions that reflect a response to something taking place. A person's attitude is, in essence, a judgment about the wisdom of a particular course of events. Negative employee attitudes also cause less effective utilization of the employee's KSAs. Negative employee attitudes about the direction being taken by the organization indicate that the employee either questions the wisdom of the proposed changes, or doubts the sincerity of the leadership. Regardless, it represents a problem that must be addressed by the training plan.

The assessments above can be conducted using audits or the survey techniques described in Chapter 3. Assessments can be conducted by either internal or external personnel. In general, employees are more likely to be open and honest when confidentiality is assured, which is more likely when assessments are conducted by outside parties. However, internal assessments can reveal valuable information if proper safeguards are observed to assure the employee's privacy.

It is important that follow-up assessments be made to determine if the training conducted closed the gap between the "is" and the "should be." The follow up will also provide a basis for additional training. Reassessment should be conducted first to assure that the desired KSAs were acquired by the target group of employees, then the process should be reassessed to determine if the new KSAs improved the process as predicted. It's common to discover that a mistake was made in assuming that the root cause of the process "is/should-be" gap is a KSA deficiency. If the reassessments indicate that the KSA gap was closed but the process gap persists, another approach must be taken to close the process gap.

POST-TRAINING EVALUATION AND REINFORCEMENT

Training is said to have "worked" if it accomplishes its objectives. Since the training objectives are (or should be) derived from the strategic plan, the ultimate test is whether or not the organization has accomplished its strategic objectives. However, training is only one of dozens of factors that determine if an organization accomplishes its strategic objectives, and one that is often far removed in time from the final result. To assess training effectiveness more direct measures of success are needed, with measurements near the time the training has been completed.

Except in academic settings, imparting knowledge or wisdom is seldom the ultimate goal of training. Instead, it is assumed that the knowledge or wisdom will result in improved judgments, lower costs, better quality, higher levels of customer satisfaction, etc. In other words, the training will produce *observable* results. These results were the focus of the training plan development and training needs analysis described earlier in this chapter. Training evaluation requires that they be converted to training measurables or objectives.

Regardless of the format of the presentation, the basic unit of training is the *lesson*. A lesson is a discrete "chunk" of information to be conveyed to a learner. The training objectives form the basis of each lesson, and the lessons provide guidance for development of measurements of success.

Lesson plans (see below) provide the basis for measurement at the lowest level. The objectives in the lesson plan are specific and the lesson is designed to accomplish these specific objectives. The assumption is made that by accomplishing the set of objectives for each lesson, the objectives of the seminar or other training activity will be met. A further assumption is made that by meeting the objectives of all of the training activities, the objectives of the training plan will be met. Finally, it is assumed that by meeting the objectives of the training plan, the objectives of the strategic plan (or strategic quality plan) will be met, or at least will not be compromised due to training inadequacies. All of these assumptions should be subjected to evaluation.

EVALUATION

The evaluation process involves four elements (Kirkpatrick, 1996):

1. **Reaction**—How well did the conferees like the program? This is essentially customer satisfaction measurement. Reaction is usually measured using comment sheets, surveys, focus groups and other customer communication techniques. See Chapter 3 for additional information.

2. **Learning**—What principles, facts, and techniques were learned? What attitudes were changed? It is entirely possible that conferees react favorably to training, even if learning does not occur. The learning of each conferee should be quantified using pre- and post-tests to identify learning imparted by the training. Results should be analyzed using proper statistical methods. In exceptional cases, e.g., evaluating a consulting company for a large training contract, a formal designed experiment may be justified.

3. **Behavior**—What changes in behavior on-the-job occurred? If the conferee leaves the SPC seminar and immediately begins to effectively apply control charts where none were used before, then the training had the desired effect on behavior. However, if the conferee's tests indicate that competence was gained in the subject matter from the training, but no change in behavior took place, the training investment was wasted. Note that behavior change is dependent on a great number of factors besides the training; e.g., management must create systems where the newly learned behaviors are encouraged.

4. **Results**—What were the tangible results of the program in terms of reduced cost, improved quality, improved quantity, etc.? This is the real payback on the training investment. The metrics used for measuring results are typically built into the action plans, project plans, budgets, etc. Again, as with behavior change, there are many factors other than training that produce the desired results.

Phillips adds a fifth item to the above list (Phillips, 1996, p. 316):

5. **Return on investment**—Did the monetary value of the results exceed the cost for the program?

Phillips considers these five items to be different *levels* of evaluation. Each evaluation level has a different value, as shown in Figure 2.2.

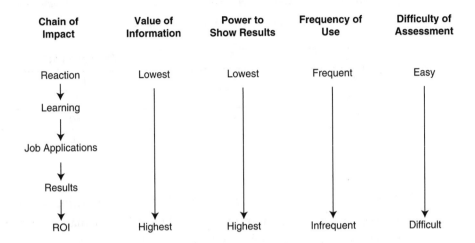

Chain of Impact	Value of Information	Power to Show Results	Frequency of Use	Difficulty of Assessment
Reaction	Lowest	Lowest	Frequent	Easy
Learning				
Job Applications				
Results				
ROI	Highest	Highest	Infrequent	Difficult

Figure 2.2. Characteristics of evaluation levels.

From Phillips, J.J. (1996). "Measuring the Results of Training," in Craig, R.L., editor in chief. *The ASTD Training & Development Handbook: A Guide to Human Resources Development.* New York: McGraw-Hill, p. 317.

Due to the difficulty and cost involved, it is impractical and uneconomical to insist that every program be evaluated at all five levels. Sampling can be used to obtain evaluations at the higher levels. As an example, one large electric utility set the following sampling targets.

Table 2.1. Targets for percentages of programs to be evaluated.

From Phillips, J.J. (1996). "Measuring the Results of Training," in Craig, R.L., editor in chief. *The ASTD Training & Development Handbook: A Guide to Human Resources Development.* New York: McGraw-Hill, p. 317.

LEVEL	PERCENTAGE
Participant's satisfaction	100
Learning	70
On-the-job-applications (behavior)	50
Results	10
ROI	5

Where sampling is used, programs should be selected using a randomization procedure such as random numbers tables. ROI calculations are not difficult and they are described in Chapter 4. However, to make the results credible, finance and accounting personnel should be involved in calculating financial ratios of this type.

REINFORCEMENT

When the subject of reinforcement is raised, monetary remuneration usually comes to mind first. Skill-based pay is gaining favor in some quarters for a variety of reasons:

- as encouragement to employees to acquire additional skills
- as reward for people for training and education
- as a reaction to the negative aspects of performance-based pay

While skill-based pay may have merit, cash awards and other such "rewards" are of dubious value and should probably not be used. Rather than assuming that employees will only engage in training if they receive an immediate tangible reward, research and experience indicate that most employees find value in training that helps them better achieve their personal, job, and career goals. Thus, reinforcement is accomplished by providing the trainee with the opportunity to use the skills learned. Proficiency is gained with practice soon after the learning has taken place. Management should provide an environment where the new skills can be honed without pressure and distraction. The "just-in-time" (JIT) principle applies here. Don't provide training for skills that won't be used in the near future.

People who have just learned something new, be it a job skill or a new philosophy such as quality-focus, often have questions arise as they attempt to integrate their new knowledge into their daily thoughts and routine. User groups are very helpful. A user group consists of a number of people who have received similar training. User groups meet from time to time to discuss their understanding of the material with others. The focus of the group varies from "How are you using this?" to "I don't understand this" to "Here's what I am doing!" At times, well-versed speakers will be invited to clarify particular aspects of the subject. Presentations of successful applications may be made. Management can encourage user groups by providing facilities, helping with administrative details, and, especially, by attending meetings on occasion.

Electronic forums are gaining in popularity. Trainers will often make themselves available to answer questions via e-mail. Forum subscribers will send their questions or comments to a "list server." The list server then automatically broadcasts the question or comment to other subscribers on the list. Every subscriber receives every user's message, along with the responses to the message. This often produces "threads." A thread is an exchange of information on a particular topic. E.g., subscriber A has a question about using control charts on financial data, subscriber B responds, then C responds to B and so on. These threads look remarkably like a free-wheeling face-to-face discussion. The result is that a great deal of learning takes place in a format that everyone finds to be more natural (and more interesting) than a traditional classroom environment.

REFRESHERS

Learning that isn't used right away tends to fade. Even when just-in-time training (JITT) is used, it is unlikely that every skill will be put to immediate and routine use. It is wise to plan for periodic refresher courses to hone the skills acquired during prior training. A refresher course is usually shorter, faster, and more intense than new learning. Instructors need not have the same subject matter mastery as those teaching new material. In fact, it may not even be necessary to have an instructor available. Media such as video and audio tape programs, CD ROM, slide presentations, etc., may be sufficient. These self-study media offer a number of cost and scheduling advantages.

If in-house instructors are used, they may be available to answer occasional questions from previous trainees. Of course, when the instructor is not a full-time trainer, this must be strictly limited. There are a number of ways to reduce the demands on the trainer's time while still answering most of the questions from participants. If the need is not urgent, the question may be asked using mail or an online forum. House newsletters or bulletins can be used to provide answers to frequently asked questions. More companies now have "intranets" where such information is made available. The trainee may be able to find an Internet news group devoted to the subject of concern. There are thousands of news groups covering a huge variety of subjects, many relating to quality and training.

TOOLS

This section covers some of the technical aspects of effective training and education. However, the reader should understand that training and education are, in essence, *communication.*

Lectures, workbooks, case studies, on-the-job training

TYPES OF INSTRUCTION

There are three basic types of instructional formats:

1. **Learner-centered instruction**—Learner-centered instruction begins with the needs of the learner and tailors the course accordingly. This approach creates challenges for instructors and administrators when learners bring a wide variety of abilities, backgrounds, and needs to the class. Barring strong reasons to the contrary, this approach should be the first choice for most training programs.

2. **Instructor-centered**—The instructor determines the direction and pace of the learning. Instructor-centered training takes a "one size fits all" approach to learning. Since student-to-student variability exists, this approach fails a high percentage of students.

3. **Material-centered**—This includes most self-paced instruction such as programmed learning, interactive CD ROM, videotape, etc. Students trained using this approach have no instructor with whom they interact.

LESSON PLANS

Lesson plans are "roadmaps" of the training material to be presented during a particular training session. Johnson (1993b) provides the following guidelines for developing lesson plans:

1. Lesson plans are crucial for training success.
2. Every subject must be adequately researched.
3. Develop twice as much material as you think you will need.

4. Ensure trainees know "what's in it for me" early on so they are motivated to learn.
5. Practice, practice, practice prior to presentation.
6. Use examples that pertain to the operation where possible.
7. Stimulate questions.
8. Use training aids.
9. Adapt the training to the group's level.
10. Never make excuses (e.g., "I've never taught this material before.").
11. Remain positive.
12. Follow your lesson plan.

There are four main types of lesson plans:
- **Topical outline**—A lesson plan set up in a standard outline format, i.e., major sections are identified using Roman numerals, topics by upper case letters, etc. This is most useful when the instructor is intimately familiar with the subject matter and has presented it previously. These lesson plans are easy to construct and can be used as agendas to help keep the class oriented.
- **Manuscript**—Lessons are described in prose in detail. This is most useful when teaching complex subjects for the first time. While this format provides a lot of information, the sheer volume of information may make it difficult to locate specific information when required. Careful organization (e.g., tab indexing) is essential. Development time can be considerable.
- **Sentence**—This is an abbreviated version of the manuscript type of lesson plan and is used for less complex subjects. While providing less information than the manuscript format, this approach is easier to prepare and it is less difficult to find the information.
- **Key word**—This is a "memory jogger" for the experienced instructor to use to pace the presentation and assure that all subjects are covered. This type of lesson plan normally does not provide information on sequence or time-per-topic. This "quick-and-dirty" approach provides little detail and should not be used unless the instructor is intimately familiar with

the material. An advantage to this approach is that it tends to produce less formal presentations.

EXAMPLE OF A LESSON PLAN

The lesson plan in Figure 2.3 was actually used by the author to conduct in-house training for a client, an integrated health-care provider. The lessons in the lesson plan were selected from a longer seminar that was provided to another group of employees. The lesson numbers were left as they were in the longer seminar to allow this group of trainees to easily cross-reference their learning with others who had taken the complete course. (Only a portion of the lesson plan is shown here.)

HEALTHCARE QUALITY IMPROVEMENT SEMINAR

This document describes the seminar to be conducted for Healthcare of Arizona by Thomas Pyzdek, an internationally known author, lecturer, and consultant on quality. The seminar will be conducted on Friday, May 5 and Monday, May 15, 1995. The seminar's objective is to provide participants with the knowledge and skills necessary to systematically improve quality and productivity in their area of responsibility. Participants will learn the principles of variation and understand the importance of these principles to all decision-making.

DAY #1
Lesson 4. DATA COLLECTION
Approximate start: Day 1, 8 a.m.
Approximate duration: 1:00 hour total
Objectives
- understand the importance of data collection
- learn to locate existing data
- know how to validate data
- know how to construct data collection sheets
- understand the different types of data and their uses
- know how data-collection activities typically occur in quality improvement

---

Figure 2.3—*Continued on next page . . .*

Figure 2.3—*Continued . . .*

Key topics
- why collect data
- sources of data
- obtaining new data
- variables, attributes, and ordinal data
- data collection tools
- layout of data sheets
- location diagrams
- check sheets

Discussion

The process generates data that can be used to facilitate continuous improvement. Knowing what data to look for and where to look for the data makes valuable information accessible to the quality team and utilizes existing data to maximum advantage.

Lesson plan

0:30   Tom Pyzdek lecture
0:30   IS department presentation

Lesson 7. FUNDAMENTAL CONCEPTS OF STATISTICAL CONTROL
Approximate start: Day 1, 9:00 a.m.
Approximate duration: 1:30
Objectives
- understand the difference between variation from special causes and variation from common causes
- understand the effect of tampering with a controlled process
- understand the concept of distributions
- know how to represent variation in a process
- understand the difference between problem prevention and problem management
- understand why meeting requirements isn't good enough to remain competitive
- understand the meaning of the term "requirements"
- understand the value of managing processes rather than managing outcomes

---

Figure 2.3—*Continued on next page . . .*

Figure 2.3—*Continued . . .*

---

     directly

Key topics

- history of SPC
- special and common causes
- distributions; normal distribution
- central-limit theorem
- measures of central tendency; measures of dispersion
- prevention-versus-detection strategies
- process control and continuous improvement versus meeting requirements
- Taguchi's loss function concept as a rationale for continuous improvement

Discussion

    This lesson presents the fundamental principles of variation and relates these principles to the philosophy of continuous improvement. Several populations are represented using colored chips to illustrate the distribution concepts of central tendency, shape, and spread. After presentation of the material, participants will be given an in-class exercise and a quiz.

Lesson plan

0:30 Tom Pyzdek lecture

0:10 Quiz

0:50 Group discussion, topic: discuss the fundamental principles of variation as they relate to the conclusions shown on form entitled "Nursing services patient education quality improvement monitor"

Figure 2.3. Sample lesson plan.

    The lesson plan shown in Figure 2.3 is a composite of the common types of lesson plans discussed above.

LECTURES AND PRESENTATIONS

In the lecture method an instructor transmits information to students. The lecture method is one of the most frequently used of all presentation methods. It is suitable for conveying information such as procedures, etc. Lectures can be effective providing the speaker keeps in mind that listeners' attention spans are limited to 15–30 minutes. Attention spans vary depending on the skill of the speaker, the topic, and the age and education level of the audience. A number of techniques can help increase the retention rate and extend the attention span:

- cover only one point per lecture; leave out anything not *directly* related to your point
- vary voice tone
- have material presented by multiple speakers
- assure that the room environment is comfortable
- avoid lecturing after the audience has eaten a meal
- avoid lecturing late in the evening
- do not schedule the lecture just prior to another significant event (e.g., 5 p.m. on Christmas eve)

Presentations include lectures, but they can also include oral, visual, and multimedia formats.

COACHING

In modern, quality-focused organizations a supervisor may spend up to 60% of his or her time coaching. On a one-on-one basis, coaching refers to the process of helping a single employee improve some aspect of his or her performance. On a group level, coaching is a process of developing effective teams and work-groups. The successful coach needs the following skills:

- communication skills
- listening skills
- analysis skills
- negotiation skills
- conflict resolution skills

The coach must also possess sufficient subject matter knowledge to assist the employee in achieving results. Expert knowledge of the task enables the coach to describe and demonstrate the desired behavior and to observe the employee performing the task and give feedback. Just as an NBA coach must be an expert in basketball, business coaches must be experts on the subjects they are coaching.

Coaches must also understand how adults learn and grow. Brookfield (1986) identified six factors that influence adult learning:

1. More learning takes place if learning is seen as voluntary, self-initiated activity.
2. More learning takes place in a climate of mutual respect.
3. The best learning takes place in an environment characterized by a spirit of collaboration.
4. Learning involves a balance between action and self-reflection.
5. People learn best when their learning is self-directed (see the next section for information on self-directed learning).

Coaches should be aware of the essentials of motivation theory, such as Maslow's needs hierarchy, McGregor's theory X and theory Y models of management, and Hertzberg's hygiene theory.

There are many variations on the coaching process, but all involve similar steps (Finnerty, 1996):

- Define performance goals.
- Identify necessary resources for success.
- Observe and analyze current performance.
- Set expectations for performance improvement.
- Plan a coaching schedule.
- Meet with the individual or team to get commitment to goals, demonstrate the desired behavior, and establish boundaries.
- Give feedback on practice and performance.
- Follow up to maintain goals.

SITUATIONS THAT REQUIRE COACHING TO IMPROVE PERFORMANCE

Coaching discussions may be initiated as a result of an administrative situation or management's awareness of an event or incident of concern in relation to a task or project. In their publication, *Coaching Skills*, The Center for Management and Organization Effectiveness lists the following situations where coaching may be required:

Administrative situations
- setting objectives
- reviewing performance
- discussing salary
- discussing career planning-development
- discussing job posting and bidding

Project or task situations
- a specific project or assignment problem: e.g., delays, quality problems, quantity problems, lack of follow-through on commitments.
- absenteeism and/or tardiness
- deficiency in effort or motivation
- behavior which causes problems, e.g., aggressiveness
- training: opportunity or assignment
- when someone new joins your group or team
- conflicts between employees or within groups
- communication problems or breakdowns
- when your own supervisor makes you aware that one of your employees has a problem

FORMS OF COACHING

Coaching can take on a variety of forms. The traditional form is, as described above, a supervisor coaching a subordinate or a sponsor coaching a team. However, other forms do occur on occasion and should probably occur more often than they do. A number of the more common alternative forms of coaching are described here (Finnerty, 1996):

Mentoring—Mentoring involves a relationship between a senior manager and a less-experienced employee. The mentor is a trusted friend as well as a source of feedback. Mentors provide employees with information and feedback they may not otherwise receive. It was stated earlier that coaches must be subject-matter experts in the area they are coaching. Mentors are experts on the *organization itself.* Because of their superior knowledge of the written and unwritten rules of the organization, the mentor can help the employee traverse the often perplexing maze that must be negotiated to achieve success. Knowledge of the organization's informal leadership, norms, values, and culture can usually only be acquired from either a mentor, or by experience. *"Experience is a stern school, 'tis a fool that will learn in no other."*

Peer coaching—Traditional, vertically structured organizations have been the model for mentoring. Typically, the mentor or coach is above the employee in the organizational hierarchy and has formal command authority over her. Peer coaching relationships are those where all parties are approximately at the same level within the organization or, at least, where no party in the relationship has command authority over any other party. For all the talk of formal training, policy, and procedure manuals, etc., the truth is that in the real world, most "training" takes the form of a coworker telling the employee "the way it's *really* done around here . . ." Peer coaching recognizes that this approach has tremendous value. There is less hesitancy in asking a peer for help for fear of revealing ignorance or bothering one's superior with a minor problem.

Peer coaching can be facilitated by putting people together for the purpose of learning from one another. Peer coaches are provided with training in the skills of coaching.

Executive coaching—By its nature a command hierarchy discourages upward communication of "bad news." The result of this is that the higher one's position in the hierarchy, the less feedback one obtains on their performance. This is especially true for negative feedback. Employees quickly learn that it is not in their best interest to criticize the boss. While these problems are partially alleviated by such innovations as anonymous 360-degree performance assessments, it may also be useful for the executive to have a coach. The executive coach is usually a consultant hired from outside of the firm. The coaching role is typically to act as coach to the executive team, rather than to a particular executive.

SELF-DIRECTED LEARNING

Self-directed learning (SDL) is defined as a training design in which trainees work at their own pace, without the aid of an instructor, to master predetermined material. SDL is only one of a number of approaches that can be employed to meet the training goal. The choice to use SDL is made after evaluating the various options available. Mastery can be measured via testing, interview, demonstration, or some other method.

SDL is the theory that underlies such concepts as self-directed teams and learning organizations. The basis of SDL is "self-directedness." Self-directedness in the SDL context refers to allowing the trainee to make learning decisions and to follow through on them. The concept of self-directedness has gained in importance with the advent of large *learning centers*. In these facilities, large numbers of training programs are available to meet company and individual needs. The advent of *desktop-learning* integrates many of the features of learning centers with modern desktop technology to allow, literally, learning on the trainee's desktop. Technological innovations such as full-screen computer video and network accessible audio-visual presentations continue to expand the availability of SDL materials. Thousands of subjects are available in software and video formats, with more being added every day. These developments increase the importance and effectiveness of SDL.

There are numerous situations where SDL should be considered (Piskurich, 1996):

- large employee populations with diverse training requirements
- need for individualized development

- multiple training sites where the same training must occur concurrently
- need for a high degree of training consistency
- high turnover rates require continuous training

Not all people are good candidates for SDL. Not all people are self-directed. Even a particular individual will have varying degrees of self-directedness based on current job circumstances, self-esteem and other factors. Many people have been conditioned to a decidedly "other-directed" approach to learning by years of experience with an education system that totally controls what, when and how material is presented as well as how the learner is expected to demonstrate familiarity with that material. At best, many people will need to be coached in SDL; some individuals will simply not be able to succeed in using SDL. Fortunately, instruments exist that make it possible to measure the degree of self-directedness of an individual employee. One such instrument is the Gugliamino Self-Directed Learning Readiness Scale (SDLRS). This instrument considers factors such as inner-directedness, achievement motivation, goal-setting skills, and listening ability. It also includes other characteristics of self-directedness such as self-confidence and observational ability which may have a more indirect relationship with SDL readiness.

Self-directedness can be enhanced. There are three components to the process:

1. **Prepare the learner for the SDL experience**—Preparation includes providing an organizational culture where SDL is accepted. Supervisors, managers, and training professionals must become knowledgeable about SDL and accept its value. Learners can be introduced to the subject through training or less intensive mechanisms, such as brochures.

2. **Develop support systems**—Facilitators or counselors should be available to help learners make the transition from other-directed to self-directed learning.

3. **Success breeds success**—Work especially hard to assure that early SDL experiences are successful. Start with simple SDL assignments and provide high levels of support to participants.

SDL ASSESSMENT

The decision to use the SDL approach should be made only after considering its advantages and disadvantages. Figure 2.4 lists advantages and disadvantages of the SDL approach (Piskurich, 1996).

	ADVANTAGES	DISADVANTAGES
Trainee	• Available when trainee is ready • Individual choice of material • Immediate feedback • Work at own pace • No surprises • Provides review and reference	• Not accustomed to SDL • No instructor • No group interaction • Not comfortable setting objectives
Trainer-developer	• No constantly repeated classes • More time to develop • Less time on the road	• Difficult to develop properly • Must revise more frequently • More trainee preparation needed • Limited choice of media • Must sell concept to others
Corporation	• Multiple-site training • Fewer trainers • Reduced travel expenses • Reduced meeting room costs • Eliminates trainee travel costs • Reduced training downtime • Easier to schedule • Enables cross-training • Just-in-time training • Greater training consistency • Reduced training time in the aggregate	• Initial production costs higher • Higher reproduction costs • Higher distribution costs • Higher revision costs • Possible logistical problems

Figure 2.4. Advantages and disadvantages of Self-Directed Learning.

DISCUSSION FORMAT

This learning format is based on a Q&A approach. The instructor develops a set of questions that cover the material of interest, then works to get the class to ask these questions. The approach is based on engaging the students in a discussion of their work, then directing the discussion towards the material the instructor wants to present to the class.

For example, assume that the instructor wants to present material on the theory of variation to a class of machine operators. The discussion might go as follows:

Instructor:	Tell me about your work, Joan.
Joan:	I run a milling machine. The milling process involves machining a surface of a casting so that it's flat.
Instructor:	Are all of the castings that you start with exactly the same?
Joan:	Oh, no! There are no two alike!
Instructor:	In what way are they different?
Joan:	Gosh, in every way you can think of. The hardness varies, so does the thickness. Sometimes the castings are warped.
Instructor:	Thanks Joan. Has anyone else ever seen variation in the raw materials?

Of course, everyone will say "yes" and the stage is set for the instructor to make a presentation on the theory of variation. Using the discussion format, a small amount of material will be presented, followed by a discussion guided to create a foundation for the next piece of material.

The discussion format approach makes the class far more interesting to the participants than a simple lecture or presentation. It connects the classroom to the workplace. Discussion classes must be led by very knowledgeable and experienced instructors. Instructors should plan to have supporting material on hand (examples, etc.) to stimulate the discussion. Facilitation techniques should be used to ensure participation and maintain focus. Care should be taken to assure that discussions do not become bogged down in technical details rather than focusing on the training material. The instructor should summarize at the close of the discussion session.

CASE STUDIES

Many different kinds of learning exercises are often referred to as cases (Alden and Kirkhorn, 1996):

1. A predicament facing an organization is explained in great detail and students are expected to pose a solution or strategy for dealing with that complex situation.
2. A story is told about how some person or some organization dealt with a difficult situation, and students analyze and critique the actions taken, indicating what was appropriate and what might have been done differently.
3. Students are placed in a dynamic situation in which things change as a result of their actions and they work the situation toward a satisfactory outcome.

Case study materials vary a great deal in content, but most follow a similar structure.

Opening scenario—This introductory section describes the problem and recaps the major actions.

Questions—This section provides the explicit questions that the students are required to answer. Three kinds of questions may be asked:

1. Summarize and translate what has been learned.
2. Assess the situation and critique the actions taken by the characters.
3. Focus on the decision point and determine what the characters should do.

References—Call attention to the background documents on the case. References might include items such as policies, procedures, grievances, regulations, reports, and so on.

Case information—This section provides the details of the story.

Exhibits—This section includes actual samples of materials that convey important information about the case: promotions materials, memos, letters, etc.

Not all case studies will include all five elements.

WHEN TO USE CASE STUDIES

While research on the effectiveness of case studies is skimpy, and the results mixed, there is general agreement on two points: 1) case studies are an effective means for developing problem-solving skills, but 2) they add no value when trying to increase factual knowledge. One survey of training managers produced the following top five reasons for using case studies:

1. exercise problem-solving skills
2. simulate real life
3. sharpen decision-making skills
4. generate discussion
5. develop judgment

THE INSTRUCTOR'S ROLE

When using case studies, the instructor's role is primarily one of orchestration. The instructor sets up the process and assures that the students have the appropriate information and know what is expected of them. The instructor should orient the students by explaining the purpose of the case, explaining the procedures they should follow, and how they will be evaluated. Students are told how they will receive the case information (e.g., self-study, group study, presentation by instructor, etc.). Then students are told what questions they must answer. Finally, the instructor leads the class discussion of the case—questioning, steering, clarifying, expanding, controlling, protecting, synthesizing, and summarizing—so that the class discussion builds to a successful learning outcome for as many students as possible.

It is important to come to some type of closure before ending the session. The case study approach doesn't permit any one "right" answer (Alden and

Kirkhorn, 1996, p. 508). However, the instructor can comment on the discussion, showing how the points related to the course content, where the discussion was especially relevant and where it was superficial.

AVAILABILITY OF CASES

Case studies can be developed in-house or purchased from a variety of sources. Many of the organizations that offer case studies also provide assistance in selecting appropriate case studies, teaching notes, and other assistance to instructors. Here is a brief listing of sources:

> **Harvard Business School**—Over 3,000 business cases are included in their catalog. 1-800-545-7685.
> **The Kennedy School**—1,000 cases. 1-617-495-9523.
> **Institute for the Study of Diplomacy**—200 cases. 1-202-687-8971.
> **Hartwick Humanities in Management Institute**—Leadership cases. 1-800-94-CASES.

CRITICISMS OF THE CASE STUDY METHOD

Critics of the case study method believe that it is based on a number of false premises and leads to a number of problems (Kirkpatrick 1992-1993):

- The case study method is based on a psycho-epistemology that is concrete-bound, anti-conceptual empiricism—the precise opposite of what today's managers need.
- It leads to people who are concrete-bound and short-range in their thinking and who act as if they are incapable of grasping principles.
- With the case study approach, "thinking" does not mean the identification and integration of facts, nor especially does it mean the conceptual grasp and application of principles. Case studies discard at the outset precisely what managers need to learn in order to solve business problems: namely, a body of absolute, abstract principles, which are the essential tools for conceptual thought.
- Business cases are contrived problems, not case histories.

- Cases are almost always developed from recent situations, thus ignoring the lessons of hundreds of years of business history.
- Despite what proponents say, cases are not real-world simulations. Real-world business decisions are made by managers who have been steeped in the concrete detail of their particular company for, at a minimum, usually, years. This familiarity enables managers to separate essentials from details. Students are given only a short time to assimilate a vast number of details, leading to information overload. Yet, decisions are required by the end of the class period. By suggesting that this artificial approach in any way resembles reality, students are being taught to make snap judgments.

There is no fundamental difference between, say, engineering and management sciences (e.g., accounting, advertising). They are all "practical" disciplines. Yet engineering is not taught using the case method. Imagine if it were. The students read a case that provides the detailed description of a highway leading up to a river; the engineer's objective in the case is to design a bridge to span the river. A problem has to be solved, decisions have to be made. No textbooks are provided or lectures given to the students—that would be a "telling" or "dictatorial" method of education. The students engage in "democratic" discussions about the design of the bridge and the materials to be used. There is no "right answer" because a variety of materials and designs would equally solve the problem—and the professor boasts that his answers are no better than the students'. Presumably, thought would be achieved through the social interaction of the discussions and the "currently useful generalizations" of civil engineering would emerge inductively.

Would you want to be the first to drive across this bridge?

WORKBOOKS

Workbooks present the trainee with a collection of discussion topics and exercises. Workbooks are usually used as supplements to classroom presentations or self-study materials. Workbooks serve two purposes: 1) to act as a learning tool, 2) to demonstrate mastery.

A common role of workbooks is as a customized supplement to textbooks. Textbooks are available on most quality subjects and they have the advantage of having been prepared by experts and subjected to peer review. The time invested in creating a textbook is enormous; many textbooks require several thousand man-hours to prepare. In addition, the typesetting, printing, and storage costs runs into tens of thousands of dollars. Most organizations do not have the resources to produce their own textbooks. However, to recoup their costs and make a profit, publishers must target their books to a large audience. Thus textbooks tend to be "general" in nature. This makes it more difficult for trainers who have a specific training need. Workbooks can help to bridge this gap.

Workbooks are often designed around the more general textbook. They contain specific examples of how the material in the textbook applies to particular situations encountered by the trainee. Ideally, workbooks will not only be specific to the organization, but to the trainee as well. Workbooks are used to allow the learner to practice the material presented in a classroom. The instructor can review workbooks with the trainee to identify any errors and help the trainee better understand the material.

JOB TRAINING

Job training is the vehicle through which the vast majority of training occurs. Job training involves assigning the learners to work with a more experienced employee, either a supervisor, peer, or lead hand, to learn specific tasks in the actual workplace. The learner is usually a new employee who has been either recently hired, transferred, or promoted into the position and who lacks the knowledge and skill to perform some components of her or his job. The experienced employee normally demonstrates and discusses new areas of knowledge and skill and then provides opportunities for practice and feedback. There are three common methods used in job training (Nolan, 1996):

1. **Structured on-the-job training (OJT)**—Structured OJT allows the learner to acquire skills and knowledge needed to perform the job through a series of structured or planned activities at the work site. All activities are performed under the careful observation and supervision

of the OJT instructor.

The structured process is based on a thorough analysis of the job and the learner. The OJT instructor introduces the learner systematically to what he or she needs to know to perform competently and meet performance standards and expectations.

2. **Unstructured OJT**—Unstructured OJT often means sink or swim. Most activities in unstructured OJT have not been thought through and are done in a haphazard way. A common method of unstructured OJT is to have the learner "sit" with another employee or "follow the employee around" for a few days to see what the employee does and how it is done. This "sit-and-see" technique often leads the learner to pick up as much by trial and error as by any instruction given by the more experienced employee. The learner is typically inundated with reading assignments concerning policies, procedures, and other assorted documentation which, when not put into the right context, can cause more confusion than assistance.

    The learner is often thrust on the experienced employee without notice and is seen as a hindrance, since this training time is interrupting the experienced employee's normal work load and performance outputs. The major drawback of the unstructured approach is that objectives, expectations, and outcomes are not defined in advance and, therefore, results are unpredictable.

3. **Job instruction training**—Job instruction training was originally developed for use with World War II production workers and is based on a mechanical step procedure requiring the instructor to present the material in an orderly, disciplined manner. It is most frequently used to teach motor skills. Since a systematic approach is involved, components of it are often found in today's structured OJT.

DEVELOPING A STRUCTURED OJT PROGRAM

Structured OJT has proven to be an efficient and effective means of teaching employees about the skills required to do their job. Developing structured OJT programs is a process that involves the following steps:

1. **Needs analysis**—This was described above.
2. **Job analysis**—Job analysis is part of the job design and employee selection processes. Job requirements are matched to the employee's knowledge, skills, and abilities during the selection process. When designing structured OJT programs the characteristics of trainees must be examined in order to target the OJT accurately and develop effective instructional materials; e.g., what works for new hires may not be best for transfers. Trainees should complete employee profile surveys to provide the instructional designer with the information needed to customize the training to the employee's needs.
3. **Course design**—This step will produce a course training plan that serves as the blueprint to be used to construct training support materials. The course training plan should include:
   - a purpose statement
   - performance objectives
   - criterion tests
   - presentation
   - application and feedback methods
   - course content outline
   - lesson plan
   - training schedule
4. **Material preparation.**
5. **Validation**—After training materials have been developed for the OJT program, they must be tested to ensure that they fulfill their mandate to train the individual to perform the job. This involves pilot studies with selected individuals to "shake down" the materials. Final validation can only occur by monitoring the program's effectiveness with actual trainees.

6. **Presentation**—Effective instructional presentations incorporate a systematic learning process of *presentation, application, and feedback* (PAF) (Nolan, 1996, p. 764). Prior to actual delivery, the OJT instructor needs to review the structured process and methods, collect all materials and tools necessary, and develop a schedule of training.

   Presentation—The OJT instructor
   - states objective
   - motivates trainee
   - overviews key steps
   - presents tasks (tell and show)
   - tests for understanding

   Application—Trainee applies new knowledge and skill through
   - directed practice
   - undirected, yet supervised, practice

   Feedback—OJT trainer observes and communicates to trainee
   - what was done well
   - what needs improvement
   - how to improve

7. The final step in a structured OJT program is to evaluate it. The method of evaluation is the same five-level process as described above for evaluating training in general: *reaction, learning, behavior, results, and return on investment.*

INSTRUCTIONAL GAMES, SIMULATIONS, AND ROLE-PLAYS

These techniques are based on two premises: 1) people learn better through active experience than passive listening; and 2) people learn better through interacting with one another than alone.

Instructional games. An instructional game is an activity that is deliberately designed to produce certain learning outcomes. Instructional games incorporate five characteristics (Thiagarajan, 1996):

1. **Conflict**—Games specify a goal to be achieved and throw in obstacles to its achievement. A game may involve competition among players, or it may involve player cooperation to achieve a group goal.

2. **Control**—Games are governed by rules that specify how to play the game.

3. **Closure**—Games have an ending rule, which may be a time limit, completion of a set of tasks, elimination of players from the game, etc. Most effective instructional games use multiple criteria for closure and permit different players or teams to win along different dimensions.

4. **Contrivance**—Games contain elements, such as chance, to assure that the game retains a playful character and isn't taken too seriously.

5. **Competency base**—The game is designed to help players improve their competencies in specific areas. Learning objectives range from rote recall to complex problem-solving and may deal with motor, informational, conceptual, interpersonal, and affective domains.

Simulation games. A simulation game contains the five characteristics of instructional games, but in addition it includes a correspondence between some aspect of the game and reality. Some examples of simulation games that have been used in teaching quality concepts are the following:

- Senge's "Beer Game" in *The Fifth Discipline* (Senge, 1990, pp. 26–53). The beer game is designed to teach systems thinking.

- Deming's *funnel experiment*. Boardman and Boardman (1990) provide a detailed description of how to set up and conduct the funnel experiment. The funnel experiment illustrates statistical thinking and decision-making.

- "The Card Drop Shop." The card drop shop is a small enterprise that has customers, a president, a supervisor, an inspector, a rework operator, several line operators, and an accountant. There is only one process: dropping playing cards onto a target on the floor. The customer ideally wants all cards on the target but will accept the product provided that the total deviation from the target is "not too bad." The customer also specifies that each card is to be held by its center and dropped individually. Like the funnel experiment, the card drop shop illustrates the effects of tampering with a stable process. However, it does so using simpler tools and materials (Alloway, 1994).

- Geometric dimensioning and tolerancing simulation (Wearring and Karl, 1995).
- Additional applications of simulation to quality are described in Simon and Bruce (1992).

In addition to simulation games, simulation tools such as quincunxes and sampling bead boxes are commonly used in quality training. Simple simulations create a concrete link to abstract concepts, making it easier for people to understand the concept.

Role-plays. In a role-play, players spontaneously act out characters assigned to them in a scenario. Role-plays take a variety of forms, for example:

- **Media**—The scenario for a role-play may be presented through a printed handout, an audiotape, videotape, etc.
- **Characters**—The characters in a role-play may be identified in terms of job functions, personality variables, or attitudes. Some role-plays require people to play their own roles in a different situation (as in a desert survival exercise).
- **Responses**—Most role-plays involve face-to-face communication among the characters, but written or phone communications are also used.
- **Mode of usage**—Groups may be divided into smaller groups or pairs, or a group can watch as others participate. Role-players may be substituted as the role-play progresses. Coaches may be assigned to help the role-players.
- **Number of players**—Most role-plays involve two characters, but there is no fixed limit on the number of players that can be involved.
- **Replay**—The effectiveness of some role-plays can be improved through repetition. Repetition can take place after a presentation of new material by the instructor, or after changing some aspect of the game.

An excellent example of a role-play game is Deming's "Red bead experiment" (Deming, 1986, p. 346ff). The red bead experiment is designed to teach statistical thinking and the use of simple statistical tools.

CORRESPONDENCE FORMAT

Correspondence schools have been around for a long time. This style of learning is self-directed. Traditionally, the student completes a lesson and then mails assignments to an instructor. The instructor reviews the assignment and returns it to the student with comments and suggestions.

The availability of computer networks has greatly expanded the scope of correspondence learning. It is now possible to do most of the work required for college degrees, from the associate degree level to the Ph.D. level, via computer. Students and instructors interact via computer networks. Assignments are posted online, students download the assignments and post their results. Computer communication takes place much faster than mail correspondence, while retaining the advantage of letting students and instructors work at times convenient to them.

Online correspondence is not limited to formal, structured lessons. A great deal of learning takes place on online forums, internet newsgroups, chat sessions, etc. Magazines such as *Quality Digest* publish lists of online resources for quality professionals. On the World-Wide Web most quality sites are linked to other quality-related sites, making it a simple matter to build an extensive list of online quality resources.

Use of technology in training

Most training is still conducted using traditional technologies. Human teachers stand in a room before a group of learners and use presentations and lectures to deliver instructional materials. Learners use pens, paper, and books. The most advanced technology is usually the overhead projector.

This situation is changing rapidly. The tremendous advances in computer technology and widespread availability of low-cost desktop computers are creating a revolution in learning that is likely to dramatically change the way people will learn in the future. Interactive multimedia training programs represent a synergistic marriage of audiovisual (AV) media and computer-based training (CBT). These programs are designed to integrate text, graphics, animation, audio, and motion video so that each unit of content can be delivered in the medium that's best for it. Because these programs are computer-based, learners can interact with them and go through them in a sequence and depth that meets their particular requirements. And, because their delivery systems are designed primarily for micro or personal computers, interactive multimedia training programs can be used at point of need. The interactive multimedia program does the following (Howell and Silvey, 1996):

1. Meets the individual needs of many learners, accommodating users at all levels of expertise
2. Lets each user work at the pace that best suits him or her
3. Offers the best presentation for different subjects
4. Reverses the traditional student-teacher ratio, bringing many teachers or experts to the individual student
5. Provides "creative" learning experiences that give each student a continuing functional reason to learn, beyond merely studying for a test
6. Can be designed to encourage learners to explore a topic rather than simply seek a single right answer
7. Allows learners at different levels to bring their own expertise and creative capabilities into the learning process
8. Can create a "virtual classroom" wherever a microcomputer or workstation can be placed
9. Permits small groups of two or three learners to engage in team problem-solving activities
10. Can function as an in-class electronic performance-support system, containing the information, guidance, and tools needed to complete complex case activities

Some interactive multimedia training programs are actually integrated into computer systems used by workers, so that small units of training can be delivered the moment they are needed to support job performance. In fact, the training functions of these systems are so well-integrated that it is often difficult to separate the training functions from the operational aspects of the programs.

DESIGN OF MULTIMEDIA TRAINING PROGRAMS

It is as easy to create a bad multimedia training program as it is with traditional media, if not more so. There are five basic guidelines to developing effective multimedia training programs (Howell and Silvey, 1996):

1. **Determine the training goals**—Interactive multimedia programs are often assigned goals that fall into one of the following categories:
   - **Transfer of knowledge**—The learner acquires information and learns what to do with it, e.g., how to plot an x-bar chart and how to interpret it.
   - **Skill building**—The learner acquires certain capabilities by learning steps that address performance. Simulation is one vehicle for achieving this goal.
   - **Performance support**—The worker acquires the skill or knowledge to solve a specific job problem without leaving the work environment.
   - **Integrating goals**—Assignments require that the student perform complex activities that use the material as it is presented. For example, a lesson might place the learner in the role of a department manager and ask that they use quality tools to reduce variation in a process. The learner would be provided with information on how to do this, e.g., a lesson on run charts.
2. **Understand your customers**—In addition to the training needs assessment, the customers' willingness to accept this new approach to learning must be understood.
3. **Decide on best learner experience**—Which types of learner experiences will best achieve the goals of the training? It isn't necessary, or desirable, to use every aspect of the medium for every lesson.
4. **Key the design to content stability**—Match the program design cycle time to the stability of the content. If a program's design takes too long, the content may be obsolete before the program design is completed.

5. **Use a team approach**—Teams should include experts in subject-matter, instructional design, graphics design, programming, and, of course, learners. Design strategy should include a plan and schedule.

OTHER TRAINING TECHNOLOGY

In addition to multimedia training, there are a number of other training technologies that should be considered:

- satellite broadcasts
- cable broadcasts
- video-conferencing and virtual classrooms
- videotape
- narrated slide presentations
- audio tape

3

Principles of Six Sigma

ELEMENTS OF CUSTOMER-DRIVEN ORGANIZATIONS

The proper place of the customer in the organization's hierarchy is illustrated in Figure 3.1.

Figure 3.1. The "correct" view of the company organization chart.
From *Marketing Management: Analysis, Planning, Implementation, and Control,*
Figure 1-7, p. 21, by Philip Kotler, copyright © 1991 by Prentice-Hall, Inc.
Reprinted by permission.

Note that this perspective is precisely the opposite of the traditional view of the organization. The difficulties involved in making such a radical change should not be underestimated. Problems exist even within the quality community itself. For example, the original Malcolm Baldrige National Quality Award criteria allocated 30% of the total points to customer satisfaction, the highest of any criteria. However, in recent years the point allocation was lowered to 25%, equal to the business results category. It seems that the customer's position atop the organization may be threatened.

The importance of the quality activity within the organization has been evolving along with that of the importance of the customer. Figure 3.2 illustrates the evolution of the quality function's role since the mid-1970s.

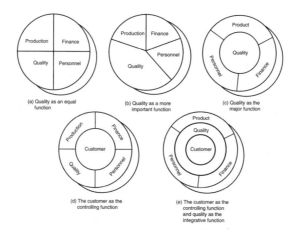

Figure 3.2. Evolving views of quality's role in the company.
Adapted from *Marketing Management: Analysis, Planning, Implementation, and Control*,
Figure 1-8, p. 24, by Philip Kotler, copyright © 1991 by Prentice-Hall, Inc.
Reprinted by permission.

Marketing has traditionally claimed jurisdiction over activities directed at acquiring and retaining customers. The roles of the quality function and marketing function are overlapping and complementary. Recent research provides evidence that quality is a primary driver in the effort to get new customers and keep existing customers. Thus, the evolution shown in Figure 3.2 holds for the marketing function as well as the quality function. In fact, it is fair to say that a great deal of what is commonly called "TQM" merely represents the quality profession discovering principles which the marketing profession knew long ago. What is new about TQM is the convergence of quality principles and marketing principles. TQM represents a perspective of the organization that combines cause (process management for quality) and effect (product quality, customer satisfaction.)

Becoming a customer- and market-driven enterprise

Edosomwan (1993) defines a customer- and market-driven enterprise as one that is committed to providing excellent quality and competitive products and services to satisfy the needs and wants of a well-defined market segment. This approach is in contrast to that of the traditional organization, as shown in Table 3.1.

Table 3.1. Traditional organizations vs. customer-driven organizations.
From *Customer and Market-Driven Quality Management*, Table 1.1. by
Johnson A. Edosomwan, copyright © 1993 by ASQ. Reprinted by permission.

	TRADITIONAL ORGANIZATIONS	CUSTOMER-DRIVEN ORGANIZATIONS
Product and service planning	−Short-term focus −Reactionary management −Management by objectives planning process	−Long-term focus −Prevention-based management −Customer-driven strategic
Measures of performance	−Bottom-line financial results −Quick return on investment	−Customer satisfaction −Market share −Long-term profitability −Quality orientation −Total productivity
Attitudes toward customers	−Customers are irrational and a pain −Customers are a bottleneck to profitability −Hostile and careless −"Take it or leave it" attitude	−Voice of the customer is important −Professional treatment and attention to customers is required −Courteous and responsive −Empathy and respectful attitude

Continued on next page . . .

Table 3.1—*Continued . . .*

	TRADITIONAL ORGANIZATIONS	CUSTOMER-DRIVEN ORGANIZATIONS
Quality of products and services	−Provided according to organizational requirements	−Provided according to customer requirements and needs
Marketing focus	−Seller's market −Careless about lost customers through customer satisfaction	−Increased market share and financial growth achieved
Process management approach	−Focus on error and defect detection	−Focus on error and defect prevention
Product and service delivery attitude	−It is OK for customers to wait for products and services	−It is best to provide fast time-to-market products and services
People orientation	−People are the source of problems and are burdens on the organization	−People are an organization's greatest resource
Basis for decision-making	−Product-driven −Management by opinion	−Customer-driven −Management by data
Improvement strategy	−Crisis management −Management by fear and intimidation	−Continuous process improvement −Total process management
Mode of operation	−Career-driven and independent work −Customers, suppliers, and process owners have nothing in common	−Management-supported improvement −Teamwork between suppliers, process owners, and customers practiced

The journey from a traditional to a customer-driven organization has been made by enough organizations to allow us to identify a number of distinct milestones that mark the path to success. Generally, the journey begins with recognition that a crisis is either upon the organization, or imminent. This wrenches the organization's leadership out of denial and forces them to abandon the status-quo.

When the familiar ways of the past are no longer acceptable, the result is a feeling of confusion among the leaders. At this stage the leadership must answer some very basic questions:

- What is the organization's purpose?
- What are our values?
- What does an organization with these values look like?

A "value" is that which one acts to gain and/or keep. It presupposes an entity capable of acting to achieve a goal in the face of an alternative. Values are not simply nice-sounding platitudes; they represent *goals*. Pursuing the organization's values implies building an organization which embodies these values. This is the leadership's *vision*, to create a reality where their values have been achieved.

After the vision has been clearly developed, the next step is to develop a strategy for building the new organization (see Chapter 1). The process of implementing the strategic plan is the *turnaround stage*.

Elements of the transformed organization

Customer-driven organizations share certain common features.

- **Flattened hierarchies**—Getting everyone closer to the customer involves reducing the number of bureaucratic "layers" in the organizational structure. It also involves the "upside-down" perspective of the organizational structure shown in Figure 3.1. The customer comes first, not the boss. Everyone serves the customer.
- **Risk-taking**—Customers' demands tend to be unpredictable. Responsiveness requires that organizations be willing to change quickly, which involves uncertainty and risk. Customer-driven organizations

encourage risk-taking in a variety of ways. One important aspect is to celebrate mistakes made by individuals who engage in risky behavior. Bureaucratic impediments such as excessive dependence on written procedures are minimized or eliminated. Employees are encouraged to act on their own best judgments and not to rely on formal approval mechanisms.

- **Communication**—During the transformation the primary task of the leadership team is the clear, consistent, and unambiguous transmission of their vision to others in the organization. One way this is accomplished is through "internal marketing" which involves using the principles of marketing to get the message to the target "market": the employees. It is vital that the leaders' actions are completely consistent with their words. The assistance of outside consultants may be helpful in identifying inconsistencies.

  Leaders should realize that their behavior carries tremendous symbolic meaning. This can contribute to the failure of convincing employees; a single action which is inconsistent with the stated message is sufficient to destroy all credibility. On the plus side, an action that clearly shows a commitment to the vision can help spread the word that "They're serious this time." The leadership should seek out stories that capture the essence of the new organization and repeat these stories often. For example, Nordstrom employees all hear the story of the sales clerk who allowed the customer to return a tire (Nordstrom's doesn't sell tires). This story captures the essence of the Nordstrom "rule book" which states:

  > Rule #1-Use your own best judgment.
  > Rule #2-There are no other rules.

  Leaders should expect to devote a minimum of 50% of their time to communication during the transition.

- **Boards of directors**—It is vital to obtain the enthusiastic endorsement of the new strategy by the board. Management cannot focus their attention until this support has been received. This will require that management educate their board and ask them for their approval. However, boards are responsible for governance, not management. Don't ask the Board to approve tactics. This bogs down the board, stifles creativity in the ranks, and slows the organization down.

- **Unions**—In the transformed organization, everyone's job changes. If the organization's employees are unionized, changing jobs requires that the union become management's partner in the transformation process. In the flat organization union employees will have greater authority. Union representation should be involved in all phases of the transformation, including planning and strategy development. By getting union input, the organization can be assured that during collective bargaining the union won't undermine the company's ability to compete or sabotage the strategic plan. Unions also play a role in auditing the company's activities to assure that they comply with contracts and labor laws.

- **Measuring results**—It is important that the right things be measured. The "right things" are measurements that determine that the organization is delivering on its promises to customers, investors, employees, and other stakeholders. Measurements must be made for the right reasons. This means that measurements are used to learn about how to improve, not for judgment. Finally, measurements must be made the right way. Measurements should cover processes as well as outcomes. Data must be available quickly to the people who use them. Measurements must be easy to understand.

- **Rewarding employees**—Care must be taken to avoid punishing with rewards. Rewarding individuals with financial incentives for simply doing their jobs well implies that the employee wouldn't do the job without the reward. It is inherently manipulative. The result is to destroy the very behavior you seek to encourage (Kohn, 1993). The message is that rewards should not be used as control mechanisms. Employees should be treated like adults and provided with adequate and fair compensation for doing their jobs. Recognizing exceptional performance or effort should be done in a way that encourages cooperation and team spirit, such as parties and public expressions of appreciation. Leaders should assure fairness: e.g., management bonuses and worker pay cuts don't mix.

SIX SIGMA VERSUS THREE SIGMA

The traditional quality model of process capability differed from Six Sigma in two fundamental respects:

1. It was applied only to manufacturing processes, while Six Sigma is applied to all important business processes.
2. It stipulated that a "capable" process was one that had a process standard deviation of no more than one-sixth of the total allowable spread, where Six Sigma requires the process standard deviation be no more than one-twelfth of the total allowable spread.

These differences are far more profound than one might realize. By addressing all business processes, Six Sigma not only treats manufacturing as part of a larger system, it removes the narrow, inward focus of the traditional approach. Customers care about more than just how well a product is manufactured. Price, service, financing terms, style, availability, frequency of updates and enhancements, technical support, and a host of other items are also important. Also, Six Sigma benefits others besides customers. When operations become more cost-effective and the product design cycle shortens, owners or investors benefit too. When employees become more productive their pay can be increased. Six Sigma's broad scope means that it provides benefits to all stakeholders in the organization.

The second point also has implications that are not obvious. Six Sigma is, basically, a process quality goal, where sigma is a statistical measure of variability in a process (see Chapter 7). As such it falls into the category of a process capability technique. The traditional quality paradigm defined a process as capable if the process natural spread, plus and minus Three Sigma, was less than the engineering tolerance. Under the assumption of normality, this Three Sigma quality level translates to a process yield of 99.73%. A later refinement considered the process location as well as its spread and tightened the minimum acceptance criterion so that the process mean was at least four sigma from the nearest engineering requirement. Six Sigma requires that processes operate such that the nearest engineering requirement is at least Six Sigma from the process mean.

Six Sigma also applies to attribute data, such as counts of things gone wrong. This is accomplished by converting the Six Sigma requirement to equivalent conformance levels, as illustrated in Figure 3.3.

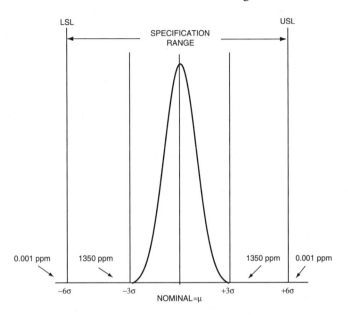

Figure 3.3. Sigma levels and equivalent conformance rates.

One of Motorola's most significant contributions was to change the discussion of quality from one where quality levels were measured in percent (parts-per-hundred), to a discussion of parts-per-million or even parts-per-billion. Motorola correctly pointed out that modern technology was so complex that old ideas about "acceptable quality levels" could no longer be tolerated. Modern business requires near perfect quality levels.

One puzzling aspect of the "official" Six Sigma literature is that it states that a process operating at Six Sigma will produce 3.4 parts-per-million (PPM) non-conformances. However, if a special normal distribution table is consulted (very few go out to Six Sigma) one finds that the expected non-conformances are 0.002 PPM (2 parts-per-billion, or PPB). The difference occurs because Motorola presumes that the process mean can drift 1.5 sigma in either direction. The area of a normal distribution beyond 4.5 sigma from the mean is indeed 3.4 PPM. Since control charts will easily detect any process shift of this magnitude in a single sample, the 3.4 PPM represents a very conservative upper bound on the non-conformance rate. See Appendix Table 18.

In contrast to Six Sigma quality, the old Three Sigma quality standard of 99.73% translates to 2,700 PPM failures, even if we assume zero drift. For processes with a series of steps, the overall yield is the *product* of the yields of the different steps. For example, if we had a simple two step process where step #1 had a yield of 80% and step #2 had a yield of 90%, then the overall yield would be 0.8 x 0.9 = 0.72 = 72%. Note that the overall yield from processes involving a series of steps is always less than the yield of the step with the *lowest* yield. If Three Sigma quality levels (99.97% yield) are obtained from every step in a ten step process, the quality level at the end of the process will contain 26,674 defects per million! Considering that the complexity of modern processes is usually far greater than ten steps, it is easy to see that Six Sigma quality isn't optional; it's required if the organization is to remain viable.

The requirement of extremely high quality is not limited to multiple-stage manufacturing processes. Consider what Three Sigma quality would mean if applied to other processes:

- Virtually no modern computer would function.
- 10,800,000 healthcare claims would be mishandled each year.
- 18,900 US Savings bonds would be lost every month.
- 54,000 checks would be lost each night by a single large bank.
- 4,050 invoices would be sent out incorrectly each month by a modest-sized telecommunications company.
- 540,000 erroneous call details would be recorded each day from a regional telecommunications company.
- 270,000,000 (270 million) erroneous credit card transactions would be recorded each year in the United States.

With numbers like these, it's easy to see that the modern world demands extremely high levels of error free performance. Six Sigma arose in response to this realization.

KANO MODEL OF CUSTOMER EXPECTATIONS
Customer expectations, priorities, needs, and "voice"

Although customers seldom spark true innovation (for example, they are usually unaware of state-of-the art developments), their input is extremely valuable. Obtaining valid customer input is a science itself. Market research firms use scientific methods such as critical incident analysis, focus groups, content analysis and surveys to identify the "voice of the customer." Noritaki Kano developed the following model of the relationship between customer satisfaction and quality.

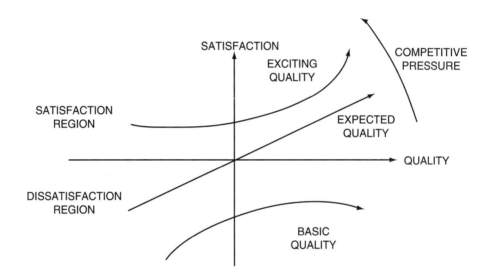

Figure 3.4. Kano model.

The Kano model shows that there is a basic level of quality that customers assume the product will have. For example, all automobiles have windows and tires. If asked, customers don't even mention the basic quality items, they take them for granted. However, if this quality level *isn't* met the customer will be dissatisfied; note that the entire "Basic Quality" curve lies in the lower half of the chart, representing dissatisfaction. However, providing basic quality isn't enough to create a satisfied customer.

The expected quality line represents those expectations which customers explicitly consider, for example, the length of time spent waiting in line at a checkout counter. The model shows that customers will be dissatisfied if their quality expectations are not met; satisfaction increases as more expectations are met.

The exciting quality curve lies entirely in the satisfaction region. This is the effect of innovation. Exciting quality represents *unexpected* quality items; the customer receives more than expected. For example, Cadillac pioneered a system where the headlights stay on long enough for the owner to walk safely to the door.

Competitive pressure will constantly raise customer expectations. Today's exciting quality is tomorrow's basic quality. Firms that seek to lead the market must innovate constantly. Conversely, firms that seek to offer standard quality must constantly research customer expectations to determine the currently accepted quality levels. It is not enough to track competitors since expectations are influenced by outside factors as well. For example, the quality revolution in manufacturing has raised expectations for service quality as well.

Some people, including your author, believe that even Six Sigma doesn't go far enough. In fact, even "zero defects" falls short. Defining quality as only the lack of non-conforming product reflects a limited view of quality. Motorola, of course, never intended to define quality as merely the absence of defects; however, some have misinterpreted the Six Sigma program in this way.

Garden variety Six Sigma only addresses half of the Kano customer satisfaction model

One problem with "garden variety" Six Sigma is that it addresses only half of the Kano model. By focusing on customer expectations and prevention of non-conformances and defects, Six Sigma addresses the portion of the Kano model on and below the line labeled "Expected Quality." While there is nothing wrong with improving these aspects of business performance, they will not assure that the organization remains viable in the long term. Long-term success requires that the organization innovate. Innovation is the result of creative activity, not analysis. Creativity is not something that can be done 'by the numbers.' In fact, excessive attention to a rigorous process such as Six Sigma can detract from creative activities if not handled carefully. As discussed above, the creative organization is one which exhibits variability, redundancy, quirky design, and slack. It is vital that the organization keep the Six Sigma Management Paradox in mind.

QFD to relate customer requirements to internal specifications

Once information about customer expectations has been obtained, techniques such as quality function deployment (QFD) can be used to link the voice of the customer directly to internal processes.

Tactical quality planning involves developing an approach to implementing the strategic quality plan. One of the most promising developments in this area has been policy deployment. Sheridan (1993) describes policy deployment as the development of a measurement-based system as a means of planning for continuous quality improvement throughout all levels of an organization. Originally developed by the Japanese, policy deployment has been used by American companies because it clearly defines the long-range direction of company development, as opposed to short-term.

QFD is a customer-driven process for planning products and services. It starts with the voice of the customer, which becomes the basis for setting requirements. QFD matrices, sometimes called "the house of quality," are graphical displays of the result of the planning process. QFD matrices vary a great deal and may show such information as competitive targets and process priorities. The matrices are created by inter-departmental teams, thus overcoming some of the barriers which exist in functionally organized systems.

QFD is also a system for design of a product or service based on customer demands, a system that moves methodically from customer requirements to specifications for the product or service. QFD involves the entire company in the design and control activity. Finally, QFD provides documentation for the decision-making process. The QFD approach involves four distinct phases (King, 1987):

Organization phase—Management selects the product or service to be improved, the appropriate interdepartmental team, and defines the focus of the QFD study.

Descriptive phase—The team defines the product or service from several different directions such as customer demands, functions, parts, reliability, cost, and so on.

Breakthrough phase—The team selects areas for improvement and finds ways to make them better through new technology, new concepts, better reliability, cost reduction, etc., and monitors the bottleneck process.

Implementation phase—The team defines the new product and how it will be manufactured.

QFD is implemented through the development of a series of matrices. In its simplest form QFD involves a matrix that presents customer requirements as rows and product or service features as columns. The cell, where the row and column intersect, shows the correlation between the individual customer requirement and the product or service requirement. This matrix is sometimes called the "requirement matrix." When the requirement matrix is enhanced by showing the correlation of the columns with one another, the result is called the "house of quality." Figure 3.5 shows one commonly used house of quality layout.

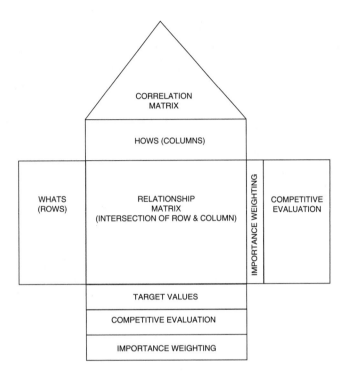

Figure 3.5. The house of quality.

The house of quality relates, in a simple graphical format, customer requirements, product characteristics, and competitive analysis. It is crucial that this matrix be developed carefully since it becomes the basis of the entire QFD process. By using the QFD approach, the customer's demands are "deployed" to the final process and product requirements.

One rendition of QFD, called the Macabe approach, proceeds by developing a series of four related matrices (King, 1987): product planning matrix, part deployment matrix, process planning matrix, and production planning matrix. Each matrix is related to the previous matrix as shown in Figure 3.6.

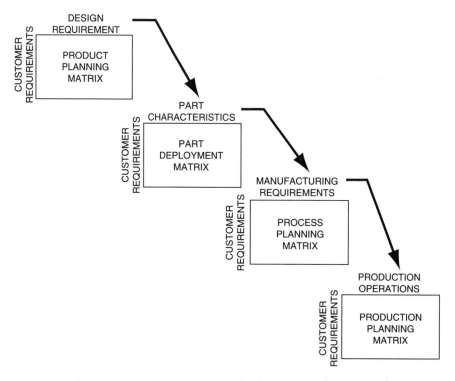

Figure 3.6. QFD methodology: Macabe approach.

Figure 3.7 shows an example of an actual QFD matrix.

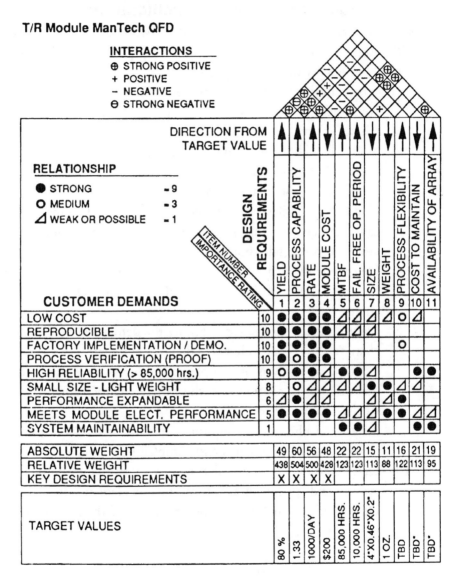

Figure 3.7. QFD matrix for an aerospace firm.

From Wahl, P.R. and Bersbach, P.L. (1991), "TQM Applied—Cradle to Grave,"
ASQ 45th Quality Congress Transactions. Reprinted with permission.

Data collection and review of customer expectations, needs, requirements, and specifications

Another approach to QFD is based on work done by Yoji Akao. Akao (1990, pp. 7–8) presents the following 11-step plan for developing the quality plan and quality design, using QFD.

1. First, survey both the expressed and latent quality demands of consumers in your target marketplace. Then decide what kinds of "things" to make.

2. Study the other important characteristics of your target market and make a demanded quality function deployment chart that reflects both the demands and characteristics of that market.

3. Conduct an analysis of competing products on the market, which we call a competitive analysis. Develop a quality plan and determine the selling features (sales points).

4. Determine the degree of importance of each demanded quality.

5. List the quality elements and make a quality elements deployment chart.

6. Make a quality chart by combining the demanded quality deployment chart and the quality elements deployment chart.

7. Conduct an analysis of competing products to see how other companies perform in relation to each of these quality elements.

8. Analyze customer complaints.

9. Determine the most important quality elements as indicated by customer quality demands and complaints.

10. Determine the specific design quality by studying the quality characteristics and converting them into quality elements.

11. Determine the quality assurance method and the test methods.

4

Six Sigma Organizational Performance Goals and Metrics

ATTRIBUTES OF GOOD METRICS

The choice of what to measure is crucial to the success of the organization. Improperly chosen metrics lead to suboptimal behavior and can lead people away from the organization's goals instead of towards them. Joiner (1994) suggests three systemwide measures of performance: overall customer satisfaction, total cycle time, and first-pass quality. An effective metric for quantifying first pass quality is total cost of poor quality (later in this chapter). Once chosen, the metrics must be communicated to the members of the organization. To be useful, the employee must be able to influence the metric through his performance, and it must be clear precisely how the employee's performance influences the metric.

Rose (1995) lists the following attributes of good metrics:

- They are either customer centered and focused on indicators that provide value to customers, such as product quality, service dependability, and timeliness of delivery, or they are associated with internal work processes that address system cost reduction, waste reduction, coordination and teamwork, innovation, and customer satisfaction.

- They measure performance across time, which shows trends rather than snapshots.
- They provide direct information at the level at which they are applied. No further processing or analysis is required to determine meaning.
- They are linked with the organization's mission, strategies, and actions. They contribute to organizational direction and control.
- They are collaboratively developed by teams of people who provide, collect, process, and use the data.

Rose also presents a performance measurement model consisting of eight steps:

Step 1: performance category—This category is the fundamental division of organizational performance that answers the question: What do we do? Sources for determining performance categories include an organization's strategic vision, core competencies, or mission statement. An organization will probably identify several performance categories. These categories define the organization at the level at which it is being measured.

Step 2: performance goal—The goal statement is an operational definition of the desired state of the performance category. It provides the target for the performance category and, therefore, should be expressed in explicit, action-oriented terms. An initial goal statement might be right on the mark, so complex that it needs further division of the performance category, or so narrowly drawn that it needs some combination of performance categories. It might be necessary to go back and forth between the performance goals in this step and the performance categories in step 1 before a satisfactory result is found for both.

Step 3: performance indicator—This is the most important step in the model because here progress toward the performance goal is disclosed and irrelevant measures are swept aside if they do not respond to an organizational goal. Here, also, the critical measures—those that communicate what is important and set the course toward organizational success—are established. Each goal will have one or more indicators, and each indicator must include an operational definition that prescribes the indicator's intent and makes its role in achieving the performance goal clear. The scope of the indicator might be viewed differently at various levels in the organization.

Step 4: elements of measure—These elements are the basic components that determine how well the organization meets the performance indicator. They are the measurement data sources—what is actually measured—and are controlled by the organization. Attempting to measure things that are beyond organizational control is a futile diversion of resources and energy because the organization is not in a position to respond to the information collected. This would be best handled in the next step.

Step 5: parameters—These are the external considerations that influence the elements of measure in some way, such as context, constraint, and boundary. They are not controlled by the organization but are powerful factors in determining how the elements of measure will be used. If measurement data analysis indicates that these external considerations present serious roadblocks for organizational progress, a policy change action could be generated.

Step 6: means of measurement—This step makes sense out of the preceding pieces. A general, how-to action statement is written that describes how the elements of measure and their associated parameters will be applied to determine the achievement level in the performance indicator. This statement can be brief, but clarifying intent is more important than the length.

Step 7: notional metrics—In this step, conceptual descriptions of possible metrics resulting from the previous steps are put in writing. This step allows everyone to agree on the concept of how the information compiled in the previous steps will be applied to measuring organizational performance. It provides a basis for validating the process and for subsequently developing specific metrics.

Step 8: specific metrics—In this final step, an operational definition and functional description of the metrics to be applied are written. The definition and description describe the data, how they are collected, how they are used, and, most important, what the data mean or how they affect organizational performance. A prototype display of real or imaginary data and a descriptive scenario are made to show what actions might be taken as a result of the measurement. This last step is the real test of any metric. It must identify what needs to be done and disclose conditions in sufficient detail to enable subsequent improvement actions.

Rose presents an application of his model used by the U.S. Army Materiel Command, which is shown in Figure 4.1.

Application of the Performance Measurement Model

Organizational performance metrics

Performance category: Material acquisition

Performance goal: Provide technologically superior equipment in the shortest possible time, while ensuring best value in all procurements.

Performance indicator	Elements of measure	Parameters	Means of measurement	Notional metrics	Specific metrics
Industrial base management (assessing and assuring adequate industrial facilities to meet military needs) **(Other performance indicators)**	Source of supply for material and services Quality of suppliers	Material and services requirements Procurement policy	Determine the level of industrial base support for required material and services Certify the quality of existing and potential suppliers	Number and capacity of existing and potential sector suppliers vs. material requirements Percentage of quality-certified sector suppliers	(Separate package containing operational definitions; functional descriptions of data collection, use, and meaning; and prototype display)

(Other performance categories and goals)

(Optional: subordinate organizational performance metrics)

Figure 4.1. Organizational performance metrics.
From "A performance measurement model," by Kenneth H. Rose. *Quality Progress*, February 1995, p. 65. Reprinted by permission.

FINANCIAL ANALYSIS
Time value of money
FINANCIAL ANALYSIS OF BENEFIT AND COST

In performing benefit-cost analysis it is helpful to understand some of the basic principles of financial analysis, in particular, break-even analysis and the time value of money (TVM).

Let's assume that there are two kinds of costs:

1. *Variable costs* are those costs which are expected to change at the same rate as the firm's level of sales. As more units are sold, total variable costs will rise. Examples include sales commissions, shipping costs, hourly wages and raw materials.

2. *Fixed costs* are those costs that are constant, regardless of the quantity produced, over some meaningful range of production. Total fixed cost *per unit* will decline as the number of units increases. Examples of fixed costs include rent, salaries, depreciation of equipment, etc.

These concepts are illustrated in Figure 4.2.

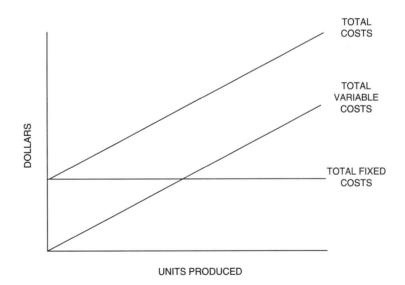

Figure 4.2. Fixed and variable costs.

BREAK-EVEN POINTS

We can define the *break-even point*, or *operating break-even point*, as the level of unit sales required for interest and taxes (EBIT) to be equal to zero, i.e., the level of sales where profits cover both fixed and variable costs.

Let Q be the quantity sold, P the price per unit, V the variable cost per unit, and F the total fixed costs. Then the quantity $P–V$ represents the variable profit per unit and

$$Q(P–V)– F = EBIT \qquad (4.1)$$

If we set EBIT equal to zero in Equation 4.1 and solve for the break-even quantity Q^* we get:

$$Q^* = \frac{F}{P - V} \qquad (4.2)$$

EXAMPLE OF BREAK-EVEN ANALYSIS

A publishing firm is selling books for $30 per unit. The variable costs are $10 per unit and fixed costs total $100,000. The break-even point is:

$$Q^* = \frac{F}{P-V} = \frac{\$100,000}{\$30-\$10} = 5,000 \; units$$

Of course, management usually wishes to earn a profit rather than to merely break even. In this case, simply set EBIT to the desired profit rather than zero in Equation 4.1 and we get the production quantity necessary to meet management's target:

$$Q^*_{TARGET} = \frac{F + EBIT_{TARGET}}{P - V} \qquad (4.3)$$

For example, if the publisher mentioned above wishes to earn a $5,000 profit then the break-even level of sales becomes

$$Q^*_{TARGET} = \frac{F + EBIT_{TARGET}}{P - V} = \frac{\$100,000 + \$5,000}{\$30 - \$10} = 5,250 \; units$$

In project benefit-cost analysis these break-even quantities are compared to the sales forecasts to determine the probability that the expected return will actually be earned.

THE TIME VALUE OF MONEY

Because money can be invested to grow to a larger amount, we say that money has a "time value." The concept of time value of money underlies much of the theory of financial decision making. We will discuss two TVM concepts: future value and present value.

Future value. Assume that you have $1,000 today and that you can invest this sum and earn interest at the rate of 10% per year. Then, one year from today, your $1,000 will have grown by $100 and it will be worth $1,100. The $1,100 figure is the *future value* of your $1,000. The $1,000 is the *present value*. Let's call the future value *FV*, the present value *PV* and the interest rate *i*, where *i* is expressed as a proportion rather than as a percentage. Then we can write this example algebraically as follows:

$$FV = PV + PV \times i = PV(1+i)$$

Now, let's say that you could invest at the 10% per year rate for two years. Then your investment would grow as follows:

YEAR	STARTING AMOUNT	INTEREST	ENDING AMOUNT
1	$1,000	$100	$1,100
2	$1,100	$110	$1,210

Observe that in year #2 you earned interest on your original $1,000 *and* on the $100 interest you earned in year #1. The result is that you earned more interest in year #2 than in year #1. This is known as *compounding*. The year time interval is know as the *compounding period*. Thus, the *FV* after two years is $1,210. Algebraically, here's what happened:

$$FV = [\$1,000(1.10)](1.10) = \$1,000(1.10)^2$$

In this equation the value between the [ ] characters represents the value at the end of the first year. This approach can be used for any number of *N* compounding periods. The equation is:

$$FV = PV(1+i)^N \qquad (4.4)$$

Of course, Equation 4.4 can be solved for *PV* as well, which gives us the present value of some future amount of money at a given rate of interest.

$$PV = \frac{FV}{(1+i)^N} \qquad (4.5)$$

NON-ANNUAL COMPOUNDING PERIODS

Note that *N* can be stated in any time interval, it need not be in years. For example, with a quarterly compounding period then *N* would be the number of quarters. Of course, the interest rate would also need to be stated in quarters. For example, if the $1,000 were invested for two years at 10% per year, compounded quarterly, then

$$FV = PV(1+i)^N = \$1,000\left(1+\frac{0.1}{4}\right)^{2*4} = \$1,000(1+0.025)^8 = \$1,218.40$$

CONTINUOUS COMPOUNDING

Note that the *FV* is greater when a greater number of compounding periods are used. The limit is an infinite number of compounding periods, known as continuous compounding. For continuous compounding the PV and FV equations are:

$$FV = PV \times e^{i \times t} \tag{4.6}$$

$$PV = \frac{FV}{e^{i \times t}} \tag{4.7}$$

Where *t* is the length of time (in years) the sum is compounded, *e* is a constant 2.71828, and all other terms are as previously defined. For our example, we have a two-year compounding period which gives

$$FV = PV \times e^{i \times t} = \$1,000 \times 2.7182818^{0.1 \times 2} = \$1,221.40$$

NET PRESENT VALUE

When evaluating project costs and benefits, it often happens that both costs and benefits come in *cash flow streams*, rather than in lump sums. Furthermore, the cash flow streams are uneven; i.e., the amounts vary from one period to the next. The approach described above can be used for uneven cash flow streams as well. Simply compute the *PV* (or *FV*) of each cash flow separately and add the various results together. The result of applying this procedure is called *the net present value*, or NPV. The procedure, while conceptually easy to grasp, becomes tedious quite quickly. Fortunately, most spreadsheets have a built in capability to perform this analysis.

Assume that a proposed project has the projected costs and benefits shown in the table below.

YEAR	COST	BENEFIT
1	$10,000	$0
2	$2,000	$500
3	$0	$5,000
4	$0	$10,000
5	$0	$15,000

Also assume that management wants a 12% return on their investment. What is the NPV of this project?

There are two ways to approach this question, both of which produce the same result. One method would be to compute the net difference between the cost and benefit for each year of the project, then find the NPV of this cash flow stream. The other method is to find the NPV of the cost cash flow stream and benefit cash flow stream, then subtract.

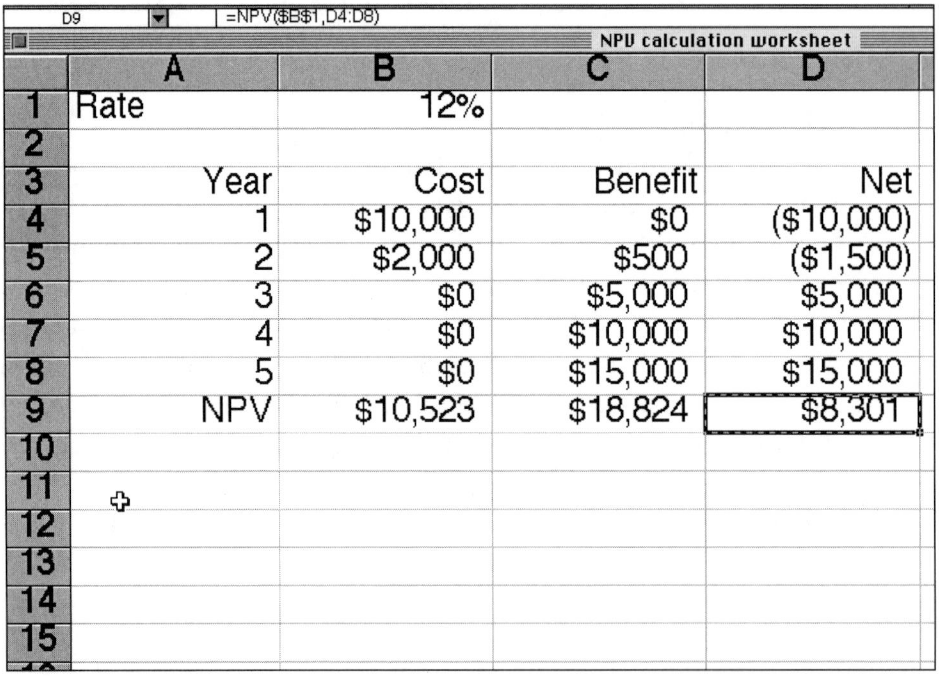

	A	B	C	D
	Rate	12%		
1				
2				
3	Year	Cost	Benefit	Net
4	1	$10,000	$0	($10,000)
5	2	$2,000	$500	($1,500)
6	3	$0	$5,000	$5,000
7	4	$0	$10,000	$10,000
8	5	$0	$15,000	$15,000
9	NPV	$10,523	$18,824	$8,301
10				
11				
12				
13				
14				
15				

D9   =NPV(B1,D4:D8)   NPV calculation worksheet

Figure 4.3. Using Excel to find the net present value of a project.

The NPV of the cost column is $10,523; the NPV of the benefits is $18,824. The project NPV can be found by subtracting the cost NPV from the benefit NPV, or by finding the NPV of the yearly benefit minus the yearly cost. Either way, the NPV analysis indicates that this project's net present value is $8,301.

INTERNAL RATE OF RETURN

Often in financial analysis of projects, it is necessary to determine the yield of an investment in a project given its price and cash flows. For example, this may be the way by which projects are prioritized. When faced with uneven cash flows, the solution to this type of problem is usually done by computer. For example, with Microsoft Excel, we need to make use of the internal rate of return (IRR) function. The IRR is defined as the rate of return which equates the present value of future cash flows with the cost of the investment. To find the IRR the computer uses an iterative process. In other words, the computer starts by taking an initial "guess" for the IRR, determines how close the computed *PV* is to the cost of the investment, then adjusts its estimate of the IRR either upward or downward. The process is continued until the desired degree of precision has been achieved.

Example

A quality improvement team in a hospital has been investigating the problem of lost surgical instruments. They have determined that in the rush to get the operating room cleaned up between surgeries many instruments are accidentally thrown away with the surgical waste. A test has shown that a $1,500 metal detector can save the following amounts:

Year	Savings
1	$750
2	$1,000
3	$1,250
4	$1,500
5	$1,750

After five years of use the metal detector will have a scrap value of $250. To find the IRR for this cash flow stream we set up the Excel spreadsheet and solve the problem as illustrated in Figure 4.4.

	B8 ▼	=IRR(B2:B7,0.1)	
	A	**B**	**C**
1	Year	Cash Flow	
2	0	($1,500)	
3	1	$750	
4	2	$1,000	
5	3	$1,250	
6	4	$1,500	
7	5	$2,000	
8	IRR	63%	

Figure 4.4. Using Excel to find the internal rate of return for a project

The Excel formula, shown in the window at the top of the figure, was built using the Insert Formula "wizard," with the cash flows in cells B2:B7 and an initial guess of 0.1 (10%). Note that in year #5 the $250 salvage value is added to the expected $1,750 in savings on surgical instruments. The cost is shown as a negative cash flow in year 0. Excel found the IRR to be 63%. The IRR can be one of the criteria for prioritizing projects, as an alternative to, or in addition to, using the Pareto Priority Index (see Chapter 5).

Cost of quality

The history of quality costs dates back to the first edition of *Juran's QC Handbook* in 1951. Today, quality cost accounting systems are part of every modern organization's quality improvement strategy. Indeed, quality cost accounting and reporting are part of many quality standards. Quality cost systems help management plan for quality improvement by identifying opportunities for greatest return on investment. However, the quality manager should keep in mind that quality costs address only half of the quality equation. The quality equation states that quality consists of doing the right things and not doing the wrong things. "Doing the right things" means including product and service features that satisfy or delight the customer. "Not doing the wrong things" means avoiding defects and other behaviors that cause customer *dissatisfaction*. Quality costs address only the latter aspect of quality. It is conceivable that a firm could drive quality costs to zero and still go out of business.

A problem exists with the very name "cost of quality." By using this terminology, we automatically create the impression that quality is a cost. However, our modern understanding makes it clear that quality is *not* a cost. Quality represents a driver that produces higher *profits* through *lower* costs and the ability to command a premium price in the marketplace. This author concurs with such quality experts as H.J. Harrington and Frank M. Gryna that a better term would be "cost of poor quality." However, we will bow to tradition and use the familiar term "cost of quality" throughout this book.

The fundamental principle of the cost of quality is that any cost that would not have been expended if quality were perfect is a cost of quality. This includes such obvious costs as scrap and rework, but it also includes many costs that are far less obvious, such as the cost of reordering to replace defective material. Service businesses also incur quality costs; for example, a hotel incurs a quality cost when room service delivers missing soap or towels to a guest. Quality costs are a measure of the costs specifically associated with the achievement or nonachievement of product or service quality—including all product or service requirements established by the company and its contracts with customers and society. Requirements include marketing specifications, end-product and process specifications, purchase orders, engineering drawings, company procedures, operating instructions, professional or industry standards, government regulations, and any other document or customer needs that can affect the definition of product or service. More specifically, quality costs are the total of the cost incurred by a) investing in the *prevention* of nonconformances to requirements; b) *appraising* a product or service for conformance to requirements; and c) *failure* to meet requirements (Figure 4.5).

PREVENTION COSTS

The costs of all activities specifically designed to prevent poor quality in products or services. Examples are the costs of new product review, quality planning, supplier capability surveys, process capability evaluations, quality improvement team meetings, quality improvement projects, quality education and training.

APPRAISAL COSTS

The costs associated with measuring, evaluating or auditing products or services to assure conformance to quality standards and performance requirements. These include the costs of incoming and source inspection/test of purchased material, in process and final inspection/test, product, process, or service audits, calibration of measuring and test equipment, and the costs of associated supplies and materials.

FAILURE COSTS

The costs resulting from products or services not conforming to requirements or customer/user needs. Failure costs are divided into internal and external failure cost categories.

INTERNAL FAILURE COSTS

Failure costs occurring prior to delivery or shipment of the product, or the furnishing of a service, to the customer. Examples are the costs of scrap, rework, reinspection, retesting, material review, and down grading.

EXTERNAL FAILURE COSTS

Failure costs occurring after delivery or shipment of the product, and during or after furnishing of a service, to the customer. Examples are the costs of processing customer complaints, customer returns, warranty claims, and product recalls.

Figure 4.5—*Continued on next page . . .*

Figure 4.5—*Continued . . .*

TOTAL QUALITY COSTS
The sum of the above costs. It represents the difference between the actual cost of a product or service, and what the reduced cost would be if there was no possibility of substandard service, failure of products, or defects in their manufacture.

Figure 4.5. Quality costs—general description.
From *Principles of Quality Costs, 3rd Edition* p. 5, Jack Campanella, Editor.
Copyright © 1999 by ASQ Quality Press.

For most organizations, quality costs are hidden costs. Unless specific quality cost identification efforts have been undertaken, few accounting systems include provision for identifying quality costs. Because of this, unmeasured quality costs tend to increase. Poor quality impacts companies in two ways: higher cost and lower customer satisfaction. The lower satisfaction creates price pressure and lost sales, which results in lower revenues. The combination of higher cost and lower revenues eventually brings on a crisis that may threaten the very existence of the company. Rigorous cost of quality measurement is one technique for preventing such a crisis from occurring. Figure 4.6 illustrates the hidden cost concept.

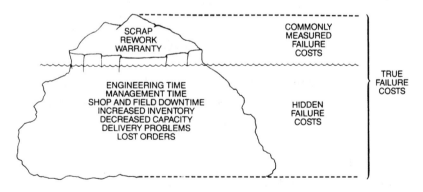

Figure 4.6. Hidden cost of quality and the multiplier effect.
From *Principles of Quality Costs, 2nd Edition* p. 11, Jack Campanella, Editor.
Copyright © 1990 by ASQ Quality Press.

GOAL OF QUALITY COST SYSTEM

The goal of any quality cost system is to reduce quality costs to the lowest practical level. This level is determined by the total of the costs of failure and the cost of appraisal and prevention. Juran and Gryna (1988) present these costs graphically as shown in Figure 4.7. In the figure it can be seen that the cost of failure declines as conformance quality levels improve toward perfection, while the cost of appraisal plus prevention increases. There is some "optimum" target quality level where the sum of prevention, appraisal, and failure costs is at a minimum. Efforts to improve quality to better than the optimum level will result in increasing the total quality costs.

Figure 4.7. Classical model of optimum quality costs.
From *Juran's Quality Control Handbook, 4th edition.* J.M. Juran, editor.
Copyright © 1988, McGraw-Hill.

Juran acknowledged that in many cases the classical model of optimum quality costs is flawed. It is common to find that quality levels can be economically improved to literal perfection. For example, millions of stampings may be produced virtually error-free from a well-designed and built stamping die. The classical model created a mindset that resisted the idea that perfection was a possibility. No obstacle is as difficult to surmount as a mindset. The new model of optimum quality cost incorporates the possibility of zero defects and is shown in Figure 4.8.

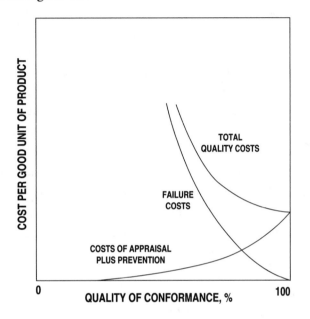

Figure 4.8. New model of optimum quality costs.
From *Juran's Quality Control Handbook, 4th edition.* J.M. Juran, editor.
Copyright © 1988, McGraw-Hill.

Quality costs are lowered by identifying the root causes of quality problems and taking action to eliminate these causes. The tools and techniques described in Chapter 7 are useful in this endeavor. KAIZEN, reengineering, and other continuous improvement approaches are commonly used.

STRATEGY FOR REDUCING QUALITY COSTS

As a general rule, quality costs increase as the detection point moves further up the production and distribution chain. The lowest cost is generally obtained when nonconformances are prevented in the first place. If nonconformances occur, it is generally least expensive to detect them as soon as possible after their occurrence. Beyond that point there is loss incurred from additional work that may be lost. The most expensive quality costs are from nonconformances detected by customers. In addition to the replacement or repair loss, a company can lose customer goodwill and find that their reputation has been damaged when the customer relates his experience to others. In extreme cases, litigation may result, adding even more cost and loss of goodwill.

Another advantage of early detection is that it provides more meaningful feedback to help identify root causes. The time lag between production and field failure makes it very difficult to trace the occurrence back to the process state that produced it. While field failure tracking is useful in *prospectively* evaluating a "fix," it is usually of little value in *retrospectively* evaluating a problem.

ACCOUNTING SUPPORT

We have said it before, but it bears repeating, that the support of the accounting department is vital whenever financial and accounting matters are involved. In fact, the accounting department bears *primary* responsibility for accounting matters, including cost of quality systems. The quality department's role in development and maintenance of the cost of quality system is to provide guidance and support to the accounting department.

The cost of quality system must be integrated into the larger cost accounting system. It is, in fact, merely a subsystem. Terminology, format, etc., should be consistent between the cost of quality system and the larger system. This will speed the learning process and reduce confusion. Ideally, the cost of quality will be so fully integrated into the cost accounting system that it will not be viewed as a separate accounting system at all, it will be a routine part of cost reporting and reduction. The ideal cost of quality accounting system will simply aggregate quality costs to enhance their visibility to management and facilitate efforts to reduce them. For most companies, this task falls under the jurisdiction of the controller's office.

Quality cost measurement need not be accurate to the penny to be effective. The purpose of measuring such costs is to provide broad guidelines for management decision-making and action. The very nature of cost of quality makes such accuracy impossible. In some instances it will only be possible to obtain periodic rough estimates of such costs as lost customer goodwill, cost of damage to the company's reputation, etc. These estimates can be obtained using special audits, statistical sampling, and other market studies and can be jointly conducted by teams of marketing, accounting, and quality personnel. Since these costs are often huge, these estimates must be obtained; however, they need not be obtained every month. Annual studies are usually sufficient to indicate trends in these measures.

MANAGEMENT OF QUALITY COSTS

In our discussion of the cost of quality subsystem, we emphasized the importance of not creating a unique accounting system. The same holds true when discussing management of quality costs. Quality cost management should be part of the charter of the senior level cross-functional cost management team. It is one part of the broader business effort to control costs. In all likelihood, however, the business will find that quality cost reduction has greater potential to contribute to the bottom line than the reduction of other costs because, unlike other costs, quality costs are *waste costs* (Pyzdek, 1976). As such, quality costs contribute no value to the product or service purchased by the customer. Indeed, quality costs are often indicators of *negative customer value.* The customer who brings his car in for a covered warranty expense suffers uncompensated inconvenience, the cost of which is not captured by most quality cost systems (although, as discussed above, we recommend that such costs be estimated from time-to-time). All other costs incurred by the firm purchase at least some value.

Effective cost of quality programs consist of taking the following steps (Campanella, 1990, p. 34):

- Establish a quality cost measurement system.
- Develop a suitable long-range trend analysis.
- Establish annual improvement goals for total quality costs.
- Develop short-range trend analyses with individual targets which, when combined, meet the annual improvement goal.
- Monitor progress towards the goals and take action when progress falls short of targets.

The tools and techniques described in Chapter 5 are useful for managing cost of quality reduction projects.

Quality cost management helps firms establish priorities for corrective action. Without such guidance, it is likely that firms will misallocate their resources, thereby getting less than optimal return on investment. If such experiences are repeated frequently, the organization may even question or abandon their quality cost reduction efforts. The most often-used tool in setting priorities is Pareto analysis (see Chapter 7). Typically at the outset of the quality cost reduction effort, Pareto analysis is used to evaluate failure costs to identify those "vital few" areas in most need of attention. Documented failure costs, especially external failure costs, almost certainly understate the true cost and they are highly visible to the customer. Pareto analysis is combined with other quality tools, such as control charts and cause-and-effect diagrams, to identify the root causes of quality problems. Of course, the analyst must constantly keep in mind the fact that most costs are hidden. Pareto analysis cannot be effectively performed until the hidden costs have been identified. Analyzing only those data easiest to obtain is an example of the GIGO (garbage-in, garbage-out) approach to analysis.

After the most significant failure costs have been identified and brought under control, appraisal costs are analyzed. Are we spending too much on appraisal in view of the lower levels of failure costs? Here quality cost analysis must be supplemented with risk analysis to assure that failure and appraisal cost levels are in balance. Appraisal cost analysis is also used to justify expenditure in prevention costs.

Prevention costs of quality are investments in the discovery, incorporation, and maintenance of defect prevention disciplines for all operations affecting the quality of product or service (Campanella, 1990). As such, prevention needs to be applied correctly and *not* evenly across the board. Much improvement has been demonstrated through reallocation of prevention effort from areas having little effect to areas where it really pays off; once again, the Pareto principle is demonstrated in action.

COST OF QUALITY EXAMPLES

I.   **Prevention costs**—Costs incurred to prevent the occurrence of non-conformances in the future, such as*

      A. Marketing/customer/user
- 1. Marketing research
- 2. Customer/user perception surveys/clinics
- 3. Contract/document review

      B. Product/service/design development
- 1. Design quality progress reviews
- 2. Design support activities
- 3. Product design qualification test
- 4. Service design qualification
- 5. Field tests

      C. Purchasing
- 1. Supplier reviews
- 2. Supplier rating
- 3. Purchase order tech data reviews
- 4. Supplier quality planning

---

*All detailed quality cost descriptions are from *Principles of Quality Costs*, 3rd edition, J. Campanella, Editor, Milwaukee, WI: ASQ Quality Press, appendix B.

D. Operations (manufacturing or service)
  1. Operations process validation
  2. Operations quality planning
      a. Design and development of quality measurement and control equipment
  3. Operations support quality planning
  4. Operator quality education
  5. Operator SPC/process control
E. Quality administration
  1. Administrative salaries
  2. Administrative expenses
  3. Quality program planning
  4. Quality performance reporting
  5. Quality education
  6. Quality improvement
  7. Quality audits
  8. Other prevention costs

II. **Appraisal costs**—Costs incurred in measuring and controlling current production to assure conformance to requirements, such as
  A. Purchasing appraisal costs
    1. Receiving or incoming inspections and tests
    2. Measurement equipment
    3. Qualification of supplier product
    4. Source inspection and control programs
  B. Operations (manufacturing or service) appraisal costs
    1. Planned operations inspections, tests, audits
        a. Checking labor
        b. Product or service quality audits
        c. Inspection and test materials
    2. Set-up inspections and tests
    3. Special tests (manufacturing)
    4. Process control measurements

 5. Laboratory support
 6. Measurement equipment
     a. Depreciation allowances
     b. Measurement equipment expenses
     c. Maintenance and calibration labor
 7. Outside endorsements and certifications
C. External appraisal costs
 1. Field performance evaluation
 2. Special product evaluations
 3. Evaluation of field stock and spare parts
D. Review of tests and inspection data
E. Miscellaneous quality evaluations

III. **Internal failure costs**—Costs generated before a product is shipped as a result of non-conformance to requirements, such as
A. Product/service design failure costs (internal)
 1. Design corrective action
 2. Rework due to design changes
 3. Scrap due to design changes
B. Purchasing failure costs
 1. Purchased material reject disposition costs
 2. Purchased material replacement costs
 3. Supplier corrective action
 4. Rework of supplier rejects
 5. Uncontrolled material losses
C. Operations (product or service) failure costs
 1. Material review and corrective action costs
     a. Disposition costs
     b. Troubleshooting or failure analysis costs (operations)
     c. Investigation support costs
     d. Operations corrective action

2. Operations rework and repair costs
   a. Rework
   b. Repair
3. Reinspection/retest costs
4. Extra operations
5. Scrap costs (operations)
6. Downgraded end product or service
7. Internal failure labor losses
D. Other internal failure costs

IV. **External failure costs**—Costs generated after a product is shipped as a result of non-conformance to requirements, such as
   A. Complaint investigation/customer or user service
   B. Returned goods
   C. Retrofit costs
   D. Recall costs
   E. Warranty claims
   F. Liability costs
   G. Penalties
   H. Customer/user goodwill
   I. Lost sales
   J. Other external failure costs

QUALITY COST BASES

The following are guidelines for selecting a base for analyzing quality costs:
- The base should be related to quality costs in a meaningful way.
- The base should be well-known to the managers who will receive the quality cost reports.
- The base should be a measure of business volume in the area where quality cost measurements are to be applied.
- Several bases are often necessary to get a complete picture of the relative magnitude of quality costs.

Some commonly used bases are (Campanella, 1990, p. 26):
- A labor base (such as total labor, direct labor, or applied labor)
- A cost base (such as shop cost, operating cost, or total material and labor)
- A sales base (such as net sales billed, or sales value of finished goods)
- A unit base (such as the number of units produced, or the volume of output).

While actual dollars spent are usually the best indicator for determining where quality improvement projects will have the greatest impact on profits and where corrective action should be taken, unless the production rate is relatively constant, it will not provide a clear indication of quality cost improvement trends. Since the goal of the cost of quality program is improvement over time, it is necessary to adjust the data for other time-related changes such as production rate, inflation, etc. Total quality cost compared to an applicable base results in an index which may be plotted and analyzed using control charts, run charts, or one of the other tools described in this chapter.

For long-range analyses and planning, net sales is the base most often used for presentations to top management (Campanella, 1990, p. 24). If sales are relatively constant over time, the quality cost analysis can be performed for relatively short spans of time. In other industries this figure must be computed over a longer time interval to smooth out large swings in the sales base. For example, in industries such as shipbuilding or satellite manufacturing, some periods may have no deliveries, while others have large dollar amounts. It is important that the quality costs incurred be related to the sales for the same period. Consider the sales as the "opportunity" for the quality costs to happen.

Some examples of cost of quality bases are (Campanella, 1990):
- Internal failure costs as a percent of total production costs
- External failure costs as an average percent of net sales
- Procurement appraisal costs as a percent of total purchased material cost
- Operations appraisal costs as a percent of total productions costs
- Total quality costs as a percent of production costs

An example of a cost of quality report that employs some of these bases is shown in Figure 4.9.

QUALITY COST SUMMARY REPORT
FOR THE MONTH ENDING _____
(In Thousands of U.S. Dollars)

DESCRIPTION	CURRENT MONTH			YEAR TO DATE		
	QUALITY COSTS	AS A PERCENT OF		QUALITY COSTS	AS A PERCENT OF	
		SALES	OTHER		SALES	OTHER
1.0 PREVENTION COSTS						
1.1 Marketing/Customer/User						
1.2 Product/Service/Design Development						
1.3 Purchasing Prevention Costs						
1.4 Operations Prevention Costs						
1.5 Quality Administration						
1.6 Other Prevention Costs						
TOTAL PREVENTION COSTS						
PREVENTION TARGETS						
2.0 APPRAISAL COSTS						
2.1 Purchasing Appraisal Costs						
2.2 Operations Appraisal Costs						
2.3 External Appraisal Costs						
2.4 Review Of Test And Inspection Data						
2.5 Misc. Quality Evaluations						
TOTAL APPRAISAL COSTS						
APPRAISAL TARGETS						
3.0 INTERNAL FAILURE COSTS						
3.1 Product/Service Design Failure Costs						
3.2 Purchasing Failure Costs						
3.3 Operations Failure Costs						
3.4 Other Internal Failure Costs						
4.0 EXTERNAL FAILURE COSTS						
TOTAL FAILURE COSTS						
FAILURE TARGETS						
TOTAL QUALITY COSTS						
TOTAL QUALITY TARGETS						

BASE DATA	CURRENT MONTH		YEAR TO DATE		FULL YEAR	
	BUDGET	ACTUAL	BUDGET	ACTUAL	BUDGET	ACTUAL
Net Sales						
Other Base (Specify)						

Figure 4.9. Quality costs summary report.
From *Principles of Quality Costs, 2nd Edition* p. 48, Jack Campanella, editor.
Copyright © 1990 by ASQ Quality Press.

QUALITY COST TREND ANALYSIS

As stated above, the purpose of collecting quality cost data is to provide a sound basis for taking the necessary action to eliminate the causes of these costs, and thereby eliminate the costs themselves. If the action taken is effective, the data will indicate a positive trend. Trend analysis is most often performed by presenting the data in run chart form and analyzing the runs (see Chapter 7). It is common to combine all of the cost of quality data on a single graph, as shown in Figure 4.10.

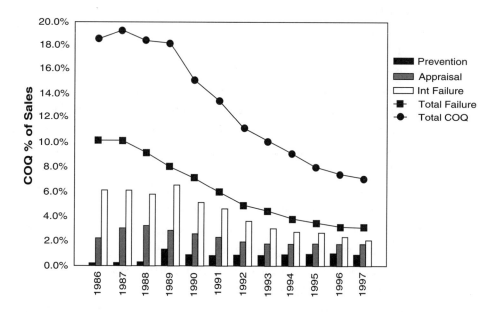

Figure 4.10. Cost of quality history.

If the runs are subjected to the run tests described below, it can be shown that the total failure and total COQ (cost of quality) trends are statistically significant. However, for these data, the use of formal statistical rules is superfluous—the improvement is obvious.

While such aggregate analysis is useful for senior management, it is of little value to those engaged in more focused cost of quality projects. In these cases the trend data should be as specific as possible to the area being studied. Also, the measurement may be something more directly related to the work being done by the improvement team rather than dollars, and the time interval should be shorter. For example, if it has been determined that a major internal failure cost item is defective solder joints, then the team should plot a control chart of the solder defect rate and analyze the process in real-time. Obviously, reducing solder defects should reduce the cost associated with solder defects.

IMPLEMENTING THE QUALITY COST PROGRAM

Quality cost program introduction is a major project and should utilize the tools and techniques described in Chapter 5. Prior to implementation, a needs analysis should be performed to determine if, in fact, a cost of quality program can benefit the company. The needs assessment should also include a benefit/cost analysis and a plan for the implementation. The plan should include:

- the management presentation, designed to identify the overall opportunity and show an example of how the program will achieve its benefits
- a description of the pilot program
- material designed to educate and involve all functions in the program
- an outline of the internal cost of quality accounting procedures
- a description of the data collection and analysis of cost of quality data at the highest level of aggregation
- a description of the cost of quality reporting system and how the data will be used to improve quality

As with any major quality project, a sponsor should be found and management support secured. In the case of cost of quality, the sponsor should be the Controller or a subordinate.

USE OF QUALITY COSTS

The principal use of quality cost data is to justify and support quality performance improvement. Quality cost data help identify problem areas and direct resources to these areas. To be effective, the cost of quality system has to be integrated with other quality information systems to assure that root causes will be addressed. Statistical analysis can be used to correlate quality cost trends with other quality data to help direct attention to problem causes.

One mission of the quality management function is to educate top management about the long-range effects of total quality performance on the profits and quality reputation of the company. Management must understand that strategic planning for quality is as important as strategic planning for any other functional area. When the strategic plan addresses cost issues, quality cost consideration should be prominent. Quality costs should be considered first because, since they are waste costs, their reduction is always taken from the "fat" of the organization. The role of the quality manager in this process should be to (Campanella, 1990, p. 56)

- analyze major trends in customer satisfaction, defects or error rates, and quality costs, both generally and by specific program or project. These trends should also be used to provide inputs for setting objectives;
- assist the other functions to ensure that costs related to quality are included in their analyses for setting objectives;
- develop an overall quality strategic plan which incorporates all functional quality objectives and strategic action plans, including plans and budgets for the quality function.

BENEFITS OF QUALITY COST REDUCTION

Quality cost reductions can have a significant impact on a company's growth rate and bottom line. Research done by the Chicago Graduate School of Business showed that companies using TQM for an average of 6.5 years increased revenues at an annual rate of 8.3% annually, versus 4.2% annually for all U.S. manufacturers. Suminski (1994) reports that the average manufacturer's price of nonconformance is 25% of operating costs; for service businesses the figure is 35%. These costs represent a direct charge against a company's profitability. A New England heavy equipment manufacturer reports that their price of nonconformance was 31% of total sales when they undertook a quality cost reduction project. In just one year they were able to

lower these costs to 9%. Among their accomplishments:
- Scrap and rework reduced 30%.
- Manufacturing cost variance reduced 20%.
- Late collections reduced 46%.
- Average turnaround on receivables reduced from 62 days to 35 days.

Calculating the value of retention of customers

Customers have value. This simple fact is obvious when one looks at a customer making a single purchase. The transaction provides revenue and profit to the firm. However, when the customer places a demand on the firm, such as a return of a previous purchase or a call for technical support, there is a natural tendency to see this as a loss. At these times it is important to understand that customer value must not be viewed on a short-term transaction-by-transaction basis. Customer value must be measured *over the lifetime of the relationship*. One method of calculating the lifetime value of a loyal customer, based on work by Frederick Reichheld of Bain and Co. and the University of Michigan's Claes Fornell, is as follows (Stewart, 1995):

1. Decide on a meaningful period of time over which to do the calculations. This will vary depending on your planning cycles and your business: A life insurer should track customers for decades, a disposable diaper maker for just a few years, for example.

2. Calculate the profit (net cash flow) customers generate each year. Track several samples—some newcomers, some old-timers—to find out how much business they gave you each year, and how much it cost to serve them. If possible, segment them by age, income, sales channel, and so on. For the first year, be sure to subtract the cost of acquiring the pool of customers, such as advertising, commissions, back-office costs of

setting up a new account. Get specific numbers—profit per customer in year one, year two, etc.—not averages for all customers or all years. Long-term customers tend to buy more, pay more (newcomers are often lured by discounts), and create less bad debt.

3. Chart the customer "life expectancy," using the samples to find out how much your customer base erodes each year. Again, specific figures are better than an average like "10% a year"; old customers are much less likely to leave than freshmen. In retail banking, 26% of account holders defect in the first year; in the ninth year, the rate drops to 9%.

4. Once you know the profit per customer per year and the customer-retention figures, it's simple to calculate net present value. Pick a discount rate—if you want a 15% annual return on assets, use that. In year one, the NPV will be profit $\div$ 1.15. Next year, NPV = (year-two profit $\times$ retention rate) $\div$ 1.15^2. In year n, the last year in your figures, the NPV is the n year's adjusted profit $\div$ 1.15^n. The sum of the years one through n is how much your customer is worth—the net present value of all the profits you can expect from his tenure.

This is very valuable information. It can be used to find out how much to spend to attract new customers, and which ones. Better still, you can exploit the leverage customer satisfaction offers. Take your figures and calculate how much more customers would be worth if you increased retention by 5%. Figure 4.11 shows the increase in customer NPV for a 5% increase in retention for three industries.

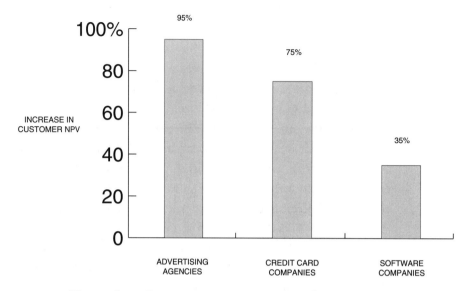

Figure 4.11. Increase in customer NPV for a 5% increase
in customer retention.

Once the lifetime value of the customer is known, it forms the basis of loyalty-based management[SM] of the customer relationship. According to Reichheld (1996), loyalty-based management is the practice of carefully selecting customers, employees, and investors, and then working hard to retain them. There is a tight, cause-and-effect connection between investor, employee and customer loyalty. These are the human assets of the firm.

COMPLAINT HANDLING

When a customer complaint has been received it represents an opportunity to increase customer loyalty or to risk losing the customer. The way the complaint is handled is crucial. The importance of complaint handling is illustrated in Figure 4.12. These data illustrate that the decision as to whether a customer who complains plans to repurchase is highly dependent on how well they felt their complaint was handled. Add to this the fact that customers who complain are likely to tell as many as 14 others of their experience, and the importance of complaint handling in customer relations becomes obvious.

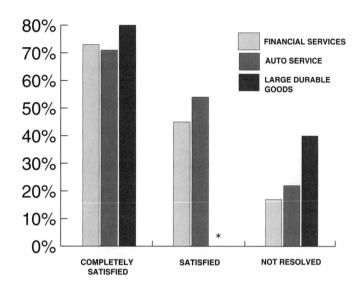

Figure 4.12. Percent planning to repurchase vs. how complaint was handled. (*Note: The large durable goods survey did not include a response category of "satisfied".)

Despite the impressive nature of Figure 4.12, even these figures dramatically understate the true extent of the problem. Complaints represent people who were not only unhappy, they notified the company. Research indicates that up to 96% of unhappy customers never tell the company. This is especially unfortunate since it has been shown that customer loyalty is *increased* by proper resolution of complaints. Given the dramatic impact of a lost customer, it makes sense to maximize the opportunity of the customer to complain. Complaints should be actively sought, an activity decidedly against human nature. This suggests that a system must be developed and implemented to force employees to seek out customer complaints. In addition to actively soliciting customer complaints, the system should also provide every conceivable way for an unhappy customer to contact the company on their own, including toll-free hotlines, email, comment cards, etc.

♦ ♦ ♦
CHAPTER

5

Managing
Six Sigma Projects

The dictionary defines the word *project* as follows:

1. A plan or proposal; a scheme. See synonyms at *plan*.
2. An undertaking requiring concerted effort.

Under the synonym *plan* we find the following:

1. A scheme, program, or method worked out beforehand for the accomplishment of an objective: a plan of attack.
2. A proposed or tentative project or course of action.
3. A systematic arrangement of important parts.

Although truly dramatic improvement in quality often requires transforming the management philosophy and organization culture, the fact is that, sooner or later, projects must be undertaken to make things happen. Projects are the means through which things are systematically changed; projects are the bridge between the planning and the doing.

Frank Gryna makes the following observations about projects (Juran and Gryna, 1988, pp. 22.18–22.19):

- An agreed-upon project is also a legitimate project. This legitimacy puts the project on the official priority list. It helps to secure the needed budgets, facilities, and personnel. It also helps those guiding the project to secure attendance at scheduled meetings, to acquire requested data, to secure permission to conduct experiments, etc.

- The project provides a forum of converting an atmosphere of defensiveness or blame into one of constructive action.
- Participation in a project increases the likelihood that the participant will act on the findings.
- All breakthrough is achieved *project by project*, and in no other way.

The last item represents both good news and bad news. The bad news is that few projects are truly successful; the good news is that companies can and do become proficient at implementing projects without the need for mystical powers. What is needed is effective project management.

USEFUL PROJECT MANAGEMENT TOOLS AND TECHNIQUES

Project management is a system for planning and implementing change that will produce the desired result most efficiently. There are a number of tools and techniques that have been found useful in project management. Brief descriptions of the major project management methods are provided here. Techniques specific to project management are covered in greater detail elsewhere in this chapter. Many of these tools are used in a wide variety of quality improvement and quality control situations in addition to project management; additional information on each of these more general techniques is found elsewhere in this book; consult the index for details.

Project plan—The project plan shows the "why" and the "how" of a project. A good project plan will include a statement of the goal, a cost/benefit analysis, a feasibility analysis, a listing of the major steps to be taken, a timetable for completion, and a description of the resources required (including human resources) to carry out the project. The plan will also identify objective measures of success that will be used to evaluate the effectiveness of the proposed changes; these are sometimes called the "deliverables" of the project.

Gantt chart—A Gantt chart shows the relationships among the project tasks, along with time constraints. See below for a discussion of Gantt charts.

Milestone charts—These are Gantt charts modified to provide additional information on project status. See below for a discussion of Milestone charts.

Pareto analysis—Pareto analysis is a technique that helps one to rank opportunities to determine which of many potential projects should be pursued first. It can also be used sequentially to determine which step to take next. The Pareto principle has been described by Juran as separating the "vital few" from the "trivial many." It is the "why" and the "benefit" of the project plan. See Chapter 7 for additional discussion.

Budget—A budget is an itemized summary of estimated or intended expenditures for a given project along with proposals for financing them. Project budgets present management with a systematic plan for the expenditure of the organization's resources, such as money or time, during the course of the project. The resources spent include time of personnel, money, equipment utilization and so on. The budget is the "cost" portion of the project plan. Also see below.

Process decision program chart (PDPC)—The PDPC technique is used to develop contingency plans. It is modeled after reliability engineering methods such as failure mode, effects, and criticality analysis (FMECA) and fault-tree analysis (FTA). The emphasis of PDPC is the impact of problems on project plans. PDPCs include the identification of specific actions to mitigate the impact of problems, should they occur. PDPCs are useful in developing a project plan with a minimum chance of encountering serious problems. Also see Chapter 7.

Quality function deployment (QFD)—Traditionally, QFD is a system for design of a product or service based on customer demands; it is a system that moves methodically from customer requirements to product or service requirements. QFD provides the documentation for the decision-making process. QFD can also be used to show the "whats" and "hows" of a project. Used in this way QFD becomes a powerful project planning tool. Also see Chapter 3.

Matrix chart—A matrix chart is a simplified application of QFD (or, perhaps, QFD is an elaborate application of matrix charts). This chart is constructed to systematically analyze the correlation's between two groups of ideas. When applied to project management the two ideas might be, for example 1) what is to be done? 2) who is to do it? Also see Chapter 7.

Arrow diagrams—Arrow diagrams are simple network representations of project flows. They show which tasks must be completed in the project and the order in which the tasks must be completed. See Chapter 7. Arrow diagrams are a simplification of PERT-type systems (see below).

PLANNING

There are several reasons why one should plan carefully before starting a project (Ruskin and Estes, 1995, p. 44):

1. The plan is a simulation of prospective project work, which allows flaws to be identified in time to be corrected.
2. The plan is a vehicle for discussing each person's role and responsibilities, thereby helping direct and control the work of the project.
3. The plan shows how the parts fit together, which is essential for coordinating related activities.
4. The plan is a point of reference for any changes of scope, thereby helping project managers deal with their customers.
5. The plan helps everyone know when the objectives have been reached and, therefore, when to stop.

The project plan shows the "why" and the "how" of a project. A good project plan will include the following elements:

- statement of the goal
- cost/benefit analysis
- feasibility analysis
- listing of the major steps to be taken
- timetable for completion
- description of the resources required (including human resources) to carry out the project

The plan will also identify objective measures of success that will be used to evaluate the effectiveness of the proposed changes; these are sometimes called the "deliverables" of the project.

PROJECT DECOMPOSITION

Most projects important enough to have a significant impact on quality are too large to tackle all at once. Instead, large projects must be broken down into smaller projects and, in turn, into specific work elements and tasks. The process of going from project objectives to tasks is called decomposition. Project decomposition begins with the preparation of a preliminary plan. A preliminary project plan will identify, in broad high-level terms, the objectives of the project and constraints in terms of time and resources. The work to be performed should be described and precedence relationships should be sketched out. Preliminary budgets and schedules will be developed. Finally, subplans will be developed for each subproject for the following:

- Control plans
  - Quality control plans
  - Cost control plans
  - Schedule control plans
- Staffing plans
- Material plans
- Reporting plans
- Other plans as deemed necessary

These subplans are developed in parallel for the various subprojects.

Integrated quality initiatives

Also see cross-functional collaboration, below.

Projects should be selected consistent with the organization's overall strategy and mission. Because of this global perspective most projects involve the efforts of several different functional areas. Not only do individual quality projects tend to cut across organizational boundaries, different projects are often related to one another. To effectively manage this complexity it is necessary to integrate the planning and execution of projects organization-wide.

(For additional details on teams see Chapter 1.)

Teams are chartered by senior leadership, generally the only group with the necessary authority to designate cross-functional responsibilities and allow access to interdepartmental resources. The team facilitator should ask senior leadership to put the problem statement in writing. The problem statement should be specific enough to help the team identify the scope of the project and the major stakeholders. Problems of gargantuan proportions should be subdivided into smaller projects.

There are six steps in the chartering process:
1. Obtaining a problem statement
2. Identifying the principal stakeholders
3. Creating a macro flowchart of the process
4. Selecting the team members
5. Training the team
6. Selecting the team leader

The project charter should include a statement indicating the mission of the project team.

If the team has not received its mission statement as part of its charter, it should prepare its own team mission statement. The mission statement should be linked to the larger organization's mission via the charter. Scholtes (1988) lists a number of situations which require that the team spend time developing its own mission statement:

- Teams with a mission statement from management which is too broad ("reduce customer complaints")
- Teams with an unclear or undefined mission ("get a team together to work in the shipping department")
- Teams who need to describe the nature and severity of a problem before they can decide how to proceed with their project ("are scratches really a big problem?")
- Teams whose sole mission is to identify and describe problems so that more focused projects can be designed; probably involving different teams
- Teams who have the leeway to select their own project

The mission statements of various project teams should clearly identify the boundaries between them. Where confusion exists, teams should meet to clarify responsibilities.

Several problems with mission statements appear repeatedly:

- Projects have little or no impact on the organization's success; even if successful, no one will really care.
- Missions overlap the missions of other teams. E.g., Team A's mission is to reduce solder rejects; Team B's mission is to reduce wave solder rejects, Team C's mission is to reduce circuit board assembly problems.
- Projects improve processes that are scheduled for extensive redesign or discontinuation. For example, working on improving work flow for a production process that is to be relocated to another factory.
- Studying a huge system ("patient admitting"), rather than a manageable process ("outpatient surgery preadmission").
- Studying symptoms ("touch-up of defective solder joints") rather than root causes ("wave solder defects")
- Project deliverables are undefined. E.g., "Study TQM" rather than "Reduce waiting time in Urgent Care."

Short- and long-term quality plans and objectives

The discussion here will focus on the role of quality plans in project management.

In general, long-term planning addresses issues of strategy and mission. Projects involve the actual implementation of strategic programs and should be considered short-term and tactical, even projects that take a relatively long time to complete.

WORK BREAKDOWN STRUCTURES

Ruskin and Estes (1995) define work breakdown structures (WBS) as a process for defining the final and intermediate products of a project and their relationships. Defining project tasks is typically complex and accomplished by a series of decompositions followed by a series of aggregations. For example, a software project to develop an SPC software application would disaggregate the customer requirements into very specific engineering requirements (e.g., the customer's requirement that the product create x-bar charts would be decomposed into engineering requirements such as subroutines for computing subgroup means and ranges, plotting data points, drawing lines, etc.). Aggregation would involve linking the various modules to produce an x-bar chart displayed on the screen.

The WBS can be represented in a tree-diagram, as shown in Figure 5.1.

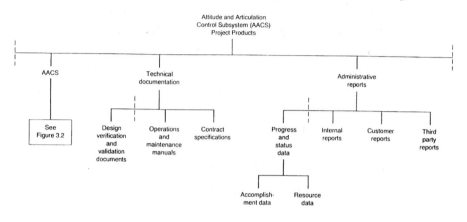

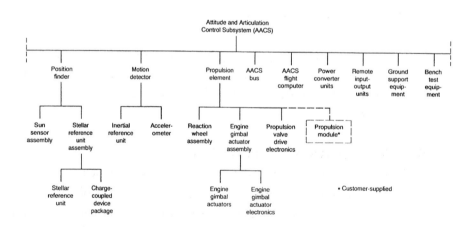

Figure 5.1. WBS of a spacecraft system.

From Ruskin, A.M. and Estes, W.E. *What Every Engineer Should Know About Project Management*, Second Edition. Copyright © 1995 by Marcel Dekker, Inc.

Reprinted with permission.

Preliminary requirements WBS—is a statement of the overall requirements for the project as expressed by the customer (e.g., the deliverables or "product"), and subsidiary requirements as expressed by management (e.g., billing, reports required).

Detailed plan WBS—breaks down the product into subproducts. Requirements are listed for each subproduct (e.g., tooling, staff). The subproducts are, in turn, broken down into their subproducts, etc., until a reasonable limit is reached. All work begins at the lowest level. Detailed plans for each subsystem include control plans for quality, cost and schedule, staffing plans, materials plans, reporting plans, contingency plans and work authorization plans. In addition, the overall detailed plan covers objectives, constraints, precedence relationships, timetables, budgets, and review and reporting criteria.

Typical subsystem WBS—is created, i.e., the process just described is performed for each subsystem. Subsytems are then built.

Integration WBS—details how the various subsystems will be assembled into the product deliverables. This usually involves integrating into larger subsystems, then still larger subsystems, etc., to the highest level of integration.

Validation WBS—plans explain how the various systems integrations will be measured and tested to assure that the final requirements will be met.

Feedback loops

The project plan is itself an important feedback tool. It provides details on the tasks that are to be performed, when they are to be performed, and how much resource is to be consumed. The plan should also include explicit provisions for feedback. Typical forms of feedback are the following:

- **Status reports**—Formal, periodic written reports, often with a standardized format, telling what the project is based on, and where it is supposed to be relative to the plan. Where project performance does not match planned performance, the reports include additional information as to the cause of the problem and what is being done to bring the project into alignment with the plan. Remedial action may, at times, involve revising the plan. When the project is not meeting the plan due to obstacles which the project team cannot overcome, the status report will request senior management intervention.

- **Management reviews**—These are meetings, scheduled in advance, where the project leader will have the opportunity to interact with key members of the management team. The chief responsibility for these meetings is management's. The purpose is to brief management on the status of the project, review the project charter and project team mission, discuss those management activities likely to have an impact on the progress of the team, etc. This is the appropriate forum for addressing systems barriers encountered by the team: while the team must work within existing systems, management has the authority to change the systems. At times a minor system change can dramatically enhance the ability of the team to progress.

- **Budget reviews**—While budget *reports* are included in each status report, a budget review is a formal evaluation of actual resource utilization with respect to budgeted utilization. Budget review may also involve revising budgets, either upward or downward, based on developments since the original budget approval. Among those unschooled in the science of statistics there is an unfortunate tendency to react to every random tick in budget variances as if they were due to a special cause of variation. Quality managers should coach finance and management personnel on the principles of variation to preclude tampering with the budgeting process (also see below).

- **Customer audits**—The "customer" in this context means the principal stakeholder in the project. This person is the "owner" of the process being modified by the project. The project deliverables are designed to meet the objectives of this customer, and the customer should play an active role in keeping the project on track to the stated goals.

- **Updating plans and timetables**—The purpose of feedback is to provide information to form a basis for modifying future behavior. Since that behavior is documented in the project plans and schedules, these documents must be modified to ensure that the appropriate action is taken. Remember, in the PDCA cycle, *plans* change first.

- **Resource redirection**—The modifications made to the plans and timetables will result in increasing or decreasing resource allocation to the project, or accelerating or decelerating the timetable for resource utilization. The impact of these resource redirections on other projects should be evaluated by management in view of the organization's overall objectives.

Performance measures

TIMELINESS

A wide variety of tools and techniques are available to help the project manager develop a realistic project timetable, to use the timetable to time the allocation of resources, and to track progress during the implementation of the project plan. We will review two of the most common here: Gantt charts and PERT-type systems.

Gantt charts

Gantt chart—A Gantt chart shows the relationships among the project tasks, along with time constraints. The horizontal axis of a Gantt chart shows the units of time (days, weeks, months, etc.). The vertical axis shows the activities to be completed. Bars show the estimated start time and duration of the various activities. Figure 5.2 illustrates a simple Gantt chart.

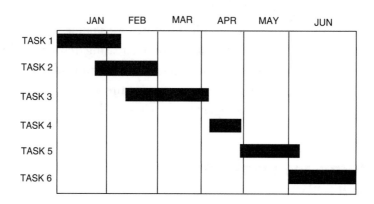

Figure 5.2. Gantt chart.

Milestone charts—Gantt charts are often modified in a variety of ways to provide additional information. One common variation is shown in Figure 5.3. The *milestone* symbol represents an event rather than an activity; it does not consume time or resources. When Gantt charts are modified in this way they are sometimes called "milestone charts."

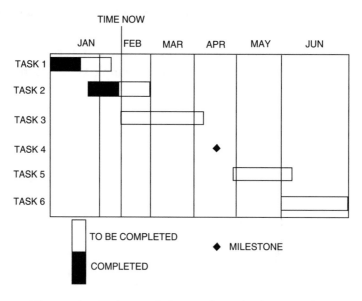

Figure 5.3. Enhanced Gantt chart (milestone chart).

Gantt charts and milestone charts can be modified to show additional information, such as who is responsible for a task, why a task is behind schedule, remedial action planned or already taken, etc.

PERT-CPM-type project management systems

While useful, Gantt charts and their derivatives provide limited project schedule analysis capabilities. The successful management of large-scale projects requires more rigorous planning, scheduling and coordinating of numerous interrelated activities. To aid in these tasks, formal procedures based on the use of networks and network techniques were developed beginning in the late 1950s. The most prominent of these procedures have been PERT (Program Evaluation and Review Technique) and CPM (Critical Path Method). The two approaches are usually referred to as PERT-type project management systems. The most important difference between PERT and CPM is that originally the time estimates for the activities were assumed deterministic in CPM and were probabilistic in PERT. Today, PERT and CPM actually comprise one technique and the differences are mainly historical.

Project scheduling by PERT-CPM consists of four basic phases: planning, scheduling, improving, and controlling. The planning phase involves breaking the project into distinct activities. The time estimates for these activities are then determined and a network (or arrow) diagram is constructed with each activity being represented by an arrow.

PERT-type systems are used to:
- Aid in planning and control of projects
- Determine the feasibility of meeting specified deadlines
- Identify the most likely bottlenecks in a project
- Evaluate the effects of changes in the project requirements or schedule
- Evaluate the effects of deviating from schedule
- Evaluate the effect of diverting resources from the project, or redirecting additional resources to the project.

The ultimate objective of the scheduling phase is to construct a time chart showing the start and finish times for each activity as well as its relationship to other activities in the project. The schedule must identify activities that are "critical" in the sense that they *must* be completed on time to keep the project on schedule.

It is vital not to merely accept the schedule as a given. The information obtained in preparing the schedule can be used to improve the project schedule. Activities that the analysis indicates to be critical are candidates for improvement. Pareto analysis can be used to identify those critical elements that are most likely to lead to significant improvement in overall project completion time. Cost data can be used to supplement the time data, and the combined time/cost information analyzed using Pareto analysis.

The final phase in PERT-CPM project management is project control. This includes the use of the network diagram and time chart for making periodic progress assessments.

Constructing PERT-CPM network charts

All PERT-type systems use a project network chart to graphically portray the interrelationships among the elements of a project. This network representation of the project plan shows all the precedence relationships, i.e., the order in which the tasks must be completed. On the network chart arrows represent *activities*, while boxes or circles represent *events*; in preparing and understanding this technique it is very important to keep these two terms distinct. An arrow goes from one event to another only if the first event is the immediate predecessor of the second. If more than one activity must be completed before an event can occur, then there will be several arrows entering the box corresponding to that event. Sometimes one event must wait for another event, but no activity intervenes between the two events. In this case, the two events are joined with a dotted arrow, representing a *dummy activity*. Dummy activities take no time to complete; they merely show precedence relationships.

These drawing conventions are illustrated in Figure 5.4.

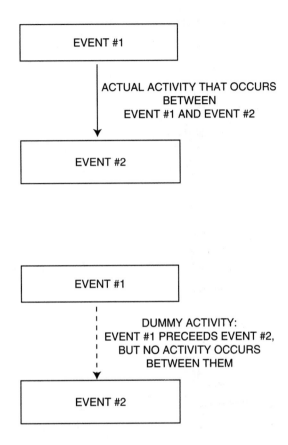

Figure 5.4. Network diagram terms and drawing conventions.

The node towards which all activities lead, the final completion of the project, is called the *sink* of the network.

Taha (1976) offers the following rules for constructing the arrow diagram:

Rule 1—*Each activity is represented by one and only one arrow in the network.* No single activity can be represented twice in the network. This does not mean that one activity cannot be broken down into segments.

Rule 2—*No two activities can be identified by the same head-and-tail events.* This situation may arise when two activities can be performed concurrently. The proper way to deal with this situation is to introduce *dummy events* and activities, as shown in Figure 5.5.

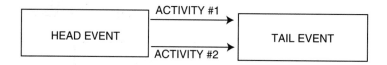

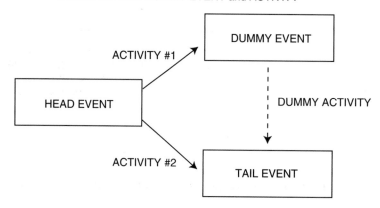

Figure 5.5. Parallel activities: network representation.

Rule #2 facilitates the analysis of network diagrams with computer programs for project analysis.

Rule 3—*In order to ensure the correct precedence relationship in the arrow diagram the following questions must be answered as each activity is added to the network:*
   a. What activities must be completed immediately before this activity can start?
   b. What activities immediately follow this activity?
   c. What activities must occur concurrently with this activity?

Example of PERT

The following is based on an example from Hillier and Lieberman (1980). Let's say that we wish to use PERT on a project for constructing a house. The following activities, and their estimated completion times, are presented in Table 5.1.

Table 5.1. Activities involved in constructing a house.

ACTIVITY	TIME TO COMPLETE (DAYS)
Excavate	2
Foundation	4
Rough wall	10
Rough electrical work	7
Rough exterior plumbing	4
Rough interior plumbing	5
Wall board	8
Flooring	4
Interior painting	5
Interior fixtures	6
Roof	6
Exterior siding	7
Exterior painting	9
Exterior fixtures	2

Now, it is important that certain of these activities be done in a particular order. For example, one cannot put on the roof until the walls are built. This is called a *precedence relationship*, i.e., the walls must *precede* the roof. The network diagram graphically displays the precedence relationships involved in constructing a house. A PERT network for constructing a house is shown in the Figure 5.6 (incidentally, the figure is also an arrow diagram).

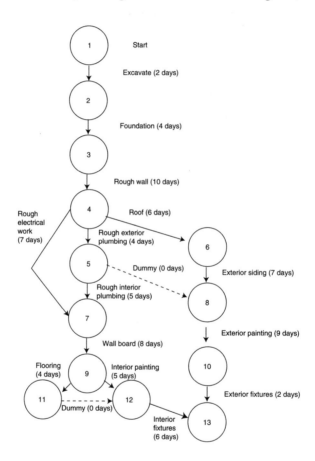

Figure 5.6. Project network for constructing a house.

Source: Based on *Introduction to Operations Research*, 3rd Edition, Hillier and Lieberman. Copyright © 1980 by Holden-Day, Inc. San Francisco, California

Finding the critical path

There are two time-values of interest for each event: its *earliest time of completion* and its *latest time of completion*. The earliest time for a given event is the estimated time at which the event will occur if the preceding activities are started as early as possible. The latest time for an event is the estimated time the event can occur without delaying the completion of the project beyond its earliest time. Earliest times of events are found by starting at the initial event and working forward, successively calculating the time at which each event will occur if each immediately preceding event occurs at its earliest time and each intervening activity uses only its estimated time. Table 5.2 shows the process of finding the earliest completion time for the house construction example. (Event numbers refer to the network diagram in Figure 5.6.) The reader is advised to work through the results in Table 5.2, line-by-line, using Figure 5.6.

Table 5.2. Calculation of earliest completion times
for house construction example.

Event	Immediately Preceding Event	Earliest Time + Activity Time	Maximum = Earliest Completion Time
1	—	—	0
2	1	0+2	2
3	2	2+4	6
4	3	6+10	16
5	4	16+4	20
6	4	16+6	22
7	4	16+7	*
	5	20+5	25

Continued on next page . . .

---

*The answer in this cell is 23, which is *not* the earliest time which event #7 will occur. Event #7 occurs when *both* events #4 and #5 have been completed.

Table 5.2—*Continued . . .*

Event	Immediately Preceding Event	Earliest Time + Activity Time	Maximum = Earliest Completion Time
8	5	20+0	*
	6	22+7	29
9	7	25+8	33
10	8	29+9	38
11	9	33+4	37
12	9	33+5	38
	11	37+0	*
13	10	38+2	*
	12	38+6	44

Thus, for example, the earliest time event #8 can be completed is 29 days. Latest times are found by starting at the final event and working backwards, calculating the latest time an event will occur if each immediately following event occurs at its latest time.

---

*The answers in these cells are *not* the earliest times which events #8, #12, and #13 will occur. Events #8, #12, and #13 occur when *all* respective immediately preceding events have been completed.

Table 5.3. Calculation of latest completion times for house construction example.

Event	Immediately Following Event	Latest Time – Activity Time	Minimum = Latest Time
13	—	—	44
12	13	44–6	38
11	12	38–0	38
10	13	44–2	42
9	12	38–5	33
	11	38–4	*
8	10	42–9	33
7	9	33–8	25
6	8	33–7	26
5	8	33–0	*
	7	25–5	20
4	7	25–7	*
	6	26–6	*
	5	20–4	16
3	4	16–10	6
2	3	6–4	2
1	2	2–2	0

*The answer in these cells are not the latest completion times since they are not the minimum time for completing each event without delaying the project. (Note that if it took 34 days to complete event #9 the project would take 45 days to complete, i.e., it would be delayed by 1 day.)

Slack time for an *event* is the difference between the latest and earliest times for a given event. Thus, assuming everything else remains on schedule, the slack for an event indicates how much delay in reaching the event can be tolerated without delaying the project completion. Slack times for the events in the house construction project are shown in Table 5.4.

Table 5.4. Calculation of slack times for house construction events.

EVENT	SLACK	EVENT	SLACK
1	0–0=0	7	25–25=0
2	2–2=0	8	33–29=4
3	6–6=0	9	33–33=0
4	16–16=0	10	42–38=4
5	20–20=0	11	38–37=1
6	26–22=4	12	38–38=0
Continued . . .	Continued . . .	13	44–44=0

The slack time for an *activity x,y* is the difference between
1. The latest time of event y.
2. The earliest time of event x plus the estimated activity time.

Slack time for an *activity* is the difference between the latest and earliest times for a given activity. Thus, assuming everything else remains on schedule, the slack for an activity indicates how much delay in reaching the activity can be tolerated without delaying the project completion. Slack times for the activities in the house construction project are shown in Table 5.5.

Table 5.5. Calculation of slack times for house construction activities.

ACTIVITY	SLACK
Excavate (1,2)	2–(0+2)=0
Foundation (2,3)	6–(2+4)=0
Rough wall (3,4)	16–(6+10)=0
Rough exterior plumbing (4,5)	20–(16+4)=0
Roof (4,6)	26–(16+6)=4
Rough electrical work (4,7)	25–(16+7)=2
Rough interior plumbing (5,7)	25–(20+5)=0
Exterior siding (6,8)	33–(22+7)=4
Wall board (7,9)	33–(25+8)=0
Exterior painting (8,10)	42–(29+9)=4
Flooring (9,11)	38–(33+4)=1
Interior painting (9,12)	38–(33+5)=0
Exterior fixtures (10,13)	44–(38+2)=4
Interior fixtures (12,13)	44–(38+6)=0

Events and activities with slack times of zero are said to lie on the *critical path* for the project. A critical path for a project is defined as a path through the network such that the activities on this path have *zero slack*. All activities and events having zero slack must lie on a critical path, but no others can. Figure 5.7 shows the activities on the critical path for the housing construction project as thick lines.

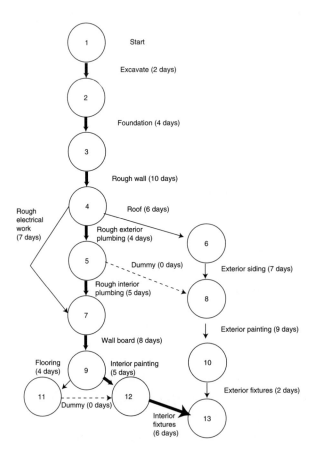

Figure 5.7. Critical path for house construction example.

Control and prevention of schedule slippage

Project managers can use the network and the information obtained from the network analysis in a variety of ways to help them manage their projects. One way is, of course, to pay close attention to the activities that lie on the critical path. Any delay in these activities will result in a delay for the project. However, the manager should also consider assembling a team to review the network with an eye towards modifying the project plan to reduce the total time needed to complete the project. The manager should also be aware that the network times are based on *estimates*. In fact, it is likely that the completion times will vary. When this occurs it often happens that a new critical path appears. Thus, the network should be viewed as a dynamic entity which should be revised as conditions change.

Primary causes of slippage include poor planning and poor management of the project. Outside forces beyond the control of the project manager will often play a role. However, it isn't enough to be able to simply identify "outside forces" as the cause and beg forgiveness. Astute project managers will anticipate as many such possibilities as possible and prepare contingency plans to deal with them. The PDPC technique is useful in this endeavor. Schedule slippage should also be addressed rigorously in the schedule control plan, which was mentioned earlier as a primary deliverable from the project planning process. The control plan should make provision for reviews conducted at intervals frequent enough to assure that any unanticipated problems are identified before schedule slippage becomes a problem.

RESOURCES

Resources are those assets of the firm, including the time of employees, that are used to accomplish the objectives of the project. The project manager should define, negotiate, and secure resource commitments for the personnel, equipment, facilities, and services needed for the project. Resource commitments should be as specific as possible. Generally, resource utilization is specified in the project budget (see below).

The following items should be defined and negotiated:
- What will be furnished?
- By whom?
- When?
- How will it be delivered?
- How much will it cost?
    - Who will pay?
    - When will payment be made?

Resource conflicts

Of course, there are always other opportunities for utilizing resources. On large projects, conflicts over resource allocation are inevitable. It is best if resource conflicts can be resolved between those managers directly involved; however, in some cases, resource conflicts must be addressed by higher levels of management. Senior managers should view resource conflicts as potential indications that the management system for allocating resources must be modified or redesigned. Often, such conflicts create ill will among managers and lead to lack of support, or even active resistance to the project. Too many such conflicts can lead to resentment towards quality improvement efforts in general.

METHODOLOGY
Cost considerations in project scheduling

Most project schedules can be compressed, if one is willing to pay the additional costs. For the analysis here, costs are defined to include direct elements only. Indirect costs (administration, overhead, etc.) will be considered in the final analysis. Assume that a straight line relationship exists between the cost of performing an activity on a *normal schedule*, and the cost of performing the activity on a *crash schedule*. Also assume that there is a crash time beyond which no further time savings are possible, regardless of cost. Figure 5.8 illustrates these concepts.

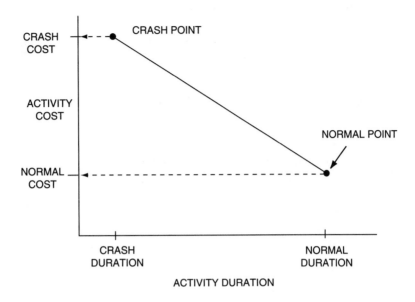

Figure 5.8. Cost-time relationship for an activity.

For a given activity the cost-per-unit-of-time saved is found as

$$\frac{crash\ cost\ -\ normal\ cost}{normal\ time\ -\ crash\ time} \quad\quad (5.1)$$

When deciding which activity on the critical path to improve, one should begin with the activity that has the smallest cost-per-unit-of-time saved. The project manager should be aware that once an activity time has been reduced there may be a new critical path. If so, the analysis should proceed using the updated information, i.e., activities on the new critical path should be analyzed.

The data for the house construction example is shown below, with additional data for costs and crash schedule times for each activity.

Table 5.6. Schedule costs for activities involved in constructing a house.

ACTIVITY	Normal Schedule Time (days)	Normal Schedule Cost	Crash Schedule Time (days)	Crash Schedule Cost	Slope
Excavate	2	1000	1	2000	1000
Foundation	4	1600	3	2400	800*
Rough wall	10	7500	6	14000	1625
Rough electrical work	7	7000	4	14000	2333
Rough exterior plumbing	4	4400	3	6000	1600
Rough interior plumbing	5	3750	3	7500	1875
Wall board	8	3500	3	7000	1750
Flooring	4	3200	2	5600	1200
Interior painting	5	3000	3	5500	1250
Interior fixtures	6	4800	2	11000	1550
Roof	6	4900	2	12000	1775
Exterior siding	7	5600	3	12000	1600
Exterior painting	9	4500	5	9000	1125
Exterior fixtures	2	1800	1	3200	1400

Activities shown in bold are on the critical path; only critical path activities are being considered since only they can produce an improvement in overall project duration. Thus, the first activity to consider improving would be foundation work, which costs $800 per day saved on the schedule (identified with an asterisk [*] in Table 5.6). If additional resources could be directed towards this activity it would produce the best "bang for the buck" in terms of reducing the total time of the project. Next, assuming the critical path doesn't change, would be excavation, then exterior painting, etc.

As activities are addressed one-by-one, the time it takes to complete the project will decline, while the direct costs of completing the project will increase. Figure 5.9 illustrates the cost-duration relationship graphically.

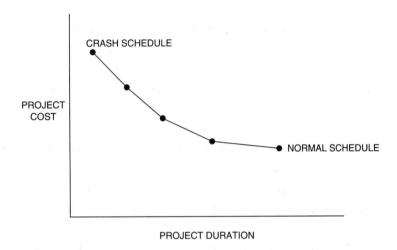

Figure 5.9. Direct costs as a function of project duration.

Conversely, *indirect costs* such as overhead, etc., are expected to *increase* as projects take longer to complete. When the indirect costs are added to the direct costs, total costs will generally follow a pattern similar to that shown in Figure 5.10 results.

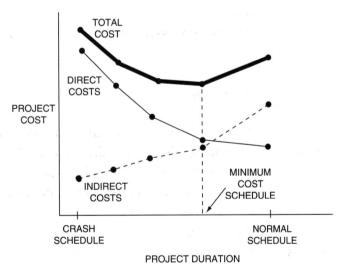

Figure 5.10. Total costs as a function of project duration.

To optimize resource utilization, the project manager will seek to develop a project plan that produces the minimum cost schedule. Of course, the organization will likely have multiple projects being conducted simultaneously, which places additional constraints on resource allocation.

Other performance measurement methodology

Project information should be collected on an ongoing basis as the project progresses. Information obtained should be communicated in a timely fashion to interested parties and decision-makers. The people who receive the information can often help the project manager to maintain or recover the schedule. There are two types of communication involved: feedback and feedforward. Feedback is historical in nature and includes such things as performance to schedule, cost variances (relative to the project budget), and quality variances (relative to the quality plan). The reader will recall that initial project planning called for special control plans in each of these three areas. Feedforward is oriented towards the future and is primarily concerned with heading off future variances in these three areas. Information reporting formats commonly fall into one of the following categories:

- formal, written reports
- informal reports and correspondence
- presentations
- meetings
- guided tours of the project, when feasible
- conversations

The principles of effective communication should be kept constantly in mind. In choosing a format for the communication consider the nature of the audience and their needs as well as the time and resources available. Audiences can be characterized along five dimensions (Ruskin and Estes, 1995, p. 193):

1. Audience diversity
2. Audience sophistication
3. Audience familiarity with the subject matter

4. Audience size and geographic location
5. Audience need to know

The report or presentation should be planned to avoid wasting the time of the audience members, or the time of those preparing the report or presentation. Objectives should be stated and the steps necessary to meet the objectives should be clearly stated in the plan. It may help to consider the communication as a "lesson" and the plan as a "lesson plan." Provision should be made for assuring that the objectives were, in fact, met.

Project communication is a process and, like all processes, it can be improved. The tools of CQI are designed for just this purpose. Measurements can be analyzed using the quality control tools described in Chapters 7 and 8 and used to improve the process of project management. The PDCA cycle also applies to project management.

Relevant stakeholders

Large quality improvement projects impact large numbers of people within the organization. Those impacted are known as "stakeholders" in the project. As far as is practicable, the interests of stakeholders should be aligned with the objectives of the project. If this is not the case, when stakeholders act according to their own interests they will be acting to sabotage the project, intentionally or unintentionally.

Identifying project stakeholders begins with obtaining a project charter. Once the project charter has been finalized, the project team should prepare a list of potential stakeholders and their roles. If the project will have significant impact on hourly employees, they should be involved as well. If the workers are unionized, the union should be informed. Sell all stakeholders on the merits of the project. People resist changes unless they see the value in them and the urgency to take action. Stakeholders must be identified and their needs analyzed so that an action plan can be created to meet the needs and gain commitment. To avoid problems, the project team must constantly communicate with the stakeholders.

Stakeholder focus groups allow group members to evaluate the potential impact of a plan by identifying the stakeholders affected by or having influence over the project plan. The focus group approach is a highly structured method in which the project team first identifies the stakeholders and their assumptions, then brings those identified together to elicit their responses to the proposed project (see Chapter 1 for a discussion of the focus group technique). The team then rates these assumptions for importance to the stakeholders and importance to the plan. A stakeholder satisfaction plan may be developed to assure the support of key individuals and groups.

As soon as possible the project manager should arrange a short, informal meeting with all of these individuals identified as being impacted, including the executive who sits on the quality council (but no other council members). The project manager and process owner are letting the stakeholders know that a project is about to be undertaken in "their" area, with the permission and direction of the senior executives. This meeting also represents an informal invitation for the middle managers to challenge the decision to conduct the project. It is important to allow the managers about a week to attempt to reverse the leadership's decision to pursue the project. If concrete information suggests that tampering or sabotage is occurring, the project manager or process owner should immediately bring it to the attention of the senior executives who approved the project charter. The senior leadership should resolve the issue promptly.

If a week or so passes without clear opposition to the project, the project manager should proceed with the implementation of the project plan. Of course, the lines of communication should remain open throughout the implementation of the project plan.

Benchmarking

Benchmarking is a topic of general interest in quality management. Thus, the discussion here goes beyond the use of benchmarking in project management alone.

Benchmarking is a popular method for developing requirements and setting goals. In more conventional terms, benchmarking can be defined as measuring your performance against that of best-in-class companies, determining how the best-in-class achieve those performance levels, and using the information as the basis for your own company's targets, strategies, and implementation. Benchmarking involves research into the best practices at the industry, firm, or process level. Benchmarking goes beyond a determination of the "industry standard;" it breaks the firm's activities down to process operations and looks for the best-in-class for a particular operation. For example, to achieve improvement in their parts distribution process Xerox Corporation studied the retailer L.L. Bean.

Benchmarking goes beyond the mere setting of goals. It focuses on practices that produce superior performance. Benchmarking involves setting up partnerships that allow both parties to learn from one another. Competitors can also engage in benchmarking, providing they avoid proprietary issues.

Benchmarking projects are like any other major project. Benchmarking must have a structured methodology to ensure successful completion of thorough and accurate investigations. However, it must be flexible to incorporate new and innovative ways of assembling difficult-to-obtain information. It is a discovery process and a learning experience. It forces the organization to take an external view, to look beyond itself.

THE BENCHMARKING PROCESS

Camp (1989) lists the following steps for the benchmarking process:
1. Planning
   1.1. Identify what is to be benchmarked
   1.2. Identify comparative companies
   1.3. Determine data collection method and collect data
2. Analysis
   2.1. Determine current performance "gap"
   2.2. Project future performance levels
3. Integration
   3.1. Communicate benchmark findings and gain acceptance

3.2. Establish functional goals
4. Action
   4.1. Develop action plans
   4.2. Implement specific actions and monitor progress
   4.3. Recalibrate benchmarks
5. Maturity
   5.1. Leadership position attained
   5.2. Practices fully integrated into process

The first step in benchmarking is determining what to benchmark. To focus the benchmarking initiative on critical issues, begin by identifying the process outputs most important to the customers of that process (i. e., the key quality characteristics). This step applies to every organizational function, since each one has outputs and customers. The QFD/customer needs assessment is a natural precursor to benchmarking activities.

GETTING STARTED WITH BENCHMARKING

The essence of benchmarking is the acquisition of information. The process begins with the identification of the process that is to be benchmarked. The process chosen should be one that will have a major impact on the success of the business.

Once the process has been identified, contact a business library and request a search for the information relating to your area of interest. The library will identify material from a variety of external sources, such as magazines, journals, special reports, etc. You should also conduct research using the Internet and other electronic networking resources. However, be prepared to pare down what will probably be an extremely large list of candidates (e.g., an Internet search on the word "benchmarking" produced 20,000 hits). Don't forget your organization's internal resources. If your company has an "Intranet" use it to conduct an internal search. Set up a meeting with people in key departments, such as R&D. Tap the expertise of those in your company who routinely work with customers, competitors, suppliers, and other "outside" organizations. Often your company's board of directors will have an extensive network of contacts.

The search is, of course, not random. Look for the best of the best, not the average firm. There are many possible sources for identifying the elites. One approach is to build a compendium of business awards and citations of merit that organizations have received in business process improvement. Sources to consider are *Industry Week*'s Best Plant's Award, National Institute of Standards and Technology's Malcolm Baldrige Award, *USA Today* and the Rochester Institute of Technology's Quality Cup Award, European Foundation for Quality Management Award, Occupational Safety and Health Administration (OSHA), Federal Quality Institute, Deming Prize, Competitiveness Forum, *Fortune* magazine, United States Navy's Best Manufacturing Practices, to name just a few. You may wish to subscribe to an "exchange service" that collects benchmarking information and makes it available for a fee. Once enrolled, you will have access to the names of other subscribers—a great source for contacts.

Don't overlook your own suppliers as a source for information. If your company has a program for recognizing top suppliers, contact these suppliers and see if they are willing to share their "secrets" with you. Suppliers are predisposed to cooperate with their customers; it's an automatic door-opener. Also contact your customers. Customers have a vested interest in helping you do a better job. If your quality, cost, and delivery performance improve, your customers will benefit. Customers may be willing to share some of their insights as to how their other suppliers compare with you. Again, it isn't necessary that you get information about direct competitors. Which of your customer's suppliers are best at billing? Order fulfillment? Customer service? Keep your focus at the process level and there will seldom be any issues of confidentiality. An advantage to identifying potential benchmarking partners through your customers is that you will have a referral that will make it easier for you to start the partnership.

Another source for detailed information on companies is academic research. Companies often allow universities access to detailed information for research purposes. While the published research usually omits reference to the specific companies involved, it often provides comparisons and detailed analysis of what separates the best from the others. Such information, provided by experts whose work is subject to rigorous peer review, will often save you thousands of hours of work.

After a list of potential candidates is compiled, the next step is to choose the best three to five targets. A candidate that looked promising early in the process might be eliminated later based on the following criteria (Vaziri, 1992):

- Not the best performer
- Unwilling to share information and practices (i.e., doesn't view the benchmarking process as a mutually beneficial learning opportunity)
- Low availability and questionable reliability of information on the candidate

As the benchmarking process evolves, the characteristics of the most desirable candidates will be continually refined. This occurs as a result of a clearer understanding of your organization's key quality characteristics and critical success factors and an improved knowledge of the marketplace and other players. This knowledge and the resulting actions tremendously strengthen an organization.

WHY BENCHMARKING EFFORTS FAIL

The causes of failed benchmarking projects are the same as those for other failed projects (DeToro, 1995):

☐ **Lack of sponsorship**—A team should submit to management a one- to four-page benchmarking project proposal that describes the project, its objectives, and potential costs. If the team can't gain approval for the project or get a sponsor, it makes little sense to proceed with a project that's not understood or appreciated or that is unlikely to lead to corrective action when completed.

☐ **Wrong people on team**—Who are the right people for a benchmarking team? Individuals involved in benchmarking should be the same ones who own or work in the process. It's useless for a team to address problems in business areas that are unfamiliar or where the team has no control or influence.

☐ **Teams don't understand their work completely**—If the benchmarking team didn't map, flowchart, or document its work process, and if it didn't benchmark with organizations that also documented their processes, there can't be an effective transfer of techniques. The intent in every benchmarking project is for a team to understand how its process works and compare it to another company's process at a detailed level. The exchange of process steps is essential for improved performance.

☐ **Teams take on too much**—The task a team undertakes is often so broad that it becomes unmanageable. This broad area must be broken into smaller, more manageable projects that can be approached logically. A suggested approach is to create a functional flowchart of an entire area, such as production or marketing, and identify its processes. Criteria can then be used to select a process to be benchmarked that would best contribute to the organization's objectives.

☐ **Lack of long-term management commitment**—Since managers aren't as familiar with specific work issues as their employees, they tend to underestimate the time, cost, and effort required to successfully complete a benchmarking project. Managers should be informed that while it's impossible to know the exact time it will take for a typical benchmarking project, there is a rule of thumb that a team of four or five individuals requires a third of their time for five months to complete a project.

☐ **Focus on metrics rather than processes**—Some firms focus their benchmarking efforts on performance targets (metrics) rather than processes. Knowing that a competitor has a higher return on assets doesn't mean that its performance alone should become the new target (unless an understanding exists about how the competitor differs in the use of its assets and an evaluation of its process reveals that it can be emulated or surpassed).

☐ **Not positioning benchmarking within a larger strategy**—Benchmarking is one of many total quality management tools—such as problem solving, process improvement, and process reengineering—used to shorten cycle time, reduce costs, and minimize variation. Benchmarking is compatible with and complementary to these tools, and they should be used together for maximum value.

☐ **Misunderstanding the organization's mission, goals, and objectives**— All benchmarking activity should be launched by management as part of an overall strategy to fulfill the organization's mission and vision by first attaining the short-term objectives and then the long-term goals.

☐ **Assuming every project requires a site visit**—Sufficient information is often available from the public domain, making a site visit unnecessary. This speeds the benchmarking process and lowers the cost considerably.

☐ **Failure to monitor progress**—Once benchmarking has been completed for a specific area or process benchmarks have been established and process changes implemented, managers should review progress in implementation and results.

The issues described here are discussed in other parts of this chapter and in other parts of this book. The best way of dealing with them is to prevent their occurrence by carefully planning and managing the project from the outset. This list can be used as a checklist to evaluate project plans; if the plans don't clearly preclude these problems, then the plans are not complete.

THE BENEFITS OF BENCHMARKING

The benefits of competitive benchmarking include:

- Creating a culture that values continuous improvement to achieve excellence
- Enhancing creativity by devaluing the not-invented-here syndrome
- Increasing sensitivity to changes in the external environment
- Shifting the corporate mind-set from relative complacency to a strong sense of urgency for ongoing improvement
- Focusing resources through performance targets set with employee input
- Prioritizing the areas that need improvement
- Sharing the best practices between benchmarking partners

SOME DANGERS OF BENCHMARKING

Benchmarking is based on learning from others, rather than developing new and improved approaches. Since the process being studied is there for all to see, benchmarking cannot give a firm a sustained competitive advantage. Although helpful, benchmarking should never be the *primary* strategy for improvement.

Competitive analysis is an approach to goal setting used by many firms. This approach is essentially benchmarking confined to one's own industry. Although common, competitive analysis virtually guarantees second-rate quality because the firm will always be following their competition. If the entire industry employs the approach it will lead to stagnation for the entire industry, setting them up for eventual replacement by outside innovators.

Budgeting

In this section we will provide an overview of budgeting as it applies to project management.

The project manager must know where he stands in terms of expenditures. Once he is informed that a given amount of future expense is allocated to him for a particular project, it is his job to run the project so that this allowance is not exceeded. The process of allocating resources to be expended in the future is called *budgeting*. Budgets should be viewed as forecasts of future events; in this case the events are expenditures. A listing of these expenditures, broken out into specific categories, is called the budget.

TYPES OF PROJECT BUDGETS

Ruskin and Estes (1995) list the following types of project-related budgets:

Direct labor budgets are usually prepared for each work element in the project plan, then aggregated for the project as a whole. Control is usually maintained at the work element level to assure that the aggregate budget allowance is not exceeded. Budgets may be in terms of dollars or some other measure of value, such as direct labor hours expended.

Support services budgets need to be prepared because, without budgets, support services tend to charge based-on-actual, without allowances for errors, rework, etc. The discipline imposed by making budget estimates and being held to them often leads to improved efficiency and higher quality.

Purchased items budgets cover purchased materials, equipment, and services. The budgets can be based on negotiated or market prices. The issues mentioned for support services also apply here.

TYPES OF BUDGET REPORTS

Budgets allocate resources to be used in the future. No one can predict the future with certainty. Thus, an important element in the budgeting process is tracking actual expenditures after the budgets have been prepared. The following techniques are useful in monitoring actual expenditures versus budgeted expenditures.

Expenditure reports which compare actual expenditures to budgeted expenditures are periodically submitted to the budget authority, e.g., finance, sponsor.

Expenditure audits are conducted to verify that charges to the project are legitimate and that the work charged was actually performed. In most large organizations with multiple projects in work at any given time it is possible to find projects being charged for work done on other projects, for work not yet done, etc. While these charges are often inadvertent, they must still be identified.

Variance reporting compares actual expenditures directly to budgeted expenditures. The term "variance" is used here in the accounting sense, not the statistical sense. In accounting, a variance is simply a comparison of a planned amount with an actual amount. An accounting variance may or may not indicate a special cause of variation; statistical techniques are required to make this determination. The timing of variance reporting varies depending on the need for control. The timing of variance reports should be determined in advance and written into the project plan.

Variance tables: Variance reports can appear in a variety of formats. Most common are simple tables that show the actual/budgeted/variances by budget item, overall for the current period, and cumulatively for the project. Since it is unlikely that variances will be zero, an allowance is usually made; e.g., 5% over or under is allowed without the need for explanations. For longer projects, historical data can be plotted on control charts and used to set allowances.

Variance graphs: When only tables are used it is difficult to spot patterns. To remedy this, tables are often supplemented with graphs. Graphs generally show the budget variances in a time-ordered sequence on a line chart. The allowance lines can be drawn on the graph to provide a visual guide to the eye.

ANALYSIS OF BUDGET REPORTS

The project manager should review the variance data for patterns which contain useful information. Ideally, the pattern will be a mixture of positive and negative but minor variances. Assuming that this pattern is accompanied by an on-schedule project, this indicates a reasonably good budget, i.e., an accurate forecasting of expenditures. Variances should be evaluated separately for each type of budget (direct labor, materials, etc.). However, the variance report for the entire project is the primary source of information concerning the status of the project in terms of resource utilization. Reports are received and analyzed periodically. For most quality improvement projects, monthly or weekly reports are adequate. Budget variance analysis[*] should include the following:

Trends: Occasional departures from budget are to be expected. Of greater concern is a pattern that indicates a fundamental problem with the budget. Trends are easier to detect from graphic reports.

Overspending: Since budgeted resources are generally scarce, overspending represents a serious threat to the project and, perhaps, to the organization itself. When a project overspends its budget, it depletes the resources available for other activities and projects. The project team, team leader and sponsors should design monitoring systems to detect and correct overspending before

---

[*]This is not to be confused with the statistical technique Analysis of Variance (ANOVA).

it threatens the project or the organization. Overspending is often a symptom of other problems with the project, e.g., paying extra in an attempt to "catch up" after falling behind schedule, additional expenses for rework, etc.

Underspending is potentially as serious as overspending. If the project budget was prepared properly then the expenses reflect a given schedule and quality level. Underspending may reflect "cutting corners" or allowing suppliers an allowance for slower delivery. The reasons for any significant departure from the plan should be explained.

Benefit-cost analysis

Benefit-cost analysis can be as elaborate or as simple as the magnitude of the project expenditures demands. The quality manager is advised that most such analyses are easier to "sell" to senior management if done by (or reviewed and approved by) experts in the finance and accounting department. The plain fact is that the finance department has credibility in estimating cost and benefit that the quality department, and any other department, lacks. The best approach is to get the finance department to conduct the benefit-cost analysis with support from the other departments involved in the project. An overview will be given of some principles and techniques that are useful in benefit-cost analysis.

A fundamental problem with performing benefit-cost analysis is that, in general, it is easier to accurately estimate costs than benefits. Costs can usually be quantified in fairly precise terms in a budget. Costs are claims on resources the firm already has. In contrast, benefits are merely predictions of future events, which may or may not actually occur. Also, benefits are often stated in units other than dollars, making the comparison of cost and benefit problematic. The problem is especially acute where quality improvement projects are concerned. For example, a proposed project may involve placing additional staff on a customer "hot line." The cost is easy to compute: X employees at a salary of $Y each, equipment, office space, supervision, etc. The benefit is much more difficult to determine. Perhaps data indicate that average time-on-hold will be improved, but the amount of the improvement and the probability that it will occur are speculations. Even if the time-on-hold improvement were precise, the impact on customer satisfaction would be an estimate. And the association between customer satisfaction and revenues is yet another estimate. Still, the intelligent manager will realize that despite these difficulties, reasonable cause-and-effect linkages can be established to form the basis for benefit-cost analysis. Such is often the best one can expect. To compensate for the uncertainties associated with estimates of benefits, it makes sense to demand a relatively high ratio of benefit to cost. For example, it is not unusual to have senior leadership demand a ROI of 100% in the first year on a quality improvement project. Rather than becoming distressed at this "injustice," the quality manager should realize that such demands are a response to the inherent difficulties in quantifying benefits.

SELECTING PROJECTS

Projects designed to improve processes should be limited to processes that are important. Important processes impact such things as product cost, delivery schedules and product features, things that customers notice. Customers cannot help identify these processes because they aren't familiar with your internal operations. However, customers can help identify what's important to them; then this must be related to the processes. Furthermore, projects should be undertaken only when success is feasible. Feasibility is determined by considering the scope and cost of a project and the support it is likely to receive from the process owner.

Pareto principle refers to the fact that a small percentage of processes cause a large percentage of the problems. The Pareto principle is useful in narrowing a list of choices to those few projects that offer the greatest potential. See Chapter 7 for Pareto analysis procedures.

Hidden pain signals: Initially problems create "pain signals" such as schedule disruptions and customer complaints. Often these symptoms are treated rather than their underlying causes; for example, if quality problems cause schedule slippages which lead to customer complaints, the "solution" might be to keep a large inventory and sort the good from the bad. The result is that the schedule is met and customers stop complaining, but at huge cost. These opportunities are often greater than those causing current problems, but they are built into the process and difficult to see. One solution to the hidden problem phenomenon is reengineering, which is focused on processes rather than symptoms. Some guidelines for identifying dysfunctional processes for potential improvement are shown in Table 5.7 (Hammer and Champy, 1993).

Table 5.7. Dysfunctional process symptoms and diseases.

SYMPTOM	DISEASE	CURE
Extensive information exchange, data redundancy, rekeying	Arbitrary fragmentation of a natural process	Discover why people need to communicate with each other so often
Inventory, buffers, and other assets stockpiled	System slack to cope with uncertainty	Remove the uncertainty
High ratio of checking and control to value-added work (internal controls, audits, etc.)	Fragmentation	Eliminate the fragmentation, integrate processes
Rework and iteration	Inadequate feedback in a long work process	Process control
Complexity, exceptions, and special causes	Accretion onto a simple base	Uncover original "clean" process and create new process(es) for special situations; eliminate excessive standardization of processes

The "symptom" column is useful in identifying problems and setting priorities. The "disease" column focuses attention on the underlying causes of the problem, and the "cure" column is helpful in chartering quality improvement project teams and preparing mission statements.

Prioritizing projects. After a serious search for improvement opportunities, the organization's leaders will probably find themselves with more projects to pursue than they have resources. The Pareto Priority Index (PPI) is a simple way of prioritizing these opportunities. The PPI is calculated as follows (Juran and Gryna, 1993, p. 49):

$$PPI = \frac{Savings \times probability\ of\ success}{Cost \times time\ to\ completion\ (years)} \tag{5.2}$$

The inputs are, of course, estimates and the result is totally dependent on the accuracy of the inputs. The resulting number is an index value for a given project. The PPI values allow comparison of various projects; they have no intrinsic meaning in and of themselves. If there are clear standouts, the PPI can make it easier to select a project. Table 5.8 shows the PPIs for several hypothetical projects.

Table 5.8. Illustration of the Pareto Priority Index (PPI).

PROJECT	Savings $ 1,000's	Probabi- lity	Cost, $ 1,000's	Time, years	PPI
Reduce wave solder defects 50%	$70	0.7	$25	0.75	2.61
NC machine capability improvement	$50	0.9	$20	1.00	2.25
ISO 9001 certification	$150	0.9	$75	2.00	0.90
Eliminate customer delivery complaints	$250	0.5	$75	1.50	1.11
Reduce assembly defects 50%	$90	0.7	$30	1.50	1.40

The PPI would indicate that resources be allocated first to reducing wave solder defects, then to improving NC machine capability, and so on. The PPI may not always give such a clear ordering of priorities. When two or more projects have similar PPIs, a judgment must be made on other criteria.

PROJECT MANAGEMENT IMPLEMENTATION
Management support and organizational roadblocks
INTERNAL ROADBLOCKS

Most organizations still have a hierarchical, command-and-control organizational structure, sometimes called "smoke stacks" or "silos." The functional specialists in charge of each smoke stack tend to focus on optimizing their own functional area, often to the detriment of the organization as a whole. In addition, the hierarchy gives these managers a monopoly on the authority to act on matters related to their functional specialty. The combined effect is both a desire to resist change and the authority to resist change, which often creates insurmountable roadblocks to quality improvement projects.

It is important to realize that organizational rules are, by their nature, a barrier to change. The formal rules take the form of written standard operating procedures (SOPs). The very purpose of SOPs is to standardize behavior. The quality profession has (in this author's opinion) historically overemphasized formal documentation, and it continues to do so by advocating such approaches as ISO 9000 and ISO 14000. Formal rules are often responses to past problems and they frequently continue to exist long after the reason for their existence has passed. In an organization that is serious about its written rules even senior leaders find themselves helpless to act without submitting to a burdensome rule-changing process. The true power in such an organization is the bureaucracy that controls the procedures. If the organization falls into the trap of creating written rules for too many things, it can find itself moribund in a fast-changing external environment. This is a recipe for disaster.

Restrictive rules need not take the form of management limitations on itself; procedures that define hourly work in great detail also produce barriers, e.g., union work rules. Projects almost always require that work be done differently but restrictive procedures prohibit change. Organizations that tend to be excessive in SOPs also tend to be heavy on work rules. The combination is often deadly to quality improvement efforts.

Organization structures preserve the status quo in other ways besides formal, written restrictions in the form of procedures and rules. Another effective method of limiting change is to require permission from various departments, committees, councils, boards, experts, etc. Even though the organization may not have a formal requirement, that "permission" be obtained, the effect may be the same, e.g., "You should run that past accounting" or "Ms. Reimer and Mr. Evans should be informed about this project." When permission for vehicles for change (e.g., project budgets, plan approvals) is required from a group that meets infrequently it creates problems for project planners. Plans may be rushed so they can be presented at the next meeting, lest the project be delayed for months. Plans that need modifications may be put on hold until the next meeting, months away. Or, projects may miss the deadline and be put off indefinitely.

EXTERNAL ROADBLOCKS

Modern organizations do not exist as islands. Powerful external forces take an active interest in what happens within the organization. Government bodies have created a labyrinth of rules and regulations that the organization must negotiate to utilize its human resources without incurring penalties or sanctions. The restrictions placed on modern businesses by outside regulators is challenging to say the least. When research involves people, ethical and legal concerns sometimes require that external approvals be obtained. The approvals are contingent on such issues as informed consent, safety, cost and so on.

Many industries have "dedicated" agencies to deal with. For example, the pharmaceutical industry must deal with the Food and Drug Administration (FDA). These agencies must often be consulted before undertaking projects. For example, a new treatment protocol involving a new process for treatment of pregnant women prior to labor may involve using a drug in a new way (e.g., administered on an outpatient basis instead of on an inpatient basis).

Many professionals face liability risks that are part of every decision. Often these fears create a "play it safe" mentality that acts as a barrier to change. The fear is even greater when the project involves new and untried practices and technology.

INDIVIDUAL BARRIERS TO CHANGE

Perhaps the most significant change, and therefore the most difficult, is to change ourselves. It seems to be a part of human nature to resist changing oneself. By and large, we worked hard to get where we are, and our first impulse is to resist anything that threatens our current position. Forsha (1992) provides the process for personal change shown in Figure 5.11.

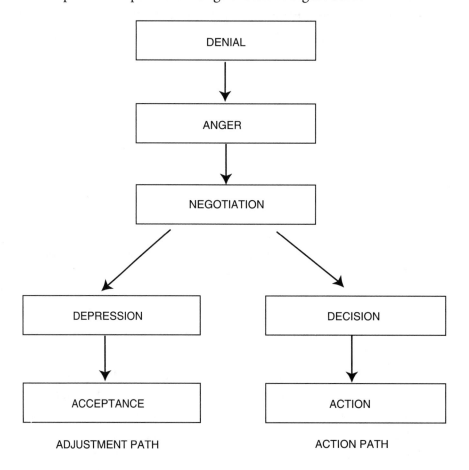

Figure 5.11. The process of personal change.

From *The Pursuit of Quality Through Personal Change*, by H.I. Forsha, Copyright © 1992 by ASQ Quality Press, Milwaukee, WI. Used by permission.

The adjustment path results in preservation of the status quo. The action path results in change. The well-known PDCA cycle can be used once a commitment to action has been made by the individual. The goal of such change is continuous *self*-improvement.

Within an organizational context, the individual's reference group plays a part in personal resistance to change. A reference group is the aggregation of people a person thinks of when using the word "we." If "we" refers to the company, then the company is the individual's reference group and he or she feels connected to the company's success or failure. However, "we" might refer to the individual's profession or trade group, e.g., "We doctors," "We engineers," "We union members." In this case the leaders shown on the formal organization chart will have little influence on the individual's attitude towards the success or failure of the project. When a project involves external reference groups with competing agendas, the task of building buy-in and consensus is daunting indeed.

INEFFECTIVE MANAGEMENT SUPPORT STRATEGIES

Strategy #1: command people to act as you wish—With this approach the senior leadership simply commands people to act as the leaders wish. The implication is that those who do not comply will be subjected to disciplinary action. People in less senior levels of an organization often have an inflated view of the value of raw power. The truth is that even senior leaders have limited power to rule by decree. Human beings by their nature tend to act according to their own best judgment. Thankfully, commanding that they do otherwise usually has little effect. The result of invoking authority is that the decision-maker must constantly try to divine what the leader wants done in a particular situation. This leads to stagnation and confusion as everyone waits on the leader. Another problem with commanding as a form of "leadership" is the simple communication problem. Under the best of circumstances people will often simply misinterpret the leadership's commands.

Strategy #2: change the rules by decree—When rules are changed by decree the result is again confusion. What are the rules today? What will they be tomorrow? This leads again to stagnation because people don't have the ability to plan for the future. Although rules make it difficult to change, they also provide stability and structure that may serve some useful purpose. Arbitrarily changing the rules based on force (which is what "authority" comes down to) instead of a set of guiding principles does more harm than good.

Strategy #3: authorize circumventing of the rules—Here the rules are allowed to stand, but exceptions are made for the leader's "pet projects." The result is general disrespect for and disregard of the rules, and resentment of the people who are allowed to violate rules that bind everyone else. An improvement is to develop a formal method for circumventing the rules, e.g., deviation request procedures. While this is less arbitrary, it adds another layer of complexity and still doesn't change the rules that are making change difficult in the first place.

Strategy #4: redirect resources to the project—Leaders may also use their command authority to redirect resources to the project. A better way is to develop a fair and easily understood system to assure that projects of strategic importance are adequately funded as a matter of policy. In our earlier discussion of project scheduling we discussed "crash scheduling" as a means of completing projects in a shorter time frame. However, the assumption was made that the basis for the allocation was cost or some other objective measure of the organ-ization's best interest. Here we are talking about political clout as the basis of the allocation.

EFFECTIVE MANAGEMENT SUPPORT STRATEGIES

Strategy #1: transform the formal organization and the organization's culture—By far the best solution to the problems posed by organizational roadblock is to transform the organization to one in which these roadblocks no longer exist. As discussed earlier, this process can't be implemented by decree. As the leader helps project teams succeed, he will learn about the need for transformation. Using his persuasive powers the leader-champion can undertake the exciting challenge of creating a culture that embraces change instead of fighting it.

Strategy #2: mentoring—In Greek mythology, Mentor was an elderly man, the trusted counselor of Odysseus, and the guardian and teacher of his son Telemachus. Today the term, "mentor" is still used to describe a wise and trusted counselor or teacher. When this person occupies an important position in the organization's hierarchy, he or she can be a powerful force for eliminating roadblocks. Modern organizations are complex and confusing. It is often difficult to determine just where one must go to solve a problem or obtain a needed resource. The mentor can help guide the project manager through this maze by clarifying lines of authority. At the same time, the mentor's senior position enables him to see the implications of complexity and to work to eliminate unnecessary rules and procedures.

Strategy #3: identify informal leaders and enlist their support—Because of their experience, mentors often know that the person whose support the project really needs is not the one occupying the relevant box on the organization chart. The mentor can direct the project leader to the person whose opinion really has influence. For example, a project may need the approval of, say, the vice-president of engineering. The engineering VP may be balking because his senior metallurgist hasn't endorsed the project.

Strategy #4: find legitimate ways around people, procedures, resource constraints and other roadblocks—It may be possible to get approvals or resources through means not known to the project manager. Perhaps a minor change in the project plan can bypass a cumbersome procedure entirely. For example, adding an engineer to the team might automatically place the authority to approve process experiments within the team rather than in the hands of the engineering department.

Short-term (tactical) plans

Conceptually, project plans are subsets of bigger plans, all of which are designed to carry out the organization's mission. The project plan must be broken down further. The objective is to reach a level where projects are "tiny." A tiny project is reached when it is possible to easily answer two questions:

1. Is the project complete?
2. Is the project done correctly?

For example, a software development team concluded that a tiny computer module had the following characteristics: 1) it implemented only one concept; 2) it could be described in 6 lines or less of easily understood pseudo-code (English-like descriptions of what the program would do); and 3) the programming would fit on a single sheet of paper. By looking at the completed programming for the module, the team felt that it could answer the two questions.

On quality improvement projects, tactical plans are created by developing work breakdown structures. The process of creating work breakdown structures was discussed above. Tactical planning takes place at the bottom-most level of the work breakdown structures. If the project team doesn't agree that the bottom level is tiny, then additional work breakdown must take place.

Creating WBS employs the tree diagram technique, described in Chapter 7. Tree diagrams are used to break down or stratify ideas in progressively greater detail. The objective is to partition a big idea or problem into its smaller components to make the idea easier to understand, or the problem easier to solve. The basic idea behind this is that, at some level, a problem's solution becomes relatively easy to find. This is the tiny level. Work takes place on the smallest elements in the tree diagram.

Tactical plans are still project plans, albeit for tiny projects. As such, they should include all of the elements of any well-designed project plan.

Contingency plans should be prepared to deal with unexpected but potentially damaging events. The process decision program chart (PDPC) is a useful tool for identifying possible events that might be encountered during the project. The emphasis of PDPC is the impact of the "failures" (problems) on project schedules. Also, PDPC seeks to describe specific actions to be taken to prevent the problems from occurring in the first place, and to mitigate the impact of the problems if they do occur. An enhancement to classical PDPC is to assign subjective probabilities to the various problems and to use these to help assign priorities. The amount of detail that should go into contingency plans is a judgment call. The project manager should consider both the seriousness of the potential problem and the likelihood of its occurring. See Chapter 7 for additional information on PDPC.

Cross-functional collaboration

This section will address the impact of organizational structures on management of quality improvement projects.

Quality improvement projects are process-oriented and most processes that have significant impact on quality cut across several different departments. Modern organizations, however, are hierarchical; i.e., they are defined by superior/subordinate relationships. These organizations tend to focus on specialized functions (e.g., accounting, engineering). But adding value for the customer requires that several different functions work together. The ideal solution is the transformation of the organization into a structure designed to produce value without the need for a hierarchical structure. However, until that is accomplished, QI project managers will need to deal with the conflicts inherent in doing cross-functional projects in a hierarchical environment.

Project managers "borrow" people from many departments for their projects, which creates matrix organizational structures. The essential feature of a matrix organization is that some people have two or more bosses or project customers. These people effectively report to multiple bosses, e.g., the project manager and their own boss. Ruskin and Estes refer to people with more than one boss as *multibossed individuals*, and their bosses and customers as *multiple bosses*. Somewhere in the organization is a *common boss*, who resolves conflicts between multiple bosses when they are unable to do so on their own. Of course, multiple bosses can prevent conflicts by cooperation and collaboration before problems arise.

Often multibossed individuals are involved with several projects, further complicating the situation. Collaborative planning between the multi-bosses is necessary to determine how the time of multi-bossed individuals, and other resources, will be shared. Figure 5.12 illustrates the simplest multi-bossing structure where the multibossed individual has just two multiple bosses, and the common boss is directly above the multiple bosses on the organizational hierarchy. For additional discussion of more complex matrix structures see Ruskin and Estes, 1995, pp. 169–182.

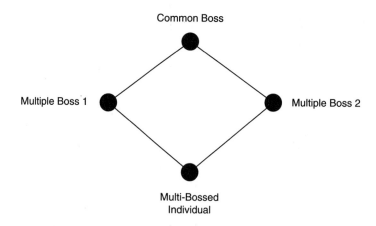

Figure 5.12. Multi-boss collaborative planning.

The matrix structure raises a number of questions regarding project planning and coordination. What should be planned? Who should organize planning activities? Who should participate in the planning? These issues were addressed earlier in this chapter, especially in the section entitled Relevant Stakeholders.

Good communication is helpful in preventing problems. Perhaps the most important communication is frequent, informal updates of all interested parties by the project manager. More formal status reports should also be specified in the project plan and sent to people with an interest in the project. The project manager should determine who gets what information, which is often tricky due to the multi-boss status of the project manager. Some managers may not want "too much" information about their department's "business" shared with their peers from other areas. Other managers may be offended if they receive less information than everyone else. The project manager's best diplomatic skills may be required to find the right balance.

Status reports invariably indicate that the project plan is less than perfect. The process by which the plans will be adjusted should be understood in advance. The process should specify who will be permitted to make adjustments, when the adjustments will be allowed and how much authority the bosses and project manager have in making adjustments.

Negotiated agreements should be documented, while generating the minimum possible amount of additional red tape and paperwork. The documentation will save the project manager a great deal of time in resolving disputes down the road regarding who agreed to what.

Continuous review and enhancement of quality process

The project management system can be improved, just as any system can be improved. The quality management professional's arsenal of tools and principles offer the means. Address such issues as cycle time, supplier management, customer service, etc., just as you would for any other critical management system. Continuous improvement principles, tools, and techniques are described in detail in Chapter 7.

Projects have customers, usually internal. The techniques described in Chapter 1 can be used to evaluate the satisfaction of the customers whose needs are being addressed by the project.

The records of the project provide the raw data for process improvement. These records, combined with customer satisfaction analysis, tell management where the project planning and implementation process can be improved. The project manager should include recommendations for process improvement in the final project report. Organizational management, in particular common bosses, should aggregate the recommendations from several projects to identify systemic problems. Project schedules and budgets should be compared to actual results to evaluate the accuracy of these forecasts. The results can be analyzed using the techniques described in Chapter 8. Where special causes of variation in the results are present, they should be identified and corrected quickly. Common causes of variation indicate systemic problems.

Documentation and procedures

Project records provide information that is useful both while the project is underway, and afterwards. Project records serve three basic purposes:

- cost accounting requirements
- legal requirements
- learning

Project records should be organized and maintained as if they were part of a single database, even if it isn't possible to keep all of the records in a single location. There should be one "official" copy of the documentation, and a person designated to act as the caretaker of this information while the project is active. Upon completion of the project, the documentation should be sent to the organization's archives. Large quality improvement projects are expensive, time-consuming undertakings. The process involved is complex and often confusing. However, a great deal can be learned from studying the "project process." To do this requires that there be data. Archives of a number of projects can be used to identify common problems and patterns between the various projects. For example, project schedules may be consistently too optimistic or too pessimistic.

The following records should be kept:

- statement of work
- plans and schedules for projects and subprojects
- correspondence (written and electronic)
- written agreements
- meeting minutes
- action items and responsibilities
- budgets and financial reports
- cost-benefit analyses
- status reports
- presentation materials

- documentation of changes made to plans and budgets
- procedures followed or developed
- notes of significant lessons learned

It is good practice for the project team to have a final meeting to perform a "post mortem" of the project. The meeting should be conducted soon after the project's completion, while memories are still fresh. The meeting will cover the lessons learned from conducting the project, and recommendations for improving the process. The minutes from these meetings should be used to educate project managers.

The author believes that former guidelines for record retention are now outdated. In the past, record storage involved warehousing costs, insurance, aging of the paper, protecting the records from damage, etc. Furthermore, using the records required that one sift through endless boxes of disorganized material thrown haphazardly in a box. Today it is possible to reduce mountains of paper to electronic form. Low-cost software can automatically catalog the information and provide the ability to search the entire database quickly and easily. There seems to be little reason not to store complete project information indefinitely.

FORMAL VERSUS INFORMAL REPORTS

When people speak of "reports," they usually mean formal written reports or, perhaps, formal verbal presentations. These forms of communication have certain advantages. They are relatively self-contained and complete and thus useful to personnel not intimately involved with the project. Their form lends itself to long-term retention. They usually include additional background materials. Finally, formal written reports are usually designed to address the concerns of all parties. However, formal written reports also have some drawbacks. Their preparation takes considerable time and effort, which makes them costly. Also, by trying to address everyone's concern the formal written report usually contains a lot of information that is of little interest to the majority of the recipients. Of course, this latter drawback can be mitigated by creating a good table of contents and index and by carefully organizing the material.

Informal reports and correspondence are used to keep everyone up to date on the project. Unlike formal reports, this form of communication generally addresses a specific issue involving both the sender and the receiver. Because the parties to the communication usually bring a great deal of background information to the communication, informal reports tend to do poorly as stand-alone documents. However, informal reports can be prepared quickly and inexpensively and they tend to be short.

6

Principles of Measurements and Data

MEASUREMENT

An argument can be made for asserting that quality begins with measurement. Only when quality is quantified can meaningful discussion about improvement begin. Conceptually, measurement is quite simple: measurement is the assignment of numbers to observed phenomena according to certain rules. Measurement is a *sine qua non* of any science, including management science.

Scales of measurement

A *measurement* is simply a numerical assignment to something, usually a non-numerical element. Measurements convey certain information about the relationship between the element and other elements. Measurement involves a theoretical domain, an area of substantive concern represented as an empirical relational system, and a domain represented by a particular selected numerical relational system. There is a mapping function that carries us from the empirical system into the numerical system. The numerical system is manipulated and the results of the manipulation are studied to help the manager better understand the empirical system.

In reality, measurement is problematic: the manager can never know the "true" value of the element being measured. The numbers provide information on a certain scale and they represent measurements of some unobservable variable of interest. Some measurements are richer than others; i.e., some measurements provide more information than other measurements. The information content of a number is dependent on the scale of measurement used. This scale determines the types of statistical analyses that can be properly employed in studying the numbers. Until one has determined the scale of measurement, one cannot know if a given method of analysis is valid.

There are four measurement scales: nominal, ordinal, interval, and ratio. Harrington (1992) summarizes the properties of each scale in Table 6.1.

Table 6.1. Types of measurement scales and permissible statistics.
From *Quality Engineering Handbook*, p. 516. Copyright © 1992. Used by permission of the publisher, ASQ Quality Press, Milwaukee, Wisconsin.

SCALE	DEFINITION	EXAMPLE	STATISTICS
Nominal	Only the presence/absence of an attribute; can only count items	go/no go; success/fail; accept/reject	percent; proportion; chi-square tests
Ordinal	Can say that one item has more or less of an attribute than another item; can order a set of items	taste; attractiveness	rank-order correlation
Interval	Difference between any two successive points is equal; often treated as a ratio scale even if assumption of equal intervals is incorrect; can add, subtract, order objects	calendar time; temperature	correlations; t-tests; F-tests; multiple regression
Ratio	True zero point indicates absence of an attribute; can add, subtract, multiply and divide	elapsed time; distance; weight	t-test; F-test; correlations; multiple regression

Numbers on a *nominal scale* aren't measurements at all; they are merely *category labels* in numerical form. Nominal measurements might indicate membership in a group (1=male, 2=female) or simply represent a designation (John Doe is #43 on the team). Nominal scales represent the simplest and weakest form of measurement. Nominal variables are perhaps best viewed as a form of classification rather than as a measurement scale. Ideally, categories on the nominal scale are constructed in such a way that all objects in the universe are members of one and only one class. Data collected on a nominal scale are called *attribute data*. The only mathematical operations permitted on nominal scales are = (which shows that an object possesses the attribute of concern) or $\neq$.

An *ordinal* variable is one that has a natural ordering of its possible values, but for which the distances between the values are undefined. An example is product preference rankings such as good, better, best. Ordinal data can be analyzed with the mathematical operators, = (equality), $\neq$ (inequality), > (greater than) and < (less than). There are a wide variety of statistical techniques which can be applied to ordinal data including the Pearson correlation. Other ordinal models include odds-ratio measures, log-linear models and logit models, both of which are used to analyze cross-classifications of ordinal data presented in contingency tables. In quality management, ordinal data is commonly converted into nominal data and analyzed using binomial or Poisson models. For example, if parts were classified using a poor-good-excellent ordering, the quality engineer might plot a *p* chart of the proportion of items in the poor category.

Interval scales consist of measurements where the ratios of *differences* are invariant. For example, 90°C = 194°F, 180°C = 356°F, 270°C = 518°F, 360°C = 680°F. Now 194°F/90°C $\neq$356°F/180°C but

$$\frac{356°F - 194°F}{680°F - 518°F} = \frac{180°C - 90°C}{360°C - 270°C}$$

Conversion between two interval scales is accomplished by the transformation $y=ax+b$, $a>0$. For example, °F=32+9/5(°C), where a=9/5, b=32. As with ratio scales, when permissible transformations are made statistical, results are unaffected by the interval scale used. Also, 0° (on either scale) is arbitrary. In this example, zero does not indicate an absence of heat.

Ratio scale measurements are so-called because measurements of an object in two different metrics are related to one another by an invariant ratio. For example, if an object's mass was measured in pounds (x) and kilograms (y), then $x/y=2.2$ for all values of x and y. This implies that a change from one ratio measurement scale to another is performed by a transformation of the form $y=ax$, $a>0$; e.g., pounds = 2.2 x kilograms. When permissible transformations are used, statistical results based on the data are identical regardless of the ratio scale used. Zero has an inherent meaning: in this example it signifies an absence of mass.

Reliability and validity of data

Fundamentally, any item measure should meet two tests:

1. The item measures what it is intended to measure (i.e., it is *valid*).
2. A remeasurement would order individual responses in the same way (i.e., it is *reliable*).

The remainder of this section describes techniques and procedures designed to assure that measurement systems produce numbers with these properties. A good measurement system possesses certain properties. First, it should produce a number that is "close" to the actual property being measured, i.e., it should be *accurate*. Second, if the measurement system is applied repeatedly to the same object, the measurements produced should be close to one another; i.e., the measurements should be *repeatable*. Third, the measurement system should be able to produce accurate and consistent results over the entire range of concern; i.e., it should be *linear*. Fourth, the measurement system should produce the same results when used by any properly trained individual; i.e., the results should be *reproducible*. Finally, when applied to the same items the measurement system should produce the same results in the future as it did in the past; i.e., it should be *stable*. The remainder of this section is devoted to discussing ways to ascertain these properties for particular measurement systems. In general, the methods and definitions presented here are consistent with those described by the Automotive Industry Action Group (AIAG) (Daugherty, R. et al, 1995).

DEFINITIONS

Bias—The difference between the average measured value and a reference value is referred to as *bias*. The reference value is an agreed-upon standard, such as a standard traceable to a national standards body (see below). When applied to attribute inspection, bias refers to the ability of the attribute inspection system to produce agreement on inspection standards. Bias is controlled by *calibration*, which is the process of comparing measurements to standards. The concept of bias is illustrated in Figure 6.1.

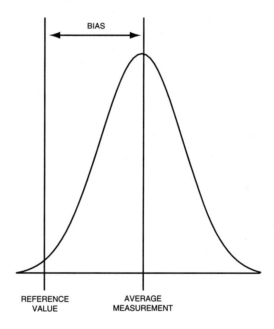

Figure 6.1. Bias illustrated.

Repeatability—AIAG defines repeatability as the variation in measurements obtained with one measurement instrument when used several times by one appraiser, while measuring the identical characteristic on the same part. Variation obtained when the measurement system is applied repeatedly under the same conditions is usually caused by conditions inherent in the measurement system.

ASQ defines *precision* as "The closeness of agreement between randomly selected individual measurements or test results. NOTE: The standard deviation of the error of measurement is sometimes called 'imprecision'." This is similar to what we are calling repeatability. Repeatability is illustrated in Figure 6.2.

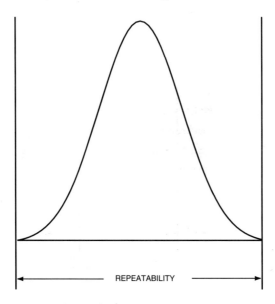

Figure 6.2. Repeatability illustrated.

Reproducibility—Reproducibility is the variation in the average of the measurements made by different appraisers using the same measuring instrument when measuring the identical characteristic on the same part. Reproducibility is illustrated in Figure 6.3.

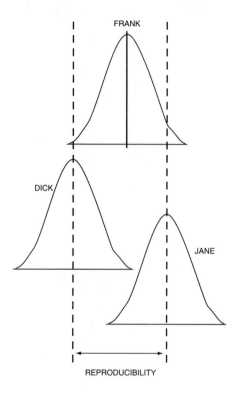

Figure 6.3. Reproducibility illustrated.

Stability—Stability is the total variation in the measurements obtained with a measurement system on the same master or parts when measuring a single characteristic over an extended time period. A system is said to be stable if the results are the same at different points in time. Stability is illustrated in Figure 6.4.

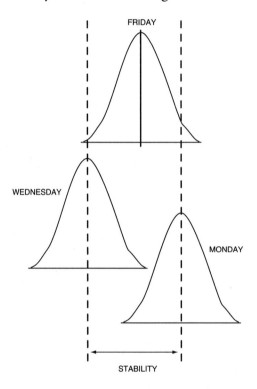

Figure 6.4. Stability illustrated.

Linearity—Linearity is the difference in the bias values through the expected operating range of the gage. Linearity is illustrated in Figure 6.5.

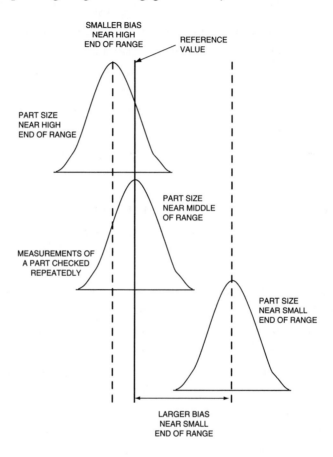

Figure 6.5. Linearity illustrated.

Repeatability and reproducibility studies

Modern measurement system analysis goes well beyond calibration. A gage can be perfectly accurate when checking a standard and still be entirely unacceptable for measuring a product or controlling a process. This section illustrates techniques for quantifying discrimination, stability, bias, repeatability, reproducibility and linearity for a measurement system. This section also shows how to express measurement error relative to the product tolerance or the process variation. For the most part, the methods shown here use control charts. Control charts provide graphical portrayals of the measurement process that enable the engineer to detect special causes that numerical methods alone would not detect.

MEASUREMENT SYSTEM DISCRIMINATION

Discrimination, sometimes called *resolution*, refers to the ability of the measurement system to divide measurements into "data categories." All parts within a particular data category will measure the same. For example, if a measurement system has a resolution of 0.001-inches, then items measuring 1.0002, 1.0003, 0.9997 would all be placed in the data category 1.000; i.e., they would all measure 1.000-inches with this particular measurement system. A measurement system's discrimination should enable it to divide the region of interest into many data categories. In quality engineering, the region of interest is the smaller of the engineering tolerance (the high specification minus the low specification) or six standard deviations. A measurement system should be able to divide the region of interest into at least five data categories. For example, if a process was capable (i.e., six sigma is less than the engineering tolerance) and $\sigma = 0.0005$, then a gage with a discrimination of 0.0005 would be acceptable (six data categories), but one with a discrimination of 0.001 would not (three data categories). When unacceptable discrimination exists, the range chart shows discrete "jumps" or "steps." This situation is illustrated in Figure 6.6.

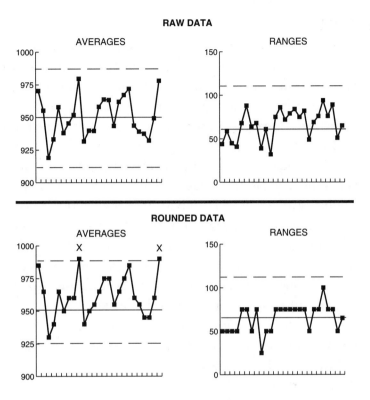

Figure 6.6 Inadequate gage discrimination on a control chart.

Note that on the control charts shown in Figure 6.6, the data plotted are the same, except that the data on the bottom two charts were rounded to the nearest 25. The effect is most easily seen on the R chart, which appears highly stratified. As sometimes happens (but not always), the result is to make the X-bar chart go out of control, even though the process is in control, as shown by the control charts with unrounded data. The remedy is to use a measurement system capable of additional discrimination; i.e., add more significant digits. If this cannot be done, it is possible to adjust the control limits for the round-off error by using a more involved method of computing the control limits, see Pyzdek (1992, 37–42) for details.

STABILITY

Measurement system stability is the change in bias over time when using a measurement system to measure a given master part or standard. *Statistical stability* is a broader term that refers to the overall consistency of measurements over time, including variation from *all causes*, e.g. bias, repeatability, reproducibility, etc. A system's statistical stability is determined through the use of control charts. Averages and range charts are typically plotted on measurements of a standard or a master part. The standard is measured repeatedly over a short time, e.g. an hour; then the measurements are repeated at predetermined intervals, e.g. weekly. Subject matter expertise is needed to determine the subgroup size, sampling intervals and measurement procedures to be followed. Control charts are then constructed and evaluated. A (statistically) stable system will show no out-of-control signals on an X-control chart of the averages readings. No "stability number" is calculated for statistical stability; the system either is or is not statistically stable.

Once statistical stability has been achieved, but not before, measurement system stability can be determined. One measure is the process standard deviation based on the R or *s* chart.

R chart method:

$$\hat{\sigma} = \overline{R}/d_2$$

s chart method:

$$\hat{\sigma} = \overline{s}/c_4$$

The values d_2 and c_4 are constants from Table 11 in the Appendix.

BIAS

Bias is the difference between an observed average measurement result and a reference value. Estimating bias involves identifying a standard to represent the reference value, then obtaining multiple measurements on the standard. The standard might be a master part whose value has been determined by a measurement system with much less error than the system under study, or by a standard traceable to NIST. Since parts and processes vary over a range, bias is measured at a point within the range. If the gage is non-linear, bias will not be the same at each point in the range (see the definition of linearity above).

Bias can be determined by selecting a single appraiser and a single reference part or standard. The appraiser then obtains a number of repeated measurements on the reference part. Bias is then estimated as the difference between the average of the repeated measurement and the known value of the reference part or standard.

Example of computing bias

A standard with a known value of 25.4mm is checked 10 times by one mechanical inspector using a dial caliper with a resolution of 0.025mm. The readings obtained are as follows:

25.425	25.425	25.400	25.400	25.375
25.400	25.425	25.400	25.425	25.375

The average is found by adding the 10 measurements together and dividing by 10,

$$\overline{X} = \frac{254.051}{10} = 25.4051mm$$

The bias is the average minus the reference value, i.e.,

$$bias = average - reference\ value$$
$$= 25.4051mm - 25.400mm = 0.0051mm$$

The bias of the measurement system can be stated as a percentage of the tolerance or as a percentage of the process variation. For example, if this measurement system were to be used on a process with a tolerance of ±0.25mm then

$$\% \ bias = 100 * |bias| \ / \ tolerance$$
$$= 100 * 0.0051 \ / \ 0.5 = 1\%$$

This is interpreted as follows: this measurement system will, on average, produce results that are 0.0051mm larger than the actual value. This difference represents 1% of the allowable product variation. The situation is illustrated in Figure 6.7.

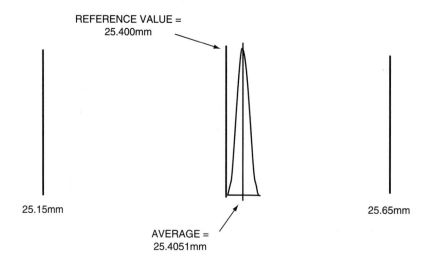

Figure 6.7. Bias example illustrated.

REPEATABILITY

A measurement system is repeatable if its variability is consistent. Consistent variability is operationalized by constructing a range or sigma chart based on repeated measurements of parts that cover a significant portion of the process variation or the tolerance, whichever is greater. If the range or sigma chart is out of control, then special causes are making the measurement system inconsistent. If the range or sigma chart is in control then repeatability can be estimated by finding the standard deviation based on either the average range or the average standard deviation. The equations used to estimate sigma are shown in Chaper 8.

Example of estimating repeatability

The data in Table 6.2 are from a measurement study involving two inspectors. Each inspector checked the surface finish of five parts; each part was checked twice by each inspector. The gage records the surface roughness in μ-inches (micro-inches). The gage has a resolution of 0.1 μ-inches.

Table 6.2. Measurement system repeatability study data.

PART	READING #1	READING #2	AVERAGE	RANGE
INSPECTOR #1				
1	111.9	112.3	112.10	0.4
2	108.1	108.1	108.10	0.0
3	124.9	124.6	124.75	0.3
4	118.6	118.7	118.65	0.1
5	130.0	130.7	130.35	0.7
INSPECTOR #2				
1	111.4	112.9	112.15	1.5
2	107.7	108.4	108.05	0.7
3	124.6	124.2	124.40	0.4
4	120.0	119.3	119.65	0.7
5	130.4	130.1	130.25	0.3

We compute:

Ranges chart

$$\overline{R} = 0.51$$

$$UCL = D_4\overline{R} = 3.267 \times 0.51 = 1.67$$

Averages chart

$$\overline{\overline{X}} = 118.85$$

$$LCL = \overline{\overline{X}} - A_2\overline{R} = 118.85 - 1.88 \times 0.51 = 117.89$$

$$UCL = \overline{\overline{X}} + A_2\overline{R} = 118.85 + 1.88 \times 0.51 = 119.81$$

The data and control limits are displayed in Figure 6.8. The R chart analysis shows that all of the R values are less than the upper control limit. This indicates that the measurement system's variability is consistent, i.e., there are no special causes of variation.

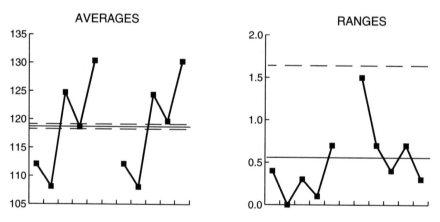

Figure 6.8. Repeatability control charts.

Note that many of the averages are outside of the control limits. This is the way it should be! Consider that the spread of the X-bar chart's control limits are based on the average range, which is based on the repeatability error. If the averages *were* within the control limits it would mean that the part-to-part variation was less than the variation due to gage repeatability error, an undesirable situation. Because the R chart is in control we can now estimate the standard deviation for repeatability or gage variation:

$$\sigma_e = \frac{\overline{R}}{d_2^*} \qquad (6.1)$$

where d_2^* is obtained from Table 13 in the Appendix. Note that we are using d_2^* and not d_2. The d_2^* values are adjusted for the small number of subgroups typically involved in gage R&R studies. Table 13 is indexed by two values: *m* is the number of repeat readings taken (*m=2* for the example), and *g* is the number of parts times the number of inspectors (*g=5x2=10* for the example). This gives, for our example

$$\sigma_e = \frac{\overline{R}}{d_2^*} = \frac{0.51}{1.16} = 0.44$$

The repeatability from this study is calculated by $5.15\sigma_e = 5.15 \times 0.44 = 2.26$. The value 5.15 is the Z ordinate which includes 99% of a standard normal distribution (see Chapter 8).

REPRODUCIBILITY

A measurement system is reproducible when different appraisers produce consistent results. Appraiser-to-appraiser variation represents a bias due to appraisers. The appraiser bias, or reproducibility, can be estimated by comparing each appraiser's average with that of the other appraisers. The standard deviation of reproducibility (σ_o) is estimated by finding the range between appraisers (R_o) and dividing by d_2^*. Reproducibility is then computed as $5.15\sigma_o$.

Reproducibility example (AIAG method)

Using the data shown in the previous example, each inspector's average is computed and we find:

> *Inspector #1 average = 118.79 μ-inches*
> *Inspector #2 average = 118.90 μ-inches*
> *Range = R_o = 0.11 μ-inches*

Looking in Table 13 in the Appendix for one subgroup of two appraisers we find d_2^*=1.41 (*m*=2, *g*=1), since there is only one range calculation *g*=1. Using these results we find R_o/d_2^*=0.11/1.41=0.078.

This estimate involves averaging the results for each inspector over all of the readings for that inspector. However, since each inspector checked each part repeatedly, this reproducibility estimate includes variation due to repeatability error. The reproducibility estimate can be adjusted using the following equation:

$$\sqrt{\left(5.15\frac{R_0}{d_2^*}\right)^2 - \frac{(5.15\sigma_e)^2}{nr}} = \sqrt{\left(5.15\times\frac{0.11}{1.41}\right)^2 - \frac{(5.15\times0.44)^2}{5\times2}} = \sqrt{0.16 - 0.51} = 0$$

As sometimes happens, the estimated variance from reproducibility exceeds the estimated variance of repeatability + reproducibility. When this occurs the estimated reproducibility is set equal to zero, since negative variances are theoretically impossible. Thus, we estimate that the reproducibility is zero.

The measurement system standard deviation is

$$\sigma_m = \sqrt{\sigma_e^2 + \sigma_o^2} = \sqrt{(0.44)^2 + 0} = 0.44 \tag{6.2}$$

and the measurement system variation, or gage R&R, is $5.15\sigma_m$. For our data gage R&R = 5.15x0.44 = 2.27.

Reproducibility example (alternative method)

One problem with the above method of evaluating reproducibility error is that it does not produce a control chart to assist the engineer with the evaluation. The method presented here does this. This method begins by rearranging the data in Table 6.2 so that all readings for any given part becomes a single row. This is shown in Table 6.3.

Table 6.3. Measurement error data for reproducibility evaluation.

Part	INSPECTOR #1		INSPECTOR #2		X-bar	R
	Reading 1	Reading 2	Reading 1	Reading 2		
1	111.9	112.3	111.4	112.9	112.125	1.5
2	108.1	108.1	107.7	108.4	108.075	0.7
3	124.9	124.6	124.6	124.2	124.575	0.7
4	118.6	118.7	120	119.3	119.15	1.4
5	130	130.7	130.4	130.1	130.3	0.7
				Averages ➤	118.845	1

Observe that when the data are arranged in this way, the R value measures the combined range of repeat readings plus appraisers. For example, the smallest reading for part #3 was from inspector #2 (124.2) and the largest was from inspector #1 (124.9). Thus, R represents two sources of measurement error: repeatability and reproducibility.

The control limits are calculated as follows:

Ranges chart

$$\bar{R} = 1.00$$

$$UCL = D_4 \bar{R} = 2.282 \times 1.00 = 2.282$$

Note that the subgroup size is 4.

Averages chart

$$\bar{\bar{X}} = 118.85$$

$$LCL = \bar{\bar{X}} - A_2 \bar{R} = 118.85 - 0.729 \times 1 = 118.12$$

$$UCL = \bar{\bar{X}} + A_2 \bar{R} = 118.85 + 0.729 \times 1 = 119.58$$

The data and control limits are displayed in Figure 6.9. The R chart analysis shows that all of the R values are less than the upper control limit. This indicates that the measurement system's variability due to the combination of repeatability and reproducibility is consistent; i.e., there are no special causes of variation.

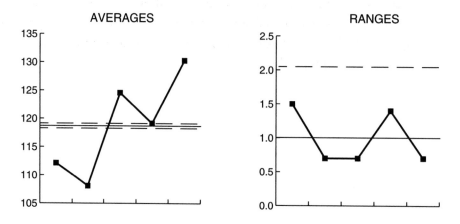

Figure 6.9. Reproducibility control charts.

Using this method, we can also estimate the standard deviation of reproducibility plus repeatability as find $\sigma_0 = R_0/d_2^* = 1/2.08 = 0.48$. Now we know that variances are additive, so

$$\sigma^2_{repeatability+reproducibility} = \sigma^2_{repeatability} + \sigma^2_{reproducibility} \qquad (6.3)$$

which implies that

$$\sigma_{reproducibility} = \sqrt{\sigma^2_{repeatability+reproducibility} - \sigma^2_{repeatability}}$$

In a previous example, we computed $\sigma_{repeatability} = 0.44$. Substituting these values gives

$$\sigma_{reproducibility} = \sqrt{\sigma^2_{repeatability+reproducibility} - \sigma^2_{repeatability}} = \sqrt{(0.48)^2 - (0.44)^2} = 0.19$$

Using this we estimate reproducibility as 5.15 x 0.19 = 1.00.

PART-TO-PART VARIATION

The X-bar charts show the part-to-part variation. To repeat, if the measurement system is adequate, *most of the parts will fall outside of the X-bar chart control limits.* If fewer than half of the parts are beyond the control limits, then the measurement system is not capable of detecting normal part-to-part variation for this process.

Part-to-part variation can be estimated once the measurement process is shown to have adequate discrimination and to be stable, accurate, linear (see below), and consistent with respect to repeatability and reproducibility. If the part-to-part standard deviation is to be estimated from the measurement system study data, the following procedures are followed:

1. Plot the average for each part (across all appraisers) on an averages control chart, as shown in the reproducibility error alternate method.
2. Confirm that at least 50% of the averages fall outside the control limits. If not, find a better measurement system for this process.
3. Find the range of the part averages, R_p.

4. Compute $\sigma_p = \dfrac{R_p}{d_2^*}$, the part-to-part standard deviation. The value of

d_2^* is found in Table 13 in the Appendix using $m=$ the number of parts and $g=1$, since there is only one R calculation.

5. The 99% spread due to part-to-part variation (PV) is found as $5.15\sigma_p$.

Once the above calculations have been made, the overall measurement system can be evaluated.

1. The total process standard deviation is found as $\sigma_t = \sqrt{\sigma_m^2 + \sigma_p^2}$, where $\sigma_m =$the standard deviation due to measurement error.

2. Total variability (TV) is $5.15\sigma_t$.

3. The percent repeatability and reproducibility (R&R) is $100\dfrac{\sigma_m}{\sigma_t}\%$.

4. The number of distinct data categories that can be created with this measurement system is 1.41x(PV/R&R).

EXAMPLE OF MEASUREMENT SYSTEM ANALYSIS SUMMARY

1. Plot the average for each part (across all appraisers) on an averages control chart, as shown in the reproducibility error alternate method.
   See Figure 6.8.
2. Confirm that at least 50% of the averages fall outside the control limits. If not, find a better measurement system for this process.
   4 of the 5 part averages, or 80%, are outside of the control limits. Thus, the measurement system error is acceptable.
3. Find the range of the part averages, R_p.
   $$R_p = 130.3 - 108.075 = 22.23.$$

4. Compute $\sigma_p = \dfrac{R_p}{d_2^*}$, the part-to-part standard deviation. The value of

d_2^* is found in Table 13 in the Appendix using $m=$ the number of parts and $g=1$, since there is only one R calculation.

$$m = 5, \ g = 1, \quad d_2^* = 2.48, \ \sigma_p = 22.23/2.48 = 8.96.$$

5. The 99% spread due to part-to-part variation (PV) is found as $5.15\sigma_p$.

$$5.15 \times 8.96 = PV = 46.15$$

Once the above calculations have been made, the overall measurement system can be evaluated.

1. The total process standard deviation is found as $\sigma_t = \sqrt{\sigma_m^2 + \sigma_p^2}$

$$\sigma_t = \sqrt{\sigma_m^2 + \sigma_p^2} = \sqrt{(0.44)^2 + (8.96)^2} = \sqrt{80.5} = 8.97$$

2. Total variability (TV) is $5.15\sigma_t$.

$$5.15 \times 8.97 = 46.20$$

3. The percent R&R is $100\dfrac{\sigma_m}{\sigma_t}\%$

$$100\frac{\sigma_m}{\sigma_t}\% = 100\frac{0.44}{8.97} = 4.91\%$$

4. The number of distinct data categories that can be created with this measurement system is 1.41x(PV/R&R).

$$1.41 \times \frac{46.15}{5.15 \times 0.44} = 28.72 = 28$$

Since the minimum number of categories is five, the analysis indicates that this measurement system is more than adequate for process analysis or process control.

LINEARITY

Linearity can be determined by choosing parts or standards that cover all or most of the operating range of the measurement instrument. Bias is determined at each point in the range and a linear regression analysis is performed.

Linearity is defined as the slope times the process variance (PV) or the slope times the tolerance, whichever is greater. A scatter diagram should also be plotted from the data.

Linearity example

The following example is taken from *Measurement Systems Analysis*, published by the Automotive Industry Action Group.

A plant foreman was interested in determining the linearity of a measurement system. Five parts were chosen throughout the operating range of the measurement system based upon the process variation. Each part was measured by a layout inspection to determine its reference value. Each part was then measured twelve times by a single appraiser. The parts were selected at random. The part average and bias average were calculated for each part as shown in Figure 6.10. The part bias was calculated by subtracting the part reference value from the part average.

PART ➔	1	2	3	4	5
Average	2.49	4.13	6.03	7.71	9.38
Ref. Value	2.00	4.00	6.00	8.00	10.00
Bias	+0.49	+0.13	+0.03	-0.29	-0.62

Figure 6.10. Gage data summary.

A linear regression analysis was performed using the methods described in Chapter 9. In the regression, x is the reference values and y is the bias. The results are shown below:

SUMMARY OUTPUT					
Regression statistics					
Multiple R	0.98877098				
R Square	0.97766805				
Adjusted R Square	0.97022407				
Standard Error	0.07284687				
Observations	5				
ANOVA					
	df	*ss*	*ms*	*F*	*Significance F*
Regression	1	0.69696	0.69696	131.336683	0.00142598
Residual	3	0.01592	0.00530667		
Total	4	0.71288			
	Coefficients	*Standard error*	*t Stat*	*P-value*	
Intercept	0.74	0.07640244	9.68555413	0.0023371	
Ref. Value	-0.132	0.0115181	-11.460222	0.00142598	

Figure 6.11. Regression analysis of linearity summary data.

The p-values indicate that the result is statistically significant, i.e., there is actually a bias in the gage. The slope of the line is –0.132, and the intercept is 0.74. R^2=0.98, indicating that the straight line explains about 98% of the variation in the bias readings. The results can be summarized as follows:

Bias   b + ax = 0.74 - 0.132 (Reference Value)
Linearity |slope| x Process Variation = 0.132 x 6 = 0.79, where 6 is the tolerance
% linearity   100% x |slope| = 13.2%

Note that the zero bias point is found at

$$x = -\left(\frac{intercept}{slope}\right) = -\left(\frac{0.74}{-0.132}\right) = 5.61.$$

In this case, this is the point of least bias. Greater bias exists as you move further from this value.

This information is summarized graphically in Figure 6.12.

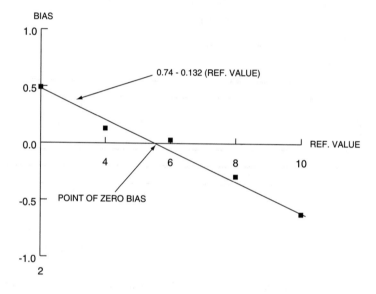

Figure 6.12. Graphical analysis of linearity.

7

Basic Six Sigma Methods

PROBLEM SOLVING TOOLS
Process mapping

Just as companies have organization charts, they can have process maps that give a picture of how work flows through the company. A process map creates a vocabulary to help people discuss process improvement. A *process map* is a graphic representation of a process, showing the sequence of tasks using a modified version of standard flowcharting symbols. The map of a work process is a picture of how people do their work. Work process maps are similar to road maps in that there are many alternative routes that will accomplish the objective. In any given circumstance, one route may be better than others. By creating a process map, the various alternatives are displayed and effective planning is facilitated. The steps involved are as follows (Galloway, 1994):

1. Select a process to be mapped.
2. Define the process.
3. Map the primary process.
4. Map alternative paths.
5. Map inspection points.
6. Use the map to improve the process.

Processes correspond to natural business activities. However, in modern organizations these natural processes are fragmented among many different departments. A process map provides an integrated picture of the natural process. Because of the focus on organizational hierarchies, processes tend to be unmanaged. People are responsible for departments and budgets, but no one is responsible for the processes.

Because organizations are arranged as departments rather than processes, it is often difficult for people to see the processes that make up the business. To get a better handle on the processes that make up a business, Hammer and Champy (1993, p. 118) suggest that the processes be given names that express their beginning and ending states. These names should imply all the work done between the processes' start and finish. Manufacturing, which sounds like a department name, is better called the procurement-to-shipment process. Some other recurring processes and their state-change names are suggested:

- Product development: concept to prototype
- Sales: prospect to order
- Order fulfillment: order to payment
- Service: inquiry to resolution

CYCLE TIME REDUCTION THROUGH CROSS FUNCTIONAL PROCESS MAPPING

Hurley and Loew (1996) describe how Motorola uses process mapping to help them reduce cycle times. Cross functional process mapping involves creating teams whose members are selected from every department involved in the new product development cycle—from marketing to manufacturing to research and development. The next phase involves mapping each step within the product development process from start to finish. Team members are divided into four categories:

- **Project champion**—provide resources and remove barriers.
- **Team leader**—organize and conduct meetings, insure that information exchange occurs.
- **Action item owner**—complete assigned tasks.
- **Team member**—complete assigned tasks.

The teams develop two maps: an "as-is" map and a "should-be" map. The As-is may detail the way the new product-development process is currently run and identifies all the problematic issues that exist in the current way that new product development is accomplished. Using the cross-functional format, each step of the process is mapped out, along with the time each step takes. The result of the exercise is twofold: a map that shows the current process, and an appreciation among team members of the contributions of their fellow team members. The As-is map can be used to improve the current process (KAIZEN). If possible, any steps that do not add value in the customer's eyes, or that are redundant, should be deleted. The techniques described in Chapter 5 can be used to identify process steps on the *critical path*, and attention can be focused on streamlining these activities first.

The Should-be map forms the basis of reengineering the product development process. The Should-be map details each step in the new, more efficient process. A list of action items is created during this mapping session. Action items define and detail what needs to be changed in order to move from the As-is state to the Should-be state. The project management tools and techniques described in Chapter 5 are then used to plan and implement the necessary steps. A Should-be process map is shown in Figure 7.1.

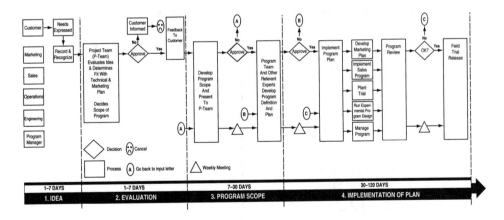

Figure 7.1. New product/service development "should-be" process map.
From Hurley, H. and Loew, C. (1996). "A quality change for new product development," *The Quality Observer*, January, pp. 10–13.

Flow charts

A process flow chart is simply a tool that graphically shows the inputs, actions, and outputs of a given system. These terms are defined as follows:

Inputs—the factors of production: land, materials, labor, equipment, and management.

Actions—the way in which the inputs are combined and manipulated in order to add value. Actions include procedures, handling, storage, transportation, and processing.

Outputs—the products or services created by acting on the inputs. Outputs are delivered to the customer or other user. Outputs also include *unplanned* and *undesirable* results, such as scrap, rework, pollution, etc. Flow charts should contain these outputs as well.

Flow charting is such a useful activity that the symbols have been standardized by various ANSI standards. There are special symbols for special processes, such as electronics or information systems. However, in most cases the symbols shown in Figure 7.2. are used:

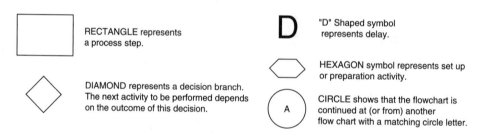

Figure 7.2. Selected flow chart symbols.

The flow chart in Figure 7.3 shows a high-level view of a process capability analysis. The flow chart can be made either more complex or less complex. As a rule of thumb, to paraphrase Albert Einstein, "Flow charts should be as simple as possible, but not simpler." The purpose of the flow chart is to help people understand the process and this is not accomplished with flow charts that are either too simple or too complex.

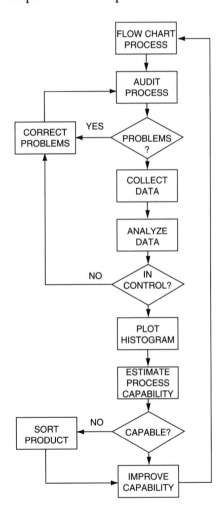

Figure 7.3. Flow chart of process capability analysis.

Check sheets

Check sheets are devices which consist of lists of items and some indicator of how often each item on the list occurs. In their simplest form, checklists are tools that make the data collection process easier by providing pre-written descriptions of events likely to occur. A well-designed check sheet will answer the questions posed by the investigator. Some examples of questions are: "Has everything been done?" "Have all inspections been performed?" "How often does a particular problem occur?" "Are problems more common with part X than with part Y?" They also serve as reminders that direct the attention of the data collector to items of interest and importance. Such simple check sheets are called *confirmation check sheets*. Check sheets have been improved by adding a number of enhancements, a few of which are described below.

Although they are simple, check sheets are extremely useful process-improvement and problem-solving tools. Their power is greatly enhanced when they are used in conjunction with other simple tools, such as histograms and Pareto analysis. Ishikawa estimated that 80% to 90% of all workplace problems could be solved using only simple quality improvement tools.

Process check sheets

These check sheets are used to create frequency distribution tally sheets that are, in turn, used to construct histograms (see below). A process check sheet is constructed by listing several ranges of measurement values and recording a mark for the actual observations. An example is shown in Figure 7.4. Notice that if reasonable care is taken in recording tick marks, the check sheet gives a graphical picture similar to a histogram.

RANGE OF MEASUREMENTS	FREQUENCY
0.990-0.995 INCHES	////
0.996-1.000 INCHES	7H/
1.001-1.005 INCHES	7H/ ////
1.006-1.010 INCHES	7H/ 7H/ //
1.011-1.015 INCHES	////
1.016-1.020 INCHES	//

Figure 7.4. Process check sheet.

Defect check sheets

Here the different types of defects are listed and the observed frequencies observed. An example of a defect check sheet is shown in Figure 7.5. If reasonable care is taken in recording tick marks, the check sheet resembles a bar chart.

DEFECT	FREQUENCY
COLD SOLDER	////
NO SOLDER IN HOLE	7H/ 7H/ ////
GRAINY SOLDER	7H/ ////
HOLE NOT PLATED THROUGH	7H/ 7H/ ///
MASK NOT PROPERLY INSTALLED	7H/ ////
PAD LIFTED	/

Figure 7.5. Defect check sheet.

Stratified defects check sheets

These check sheets stratify a particular defect type according to logical criteria. This is helpful when the defect check sheet fails to provide adequate information regarding the root cause or causes of a problem. An example is shown in Figure 7.6.

SAMPLES OF 1,000 SOLDER JOINTS	PART NUMBER X-1011	PART NUMBER X-2011	PART NUMBER X-3011	PART NUMBER X-4011	PART NUMBER X-5011
COLD SOLDER	////			⑤	
NO SOLDER IN HOLE	⑤		//	//	
GRAINY SOLDER	⑤	/		///	
HOLE NOT PLATED THROUGH	⑤			///	
MASK NOT PROPERLY INSTALLED	⑤		////	⑤	
PAD LIFTED	/				

Figure 7.6. Stratified defect check sheet.

Defect location check sheet

These "check sheets" are actually drawings, photographs, layout diagrams or maps which show where a particular problem occurs. The spatial location is valuable in identifying root causes and planning corrective action. In Figure 7.7, the location of complaints from customers about lamination problems on a running shoe are shown with an "X." The diagram makes it easy to identify a problem area that would be difficult to depict otherwise. In this case, a picture is truly worth a thousand words of explanation.

Figure 7.7. Defect location check sheet lamination complaints.

Cause and effect diagram check sheet

Cause and effect diagrams can also serve as check sheets. Once the diagram has been prepared, it is posted in the work area and the appropriate arrow is marked whenever that particular cause or situation occurs. Teams can also use this approach for historic data, when such data is available.

Pareto analysis

Definition—Pareto analysis is the process of ranking opportunities to determine which of many potential opportunities should be pursued first. It is also known as "separating the vital few from the trivial many."

Usage—Pareto analysis should be used at various stages in a quality improvement program to determine which step to take next. Pareto analysis is used to answer such questions as "What department should have the next SPC team?" or "On what type of defect should we concentrate our efforts?"

HOW TO PERFORM A PARETO ANALYSIS

1. Determine the classifications (Pareto categories) for the graph. If the desired information does not exist, obtain it by designing checksheets and logsheets.

2. Select a time interval for analysis. The interval should be long enough to be representative of typical performance.

3. Determine the total occurrences (i.e., cost, defect counts, etc.) for each category. Also determine the grand total. If there are several categories which account for only a small part of the total, group these into a category called "other."

4. Compute the percentage for each category by dividing the category total by the grand total and multiplying by 100.

5. Rank-order the categories from the largest total occurrences to the smallest.

6. Compute the "cumulative percentage" by adding the percentage for each category to that of any preceding categories.

7. Construct a chart with the left vertical axis scaled from 0 to at least the grand total. Put an appropriate label on the axis. Scale the right vertical axis from 0 to 100%, with 100% on the right side being the same height as the grand total on the left side.

8. Label the horizontal axis with the category names. The left-most category should be the largest, second largest next, and so on.

9. Draw in bars representing the amount of each category. The height of the bar is determined by the left vertical axis.

10. Draw a line that shows the cumulative percentage column of the Pareto analysis table. The cumulative percentage line is determined by the right vertical axis.

EXAMPLE OF PARETO ANALYSIS

The data in Table 7.1 has been recorded for peaches arriving at Super Duper Market during August.

Table 7.1. Raw data for Pareto analysis.

PROBLEM	PEACHES LOST
Bruised	100
Undersized	87
Rotten	235
Underripe	9
Wrong variety	7
Wormy	3

The Pareto table for the data in Table 7.1 is shown in Table 7.2.

Table 7.2. Data organized for Pareto analysis.

RANK	CATEGORY	COUNT	PERCENTAGE	CUM %
1	Rotten	235	53.29	53.29
2	Bruised	100	22.68	75.97
3	Undersized	87	19.73	95.70
4	Other	19	4.31	100.01

Note that, as often happens, the final percentage is slightly different than 100%. This is due to round-off error and is nothing to worry about. The finished diagram is shown in Figure 7.8.

Figure 7.8. The completed Pareto diagram.

Cause and effect diagrams

Process improvement involves taking action on the causes of variation. With most practical applications, the number of possible causes for any given problem can be huge. Dr. Kaoru Ishikawa developed a simple method of graphically displaying the causes of any given quality problem. His method is called by several names: the Ishikawa diagram, the fishbone diagram, and the cause and effect diagram.

Cause and effect diagrams are tools that are used to organize and graphically display all of the knowledge a group has relating to a particular problem. Usually, the steps are:

1. Develop a flow chart of the area to be improved.
2. Define the problem to be solved.
3. Brainstorm to find all possible causes of the problem.
4. Organize the brainstorming results in rational categories.
5. Construct a cause and effect diagram that accurately displays the relationships of all the data in each category.

Once these steps are complete, constructing the cause and effect diagram is very simple. The steps are:

1. Draw a box on the far right-hand side of a large sheet of paper and draw a horizontal arrow that points to the box. Inside of the box, write the description of the problem you are trying to solve.
2. Write the names of the categories above and below the horizontal line. Think of these as branches from the main trunk of the tree.
3. Draw in the detailed cause data for each category. Think of these as limbs and twigs on the branches.

A good cause and effect diagram will have many "twigs," as shown in Figure 7.9. If your cause and effect diagram doesn't have a lot of smaller branches and twigs, it shows that the understanding of the problem is superficial. Chances are you need the help of someone outside of your group to aid in the understanding, perhaps someone more closely associated with the problem.

Cause and effect diagrams come in several basic types. The dispersion analysis type is created by repeatedly asking "why does this dispersion occur?" For example, we might want to know why all of our fresh peaches don't have the same color.

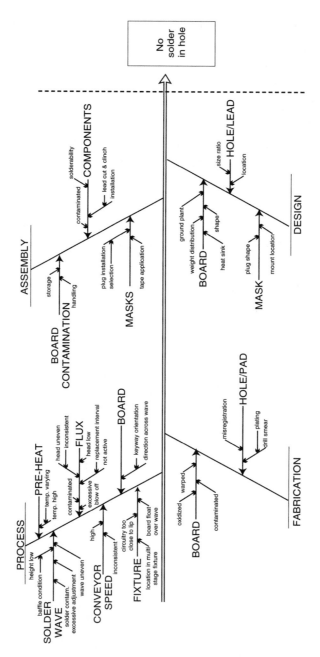

Figure 7.9. Cause and effect diagram.

The production process class cause and effect diagram uses production processes as the main categories, or branches, of the diagram. The processes are shown joined by the horizontal line. Figure 7.10 is an example of this type of diagram.

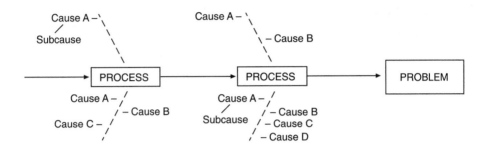

Figure 7.10. Process production class cause and effect diagram.

The cause enumeration cause and effect diagram simply displays all possible causes of a given problem grouped according to rational categories. This type of cause and effect diagram lends itself readily to the brainstorming approach we are using.

Cause and effect diagrams have a number of uses. Creating the diagram is an education in itself. Organizing the knowledge of the group serves as a guide for discussion and frequently inspires more ideas. The cause and effect diagram, once created, acts as a record of your research. Simply record your tests and results as you proceed. If the true cause is found to be something that wasn't on the original diagram, write it in. Finally, the cause and effect diagram is a display of your current level of understanding. It shows the existing level of technology as understood by the team. It is a good idea to post the cause and effect diagram in a prominent location for all to see.

A variation of the basic cause and effect diagram, developed by Dr. Ryuji Fukuda of Japan, is cause and effect diagrams with the addition of cards, or CEDAC. The main difference is that the group gathers ideas outside of the meeting room on small cards, as well as in group meetings. The cards also serve as a vehicle for gathering input from people who are not in the group;

they can be distributed to anyone involved with the process. Often the cards provide more information than the brief entries on a standard cause and effect diagram. The cause and effect diagram is built by actually placing the cards on the branches.

Scatter plots

Definition—A scatter diagram is a plot of one variable versus another. One variable is called the *independent variable* and it is usually shown on the horizontal (bottom) axis. The other variable is called the *dependent variable* and it is shown on the vertical (side) axis.

Usage—Scatter diagrams are used to evaluate cause and effect relationships. The assumption is that the independent variable causes a change in the dependent variable. Scatter plots are used to answer such questions as "Does vendor A's material machine better than vendor B's?" "Does the length of training have anything to do with the amount of scrap an operator makes?" and so on.

HOW TO CONSTRUCT A SCATTER DIAGRAM

1. Gather several paired sets of observations, preferably 20 or more. In a paired set the dependent variable can be directly tied to the independent variable.

2. Find the largest and smallest independent variable and the largest and smallest dependent variable.

3. Construct the vertical and horizontal axes so that the smallest and largest values can be plotted. Figure 7.11 shows the basic structure of a scatter diagram.

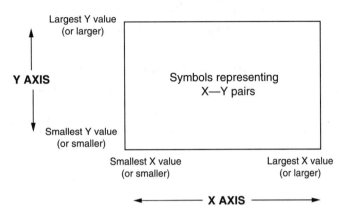

Figure 7.11. Layout of a scatter diagram.

4. Plot the data by placing a mark at the point corresponding to each X-Y pair, as illustrated by Figure 7.12. If more than one classification is used, you may use different symbols to represent each group.

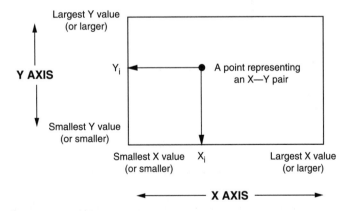

Figure 7.12. Plotting points on a scatter diagram.

From *Pyzdek's Guide to SPC-Volume One: Fundamentals*, p. 66. Copyright © 1990 by Thomas Pyzdek.

EXAMPLE OF A SCATTER DIAGRAM

The orchard manager has been keeping track of the weight of peaches on a day by day basis. The data are provided in Table 7.3.

Table 7.3. Raw data for scatter diagram.

From *Pyzdek's Guide to SPC-Volume One: Fundamentals*, p. 67. Copyright © 1990 by Thomas Pyzdek.

NUMBER	DAYS ON TREE	WEIGHT (OUNCES)
1	75	4.5
2	76	4.5
3	77	4.4
4	78	4.6
5	79	5.0
6	80	4.8
7	80	4.9
8	81	5.1
9	82	5.2
10	82	5.2
11	83	5.5
12	84	5.4
13	85	5.5
14	85	5.5
15	86	5.6
16	87	5.7
17	88	5.8
18	89	5.8
19	90	6.0
20	90	6.1

1. Organize the data into X-Y pairs, as shown in Table 7.3. The independent variable, X, is the number of days the fruit has been on the tree. The dependent variable, Y, is the weight of the peach.

2. Find the largest and smallest values for each data set. The largest and smallest values from Table 7.3 are shown in Table 7.4.

Table 7.4. Smallest and largest values.

From *Pyzdek's Guide to SPC-Volume One: Fundamentals*, p. 68. Copyright © 1990 by Thomas Pyzdek.

VARIABLE	SMALLEST	LARGEST
Days on tree (X)	75	90
Weight of peach (Y)	4.4	6.1

3. Construct the axes. In this case, we need a horizontal axis that allows us to cover the range from 75 to 90 days. The vertical axis must cover the smallest of the small weights (4.4 ounces) to the largest of the weights (6.1 ounces). We will select values beyond these minimum requirements, because we want to estimate how long it will take for a peach to reach 6.5 ounces.

4. Plot the data. The completed scatter diagram is shown in Figure 7.13.

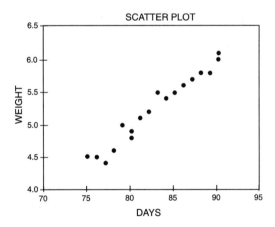

Figure 7.13. Completed scatter diagram.

From *Pyzdek's Guide to SPC-Volume One: Fundamentals*, p. 68. Copyright © 1990 by Thomas Pyzdek.

POINTERS FOR USING SCATTER DIAGRAMS

- Scatter diagrams display different patterns that must be interpreted; Figure 7.14 provides a scatter diagram interpretation guide.

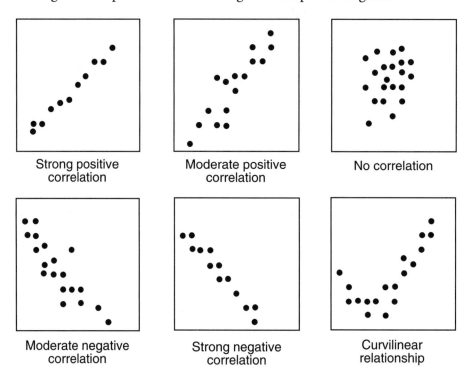

Figure 7.14. Scatter diagram interpretation guide.

From *Pyzdek's Guide to SPC-Volume One: Fundamentals*, p. 69. Copyright © 1990 by Thomas Pyzdek.

- Be sure that the independent variable, X, is varied over a sufficiently large range. When X is changed only a small amount, you may not see a correlation with Y, even though the correlation really does exist.
- If you make a prediction for Y, for an X value that lies outside of the range you tested, be advised that the prediction is highly questionable and should be tested thoroughly. Predicting a Y value beyond the X range actually tested is called extrapolation.

- Watch for the effect of variables you didn't evaluate. Often, an uncontrolled variable will wipe out the effect of your X variable. It is also possible that an uncontrolled variable will be causing the effect and you will mistake the X variable you are controlling as the true cause. This problem is much less likely to occur if you choose X levels at random. An example of this is our peaches. It is possible that any number of variables changed steadily over the time period investigated. It is possible that these variables, and not the independent variable, are responsible for the weight gain (e.g., was fertilizer added periodically during the time period investigated?).

- Beware of "happenstance" data! Happenstance data is data that was collected in the past for a purpose different than constructing a scatter diagram. Since little or no control was exercised over important variables, you may find nearly anything. Happenstance data should be used only to get ideas for further investigation, never for reaching final conclusions. One common problem with happenstance data is that the variable that is truly important is not recorded. For example, records might show a correlation between the defect rate and the shift; however, perhaps the real cause of defects is the ambient temperature, which also changes with the shift.

- If there is more than one possible source for the dependent variable, try using different plotting symbols for each source. For example, if the orchard manager knew that some peaches were taken from trees near a busy highway, he could use a different symbol for those peaches. He might find an interaction; perhaps the peaches from trees near the highway have a different growth rate than those from trees deep within the orchard.

Although it is possible to do advanced analysis without plotting the scatter diagram, this is generally bad practice. This misses the enormous learning opportunity provided by the graphical analysis of the data.

7M TOOLS

Since Dr. Shewhart launched modern quality control practice in 1931, the pace of change in recent years has been accelerating. The 7M tools are an example of the rapidly changing face of quality technology. While the traditional QC tools (Pareto analysis, control charts, etc.) are used in the analysis of quantitative data analysis, the 7M tools apply to qualitative data as well. The "M" stands for Management, and the tools are focused on managing and planning quality improvement activities. In recognition of the planning emphasis, these tools are often referred to as the "7 MP" tools. This section will provide definitions of the 7M tools. The reader is referred to Mizuno (1988) for additional information on each of these techniques.

Affinity diagrams

The word *affinity* means a "natural attraction" or kinship. The affinity diagram is a means of organizing ideas into meaningful categories by recognizing their underlying similarity. It is a means of *data reduction* in that it organizes a large number of qualitative inputs into a smaller number of major dimensions, constructs, or categories. The basic idea is that, while there are many *variables*, the variables are measuring a smaller number of important factors. For example, if patients are interviewed about their hospital experience they may say "the doctor was friendly," "the doctor knew what she was doing," and "the doctor kept me informed." Each of these statements relates to a single thing, the doctor. Many times affinity diagrams are constructed using existing data, such as memos, drawings, surveys, letters, and so on. Ideas are sometimes generated in brainstorming sessions by teams. The technique works as follows:

1. Write the ideas on small pieces of paper (Post-its™ or 3x5 cards work very well).

2. The team works *in silence* to arrange the ideas into separate categories. Silence is believed to help because the task involves pattern recognition and some research shows that for some people, particularly males, language processing involves the left side of the brain. Research also shows that left-brain thinking tends to be more linear, which is thought to inhibit creativity and pattern-recognition. Thus, by working silently, the right brain is more involved in the task. To put an idea into a category a person simply picks up the Post-it™ and moves it.

3. The final groupings are then reviewed and discussed by the team. Usually, the grouping of ideas helps the team to develop a coherent plan.

Affinity diagrams are useful for analysis of quality problems, defect data, customer complaints, survey results, etc. They can be used in conjunction with other techniques such as cause and effect diagrams or interrelationship diagraphs (see below). Figure 7.15 is an example of an affinity diagram.

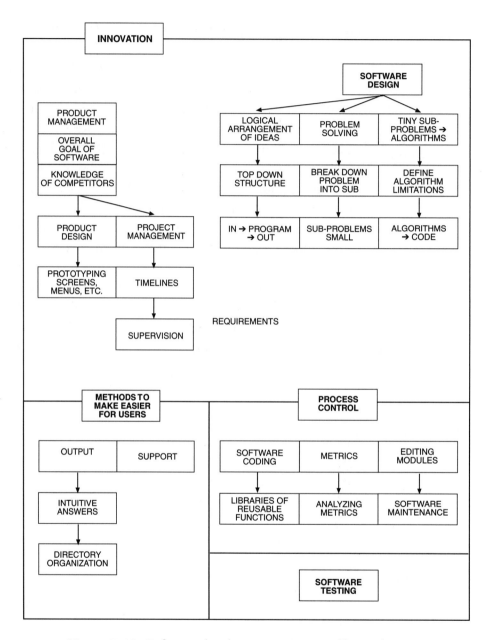

Figure 7.15. Software development process affinity diagram.

From "Modern approaches to software quality improvement," figure 3. *Australian Organization for Quality: Qualcon 90.* Copyright © 1990 by Thomas Pyzdek.

Tree diagrams

Tree diagrams are used to break down or stratify ideas in progressively greater detail. The objective is to partition a big idea or problem into its smaller components, making the idea easier to understand, or the problem easier to solve. The basic idea behind this is that, at some level, a problem's solution becomes relatively easy to find. Figure 7.16 shows an example of a tree diagram. Quality improvement would progress from the rightmost portion of the tree diagram to the left-most. Another common usage of tree diagrams is to show the goal or objective on the left side and the means of accomplishing the goal, to the right.

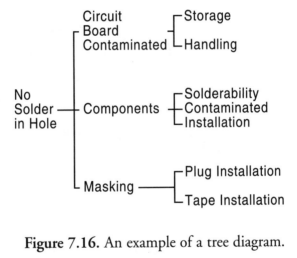

Figure 7.16. An example of a tree diagram.

Process decision program charts

The process decision program chart (PDPC) is a technique designed to help prepare contingency plans. It is modeled after reliability engineering methods of Failure Mode, Effects, and Criticality Analysis (FMECA) and Fault Tree Analysis (see Chapter 9). The emphasis of PDPC is the impact of the "failures" (problems) on project schedules. Also, PDPC seeks to describe specific actions to be taken to prevent the problems from occurring in the first place, and to mitigate the impact of the problems if they do occur. An enhancement to classical PDPC is to assign subjective probabilities to the various problems and to use these to help assign priorities. Figure 7.17 shows a PDPC.

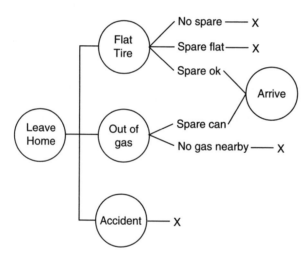

Figure 7.17. Process decision program chart.

Matrix diagrams

A matrix diagram is constructed to analyze the correlations between two groups of ideas. Actually, quality function deployment (QFD) is an enhanced matrix diagram (see Chapter 3 for a discussion of QFD). The major advantage of constructing matrix diagrams is that it forces one to *systematically* analyze correlations. Matrix diagrams can be used in conjunction with decision trees. To do this, simply use the most detailed level of two decision trees as the contents of rows and columns of a matrix diagram. An example of a matrix diagram is shown in Figure 7.18.

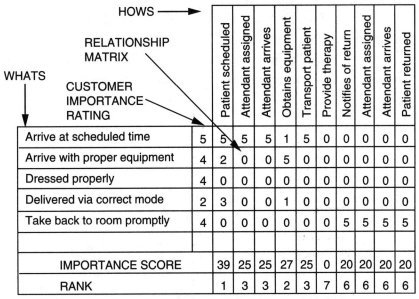

WHATS		Patient scheduled	Attendant assigned	Attendant arrives	Obtains equipment	Transport patient	Provide therapy	Notifies of return	Attendant assigned	Attendant arrives	Patient returned
Arrive at scheduled time	5	5	5	5	1	5	0	0	0	0	0
Arrive with proper equipment	4	2	0	0	5	0	0	0	0	0	0
Dressed properly	4	0	0	0	0	0	0	0	0	0	0
Delivered via correct mode	2	3	0	0	1	0	0	0	0	0	0
Take back to room promptly	4	0	0	0	0	0	0	5	5	5	5
IMPORTANCE SCORE		39	25	25	27	25	0	20	20	20	20
RANK		1	3	3	2	3	7	6	6	6	6

5 = high importance, 3 = average importance, 1 = low importance

Figure 7.18. An example of a matrix diagram.

Interrelationship diagraphs

Like affinity diagrams, interrelationship diagraphs are designed as a means of organizing disparate ideas, usually (but not always) ideas generated in brainstorming sessions. However, while affinity diagrams seek to simply arrange related ideas into groups, interrelationship diagraphs attempt to define the ways in which ideas influence one another. It is best to use both affinity diagrams and interrelationship diagraphs.

The interrelationship diagraph begins with ideas written on small pieces of paper, such as Post-its™. The pieces of paper are then placed on a large sheet of paper, such as a flip-chart sheet or a piece of large-sized blueprint paper. Arrows are drawn between related ideas. An idea that has arrows leaving it but none entering is a "root idea." Evaluating the relationships between ideas gives a better picture of the way things happen. The root ideas are often keys to improving the system. Figure 7.19 illustrates a simple interrelationship diagraph.

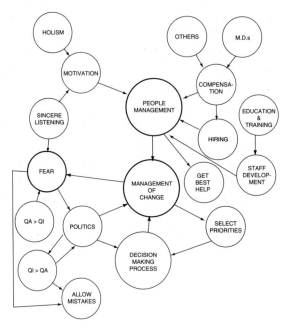

Figure **7.19.** How does "people management" impact change?

Prioritization matrices*

To prioritize is to arrange or deal with in order of importance. A prioritization matrix is a combination of a tree diagram and a matrix chart and it is used to help decision makers determine the order of importance of the activities or goals being considered. Prioritization matrices are designed to rationally narrow the focus of the team to those key issues and options which are most important to the organization. Brassard (1989, 102–103) presents three methods for developing prioritization matrices: the full analytical criteria method, the combination interrelationship diagraph (ID)/matrix method, and the consensus criteria method. Three different methods will be discussed in the following sections.

FULL ANALYTICAL CRITERIA METHOD

The full analytical criteria method is based upon work done by Saaty (1988). Saaty's approach is called the analytic hierarchy process (AHP). While analytically rigorous, AHP is cumbersome in both data collection procedures and the analysis. This author recommends that the AHP approach be reserved for truly "heavy-duty" decisions of major strategic importance to the organization. In those cases, consulting assistance may be obtained to assure that the approach is properly applied. In addition, software may be acquired to assist in the analysis**. Brassard (1989) and Saaty (1988) provide detailed examples of the application of the full analytical criteria approach.

---

*This chart replaces the matrix data analysis chart, formerly one of the 7M tools. The matrix data analysis chart was based on factor analysis or principal components analysis. This dependence on heavy-duty statistical methods made it unacceptable as a tool for use by nonstatisticians on a routine basis.

**At the time of this writing, software was available from Quality America, Inc. in Tucson, Arizona, and Expert Choice, Inc., in Pittsburgh, Pennsylvania.

COMBINATION ID/MATRIX METHOD

The interrelationship diagraph (ID) is a method used to uncover patterns in cause and effect relationships (see above). This approach to creating a prioritization matrix begins with a tree diagram (see above). Items at the rightmost level of the tree diagram (the most detailed level) are placed in a matrix (i.e., both the rows and columns of the matrix are the items from the rightmost position of the tree diagram) and their impact on one another evaluated. The ID matrix is developed by starting with a single item, then adding items one-by-one. As each item is added, the team answers the question "is this item caused by X? where X is another item?" The process is repeated item-by-item until the relationship between each item and every other item has been determined. If the answer is "yes," then an arrow is drawn between the "cause" item and the "effect" item. The strength of the relationship is determined by consensus. The final result is an estimate of the relative strength of each item and its effect on other items.

Legend:
- ◎ (9) = Strong influence
- ○ (3) = Some influence
- △ (1) = Weak/possible influence
- ↑ Means row leads to column item
- ← Means column leads to row item

	Add features to existing products	Make existing product faster	Make existing product easier to use	Leave as-is and lower price	Devote resources to new products	Increase technical support budget	Out arrows	In arrows	Total arrows	Strength
Add features to existing products	■	↑◎	↑◎	↑◎	↑◎	↑◎	5	0	5	45
Make existing product faster	←◎	■	↑◎	↑◎			2	1	3	27
Make existing product easier to use	←◎	←◎	■	↑○			1	2	3	21
Leave as-is and lower price	←◎	←◎	←○	■			0	3	3	21
Devote resources to new products	←◎				■	↑◎	1	1	2	18
Increase technical support budget	←◎				←◎	■	0	2	2	18

Figure 7.20. Combination I.D./matrix method.
Use the best mix of marketing medium.

In Figure 7.20, an "in" arrow points left and indicates that the column item leads to the row item. On the ID, this would be indicated by an arrow *from* the column item *to* the row item. An "out" arrow points upward and indicates the opposite of an "in" arrow. To maintain symmetry, if an in arrow appears in a row/column cell, an out arrow must appear in the corresponding column/row cell, and vice versa.

Once the final matrix has been created, priorities are set by evaluating the strength column, the total arrows column, and the relationship between the number of in and out arrows. An item with a high strength and a large number of out arrows would be a strong candidate because it is important (high strength) and it influences a large number of other options (many arrows, predominately out arrows). Items with high strength and a large number of in arrows are candidates for outcome measures of success.

CONSENSUS CRITERIA METHOD

The consensus criteria method is a simplified approach to selecting from several options according to some criteria. It begins with a matrix where the different options under consideration are placed in rows and the criteria to be used are shown in columns. The criteria are given weights by the team using the consensus decision rule. For example, if criterion #1 were given a weight of 3 and the group agreed that criterion #2 was twice as important, then criterion #2 would receive a weight of 6. Another way to do the weighting is to give the team $1 in nickels and have them "spend" the dollar on the various criteria. The resulting value allocated to each criterion is its weight. The group then rank orders the options based on each criterion. Ranks are labeled such that the option that best meets the criterion gets the highest rank; e.g., if there are five options being considered for a given criterion, the option that best meets the criterion is given a rank of 5.

The options are then prioritized by adding up the option's rank for each criterion multiplied by the criterion weight.

Example of consensus criteria method

A team had to choose which of four projects to pursue first. To help them decide, they identified four criteria for selection and their weights as follows: high impact on bottom line (weight=0.25), easy to implement (0.15), low cost to implement (0.20) and high impact on customer satisfaction (0.40). The four projects were then ranked according to each of the criterion; the results are shown in the table below.

	CRITERIA AND WEIGHTS				
WEIGHT →	0.25	0.15	0.2	0.4	
	Bottom line	Easy	Low cost	Customer satisfaction	Total
Project 1	1	2	2	1	1.35
Project 2	3	4	4	3	3.35
Project 3	2	1	3	4	2.85
Project 4	4	3	1	2	2.45

In the above example, the team would begin with project #2 because it has the highest score. If the team had difficulty reaching consensus on the weights or ranks, they could use totals or a method such as the nominal group technique described below.

Activity network diagram

Activity network diagrams, sometimes called arrow diagrams, have their roots in well-established methods used in operations research. The arrow diagram is directly analogous to the Critical Path Method (CPM) and the Program Evaluation and Review Technique (PERT) discussed in Chapter 5. These two project management tools have been used for many years to determine which activities must be performed, when they must be performed, and in what order. Unlike CPM and PERT, which require training in project management or systems engineering, arrow diagrams are greatly simplified so that they can be used with a minimum of training. Figure 7.21, an illustration of an arrow (PERT) diagram, is reproduced here.

ACTIVITIES LIST

1. Excavate
2. Foundation
3. Rough wall
4. Roof
5. Rough exterior plumbing
6. Exterior siding
7. Rough interior plumbing
8. Exterior painting
9. Wall boards
10. Exterior fixtures
11. Flooring
12. Interior painting
13. Interior fixtures

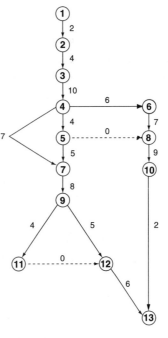

Figure 7.21. PERT network for constructing a house.

Other continuous improvement tools

Over the years, the tools of quality improvement have proliferated. By some estimates there are now over 400 tools in the "TQM Toolbox." This author believes that it is possible to make dramatic improvements with the tools already described, combined with the powerful statistical techniques described in other parts of this book. However, in addition to the tools already discussed, there are two more simple tools that the author believes deserve mention: the nominal group technique, and force field analysis. These tools are commonly used to help teams move forward by obtaining input from all interested parties and identifying the obstacles they face.

NOMINAL GROUP TECHNIQUE

The nominal group technique (NGT) is a method for generating a "short list" of items to be acted upon. NGT uses a highly structured approach designed to reduce the usual give-and-take among group members. Usage of NGT is indicated when 1) the group is new or has several new members, 2) when the topic under consideration is controversial, or 3) when the team is unable to resolve a disagreement. Scholtes (1988) describes the steps involved in the NGT. A summary of the approach is shown below.

Part I—Formalizing the brainstorm:

1. Define the task in the form of a question.
2. Describe the purpose of this discussion and the rules and procedures of the NGT.
3. Introduce and clarify the question.
4. Generate ideas. Do this by having the team write down their ideas in silence.
5. List the ideas obtained.
6. Clarify and discuss the ideas.

Part II—Making the selection:

1. Choose the top 50 ideas. Note: members can remove their ideas from consideration if they wish, but no member can remove another's idea.
2. Pass out index cards to each member, using the following table as a guide:

IDEAS	INDEX CARDS
less than 20	4 cards
20–35	6 cards
36–50	8 cards

3. Individual members write down their choices from the list, one choice per card.
4. Individual members rank-order their choices and write the rank on the cards.
5. Record the group's choices and ranks.
6. Group reviews and discusses the results. Consider: How often was an item selected? What is the total of the ranks for each item?

If the team can agree on the importance of the item(s) that got the highest score(s) (sum of ranks), then the team moves on to preparing an action plan to deal with the item or items selected.

FORCE-FIELD ANALYSIS

Force-field analysis (FFA) is a method borrowed from the mechanical engineering discipline known as free-body diagrams. Free-body diagrams are drawn to help the engineer identify all the forces surrounding and acting on a body. The objective is to ascertain the forces leading to an *equilibrium state* for the body.

In FFA the "equilibrium" is the status quo. FFA helps the team understand the forces that keep things the way they are. Some of the forces are "drivers" that move the system towards a desired goal. Other forces are "restrainers" that prevent the desired movement and may even cause movement away from the goal. Once the drivers and restrainers are known, the team can design an action plan which will 1) reduce the forces restraining progress and 2) increase the forces which lead to movement in the desired direction.

FFA is useful in the early stages of planning. Once restrainers are explicitly identified, a strategic plan can be prepared to develop the drivers necessary to overcome them. FFA is also useful when progress has stalled. By performing FFA, people are brought together and guided toward consensus, an activity that, by itself, often overcomes a number of obstacles. Pyzdek (1994) lists the following steps for conducting FFA.

1. Determine the goal.
2. Create a team of individuals with the authority, expertise, and interest needed to accomplish the goal.
3. Have the team use brainstorming or the NGT to identify restrainers and drivers.
4. Create a force-field diagram or table which lists the restrainers and drivers.
5. Prepare a plan for removing restrainers and increasing drivers.

An example of a force-field diagram is shown in Figure 7.22.

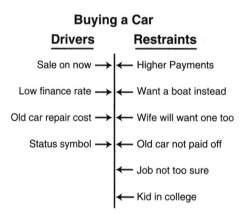

Figure 7.22. Example of a force-field diagram.

From *Pocket Guide to Quality Tools*, p. 10. Copyright © 1995 by Thomas Pyzdek.

It may be helpful to assign "strength weights" to the drivers and restrainers (e.g., weak, moderate, strong).

KNOWLEDGE DISCOVERY TOOLS

Getting the correct answer begins with asking the right question. The tools and techniques described in this section help the Six Sigma team learn which questions to ask. These simple tools are properly classified as *data presentation tools*. Many are graphically based, creating pictures that are easy to understand from the numbers and categories in the data. Others summarize the data, reducing incomprehensible data in massive tables to a few succinct numbers that convey essential information.

In addition to these traditional tools of the trade, the reader should determine if they have access to on-line analytic processing tools (OLAP). OLAP is discussed briefly in Chapter 1 (see Integrating Six Sigma With Other Information Systems Technologies). Contact your organization's Information Systems department for additional information regarding OLAP.

This section addresses the subject of time series analysis on a relatively simple level with a look at statistical methods that can be used with data from a stable process. This involves the analysis of patterns in runs of data in a time-ordered sequence. The problem of autocorrelation in time series data is discussed in Chapter 8 with a method of dealing with the problem shown in EWMA charts.

Run charts

Run charts are plots of data arranged in time sequence. Analysis of run charts is performed to determine if the patterns can be attributed to common causes of variation, or if special causes of variation were present. Run charts should be used for preliminary analysis of any data measured on a continuous scale that can be organized in time sequence. Run chart candidates include such things as fuel consumption, production throughput, weight, size, etc. Run charts answer the question "was this process in statistical control for the time period observed?" If the answer is "no," then the process was influenced by one or more special causes of variation. If the answer is "yes," then the long-term performance of the process can be estimated using process capability analysis methods. The run chart tests shown are all *non-parametric*, i.e., there are no assumptions made regarding the underlying distribution.

HOW TO PREPARE AND ANALYZE RUN CHARTS

1. Plot a line chart of the data in time sequence.
2. Find the median of the data. This can be easily done by using the line chart constructed in the above step. Simply place a straightedge or a piece of paper across the top of the chart, parallel to the bottom axis. Lower the straightedge until half of the data points appear above the straightedge, or on it. Draw a horizontal line across the chart at that point and label the line "Median" or $\tilde{X}$. This procedure is shown in Figure 7.23.

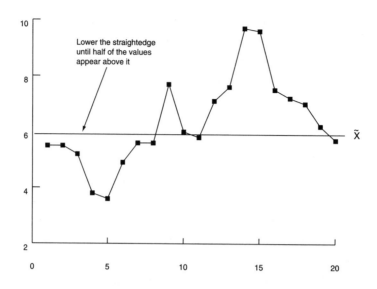

Figure 7.23. Using a straightedge to find the median.

As might be expected, run charts are evaluated by examining the "runs" on the chart. A "run" is a time-ordered sequence of points. There are several different statistical tests that can be applied to the runs.

RUN LENGTH

A *run to the median* is a series of consecutive points on the same side of the median. Unless the process is being influenced by special causes, it is unlikely that a long series of consecutive points will all fall on the same side of the median. Thus, checking run length is one way of checking for special causes of variation. The length of a run is found by simply counting the number of consecutive points on the same side of the median. However, it may be that some values are exactly equal to the median. If only one value is exactly on the median line, ignore it. There will always be at least one value exactly on the median with an odd number of data points. If more than one value is on the line, assign them to one side or the other in a way that results in 50% being on one side and 50% on the other. On the run chart, mark those that will be counted as above the median with an *a* and those that will be counted below the median with a *b*. The run length concept is illustrated in Figure 7.24.

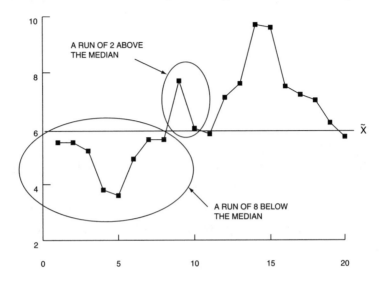

Figure 7.24. Determination of run length.

After finding the longest run, compare the length of the longest run to the values in Table 7.5. If the longest run is longer than the maximum allowed, then the process was probably influenced by a special cause of variation ($\alpha=0.05$). With the example, there are 20 values plotted and the longest run was 8. Table 7.5 indicates that a run of 7 would not be too unusual for 20 plotted points but a run of 8 would be. Since our longest run is 8, we conclude that a special cause of variation is indicated and conduct an investigation to identify the special cause.

Table 7.5. Maximum run length.

NUMBER OF PLOTTED VALUES	MAXIMUM RUN LENGTH
10	5
15	6
20	7
30	8
40	9
50	10

NUMBER OF RUNS

The number of runs expected from a controlled process can also be mathematically determined. A process that is not being influenced by special causes will not have either too many runs or too few runs. The number of runs is found by simple counting. Referring to Figure 7.25, it can be seen that there are 5 runs.

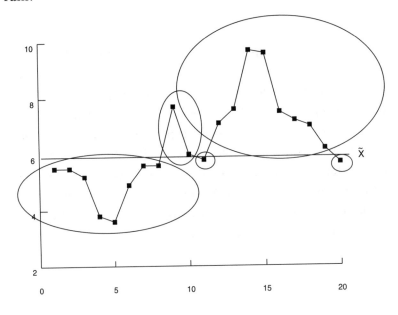

Figure 7.25. Determination of number of runs.

Table 7.6 is used to evaluate the number of runs. If there are fewer runs than the smallest allowed or more runs than the largest allowed, then there is a high probability (α=0.05) that a special cause is present. With the example, there are 20 values plotted and 5 runs. Table 7.6 indicates that for 20 plotted points, 6 to 15 runs are expected; therefore the conclusion is reached that a special cause was present.

Table 7.6. Limits on the number of runs.

Number of Plotted Values	Smallest Run Count	Largest Run Count
10	3	8
12	3	10
14	4	11
16	5	12
18	6	13
20	6	15
22	7	16
24	8	17
26	9	18
28	10	19
30	11	20
32	11	22
34	12	23
36	13	24
38	14	25
40	15	26
42	16	27
44	17	28
46	17	30
48	18	31
50	19	32

TRENDS

The run chart should not have any unusually long series of consecutive increases or decreases. If it does, then a trend is indicated and it is probably due to a special cause of variation ($\alpha=0.05$). Compare the longest count of consecutive increases or decreases to the longest allowed shown in Table 7.7, and if the count exceeds the table value then it is likely that a special cause of variation caused the process to drift.

Table 7.7. Maximum consecutive increases/decreases.

NUMBER OF PLOTTED VALUES	MAXIMUM CONSECUTIVE INCREASES/DECREASES
5 to 8	4
9 to 20	5
21 to 100	6
101 or more	7

Figure 7.26 shows the analysis of trends. Note that the trend can extend on both sides of the median, i.e., for this particular run test the median is ignored.

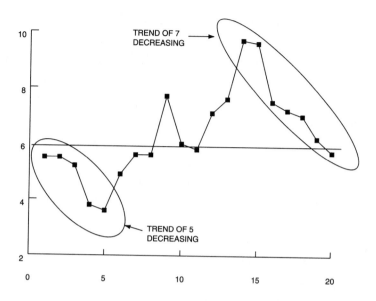

Figure 7.26. Determination of trend length.

When counting increases or decreases, ignore "no change" values. For example, the trend length in the series 2, 3, 3, 5, 6 is four.

POINTERS FOR USING RUN CHARTS

Run charts should not be used if too many of the numbers are the same. As a rule of thumb, don't use run charts if more than 30% of the values are the same. For example, in the data set 1, 2, 3, 3, 6, 7, 7, 11, 17, 19, the number 3 appears twice and the number 7 appears twice. Thus, 4 of the 10, or 40% of the values are the same.

Run charts are preliminary analysis tools, so with continuous data in time-order always sketch a quick run chart before doing any more complex analysis. Often the patterns on a run chart will point in the right direction without any further work.

Run charts are one of the least sensitive SPC techniques. They are unable to detect "freaks," i.e., single points dramatically different from the rest. Thus, run charts may fail to find a special cause even if a special cause was present. In statistical parlance, run charts tend to have large Type II errors, i.e., they have a high probability of accepting the hypothesis of no special cause even when the special cause actually exists. Use run charts to aid in troubleshooting. The different run tests indicate different types of special causes. A long run on the same side of the median indicates a special cause that created a process shift. A long series of consecutively increasing or decreasing values indicates a special cause that created a trend. Too many runs often indicates mixture of several sources of variation in the sample. Too few runs often occur in conjunction with a process shift or trend. If there are too few runs and they are not caused by a process shift or trend, then too few runs may indicate mixture that follows a definite pattern (e.g., an operator who is periodically changed).

Descriptive statistics

Typically, descriptive statistics are computed to describe properties of empirical distributions, that is, distributions of data from samples. There are three areas of interest: the distribution's location or central tendency, its dispersion, and its shape. The analyst may also want some idea of the magnitude of possible error in the statistical estimates. Table 7.8 describes some of the more common descriptive statistical measures.

Table 7.8. Common descriptive statistics.

SAMPLE STATISTIC	DISCUSSION	EQUATION/SYMBOL
Measures of location		
Population mean	The center of gravity or centroid of the distribution.	$\mu = \dfrac{1}{N} \sum\limits_{i=1}^{N} x_i$, where x is an observation, N is the population size.
Sample mean	The center of gravity or centroid of a sample from a distribution.	$\overline{X} = \dfrac{1}{n} \sum\limits_{i=1}^{n} x_i$, where x is an observation, n is the sample size.

Continued on next page . . .

Table 7.8—*Continued . . .*

SAMPLE STATISTIC	DISCUSSION	EQUATION/SYMBOL
Measures of location		
Median	The 50%/50% split point. Precisely half of the data set will be above the median, and half below it.	$\tilde{X}$
Mode	The value that occurs most often. If the data are grouped, the mode is the group with the highest frequency.	None
Measures of dispersion		
Range	The distance between the sample extreme values.	R=Largest–Smallest
Population variance	A measure of the variation around the mean, units are the square of the units used for the original data.	$\sigma^2 = \sum_{i=1}^{N} \frac{(x_i - \mu)^2}{N}$
Population standard deviation	A measure of the variation around the mean, in the same units as the original data.	$\sigma = \sqrt{\sigma^2}$
Sample variance	A measure of the variation around the mean, units are the square of the units used for the original data.	$s^2 = \sum_{i=1}^{n} \frac{(x_i - \overline{X})^2}{n-1}$
Sample standard deviation	A measure of the variation around the mean, in the same units as the original data.	$s = \sqrt{s^2}$

Continued on next page . . .

Table 7.8—Continued . . .

SAMPLE STATISTIC	DISCUSSION	EQUATION/SYMBOL
Measures of shape		
Skewness	A measure of asymmetry. Zero indicates perfect symmetry; the normal distribution has a skewness of zero. Positive skewness indicates that the "tail" of the distribution is more stretched on the side above the mean. Negative skewness indicates that the tail of the distribution is more stretched on the side below the mean. The normal distribution has a skewness of 0.	$$k = \dfrac{\dfrac{\sum_{i=1}^{n} x_i^3}{n} - \dfrac{3\overline{X}\sum_{i=1}^{n} x_i^2}{n} + 2\overline{X}^3}{s^3}$$
Kurtosis	Kurtosis is a measure of flatness of the distribution. Heavier tailed distribution have larger kurtosis measures. The normal distribution has a kurtosis of 3.	$$\beta_2 = \dfrac{\dfrac{\sum_{i=1}^{n} x_i^4}{n} - 4\overline{X}\dfrac{\sum_{i=1}^{n} x_i^3}{n} + 6\overline{X}^2\dfrac{\sum_{i=1}^{n} x_i^2}{n} - 3\overline{X}^4}{s^4}$$

The figures below illustrate distributions with different descriptive statistics.

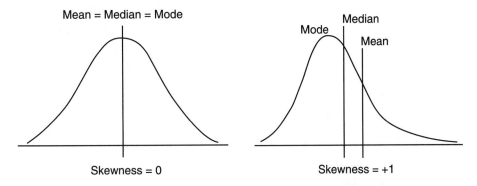

Figure 7.27. Illustration of mean, median, and mode.

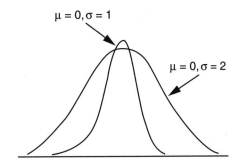

Figure 7.28. Illustration of sigma.

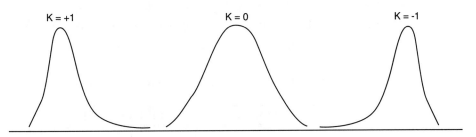

Figure 7.29. Illustration of skewness.

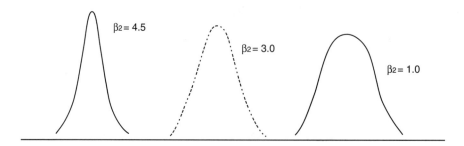

Figure 7.30. Illustration of kurtosis.

Histograms

A histogram is a pictorial representation of a set of data. It is created by grouping the measurements into "cells." Histograms are used to determine the shape of a data set. Also, a histogram displays the numbers in a way that makes it easy to see the dispersion and central tendency and to compare the distribution to requirements. Histograms can be valuable troubleshooting aids. Comparisons between histograms from different machines, operators, vendors, etc., often reveal important differences.

HOW TO CONSTRUCT A HISTOGRAM

1. Find the largest and the smallest value in the data.
2. Compute the range by subtracting the smallest value from the largest value.
3. Select a number of cells for the histogram. Table 7.9 provides some useful guidelines. The final histogram may not have exactly the number of cells you choose here, as explained below.

Table 7.9. Histogram cell determination guidelines.

SAMPLE SIZE	NUMBER OF CELLS
100 or less	7 to 10
101–200	11 to 15
201 or more	13 to 20

As an alternative, the number of cells can be found as the square root of the number in the sample. For example, if n=100, then the histogram would have 10 cells. Round to the nearest integer.

4. Determine the width of each cell. Use the letter W to stand for the cell width. W is computed from Equation 7.1.

$$W = \frac{Range}{Number\ of\ Cells} \tag{7.1}$$

The number W is a starting point. Round W to a convenient number. Rounding W will affect the number of cells in the histogram.

5. Compute "cell boundaries." A cell is a range of values and cell boundaries define the start and end of each cell. Cell boundaries should have one more decimal place than the raw data values in the data set; for example, if the data are integers, the cell boundaries would have one decimal place. The low boundary of the first cell must be less than the smallest value in the data set. Other cell boundaries are found by adding W to the previous boundary. Continue until the upper boundary is larger than the largest value in the data set.

6. Go through the raw data and determine into which cell each value falls. Mark a tick in the appropriate cell.

7. Count the ticks in each cell and record the count, also called the frequency, to the right of the tick marks.

8. Construct a graph from the table. The vertical axis of the graph will show the frequency in each cell. The horizontal axis will show the cell boundaries. Figure 7.31 illustrates the layout of a histogram.

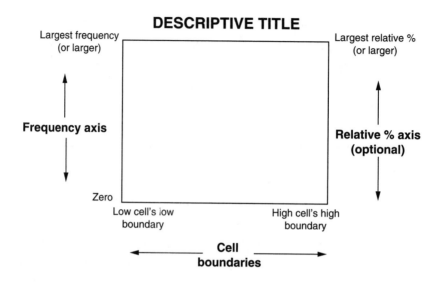

Figure 7.31. Layout of a histogram.

From *Pyzdek's Guide to SPC-Volume One: Fundamentals*, p. 61. Copyright © 1990 by Thomas Pyzdek.

9. Draw bars representing the cell frequencies. The bars should all be the same width; the height of the bars should equal the frequency in the cell.

HISTOGRAM EXAMPLE

Assume that the data in Table 7.10 represent the size of a metal rod. The rods were sampled every hour for 20 consecutive hours and 5 consecutive rods were checked each time (20 subgroups of 5 values per group).

Table 7.10. Data for histogram.

From *Pyzdek's Guide to SPC-Volume One: Fundamentals*, p. 62. Copyright © 1990 by Thomas Pyzdek.

ROW	SAMPLE 1	SAMPLE 2	SAMPLE 3	SAMPLE 4	SAMPLE 5
1	1.002	0.995	1.000	1.002	1.005
2	1.000	0.997	1.007	0.992	0.995
3	0.997	1.013	1.001	0.985	1.002
4	0.990	1.008	1.005	0.994	1.012
5	0.992	1.012	1.005	0.985	1.006
6	1.000	1.002	1.006	1.007	0.993
7	0.984	0.994	0.998	1.006	1.002
8	0.987	0.994	1.002	0.997	1.008
9	0.992	0.988	1.015	0.987	1.006
10	0.994	0.990	0.991	1.002	0.988
11	1.007	1.008	0.990	1.001	0.999
12	0.995	0.989	0.982*	0.995	1.002
13	0.987	1.004	0.992	1.002	0.992
14	0.991	1.001	0.996	0.997	0.984
15	1.004	0.993	1.003	0.992	1.010
16	1.004	1.010	0.984	0.997	1.008
17	0.990	1.021*	0.995	0.987	0.989
18	1.003	0.992	0.992	0.990	1.014
19	1.000	0.985	1.019	1.002	0.986
20	0.996	0.984	1.005	1.016	1.012

1. Find the largest and the smallest value in the data set. The smallest value is 0.982 and the largest is 1.021. Both values are marked with an (*) in Table 7.10.

2. Compute the range, R, by subtracting the smallest value from the largest value. R = 1.021 – 0.982 = 0.039.

3. Select a number of cells for the histogram. Since there are 100 values, 7 to 10 cells are recommended. Using 10 cells the following calculations can be made.

4. Determine the width of each cell, W. Using Equation 7.1, compute W=0.039 / 10 = 0.0039. Round this to 0.004 for convenience. Thus, W= 0.004.

5. Compute the cell boundaries. The low boundary of the first cell must be below the smallest value of 0.982, and the cell boundaries should have one decimal place more than the raw data. Thus, the lower cell boundary for the first cell will be 0.9815. Other cell boundaries are found by adding W = 0.004 to the previous cell boundary until the upper boundary is greater than the largest value of 1.021. This gives the cell boundaries in Table 7.11.

Table 7.11. Histogram cell boundaries.

From *Pyzdek's Guide to SPC-Volume One: Fundamentals*, p. 63. Copyright © 1990 by Thomas Pyzdek.

CELL NUMBER	LOWER CELL BOUNDARY	UPPER CELL BOUNDARY
1	0.9815	0.9855
2	0.9855	0.9895
3	0.9895	0.9935
4	0.9935	0.9975
5	0.9975	1.0015
6	1.0015	1.0055
7	1.0055	1.0095
8	1.0095	1.0135
9	1.0135	1.0175
10	1.0175	1.0215

6. Go through the raw data and mark a tick in the appropriate cell for each data point.

7. Count the tick marks in each cell and record the frequency to the right of each cell. The results of the calculations are shown in Table 7.12. Table 7.12 is often referred to as a "frequency table" or "frequency tally sheet."

Table 7.12. Frequency tally sheet.

From *Pyzdek's Guide to SPC-Volume One: Fundamentals*, p. 64. Copyright © 1990 by Thomas Pyzdek.

CELL NUMBER	CELL START	CELL END	TALLY	FREQUENCY
1	0.9815	0.9855	|||||||	8
2	0.9855	0.9895	||||||||	9
3	0.9895	0.9935	|||| |||| |||| ||	17
4	0.9935	0.9975	|||| |||| ||||		16
5	0.9975	1.0015	||||||||	9
6	1.0015	1.0055	|||| |||| |||| ||||	19
7	1.0055	1.0095	|||| ||||		11
8	1.0095	1.0135	|||||	6
9	1.0135	1.0175	|||	3
10	1.0175	1.0215	||	2

Construct a graph from the table in step 7. The frequency column will be plotted on the vertical axis, and the cell boundaries will be shown on the horizontal (bottom) axis. The resulting histogram is shown in Figure 7.32.

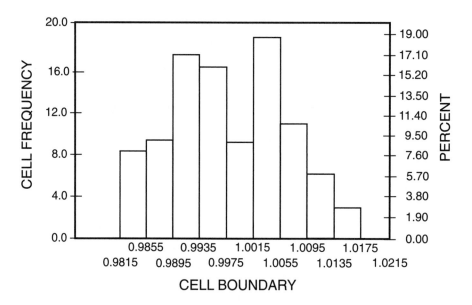

Figure 7.32. Completed histogram.

From *Pyzdek's Guide to SPC-Volume One: Fundamentals*, p. 64. Copyright © 1990 by Thomas Pyzdek.

POINTERS FOR USING HISTOGRAMS

- Histograms can be used to compare a process to requirements if the specification lines are drawn on the histogram. If this is done, be sure to scale the histogram accordingly.
- Histograms should not be used alone. Always construct a run chart or a control chart before constructing a histogram. They are needed because histograms will often conceal out of control conditions due to the fact that they don't show the time sequence of the data.
- Evaluate the pattern of the histogram to determine if changes of any kind can be detected. The changes will usually be indicated by multiple modes or "peaks" on the histogram. Most real-world processes produce histograms with a single peak. However, histograms from small samples often have multiple peaks that merely represent sampling variation. Also, multiple peaks are sometimes caused by an unfortunate choice of the number of cells. Also, processes heavily influenced by behavior patterns

are often multi-modal. For example, traffic patterns have distinct "rush-hours," and prime time is prime time precisely because more people tend to watch television at that time.

- Compare histograms from different periods of time. Changes in histogram patterns from one time period to the next can be very useful in finding ways to improve the process.

- Stratify the data by plotting separate histograms for different sources of data. For example, with the rod diameter histogram we might want to plot separate histograms for shafts made from different vendors' materials or made by different operators or machines. This can sometimes reveal things that even control charts don't detect.

Exploratory data analysis

Data analysis can be divided into two broad phases: an exploratory phase and a confirmatory phase. Data analysis can be thought of as detective work. Before the "trial" one must collect evidence and examine it thoroughly. One must have a basis for developing a theory of cause and effect. Is there a gap in the data? Are there patterns that suggest some mechanism? Or, are there patterns that are simply mysterious (e.g., are all of the numbers even or odd)? Do outliers occur? Are there patterns in the variation of the data? What are the shapes of the distributions? This activity is known as exploratory data analysis (EDA). Tukey's 1977 book with this title elevated this task to acceptability among "serious" devotees of statistics.

Four themes appear repeatedly throughout EDA: resistance, residuals, re-expression, and visual display. *Resistance* refers to the insensitivity of a method to a small change in the data. If a small amount of the data is contaminated, the method shouldn't produce dramatically different results. *Residuals* are what remain after removing the effect of a model or a summary. For example, one might subtract the mean from each value, or look at deviations about a regression line. *Re-expression* involves examination of different scales on which the data are displayed. Tukey focused most of his attention on simple power transformations such as $y = \sqrt{x}$, $y = x^2$, $y = 1/x$. *Visual display* helps the analyst examine the data graphically to grasp regularities and peculiarities in the data.

EDA is based on a simple basic premise: it is important to understand what you can do before you learn to measure how well you seem to have done it (Tukey, 1977). The objective is to investigate the appearance of the data, not to confirm some prior hypothesis. While there are a large number of EDA methods and techniques, there are two which are commonly encountered in quality engineering work: stem-and-leaf plots and boxplots. These techniques are commonly included in most statistics packages. (SPSS was used to create the figures used in this book.) However, the graphics of EDA are simple enough to be done easily by hand.

STEM-AND-LEAF PLOTS

Stem-and-leaf plots are a variation of histograms and are especially useful for smaller data sets (n<200). A major advantage of stem-and-leaf plots over the histogram is that the raw data values are preserved, sometimes completely and sometimes only partially. There is a loss of information in the histogram because the histogram reduces the data by grouping several values into a single cell.

Figure 7.33 is a stem-and-leaf plot of diastolic blood pressures. As in a histogram, the length of each row corresponds to the number of cases that fall into a particular interval. However, a stem-and-leaf plot represents each case with a numeric value that corresponds to the actual observed value. This is done by dividing observed values into two components—the leading digit or digits, called the *stem*, and the trailing digit, called the *leaf*. For example, the value 75 has a stem of 7 and a leaf of 5.

FREQUENCY	STEM & LEAF	
.00	6	*
7.00	6	. 5558889
13.00	7	* 0000111223344
32.00	7	. 55555555566777777777788888889999
44.00	8	* 00000000000000000000001111122222333333334444
45.00	8	. 555555555566666667777777777777788888999999999
31.00	9	* 0000000001111111122222222333334
27.00	9	. 556666677777788888888899999
13.00	10	* 0000122233333
11.00	10	. 55555577899
5.00	11	* 00003
5.00	11	. 55789
2.00	12	* 01
4.00	Extremes	(125), (133), (160)

Stem width: 10
Each leaf: 1 case (s)

Figure 7.33. Stem-and-leaf plot of diastolic blood pressures.

From *SPSS for Windows Base System User's Guide*, p. 183. Copyright © 1993. Used by permission of the publisher, SPSS, Inc., Chicago, IL.

In this example, each stem is divided into two rows. The first row of each pair has cases with leaves of 0 through 4, while the second row has cases with leaves of 5 through 9. Consider the two rows that correspond to the stem of 11. In the first row, there are four cases with diastolic blood pressure of 110 and one case with a reading of 113. In the second row, there are two cases with a value of 115 and one case each with a value of 117, 118, and 119.

The last row of the stem-and-leaf plot is for cases with extreme values (values far removed from the rest). In this row, the actual values are displayed in parentheses. In the frequency column, there are four extreme cases with values of 125, 133, and 160. Only distinct values are listed.

When there are few stems, it is sometimes useful to subdivide each stem even further. Consider Figure 7.34 a stem-and-leaf plot of cholesterol levels. In this figure, stems 2 and 3 are divided into five parts, each representing two leaf values. The first row, designated by an asterisk, is for leaves of 0 and 1; the next, designated by t, is for leaves of 2's and 3's; the third, designated by f, is for leaves of 4's and 5's; the fourth, designated by s is for leaves of 6's and 7's; and the fifth, designated by a period, is for leaves of 8's and 9's. Rows without cases are not represented in the plot. For example, in Figure 7.34, the first two rows for stem 1 (corresponding to 0-1 and 2-3) are omitted.

FREQUENCY	STEM & LEAF		
1.00	Extremes		(106)
2.00	1	f	55
6.00	1	s	677777
12.00	1	.	888889999999
23.00	2	*	00000000000001111111111
36.00	2	t	222222222222222223333333333333333333
35.00	2	f	44444444444444444455555555555555555
42.00	2	s	666666666666666666666677777777777777777777777
28.00	2	.	8888888888888889999999999999
18.00	3	*	000000011111111111
17.00	3	t	22222222222233333
9.00	3	f	444445555
6.00	3	s	666777
1.00	3	.	8
3.00	Extremes		(393), (425), (515)
Stem width:	100		
Each leaf:	1 case (s)		

Figure 7.34. Stem-and-leaf plot of cholesterol levels.

From *SPSS for Windows Base System User's Guide*, p. 185. Copyright © 1993. Used by permission of the publisher, SPSS, Inc., Chicago, IL.

This stem-and-leaf plot differs from the previous one in another way. Since cholesterol values have a wide range—from 105 to 515 in this example—using the first two digits for the stem would result in an unnecessarily detailed plot. Therefore, use only the hundreds digit as the stem, rather than the first two digits. The stem setting of 100 appears in the column labeled Stem width.

The leaf is then the tens digit. The last digit is ignored. Thus, from this particular stem-and-leaf plot, it is not possible to determine the exact cholesterol level for a case. Instead, each is classified by only its first two digits.

BOXPLOTS

A display that further summarizes information about the distribution of the values is the boxplot. Instead of plotting the actual values, a *boxplot* displays summary statistics for the distribution. It is a plot of the 25th, 50th, and 75th percentiles, as well as values far removed from the rest.

Figure 7.35 shows an annotated sketch of a boxplot. The lower boundary of the box is the 25th percentile. Tukey refers to the 25th and 75th percentiles as "hinges." Note that the 50th percentile is the median of the overall data set, the 25th percentile is the median of those values below the median, and the 75th percentile is the median of those values above the median. The horizontal line inside the box represents the median. 50% of the cases are included within the box. The box length corresponds to the interquartile range, which is the difference between the 25th and 75th percentiles.

The boxplot includes two categories of cases with outlying values. Cases with values that are more than 3 box-lengths from the upper or lower edge of the box are called *extreme values*. On the boxplot, these are designated with an asterisk (*). Cases with values that are between 1.5 and 3 box-lengths from the upper or lower edge of the box are called *outliers* and are designated with a circle. The largest and smallest observed values that aren't outliers are also shown. Lines are drawn from the ends of the box to these values. (These lines are sometimes called *whiskers* and the plot is then called a *box-and-whiskers plot*.)

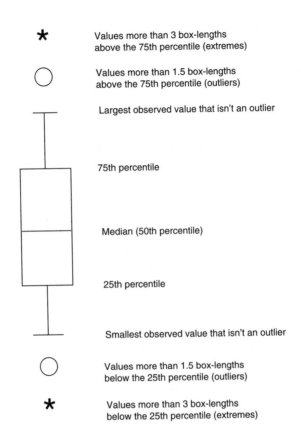

Figure 7.35. Annotated boxplot.

Despite its simplicity, the boxplot contains an impressive amount of information. From the median the central tendency, or location can be determined. From the length of the box, the spread, or variability, of your observations can be determined. If the median is not in the center of the box, then the observed values are skewed. If the median is closer to the bottom of the box than to the top, the data are positively skewed. If the median is closer to the top of the box than to the bottom, the opposite is true: the distribution is negatively skewed. The length of the tail is shown by the whiskers and the outlying and extreme points.

Boxplots are particularly useful for comparing the distribution of values in several groups. Figure 7.36 shows boxplots for the salaries for several different job titles.

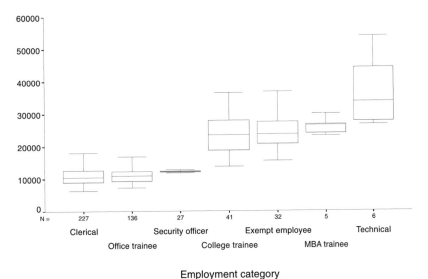

Figure 7.36. Boxplots of salary by job category.

The boxplot makes it easy to see the different properties of the distributions. The location, variability, and shapes of the distributions are obvious at a glance. This ease of interpretation is something that statistics alone cannot provide.

◆ ◆ ◆

CHAPTER

8

Intermediate Six Sigma Methods

ENUMERATIVE VERSUS ANALYTIC STATISTICAL METHODS

How would you respond to the following question?

A sample of 100 bottles taken from a filling process has an average of 11.95 ounces and a standard deviation of 0.1 ounce. The specifications are 11.9–12.1 ounces. Based on these results, should you

a. Do nothing?
b. Adjust the average to precisely 12 ounces?
c. Compute a confidence interval about the mean and adjust the process if the nominal fill level is not within the confidence interval?
d. None of the above?

The correct answer is *d*, none of the above. The other choices all make the mistake of applying enumerative statistical concepts to an analytic statistical situation. In short, *the questions themselves are wrong!* For example, based on the data, there is no way to determine if doing nothing is appropriate. "Doing something" implies that there is a known cause and effect mechanism which can be employed to reach a known objective. There is nothing to suggest that this situation exists. Thus, we can't simply adjust the process average to the nominal value of 12 ounces, even though the process appears to be 5 standard errors below this value. This might have happened because the first 50 were 10 standard errors below the nominal and the last 50 were exactly equal to the nominal (or any of a nearly infinite number of other possible scenarios). The confidence interval calculation fails for the same reason. Figure 8.1 illustrates some processes that could produce the statistics provided above.

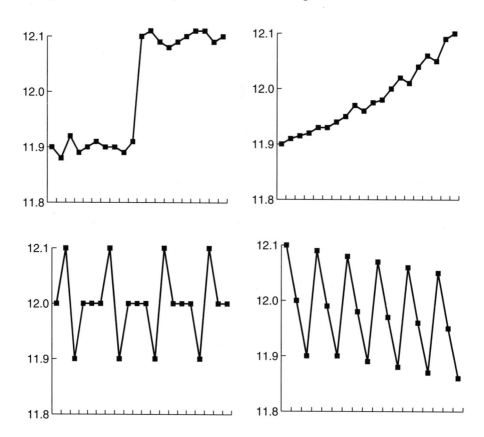

Figure 8.1. Possible processes with similar means and sigmas.

The following analytic statistics questions might be appropriate:

- Is the process central tendency stable over time?
- Is the process dispersion stable over time?
- Does the process distribution change over time?

If any of the above are answered "no," then what is the cause of the instability? To help answer this question, ask "what is the nature of the variation as revealed by the patterns?" when plotted in time-sequence and stratified in various ways.

If none of the above are answered "no," then, and only then, we can ask such questions as the following:

- Is the process meeting the requirements?
- *Can* the process meet the requirements?
- Can the process be improved by recentering it?
- How can we reduce variation in the process?

WHAT ARE ENUMERATIVE AND ANALYTIC STUDIES?

Deming (1975) defines enumerative and analytic studies as follows:

Enumerative study—a study in which action will be taken on the universe.

Analytic study—a study in which action will be taken on a process to improve performance in the future.

The term "universe" is defined in the usual way: the entire group of interest, e.g., people, material, units of product, which possess certain properties of interest. An example of an enumerative study would be sampling an isolated lot to determine the quality of the lot.

In an analytic study the focus is on a *process* and how to improve it. The focus is the *future*. Thus, unlike enumerative studies which make inferences about the universe actually studied, analytic studies are interested in a universe which has yet to be produced. Table 8.1 compares analytic studies with enumerative studies (Provost, 1988).

Table 8.1. Important aspects of analytic studies.

ITEM	ENUMERATIVE STUDY	ANALYTIC STUDY
Aim	Parameter estimation	Prediction
Focus	Universe	Process
Method of access	Counts, statistics	Models of the process (e.g., flow charts, cause and effects, mathematical models)
Major source of uncertainty	Sampling variation	Extrapolation into the future
Uncertainty quantifiable?	Yes	No
Environment for the study	Static	Dynamic

Deming (1986) points out that "Analysis of variance, t-tests, confidence intervals, and other statistical techniques taught in the books, however interesting, are inappropriate because they provide no basis for prediction and because they bury the information contained in the order of production." These traditional statistical methods have their place, but they are widely abused in the real world. When this is the case, statistics do more to cloud the issue than to enlighten.

Analytic study methods provide information for *inductive thinking*, rather than the largely *deductive* approach of enumerative statistics. Analytic methods are primarily graphical devices such as run charts, control charts, histograms, interrelationship diagraphs, etc. Analytic statistics provide operational guidelines, rather than precise calculations of probability. Thus, such statements as "There is a 0.13% probability of a Type I error when acting on a point outside a three-sigma control limit" are false. (The author admits to having made this error in the past). The future cannot be predicted with a known level of confidence. Instead, based on knowledge obtained from every source, including analytic studies, one can state with a certain degree of belief (e.g., high, low) that such and such will result from such and such action on a process.

Another difference between the two types of studies is that enumerative statistics proceed from predetermined hypotheses while analytic studies try to help the analyst generate new hypotheses. In the past, this extremely worthwhile approach has been criticized by some statisticians as "fishing" or "rationalizing." However, this author believes that using data to develop plausible explanations retrospectively is a perfectly legitimate way of creating new theories to be tested. To refuse to explore possibilities suggested by data is to take a very limited view of the scope of statistics in quality improvement and control.

ENUMERATIVE STATISTICAL METHODS

This section discusses the basic concept of statistical inference. The reader should also consult the Glossary in the Appendix for additional information. Inferential statistics belong to the enumerative class of statistical methods.

The term *inference* is defined as 1) the act or process of deriving logical conclusions from premises known or assumed to be true, or 2) the act of reasoning from factual knowledge or evidence. Inferential statistics provide information that is used in the process of inference. As can be seen from the definitions, inference involves two domains: the premises and the evidence or factual knowledge. Additionally, there are two conceptual frameworks for addressing premises questions in inference: the design-based approach and the model-based approach.

As discussed by Koch and Gillings (1983), a statistical analysis whose only assumptions are random selection of units or random allocation of units to experimental conditions results in *design-based inferences*; or, equivalently, randomization-based inferences. The objective is to structure sampling such that the sampled population has the same characteristics as the target population. If this is accomplished then inferences from the sample are said to have internal validity. A limitation on design-based inferences for experimental studies is that formal conclusions are restricted to the finite population of subjects that actually received treatment, that is, they lack *external validity*. However, if sites and subjects are selected at random from larger eligible sets, then models with random effects provide one possible way of addressing both internal and external validity considerations. One important consideration for external validity is that the sample coverage includes all relevant subpopulations; another is that treatment differences be homogeneous across subpopulations. A common application of design-based inference is the survey.

Alternatively, if assumptions external to the study design are required to extend inferences to the target population, then statistical analyses based on postulated probability distributional forms (e.g., binomial, normal, etc.) or other stochastic processes yield *model-based inferences*. A focus of distinction between design-based and model-based studies is the population to which the results are generalized rather than the nature of the statistical methods applied. When using a model-based approach, external validity requires substantive justification for the model's assumptions, as well as statistical evaluation of the assumptions.

Statistical inference is used to provide probabilistic statements regarding a scientific inference. Science attempts to provide answers to basic questions, such as can this machine meet our requirements? Is the quality of this lot within the terms of our contract? Does the new method of processing produce better results than the old? These questions are answered by conducting an experiment, which produces data. If the data vary, then statistical inference is necessary to interpret the answers to the questions posed. A statistical model is developed to describe the probabilistic structure relating the observed data to the quantity of interest (the *parameters*), i.e., a scientific hypothesis is formulated. Rules are applied to the data and the scientific hypothesis is either rejected or not. In formal tests of hypothesis, there are usually two mutually exclusive and exhaustive hypotheses formulated: a *null hypothesis* and an *alternate hypothesis*. Formal hypothesis testing is discussed later in this chapter.

Basic probability concepts

In quality engineering, most decisions involve uncertainty. Can a process meet the requirements? Is a gage accurate and repeatable enough to be used for process control? Does the quality of the lot on the receiving dock meet the contract quality requirements? Statistical methods are used to answer these questions. Probability theory forms the basis of statistical decision-making. This section discusses those probability concepts that underlie the statistical methods commonly used in quality engineering.

RANDOM VARIABLES

Every time an observation is made and recorded, a random experiment has occurred. The experiment may not have involved any deliberate change on the part of the observer, but it is an experiment nonetheless. The observation is an experimental outcome which cannot be determined in advance with certainty. However, probability theory makes it possible to define the set of all possible outcomes and to assign unique numbers to every possible outcome in the set. For example, if a die is rolled it must result in either 1, 2, 3, 4, 5, or 6. We cannot determine in advance which number will come up, but we know it will be one of these. This set of numbers is known as the *sample space* and the variable to which we assign the outcome is known as a *random variable*. If we assign the outcome of the roll of a die to the variable X, then X is a random variable and the space of X is {1, 2, 3, 4, 5, 6}.

SETS

Probability theory makes heavy use of parts of set theory. In addition to presenting important concepts, the notation used in set theory provides a useful shorthand for the discussion of probability concepts.

The *universal set* is the totality of objects under consideration and is denoted *S*. In probability theory, S is called the *sample space*. Each object in S is an *element* of S. When x is an element of the set A, it is written as $x \in$ A. If a set includes some, but not all, of the elements in S, it is termed a *subset* of S. If A is a subset of S we write A⊂S. The part of S that is not in the set A is called the *complement* of A, denoted A'. A set that contains no elements of S is called the *null* or *empty* set and is denoted by ∅ (pronounced "fee").

Let A and B be two sets. The set of elements in either A or B or both A and B is called the *union* of A and B and is denoted by A∪B. The set of elements in both A and B is called the *intersection* of A and B and is denoted by A∩B. If A and B have no elements in common, then A and B are said to be *mutually exclusive*, denoted A∩B=∅. If A and B cover the entire sample space, then they are said to be *exhaustive*, denoted A∪B=S.

A simple graphical method that is useful for illustrating many probability relationships, and other relationships involving sets, is the Venn diagram. Figure 8.2 is a Venn diagram of the flip of a coin.

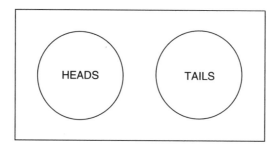

Figure 8.2. Venn diagram of two mutually exclusive events.

We say the events A and B are *independent* if A does not depend on B, and vice versa. When this is the case, the probability of two events occurring simultaneously is simply the product of them occurring individually. In fact, by definition, events A and B are independent if and only if P(A∩B)=P(A)P(B). For example, if a coin is flipped twice the probability of getting a head followed by a tail is P(H∩T)=P(H)P(T)=(0.5)(0.5)=0.25.

Figure 8.2 shows two circles that do not overlap, which means that they are mutually exclusive. If it is possible to get both events simultaneously, we have a different situation. Let's say for example, that we have a group of 1000 parts (the sample space). Let event A be that a part is defective, and event B be that the part is from Vendor A. Since it is possible to find a defective part from Vendor A, the two events can occur simultaneously. The Venn diagram in Figure 8.3 illustrates this.

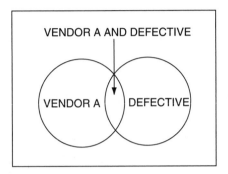

Figure 8.3. Venn diagram of two events that can occur simultaneously.

If we have the situation illustrated by Figure 8.3, then we can no longer find the probability of either event occurring by just adding the individual probabilities. Instead we must use the equation

$$P(A \cup B) = P(A) + P(B) - P(A \cap B) \qquad (8.1)$$

For example, let A be the event that the part is defective (P=0.05), and B be the event that the part is from Vendor A (P=0.50). Then, assuming the events are independent, the probability that the part is either defective or from Vendor A is .05 + .50 − (.05 x .50) = .55 − .025 = .525. The same rules can be applied to more than two events. For example, if A, B, and C are three events then

$$P(A \cup B \cup C) = P(A) + P(B) + P(C) - P(A \cap B) - P(A \cap C)$$
$$- P(B \cap C) + P(A \cap B \cap C) \qquad (8.2)$$

PROBABILITY FUNCTIONS

With this background it is now possible to define probability formally. Probability is a set function P that assigns to each event A in the sample space S a number P(A), called the probability of the event A, such that

1. $P(A) \geq 0$,
2. $P(S) = 1$,
3. If A, B, C, . . . are mutually exclusive events then $P(A \cup B \cup C \cup \ldots) = P(A) + P(B) + P(C) + \ldots$

DISCRETE AND CONTINUOUS DATA

Data are said to be *discrete* when they take on only a finite number of points that can be represented by the non-negative integers. An example of discrete data is the number of defects in a sample. Data are said to be *continuous* when they exist on an interval, or on several intervals. An example of continuous data is the measurement of pH. Quality methods exist based on probability functions for both discrete and continuous data.

METHODS OF ENUMERATION

Enumeration involves counting techniques for very large numbers of possible outcomes. This occurs for even surprisingly small sample sizes. In quality engineering, these methods are commonly used in a wide variety of statistical procedures.

The basis for all of the enumerative methods described here is the multiplication principle. The multiplication principle states that the number of possible outcomes of a series of experiments is equal to the product of the number of outcomes of each experiment. For example, consider flipping a coin twice. On the first flip there are two possible outcomes (heads/tails) and on the second flip there are also two possible outcomes. Thus, the series of two flips can result in 2x2=4 outcomes. Figure 8.4 illustrates this example.

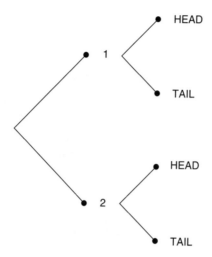

Figure 8.4. Multiplication principle applied to coin flips.

An ordered arrangement of elements is called a *permutation*. Suppose that you have four objects and four empty boxes, one for each object. Consider how many different ways the objects can be placed into the boxes. The first object can be placed in any of the four boxes. Once this is done there are three boxes to choose from for the second object, then two boxes for the third object and finally one box left for the last object. Using the multiplication principle you find that the total number of arrangements of the four objects into the four boxes is 4x3x2x1=24. In general, if there are *n* positions to be filled with *n* objects there are

$$n(n-1) \ldots (2)(1) = n! \tag{8.3}$$

possible arrangements. The symbol n! is read n factorial. By definition, 0!=1.

In applying probability theory to discrete variables in quality control we frequently encounter the need for efficient methods of counting. One counting technique that is especially useful is combinations. The combination formula is shown in Equation 8.4.

$$C_r^n = \frac{n!}{r!(n-r)!} \tag{8.4}$$

Combinations tell how many unique ways you can arrange n objects taking them in groups of r objects at a time, where r is a positive integer less than or equal to n. For example, to determine the number of combinations we can make with the letters X, Y, and Z in groups of 2 letters at a time, we note that $n = 3$ letters, $r = 2$ letters at a time and using the above formula find the following:

$$C_2^3 = \frac{3!}{2!(3-2)!} = \frac{3 \times 2 \times 1}{(2 \times 1)(1)} = \frac{6}{2} = 3$$

The 3 combinations are XY, XZ, and YZ. Notice that this method does not count reversing the letters as separate combinations, i.e., XY and YX are considered to be the same.

Theoretical expected value

The theoretical expected value, or mathematical expectation, or simply expectation, of a random variable is a theoretically defined quantity intended to be an analog of the arithmetic mean. It can be regarded as corresponding to a limit of the arithmetic mean as the sample size increases indefinitely.

The concept of mathematical expectation is useful in summarizing important characteristics of probability distributions. There are two expected values of particular importance in quality engineering: the mean and the variance; these are discussed below. An example of the application of the expected value concept is provided below.

EXAMPLE OF EXPECTATION

A contractor must reserve an expensive piece of construction equipment from a rental company at least three days in advance. The rental costs $500. If it rains, the contractor will still pay the $500 but he will not be able to use the equipment. If it does not rain, the contractor will earn $1000 for the work done. If the probability of rain is 20%, what is the expected value of renting the equipment?

The solution involves solving the following equation:

$$E = \tfrac{1}{5} \times (-\$500) + \tfrac{4}{5} \times \$1,000 = \$700$$

In other words, the contractor can expect to earn $700. Note that, in fact, the number $700 cannot actually occur; either the contractor will lose $500 or he will gain $1,000. The expectation applies *on the average*. The probabilities are "weights" applied to the different outcomes. Thus, mathematical expectation can be thought of as a weighted average of the various outcomes.

EXPECTATION FOR DISCRETE RANDOM VARIABLES

There are two different aspects to expectation: the outcome and the probability of the outcome. In the example, the outcomes were a loss of $500 or a gain of $1,000. The probabilities were 1/5 and 4/5. It can be seen that the expectation is just a sum of the outcome multiplied by its probability. If we designate the outcomes as *u(x)* and the probability function as *f(x)* then expectation can be expressed mathematically.

$$E[u(X)] = \sum_{R} u(x)f(x) \tag{8.5}$$

The subscript R indicates that the sum is taken over the entire region of x values. For our example,

$$f(x) = \begin{cases} \tfrac{1}{5}, & \textit{rain} \\ \tfrac{4}{5}, & \textit{shine} \end{cases}$$

$$u(x) = \begin{cases} -\$500, & x = \textit{rain} \\ +\$1,000, & x = \textit{shine} \end{cases}$$

PROPERTIES OF EXPECTATION

When it exists, expectation satisfies the following properties:
1. If c is a constant, $E[c]=c$.
2. If c is a constant and u is a function, $E[cu(x)]=cE[u(X)]$.
3. If c_1 and c_2 are constants and u_1 and u_2 are functions, then $E[c_1u_1(x)+c_2u_2(x)]= c_1E[u_1(x)]+ c_2E[u_2(x)]$.

THE MEAN, VARIANCE, AND STANDARD DEVIATION AS EXPECTATIONS

As mentioned above, expectation can be thought of as a weighted average. In fact, the mean itself is an expectation. In general, if X is a random variable with the discrete pdf *f(x)* defined on a region R, then

$$\mu = E(X) = \sum_R xf(x) \tag{8.6}$$

Where μ is the mean of the distribution. μ is often called the population mean. The sample mean is discussed later in this chapter.

If X is a random variable with the continuous pdf f(x) defined on a region R, then integration is used instead of summation,

$$\mu = E(X) = \int_R xf(x)dx \tag{8.7}$$

This is merely the continuous analog of the previous equation.

EXAMPLE: FINDING THE MEAN FOR A FAIR DIE

For a fair die, the probability of getting x=1, 2, 3, 4, 5, or 6 = 1/6; thus *f(x)*=1/6. Substituting x and *f(x)* into Equation 8.6,

$$\mu = \sum_{x=1}^{6} xf(x) = 1\left(\frac{1}{6}\right)+2\left(\frac{1}{6}\right)+3\left(\frac{1}{6}\right)+4\left(\frac{1}{6}\right)+5\left(\frac{1}{6}\right)+6\left(\frac{1}{6}\right)$$

$$= \frac{1+2+3+4+5+6}{6} = 3.5$$

The mean provides a measure of the center of a distribution. In mechanics, the mean is the centroid.

The *variance* of a distribution is also an expectation. Where the mean provides information about the location of a distribution, the variance provides information about the dispersion or spread of a distribution. Mathematically, for a discrete distribution,

$$\sigma^2 = E\left[(X-\mu)^2\right] = \sum_R (X-\mu)^2 f(x) \tag{8. 8}$$

When x is a continuous variable, the variance equation is found by integration,

$$\sigma^2 = E\left[(X-\mu)^2\right] = \int_R (X-\mu)^2 f(x)dx \tag{8. 9}$$

As with the mean, this is simply the continuous variable equivalent to the previous equation.

EXAMPLE: FINDING THE VARIANCE FOR A FAIR DIE

Knowing that the mean for a fair die is 3.5, the following equation can be used to find the variance:

$$\sigma^2 = E\left[(X-3.5)^2\right] = \sum_{x=1}^{6} (X-3.5)^2 \frac{1}{6} = \left[(1-3.5)^2 + (2-3.5)^2 + \cdots\right.$$

$$\left.\cdots + (6-3.5)^2\right]\frac{1}{6} = \frac{35}{12}$$

The *standard deviation* is the positive square root of the variance and is denoted by

$$\sigma = \sqrt{Var(X)} = \sqrt{\sigma^2} \tag{8.10}$$

σ is often called the *population standard deviation*. The sample standard deviation is discussed later in this chapter. For the example, the approximate value can be calculated:

$$\sigma = \sqrt{35/12} = 1.708$$

Assumptions and robustness of tests

It is important at the outset to comment on what we are *not* discussing here when we use the term "robustness." First, we are not talking about the sensitivity of a particular statistic to outliers. This concept is more properly referred to as *resistance*; it is discussed in the exploratory data analysis section of this chapter. Also we are not speaking of a product design that can perform well under a wide variety of operating conditions. This design-based definition of robustness is discussed in Chapter 9 in the Taguchi robustness concepts section.

All statistical procedures rest upon certain assumptions. For example, ANOVA assumes that the data are normally distributed with equal variances. When we use the term robustness here, we mean the ability of the statistical procedure to produce the correct final result when the assumptions are violated. A statistical procedure is said to be *robust* when it can be used even when the basic assumptions are violated to a small degree.

How large a departure from the assumptions is acceptable? Or, equivalently, how small is a "small" degree of error? For a given violation of the assumptions, how large an error in the result is acceptable? Regrettably, there is no rigorous mathematical definition of the term "robust."

In practice, robustness is commonly addressed in two ways. One approach is to test the underlying assumptions prior to using a given statistical procedure. In the case of ANOVA, for example, the practitioner would test the assumptions of normality and constant variance on the data set before accepting the results of the ANOVA.

Another approach is to use robust statistical procedures. Some ways of dealing with the issue include the following:

- Use procedures with less restrictive underlying assumptions (e.g., non-parametric procedures).
- Drop "gross outliers" from the data set before proceeding with the analysis (using an acceptable statistical method to identify the outliers).
- Use more resistant statistics (e.g., the median instead of the arithmetic mean).

Distributions

Distributions are a set of numbers collected from a well-defined universe of possible measurements arising from a property or relationship under study. Distributions show the way in which the probabilities are associated with the numbers being studied. Assuming a state of statistical control, by consulting the appropriate distribution one can determine the answer to such questions as:

- What is the probability that x will occur?
- What is the probability that a value less than x will occur?
- What is the probability that a value greater than x will occur?
- What is the probability that a value will occur that is between x and y?

By examining plots of the distribution shape, one can determine how rapidly or slowly probabilities change over a given range of values. In short, distributions provide a great deal of information.

FREQUENCY AND CUMULATIVE DISTRIBUTIONS

A frequency distribution is an empirical presentation of a set of observations. If the frequency distribution is *ungrouped*, it simply shows the observations and the frequency of each number. If the frequency distribution is *grouped*, then the data are assembled into cells, each cell representing a subset of the total range of the data. The frequency in each cell completes the grouped frequency distribution. Frequency distributions are often graphically displayed in histograms or stem-and-leaf plots (see Chapter 7).

While histograms and stem-and-leaf plots show the frequency of specific values or groups of values, analysts often wish to examine the *cumulative frequency* of the data. The cumulative frequency refers to the total up to and including a particular value. In the case of grouped data, the cumulative frequency is computed as the total number of observations up to and including a cell boundary. Cumulative frequency distributions are often displayed on an *ogive*, as depicted in Figure 8.5.

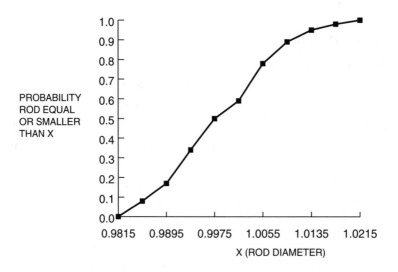

Figure 8.5. Ogive of rod diameter data.

SAMPLING DISTRIBUTIONS

In most engineering situations involving enumerative statistics, we deal with samples, not populations. In the previous section, sample data were used to construct an ogive and, earlier in this book, sample data were used to construct histograms, stem-and-leaf plots, boxplots, and to compute various statistics. We now consider the estimation of certain characteristics or parameters of the distribution from the data.

The empirical distribution assigns the probability $1/n$ to each X_i in the sample, thus the mean of this distribution is

$$\bar{X} = \sum_{i=1}^{n} X_i \frac{1}{n} \tag{8.11}$$

The symbol $\bar{X}$ is called "x bar." Since the empirical distribution is determined by a sample, $\bar{X}$ is simply called the *sample mean*.

Earlier in this chapter, the population variance was shown to be

$$\sigma^2 = E\left[(X-\mu)^2\right] = \sum_R (X-\mu)^2 f(x)$$

The equivalent variance of the empirical distribution is given by

$$S^2 = \frac{1}{n} \sum_{i=1}^{n} \left(X_i - \bar{X}\right)^2 \tag{8.12}$$

However, it can be shown that $E[S^2] \neq \sigma^2$. In other words, this statistic is a *biased estimator* of the population parameter σ^2. In fact,

$$E(S^2) = \frac{n-1}{n} \sigma^2$$

Thus, to correct for the bias, it is necessary to multiply the value found in Equation 8.12 by the factor

$$\frac{n}{n-1}$$

This gives

$$S^2 = \frac{1}{n-1} \sum_{i=1}^{n} \left(X_i - \bar{X}\right)^2 \tag{8.13}$$

This equation for S^2 is commonly referred to as the *sample variance*. The unbiased *sample standard deviation* is given by

$$S = \sqrt{S^2} = \sqrt{\frac{\sum_{i=1}^{n}\left(X_i - \bar{X}\right)^2}{n-1}} \tag{8.14}$$

Another sampling statistic of special interest in quality engineering is the standard deviation of the sample average, also referred to as the *standard error of the mean* or simply the standard error. This statistic is given by

$$S_{\bar{X}} = \frac{S}{\sqrt{n}} \qquad (8.15)$$

As can be seen, the standard error of the mean is inversely proportional to the square root of the sample size; i.e., the larger the sample size, the smaller the standard deviation of the sample average. This relationship is shown in Figure 8.6. It can be seen that averages of n=4 have a distribution half as variable as the population from which the samples are drawn.

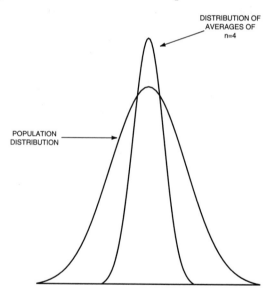

Figure 8.6. Effect of sample size on the standard error.

PROBABILITY DENSITY FUNCTIONS

Although probability density functions (pdfs) have been introduced and used previously, they have not been formally discussed. This will be done, briefly, in this section.

Discrete pdfs and cdfs

Let *f(x)* be the pdf of a random variable of the discrete type defined on the space R of X. The pdf *f(x)* is a real-valued function and satisfies the following properties.

1. $f(x) \geq 0$, $x \in R$;

2. $\sum\limits_{x \in R} f(x) = 1$;

3. $P(X \in A) = \sum\limits_{x \in A} f(x)$, where $A \subset R$.

For discrete data, *f(x)* gives the probability of obtaining an observation exactly equal to x, i.e., $P(X=x)$. The cumulative distribution function (cdf) is denoted F(x) and it gives the probability of obtaining an observation equal to or less than x, i.e., $F(x)=P(X \leq x)$.

Example of discrete pdf

Let the random variable X of the discrete type have the pdf *f(x)*=x/10, x = 1, 2, 3, 4. Then, for example

$$\sum\limits_{x \in R} f(x) = \frac{1+2+3+4}{10} = 1$$

$$F(X=1) = 1/10,$$

and

$$F(X \leq 3) = \frac{1+2+3}{10} = \frac{3}{5}.$$

The cdf and the pdf of the example are plotted in Figure 8.7.

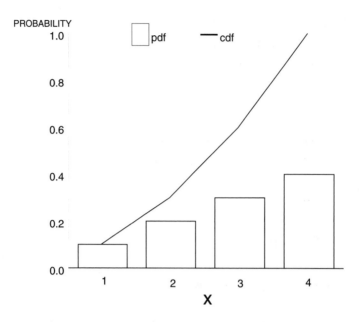

Figure 8.7. Plots of *f(x)*=x/10 and F(X).

Continuous pdfs and cdfs

Basically, the pdf and cdf concepts are the same for both continuous and discrete variables. The major difference is that calculus is required to obtain the cdf for continuous variables. One cannot merely add up a pdf for continuous data, instead, integration must be used. However, the equations for most continuous distributions commonly used in quality engineering are presented later in this section or in tabular form in the Appendix. This section presents a brief conceptual overview of pdfs and cdfs for continuous data. Although calculus is required for complete understanding, it is possible to grasp the ideas involved without a background in calculus.

Continuous pdfs

Let *f(x)* be the pdf of a random variable of the continuous type defined on the space R of *X*. The pdf *f(x)* is a real-valued function and satisfies the following properties.

1. *f(x)*>0, x∈ R;

2. $\int\limits_{x \in R} f(x)dx = 1$;

3. $P(X \in A) = \int\limits_{A} f(x)dx.$

Discussion of continuous pdf properties

Property 1 states that the pdf can never be zero or negative for the region (space) over which it applies. For example, the normal distribution (see below) covers the region from negative infinity to positive infinity, thus, theoretically at least, it is possible to obtain *any* value for *any* normally distributed random variable. Of course, extreme values have a probability that is vanishingly small and, in practice, they never appear.

Property 2 states that the total area under the pdf curve is 1. For continuous random variables probability is measured as the area under the pdf curve. Since the pdf is a probability function, and P(S)=1 is a property of probability functions (see section A above), the area under the pdf curve must equal 1.

Property 3 states that the probability of some value (X) occurring within a subset (A) of the space covered by the pdf is found by integrating the pdf over the space covered by the subset. For example, if the amount of medication in a capsule is normally distributed with a mean of 40mg and a standard deviation of 0.1mg, then the probability of obtaining a capsule which has between 40.1mg and 40.2mg is found by integrating the normal pdf between 40.1mg and 40.2mg. This is equivalent to finding the area under the curve between these two values. In practice, these probabilities are usually obtained from tables.

Continuous cdfs

The cumulative distribution function (cdf) is denoted F(x) and it gives the probability of obtaining an observation equal to or less than x, i.e., $F(x)=P(X \leq x)$. For continuous data,

$$F(X \leq x) = \int_{-\infty}^{x} f(t)dt$$

In other words, the cdf for any value is found by integrating the pdf up to that value. This is equivalent to finding the area under the pdf curve up to the value of interest. In practice, these probabilities are found by using tables.

The probability that x lies between two values a and b can be found using

$$F(a \leq X \leq b) = \int_{a}^{b} f(x)dx$$

This merely states that the probability of obtaining a result between two values is the area under the pdf that lies between the two values. Since the cdf gives the area *less than* a particular value, the probability of an observation being between two values, a and b can also be calculated as

$$F(a \leq X \leq b) = F(b) - F(a)$$

Several examples of finding probabilities for continuous distributions commonly encountered in quality engineering are shown later in this chapter.

PROBABILITY DISTRIBUTIONS FOR QUALITY ENGINEERING

This section discusses the following probability distributions often used in quality engineering:

- Hypergeometric distribution
- Binomial distribution
- Poisson distribution
- Normal distribution
- Exponential distribution
- Chi-square distribution
- Student's t distribution
- F distribution

Binomial distribution

Assume that a process is producing some proportion of non-conforming units, which we will call *p*. If we are basing p on a sample we find p by dividing the number of non-conforming units in the sample by the number of items sampled. The equation that will tell us the probability of getting x defectives in a sample of n units is shown by Equation 8.16.

$$P(x) = C_x^n p^x (1-p)^{n-x} \qquad (8.16)$$

This equation is known as the *binomial probability distribution*. In addition to being useful as the exact distribution of non-conforming units for processes in continuous production, it is also an excellent approximation to the cumbersome hypergeometric probability distribution when the sample size is less than 10% of the lot size.

Example of applying the binomial probability distribution

A process is producing glass bottles on a continuous basis. Past history shows that 1% of the bottles have one or more flaws. If we draw a sample of 10 units from the process, what is the probability that there will be 0 non-conforming bottles?

Using the above information, n = 10, p = .01, and x = 0. Substituting these values into Equation 8.16 gives us

$$P(0) = C_0^{10} 0.01^0 (1-0.01)^{10-0} = 1 \times 1 \times 0.99^{10} = 0.904 = 90.4\%$$

Another way of interpreting the above example is that a sampling plan "inspect 10 units, accept the process if no non-conformances are found" has a 90.4% probability of accepting a process that is averaging 1% non-conforming units.

Poisson distribution

Another situation encountered often in quality control is one not only concerned with *units* that don't conform to requirements, but also concerned with the number of non-conformances themselves. For example, consider quality control of a computer. A complete audit of the finished computer would almost certainly reveal some non-conformances, even though these non-conformances might be of minor importance (for example, a decal on the back panel might not be perfectly straight). Using the hypergeometric or binomial probability distributions to evaluate sampling plans for this situation, we would find they didn't work because our lot or process would be composed of 100% non-conforming units. Obviously, we are interested not in the units per se, but in the non-conformances themselves. In other cases, it isn't even possible to count sample units per se. For example, the number of accidents must be counted as occurrences.

The correct probability distribution for evaluating counts of non-conformances is the *Poisson distribution*. The pdf is given in Equation 8.17.

$$P(x) = \frac{\mu^x e^{-\mu}}{x!} \tag{8.17}$$

In Equation 8.17, μ is the average number of non-conformances per unit, x is the number of non-conformances in the sample, and e is the constant approximately equal to 2.7182818. P(x) gives the probability of exactly x occurrences in the sample.

Example of applying the Poisson distribution

A production line is producing guided missiles. When each missile is completed, an audit is conducted by an Air Force representative and every non-conformance to requirements is noted. Even though any major non-conformance is cause for rejection, the prime contractor wants to control minor non-conformances as well. Such minor problems as blurred stencils, small burrs, etc., are recorded during the audit. Past history shows that on the average each missile has 3 minor non-conformances. What is the probability that the next missile will have 0 non-conformances?

For this example μ = 3, x = 0. Substituting these values into Equation 8.17 gives

$$P(0) = \frac{3^0 e^{-3}}{0!} = \frac{1 \times 0.05}{1} = 0.05 = 5\%$$

In other words, 100% − 5% = 95% of the missiles will have at least one non-conformance.

The Poisson distribution, in addition to being the exact distribution for the number of non-conformances, is also a good approximation to the binomial distribution in certain cases. To use the Poisson approximation, simply let μ = np in Equation 8.17. Juran recommends considering the Poisson approximation if the sample size is at least 16, the population size is at least 10 times the sample size, and the probability of occurrence p on each trial is less than 0.1 (Dudewicz, 1988). The major advantage of this approach is that it allows use of the tables of the Poisson distribution, such as Table 7 in the Appendix. Also, the approach is useful for designing sampling plans.

Hypergeometric distribution

Assume that a lot of 12 parts has been received from a distributor. We need the parts badly and are willing to accept the lot if it has fewer than 3 non-conforming parts. We decide to inspect only 4 parts since we can't spare the time to check every part. Checking the sample, we find 1 part that doesn't conform to the requirements. Should we reject the remainder of the lot?

This situation involves sampling without replacement. We draw a unit from the lot, inspect it, and draw another unit from the lot. Furthermore, the lot is quite small, the sample is 25% of the entire lot. The formula needed to compute probabilities for this procedure is known as the hypergeometric probability distribution; it is shown in Equation 8.18.

$$P(x) = \frac{C_{n-x}^{N-m} C_x^m}{C_n^N} \tag{8.18}$$

In the above equation, N is the lot size, m is the number of defectives in the lot, n is the sample size, x is the number of defectives in the sample, and P(x) is the probability of getting exactly x defectives in the sample. Note that the numerator term C_{n-x}^{N-m} gives the number of combinations of non-defectives while C_x^m is the number of combinations of defectives. Thus the numerator gives the total number of arrangements of samples from lots of size N with m defectives where the sample n contains exactly x defectives. The term C_n^N in the denominator is the total number of combinations of samples of size n from lots of size N, regardless of the number of defectives. Thus, the probability is a ratio of the likelihood of getting the result under the assumed conditions.

For this example, solve the above equation for x = 0 as well as x = 1, since we would also accept the lot if we had no defectives. The solution is shown as follows.

$$P(0) = \frac{C_{4-0}^{12-3} C_0^3}{C_4^{12}} = \frac{126 \times 1}{495} = 0.255$$

$$P(1) = \frac{C_{4-1}^{12-3} C_1^3}{C_4^{12}} = \frac{84 \times 3}{495} = \frac{252}{495} = 0.509$$

P(1 or less) = P(0) + P(1).

Adding the two probabilities tells us the probability that our sampling plan will accept lots of 12 with 3 non-conforming units. The plan of inspecting 4 parts and accepting the lot if there are 0 or 1 non-conforming has a probability of .255 + .509 = .764, or 76.4%, of accepting this "bad" quality lot. This is the "consumer's risk" for this sampling plan. Such a high sampling risk would be unacceptable to most people.

Normal distribution

The most common continuous distribution encountered in quality control work is, by far, the normal distribution. Sometimes the process itself produces an approximately normal distribution; other times a normal distribution can be obtained by performing a mathematical transformation on the data or by using averages. The probability density function for the normal distribution is given by Equation 8.19.

$$f(x) = \frac{1}{\sigma\sqrt{2\pi}} e^{-(x-\mu)^2/2\sigma^2} \tag{8.19}$$

If *f(x)* is plotted versus *x*, the well-known "bell curve" results. The normal distribution is also known as the Gaussian distribution. An example is shown in Figure 8.8.

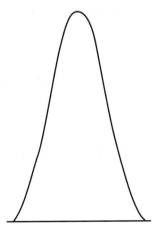

Figure 8.8. The normal/Gaussian curve.

In Equation 8.19, μ is the population average or mean and σ is the population standard deviation. These parameters have been discussed earlier in this chapter.

Example of calculating μ, σ^2 and σ

Find μ, σ^2 and σ for the following data:

i	x_i
1	17
2	23
3	5

Table 7.8 gives the equation for the population mean as

$$\mu = \frac{1}{N}\sum_{i=1}^{N} x_i$$

To find the mean for this data compute

$$\mu = \frac{1}{3}(17 + 23 + 5) = 15$$

The variance and standard deviation are both measures of dispersion or spread. The equations for the population variance σ^2 and standard deviation σ are given in Table 7.8.

$$\sigma^2 = \sum_{i=1}^{N} \frac{(x_i - \mu)^2}{N}$$

$$\sigma = \sqrt{\sigma^2}$$

Referring to the data above with a mean μ of 15, σ^2 and σ are computed as follows:

i	x_i	$x_i - \mu$	$(x_i - \mu)^2$
1	17	2	4
2	23	8	64
3	5	-10	100
			SUM 168

$$\sigma^2 = 168 / 3 = 56$$

$$\sigma = \sqrt{\sigma^2} = \sqrt{56} \approx 7.483$$

Usually there is only a sample and not the entire population. A population is the entire set of observations from which the sample, a subset, is drawn. Calculations for the sample mean, variance, and standard deviation were shown earlier in this chapter.

The areas under the normal curve can be found by integrating Equation 8.19 using numerical methods, but, more commonly, tables are used. Table 2 in the Appendix gives areas under the normal curve. The table is indexed by using the Z transformation, which is

$$Z = \frac{x_{i-\mu}}{\sigma} \qquad (8.20)$$

for population data, or

$$Z = \frac{x_{i-\bar{x}}}{s} \qquad (8.21)$$

for sample data.

By using the Z transformation, any normal distribution can be converted into a normal distribution with a mean of 0 and a standard deviation of 1. Thus, a single normal table can be used to find probabilities.

Example

The normal distribution is very useful in predicting long-term process yields. Assume that in checking the breaking strength of a gold wire bonding process used in microcircuit production the process average strength is found to be 9# and the standard deviation is 4#. The process distribution is normal. If the engineering specification is 3# minimum, what percentage of the process will be below the low specification?

Since the data are a sample, compute Z using Equation 8.21.

$$Z = \frac{3-9}{4} = \frac{-6}{4} = -1.5$$

Figure 8.9 illustrates this situation.

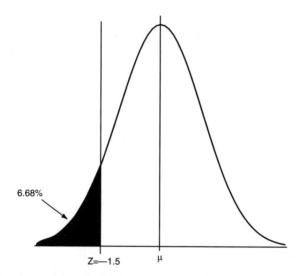

Figure 8.9. Illustration of using Z tables for normal areas.

Entering Table 2 in the Appendix for Z = −1.5, we find that 6.68% of the area is below this Z value. Thus 6.68% of the breaking strengths will be below the low specification limit of 3# for this example. In quality control applications, we usually try to have the average at least 3 standard deviations away from the specification. To accomplish this, we would have to improve the process by either raising the average breaking strength or reducing the process standard deviation, or both.

Exponential distribution

Another distribution encountered often in quality control work is the exponential distribution. The exponential distribution is especially useful in analyzing reliability (see Chapter 9). The equation for the probability density function of the exponential distribution is

$$f(x) = \frac{1}{\mu} e^{-x/\mu}, \; x \geq 0 \tag{8.22}$$

Unlike the normal distribution, the shape of the exponential distribution is highly skewed and there is a much greater area below the mean than above it. In fact, over 63% of the exponential distribution falls below the mean. Figure 8.10 shows an exponential pdf.

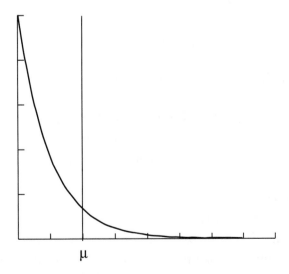

Figure 8.10. Exponential pdf curve.

Unlike the normal distribution, the exponential distribution has a closed form cumulative density function; i.e., there is an equation which gives the cumulative probabilities directly. Since the probabilities can be determined directly from the equation, no tables are necessary.

$$P(X \leq x) = 1 - e^{-x/\mu} \tag{8.23}$$

Example of using the exponential cdf

A city water company averages 500 system leaks per year. What is the probability that the weekend crew, which works from 6 p.m. Friday to 6 a.m. Monday, will get no calls?

There are μ = 500 leaks per year, which must be converted to leaks per hour. There are 365 days of 24 hours each in a year, or 8760 hours. Thus, mean time between failures (MTBF) is 8760/500 = 17.52 hours. There are 60 hours between 6 p.m. Friday and 6 a.m. Monday. Thus x_i = 60. Using Equation 8.23 gives

$$P(X \leq 60) = 1 - e^{-60/17.52} = 0.967 = 96.7\%$$

Thus, the crew will get to loaf away 3.3% of the weekends.

CHI-SQUARE, STUDENT'S t, AND F DISTRIBUTIONS

These three distributions are used in quality engineering to test hypotheses, construct confidence intervals, and to compute control limits.

Chi-square

Many characteristics encountered in quality engineering have normal or approximately normal distributions. It can be shown that in these instances the distribution of sample variances has the form (except for a constant) of a chi-square distribution, symbolized χ^2. Tables have been constructed giving abscissa values for selected ordinates of the cumulative χ^2 distribution. One such table is Table 4 in the Appendix.

The χ^2 distribution varies with the quantity v, which for these purposes is equal to the sample size minus 1. For each value of v there is a different χ^2 distribution. Equation 8.24 gives the pdf for the χ^2.

$$f(\chi^2) = \frac{e^{-\chi^2/2}\left(\chi^2\right)^{(v-2)/2}}{2^{v/2}\left(\dfrac{v-2}{2}\right)!} \tag{8.24}$$

Figure 8.11 shows the pdf for $v=4$.

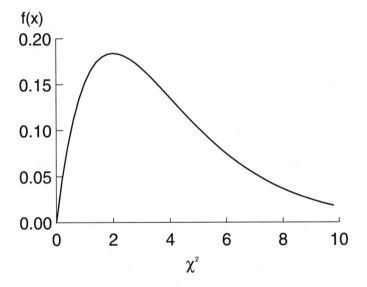

Figure 8.11. χ^2 pdf for $v=4$.

Example

The use of χ^2 is illustrated in this example to find the probability that the variance of a sample of n items from a specified normal universe will equal or exceed a given value s^2; we compute $\chi^2 = (n-1)s^2/\sigma^2$. Now, suppose that we sample $n=10$ items from a process with $\sigma^2=25$ and wish to determine the probability that the sample variance will exceed 50. Then

$$\frac{(n-1)s^2}{\sigma^2} = \frac{9(50)}{25} = 18$$

We enter Appendix Table 4 (χ^2) at the line for $v=10-1=9$ and note that 18 falls between the columns for the percentage points of 0.025 and 0.05. Thus, the probability of getting a sample variance in excess of 50 is about 3%.

It is also possible to determine the sample variance that would be exceeded only a stated percentage of the time. For example, we might want to be alerted when the sample variance exceeded a value that should occur only once in 100 times. Then we set up the χ^2 equation, find the critical value from Table 4 in the Appendix, and solve for the sample variance. Using the same values as above, the value of s^2 that would be exceeded only one in 100 times is found as follows:

$$\frac{9s^2}{\sigma^2} = \frac{9s^2}{25} = 21.7 \implies s^2 = \frac{21.7 \times 25}{9} = 60.278$$

In other words, the variance of samples of size 10, taken from this process, should be less than 60.278, 99% of the time.

Student's t distribution

The t statistic is commonly used to test hypotheses regarding means, regression coefficients and a wide variety of other statistics used in quality engineering. "Student" was the pseudonym of W.S. Gosset, whose need to quantify the results of small scale experiments motivated him to develop and tabulate the probability integral of the ratio which is now known as the t statistic and is shown in Equation 8.25.

$$t = \frac{\mu - \overline{X}}{s/\sqrt{n}} \qquad (8.25)$$

In Equation 8.25, the denominator is the standard deviation of the sample mean. Percentage points of the corresponding distribution function of t may be found in Table 3 in the Appendix. There is a t distribution for each sample size of $n>1$. As the sample size increases, the t distribution approaches the shape of the normal distribution, as shown in Figure 8.12.

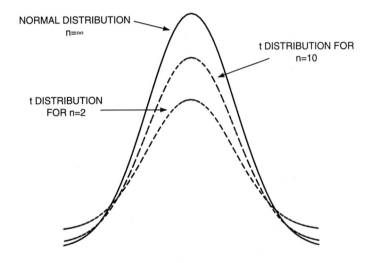

NORMAL DISTRIBUTION
$n=\infty$

t DISTRIBUTION FOR
$n=10$

t DISTRIBUTION
FOR $n=2$

Figure 8.12. Student's t distributions.

One of the simplest (and most common) applications of the Student's t test involves using a sample from a normal population with mean μ and variance σ^2.

F DISTRIBUTION

Suppose there are two random samples drawn from a normal population, with s_1^2 the variance of the first sample and s_2^2 the variance of the second sample. The two samples need not have the same sample size. The statistic F given by

$$F = \frac{s_1^2}{s_2^2}$$

(8.26)

has a sampling distribution called the *F distribution*. There are two sample variances involved and two sets of degrees of freedom, n_1-1 in the numerator and n_2-1 in the denominator. The Appendix includes tables for 1 and 5 percentage points for the F distribution. The percentages refer to the areas to the right of the values given in the tables. Figure 8.13 illustrates two *F* distributions.

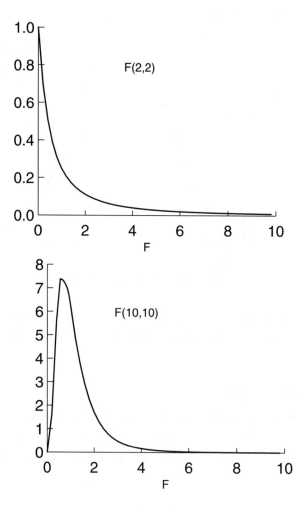

Figure 8.13. F distributions.

Statistical inference

All statements made in this section are valid only for stable processes, i.e., processes in statistical control. The statistical methods described in this section are enumerative. Although most applications of quality engineering are analytic, there are times when enumerative statistics prove useful. In reading this material, the engineer should keep in mind the fact that analytic methods should also be used to identify the underlying process dynamics and to control and improve the processes involved. The subject of statistical inference is large and it is covered in many different books on introductory statistics. In this book we review that part of the subject matter of particular interest in quality engineering.

POINT AND INTERVAL ESTIMATION

So far, a number of important statistics have been introduced including the sample mean, the sample standard deviation, and the sample variance. These sample statistics are called *point estimator*s because they are single values used to represent population parameters. It is also possible to construct an interval about the statistics that has a predetermined probability of including the true population parameter. This interval is called a *confidence interval*. Interval estimation is an alternative to point estimation that gives a better idea of the magnitude of the sampling error. Confidence intervals can be either one-sided or two-sided. A one-sided confidence interval places an upper or lower bound on the value of a parameter with a specified level of confidence. A two-sided confidence interval places both upper and lower bounds.

In almost all practical applications of enumerative statistics, including quality control applications, *inferences* are made about *populations* based on data from *samples*. In this chapter, we have talked about sample averages and standard deviations; we have even used these numbers to make statements about future performance, such as long term yields or potential failures. A problem arises that is of considerable practical importance: any estimate that is based on a sample has some amount of sampling error. This is true even though the sample estimates are the "best estimates" in the sense that they are (usually) unbiased estimators of the population parameters.

Estimates of the mean

For random samples with replacement, the sampling distribution of $\overline{X}$ has a mean μ and a standard deviation equal to $\sigma/\sqrt{n}$. For large samples the sampling distribution of $\overline{X}$ is approximately normal and normal tables can be used to find the probability that a sample mean will be within a given distance of μ. For example, in 95% of the samples a mean can be observed within $\pm 1.96\, \sigma/\sqrt{n}$ of μ. In other words, in 95% of the samples the interval from $\overline{X}-1.96\dfrac{\sigma}{\sqrt{n}}$ to $\overline{X}+1.96\dfrac{\sigma}{\sqrt{n}}$ will include μ. This interval is called a "95% confidence interval for estimating μ." It is usually shown using inequality symbols:

$$\overline{X}-1.96\frac{\sigma}{\sqrt{n}} < \mu < \overline{X}+1.96\frac{\sigma}{\sqrt{n}}$$

The factor 1.96 is the Z value obtained from the normal Table 2 in the Appendix. It corresponds to the Z value beyond which 2.5% of the population lie. Since the normal distribution is symmetric, 2.5% of the distribution lies above Z and 2.5% below -Z. The notation commonly used to denote Z values for confidence interval construction or hypothesis testing is $Z_{\alpha/2}$ where $100(1-\alpha)$ is the desired confidence level in percent. For example, if we want 95% confidence, $\alpha=0.05$, $100(1-\alpha)=95\%$, and $Z_{0.025}=1.96$. In hypothesis testing the value of α is known as the *significance level.*

Example : estimating μ when σ is known

Suppose that σ is known to be 2.8. If we collect a sample of $n=16$ and compute $\overline{X}=15.7$, using the above equation we find the 95% confidence interval for μ as follows:

$$\overline{X} - 1.96 \frac{\sigma}{\sqrt{n}} < \mu < \overline{X} + 1.96 \frac{\sigma}{\sqrt{n}}$$

$$15.7 - 1.96 \left(\frac{2.8}{\sqrt{16}} \right) < \mu < 15.7 + 1.96 \left(\frac{2.8}{\sqrt{16}} \right)$$

$$14.33 < \mu < 17.07$$

There is a 95% *level of confidence* associated with this interval. The numbers 14.33 and 17.07 are sometimes referred to as the *confidence limits*.

Note that this is a two-sided confidence interval. There is a 2.5% probability that 17.07 is lower than μ and a 2.5% probability that 14.33 is greater than μ. If we were only interested in, say, the probability that μ were greater than 14.33, then the one-sided confidence interval would be $\mu > 14.33$ and the one-sided confidence level would be 97.5%.

Example: estimating μ when σ is unknown

When σ is not known and we wish to replace σ with s in calculating confidence intervals for μ, we must replace $Z_{\alpha/2}$ with $t_{\alpha/2}$ and obtain the percentiles from tables for Student's t distribution instead of the normal tables. If we revisit the example above and assume that instead of knowing σ, it was estimated from the sample, that is, based on the sample of $n=16$, we computed $s=2.8$ and $\overline{X} = 15.7$. Then the 95% confidence interval becomes:

$$\overline{X} - 2.131 \frac{s}{\sqrt{n}} < \mu < \overline{X} + 2.131 \frac{s}{\sqrt{n}}$$

$$15.7 - 2.131 \left(\frac{2.8}{\sqrt{16}} \right) < \mu < 15.7 + 2.131 \left(\frac{2.8}{\sqrt{16}} \right)$$

$$14.21 < \mu < 17.19$$

It can be seen that this interval is wider than the one obtained for known σ. The $t_{\alpha/2}$ value found for 15 df is 2.131 (see Table 3 in the Appendix), which is greater than $Z_{\alpha/2} = 1.96$ above.

Tolerance and confidence intervals, significance level

TOLERANCE INTERVALS

We have found that confidence limits may be determined so that the interval between these limits will cover a population parameter with a certain confidence, that is, a certain proportion of the time. Sometimes it is desirable to obtain an interval which will cover a fixed portion of the population distribution with a specified confidence. These intervals are called *tolerance intervals*, and the end points of such intervals are called *tolerance limits*. For example, a manufacturer may wish to estimate what proportion of product will have dimensions that meet the engineering requirement. In quality engineering, tolerance intervals are typically of the form $\overline{X} \pm Ks$, where K is determined, so that the interval will cover a proportion P of the population with confidence γ. Confidence limits for μ are also of the form $\overline{X} \pm Ks$. However, we determine k so that the confidence interval would cover the population mean μ a certain proportion of the time. It is obvious that the interval must be longer to cover a large portion of the distribution than to cover just the single value μ. Table 8 in the Appendix gives K for P = 0.90, 0.95, 0.99, 0.999 and $\gamma = 0.90, 0.95, 0.99$ and for many different sample sizes n.

Example of calculating a tolerance interval

Assume that a sample of $n=20$ from a stable process produced the following results: $\overline{X} = 20$, $s = 1.5$. We can estimate that the interval $\overline{X} \pm Ks = 20 \pm 3.615(1.5) = 20 \pm 5.4225$, or the interval from 14.5775 to 25.4225 will contain 99% of the population with confidence 95%. The K values in the table assume normally distributed populations.

Hypothesis testing/Type I and Type II errors
HYPOTHESIS TESTING
Statistical inference generally involves four steps:
1. Formulating a hypothesis about the population or "state of nature,"
2. Collecting a sample of observations from the population,
3. Calculating statistics based on the sample,
4. Either accepting or rejecting the hypothesis based on a pre-determined acceptance criterion.

There are two types of error associated with statistical inference

Type I error (α error)—The probability that a hypothesis that is actually true will be rejected. The value of α is known as the significance level of the test.

Type II error (ß error)—The probability that a hypothesis that is actually false will be accepted.

Type II errors are often plotted in what is known as an operating characteristics curve. Operating characteristics curves will be used extensively in subsequent chapters of this book in evaluating the properties of various statistical quality control techniques.

Confidence intervals are usually constructed as part of a *statistical test of hypotheses*. The hypothesis test is designed to help us make an inference about the true population value at a desired level of confidence. We will look at a few examples of how hypothesis testing can be used in quality control applications.

Example: hypothesis test of sample mean
Experiment: The nominal specification for filling a bottle with a test chemical is 30 cc's. The plan is to draw a sample of n=25 units from a stable process and, using the sample mean and standard deviation, construct a two-sided confidence interval (an interval that extends on either side of the sample average) that has a 95% probability of including the true population mean. If the interval includes 30, conclude that the lot mean is 30, otherwise conclude that the lot mean is not 30.

Result: A sample of 25 bottles was measured and the following statistics computed

$$\overline{X} = 28 \ cc$$

$$s = 6 \ cc$$

The appropriate test statistic is t, given by the formula

$$t = \frac{\overline{X} - \mu}{s/\sqrt{n}} = \frac{28 - 30}{6/\sqrt{25}} = -1.67$$

Table 3 in the Appendix gives values for the t statistic at various degrees of freedom. There are n-1 degrees of freedom. For this example we need the $t_{.975}$ column and the row for 24 df. This gives a t value of 2.064. Since the absolute value of this t value is greater than the test statistic, we fail to reject the hypothesis that the lot mean is 30 cc's. Using statistical notation this is shown as:

H_0: μ = 30 cc's (the *null hypothesis*)

H_1: μ is not equal to 30 cc's (the *alternate hypothesis*)

α = .05 (*Type I error or level of significance*)

Critical region: -2.064 " t_0 " +2.064

Test statistic: t = −1.67.

Since t lies inside the critical region, we fail to reject H_0.

Example: hypothesis test of two sample variances

The variance of machine X's output, based on a sample of n = 25 taken from a stable process, is 100. Machine Y's variance, based on a sample of 10, is 50. The manufacturing representative from the supplier of machine X contends that the result is a mere "statistical fluke." Assuming that a "statistical fluke" is something that has less than 1 chance in 100, test the hypothesis that both variances are actually equal.

The test statistic used to test for equality of two sample variances is the F statistic, which, for this example, is given by the equation

$$F = \frac{s_1^2}{s_2^2} = \frac{100}{50} = 2 \text{ , numerator df = 24, denominator df = 9}$$

Using Table 5 in the Appendix for $F_{.99}$ we find that for 24 df in the numerator and 9 df in the denominator F = 4.73. Based on this we conclude that the manufacturer of machine X could be right; the result could be a statistical fluke. This example demonstrates the volatile nature of the sampling error of sample variances and standard deviations.

Example: hypothesis test of a standard deviation
compared to a standard value

A machine is supposed to produce parts in the range of 0.500 inches plus or minus 0.006 inches. Based on this, a statistician computes that the absolute worst standard deviation tolerable is 0.002 inches. In looking over the capability charts it is found that the best machine in the shop has a standard deviation of 0.0022, based on a sample of 25 units. In discussing the situation with the statistician and management, it is agreed that the machine will be used if a one-sided 95% confidence interval on sigma includes 0.002.

The correct statistic for comparing a sample standard deviation with a standard value is the chi-square statistic. For this example s=0.0022, n=25, and σ_0=0.002. The χ^2 statistic has n-1 = 24 degrees of freedom. Thus,

$$\chi^2 = \frac{(n-1)s^2}{\sigma^2} = \frac{24 \times (0.0022)^2}{(0.002)^2} = 29.04$$

Appendix Table 4 gives, in the 0.05 column (since we are constructing a one-sided confidence interval) and the df = 24 row, the critical value χ^2 = 36.42. Since our computed value of χ^2 is less than 36.42, we use the machine. The reader should recognize that all of these exercises involved a number of assumptions; e.g., that we "know" that the best machine has a standard deviation of 0.0022. In reality, this knowledge must be confirmed by a stable control chart.

RESAMPLING (BOOTSTRAPPING)

Criticisms have been raised regarding the methods used for estimation and hypothesis testing:

- They are not intuitive.
- They are based on strong assumptions (e.g., normality) that are often not met in practice.
- They are difficult to learn and to apply.
- They are error-prone.

In recent years a new method of performing these analyses has been developed. It is known as resampling or bootstrapping. The new methods are conceptually quite simple: using the data from a sample, calculate the statistic of interest repeatedly and examine the distribution of the statistic. For example, if you obtained a sample of $n=25$ measurements from a lot and you wished to determine a confidence interval on the statistic C_{pk}, using resampling, you would tell the computer to select a sample of $n=25$ *from the sample results*, compute C_{pk}, and repeat the process many times, say 10,000 times. You would then determine whatever percentage point value you wished by simply looking at the results. The samples would be taken "with replacement;" i.e., a particular value from the original sample might appear several times (or not at all) in a resample.

Resampling has many advantages, especially in the era of easily available, low-cost computer power. Spreadsheets can be programmed to resample and calculate the statistics of interest. Compared with traditional statistical methods, resampling is easier for most people to understand. It works without strong assumptions, and it is simple. Resampling doesn't impose as much baggage between the engineering problem and the statistical result as conventional methods. It can also be used for more advanced problems, such as modeling, design of experiments, etc.

For a discussion of the theory behind resampling, see Efron (1982). For a presentation of numerous examples using a resampling computer program see Simon (1992).

ANALYTIC STATISTICAL METHODS
Basic control charts
TERMS AND CONCEPTS
Distributions

A central concept in statistical process control is that every measurable phenomenon is a statistical distribution. In other words, an observed set of data constitutes a sample of the effects of unknown common causes. It follows that, after we have done everything to eliminate special causes of variations, there will still remain a certain amount of variability exhibiting the state of control. Figure 8.14 illustrates the relationships between common causes, special causes, and distributions.

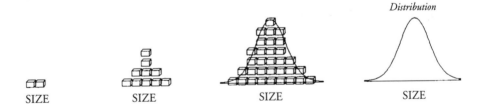

Figure 8.14. Distributions.

From *Continuing Process Control and Process Capability Improvement*, p. 4a. Copyright 1983 by Ford Motor Company. Used by permission of the publisher.

There are three basic properties of a distribution: location, spread, and shape. The *location* refers to the typical value of the distribution, such as the mean. The *spread* of the distribution is the amount by which smaller values differ from larger ones. The standard deviation and variance are measures of distribution spread. The *shape* of a distribution is its pattern—peakedness, symmetry, etc. A given phenomenon may have any one of a number of distribution shapes, e.g., the distribution may be bell-shaped, rectangular-shaped, etc.

Central limit theorem

The central limit theorem can be stated as follows:

> Irrespective of the shape of the distribution of the population or universe, the distribution of average values of samples drawn from that universe will tend toward a normal distribution as the sample size grows without bound.

It can also be shown that the average of sample averages will equal the average of the universe and that the standard deviation of the averages equals the standard deviation of the universe divided by the square root of the sample size. Shewhart performed experiments which showed that small sample sizes were needed to get approximately normal distributions from even wildly nonnormal universes. Figure 8.15 was created by Shewhart (1980) using samples of four measurements.

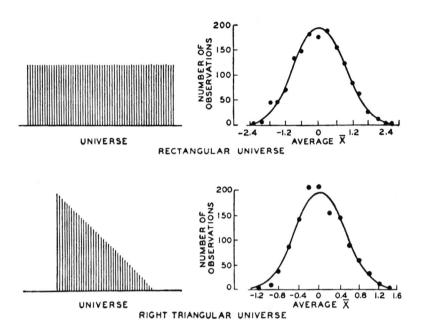

Figure 8.15. Illustration of the central limit theorem.

From *Economic Control of Quality of Manufactured Product*, figure 59. Copyright © 1980.

Used by permission of the publisher, ASQ Quality Press. Milwaukee, Wisconsin.

The practical implications of the central limit theorem are immense. Without the central limit theorem effects, a separate statistical model would need to be developed for every non-normal distribution encountered in practice. This would be the only way to determine if the system were exhibiting chance variation. Because of the central limit theorem *averages* of small samples can be used to evaluate *any* process using the normal distribution. The central limit theorem is the basis for the most powerful of statistical process control tools, Shewhart control charts.

OBJECTIVES AND BENEFITS

Without SPC, the basis for decisions regarding quality improvement are based on intuition, after-the-fact product inspection, or seat-of-the-pants "data analysis." SPC provides a scientific basis for decisions regarding process improvement.

Prevention versus detection

A process control system is essentially a feedback system that links process outcomes with process inputs. There are four main elements involved: the process itself, information about the process, action taken on the process, and action taken on the output from the process. The way these elements fit together is shown in Figure 8.16.

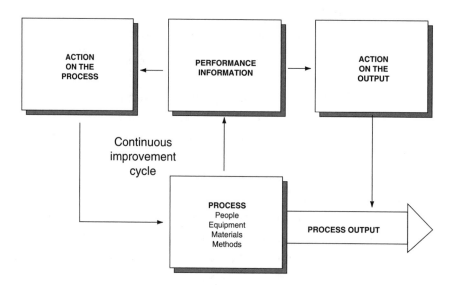

Figure 8.16. A process control system.

By the process, we mean the whole combination of people, equipment, input materials, methods, and environment that work together to produce output. The performance information is obtained, in part, from evaluation of the process output. The output of a process includes more than product, it also includes information about the operating state of the process such as temperature, cycle times, etc. Action taken on a *process* is future-oriented in the sense that it will affect output yet to come. Action on the *output* is past-oriented because it involves detecting out-of-specification output that has already been produced.

There has been a tendency in the past to concentrate attention on the detection-oriented strategy of product inspection. With this approach, once an output has been produced, then the output is inspected and either accepted or rejected. SPC takes a completely different direction: improvement in the future. A key concept is *the smaller the variation around the target, the better*. Thus, under this school of thought, it is not enough to merely meet the requirements; continuous improvement is called for even if the requirements are already being met. The concept of never-ending, continuous improvement is at the heart of SPC.

COMMON AND SPECIAL CAUSES OF VARIATION
Shewhart (1931, 1980) defined *control* as follows:

> A phenomenon will be said to be controlled when, through the use of past experience, we can predict, at least within limits, how the phenomenon may be expected to vary in the future. Here it is understood that prediction within limits means that we can state, at least approximately, the probability that the observed phenomenon will fall within the given limits.

The critical point in this definition is that control is not defined as the complete absence of variation. Control is simply a state where all variation is *predictable* variation. A controlled process isn't necessarily a sign of good management, nor is an out-of-control process necessarily producing non-conforming product.

In all forms of prediction there is an element of chance. For our purposes, any unknown random cause of variation will be called a *chance cause* or a *common cause*; the terms are synonymous and will be used as such. If the influence of any particular chance cause is very small, and if the number of chance causes of variation are very large and relatively constant, there is a situation where the variation is predictable within limits. From the definition above, a system such as this qualifies as a controlled system. Where Dr. Shewhart used the term chance cause, Dr. W. Edwards Deming coined the term *common cause* to describe the same phenomenon. Both terms are encountered in practice.

Needless to say, not all phenomena arise from constant systems of common causes. At times, the variation is caused by a source of variation that is not part of the constant system. These sources of variation were called *assignable causes* by Shewhart, *special causes* of variation by Dr. Deming. Experience indicates that special causes of variation can usually be found without undue difficulty, leading to a process that is less variable.

Statistical tools are needed to help effectively identify the effects of special causes of variation. This leads to another definition:

Statistical process control—the use of valid analytical statistical methods to identify the existence of special causes of variation in a process.

The basic rule of statistical process control is:

Variation from common-cause systems should be left to chance, but special causes of variation should be identified and eliminated.

This is Shewhart's original rule. However, the rule should not be misinterpreted as meaning that variation from common causes should be ignored. Rather, common-cause variation is explored "off-line." That is, long-term process improvements are sought to address common-cause variation.

Figure 8.17 illustrates the need for statistical methods to determine the category of variation.

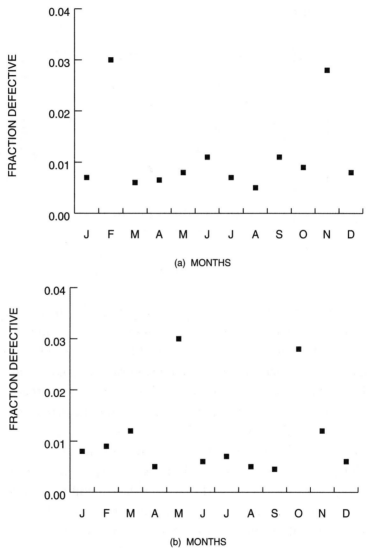

(a) MONTHS

(b) MONTHS

Figure 8.17. Should these variations be left to chance?

From *Economic Control of Quality of Manufactured Product*, p. 13. Copyright © 1931, 1980 by ASQ Quality Press. Used by permission of the publisher.

The answer to the question "should these variations be left to chance?" can be obtained only through the use of statistical methods. Figure 8.18 illustrates the basic concept.

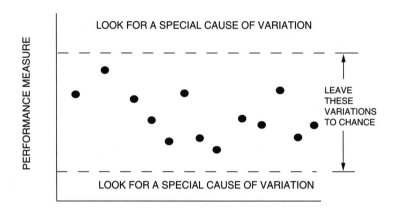

Figure 8.18. Types of variation.

In short, variation between the two "control limits" designated by the dashed lines will be deemed as variation from the common-cause system. Any variability beyond these fixed limits will be assumed to have come from special causes of variation. Any system exhibiting only common-cause variation will be called "statistically controlled." It must be noted that the control limits are not simply pulled out of the air, they are calculated from actual process data using valid statistical methods. Figure 8.17 is shown below as Figure 8.19, only with the control limits drawn on it; notice that process (a) is exhibiting variations from special causes, while process (b) is not. This implies that the type of action needed to reduce the variability in each case is of a different nature. Without statistical guidance there could be endless debate over whether special or common causes were to blame for variability.

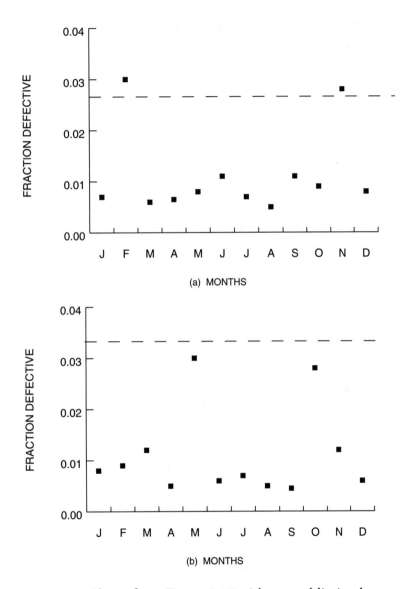

Figure 8.19. Charts from Figure 8.17 with control limits shown.

From *Economic Control of Quality of Manufactured Product*, p. 13. Copyright © 1931, 1980 by ASQ Quality Press. Used by permission of the publisher.

TYPES OF CONTROL CHARTS

There are two broad categories of control charts: those for use with continuous data (e.g., measurements) and those for use with attributes data (e.g., counts). This section describes the various charts used for these different data.

VARIABLE CHARTS

In SPC, the mean, range, and standard deviation are the statistics most often used for analyzing measurement data. Control charts are used to monitor these statistics. An out-of-control point for any of these statistics is an indication that a special cause of variation is present and that an immediate investigation should be made to identify the special cause.

Average and range control charts

Average charts are statistical tools used to evaluate the central tendency of a process over time. Range charts are statistical tools used to evaluate the dispersion or spread of a process over time.

Average charts answer the question "Has a special cause of variation caused the central tendency of this process to change over the time period observed?"

Range charts answer the question "Has a special cause of variation caused the process distribution to become more or less consistent?" Average and range charts can be applied to any continuous variable like weight, size, etc.

The basis of the control chart is the *rational subgroup*. Rational subgroups are composed of items which were produced under essentially the same conditions. The average and range are computed for each subgroup separately, then plotted on the control chart. Each subgroup's statistics are compared to the control limits, and patterns of variation between subgroups are analyzed.

Subgroup equations for average and range charts

$$\overline{X} = \frac{sum\ of\ subgroup\ measurements}{subgroup\ size} \qquad (8.27)$$

$$R = Largest\ in\ subgroup\ -\ Smallest\ in\ subgroup \qquad (8.28)$$

Control limit equations for averages and ranges charts

Control limits for both the averages and the ranges charts are computed such that it is highly unlikely that a subgroup average or range from a stable process would fall outside of the limits. All control limits are set at plus and minus three standard deviations from the center line of the chart. Thus, the control limits for subgroup averages are plus and minus three standard deviations of the mean from the grand average; the control limits for the subgroup ranges are plus and minus three standard deviations of the range from the average range. These control limits are quite robust with respect to non-normality in the process distribution.

To facilitate calculations, constants are used in the control limit equations. Table 11 in the Appendix provides control chart constants for subgroups of 25 or less. The derivation of the various control chart constants is shown in Burr (1976, pp. 97–105).

Control limit equations for range charts

$$\overline{R} = \frac{sum\ of\ subgroup\ ranges}{number\ of\ subgroups} \qquad (8.29)$$

$$LCL = D_3 \overline{R} \qquad (8.30)$$

$$UCL = D_4 \overline{R} \qquad (8.31)$$

Control limit equations for averages charts using R-bar

$$\overline{\overline{X}} = \frac{sum\ of\ subgroup\ averages}{number\ of\ subgroups} \qquad (8.32)$$

$$LCL = \overline{\overline{X}} - A_2 \overline{R} \qquad (8.33)$$

$$UCL = \overline{\overline{X}} + A_2 \overline{R} \qquad\qquad (8.34)$$

Example of averages and ranges control charts

Table 8.2 contains 25 subgroups of five observations each.

Table 8.2. Data for averages and ranges control charts.

Sample 1	Sample 2	Sample 3	Sample 4	Sample 5	AVERAGE	RANGE
110	93	99	98	109	101.8	17
103	95	109	95	98	100.0	14
97	110	90	97	100	98.8	20
96	102	105	90	96	97.8	15
105	110	109	93	98	103.0	17
110	91	104	91	101	99.4	19
100	96	104	93	96	97.8	11
93	90	110	109	105	101.4	20
90	105	109	90	108	100.4	19
103	93	93	99	96	96.8	10
97	97	104	103	92	98.6	12
103	100	91	103	105	100.4	14
90	101	96	104	108	99.8	18
97	106	97	105	96	100.2	10
99	94	96	98	90	95.4	9
106	93	104	93	99	99.0	13
90	95	98	109	110	100.4	20
96	96	108	97	103	100.0	12
109	96	91	98	109	100.6	18
90	95	94	107	99	97.0	17
91	101	96	96	109	98.6	18
108	97	101	103	94	100.6	14
96	97	106	96	98	98.6	10
101	107	104	109	104	105.0	8
96	91	96	91	105	95.8	14

The control limits are calculated from this data as follows:

Ranges control chart example

$$\bar{R} = \frac{sum\ of\ subgroup\ ranges}{number\ of\ subgroups} = \frac{369}{25} = 14.76$$

$$LCL_R = D_3\bar{R} = 0 \times 14.76 = 0$$

$$UCL_R = D_4\bar{R} = 2.115 \times 14.76 = 31.22$$

Since it is not possible to have a subgroup range less than zero, the LCL is not shown on the control chart for ranges.

Averages control chart example

$$\bar{\bar{X}} = \frac{sum\ of\ subgroup\ averages}{number\ of\ subgroups} = \frac{2,487.5}{25} = 99.5$$

$$LCL_{\bar{x}} = \bar{\bar{X}} - A_2\bar{R} = 99.5 - 0.577 \times 14.76 = 90.97$$

$$UCL_{\bar{x}} = \bar{\bar{X}} + A_2\bar{R} = 99.5 + 0.577 \times 14.76 = 108.00$$

The completed averages and ranges control charts are shown in Figure 8.20.

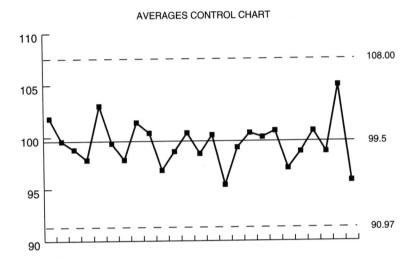

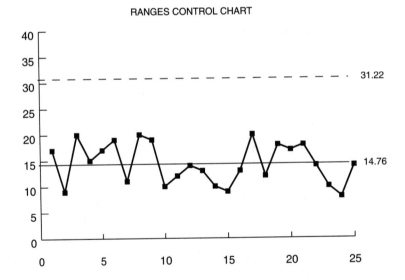

Figure 8.20. Completed averages and ranges control charts.

The above charts show a process in statistical control. This merely means that the limits of variability can be predicted for this process. To determine the capability of the process with respect to requirements the methods described later in this chapter under Process Capability Studies must be used.

Averages and standard deviation (sigma) control charts

Averages and standard deviation control charts are conceptually identical to averages and ranges control charts. The difference is that the subgroup standard deviation is used to measure dispersion rather than the subgroup range. The subgroup standard deviation is statistically more efficient than the subgroup range for subgroup sizes greater than 2. This efficiency advantage increases as the subgroup size increases. However, the range is easier to compute and easier for most people to understand. In general, this author recommends using subgroup ranges unless the subgroup size is 10 or larger. However, if the analyses are to be interpreted by statistically knowledgeable personnel and calculations are not a problem, the standard deviation chart may be preferred for all subgroup sizes.

Subgroup equations for average and sigma charts

$$\overline{X} = \frac{sum\ of\ subgroup\ measurements}{subgroup\ size} \tag{8.35}$$

$$s = \sqrt{\frac{\sum_{i=1}^{n}\left(x_i - \overline{X}\right)^2}{n-1}} \tag{8.36}$$

The standard deviation, s, is computed separately for each subgroup, using the subgroup average rather than the grand average. This is an important point; using the grand average would introduce a special cause variation if the process were out of control, thereby underestimating the process capability, perhaps significantly.

Control limit equations for averages and sigma charts

Control limits for both the averages and the sigma charts are computed such that it is highly unlikely that a subgroup average or sigma from a stable process would fall outside of the limits. All control limits are set at plus and minus three standard deviations from the center line of the chart. Thus, the control limits for subgroup averages are plus and minus three standard deviations of the mean from the grand average. The control limits for the subgroup sigmas are plus and minus three standard deviations of sigma from the average sigma. These control limits are quite robust with respect to non-normality in the process distribution.

To facilitate calculations, constants are used in the control limit equations. Table 11 in the Appendix provides control chart constants for subgroups of 25 or less.

Control limit equations for sigma charts based on s-bar

$$\bar{s} = \frac{sum\ of\ subgroup\ sigmas}{number\ of\ subgroups} \tag{8.37}$$

$$LCL = B_3\bar{s} \tag{8.38}$$

$$UCL = B_4\bar{s} \tag{8.39}$$

Control limit equations for averages charts based on s-bar

$$\bar{\bar{X}} = \frac{sum\ of\ subgroup\ averages}{number\ of\ subgroups} \tag{8.40}$$

$$LCL = \bar{\bar{X}} - A_3\bar{s} \tag{8.41}$$

$$UCL = \bar{\bar{X}} + A_3\bar{s} \tag{8.42}$$

Example of averages and standard deviation control charts

To illustrate the calculations and to compare the range method to the standard deviation results, the data used in the previous example will be reanalyzed using the subgroup standard deviation rather than the subgroup range.

Table 8.3. Data for averages and sigma control charts.

Sample 1	Sample 2	Sample 3	Sample 4	Sample 5	AVERAGE	SIGMA
110	93	99	98	109	101.8	7.396
103	95	109	95	98	100.0	6.000
97	110	90	97	100	98.8	7.259
96	102	105	90	96	97.8	5.848
105	110	109	93	98	103.0	7.314
110	91	104	91	101	99.4	8.325
100	96	104	93	96	97.8	4.266
93	90	110	109	105	101.4	9.290
90	105	109	90	108	100.4	9.607
103	93	93	99	96	96.8	4.266
97	97	104	103	92	98.6	4.930
103	100	91	103	105	100.4	5.550
90	101	96	104	108	99.8	7.014
97	106	97	105	96	100.2	4.868
99	94	96	98	90	95.4	3.578
106	93	104	93	99	99.0	6.042
90	95	98	109	110	100.4	8.792
96	96	108	97	103	100.0	5.339
109	96	91	98	109	100.6	8.081
90	95	94	107	99	97.0	6.442
91	101	96	96	109	98.6	6.804
108	97	101	103	94	100.6	5.413
96	97	106	96	98	98.6	4.219
101	107	104	109	104	105.0	3.082
96	91	96	91	105	95.8	5.718

The control limits are calculated from this data as follows:

Sigma control chart

$$\bar{s} = \frac{sum\ of\ subgroup\ sigmas}{number\ of\ subgroups} = \frac{155.45}{25} = 6.218$$

$$LCL_s = B_3\bar{s} = 0 \times 6.218 = 0$$

$$UCL_s = B_4\bar{s} = 2.089 \times 6.218 = 12.989$$

Since it is not possible to have a subgroup sigma less than zero, the LCL is not shown on the control chart for sigma.

Averages control chart

$$\bar{\bar{X}} = \frac{sum\ of\ subgroup\ averages}{number\ of\ subgroups} = \frac{2,487.5}{25} = 99.5$$

$$LCL_{\bar{x}} = \bar{\bar{X}} - A_3\bar{s} = 99.5 - 1.427 \times 6.218 = 90.63$$

$$UCL_{\bar{x}} = \bar{\bar{X}} + A_3\bar{s} = 99.5 + 1.427 \times 6.218 = 108.37$$

The completed averages and sigma control charts are shown in Figure 8.21. Note that the control limits for the averages chart are only slightly different than the limits calculated using ranges.

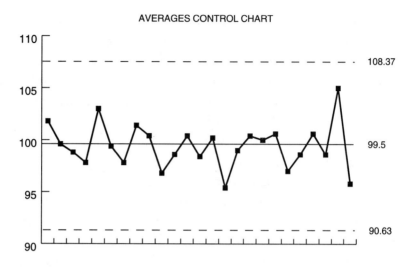

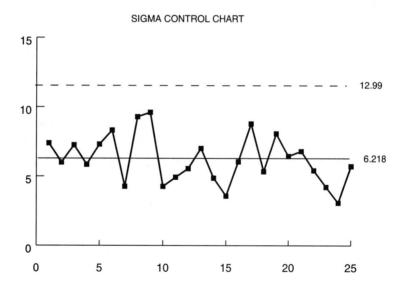

Figure 8.21. Completed average and sigma control charts.

Note that the conclusions reached are the same as when ranges were used.

Control charts for individual measurements (X charts)

Individuals control charts are statistical tools used to evaluate the central tendency of a process over time. They are also called *X charts* or *moving range charts*. Individuals control charts are used when it is not feasible to use averages for process control. There are many possible reasons why averages control charts may not be desirable: observations may be expensive to obtain (e.g., destructive testing), output may be too homogeneous over short time intervals (e.g., pH of a solution), the production rate may be slow and the interval between successive observations long, et cetera. Control charts for individuals are often used to monitor batch processes, such as chemical processes, where the within-batch variation is so small relative to between-batch variation that the control limits on a standard $\bar{X}$ chart would be too close together. Range charts are used in conjunction with individuals charts to help monitor dispersion.*

Calculations for moving ranges charts

As with averages and ranges charts, the range is computed as shown above,

$$R = Largest\ in\ subgroup\ -\ Smallest\ in\ subgroup$$

where the subgroup is a consecutive pair of process measurements. The range control limit is computed as was described for averages and ranges charts, using the D_4 constant for subgroups of 2, which is 3.267. I.e.,

$$LCL = 0 \text{ (for } n = 2)$$
$$UCL = 3.267 \text{ x R-Bar}$$

---

*There is considerable debate over the value of moving R charts. Academic researchers have failed to show statistical value in them. However, many practitioners (including the author) believe that moving R charts provide valuable additional information that can be used in troubleshooting.

Control limit equations for individuals charts

$$\overline{X} = \frac{sum\ of\ measurements}{number\ of\ measurements} \tag{8.43}$$

$$LCL = \overline{X} - E_2\overline{R} = \overline{X} - 2.66 \times \overline{R} \tag{8.44}$$

$$UCL = \overline{X} + E_2\overline{R} = \overline{X} + 2.66 \times \overline{R} \tag{8.45}$$

where E_2=2.66 is the constant used when individual measurements are plotted, and $\overline{R}$ is based on subgroups of n = 2.

Example of individuals and moving ranges control charts

Table 8.4 contains 25 measurements. To facilitate comparison, the measurements are the first observations in each subgroup used in the previous average/ranges and average/standard deviation control chart examples.

Table 8.4. Data for individuals and moving ranges control charts.

SAMPLE 1	RANGE	SAMPLE 1	RANGE
110	None	90	13
103	7	97	7
97	6	99	2
96	1	106	7
105	9	90	16
110	5	96	6
100	10	109	13
93	7	90	19
90	3	91	1
103	13	108	17
97	6	96	12
103	6	101	5
		96	5

Continued at right . . .

The control limits are calculated from this data as follows:

Moving ranges control chart control limits

$$\overline{R} = \frac{sum\ of\ ranges}{number\ of\ ranges} = \frac{196}{24} = 8.17$$

$$LCL_R = D_3\overline{R} = 0 \times 8.17 = 0$$

$$UCL_R = D_4\overline{R} = 3\ 267 \times 8\ 17 = 26\ 69$$

Since it is not possible to have a subgroup range less than zero, the LCL is not shown on the control chart for ranges.

Individuals control chart control limits

$$\overline{X} = \frac{sum\ of\ measurements}{number\ of\ measurements} = \frac{2,475}{25} = 99.0$$

$$LCL_X = \overline{X} - E_2\overline{R} = 99.0 - 2.66 \times 8.17 = 77.27$$

$$UCL_X = \overline{X} + E_2\overline{R} = 99.0 + 2.66 \times 8.17 = 120.73$$

The completed individuals and moving ranges control charts are shown in Figure 8.22.

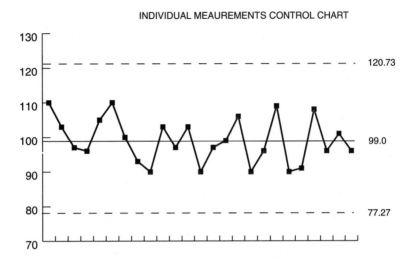

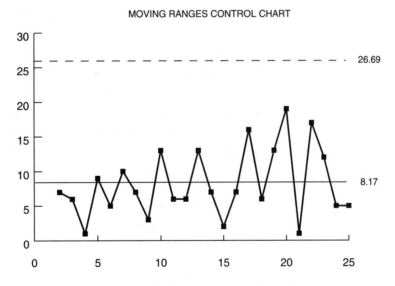

Figure 8.22. Completed individuals and moving ranges control charts.

In this case, the conclusions are the same as with averages charts. However, averages charts always provide tighter control than X charts. In some cases, the additional sensitivity provided by averages charts may not be justified on either an economic or an engineering basis. When this happens, the use of averages charts will merely lead to wasting money by investigating special causes that are of minor importance.

ATTRIBUTE CHARTS
Control charts for proportion defective (p charts)
P charts are statistical tools used to evaluate the proportion defective, or proportion non-conforming, produced by a process.

P charts can be applied to any variable where the appropriate performance measure is a unit count. P charts answer the question "Has a special cause of variation caused the central tendency of this process to produce an abnormally large or small number of defective units over the time period observed?"

P chart control limit equations
Like all control charts, p charts consist of three guidelines: center line, a lower control limit, and an upper control limit. The center line is the average proportion defective and the two control limits are set at plus and minus three standard deviations. If the process is in statistical control, then virtually all proportions should be between the control limits and they should fluctuate randomly about the center line.

$$p = \frac{subgroup\ defective\ count}{subgroup\ size} \qquad (8.46)$$

$$\bar{p} = \frac{sum\ of\ subgroup\ defective\ counts}{sum\ of\ subgroup\ sizes} \qquad (8.47)$$

$$LCL = \bar{p} - 3\sqrt{\frac{\bar{p}(1-\bar{p})}{n}} \qquad (8.48)$$

$$UCL = \bar{p} + 3\sqrt{\frac{\bar{p}(1-\bar{p})}{n}} \qquad (8.49)$$

In the above equations, n is the subgroup size. If the subgroup sizes vary, the control limits will also vary, becoming closer together as n increases.

Analysis of p charts

As with all control charts, a special cause is probably present if there are any points beyond either the upper or the lower control limit. Analysis of p chart patterns between the control limits is extremely complicated if the sample size varies because the distribution of p varies with the sample size.

Example of p chart calculations

The data in Table 8.5 were obtained by opening randomly selected crates from each shipment and counting the number of bruised peaches. There are 250 peaches per crate. Normally, samples consist of one crate per shipment. However, when part-time help is available, samples of two crates are taken.

Table 8.5. Raw data for p chart.

SHIPMENT #	CRATES	PEACHES	BRUISED	P
1	1	250	47	0.188
2	1	250	42	0.168
3	1	250	55	0.220
4	1	250	51	0.204
5	1	250	46	0.184
6	1	250	61	0.244
7	1	250	39	0.156
8	1	250	44	0.176
9	1	250	41	0.164
10	1	250	51	0.204

Continued on next page . . .

Table 8.5—*Continued . . .*

SHIPMENT #	CRATES	PEACHES	BRUISED	p
11	2	500	88	0.176
12	2	500	101	0.202
13	2	500	101	0.202
14	1	250	40	0.160
15	1	250	48	0.192
16	1	250	47	0.188
17	1	250	50	0.200
18	1	250	48	0.192
19	1	250	57	0.228
20	1	250	45	0.180
21	1	250	43	0.172
22	2	500	105	0.210
23	2	500	98	0.196
24	2	500	100	0.200
25	2	500	96	0.192
TOTALS		8,000	1,544	

Using the above data the center line and control limits are found as follows:

$$p = \frac{subgroup\ defective\ count}{subgroup\ size}$$

these values are shown in the last column of Table 8.5.

$$\overline{p} = \frac{sum\ of\ subgroup\ defective\ counts}{sum\ of\ subgroup\ sizes} = \frac{1,544}{8,000} = 0.193,$$

which is constant for all subgroups.

n=250 (*1 crate*):

$$LCL = \bar{p} - 3\sqrt{\frac{\bar{p}(1-\bar{p})}{n}} = 0.193 - 3\sqrt{\frac{0.193 \times (1-0.193)}{250}} = 0.118$$

$$UCL = \bar{p} + 3\sqrt{\frac{\bar{p}(1-\bar{p})}{n}} = 0.193 + 3\sqrt{\frac{0.193 \times (1-0.193)}{250}} = 0.268$$

n=500 (*2 crates*):

$$LCL = 0.193 - 3\sqrt{\frac{0.193 \times (1-0.193)}{500}} = 0.140$$

$$UCL = 0.193 + 3\sqrt{\frac{0.193 \times (1-0.193)}{500}} = 0.246$$

The control limits and the subgroup proportions are shown in Figure 8.23.

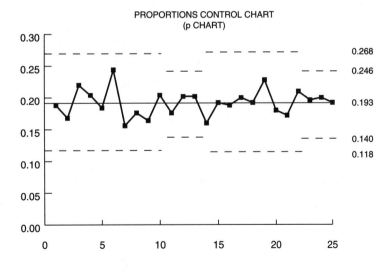

Figure 8.23. Completed *p* control chart.

404   INTERMEDIATE SIX SIGMA METHODS

Pointers for using p charts

Determine if "moving control limits" are really necessary. It may be possible to use the average sample size (total number inspected divided by the number of subgroups) to calculate control limits. For instance, with the preceding example the sample size doubled from 250 peaches to 500 but the control limits hardly changed at all. Table 8.6 illustrates the different control limits based on 250 peaches, 500 peaches, and the average sample size which is 8,000÷25 = 320 peaches.

Table 8.6. Effect of using average sample size.

SAMPLE SIZE	LOWER CONTROL LIMIT	UPPER CONTROL LIMIT
250	0.1181	0.2679
500	0.1400	0.2460
320	0.1268	0.2592

Notice that the conclusions regarding process performance are the same when using the average sample size as they are using the exact sample sizes. This is usually the case if the variation in sample size isn't too great. There are many rules of thumb, but most of them are extremely conservative. The best way to evaluate limits based on the average sample size is to check it out as shown above. SPC is all about improved decision-making. In general, use the most simple method that leads to correct decisions.

Control charts for count of defectives (np charts)

Np charts are statistical tools used to evaluate the count of defectives, or count of items non-conforming, produced by a process. Np charts can be applied to any variable where the appropriate performance measure is a unit count and the subgroup size is held constant. Note that wherever an np chart can be used, a p chart can be used too.

Control limit equations for np charts

Like all control charts, *np* charts consist of three guidelines: center line, a lower control limit, and an upper control limit. The center line is the average count of defectives-per-subgroup and the two control limits are set at plus and minus three standard deviations. If the process is in statistical control, then virtually all subgroup counts will be between the control limits, and they will fluctuate randomly about the center line.

$$np = subgroup\ defective\ count \tag{8.50}$$

$$n\bar{p} = \frac{sum\ of\ subgroup\ defective\ counts}{number\ of\ subgroups} \tag{8.51}$$

$$LCL = n\bar{p} - 3\sqrt{n\bar{p}(1 - \bar{p})} \tag{8.52}$$

$$UCL = n\bar{p} + 3\sqrt{n\bar{p}(1 - \bar{p})} \tag{8.53}$$

Note that

$$\bar{p} = \frac{n\bar{p}}{n} \tag{8.54}$$

Example of np chart calculation

The data in Table 8.7 were obtained by opening randomly selected crates from each shipment and counting the number of bruised peaches. There are 250 peaches per crate (constant *n* is required for *np* charts).

Table 8.7. Raw data for *np* chart.

SHIPMENT NUMBER	BRUISED PEACHES	SHIPMENT NUMBER	BRUISED PEACHES
1	20	16	23
2	28	17	27
3	24	18	28
4	21	19	31
5	32	20	27
6	33	21	30
7	31	22	23
8	29	23	23
9	30	24	27
10	34	25	35
11	32	26	29
12	24	27	23
13	29	28	23
14	27	29	30
15	37	30	28
		TOTAL	838

Continued at right . . .

Using the above data the center line and control limits are found as follows:

$$n\bar{p} = \frac{sum\ of\ subgroup\ defective\ counts}{number\ of\ subgroups} = \frac{838}{30} = 27.93$$

$$LCL = n\bar{p} - 3\sqrt{n\bar{p}(1-\bar{p})} = 27.93 - 3\sqrt{27.93 \times \left(1 - \frac{27.93}{250}\right)} = 12.99$$

$$UCL = n\bar{p} + 3\sqrt{n\bar{p}(1-\bar{p})} = 27.93 + 3\sqrt{27.93 \times \left(1 - \frac{27.93}{250}\right)} = 42.88$$

The control limits and the subgroup defective counts are shown in Figure 8.24.

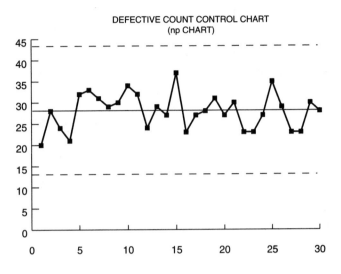

Figure 8.24. Completed *np* control chart.

Control charts for average occurrences-per-unit (u charts)

U charts are statistical tools used to evaluate the average number of occurrences-per-unit produced by a process. *U* charts can be applied to any variable where the appropriate performance measure is a count of how often a particular event occurs. *U* charts answer the question "Has a special cause of variation caused the central tendency of this process to produce an abnormally large or small number of occurrences over the time period observed?" Note that, unlike *p* or *np* charts, *u* charts do not necessarily involve counting physical items. Rather, they involve counting of *events*. For example, when using a *p* chart one would count bruised peaches. When using a *u* chart one would count the *bruises*.

Control limit equations for u charts

Like all control charts, u charts consist of three guidelines: center line, a lower control limit, and an upper control limit. The center line is the average number of occurrences-per-unit and the two control limits are set at plus and minus three standard deviations. If the process is in statistical control then virtually all subgroup occurrences-per-unit should be between the control limits and they should fluctuate randomly about the center line.

$$u = \frac{subgroup\ count\ of\ occurrences}{subgroup\ size\ in\ units} \qquad (8.55)$$

$$\bar{u} = \frac{sum\ of\ subgroup\ occurrences}{sum\ of\ subgroup\ sizes\ in\ units} \qquad (8.56)$$

$$LCL = \bar{u} - 3\sqrt{\frac{\bar{u}}{n}} \qquad (8.57)$$

$$UCL = \bar{u} + 3\sqrt{\frac{\bar{u}}{n}} \qquad (8.58)$$

In the above equations, n is the subgroup size in units. If the subgroup size varies, the control limits will also vary.

One way to determine whether a particular set of data is suitable for a u chart or a p chart is to examine the equation used to compute the center line for the control chart. If the unit of measure is the same in both the numerator and the denominator, then a p chart is indicated, otherwise a u chart is indicated. For example, if

$$Center\ Line = \frac{bruises\ per\ crate}{number\ of\ crates},$$

then the numerator is in terms of bruises while the denominator is in terms of crates, indicating a *u* chart.

The unit size is arbitrary but once determined it cannot be changed without recomputing all subgroup occurrences-per-unit and control limits. For example, if the occurrences were accidents and a unit was 100,000 hours worked, then a month with 250,000 hours worked would be 2.5 units and a month with 50,000 hours worked would be 0.5 units. If the unit size were 200,000 hours then the two months would have 1.25 and 0.2 units respectively. The equations for the center line and control limits would "automatically" account for the unit size, so the control charts would give identical results regardless of which unit size is used.

Analysis of u charts

As with all control charts, a special cause is probably present if there are any points beyond either the upper or the lower control limit. Analysis of *u* chart patterns between the control limits is extremely complicated when the sample size varies and usually is not done.

Example of u chart

The data in Table 8.8 were obtained by opening randomly selected crates from each shipment and counting the number of bruised peaches. There are 250 peaches per crate. The unit size will be taken as one full crate; i.e., crates will be counted rather than the peaches themselves. Normally, samples consist of one crate per shipment. However, when part-time help is available, samples of two crates are taken.

Table 8.8. Raw data for u chart.

SHIPMENT NO.	UNITS (CRATES)	FLAWS	FLAWS-PER-UNIT
1	1	47	47
2	1	42	42
3	1	55	55
4	1	51	51
5	1	46	46
6	1	61	61
7	1	39	39
8	1	44	44
9	1	41	41
10	1	51	51
11	2	88	44
12	2	101	50.5
13	2	101	50.5
14	1	40	40
15	1	48	48
16	1	47	47
17	1	50	50
18	1	48	48
19	1	57	57
20	1	45	45
21	1	43	43
22	2	105	52.5
23	2	98	49
24	2	100	50
25	2	96	48
TOTALS	32	1,544	

Using the above data the center line and control limits are found as follows:

$$u = \frac{subgroup\ count\ of\ occurrences}{subgroup\ size\ in\ units}$$

These values are shown in the last column of Table 8.8.

$$\bar{u} = \frac{sum\ of\ subgroup\ count\ of\ occurrences}{sum\ of\ subgroup\ unit\ sizes} = \frac{1,544}{32} = 48.25,$$

which is constant for all subgroups.

n=1 unit:

$$LCL = \bar{u} - 3\sqrt{\frac{\bar{u}}{n}} = 48.25 - 3\sqrt{\frac{48.25}{1}} = 27.411$$

$$UCL = \bar{u} + 3\sqrt{\frac{\bar{u}}{n}} = 48.25 + 3\sqrt{\frac{48.25}{1}} = 69.089$$

n=2 units:

$$LCL = 48.25 - 3\sqrt{\frac{48.25}{2}} = 33.514$$

$$UCL = 48.25 + 3\sqrt{\frac{48.25}{2}} = 62.986$$

The control limits and the subgroup occurrences-per-unit are shown in Figure 8.25.

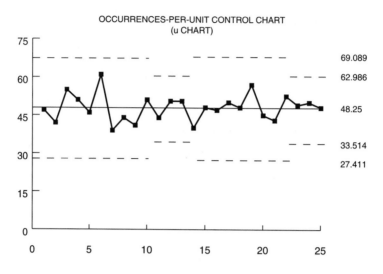

Figure 8.25. Completed *u* control chart.

The reader may note that the data used to construct the *u* chart were the same as used for the *p* chart, except that counts of occurrences (flaws) were considered instead of counts of physical items (bruised peaches). The practical implications of using a *u* chart when a *p* chart should have been used, or vice versa, are usually not serious. The decisions based on the control charts will be quite similar in most cases encountered in quality engineering regardless of whether a *u* or a *p* chart is used.

Control charts for counts of occurrences-per-unit (c charts)

C charts are statistical tools used to evaluate the number of occurrences-per-unit produced by a process. *C* charts can be applied to any variable where the appropriate performance measure is a count of how often a particular event occurs and samples of constant size are used. *C* charts answer the question "Has a special cause of variation caused the central tendency of this process to produce an abnormally large or small number of occurrences over the time period observed?" Note that, unlike *p* or *np* charts, *c* charts do not involve counting physical items. Rather, they involve counting of *events*. For example, when using an *np* chart one would count bruised peaches. When using a *c* chart one would count the *bruises*.

Control limit equations for c charts

Like all control charts, *c* charts consist of three guidelines: center line, a lower control limit, and an upper control limit. The center line is the average number of occurrences-per-unit and the two control limits are set at plus and minus three standard deviations. If the process is in statistical control then virtually all subgroup occurrences-per-unit should be between the control limits and they should fluctuate randomly about the center line.

$$\bar{c} = \frac{sum\ of\ subgroup\ occurrences}{number\ of\ subgroups} \qquad (8.59)$$

$$LCL = \bar{c} - 3\sqrt{\bar{c}} \qquad (8.60)$$

$$UCL = \bar{c} + 3\sqrt{\bar{c}} \qquad (8.61)$$

One way to determine whether a particular set of data is suitable for a *c* chart or an *np* chart is to examine the equation used to compute the center line for the control chart. If the unit of measure is the same in both the numerator and the denominator, then a *p* chart is indicated, otherwise a *c* chart is indicated. For example, if

$$Center\ Line = \frac{bruises}{number\ of\ crates},$$

then the numerator is in terms of bruises while the denominator is in terms of crates, indicating a *c* chart.

The unit size is arbitrary but, once determined, it cannot be changed without recomputing all subgroup occurrences-per-unit and control limits.

Analysis of c charts

As with all control charts, a special cause is probably present if there are any points beyond either the upper or the lower control limit. Analysis of c chart patterns between the control limits is shown later in this chapter.

Example of c chart

The data in Table 8.9 were obtained by opening randomly selected crates from each shipment and counting the number of flaws. There are 250 peaches per crate. Our unit size will be taken as one full crate; i.e., crates will be counted rather than the peaches themselves. Every subgroup consists of one crate. If the subgroup size varied, a u chart would be used.

Table 8.9. Raw data for c chart.

SHIPMENT #	FLAWS	SHIPMENT #	FLAWS
1	27	16	29
2	32	17	33
3	24	18	33
4	31	19	38
5	42	20	32
6	38	21	37
7	33	22	30
8	35	23	31
9	35	24	32
10	39	25	42
11	41	26	40
12	29	27	21
13	34	28	23
14	34	29	39
15	43	30	29
		TOTAL	1,006

Continued at right . . .

Using the above data the center line and control limits are found as follows:

$$\bar{c} = \frac{\textit{sum of subgroup occurrences}}{\textit{number of subgroups}} = \frac{1,006}{30} = 33.53$$

$$LCL = \bar{c} - 3\sqrt{\bar{c}} = 33.53 - 3\sqrt{33.53} = 16.158$$

$$UCL = \bar{c} + 3\sqrt{\bar{c}} = 33.53 + 3\sqrt{33.53} = 50.902$$

The control limits and the occurrence counts are shown in Figure 8.26.

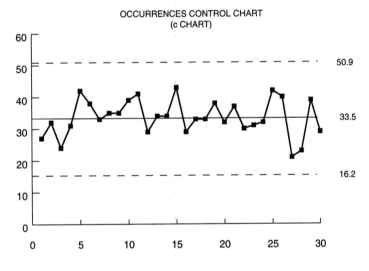

Figure 8.26. Completed c control chart.

IMPLEMENTATION

Assuming that the organization's leadership has created an environment where open and honest communication can flourish, SPC implementation becomes a matter of 1) selecting processes for applying the SPC approach and 2) selecting variables within each process. This section describes an approach to this activity.

VARIABLE SELECTION

Preparing the process control plan

Process control plans should be prepared for each key process. The plans should be prepared by teams who understand the process. The team should begin by creating a flowchart of the process using the process elements determined in creating the house of quality (see the QFD discussion in Chapter 3). The flowchart will show how the process elements relate to one another and it will help in the selection of control points. It will also show the point of delivery to the customer, which is usually an important control point. Note that the customer may be an internal customer.

For any given process there are a number of different types of process elements. Some process elements are *internal* to the process, others *external*. The rotation speed of a drill is an internal process element, while the humidity in the building is external. Some process elements, while important, are easy to hold constant at a given value so that they do not change unless deliberate action is taken. These are called *fixed* elements. Other process elements vary of their own accord and must be watched; these are called *variable* elements. The drill rotation speed can be set in advance, but the line voltage for the drill press may vary, which causes the drill speed to change in spite of its initial setting (a good example of how a correlation matrix might be useful). Figure 8.27 provides a planning guide based on the internal/external and fixed/variable classification scheme. Of course, other classification schemes may be more suitable on a given project and the engineer is encouraged to develop the approach that best serves his or her needs. For convenience, each class is identified with a Roman numeral: I = fixed–internal, II = fixed–external, III = variable–internal and IV = variable–external.

	INTERNAL	EXTERNAL
FIXED	**I**	**II**
	• Setup approval • Periodic audits • Preventive maintenance	• Audit • Certification
VARIABLE	**III**	**IV**
	• Control charts • Fool-proofing product • Fool-proofing process • Sort the output	• Supplier SPC • Receiving inspection • Supplier sorting • Fool-proof product

Figure 8.27. Guide to selecting and controlling process variables.

In selecting the appropriate method of control for each process element, it is necessary to pay particular attention to those process elements which received high importance rankings in the house of quality analysis. In some cases an important process element is very expensive to control. When this happens, the QFD correlation matrix or the statistical correlation matrix may provide assistance. The process element may be correlated with other process elements that are less costly to control. Either correlation matrix will also help to minimize the number of control charts. It is usually unnecessary to keep control charts on several variables that are correlated with one another. In these cases, it may be possible to select the process element that is least expensive (or most sensitive) to monitor as the control variable.

As Figure 8.27 indicates, control charts are not always the best method of controlling a given process element. In fact, control charts are seldom the method of choice. When process elements are important the ideal situation is that they *not vary at all!* Only when this can not be accomplished economically should the engineer resort to the use of control charts to monitor the element's variation. Control charts may be thought of as a control mechanism of last resort. Control charts are useful only when the element being monitored can be expected to exhibit measurable and "random-looking" variation when the process is properly controlled. A process element that always checks "10" if everything is okay is not a good candidate for control charting. Nor is one that checks "10" or "12," but never anything else. Ideally, the measurements being monitored with variables control charts will be capable of taking on any value; i.e., the data will be continuous. Discrete measurement data can be used if it's not too discrete; indeed, all real-world data are somewhat discrete. As a rule of thumb, at least ten different values should appear in the data set and no one value should comprise more than 20% of the data set. Measurement data too discrete for SPC should be monitored with checksheets or simple time-ordered plots.

Of course, the above discussion applies to measurement data. Attribute control charts can be used to monitor process elements that are discrete counts.

Any process control plan must include instructions on the action to be taken if problems appear. This is particularly important where control charts are being used for process control. Unlike process control procedures such as audits or setup approvals, it is not always apparent just what is wrong when a control chart indicates a problem. The investigation of special causes of variation usually consists of a number of predetermined actions (such as checking the fixture or checking a cutting tool) followed by notifying someone if the items checked don't reveal the source of the problem. It should be verified that the arithmetic was done correctly and that the point was plotted in the correct position on the control chart.

The reader may have noticed that Figure 8.27 includes "sort output" as part of the process control plan. Sorting the output implies that the process is not capable of meeting the customer's requirements, as determined by a process capability study and the application of Deming's all-or-none rules. However, even if sorting is taking place, SPC is still advisable. SPC will help assure that things don't get any worse. SPC will also reveal improvements that may otherwise be overlooked. The improvements may result in a process that is good enough to eliminate the need for sorting.

CONTROL CHART SELECTION

Selecting the proper control chart for a particular data set is a simple matter if approached properly. The proper approach is illustrated in Figure 8.28.

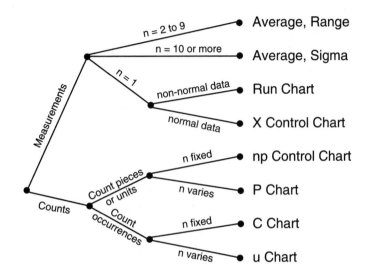

Figure 8.28. Control chart selection decision tree.

To use the decision tree, begin at the left-most node and determine if the data are measurements or counts. If measurements, then select the control chart based on the subgroup size. If the data are counts, then determine if the counts are of occurrences or pieces. An aid in making this determination is to examine the equation for the process average. If the numerator and denominator involve the same units, then a *p* or *np* chart is indicated. If different units of measure are involved, then a *u* or *c* chart is indicated. For example, if the average is in accidents-per-month, then a *c* or *u* chart is indicated because the numerator is in terms of accidents but the denominator is in terms of time.

RATIONAL SUBGROUP SAMPLING

The basis of all control charts is the *rational subgroup*. Rational subgroups are composed of items which were produced under essentially the same conditions. The statistics, for example, the average and range, are computed for each subgroup separately, then plotted on the control chart. When possible, rational subgroups are formed by using consecutive units. Each subgroup's statistics are compared to the control limits, and patterns of variation between subgroups are analyzed. Note the sharp contrast between this approach and the *random sampling* approach used for enumerative statistical methods.

The idea of rational subgrouping becomes a bit fuzzy when dealing with *x* charts, or individuals control charts. The reader may well wonder about the meaning of the term subgrouping when the "subgroup" is a single measurement. The basic idea underlying control charts of all types is to identify the capability of the process. The mechanism by which this is accomplished is careful formation of rational subgroups as defined above. When possible, rational subgroups are formed by using consecutive units. The measure of process variability, either the subgroup standard deviation or the subgroup range, is the basis of the control limits for averages. Conceptually, this is akin to basing the control limits on short-term variation. These control limits are used to monitor variation over time.

As far as possible, this approach also forms the basis of establishing control limits for individual measurements by forming quasi-subgroups using pairs of consecutive measurements. These "subgroups of 2" are used to compute ranges. The ranges are used to compute the control limits for the individual measurements.

CONTROL CHARTS INTERPRETATION

Control charts provide the operational definition of the term *special cause*. A special cause is simply anything which leads to an observation beyond a control limit. However, this simplistic use of control charts does not do justice to their power. Control charts are running records of the performance of the process and, as such, they contain a vast store of information on potential improvements. While some guidelines are presented here, control chart interpretation is an art that can only be developed by looking at many control charts and probing the patterns to identify the underlying system of causes at work.

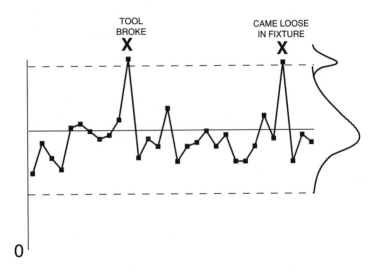

Figure 8.29. Control chart patterns: *freaks*.

Freak patterns are the classical special cause situation. Freaks result from causes that have a large effect but that occur infrequently. When investigating freak values look at the cause-and-effect diagram for items that meet these criteria. The key to identifying freak causes is timelines in collecting and recording the data. If difficulty is experienced sampling should occur more frequently.

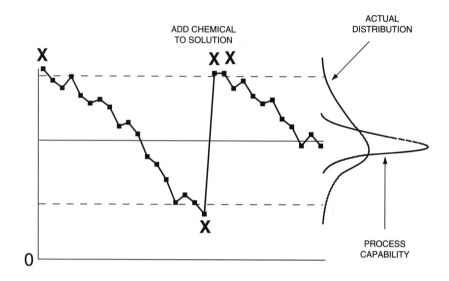

Figure 8.30. Control chart patterns: *drift*.

Drift is generally seen in processes where the current process value is part-ly determined by the previous process state. For example, if the process is a plating bath, the content of the tank cannot change instantaneously, instead it will change gradually. Another common example is tool wear: the size of the tool is related to its previous size. Once the cause of the drift has been deter-mined, the appropriate action can be taken. Whenever economically feasible, the drift should be eliminated; e.g., install an automatic chemical dispenser for the plating bath, or make automatic compensating adjustments to correct for tool wear. Note that the total process variability increases when drift is allowed, which adds cost. When this is not possible, the control chart can be modified in one of two ways:

1. Make the slope of the center line and control limits match the natural process drift. The control chart will then detect departures from the natural drift.

2. Plot *deviations* from the natural or expected drift.

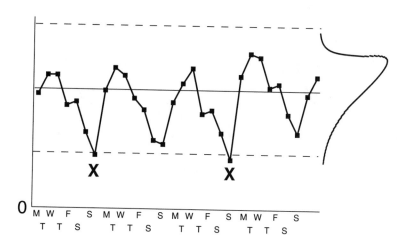

Figure 8.31. Control chart patterns: *cycles.*

Cycles often occur due to the nature of the process. Common cycles include hour of the day, day of the week, month of the year, quarter of the year, week of the accounting cycle, etc. Cycles are caused by modifying the process inputs or methods according to a regular schedule. The existence of this schedule and its effect on the process may or may not be known in advance. Once the cycle has been discovered, action can be taken. The action might be to adjust the control chart by plotting the control measure against a variable base. For example, if a day-of-the-week cycle exists for shipping errors because of the workload, shipping errors per 100 orders shipped might be plotted instead of shipping errors per day. Alternatively, the system might be changed to smooth out the cycle. Most processes operate more efficiently when the inputs are relatively stable and when methods are changed as little as possible.

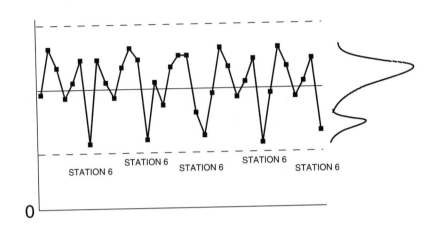

Figure 8.32. Control chart patterns: *repeating patterns.*

A controlled process will exhibit only "random looking" variation. A pattern where every nth item is different is, obviously, non-random. These patterns are sometimes quite subtle and difficult to identify. It is sometimes helpful to see if the average fraction defective is close to some multiple of a known number of process streams. For example, if the machine is a filler with 40 stations, look for problems that occur 1/40, 2/40, 3/40, etc., of the time.

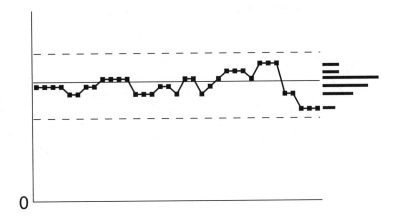

Figure 8.33. Control chart patterns: *discrete data.*

When plotting measurement data the assumption is that the numbers exist on a continuum, i.e., there will be many different values in the data set. In the real world, the data are never completely continuous. It usually doesn't matter much if there are, for example, 10 or more different numbers. However, when there are only a few numbers that appear over-and-over there can be problems with the analysis. A common problem is that the R chart will underestimate the average range, causing the control limits on both the average and range charts to be too close together. The result will be too many "false alarms" and a general loss of confidence in SPC.

The usual cause of this situation is inadequate gage resolution. The ideal solution is to obtain a gage with greater resolution. Sometimes the problem occurs because operators, inspectors, or computers are rounding the numbers. The solution here is to record additional digits.

BEFORE CHANGE   AFTER CHANGE

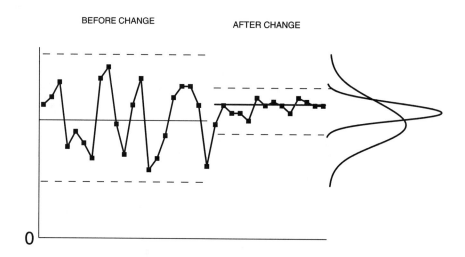

0

Figure 8.34. Control chart patterns: *planned changes.*

The purpose of SPC is to accelerate the learning process and to eventually produce an improvement. Control charts serve as historical records of the learning process and they can be used by others to improve other processes. When an improvement is realized the change should be written on the old control chart; its effect will be evident as a less variable process. These charts are also useful in communicating the results to leaders, suppliers, customers, and others interested in quality improvement.

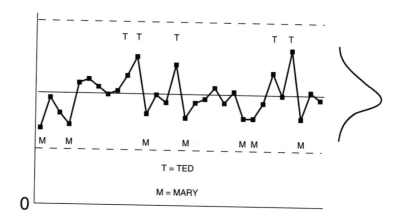

Figure 8.35. Control chart patterns: *suspected differences.*

Seemingly random patterns on a control chart are evidence of unknown causes of variation, which is not the same as *uncaused* variation. There should be an ongoing effort to reduce the variation from these so-called common causes. Doing so requires that the unknown causes of variation be identified. One way of doing this is a retrospective evaluation of control charts. This involves brainstorming and preparing cause and effect diagrams, then relating the control chart patterns to the causes listed on the diagram. For example, if "operator" is a suspected cause of variation, a label should be placed on the control chart points produced by each operator. If the labels exhibit a pattern, there is evidence to suggest a problem. An investigation should then be conducted into the reasons and controlled experiments (prospective studies) set up to test any theories proposed. If the experiments indicate a true cause and effect relationship appropriate process improvements should be made. The observed association must be backed up with solid subject-matter expertise and experimental data; a statistical *association* is not the same thing as a causal *correlation.*

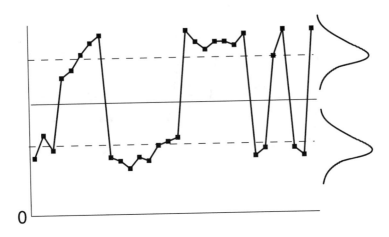

Figure 8.36. Control chart patterns: *mixture*.

Mixture exists when the data from two different cause-systems are plotted on a single control chart. It indicates a failure in creating rational subgroups. The underlying differences should be identified and corrective action taken. The nature of the corrective action will determine how the control chart should be modified.

Mixture example #1

The mixture represents two different operators who can be made more consistent. A single control chart can be used to monitor the new, consistent process.

Mixture example #2

The mixture is in the number of emergency room cases received on Saturday evening, versus the number received during a normal week. Separate control charts should be used to monitor patient-load during the two different time periods.

RULES FOR DETERMINING STATISTICAL CONTROL
Run tests

If the process is stable, then the distribution of subgroup averages will be approximately normal; therefore, the *patterns* on the control charts can be analyzed to see if they might be attributed to a special cause of variation. To do this, a normal distribution is divided into zones, with each zone one standard deviation wide. Figure 8.37 shows the approximate percentage expected in each zone from a stable process.

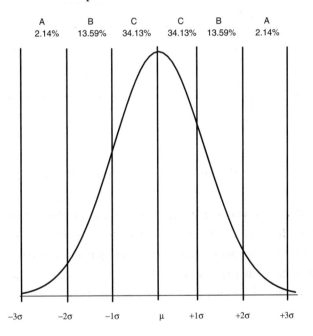

Figure 8.37. Percentiles for a normal distribution.

Zone *C* is the area from the mean to the mean plus or minus one sigma; zone B is from plus or minus one to plus or minus two sigma, and zone A is from plus or minus two to plus or minus three sigma. Of course, any point beyond three sigma (i.e., outside of the control limit) is an indication of an out-of-control process.

Since the control limits are at plus and minus three standard deviations, the one and two sigma lines on a control chart are found simply by dividing the distance between the grand average and either control limit into thirds, which can be done using a ruler. This divides each half of the control chart into three zones. The three zones are labeled A, B, and C as shown on Figure 8.38.

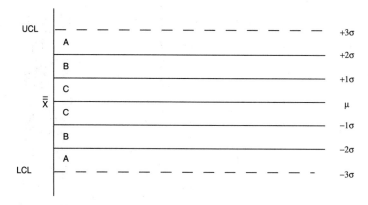

Figure 8.38. Zones on a control chart.

Based on the expected percentages in each zone, sensitive run tests can be developed for analyzing the patterns of variation in the various zones. It should be remembered that, the existence of a non-random pattern means that a special cause of variation was (or is) probably present. The averages, np and c control chart run tests are shown in Figure 8.39.

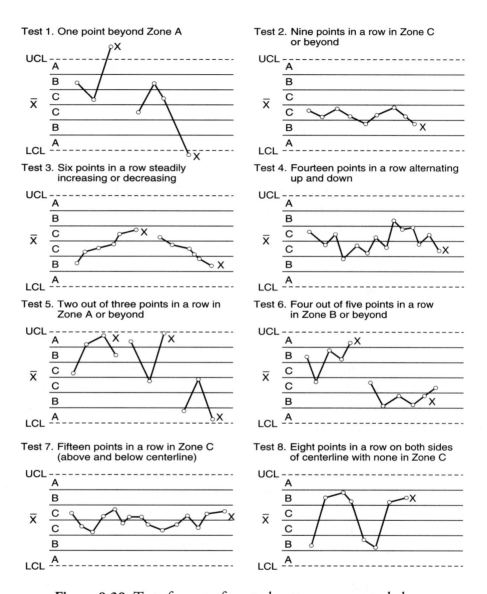

Figure 8.39. Tests for out of control patterns on control charts.

From "The Shewhart Control Chart—Tests for Special Causes," *Journal of Quality Technology*, 16(4), p 238. Copyright © 1986 by Nelson.

Note that, when a point responds to an out-of-control test it is marked with an "X" to make the interpretation of the chart easier. Using this convention, the patterns on the control charts can be used as an aid in troubleshooting.

TAMPERING EFFECTS AND DIAGNOSIS

Tampering occurs when adjustments are made to a process that is in statistical control. Adjusting a controlled process will always increase process variability, an obviously undesirable result. The best means of diagnosing tampering is to conduct a process capability study (see below) and to use a control chart to provide guidelines for adjusting the process.

Perhaps the best analysis of the effects of tampering is from Deming (1986). Deming describes four common types of tampering by drawing the analogy of aiming a funnel to hit a desired target. These "funnel rules" are described by Deming (1986, p. 328):

1. "Leave the funnel fixed, aimed at the target, no adjustment.
2. "At drop k (k = 1, 2, 3, ...) the marble will come to rest at point z_k, measured from the target. (In other words, z_k is the error at drop k.) Move the funnel the distance $-z_k$ from the last position. Memory 1.
3. "Set the funnel at each drop right over the spot z_k, measured from the target. No memory.
4. "Set the funnel at each drop right over the spot (z_k) where it last came to rest. No memory."

Rule #1 is the best rule for stable processes. If this rule is followed, the process average will remain stable and the variance will be minimized. Rule #2 produces a stable output but one with twice the variance of rule #1. Rule #3 results in a system that "explodes"; i.e., a symmetrical pattern will appear with a variance that increases without bound. Rule #4 creates a pattern that steadily moves away from the target, without limit.

At first glance, one might wonder about the relevance of such apparently abstract rules. However, upon more careful consideration, one finds many practical situations where these rules apply.

Rule #1 is the ideal situation and it can be approximated by using control charts to guide decision-making. If process adjustments are made only when special causes are indicated and identified, a pattern similar to that produced by rule #1 will result.

Rule #2 has intuitive appeal for many people. It is commonly encountered in such activities as gage calibration (the standard is checked once and the gage adjusted accordingly) or in some automated equipment (using an automatic gage, the size of the last feature produced is checked and a compensating adjustment made). Since the system produces a stable result, this situation can go unnoticed indefinitely. However, as shown by Taguchi, increased variance translates to poorer quality and higher cost.

The rationale that leads to rule #3 goes something like this: "A measurement was taken and it was found to be 10 units above the desired target. This happened because the process was set 10 units too high. I want the average to equal the target. To accomplish this I must try to get the next unit to be 10 units too low." This might be used, for example, in preparing a chemical solution. While reasonable on its face, the result of this approach is a wildly oscillating system.

A common example of rule #4 is the "train-the-trainer" method. A master spends a short time training a group of "experts," who then train others, who train others, et cetera. An example is on-the-job training. Another is creating a setup by using a piece from the last job. Yet another is a gage calibration system where standards are used to create other standards, which are used to create still others, and so on. Just how far the final result will be from the ideal depends on how many levels deep the scheme has progressed.

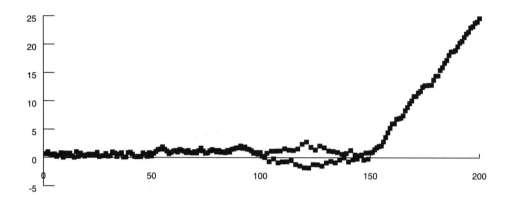

Figure 8.40. Funnel rule simulation results.

PRE-Control

The PRE-Control method was originally developed by Dorian Shainin in the 1950s. According to Shainin, PRE-Control is a simple algorithm for controlling a process based on the tolerances. It assumes the process is producing a product with a measurable and adjustable quality characteristic which varies according to some distribution. It makes no assumptions concerning the actual shape and stability of the distribution. Cautionary zones are designated just inside each tolerance extreme. A new process is qualified by taking consecutive samples of individual measurements until five in a row fall within the central zone before two in a row fall into the cautionary zones. To simplify the application, PRE-Control charts are often color-coded. On such charts the central zone is colored green, the cautionary zones yellow, and the zone outside of the tolerance red. PRE-Control is not equivalent to SPC. SPC is designed to identify special causes of variation; PRE-Control starts with a process that is known to be capable of meeting the tolerance and assures that it does so. SPC and process capability analysis should always be used before PRE-Control is applied.*

---

*Considerable controversy surrounds the use of PRE-Control. However, the discussions tend towards considerable statistical sophistication and will not be reviewed here. The reader should keep in mind that PRE-Control should not be considered a *replacement* for SPC.

Once the process is qualified, it is monitored by taking periodic samples consisting of two individuals each (called the A,B pair). Action is taken only if both A and B are in the cautionary zone. Processes must be requalified after any action is taken.

SETTING UP PRE-CONTROL

Figure 8.41 illustrates the PRE-Control zones for a two-sided tolerance (i.e., a tolerance with both a lower specification limit and an upper specification limit).

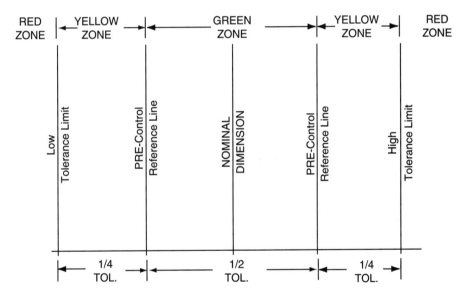

Figure 8.41. PRE-Control zones (2-sided tolerance).

Figure 8.42 illustrates the PRE-Control zones for a one-sided tolerance (i.e., a tolerance with only a lower specification limit or only an upper specification limit). Examples of this situation are flatness, concentricity, runout and other total indicator reading type features.

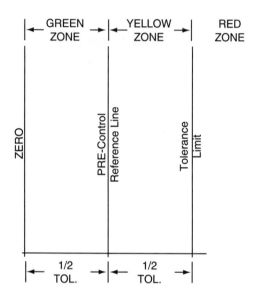

Figure 8.42. PRE-Control zones (1-sided tolerance).

Figure 8.43 illustrates the PRE-Control zones for characteristics with minimum or maximum specification limits. Examples of this situation are tensile strength, contamination levels, etc. In this situation one reference line is placed a quarter of the way from the tolerance limit toward the best sample produced during past operations.

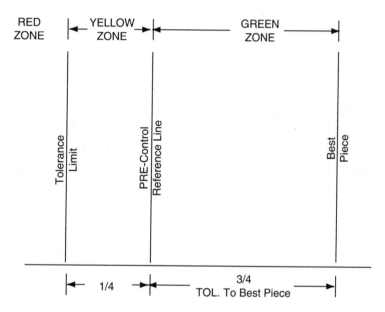

Figure 8.43. PRE-Control zones (minimum/maximum specifications).

USING PRE-CONTROL

The first step is *setup qualification*. Measure every piece produced until five greens in a row are obtained. If one yellow is encountered the count should be restarted. If two yellows in a row or any reds are encountered the process should be adjusted and the count restarted. This step replaces first-piece inspection.

After setup qualification the *run* phase will be entered. Measure two consecutive pieces periodically (the A,B pair). If both are yellow on the same side, adjustment should be made. If yellow on opposite sides, help may be needed to reduce the variability of the process. If either are red, adjustment should be made. In the case of two yellows, the adjustment must be made immediately to prevent nonconforming work. In the case of red, stop; nonconforming work is already being produced. Segregate all nonconforming product according to established procedures.

Shainin and Shainin (1988) recommend adjusting the inspection frequency such that six A,B pairs are measured on average between each process adjustment. A simple formula for this is shown in Equation 8.62.

$$\textit{minutes between measurements} = \textit{hours between adjustments} \times 10 \qquad (8.62)$$

EWMA charts

SPC TECHNIQUES FOR AUTOMATED MANUFACTURING

Many people erroneously believe that statistics are not needed when automated manufacturing processes are involved. Since we have measurements from every unit produced, they reason, sampling methods are inappropriate. We will simply correct the process when the characteristic is not on target.

This attitude reflects a fundamental misunderstanding of the relationship between a process and the output of a process. It also shows a lack of appreciation for the intrinsic variability of processes and of measurements. The fact is, even if there is a "complete" data record of every feature of every part produced, there is still only a sample of the output of the process. The process is future-oriented in time, while the record of measurements is past-oriented. Unless statistical control is attained, the data from past production cannot be used to predict the variability from the process in the future (refer to the definition of statistical control above.) And without statistical tools there is no sound basis for the belief that statistical control exists.

Another reason process control should be based on an understanding and correct use of statistical methods is the effect of making changes without this understanding. Consider, for example, the following process adjustment rule:

> Measure the diameter of the gear shaft. If the diameter is above the nominal size, adjust the process to reduce the diameter. If the diameter is below the nominal size, adjust the process to increase the diameter.

The problem with this approach is described by Deming's "funnel rules" (see above). This approach to process control will increase the variability of a statistically controlled process by 141%, certainly not what the process control engineer had in mind. The root of the problem is a failure to realize that the part measurement is a sample from the process and, although it provides information about the state of the process, the information is incomplete. Only through using proper statistical methods can the information be extracted, analyzed and understood.

PROBLEMS WITH TRADITIONAL SPC TECHNIQUES

A fundamental assumption underlying traditional SPC techniques is that the observed values are independent of one another. Although the SPC tools are quite insensitive to moderate violations of this assumption (Wheeler, 1991), automated manufacturing processes often breach the assumption by enough to make traditional methods fail (Alwan and Roberts, 1989). By using scatter diagrams, as described in the previous chapter, it can be determined if the assumption of independence is satisfied for the data. If not, the methods described below should be considered instead of the traditional SPC methods.

A common complaint about non-standard SPC methods is that they are usually more complex than the traditional methods (Wheeler, 1991). This is often true. However, when dealing with automated manufacturing processes the analysis is usually handled by a computer. Since the complexity of the analysis is totally invisible to the human operator, it makes little difference. Of course, if the operator will be required to act based on the results, he or she must understand how the results are to be used. The techniques described in this chapter which require human action are interpreted in much the same way as traditional SPC techniques.

SPECIAL AND COMMON CAUSE CHARTS

When using traditional SPC techniques the rules are always the same, namely

1. As long as the variation in the statistic being plotted remains within the control limits, leave the process alone.
2. If a plotted point exceeds a control limit, look for the cause.

This approach works fine as long as the process remains static. However, the mean of many automated manufacturing processes often drift because of inherent process factors. In other words, the drift is produced by *common causes*. In spite of this, there may be known ways of intervening in the process to compensate for the drift. Traditionalists would say that the intervention should be taken in such a way that the control chart exhibits only random variation. However, this may involve additional cost. Mindlessly applying arbitrary rules to achieve some abstract result, like a stable control chart, is poor practice. All of the options should be considered.

One alternative is to allow the drift to continue until the cost of intervention equals the cost of running off-target. This alternative can be implemented through the use of a "common cause chart." This approach, described in Alwan and Roberts (1989) and Abraham and Whitney (1990), involves creating a chart of the process mean. However, unlike traditional $\overline{X}$ charts, there are no control limits. Instead, *action limits* are placed on the chart. Action limits differ from control limits in two ways

- They are computed based on costs rather than on statistical theory.
- Since the chart shows variation from common causes, violating an action limit does not result in a search for a special cause. Instead, a prescribed action is taken to bring the process closer to the target value.

These charts are called "common cause charts" because the changing level of the process is due to built-in process characteristics. The process mean is tracked by using exponentially weighted moving averages (EWMA.) While somewhat more complicated than traditional $\overline{X}$ charts, EWMA charts have a number of advantages for automated manufacturing:

- EWMA charts can be used when processes have inherent drift.
- EWMA charts provide a forecast of where the next process measurement will be. This allows feed-forward control.
- EWMA models can be used to develop procedures for dynamic process control, as described later in this section.

EWMA COMMON CAUSE CHARTS

When dealing with a process that is essentially static, the predicted value of the average of the every sample is simply the grand average. EWMA charts, on the other hand, use the actual process data to determine the predicted process value for processes that may be drifting. If the process has trend or cyclical components, the EWMA will reflect the effect of these components. Also, the EWMA chart produces a forecast of what the *next* sample mean will be; the traditional $\overline{X}$ chart merely shows what the process was doing at the time the sample was taken. Thus, the EWMA chart can be used to take preemptive action to prevent a process from going too far from the target.

If the process has inherent non-random components, an EWMA common cause chart should be used. This is an EWMA chart with economic action limits instead of control limits. EWMA control charts, which are described in the next section, can be used to monitor processes that vary within the action limits.

The equation for computing the EWMA is

$$EWMA = \hat{y}_t + \lambda\left(y_t - \hat{y}_t\right) \tag{8.63}$$

In this equation $\hat{y}_t$ is the predicted value y at time period t, y_t is the actual value at time period t, and λ is a constant between 0 and 1. If λ is close to 1, Equation 8.63 will give little weight to historic data; if λ is close to 0 then current observations will be given little weight. EWMA can also be thought of as the forecasted process value at time period t+1, in other words, $EWMA = \hat{y}_{t+1}$.

Since most people already understand the traditional $\overline{X}$ chart, thinking about the relationship between $\overline{X}$ charts and EWMA charts can help to understand the EWMA chart. It is interesting to note that traditional $\overline{X}$ charts give 100% of the weight to the current sample and 0% to past data. This is roughly equivalent to setting $\lambda = 1$ on an EWMA chart. In other words, the traditional $\overline{X}$ chart can be thought of as a special type of EWMA chart where past data is considered to be unimportant (assuming run tests are not applied to the Shewhart chart). This is equivalent to saying that the data points are all independent of one another. In contrast, the EWMA chart uses the information from all previous samples. Although Equation 8.63 may look as though it is using only the results of the most recent data point, in reality the EWMA weighting scheme applies progressively less weight to each sample result as time passes. Figure 8.44 compares the weighting schemes of EWMA and $\overline{X}$ charts.

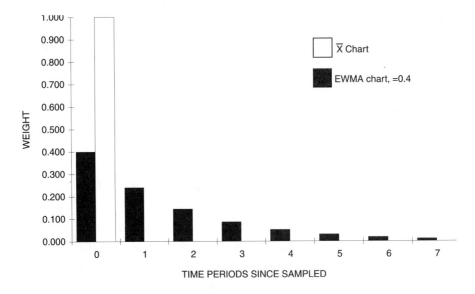

Figure 8.44. X-bar versus EWMA weigting.

In contrast, as lambda approaches 0 the EWMA chart begins to behave like a cusum chart. With a cusum chart all previous points are given equal weight. Between the two extremes the EWMA chart weights historical data in importance somewhere between the traditional Shewhart chart and the cusum chart. By changing the value of lambda the chart's behavior can be "adjusted" to the process being monitored.

In addition to the weighting, there are other differences between the EWMA and the $\overline{X}$ chart. The "forecast" from the $\overline{X}$ chart is always the same: the next data point will be equal to the historical grand average. In other words, the $\overline{X}$ chart treats all data points as coming from a process that doesn't change its central tendency (implied when the forecast is always the grand average).[*]

When using an $\overline{X}$ chart it is not essential that the sampling interval be kept constant. After all, the process is supposed to behave as if it were static. However, the EWMA chart is designed to account for process drift and, therefore, the sampling interval should be kept constant when using EWMA charts. This is usually not a problem with automated manufacturing.

EXAMPLE

Krishnamoorthi (1991) describes a mold line that produces green sand molds at the rate of about one per minute. The molds are used to pour cylinder blocks for large size engines. Application of SPC to the process revealed that the process had an assignable cause that could not be eliminated from the process. The mold sand, which was partly recycled, tended to increase and decrease in temperature based on the size of the block being produced and the number of blocks in the order. Sand temperature is important because it affects the compactability percentage, an important parameter. The sand temperature could not be better controlled without adding an automatic sand cooler, which was not deemed economical. However, the effect of the sand

---

[*] We aren't saying this situation actually exists, we are just saying that the $\overline{X}$ treats the process *as if* this were true. Studying the patterns of variation will often reveal clues to making the process more consistent, even if the process variation remains within the control limits.

temperature on the compactability percent could be made negligible by modifying the amount of water added to the sand so feed-forward control was feasible.

Although the author doesn't indicate that EWMA charts were used for this process, it is an excellent application for EWMA common cause charts. The level of the sand temperature doesn't really matter, as long as it is known. The sand temperature tends to drift in cycles because the amount of heated sand depends on the size of the casting and how many are being produced. A traditional control chart for the temperature would indicate that sand temperature is out-of-control, which we already know. What is really needed is a method to predict what the sand temperature will be the next time it is checked, then the operator can add the correct amount of water so the effect on the sand compactability percent can be minimized. This will produce an in-control control chart for compactability percent, which is what really matters.

The data in Table 8.11 show the EWMA calculations for the sand temperature data. Using a spreadsheet program, Microsoft Excel for Windows, the optimal value of λ, that is the value which provided the "best fit" in the sense that it produced the smallest sum of the squared errors, was found to be close to 0.9. Figure 8.45 shows the EWMA common cause chart for this data, and the raw temperature data as well. The EWMA is a *forecast* of what the sand temperature will be the next time it is checked. The operator can adjust the rate of water addition based on this forecast.

Table 8.11. Data for EWMA chart of sand temperature.

SAND TEMPERATURE	EWMA	ERROR
125	125.00*	0.00
123	125.00	−2.00**
118	123.20***	−5.20
116	118.52	−2.52
108	116.25	−8.25
112	108.83	3.17
101	111.68	−10.68
100	102.07	−2.07
98	100.21	−2.21
102	98.22	3.78
111	101.62	9.38
107	110.6	−3.06
112	107.31	4.69
112	111.53	0.47
122	111.95	10.05
140	121.00	19.00
125	138.10	−13.10
130	126.31	3.69
136	129.63	6.37
130	135.36	−5.36
112	130.54	−18.54
115	113.85	1.15
100	114.89	−14.89
113	101.49	11.51
111	111.85	−0.85
128	111.08	16.92
122	126.31	−4.31
142	122.43	19.57

Continued on next page . . .

Table 8.11—*Continued . . .*

SAND TEMPERATURE	EWMA	ERROR
134	140.64	–6.04
130	134.60	–4.60
131	130.46	0.54
104	130.95	–26.95
84	106.69	–22.69
86	86.27	–0.27
99	86.03	12.97
90	97.70	–7.70
91	90.77	0.23
90	90.98	–0.98
101	90.10	10.90

*   The starting EWMA is either the target, or, if there is no target, the first observation.

**   Error = Actual observation – EWMA. E.g., –2 = 123 – 125.

***   Other than the first sample, all EWMAs are commuted as
EWMA = last EWMA + λ error. E.g., 123.2 = 125 + 0.9 * (–2).

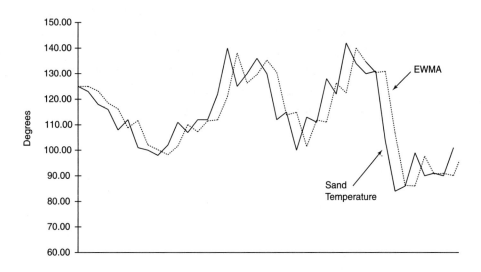

Figure 8.45. EWMA chart of sand temperature.

EWMA CONTROL CHARTS

Although it is not always necessary to put control limits on the EWMA chart, as shown by the above example, it is possible to do so when the situation calls for it. Three sigma control limits for the EWMA chart are computed based on

$$\sigma^2 EWMA = \sigma^2 \left[\frac{\lambda}{(2-\lambda)} \right] \qquad (8.64)$$

For the sand temperature example above, $\lambda = 0.9$ which gives

$$\sigma^2 EWMA = \sigma^2 \left[\frac{0.9}{(2-0.9)} \right] = 0.82\sigma^2$$

σ^2 is estimated using all of the data. For the sand temperature data $\sigma = 15.37$ so $\sigma EWMA = 15.37 \times \sqrt{0.82} = 13.92$. The 3σ control limits for the EWMA chart are placed at the grand average plus and minus 41.75. Figure 8.46 shows the control chart for this data. The EWMA line must remain within the control limits. Since the EWMA accounts for "normal drift" in the process centerline, deviations beyond the control limits imply assignable causes other than those accounted for by normal drift. Again, since the effects of changes in temperature can be ameliorated by adjusting the rate of water input, the EWMA control chart may not be necessary.

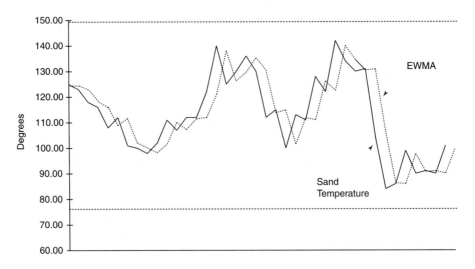

Figure 8.46. EWMA control chart of sand temperature.

CHOOSING THE VALUE OF λ

The choice of λ is the subject of much literature. A value λ of near 0 provides more "smoothing" by giving greater weight to historic data, while a λ value near 1 gives greater weight to current data. Most authors recommend a value in the range of 0.2 to 0.3. The justification for this range of λ values is probably based on applications of the EWMA technique in the field of economics, where EWMA methods are in widespread use. Industrial applications are less common, although the use of EWMA techniques is growing rapidly.

Hunter (1989) proposes an EWMA control chart scheme where $\lambda = 0.4$. This value of λ provides a control chart with approximately the same statistical properties as a traditional $\overline{X}$ chart combined with the run tests described in the *AT&T Statistical Quality Control Handbook* (commonly called the Western Electric Rules.) It also has the advantage of providing control limits that are exactly half as wide as the control limits on a traditional $\overline{X}$ chart. Thus, to compute the control limits for an EWMA chart when λ is 0.4 the traditional $\overline{X}$ chart (or X chart) control limits are computed and the distance between the upper and lower control limit divided by two. The EWMA should remain within these limits.

As mentioned above, the optimal value of λ can be found using some spreadsheet programs. The sum of the squared errors is minimized by changing the value of λ. If your spreadsheet doesn't automatically find the minimum, it can be approximated manually by changing the cell containing λ or by setting up a range of λ values and watching what happens to the cell containing the sum of the squared errors. A graph of the error sum of the squares versus different λ values can indicate where the optimum λ lies.

SPECIAL CAUSE CHARTS

Whether using an EWMA common cause chart without control limits or an EWMA control chart, it is a good idea to keep track of the forecast errors using a control chart. The special cause chart is a traditional X chart, created using the difference between the EWMA forecast and the actual observed values. Figure 8.47 shows the special cause chart of the sand temperature data analyzed above.

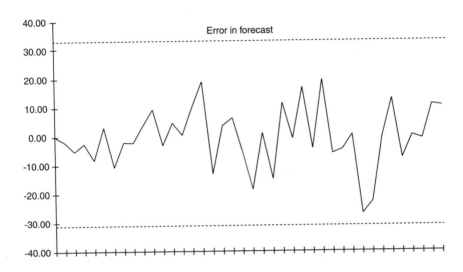

Figure 8.47. Special cause control chart of EWMA errors.

SPC AND AUTOMATIC PROCESS CONTROL

As SPC has grown in popularity its use has been mandated with more and more processes. When this trend reached automated manufacturing processes there was resistance from process control engineers who were applying a different approach with considerable success (Palm, 1990.) Advocates of SPC attempted to force the use of traditional SPC techniques as feedback mechanisms for process control. This inappropriate application of SPC was correctly denounced by process control engineers. SPC is designed to serve a purpose fundamentally different than automatic process control (APC.) SPC advocates correctly pointed out that APC was not a cure-all and that many process controllers added variation by making adjustments based on data analysis that was statistically invalid.

Both SPC and APC have their rightful place in quality improvement. APC attempts to dynamically control a process to minimize variation around a target value. This requires valid statistical analysis, which is the domain of the statistical sciences. SPC makes a distinction between special causes and common causes of variation. If APC responds to all variation as if it were the same it will result in missed opportunities to reduce variation by attacking it at the source. A process that operates closer to the target without correction will produce less variation overall than a process that is frequently returned to the target via APC. However, at times APC must respond to *common cause variation that can't be economically eliminated,* e.g., the mold process described above. Properly used, APC can greatly reduce variability in the output.

J.S. Hunter (1986) shows that there is a statistical equivalent to the PID control equation commonly used. The PID equation is

$$u(t) = Ke(t) + \frac{K}{T_I} \int_0^1 e(s)ds + KT_D \left(\frac{d_e}{d_t} \right) \tag{8.65}$$

The "PID" label comes from the fact that the first term is a proportional term, the second an integral term and the third a derivative term. Hunter modified the basic EWMA equation by adding two additional terms. The result is the *empirical control equation.*

$$\hat{y}_{t+1} = \hat{y}_t + \lambda e_t + \lambda_2 \Sigma e_t + \lambda_3 \nabla e_t \tag{8.66}$$

The term ∇e_t means the first difference of the errors e_t, i.e., $\nabla e_t = e_t - e_{t-1}$. Like the PID equation, the empirical control equation has a proportional, an integral and a differential term. It can be used by APC or the results can be plotted on a common cause chart and reacted to by human operators, as described above. A special cause chart can be created to track the errors in the forecast from the empirical control equation. Such an approach may help to bring SPC and APC together to work on process improvement.

Process capability analysis

Process capability analysis is a two-stage process that involves:

1. Bringing a process into a state of statistical control for a reasonable period of time.
2. Comparing the long-term process performance to management or engineering requirements.

Process capability analysis can be prepared with either attribute data or continuous data *if and only if the process is in statistical control,* and has been for a reasonable period of time.*

Application of process capability methods to processes that are not in statistical control results in unreliable estimates of process capability and should never be considered acceptable.

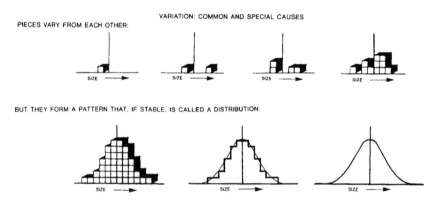

Figure 8.48—*Continued on next page . . .*

---

*Occasional freak values from known causes can usually be ignored.

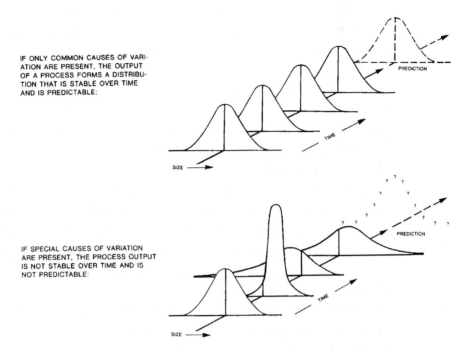

Figure 8.48—*Continued* . . .

Figure 8.48. Process control concepts illustrated.

From *Continuing Process Control and Process Capability Improvement*, p. 4a. Copyright 1983. Used by permission of the publisher, Ford Motor Company, Dearborn, Michigan.

HOW TO PERFORM A PROCESS CAPABILITY STUDY

This section presents a step-by-step approach to process capability analysis (Pyzdek, 1985). The approach makes frequent reference to materials presented elsewhere in this book.

1. **Select a candidate for the study**

   This step should be institutionalized. A goal of any organization should be ongoing process improvement. However, because a company has only a limited resource base and can't solve all problems simultaneously, it must set priorities for its efforts. The tools for this include Pareto analysis and fishbone diagrams.

2. **Define the process**

   It is all too easy to slip into the trap of solving the wrong problem. Once the candidate area has been selected in step 1, the scope of the study should be defined. A process is a unique combination of machines, tools, methods, and personnel engaged in adding value by providing a product or service. Each element of the process should be identified at this stage. This is not a trivial exercise. The input of many people may be required. There are likely to be a number of conflicting opinions about what the process actually involves.

3. **Procure resources for the study**

   Process capability studies disrupt normal operations and require significant expenditures of both material and human resources. Since it is a project of major importance, it should be managed as such. All of the usual project management techniques should be brought to bear. This includes planning, scheduling, and management status reporting.

4. **Evaluate the measurement system**

   Using the techniques described in Chapter 6, the measurement system's ability to do the job should be evaluated. Again, be prepared to spend the time necessary to get a valid means of measuring the process before going ahead.

5. **Prepare a control plan**

   The purpose of the control plan is twofold: 1) to isolate and control as many important variables as possible and, 2) to provide a mechanism for tracking variables that can not be completely controlled. The object of the capability analysis is to determine what the process can do if it is operated the way it is designed to be operated. This means that such obvious sources of *potential* variation as operators and vendors will be controlled while the study is conducted. In other words, a single well-trained operator will be used and the material will be from a single vendor.

   There are usually some variables that are important, but that are not controllable. One example is the ambient environment, such as temperature, barometric pressure, or humidity. Certain process variables may degrade as part of the normal operation; for example, tools wear and chemicals are depleted. These variables should still be tracked using logsheets and similar tools. See Chapter 1, Information systems requirements.

6. **Select a method for the analysis**
   The SPC method will depend on the decisions made up to this point. If the performance measure is an attribute, one of the attribute charts will be used. Variables charts will be used for process performance measures assessed on a continuous scale. Also considered will be the skill level of the personnel involved, need for sensitivity, and other resources required to collect, record, and analyze the data.

7. **Gather and analyze the data**
   One of the control charts described in this chapter should be used, plus common sense. It is usually advisable to have at least two people go over the data analysis to catch inadvertent errors in transcribing data or performing the analysis.

8. **Track down and remove special causes**
   A special cause of variation may be obvious, or it may take months of investigation to find it. The effect of the special cause may be good or bad. Removing a special cause that has a bad effect usually involves eliminating the cause itself. For example, if poorly trained operators are causing variability the special cause is the training system (not the operator) and it is eliminated by developing an improved training system or a process that requires less training. However, the removal of a beneficial special cause may actually involve incorporating the special cause into the normal operating procedure. For example, if it is discovered that materials with a particular chemistry produce better product the special cause is the newly discovered material and it can be made a common cause simply by changing the specification to assure that the new chemistry is always used.

9. **Estimate the process capability**
   One point can not be overemphasized: *the process capability can not be estimated until a state of statistical control has been achieved!* After this

stage has been reached, the methods described later in this chapter may be used. After the numerical estimate of process capability has been arrived at, it must be compared to management's goals for the process, or it can be used as an input into economic models. Deming's all-or-none rules provide a simple model that can be used to determine if the output from a process should be sorted 100% or shipped as-is.

10. **Establish a plan for continuous process improvement**
   Once a stable process state has been attained, steps should be taken to maintain it and improve upon it. SPC is just one means of doing this. Far more important than the particular approach taken is a company environment that makes continuous improvement a normal part of the daily routine of everyone.

STATISTICAL ANALYSIS OF PROCESS CAPABILITY DATA

This section presents several methods of analyzing the data obtained from a process capability study.

Control chart method: attributes data

1. Collect samples from 25 or more subgroups of consecutively produced units. Follow the guidelines presented in steps 1–10 above.
2. Plot the results on the appropriate control chart (e.g., c chart). If all groups are in statistical control, go to step #3. Otherwise the special cause of variation should be identified and action taken to eliminate it. Note that a special cause might be beneficial. Beneficial activities can be "eliminated" as special causes by doing them all of the time. A special cause is "special" only because it comes and goes, not because its impact is either good or bad.
3. Using the control limits from the previous step (called operation control limits), put the control chart to use for a period of time. Once you are satisfied that sufficient time has passed for most special causes to have been identified and eliminated, as verified by the control charts, go to step #4.

4. The process capability is estimated as the control chart *centerline*. The centerline on attribute charts is the long-term expected quality level of the process, e.g., the average proportion defective. This is the level created by the common causes of variation.

If the process capability doesn't meet management requirements, immediate action should be taken to modify the process for the better. "Problem solving" (e.g., studying each defective) won't help, and it may result in tampering. Whether the process meets requirements or not, always be on the lookout for possible process improvements. The control charts will provide verification of improvement.

Control chart method: variables data

1. Collect samples from 25 or more subgroups of consecutively produced units, following the 10-step plan described above.
2. Plot the results on the appropriate control chart (e.g., $\overline{X}$ and R chart). If all groups are in statistical control, go to step #3. Otherwise the special cause of variation should be identified and action taken to eliminate it.
3. Using the control limits from the previous step (called operation control limits), put the control chart to use for a period of time. Once you are satisfied that sufficient time has passed for most special causes to have been identified and eliminated, as verified by the control charts, process capability should be estimated as described below.

The process capability is estimated from the process average and standard deviation, where the standard deviation is computed based on the average range or average standard deviation. When statistical control has been achieved, the capability is the level created by the common causes of process variation. The formulas for estimating the process standard deviation are:

R chart method:

$$\hat{\sigma} = \overline{R}\big/d_2 \qquad\qquad (8.67)$$

s chart method:

$$\hat{\sigma} = \bar{s}\Big/c_4 \qquad (8.68)$$

The values d_2 and c_4 are constants from Table 11 in the Appendix.

PROCESS CAPABILITY INDEXES

Only now can the process be compared to engineering requirements. One way of doing this is by calculating "Capability Indexes." Several popular capability indexes are given in Table 8.12.

Table 8.12. Process capability analysis.

$$C_P = \dfrac{\textit{engineering tolerance}}{6\hat{\sigma}}$$	(8.69)
$$C_R = 100 \times \dfrac{6\hat{\sigma}}{\textit{engineering tolerance}}$$	(8.70)
$$C_M = \dfrac{\textit{engineering tolerance}}{8\hat{\sigma}}$$	(8.71)
$$Z_U = \dfrac{\textit{upper specification} - \overline{\overline{X}}}{\hat{\sigma}}$$	(8.72)
$$Z_L = \dfrac{\overline{\overline{X}} - \textit{lower specification}}{\hat{\sigma}}$$	(8.73)

Continued on next page . . .

Table 8.12—*Continued* . . .

$$Z_{MIN.} = Minimum\{Z_L, Z_U\} \qquad\qquad (8.74)$$

$$C_{PK} = \frac{Z_{MIN}}{3} \qquad\qquad (8.75)$$

$$C_{pm} = \frac{C_p}{\sqrt{1 + \dfrac{(\mu - T)^2}{\hat{\sigma}^2}}} \qquad\qquad (8.76)$$

INTERPRETING CAPABILITY INDEXES

Perhaps the biggest drawback of using process capability indexes is that they take the analysis a step away from the data. The danger is that the analyst will lose sight of the purpose of the capability analysis, which is to improve quality. To the extent that capability indexes help accomplish this goal, they are worthwhile. To the extent that they distract from the goal, they are harmful. The quality engineer should continually refer to this principle when interpreting capability indexes.

C_P—This is one of the first capability indexes used. The "natural tolerance" of the process is computed as 6σ. The index simply makes a direct comparison of the process natural tolerance to the engineering requirements. Assuming the process distribution is normal and the process average is exactly centered between the engineering requirements, a C_P index of 1 would give a "capable process." However, to allow a bit of room for process drift, the generally accepted minimum value for C_P is 1.33. In general, the larger C_P is, the better.

The C_P index has two major shortcomings. First, it can't be used unless there are both upper and lower specifications. Second, it does not account for process centering. If the process average is not exactly centered relative to the engineering requirements, the C_P index will give misleading results. In recent years, the C_P index has largely been replaced by C_{PK} (see below).

C_R—The C_R index is equivalent to the C_P index. The index simply makes a direct comparison of the process to the engineering requirements. Assuming the process distribution is normal and the process average is exactly centered between the engineering requirements, a C_R index of 100% would give a "capable process." However, to allow a bit of room for process drift, the generally accepted maximum value for C_R is 75%. In general, the smaller C_R is, the better. The C_R index suffers from the same shortcomings as the C_P index.

C_M—The C_M index is generally used to evaluate machine capability studies, rather than full-blown process capability studies. Since variation will increase when other sources of process variation are added (e.g., tooling, fixtures, materials, etc.), C_M uses an 8 sigma spread rather than a 6 sigma spread to represent the natural tolerance of the process.

Z_U—The Z_U index measures the process location (central tendency) relative to its standard deviation and the upper requirement. If the distribution is normal, the value of Z_U can be used to determine the percentage above the upper requirement by using Table 2 in the Appendix. The method is the same as described in Equations 8.20 and 8.21, using the Z statistic; simply use Z_U instead of using Z.

In general, the bigger Z_U is, the better. A value of at least +3 is required to assure that 0.1% or less defective will be produced. A value of +4 is generally desired to allow some room for process drift.

Z_L—The Z_L index measures the process location relative to its standard deviation and the lower requirement. If the distribution is normal, the value of Z_L can be used to determine the percentage above the upper requirement by using Table 2 in the Appendix. The method is the same as described in Equations 8.20 and 8.21, using the Z transformation, except that you use $-Z_L$ instead of using Z.

In general, the bigger Z_L is, the better. A value of at least +3 is required to assure that 0.1% or less defective will be produced. A value of +4 is generally desired to allow some room for process drift.

Z_{MIN}—The value of Z_{MIN} is simply the smaller of the Z_L or the Z_U values. It is used in computing C_{PK}.

C_{PK}—The value of C_{PK} is simply Z_{MIN} divided by 3. Since the smallest value represents the nearest specification, the value of C_{PK} tells you if the process is truly capable of meeting requirements. A C_{PK} of at least +1 is required, and +1.33 is preferred. Note that C_{PK} is closely related to C_P, the difference between C_{PK} and C_P represents the potential gain to be had from centering the process.

C_{pm}—The value of C_{pm} measures both the process spread and its central tendency relative to the Target value, T. If the process mean is equal to the target, then C_{pm} will equal C_P. The difference between C_{pm} and C_P indicates the potential gain from centering the process. C_{pm} differs from C_{PK} in that its focus is on the center of the specification range while C_{PK} is based on the specification limits.

EXAMPLE OF CAPABILITY ANALYSIS USING NORMALLY DISTRIBUTED VARIABLES DATA

Assume we have conducted a capability analysis using X bar and R charts with subgroups of 5. Also assume that we found the process to be in statistical control with a grand average of 0.99832 and an average range of 0.2205. From the table of d_2 values (Appendix Table 11), d_2 is found to be 2.326 for subgroups of 5. Thus, using Equation 8.67,

$$\hat{\sigma} = \frac{0.2205}{2.326} = 0.00948$$

Before process capability can be analyzed, the requirements must be known. For this process the requirements are a lower specification of 0.980 and an upper specification of 1.020 (1.000±0.020). With this information, plus the knowledge that the process performance has been in statistical control, the capability indexes for this process can be computed.

$$C_P = \frac{engineering\ tolerance}{6\hat{\sigma}} = \frac{1.020 - 0.9800}{6 \times 0.00948} = 0.703$$

$$C_R = 100 \times \frac{6\hat{\sigma}}{engineering\ tolerance} = 100 \times \frac{6 \times 0.00948}{0.04} = 142.2\%$$

$$C_M = \frac{engineering\ tolerance}{8\hat{\sigma}} = \frac{0.04}{8 \times 0.00948} = 0.527$$

$$Z_U = \frac{upper\ specification - \overline{\overline{X}}}{\hat{\sigma}} = \frac{1.020 - 0.99832}{0.00948} = 2.3$$

$$Z_L = \frac{\overline{\overline{X}} - lower\ specification}{\hat{\sigma}} = \frac{0.99832 - 0.980}{0.00948} = 1.9$$

$$Z_{MIN} = \text{Minimum}\{1.9, 2.3\} = 1.9$$

$$C_{PK} = \frac{Z_{MIN}}{3} = \frac{1.9}{3} = 0.63$$

Assuming that the target is precisely 1.000,

$$C_{pm} = \frac{C_p}{\sqrt{1 + \frac{\left(\overline{\overline{X}} - T\right)^2}{\hat{\sigma}^2}}} = \frac{0.703}{\sqrt{1 + \frac{(0.99832 - 1.000)^2}{0.00948^2}}} = 0.692$$

DISCUSSION

C_P—(0.703) Since the minimum acceptable value for this index is 1, the 0.703 result indicates that this process can not meet the requirements. Furthermore, since the C_P index doesn't consider the centering process, the process can't be made acceptable by merely adjusting the process closer to the center of the requirements. Thus, the Z_L, Z_U, and Z_{MIN} values are expected to be unacceptable too.

C_R—(142.2%) This value always gives the same conclusions as the C_P index. The number itself means that the "natural tolerance" of the process uses 142.2% of the engineering requirement, which is, of course, unacceptable.

C_M—(0.527) The C_M index should be 1.33 or greater. Obviously it is not. If this were a machine capability study the value of the C_M index would indicate that the machine was incapable of meeting the requirement.

Z_U—(+2.3) A Z_U value of at least +3 is desired, so this value is unacceptable. Z_U can be used to estimate the percentage of production that will exceed the upper specification. In Table 2 in the Appendix it is found that approximately 1.1% will be oversized.

Z_L—(+1.9) A Z_L value of at least +3 is desired, so this value is unacceptable. Z_L can be used to estimate the percentage of production that will be below the lower specification. In Table 2 in the Appendix it is foundthat approximately 2.9% will be undersized. When added to the 1.1% oversized a total reject rate of 4.0% is estimated with a projected yield of 96.0%.

Z_{MIN}—(+1.9) The smaller of Z_L and Z_U. Since neither of these two results were acceptable, Z_{MIN} cannot be acceptable.

C_{PK}—(0.63) The value of C_{PK} is only slightly smaller than that of C_P. This indicating that not much is gained by centering the process. The actual amount gained can be calculated by assuming the process is exactly centered at 1.000 and recalculating Z_{MIN}. This gives a predicted total reject rate of 3.6% instead of 4.0%.

C_{pm}—(0.692) The value of C_{pm} is only slightly larger than the value of C_P, indicating that not much will be gained by cenering the process. The amount of gain can be computed as indicated in the discussion for C_{PK}.

Process control for short and small runs

A starting place for understanding statistical process control (SPC) for short and small runs is to define the terms. The question "what *is* a short run?" will be answered for these purposes as an environment that has a large number of jobs per operator in a production cycle, each job involving different product. A production cycle is typically a week or a month. A *small run* is a situation where only a very few products of the same type are to be produced. An extreme case of a small run is the one-of-a-kind product, such as the Hubble Space Telescope. Short runs need not be small runs; a can manufacturing line can produce over 100,000 cans in an hour or two. Likewise small runs are not necessarily short runs; the Hubble Space Telescope took over 15 years to get into orbit (and even longer to get into orbit and working properly)! However, it is possible to have runs that are both short *and* small. Programs such as Just-In-Time inventory control (JIT) are making this situation more common all of the time.

Process control for either small or short runs involve similar strategies. Both situations involve markedly different approaches than those used in the classical mass-production environment. Thus, this text will treat both the small run and the short run situations simultaneously. However, the SPC tool that best fits a particular situation should be selected.

STRATEGIES FOR SHORT AND SMALL RUNS

Juran's famous trilogy separates quality activities into three distinct phases: (Juran and Gryna, 1988)
- Planning
- Control
- Improvement

Figure 8.49 provides a graphic portrayal of the Juran trilogy.

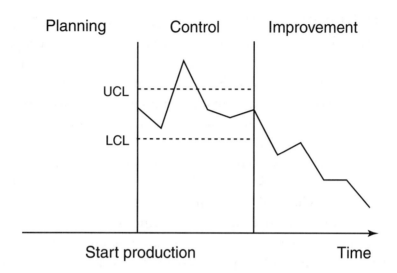

Figure 8.49. Juran's trilogy.

For small or short runs the emphasis should be placed in the planning phase. As much as possible it needs to be done *before* any product is made, because it simply isn't possible to waste time or materials "learning from mistakes" made during production. It is also helpful to realize that the Juran trilogy is usually applied to *products*, while SPC applies to *processes*. It is quite possible that the element being monitored with SPC is a process element and not a product feature at all. In this case there really is no "short run," despite appearances to the contrary.

A common problem with application of SPC to short/small runs is that people fail to realize the limitations of SPC in this application. Even the use of SPC to *long production runs* will benefit from a greater emphasis on pre-production planning. In the best of all worlds, SPC will merely confirm that the correct process has been selected and controlled in such a way that it consistently produces well-designed parts at very close to the desired target values for every dimension.

PREPARING THE SHORT RUN PROCESS CONTROL PLAN (PCP)

Plans for short runs require a great deal of up-front attention. The objective is to create a list of as many potential sources of variation as possible and to take action to deal with them *before* going into production. One of the first steps to be taken is to identify which processes may be used to produce a given part; this is called the "Approved Process List." Analogously, parts that can be produced by a given process should also be identified; this is called the "Approved Parts List." These determinations are made based on process capability studies (Pyzdek, 1992). The approach described in this guide uses process capability indices, specifically C_{pk} (the number of standard deviations between the mean and the nearest specification limit). The use of this capability index depends on a number of assumptions, such as normality of the data etc.; Pyzdek (*Quality Engineering*, 1992) describes the proper use, and some common abuses, of capability indices.

Because short runs usually involve less than the recommended number of pieces the acceptability criteria is usually modified. When less than 50 observations are used to determine the capability I recommend that the capability indices be modified by using a $\pm 4\sigma$ minimum acceptable process width (instead of $\pm 3\sigma$) and a minimum acceptable C_{pk} of 1.5 (instead of 1.33). Don't bother making formal capability estimates until you have at least 20 observations. (You will see below that these observations need not always be from 20 separate parts.)

When preparing for short runs it often happens that actual production parts are not available in sufficient quantity for process capability studies. One way of dealing with this situation is to study process elements separately and to then sum the variances from all of the known elements to obtain an estimate of the best overall variance a given process will be able to produce.

For example, in an aerospace firm that produced conventional guided missiles, each missile contained thousands of different parts. In any given month only a small number of missiles were produced. Thus, the CNC machine shop (and the rest of the plant) was faced with a small/short run situation. However it was not possible to do separate pre-production capability studies of each part separately. The approach used instead was to design a special test part that would provide estimates of the machine's ability to produce every basic type of characteristic (flatness, straightness, angularity, location, etc.). Each CNC machine produced a number of these test parts under controlled conditions and the results were plotted on a Short Run $\overline{X}$ and R chart (described later in this chapter). The studies were repeated periodically for each machine.

These studies provided pre-production estimates of the machine's ability to produce different characteristics. However, these estimates were always *better* than the process would be able to do with actual production parts. Actual production would involve different operators, tooling, fixtures, materials, and other common and special causes not evaluated by the *machine capability study*. Preliminary Approved Parts Lists and Preliminary Approved Process Lists were created from the capability analysis using the more stringent acceptability criteria described above (C_{pk} at least 1.5 based on a ±4σ process spread). When production commenced the actual results of the production runs were used instead of the estimates based on special runs. Once sufficient data were available, the parts were removed from the preliminary lists and placed on the appropriate permanent lists.

When creating Approved Parts and Approved Process lists the most stringent product requirements should be used to determine the *process requirement*. For example, if a process will be used to drill holes in 100 different parts with hole location tolerances ranging from 0.001 inches to 0.030 inches, the process requirement is 0.001 inches. The process capability estimate is based on its ability to hold the 0.001 inch tolerance.

The approach used is summarized as follows:
1. Get the process into statistical control.
2. Set the control limits *without regard to the requirement*.
3. Based on the calculated process capability, determine if the most stringent product requirement can be met.

PROCESS AUDIT

The requirements for all processes should be documented. A process audit checklist should be prepared and used to determine the condition of the process prior to production. The audit can be performed by the operator himself, but the results should be documented. The audit should cover known or suspected sources of variation. These include such things as the production plan, condition of fixtures, gage calibration, the resolution of the gaging being used, obvious problems with materials or equipment, operator changes, and so on.

SPC can be used to monitor the results of the process audits over time. For example, an audit score can be computed and tracked using an individuals control chart.

SELECTING PROCESS CONTROL ELEMENTS

Many short run SPC programs bog down because the number of control charts being used grows like Topsy. Before anyone knows what is happening the walls are plastered with charts that few understand and no one uses. The operators and inspectors wind up spending more time filling out paperwork than they spend on true value-added work. Eventually the entire SPC program collapses under its own weight.

One reason for this is that people tend to focus their attention on the *product* rather than on the *process*. Control elements are erroneously selected because they are functionally important. A great fear is that an important product feature will be produced out of specification and that it will slip by unnoticed. This is a misunderstanding of the purpose of SPC, which is to provide a means of *process* control; SPC is not intended to be a substitute for inspection or testing. The guiding rule of selecting control items for SPC is:

> SPC control items should be selected to provide a maximum amount of information regarding the state of the process at a minimum cost.

Fortunately most process elements are correlated with one another. Because of this, one process element may provide information not only about itself, but about several others as well. This means that a small number of process control elements will often explain a large portion of the process variance.

Although sophisticated statistical methods exist to help determine which groups of process elements explain the most variance, common sense and knowledge of the process can often do as well, if not better. The key is to think about the process carefully. What are the "generic process elements" that affect all parts? How do the process elements combine to affect the product? Do several process elements affect a single product feature? Do changes in one process element automatically cause changes in some other process elements? What process elements or product features are most sensitive to unplanned changes?

Example one

The CNC machines mentioned earlier were extremely complex. A typical machine had dozens of different tools and produced hundreds of different parts with thousands of characteristics. However, the SPC team reasoned that the machines themselves involved only a small number of "generic operations:" select a tool, position the tool, remove metal, and so on. Further study revealed that nearly all of the problems encountered after the initial setup involved only the ability of the machine to position the tool precisely. A control plan was created that called for monitoring no more than one variable for each axis of movement. The features selected were those farthest from the machine's "home position" which involved the most difficult to control operations. Often a single feature provided control of more than one axis of movement; for example the location of a single hole provided information on the location of the tool in both the X and Y directions.

As a result of this system no part had more than four features monitored with control charts, even though many parts had thousands of features. Subsequent sophisticated multivariate evaluation of the accumulated data by a statistician revealed that the choices made by the team explained over 90% of the process variance.

Example two

A wave solder machine was used to solder printed circuit boards for a manufacturer of electronic test equipment. After several months of applying SPC the SPC team evaluated the data and decided that they needed only a single measure of product quality for SPC purposes: defects per 1,000 solder joints. A single control chart was used for dozens of different circuit boards. The team also determined that most of the process variables being checked could be eliminated. The only process variables monitored in the future would be flux density, solder chemistry (provided by the vendor), solder temperature, and final rinse contamination. Historic data showed that one of these variables was nearly always out-of-control when process problems were encountered. Other variables were monitored with periodic audits using checksheets, but they were not charted.

Notice that in both of these examples all of the variables being monitored were related to the *process*, even though some of them were product features. The terms "short run" and "small run" refer to the product variables only; the process is in continuous operation so its run size and duration is neither small nor short.

THE SINGLE PART PROCESS

The ultimate small run is the single part. A great deal can be learned by studying single pieces, even if the situation involves more than one part.

The application of SPC to single pieces may seem incongruous. Yet when it is considered that the "P" in SPC stands for *process* and not product, perhaps it is possible after all. Even the company producing a one-of-a-kind product usually does so with the same equipment, employees, facilities, etc. In other words, the same *process* is used to produce different *products*. Also, products are usually produced that are similar, even though not identical. This is also to be expected. It would be odd indeed to find a company fabricating microchips one day and baking bread the next. The processes are too dissimilar. The company assets are, at least to a degree, product-specific.

This discussion implies that the key to controlling the quality of single parts is to concentrate on the process elements rather than on the product features.

This is the same rule applied above to larger runs. In fact, it's a good rule to apply to all SPC applications, regardless of the number of parts being produced!

Consider a company manufacturing communications satellites. The company produces a satellite every year or two. The design and complexity of each satellite is quite different than any other. How can SPC be applied at this company?

A close look at a satellite will reveal immense complexity. The satellite will have thousands of terminals, silicon solar cells, solder joints, fasteners, and so on. Hundreds, even thousands of people are involved in the design, fabrication, testing, and assembly. In other words, there are *processes* that involve massive amounts of repetition. The processes include engineering (errors per engineering drawing); terminal manufacture (size, defect rates); solar cell manufacture (yields, electrical properties); soldering (defects per 1,000 joints; strength); fastener installation quality (torque) and so on.

Another example of a single-piece run is software development. The "part" in this case is the working copy of the software delivered to the customer. Only a single unit of product is involved. How can SPC be used here?

Again, the answer comes when attention is directed to the underlying process. Any marketable software product will consist of thousands, perhaps millions of bytes of finished machine code. This code will be compiled from thousands of lines of source code. The source code will be arranged in modules; the modules will contain procedures; the procedures will contain functions; and so on. Computer science has developed a number of ways of measuring the quality of computer code. The resulting numbers, called computer metrics, can be analyzed using SPC tools just like any other numbers. The processes that produced the code can thus be measured, controlled and improved. If the process is in statistical control, the process elements, such as programmer selection and training, coding style, planning, procedures, etc. must be examined. If the process is not in statistical control, the special cause of the problem must be identified.

As discussed earlier, although the single part process is a small run, it isn't necessarily a short run. By examining the process rather than the part, improvement possibilities will begin to suggest themselves. The key is to find the process, to define its elements so they may be measured, controlled, and improved.

OTHER ELEMENTS OF THE PROCESS CONTROL PLAN

In addition to the selection of process control elements, the PCP should also provide information on the method of inspection, dates and results of measurement error studies, dates and results of process capability studies, subgroup sizes and methods of selecting subgroups, sampling frequency, required operator certifications, pre-production checklists, notes and suggestions regarding previous problems, etc. In short, the PCP provides a complete, detailed roadmap that describes how process integrity will be measured and maintained. By preparing a PCP the *inputs* to the process are controlled, thus assuring that the *outputs* from the process will be consistently acceptable.

SHORT RUN STATISTICAL PROCESS CONTROL TECHNIQUES

Short production runs are a way of life with many manufacturing companies. In the future, this will be the case even more often. The trend in manufacturing has been toward smaller production runs with product tailored to the specific needs of individual customers. Henry Ford's days of "the customer can have any color, as long as it's black" have long since passed.

Classical SPC methods, such as $\overline{X}$ and R charts, were developed in the era of mass production of identical parts. Production runs often lasted for weeks, months, or even years. Many of the "SPC rules of thumb" currently in use were created for this situation. For example, there is the rule that control limits should not be calculated until data is available from at least 25 subgroups of 5. This may not have been a problem in 1930, but it certainly is today. In fact, many *entire production runs* involve fewer parts than required to start a standard control chart!

Many times the usual SPC methods can be modified slightly to work with short and small runs. For example, $\overline{X}$ and R control charts can be created using moving averages and moving ranges (Pyzdek, 1989). However, there are SPC methods that are particularly well suited to application on short or small runs.

VARIABLES DATA

Variables data, sometimes called continuous data, involve measurements such as size, weight, Ph, temperature, etc. In theory data are variables data if no two values are exactly the same. In practice this is seldom the case. As a rough rule-of-thumb data can be considered to be variables data if at least ten different values occur and repeat values make up no more than 20% of the data set. If this is not the case, the data may be too discrete to use standard control charts. An attribute procedure such as the demerit charts described later in this text can be considered. The following approaches to SPC for short or small runs are discussed:

1. **Exact method**—Tables of special control chart constants are used to create X, $\overline{X}$ and R charts that compensate for the fact that a limited number of subgroups are available for computing control limits. The exact method is also used to compute control limits when using a code value chart or stabilized X or $\overline{X}$ and R charts (see below). The exact method allows the calculation of control limits that are correct when only a small amount of data is available. As more data becomes available the exact method updates control limits until, finally, no further updates are required and standard control chart factors can be used (Pyzdek, 1992).

2. **Code value charts**—Code value charts are control charts created by subtracting nominal or other target values from actual measurements. These charts are often standardized so that measurement units are converted to whole numbers. For example, if measurements are in thousandths of an inch a reading of 0.011 inches above nominal would be recorded simply as "11." Code value charts enable the user to plot several parts from a given process on a single chart, or to plot several features from a single part on the same control chart. The Exact Method can be used to adjust the control limits when code value charts are created with limited data.

3. **Stabilized control charts for variables**—Statisticians have known about normalizing transformations for many years. This approach can be used to create control charts that are independent of the unit of measure and

scaled in such a way that several different characteristics can be plotted on the same control chart. Since stabilized control charts are independent of the unit of measure, they can be thought of as true *process control charts*. The Exact Method adjusts the control limits for stabilized charts created with limited data.

EXACT METHOD OF COMPUTING CONTROL LIMITS FOR SHORT AND SMALL RUNS

This procedure, adapted from Hillier (1969) and Proschan and Savage (1960), applies to short runs or to any situation where a small number of subgroups will be used to set up a control chart. It consists of three stages:

1. finding the process (establishing statistical control);
2. setting limits for the remainder of the initial run;
3. setting limits for future runs.

The procedure correctly compensates for the uncertainties involved when computing control limits with small amounts of data.

Stage one: find the process

1. Collect an initial sample of subgroups (g). The factors for the recommended minimum number of subgroups are shown in Appendix Table 15 enclosed in a dark box. If it is not possible to get the minimum number of subgroups, use the appropriate control chart constant for the number of subgroups you actually have.

2. Using Table 15 compute the Range chart control limits using the equation Upper Control Limit for Ranges $(UCL_R) = D_{4F} \times \bar{R}$. Compare the subgroup ranges to the UCL_R and drop any out-of-control groups. Repeat the process until all remaining subgroup ranges are smaller than UCL_R.

3. Using the $\bar{R}$ value found in step #2, compute the control limits for the averages or individuals chart. The control limits are found by adding and subtracting $A_{2F} \times \bar{R}$ from the overall average. Drop any subgroups that have out-of-control averages and recompute. Continue until all remaining values are within the control limits. Go to stage two.

Stage two: set limits for remainder of the initial run

1. Using Table 15 compute the control limits for the remainder of the run. Use the A_{2S} factors for the $\overline{X}$ chart and the D_{4S} factors for the R chart; g = the number of groups used to compute stage one control limits.

Stage three: set limits for a future run

1. After the run is complete, combine the raw data from the entire run and perform the analysis as described in stage one above. Use the results of this analysis to set limits for the next run, following the stage two procedure. If more than 25 groups are available, use a standard table of control chart constants.

Notes

1. Stage three assumes that there are no special causes of variation between runs. If there are, the process may go out of control when using the stage three control limits. In these cases, remove the special causes. If this isn't possible, apply this procedure to each run separately (i.e., start over each time).
2. This approach will lead to the use of standard control chart tables when enough data is accumulated.
3. The control chart constants for the first stage are A_{2F} and D_{4F} (the "F" subscript stands for First-stage); for the second stage use A_{2S} and D_{4S}. These factors correspond to the A_2 and D_4 factors usually used, except that they are adjusted for the small number of subgroups actually available.

Setup approval procedure

The following procedure can be used to determine if a setup is acceptable using a relatively small number of sample units.

1. After the initial setup, run 3 to 10 pieces *without adjusting the process.*
2. Compute the average and the range of the sample.
3. Compute $T = \left[\dfrac{average - target}{range} \right]$

    using absolute values (i.e., ignore any minus signs.) The target value is usually the specification midpoint or nominal.
4. If T is less than the critical T in Table 8.13 accept the setup. Otherwise adjust the setup to bring it closer to the target. NOTE: there is approximately 1 chance in 20 that an on-target process will fail this test.

Table 8.13. Critical value for setup acceptance.

n	3	4	5	6	7	8	9	10
Critical T	0.885	0.529	0.388	0.312	0.263	0.230	0.205	0.186

Example

Assume that SPC is used for a process that involves producing a part in lots of 30 parts each. The parts are produced approximately once each month. The control feature on the part is the depth of a groove and every piece will be measured. Subgroups of size three are used and the stage one control limits are computed after the first five groups. The measurements obtained are shown in Table 8.14.

Table 8.14. Raw data for example of exact method.

SUBGROUP	SAMPLE NUMBER				
NUMBER	1	2	3	$\overline{X}$	R
1	0.0989	0.0986	01031	0.1002	0.0045
2	0.0986	0.0985	0.1059	0.1010	0.0074
3	0.1012	0.1004	0.1000	0.1005	0.0012
4	0.1023	0.1027	0.1000	0.1017	0.0027
5	0.0992	0.0997	0.0988	0.0992	0.0009

Using the data in Table 8.14 the grand average and average range can be computed:

$$\text{Grand average} = 0.10053$$
$$\text{Average range } (\overline{R}) = 0.00334$$

From Appendix Table 15 the first stage constant is obtained for the range chart of $D_{4F} = 2.4$ in the row for g = 5 groups and a subgroup size of 3. Thus,

$$UCL_R = D_{4F} \times \overline{R} = 2.4 \times 0.00334 = 0.0080$$

All of the ranges are below this control limit, so we can proceed to the analysis of the averages chart. If any R was above the control limit, we would try to determine why before proceeding.

For the averages chart the following are obtained:

$$LCL_{\overline{X}} = \text{grand average} - A_{2F} \times \overline{R}$$
$$= 0.10053 - 1.20 \times 0.00334 = 0.09652 \text{ (rounded)}$$

$$UCL_{\overline{X}} = \text{grand average} + A_{2F} \times \overline{R}$$
$$= 0.10053 + 1.20 \times 0.00334 = 0.10454 \text{ (rounded)}$$

All of the subgroup averages are between these limits. Now setting limits for the remainder of the run we use $D_{4S} = 3.4$ and $A_{2S} = 1.47$. This gives, after rounding,

$$UCL_R = 0.01136$$
$$LCL_{\overline{X}} = 0.09562$$
$$UCL_{\overline{X}} = 0.10544$$

If desired, this procedure can be repeated when a larger number of subgroups becomes available, say 10 groups. This would provide somewhat better estimates of the control limits, but it involves considerable administrative overhead. When the entire run is finished there will be 10 subgroups of 3 per subgroup. The data from all of these subgroups should be used to compute stage one and stage two control limits. The resulting stage two control limits would then be applied to the *next run* of this part number.

By applying this method in conjunction with the code value charts or stabilized charts described below, the control limits can be applied to the next parts produced on this process (assuming the part-to-part difference can be made negligible). Note that if the standard control chart factors were used the limits for *both* stages would be (values are rounded)

$$UCL_R = 0.00860$$
$$LCL_{\overline{X}} = 0.09711$$
$$UCL_{\overline{X}} = 0.10395$$

As the number of subgroups available for computing the control limits increases, the "short run" control limits approach the standard control limits. However, if the standard control limits are used when only small amounts of data are available there is a greater chance of erroneously rejecting a process that is actually in control (Hillier, 1969).

CODE VALUE CHARTS

This procedure allows the control of multiple features with a single control chart. It consists of making a simple transformation to the data, namely

$$\hat{x} = \frac{X - Target}{unit\ of\ measure} \qquad (8.77)$$

The resulting $\hat{x}$ values are used to compute the control limits and as plotted points on the $\overline{X}$ and R charts. This makes the target dimension irrelevant for the purposes of SPC and makes it possible to use a single control chart for several different features or part numbers.

Example

A lathe is used to produce several different sizes of gear blanks, as is indicated in Figure 8.50.

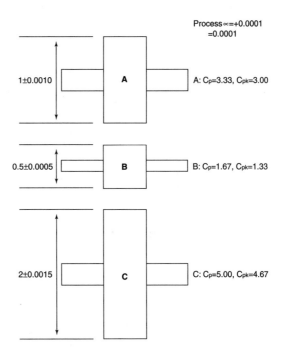

Figure 8.50. Some of the gear blanks to be machined.

Product engineering wants all of the gear blanks to be produced as near as possible to their nominal size. Process engineering believes that the process will have as little deviation for larger sizes as it does for smaller sizes. Quality engineering believes that the inspection system will produce approximately the same amount of measurement error for larger sizes as for smaller sizes. Process capability studies and measurement error studies support these conclusions. (I hope you are starting to get the idea that a number of assumptions are being made and that they must be valid before using code value charts.)

Based on these conclusions, the code value chart is recommended. By using the code value chart the amount of paperwork will be reduced and more data will be available for setting control limits. Also, the process history will be easier to follow since the information won't be fragmented among several different charts. The data in Table 8.15 show some of the early results.

Table 8.15. Deviation from target in hundred-thousandths.

| PART | NOMINAL | NO. | SAMPLE NUMBER | | | $\overline{X}$ | R |
			1	2	3		
A	1.0000	1	4	3	25	10.7	22
		2	3	3	39	15.0	36
		3	16	12	10	12.7	6
B	0.5000	4	21	24	10	18.3	14
		5	6	8	4	6.0	4
		6	19	7	21	15.7	14
C	2.0000	7	1	11	4	5.3	10
		8	1	25	8	11.3	24
		9	6	8	7	7.0	2

Note that the process must be able to produce the *tightest tolerance* of ±0.0005 inches. The capability analysis should indicate its ability to do this; i.e., C_{pk} should be at least 1.33 based on the tightest tolerance. It will *not* be allowed to drift or deteriorate when the less stringently toleranced parts are produced. *Process control* is independent of the *product requirements.*

Permitting the process to degrade to its worst acceptable level (from the product perspective) creates engineering nightmares when the more tightly toleranced parts come along again. It also confuses and demoralizes operators and others trying to maintain high levels of quality. In fact, it may be best to publish only the process performance requirements and to keep the product requirements secret.

The control chart of the data in Table 8.15 is shown in Figure 8.51. Since only nine groups were available, the exact method was used to compute the control limits. Note that the control chart shows the *deviations* on the $\overline{X}$ and R chart axes, not the actual measured dimensions; e.g., the value of Part A, subgroup #1, sample #1 was +0.00004" from the target value of 1.0000" and it is shown as a deviation of +4 hundred-thousandths; i.e., the part checked 1.00004". The stage one control chart shows that the process is obviously in statistical control, but it is producing parts that are consistently too large - regardless of the nominal dimension. If the process were on target, the grand average would be very close to 0. The setup problem would have been detected by the second subgroup if the setup approval procedure described earlier in this text had been followed.

This ability to see process performance across different part numbers is one of the advantages of Code Value Charts. It is good practice to actually identify the changes in part numbers on the charts, as is done in Figure 8.51.

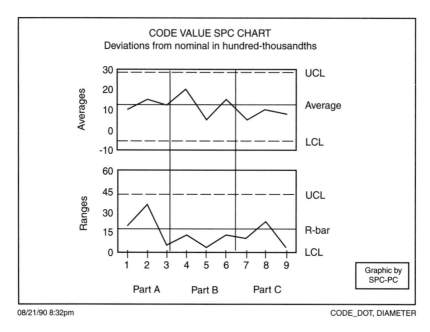

Figure 8.51. Code value chart of Table 8.15 data.

STABILIZED CONTROL CHARTS FOR VARIABLES

All control limits, for standard sized runs or short and small runs, are based on methods that determine if a process statistic falls within limits that might be expected from chance variation (common causes) alone. In most cases, the statistic is based on actual measurements from the process and it is in the same unit of measure as the process measurements. As with code value charts, it is sometimes useful to transform the data in some way. With code value charts a simple transformation was used that removed the effect of changing nominal and target dimensions. While useful, this approach still requires that all measurements be in the same units of measurement, e.g., all inches, all grams, etc. For example, all of the variables on the control chart for the different gear blanks had to be in units of hundred-thousandths of an inch. To plot, for example, the perpendicularity of two surfaces on the gear blank a separate control chart would have been needed because the units would be in degrees instead of inches.

Stabilized control charts for variables overcome the units of measure problem by converting all measurements into standard, non-dimensional units. Such "standardizing transformations" are not new; they have been around for many years and they are commonly used in all types of statistical analyses. The two transformations used here are shown in Equations 8.78 and 8.79.

$$\frac{\left(\overline{X} - grand\ average\right)}{\overline{R}} \tag{8.78}$$

$$\frac{R}{\overline{R}} \tag{8.79}$$

Equation 8.78 involves subtracting the grand average from each subgroup average (or from each individual measurement if the subgroup size is one) and dividing the result by $\overline{R}$. Note that this is not the usual statistical transformation where the denominator is σ. By using $\overline{R}$ as our denominator instead of s some desirable statistical properties are sacrificed such as normality and independence to gain simplicity. However, the resulting control charts remain valid and the false alarm risk based on points beyond the control limits is identical to standard control charts. Also, as with all transformations, this approach suffers in that it involves plotting numbers that are not in the usual engineering units people are accustomed to working with. This makes it more difficult to interpret the results and spot data entry errors.

Equation 8.79 divides each subgroup range by the average range. Since the numerator and denominator are both in the same unit of measurement, the unit of measurement cancels leaving a number that is in terms of the number of average ranges, R's. It turns out that control limits are also in the same units; i.e., to compute standard control limits simply multiply R by the appropriate table constant to determine the width between the control limits.

Hillier (1969) noted that this is equivalent to using the transformations shown in Equations 8.78 and 8.79 with control limits set at

$$-A_2 \leq \frac{\left(\overline{X} - grand\ average\right)}{\overline{R}} \leq A_2 \qquad (8.80)$$

for the individuals or averages chart. Control limits are

$$D_3 \leq \frac{R}{\overline{R}} \leq D_4 \qquad (8.81)$$

for the range chart. Duncan (1974) described a similar transformation for attribute charts, p charts in particular (see below) and called the resulting chart a "stabilized p chart." We will call charts of the transformed variables data stabilized charts as well.

Stabilized charts allow plotting multiple units of measurement on the same control chart. The procedure described in this text for stabilized variables charts requires that all subgroups be of the same size.* The procedure for stabilized attribute charts, described later in this text allows varying subgroup sizes. When using stabilized charts the control limits are always fixed. The raw data are "transformed" to match the scale determined by the control limits. When only limited amounts of data are available, the constants in Appendix Table 15 should be used for computing control limits for stabilized variables charts. As more data become available, the Appendix Table 15 constants approach the constants in standard tables of control chart factors. Table 8.16 summarizes the control limits for stabilized averages, stabilized ranges, and stabilized individuals control charts. The values for A_2, D_3 and D_4 can be found in standard control chart factor tables.

---

*The procedure for stabilized attribute charts, described later in this chapter, allows varying subgroup sizes.

Table 8.16. Control limits for stabilized charts.

STAGE	AVAILABLE GROUPS		CHART			APPENDIX TABLE
			$\overline{X}$	R	x	
One	25 or less	LCL	$-A_{2F}$	None	$-A_{2F}$	15
		Average	0	1	0	
		UCL	$+A_{2F}$	D_{4F}	$+A_{2F}$	
Two	25 or less	LCL	$-A_{2S}$	None	$-A_{2S}$	15
		Average	0	1	0	
		UCL	$+A_{2S}$	D_{4S}	$+A_{2S}$	
One	More than	LCL	$-A_2$	D_3	-2.66	11
or	25	Average	0	1	0	
Two		UCL	$+A_2$	D_4	$+2.66$	

Example

A circuit board is produced on an electroplating line. Three parameters are considered important for SPC purposes: lead concentration of the solder plating bath, plating thickness, and resistance. Process capability studies have been done using more than 25 groups; thus, based on Table 8.16 the control limits are

$$-A_2 \leq \overline{X} \leq A_2$$

for the averages control chart, and

$$D_3 \leq R \leq D_4$$

for the ranges control chart. The actual values of the constants A_2, D_3, and D_4 depend on the subgroup size, for subgroups of three A_2=1.023, D_3=0 and D_4=2.574.

The capabilities are shown in Table 8.17.

Table 8.17. Process capabilities for example.

FEATURE CODE	FEATURE	GRAND AVG.	AVG. RANGE
A	Lead %	10%	1%
B	Plating thickness	0.005"	0.0005"
C	Resistance	0.1Ω	0.0005Ω

A sample of three will be taken for each feature. The three lead concentration samples are taken at three different locations in the tank. The results of one such set of sample measurements is shown in Table 8.18, along with their stabilized values.

Table 8.18. Sample data for example.

NUMBER	LEAD % (A)	THICKNESS (B)	RESISTANCE (C)
1	11%	0.0050"	0.1000Ω
2	11%	0.0055"	0.1010Ω
3	8%	0.0060"	0.1020Ω
$\overline{X}$	10%	0.0055"	0.1010Ω
R	3%	0.0010"	0.0020Ω
$\dfrac{(x - \overline{x})}{\overline{R}}$	0	1	2
$\dfrac{R}{\overline{R}}$	3	2	4

On the control chart *only the extreme values are plotted*. Figure 8.52 shows a stabilized control chart for several subgroups. Observe that the feature responsible for the plotted point is written on the control chart. If a long series of largest or smallest values come from the same feature it is an indication that the feature has changed. If the process is in statistical control for all features, the feature responsible for the extreme values will vary randomly.

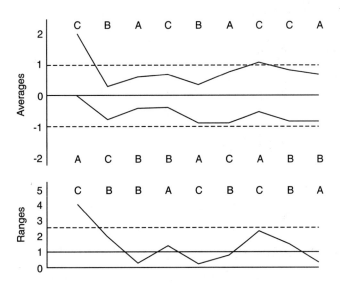

Figure 8.52. Stabilized control chart for variables.

When using stabilized charts it is possible to have a single control chart accompany a particular part or lot of parts through the entire production sequence. For example, the circuit boards described above could have a control chart that shows the results of process and product measurement for characteristics at all stages of production. The chart would then show the "processing history" for the part or lot. The advantage would be a coherent log of the production of a given part. Table 8.19 illustrates a process control plan that could possibly use this approach.

Caution is in order if the processing history approach is used. When small and short runs are common, the history of a given process can be lost among the charts of many different parts. This can be avoided by keeping a separate chart for each distinct process; additional paperwork is involved, but it might be worth the effort. If the additional paperwork burden becomes large, computerized solutions may be worth investigating.

Table 8.19. PWB fab process capabilities and SPC plan.

OPERATION	FEATURE	$\bar{X}$	$\bar{R}$	n
Clean	Bath Ph	7.5	0.1	3/hr
	Rinse contamination	100 ppm	5 ppm	3/hr
	Cleanliness quality rating	78	4	3 pcs/hr
Laminate	Riston thickness	1.5 min.	0.1mm	3 pcs/hr
	Adhesion	7 in.–lbs.	0.2 in.–lbs.	3 pcs/hr
Plating	Bath lead %	10%	1%	3/hr
	Thickness	0.005"	0.0005"	3 pcs/hr
	Resistance	0.1Ω	0.0005Ω	3 pcs/hr

ATTRIBUTE SPC FOR SMALL AND SHORT RUNS

When data is difficult to obtain, as it usually is when small or short runs are involved, variables SPC should be used if at all possible. A variables measurement on a continuous scale contains more information than a discrete attributes classification provides. For example, a machine is cutting a piece of metal tubing to length. The specifications call for the length to be between 0.990" and 1.010" with the preferred length being 1.000" exactly. There are two methods available for checking the process. Method #1 involves measuring the length of the tube with a micrometer and recording the result to the nearest 0.001". Method #2 involves placing the finished part into a "go/no-go gage." With method #2 a part that is shorter than 0.990" will go into the "no-go" portion of the gage, while a part that is longer than 1.010" will fail to go into the "go" portion of the gage. With method #1 we can determine the size of the part to within 0.001". With method #2 we can only determine the size of the part to within 0.020"; i.e. either it is within the size tolerance, it's too short, or it's long. If the process could hold a tolerance *of less than 0.020"*, method #1 would provide the necessary information to hold the process to the variability it is capable of holding. Method #2 would not detect a process drift until out of tolerance parts were actually produced.

Another way of looking at the two different methods is to consider each part as belonging to a distinct category, determined by the part's length. Method #1 allows any part that is within tolerance to be placed into one of twenty categories. When out of tolerance parts are considered, method #1 is able to place parts into even more than twenty different categories. Method #1 also tells us if the part is in the best category, namely within ±0.001" of 1.000"; if not, we know how far the part is from the best category. With method #2 a given part can be placed into only three categories: too short, within tolerance, or too long. A part that is far too short will be placed in the same category as a part that is only slightly short. A part that is barely within tolerance will be placed in the same category as a part that is exactly 1.000" long.

SPC OF ATTRIBUTES DATA FROM SHORT RUNS

In spite of the disadvantages, it is sometimes necessary to use attributes data. Special methods must be used for attributes data used to control short run processes. Two such methods will be described:

- Stabilized attribute control charts.
- Demerit control charts.

Stabilized attribute control charts

When plotting attribute data statistics from short run processes two difficulties are typically encountered:

1. Varying subgroup sizes.
2. A small number of subgroups per production runs.

Item #1 results in messy charts with different control limits for each subgroup, distorted chart scales that mask significant variations, and chart patterns that are difficult to interpret because they are affected by both sample size changes and true process changes. Item #2 makes it difficult to track long-term process trends because the trends are broken up among many different control charts for individual parts. For these reasons, many believe that SPC is not practical unless large and long runs are involved. This is not the case. In many cases stabilized attribute charts can be used to eliminate these problems. Although somewhat more complicated than classical control charts, stabilized attribute control charts offer a way of realizing the benefits of SPC with processes that are difficult to control any other way.

Stabilized attribute charts may be used if a process is producing part features that are essentially the same from one part number to the next. Production lot sizes and sample sizes can vary without visibly affecting the chart.

Example one

A lathe is being used to machine terminals of different sizes. Samples (of different sizes) are taken periodically and inspected for burrs, nicks, tool marks and other visual defects.

Example two

A printed circuit board hand assembly operation involves placing electrical components into a large number of different circuit boards. Although the boards differ markedly from one another, the hand assembly operation is similar for all of the different boards.

Example three

A job-shop welding operation produces small quantities of "one order only" items. However, the operation always involves joining parts of similar material and similar size. The process control statistic is weld imperfections per 100 inches of weld.

The techniques used to create stabilized attribute control charts are all based on corresponding classical attribute control chart methods. There are four basic types of control charts involved:

1. Stabilized p charts for proportion of defective units per sample.
2. Stabilized np charts for the number of defective units per sample.
3. Stabilized c charts for the number of defects per unit.
4. Stabilized u charts for the average number of defects per unit.

All of these charts are based on the transformation

$$Z = \frac{sample\ statistic - process\ average}{process\ standard\ deviation} \qquad (8.82)$$

In other words, stabilized charts are plots of the number of standard deviations (plus or minus) between the sample statistic and the long-term process average. Since control limits are conventionally set at ± 3 standard deviations, stabilized control charts always have the lower control limit at −3 and the upper control limit at +3. Table 8.20 summarizes the control limit equations for stabilized control charts for attributes.

Table. 8.20. Stabilized attribute chart statistics.

ATTRIBUTE	CHART	SAMPLE STATISTIC	PROCESS AVERAGE	PROCESS	Z
Proportion defective units	p chart	p	$\bar{p}$	$\sqrt{\bar{p}(1-\bar{p})}$	$(p-\bar{p})\big/\sigma$
Number of defective units	np chart	np	$\overline{np}$	$\sqrt{np(1-\bar{p})}$	$(np-\overline{np})\big/\sigma$
Defects per unit	c chart	c	$\bar{c}$	$\sqrt{\bar{c}}$	$(c-\bar{c})\big/\sigma$
Average defects per unit	u chart	u	$\bar{u}$	$\sqrt{\bar{u}\big/n}$	$(u-\bar{u})\big/\sigma$

When applied to long runs, stabilized attribute charts are used to compensate for varying sample sizes; process averages are assumed to be constant. However, stabilized attribute charts can be created even if the process average varies. This is often done when applying this technique to short runs of parts that vary a great deal in average quality. For example, a wave soldering process used for several missiles has boards that vary in complexity from less than 100 solder joints to over 1,500 solder joints. Tables 8.21 and 8.22 show how the situation is handled to create a stabilized u chart. The unit size is 1,000 leads, set arbitrarily. It doesn't matter what the unit size is set to, the calculations will still produce the correct result since the actual number of leads is divided by the unit size selected.

Table 8.21. Data from a wave solder process.

MISSILE	BOARD	LEADS	UNITS/BOARD	$\bar{u}$
Phoenix	A	1,650	1.65	16
	B	800	0.80	9
	C	1,200	1.20	9
TOW	D	80	0.08	4
	E	50	0.05	2
	F	100	0.10	1

Example one

From the process described in Table 8.21 a sample of 10 TOW missile boards of type E are sampled. Three defects were observed in the sample. Using Tables 8.20 and 8.21 Z is computed for the subgroup as follows:

$\sigma = \sqrt{\bar{u}/n}$, we get $\bar{u} = 2$ from Table 8.21.

$$n = \frac{50 \times 10}{1000} = 0.5 \; units$$

$$\sigma = \sqrt{2/0.5} = \sqrt{4} = 2$$

$$u = \frac{number\;of\;defects}{number\;of\;units} = \frac{3}{0.5} = 6\;defects\;per\;unit$$

$$Z = \frac{u - \bar{u}}{\sigma} = \frac{6 - 2}{2} = \frac{4}{2} = 2$$

Since Z is between −3 and +3 the process has not gone out of control; i.e., it is not being influenced by a special cause of variation.

Table 8.22 shows the data for several samples from this process. The resulting control chart is shown in Figure 8.53. Note that the control chart indicates that the process was better than average when it produced subgroups 2 and 3 and perhaps 4. Negative Z values mean that the defect rate is below (better than) the long-term process average. Groups 7 – 8 show an apparent deterioration in the process with group 7 being out of control. Positive Z values indicate a defect rate above (worse than) the long term process average.

Table 8.22. Stabilized u chart data for wave solder.

NO.	BOARD	$\bar{u}$	UNITS	# SAMPLED	n	σ	DEFECTS	u	Z
1	E	2	0.05	10	0.50	2.00	3	6.00	2.00
2	A	16	1.65	1	1.65	3.11	8	4.85	−3.58
3	A	16	1.65	1	1.65	3.11	11	6.67	−3.00
4	B	9	0.80	1	0.80	3.35	0	0.00	−2.68
5	F	1	0.10	2	0.20	2.24	1	5.00	1.79
6	E	2	0.05	5	0.25	2.83	2	8.00	2.12
7	C	9	1.20	1	1.20	2.74	25	20.83	4.32
8	D	4	0.08	5	0.40	3.16	5	12.50	2.69
9	B	9	0.80	1	0.80	3.35	7	8.75	−0.07
10	B	9	0.80	1	0.80	3.35	7	8.75	−0.07

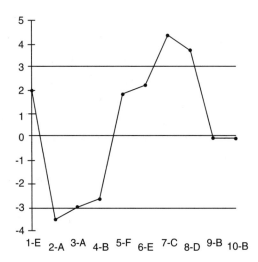

Figure 8.53. Control chart of Z values from Table 8.22.

The ability to easily see process trends and changes like these in spite of changing part numbers and sample sizes is the big advantage of stabilized control charts. The disadvantages of stabilized control charts are as follows:

1. They convert a number that is easy to understand, the number of defects or defectives, into a confusing statistic with no intuitive meaning.

2. They involve tedious calculation.

Item #1 can be corrected only by training and experience applying the technique. Item #2 can be handled with computers; the calculations are simple to perform with a spreadsheet. Table 8.22 can be used as a guide to setting up the spreadsheet. Inexpensive programmable calculators can be used to perform the calculations right at the process, thus making the results available immediately.

DEMERIT CONTROL CHARTS

As described above, there are two kinds of data commonly used to perform SPC: variables data and attributes data. When short runs are involved we can seldom afford the information loss that results from using attribute data. However, the following are ways of extracting additional information from attribute data:

1. Making the attribute data "less discrete" by adding more classification categories.
2. Assigning weights to the categories to accentuate different levels of quality.

Consider a process that involves fabricating a substrate for a hybrid microcircuit. The surface characteristics of the substrate are extremely important. The "ideal part" will have a smooth surface, completely free of any visible flaws or blemishes. However, parts are sometimes produced with stains, pits, voids, cracks and other surface defects. Although undesirable, most of the less than ideal parts are still acceptable to the customer.

If conventional attribute SPC methods are applied to this process the results would probably be disappointing. Since very few parts are actually rejected as unacceptable, a standard p chart or stabilized p chart would probably show a flat line at "zero defects" most of the time, even though the quality level might be less than the target ideal part. Variables SPC methods can't be used because attributes data such as "stains" are not easily measured on a variables scale. Demerit control charts offer an effective method of applying SPC in this situation.

To use demerit control charts it must be determined how many imperfections of each type are found in the parts. Weights are assigned to the different categories. The quality score for a given sample is the sum of the weights times the frequencies of each category. Table 8.23 illustrates this approach for the substrate example.

Table 8.23. Demerit scores for substrates.

SUBGROUP NUMBER →		1		2		3	
Attribute	Weight	Freq.	Score	Freq.	Score	Freq.	Score
Light stain	1	3	3				
Dark stain	5			1	5	1	5
Small blister	1			2	2	1	1
Medium blister	5	1	5				
Pit: 0.01–0.05 mm	1					3	3
Pit: 0.06–0.10	5			2	10		
Pit: larger than 0.10 mm	10	1	10				
TOTAL DEMERITS →		18		17		9	

If the subgroup size is kept constant, the average for the demerit control chart is computed as follows (Burr, 1976),

$$Average = \overline{D} = \frac{sum\ of\ subgroup\ demerits}{number\ of\ subgroups} s \qquad (8.83)$$

Control limits are computed in two steps. First compute the weighted average defect rate for each category. For example, there might be the following categories and weights

CATEGORY	WEIGHT
Major	10
Minor	5
Incidental	1

Three average defect rates, one each for major, minor and incidental, could be computed using the following designations:

$\bar{c}_1$ = *Average number of major defects per subgroup*

$\bar{c}_2$ = *Average number of minor defects per subgroup*

$\bar{c}_3$ = *Average number of incidental defects per subgroup*

The corresponding weights might be $W_1 = 10$, $W_2 = 5$, $W_3 = 1$. Using this notation the demerit standard deviation for this three category example would be computed.

$$\sigma_D = \sqrt{W_1^2 \bar{c}_1 + W_2^2 \bar{c}_2 + W_3^2 \bar{c}_3} \qquad (8.84)$$

For the general case the standard deviation is

$$\sigma_D = \sqrt{\sum_{i=1}^{k} W_i^2 \bar{c}_i} \qquad (8.85)$$

The control limits are

$$LCL = \bar{D} - 3\sigma_D \qquad (8.86)$$

$$UCL = \bar{D} + 3\sigma_D \qquad (8.87)$$

If the Lower Control Limit is negative, it is set to zero.

SIMPLIFIED QUALITY SCORE CHARTS

The above procedure, while correct, may sometimes be too burdensome to implement effectively. When this is the case a simplified approach may be used. The simplified approach is summarized as follows:

1. Classify each part in the subgroup into the following classes (scores are arbitrary).

CLASS	DESCRIPTION	POINTS
A	Preferred quality. All product features at or very near targets.	10
B	Acceptable quality. Some product features have departed significantly from target quality levels, but they are a safe distance from the reject limits.	5
C	Marginal quality. One or more product features are in imminent danger of exceeding reject limits.	1
D	Reject quality. One or more product features fail to meet minimum acceptability requirements.	0

2. Plot the total scores for each subgroup, keeping the subgroup sizes constant.
3. Treat the total scores as if they were variables data and prepare an individuals and moving range control chart or an $\bar{X}$ and R chart. These charts are described in (Pyzdek, 1989) and in most texts on SPC.

CONCLUSION

Small runs and short runs are common in modern business environments. Different strategies are needed to deal with these situations. Advance planning is essential. Special variables techniques were introduced which compensate for small sample sizes and short runs by using special tables or mathematically transforming the statistics and charts. Attribute short run SPC methods were introduced that make process patterns more evident when small runs are produced. Demerit and scoring systems were introduced that extract more information from attribute data.

9

Advanced Six Sigma Methods

DOE

Designed experiments play an important role in quality improvement. This section will introduce the basic concepts involved and it will contrast the statistically designed experiment with the "one variable at a time" approach that has been used traditionally. Also briefly discussed are the concepts involved in Taguchi methods, statistical methods named after their creator, Dr. Genichi Taguchi.

The traditional approach vs. statistically designed experiments

The traditional approach, which most of us learned in high school science class, is to hold all variables constant except one. When this approach is used we can be sure that the variation is due to a cause and effect relationship. However, this approach suffers from a number of problems:

- It usually isn't possible to hold all other variables constant.
- There is no way to account for the effect of joint variation of independent variables, such as interaction.
- There is no way to account for experimental error, including measurement variation.

The statistically designed experiment usually involves varying two or more variables simultaneously and obtaining multiple measurements under the same experimental conditions. The advantage of the statistical approach is three-fold:

1. Interactions can be detected and measured. Failure to detect interactions is a major flaw in the "one variable at a time" approach.
2. Each value does the work of several values. A properly designed experiment allows you to use the same observation to estimate several different effects. This translates directly to cost savings when using the statistical approach.
3. Experimental error is quantified and used to determine the confidence the experimenter has in his conclusions.

Terminology

Much of the early work on the design of experiments involved agricultural studies. The language of experimental design still reflects these origins. The experimental area was literally a piece of ground. A block was a smaller piece of ground with fairly uniform properties. A plot was smaller still and it served as the basic unit of the design. As the plot was planted, fertilized and harvested, it could be split simply by drawing a line. A treatment was actually a treatment, such as the application of fertilizer. Unfortunately for the quality engineer, these terms are still part of the language of experiments. The engineer must do his or her best to understand quality improvement experimenting using these terms. Natrella (1963) recommends the following:

> Experimental area can be thought of as the scope of the planned experiment. For us, a block can be a group of results from a particular operator, or from a particular machine, or on a particular day—any planned natural grouping which should serve to make results from one block more alike than results from different blocks. For us, a treatment is the factor being investigated (material, environmental condition, etc.) in a single factor experiment. In factorial experiments (where several variables

are being investigated at the same time) we speak of a treatment combination and we mean the prescribed levels of the factors to be applied to an experimental unit. For us, a yield is a measured result and, happily enough, in chemistry it will sometimes be a yield.

DEFINITIONS

A designed experiment is an experiment where one or more variables, called independent variables, believed to have an effect on the experimental outcome are identified and manipulated according to a predetermined plan. Data collected from a designed experiment can be analyzed statistically to determine the effect of the independent variables, or combinations of more than one independent variable. An experimental plan must also include provisions for dealing with extraneous variables, that is, variables not explicitly identified as independent variables.

Response variable—The variable being investigated, also called the *dependent variable.*

Primary variables—The controllable variables believed most likely to have an effect. These may be quantitative, such as temperature, pressure, or speed, or they may be qualitative such as vendor, production method, or operator.

Background variables—Variables, identified by the designers of the experiment, which may have an effect but either can not or should not be deliberately manipulated or held constant. The effect of background variables can contaminate primary variable effects unless they are properly handled. The most common method of handling background variables is blocking (blocking is described later in this section).

Experimental error—In any given experimental situation, a great many variables may be potential sources of variation. So many, in fact, that no experiment could be designed that deals with every possible source of variation explicitly. Those variables that are not considered explicitly are analogous to common causes of variation. They represent the "noise level" of the process and their effects are kept from contaminating the primary variable effects by *randomization*. Randomization is a term meant to describe a procedure that assigns test units to test conditions in such a way that any given unit has an equal probability of being processed under a given set of test conditions.

Interaction—A condition where the effect of one factor depends on the level of another factor. Interaction is illustrated in Figure 9.1.

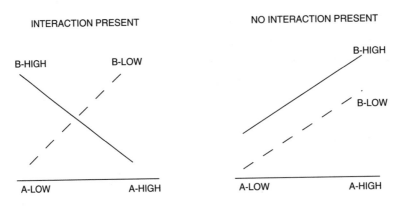

Figure 9.1. Illustration of interaction.

Power and sample size

In designed experiments, the term *power of the test* refers to the probability that the *F* test will lead to accepting the alternative hypothesis when in fact the alternative hypothesis holds, i.e., 1-ß. To determine power probabilities we use the non-central *F* distribution. Charts have been prepared to simplify this task (see Appendix Table 14). The tables are indexed by values of φ. When all sample sizes are of equal size *n*, φ is computed using Equation 9.1.

$$\phi = \frac{1}{\sigma}\sqrt{\frac{n}{r}\sum\left(\mu_i - \mu_.\right)^2}$$

where:

$$\mu_. = \frac{\sum \mu_{i.}}{r}$$

(9.1)

and r is the number of factor levels being studied.

The tables in Appendix 14 are used as follows:

1. Each page refers to a different $v_1 = r-1$, the number of degrees of freedom for the numerator of the F statistic.
2. Two levels of significance are shown, $\alpha = 0.01$ and $\alpha = 0.05$. The left set of curves are used for $\alpha = 0.05$ and the right set when $\alpha = 0.01$.
3. There are separate curves for selected values of $v_2 = \Sigma n - r$, the number of degrees of freedom for the denominator of the F statistic.
4. The X scale is in units of ϕ.
5. The Y scale gives the power, $1-\beta$.

EXAMPLE

Consider the curve on the second page of Appendix Table 14 for $\alpha = 0.05$, $v_1 = 3$, $v_2 = 12$. This ANOVA tests the hypothesis that four ($v_1 = 4-1 = 3$) populations have equal means with sample sizes of $n = 4$ from each population ($v_2 = 16-4 = 12$). Reading above $\phi = 2$, we see that the chance of recognizing that the four populations do not actually have equal means when $\phi = 2$ is 0.82. It must be understood that there are many combinations of four unequal means that would produce $\phi = 2$.

Design characteristics

Good experiments don't just happen, they are a result of careful planning. A good experimental plan depends on the following (Natrella 1963):

- The purpose of the experiment
- Physical restrictions on the process of taking measurements
- Restrictions imposed by limitations of time, money, material, and personnel.

The engineer must explain clearly why the experiment is being done, why the experimental treatments were selected, and how the completed experiment will accomplish the stated objectives. The experimental plan should be in writing and it should be endorsed by all key participants. The plan will include a statement of the objectives of the experiment, the experimental treatments to be applied, the size of the experiment, the time frame, and a brief discussion of the methods to be used to analyze the results. Two concepts are of particular interest to the quality engineer, replication and randomization.

Replication—The collection of more than one observation for the same set of experimental conditions. Replication allows the experimenter to estimate experimental error. If variation exists when all experimental conditions are held constant, the cause must be something other than the variables being controlled by the experimenter. Experimental error can be estimated without replicating the entire experiment. If a process has been in statistical control for a period of time, experimental error can be estimated from the control chart. Replication also serves to decrease bias due to uncontrolled factors.

Randomization—In order to eliminate bias from the experiment, variables not specifically controlled as factors should be randomized. This means that allocations of specimens to treatments should be made using some mechanical method of randomization, such as a random numbers table. Randomization also assures valid estimates of experimental error.

Types of design

Experiments can be designed to meet a wide variety of experimental objectives. A few of the more common types of experimental designs are defined here.

Fixed-effects model—An experimental model where all possible factor levels are studied. For example, if there are three different materials, all three are included in the experiment.

Random-effects model—An experimental model where the levels of factors evaluated by the experiment represent a sample of all possible levels. For example, if we have three different materials but only use two materials in the experiment.

Mixed model—An experimental model with both fixed and random effects.

Completely randomized design—An experimental plan where the order in which the experiment is performed is completely random, e.g.,

LEVEL	TEST SEQUENCE NUMBER
A	7, 1, 5
B	2, 3, 6
C	8, 4

Randomized-block design—An experimental design is one where the experimental observations are divided into "blocks" according to some criteria. The blocks are filled sequentially, but the order within the block is filled randomly. For example, assume that a painting test is conducted with different materials, material A and material B. There are four test pieces of each material. Ideally all of the pieces should be cleaned at the same time to assure that the cleaning process doesn't have an effect on the results; but what if the test requires that a cleaning tank be used that cleans two test pieces at a time? The tank load then becomes a "blocking factor." There will be four blocks, which might look like this:

MATERIAL	TANK LOAD	TEST PIECE NUMBER
A	1	7
B		1
B	2	5
A		2
B	3	3
A		6
B	4	4
A		8

Since each material appears exactly once per cleaning tank load the design is *balanced*. The material totals or averages can be compared directly. The reader should be aware that statistical designs exist to handle more complicated "unbalanced designs."

Latin-square designs—These are designs where each treatment appears once and only once in each row and column. A Latin-square plan is useful when it is necessary or desirable to allow for two specific sources on non-homogeneity in the conditions affecting test results. Such designs were originally applied in agricultural experimentation when the two sources of non-homogeneity were the two directions on the field and the "square" was literally a square piece of ground. Its usage has been extended to many other applications where there are two sources of non-homogeneity that may affect experimental results—for example, machines, positions, operators, runs, days. A third variable is then associated with the other two in a prescribed fashion. The use of Latin squares is restricted by two conditions:

1. the number of rows, columns and treatments must all be the same;

2. there must be no interactions between row and column factors.

Natrella (1963, p. 13–30) provides the following example of a Latin square. Suppose materials are to be compared with regard to their wearing qualities. Suppose further that there is a wear-testing machine which can handle four samples simultaneously. Two sources of inhomogeneity might be the variations from run to run, and the variation among the four positions on the wear machine. In this situation a 4 x 4 Latin square will allow for both sources of inhomogeneity if four runs can be made. The Latin square plan is as follows: (The four materials are labeled A, B, C, D).

Run	Position Number			
	(1)	(2)	(3)	(4)
1	A	B	C	D
2	B	C	D	A
3	C	D	A	B
4	D	A	B	C

Figure 9.2. A 4 x 4 Latin square.

The procedure to be followed in using a given Latin square is as follows:
1. Permute the columns at random;
2. Permute the rows at random;
3. Assign letters randomly to the treatments.

ONE-FACTOR
Example of a one-way ANOVA
The following example will be used to illustrate the interpretation of a single factor analysis of variance. With the widespread availability of computers, few people actually perform such complex calculations by hand. The analysis below was performed using Microsoft Excel. Commonly used statistical methods such as regression and ANOVA are included in most high-end spreadsheets.

The coded results in Table 9.1 were obtained from a single factor, completely randomized experiment, in which the production outputs of three machines (A, B, and C) were to be compared.

Table 9.1. Experimental raw data (coded).

A	B	C
4	2	-3
8	0	1
5	1	-2
7	2	-1
6	4	0

An ANOVA of these results produced the results shown in Table 9.2:

Table 9.2. Results of the analysis.

ANOVA: SINGLE FACTOR						
SUMMARY						
Groups	*Count*	*Sum*	*Average*	*Variance*		
A	5	30.000	6.000	2.500		
B	5	9.000	1.800	2.200		
C	5	-5.000	-1.000	2.500		
ANOVA						
Source of variation	*SS*	*df*	*MS*	*F*	*P-value*	*F crit*
Between groups	124.133	2	62.067	25.861	0.000	3.885
Within groups	28.800	12	2.400			
Total	152.933	14				

The first part of Table 9.2 shows descriptive statistics for the data; the engineer should always look carefully at these easily understood results to check for obvious errors. The results show that the means vary from a low of -1 for machine *C* to a high of 6 for machine *A*.

ANOVA procedure

ANOVA proceeds as follows:

1. State the null and alternative hypotheses. The ANOVA table tests the hypothesis H_0: All means are equal versus H_a: At least two of the means are different.

2. Choose the level of significance. For this analysis a significance level $\alpha=0.05$ was selected.

3. Compute the F statistic, the ratio of the mean square between groups to the mean square within groups.

4. Assuming that the observations are random samples from normally distributed populations with equal variances, and that the hypothesis is true, the critical value of F is found in Table 5 or 6 in the Appendix. The numerator will have the degrees of freedom shown in the *df* column for the Between Groups row. The denominator will have the degrees of freedom shown in the *df* column for the Within Groups row.

5. If the computed $F > F_{1-\alpha}$ then reject the null hypothesis and conclude the alternate hypothesis. Otherwise fail to reject the null hypothesis.

The ANOVA table shows that for these data F computed is 62.067/2.4=25.861 and F critical at $\alpha=0.05$ with numerator *df*=2 and denominator *df*=12 is 3.885.* Since 25.861>3.885 the null hypothesis is rejected and the conclusion is made that the machines produce different results. Note that all that is known is that at least the two extreme machines (A and *C*) are different. The ANOVA does *not* tell if A and B or B and *C* are significantly different. There are methods which can make this determination, such as *contrasts*. The reader is referred to a text on design of experiments, e.g., Montgomery (1984) for additional information.

---

*Referring to the critical value is actually unnecessary; the P-value of 0.000 indicates that the probability of getting an F value as large as that computed is less than 1 in 1,000.

Performing ANOVA manually

On rare occasions (such as taking a CQE exam), the engineer may find that computers are not available and the analysis must be performed "by hand." The analysis is illustrated below.

		Total	N	Sum of Squares
Treatment A	4, 8, 5, 7,6	30	5	190
Treatment B	2, 0, 1, 2, 4	9	5	25
Treatment C	-3, 1, -2, -1, 0	-5	5	15
	Totals	34	15	230

$$Total\ sum\ of\ squares\ =\ 230 - \frac{(34)^2}{15} = 152.933$$

$$Treatment\ sum\ of\ squares = \frac{(30)^2}{5} + \frac{(9)^2}{5} + \frac{(-5)^2}{5} - \frac{(34)^2}{15} = 124.133$$

$$Error\ sum\ of\ squares$$
$$= Total\ sum\ of\ squares - Treatment\ sum\ of\ squares$$
$$= 152.933 - 124.133 = 28.8$$

These values are placed in the Sum of Squares (SS) column in the ANOVA table (Table 9.2). The remainder of the ANOVA table is obtained through simple division.

EXAMPLES OF APPLYING COMMON DOE METHODS USING SOFTWARE

This section includes examples of the most commonly used design of experiment methods using software. Whenever possible the examples employ popular software, such as Microsoft Excel. For detailed mathematical background on these methods, the reader is referred to any of the many fine books on the subject.* DOE PC, a full-featured commercial software for design and analysis of experiments, is available from http://www.qualityamerica.com. A statistical analysis shareware package for Windows operating systems can be downloaded from http://www.dagonet.com/scalc.htm.

Two way ANOVA with no replicates

When experiments are conducted which involve two factors, and it is not possible to obtain repeat readings for a given set of experimental conditions, a two-way analysis of variance may be used. The following example assumes that experimental treatments are assigned at random. Note that if the factors involved are each tested at only two levels, the full factorial analysis method described below could also be used.

EXAMPLE OF TWO WAY ANOVA WITH NO REPLICATES

An experiment was conducted to evaluate the effect of different detergents and water temperatures on the cleanliness of ceramic substrates. The experimenter selected three different detergents, based on their pH levels, and conducted a series of experiments at four different water temperatures. Cleanliness was quantified by measuring the contamination of a distilled water beaker after rinsing the parts cleaned using each treatment combination. The coded data are shown in Table 9.3.

---

*Montgomery, Douglas C., 1996; Box, Hunter and Hunter, 1978; Hicks, Charles R., 1993.

Table 9.3. Cleaning experiment raw data.

	DETERGENT A	DETERGENT B	DETERGENT C
Cold	15	18	10
Cool	12	14	9
Warm	10	18	7
Hot	6	12	5

Table 9.4. Cleaning experiment two-way ANOVA output from Microsoft Excel. (Two-factor without replication.)

SUMMARY OUTPUT						
	Count	*Sum*	*Average*	*Variance*		
Cold water	3	43	14.333333	16.33333		
Cool water	3	35	11.666667	6.333333		
Warm water	3	35	11.666667	32.33333		
Hot water	3	23	7.6666667	14.33333		
Detergent A	4	43	10.75	14.25		
Detergent B	4	62	15.5	9		
Detergent C	4	31	7.75	4.916667		
ANOVA						
Source of variation	*SS*	*df*	*MS*	*F*	*P-value*	*F crit*
Rows	68	3	22.666667	8.242424	0.015043179	4.757055
Columns	122.1666667	2	61.083333	22.21212	0.001684751	5.143249
Error	16.5	6	2.75			
Total	206.6666667	11				

Part one of the Excel output provides descriptive statistics on the different treatment levels. The ANOVA table is shown in part two. Note that in the previously presented raw data table the rows represent the different temperatures and the columns the different detergents. Because there are no replicates, Excel is not able to provide an estimate of the interaction of detergent and water temperature. If it is suspected that an interaction may be present, then the experiment should be replicated to estimate this effect. For this experiment, any P-value less than 0.05 would indicate a significant effect. The ANOVA table indicates that there are significant differences between the different detergents and the different water temperatures. To identify *which* differences are significant the experimenter can examine the means of the different detergents and water temperatures using *t*-tests. (Excel's data analysis tools add-in includes these tests). Be aware that the Type I error is affected by conducting multiple *t*-tests. If the Type I error on a single *t*-test is α, then the overall Type I error for k such tests is $1-(1-\alpha)^k$. For example, if $\alpha=0.01$ and three pairs of means are examined, then the combined Type I error for all three *t*-tests is $1-(1-0.01)^3 = 1-(0.99)^3 = 0.03$. Statistical methods exist that guarantee an overall level of Type I error for simultaneous comparisons (Hicks, 1973; pp. 31–38).

Two way ANOVA with replicates

If two factors are investigated which might interact with one another, and more than one result can be obtained for each combination of experimental treatments, then two-way analysis of variance with replicates may be used for the analysis. Spreadsheets such as Microsoft Excel include functions that perform this analysis.

EXAMPLE OF TWO WAY ANOVA WITH REPLICATES

An investigator is interested in improving a process for bonding photoresist to copper clad printed circuit boards. Two factors are to be evaluated: the pressure used to apply the photoresist material and the preheat temperature of the photoresist. Three different pressures and three different temperatures are to be evaluated; the number of levels need not be the same for each factor and there is no restriction on the total number of levels. Each experimental combination of variables is repeated five times. Note that while Excel requires equal numbers of replicates for each combination of treatments, most statistical analysis packages allow different sample sizes to be used. The experimenter recorded the number of photoresist defects per batch of printed wiring boards. The coded data are shown in Table 9.5.

Table 9.5. Photoresist experiment raw data. ANOVA results.

	HIGH PRESSURE	MED PRESSURE	LOW PRESSURE
High temp	39	32	18
	30	31	20
	35	28	21
	43	28	25
	25	29	26
Med temp	38	10	22
	31	15	28
	31	25	29
	30	31	26
	35	36	20
Low temp	30	21	25
	35	22	24
	36	25	20
	37	24	21
	39	27	21

These data were analyzed using Excel's two-way ANOVA with replicates function. The results are shown in Table 9.6.

Table 9.6. Cleaning experiment two-way ANOVA
output from Microsoft Excel. (Two-factor with replication.)

SUMMARY OUTPUT				
	High pressure	*Med pressure*	*Low pressure*	*Total*
High temp				
Count	5	5	5	15
Sum	172	148	110	430
Average	34.4	29.6	22	28.66667
Variance	50.8	3.3	11.5	46.66667
Med temp				
Count	5	5	5	15
Sum	165	117	125	407
Average	33	23.4	25	27.13333
Variance	11.5	117.3	15	59.98095
Low temp				
Count	5	5	5	15
Sum	177	119	111	407
Average	35.4	23.8	22.2	27.13333
Variance	11.3	5.7	4.7	43.26667
Total				
Count	15	15	15	
Sum	514	384	346	
Average	34.26666667	25.6	23.06666667	
Variance	22.06666667	44.68571429	10.92380952	

ANOVA						
Source of variation	*SS*	*df*	*MS*	*F*	*P-value*	*F crit*
Sample	23.5111111	2	11.7555556	0.45781	0.6363	3.259444
Columns	1034.84444	2	517.422222	20.1506	1.34E-06	3.259444
Interaction	139.555556	4	34.8888889	1.35872	0.267501	2.633534
Within	924.4	36	25.6777778			
Total	2122.31111	44				

As before, part one of the Excel output provided descriptive statistics on the different treatment levels. The ANOVA table is shown in part two. Because there were now replicates, Excel was able to provide an estimate of the interaction of pressure and temperature. For this experiment, the experimenter decided that any P-value less than 0.05 would indicate a significant effect. The ANOVA table p-value of less than 0.001 indicates that there were significant differences between the different columns (pressure), but the p-value of 0.6363 indicated that there was not a significant difference between the rows (temperature). The interaction of pressure and temperature was also not significant, as indicated by the p-value of 0.267501.

Since the p-value indicated that at least one difference was significant, the largest difference of 34.26666667–23.06666667 = 11.2 is known to be significant. To identify *which other* differences are significant the experimenter can examine the means of the different pressures using t-tests. (Excel's data analysis tools add-in includes these tests). Be aware that the Type I error is affected by conducting multiple t-tests. If the Type I error on a single t-test is α, then the overall Type I error for k such tests is $1-(1-\alpha)^k$. For example, if $\alpha=0.01$ and three pairs of means are examined, then the combined Type I error for all three t-tests is $1-(1-0.01)^3 = 1-(0.99)^3 = 0.03$.

FULL AND FRACTIONAL FACTORIAL

Full factorial experiments are those where at least one observation is obtained for every possible combination of experimental variables. For example, if A has 2 levels, B has 3 levels and C has 5 levels, a full factorial experiment would have at least 2x3x5=30 observations.

Fractional factorial or *fractional replicate* are experiments where there are some combinations of experimental variables where observations were not obtained. Such experiments may not allow the estimation of every interaction. However, when carefully planned, the experimenter can often obtain all of the information needed at a significant savings.

Analyzing factorial experiments

A simple method exists for analyzing the common 2^n experiment. The method, known as the Yates method, can be performed easily with a pocket calculator or programmed into a spreadsheet. It can be used with any properly designed 2^n experiment, regardless of the number of factors being studied.

To use the Yates algorithm, the data are first arranged in standard order (of course, the actual running order is random). The concept of standard order is easier to understand if demonstrated. Assume that an experiment has been conducted with three factors, A, B, and C. Each of the three factors is evaluated at two levels, which will be called low and high. A factor held at a low level will be identified with a "−" sign, one held at a high level will be identified with a "+" sign. The eight possible combinations of the three factors are identified using the scheme shown in the table below.

I.D.	A	B	C
(1)	−	−	−
a	+	−	−
b	−	+	−
ab	+	+	−
c	−	−	+
ac	+	−	+
bc	−	+	+
abc	+	+	+

Note that the table begins with all factors at their low level. Next, the first factor is high and all others are low. When a factor is high, it is shown in the identification column, otherwise it is not; e.g., whenever "*a*" appears it indicates that factor A is at its high level. To complete the table, as each factor is added to the table it is "multiplied" by each preceding row. Thus, when *b* is added it is multiplied by *a*, giving the row *ab*. When *c* is added it is multiplied by, in order, *a*, *b*, and *ab*, giving the remaining rows in the table. (As an exercise, the reader should add a fourth factor D to the above table. Hint: the result will be a table with eight more rows.) Once the data are in standard order, add a column for the data and one additional column for each variable, e.g., for the three variables four columns will be added.

I.D.	A	B	C	DATA	1	2	3
(1)	−	−	−				
a	+	−	−				
b	−	+	−				
ab	+	+	−				
c	−	−	+				
ac	+	−	+				
bc	−	+	+				
abc	+	+	+				

Record the data in the data column (if the experiment has been replicated, record the totals). Now record the sum of the data values in the first two rows i.e., (1)+a in the first cell of the column labeled column 1. Record the sum of the next two rows in the second cell (i.e., b+ab). Continue until the top half of column 1 is completed. The lower half of column 1 is completed by subtracting one row from the next, e.g., the fifth value in column 1 is found by subtracting −5−2=−7. After completing column 1 the same process is completed for column 2, using the values in column 1. Column 3 is created using the value in column 2. The result is shown below.

I.D.	A	B	C	DATA	1	2	3
(1)	−	−	−	−2	−7	21	−17
a	+	−	−	−5	28	−38	−15
b	−	+	−	15	−29	−5	55
ab	+	+	−	13	−9	−10	1
c	−	−	+	−12	−3	35	−59
ac	+	−	+	−17	−2	20	−5
bc	−	+	+	−2	−5	1	−15
abc	+	+	+	−7	−5	0	−1

Example of Yates method

The table below shows sample data from an actual experiment. The experiment involved a target shooter trying to improve the number of targets hit per box of 25 shots. Three variables were involved: a=the gauge of the shotgun (12-gauge and 20-gauge), b=the shot size (6 shot and 8 shot), and c=the length of the handle on the target thrower (short or long). The shooter ran the experiment twice. The column labeled "1st" is the number of hits the first time the combination was tried. The column labeled "2nd" is the number of hits the second time the combination was tried. The Yates analysis begins with the sums shown in the column labeled Sum.

ID	1st	2nd	Sum	1	2	3	Effect	df	SS	MS	F ratio
1	22	19	41	86	167	288	18	Avg.			
a	21	24	45	81	121	20	2.5	1	25.00	25.00	3.64
b	20	18	38	58	9	0	0	1	0.00	0.00	0.00
ab	21	22	43	63	11	4	0.5	1	1.00	1.00	0.15
c	12	15	27	4	-5	-46	-5.75	1	132.25	132.25	19.24
ac	12	19	31	5	5	2	0.25	1	0.25	0.25	0.04
bc	13	15	28	4	1	10	1.25	1	6.25	6.25	0.91
abc	20	15	35	7	3	2	0.25	1	0.25	0.25	0.04
Error								8	55.00	6.88	
Total	141	147						15	220.00		

The first row in the Effect column is simply the first row of column 3 (288) divided by the count ($r*2^n$); this is simply the average. Subsequent rows in the Effect column are found by dividing the numbers in column 3 by $r*2^{n-1}$. The Effect column provides the impact of the given factor on the response; thus, the shooter hit, on average, 2.5 more targets per box when shooting a 12-gauge than he did when shooting a 20-gauge.

The next question is whether or not these differences are statistically significant; i.e., could they be due to chance alone? To answer this question the F-ratio of the effect MS for each factor to the error MS will be used. The degrees of freedom (df) for each effect is simply 1 (the number of factor levels minus 1), the total df is N–1, and the error df is the total df minus the sum of the factor dfs. The sum of squares (SS) for each factor is the column 3 value squared divided by $r*2^n$; e.g., $SS_A=20^2/16=25$. The total SS is the sum of the individual values squared, minus the first row in column 3 squared, divided by $r*2^n$; e.g.,

$$\left(22^2 + 21^2 + \dots + 15^2\right) - \frac{288^2}{16} = 220.$$

The error SS is the total SS minus the factor SS. The MS and F columns are computed using the same approach as shown above for one-way ANOVA. For the example the F-ratio for factor c (thrower) is significant at $\alpha<0.01$ and the F-ratio for factor a (gauge) is significant at $\alpha<0.10$; no other F-ratios are significant.

EMPIRICAL MODEL BUILDING AND SEQUENTIAL LEARNING

If you are new to design of experiments and empirical model building, a metaphor may prove helpful. Imagine that you suddenly wake up in a strange wilderness. You don't know where you are, but you'd like to climb to the top of the nearest hill to see if there are any signs of civilization. What would you do?

A first step might be to take a good look around you. Is there anything you should know before starting out? You would probably pay particular attention to things that might be dangerous. If you are in a jungle these might be dangerous animals, quicksand, and other things to avoid. You'd also look for things that could be used for basic survival, such as food, shelter, and clothing. You may wish to establish a "base camp" where you can be assured that all the basic necessities are available; a safe place to return to if things get a bit too exciting. In empirical modeling we also need to begin by becoming oriented with the way things are, before we proceed to changing them. We will call this *knowledge discovery* activity phase 0.

Now that you have a feel for your current situation and you feel confident that you know something about where you are, you may begin planning your trip to the highest hill. Before starting out you will probably try to determine what you will need to make the trip. You are only interested in things that are truly important. However, since you are new to jungle travel, you decide to make a few short trips to be sure that you have what you need. For your first trip you pack up every conceivable item and set out. In all likelihood you will discover that you have more than you need. Those things that are not important you will leave at your camp. As part of your short excursions you also learn something about the local terrain close to your camp, not much, of course, but enough to identify which direction is uphill. This phase is equivalent to a *screening experiment*, which we call Phase I.

You now feel that you are ready to begin your journey. You take only those things you will need and head out into the jungle in the uphill direction. From time to time you stop to get your bearings and to be sure that you are still moving in the right direction. We call this hill-climbing *steepest ascent*, or Phase II.

At some point you notice that you are no longer moving uphill. You realize that this doesn't mean that you are at the highest point in your area of the jungle, only that you are no longer moving in the right direction. You decide to stop and make camp. The next morning you begin to explore the local area more carefully, making a few short excursions from your camp. The jungle is dense and you learn that the terrain in the immediate vicinity is irregular, sometimes steep, sometimes less steep. This is in contrast to the smooth and consistent uphill slope you were on during your ascent. We call this phase of your journey the *factorial experiment*, or Phase III.

Now you decide that a more organized approach will be needed to locate the nearby peak. You break out the heavy artillery, the GPS you've been carrying since the beginning! (one of those cheap ones that doesn't have built-in maps) You take several altitude readings from near your camp, and others at a carefully measured distance on all major compass headings. Each time you carefully record the altitude on a hand-drawn map. You use the map to draw contour lines of equal altitude and eventually a picture emerges that clearly shows the location of the top of the hill. This is the *composite design phase*, which we call Phase IV.

At last you reach the top of the hill. You climb to the top of a tree and are rewarded with a spectacular view, the best for miles around. You decide that you love the view so much, you will build your home on this hill and live there permanently. You make your home sturdy and strong, able to withstand the ravages of wind and weather that are sure to come to your little corner of the jungle. In other words, your home design is *robust,* or impervious to changes in its environment. We call the activity of building products and processes that are insensitive to changes in their operating parameters *robust product and process design,* which is Phase V of the journey.

Now that this little tale has been told, let's go on to the real thing, improving your products, processes, and services!

Phase 0: Getting your bearings
"WHERE ARE WE ANYWAY?"

Before any experimentation can begin the team should get an idea of the major problems, important measures of performance, costs, time and other resources available for experimentation, etc. Methods and techniques for conducting Phase 0 research are described in Chapters 7 and 8. The author recommends that SPC be applied to the process before experimentation. SPC allows the separation of factors into the categories of special and common causes. The process of discovering which variables belong to which class is extremely valuable in development of an experimental plan.

The central premise of the approach described in this section is that learning is, by its very nature, a sequential process. The experimenter, be it an individual or a team, begins with relatively little specific knowledge and proceeds to gain knowledge by conducting experiments on the process. As new knowledge is acquired, the learner is better able to determine which step is most appropriate to take next. In other words, experimentation always involves guesswork; but guesses become more educated as experimental data become available for analysis.

This approach is in contrast to the classical approach where an effort is made to answer all conceivably relevant questions in one large experiment.

The classical approach to experimentation was developed primarily for agricultural experiments. Six Sigma applications are unlike agricultural applications in many ways, especially in that results become available quickly. The approach described here takes advantage of this to accelerate and direct learning.

An example from electronic manufacturing will be used. At the outset, a team of personnel involved in a soldering process received a mission from another team that had been evaluating problems for the factory as a whole. The factory team had learned that a leading reason for customer returns was solder problems. Another team discovered that the solder area spent more resources in terms of floor space than other areas; a major usage of floor space was for the storage of defective circuit boards and the repair of solder defects. Thus, the solder process improvement team was formed and asked to find ways to eliminate solder defects if possible, or to at least reduce them by a factor of 10. Team members included a Six Sigma technical leader, a process engineer, an inspector, a production operator, and a product engineer.

The team spent several meetings reviewing Pareto charts and problem reports. It also performed a process audit which uncovered several obvious problems. When the problems were repaired the team conducted a process capability study, which revealed a number of special causes of variation, which were investigated and corrected. Over a four-month period, this preliminary work resulted in a 50% reduction in the number of solder defects, from about 160 defects per standard unit to the 70–80 defect range. The productivity of the solder area nearly doubled as a result of these efforts. While impressive, the results were still well short of the 10X minimum improvement the team was asked to deliver.

Phase I: The screening experiment
"WHAT'S IMPORTANT HERE?"
At this point the process was stable and the team was ready to move from the process control stage to the process improvement stage. This involved conducting designed experiments to measure important effects. The solder team

decided to list as many items as possible that might be causing solder problems. Since many variables had already been studied as part of the Phase 0 work, the list was not unreasonably long. The team looked at ways to control the variables listed and was able to develop methods for eliminating the effects of many variables on their list. The remaining list included the following factors:

VARIABLE	LOW LEVEL (–)	HIGH LEVEL (+)
A: Pre-baking of boards in an oven	No	Yes
B: Pre-heat time	10 seconds	20 seconds
C: Pre-heat temperature	150 °F	200 °F
D: Distance from pre-heat element to board surface	25cm	50 cm
E: Line speed	3 fpm	5 fpm
F: Solder temperature	495 °F	505 °F
G: Circuit density	Low	High
H: Was the board in a fixture?	No	Yes

This information was used to create an experimental design using a statistical software package. There are many packages on the market that perform similar analyses to the one shown here.

Since this was only to be a screening experiment, the team was not interested in obtaining estimates of factor interactions. The focus was to identify important main effects. The software allowed selection from among several designs. The Black Belt decided upon the design which would estimate the main effects with the smallest number of test units. This design involved testing 16 units. The data matrix produced by the computer is shown in Table 9.7. The run order had been randomized by the computer. If the experiment could not be conducted in that particular order, the computer software would allow the data to be run in blocks and it would adjust the analysis accordingly. The program also tells us that the design is of resolution IV, which means that main effects are not confounded with each other or any two factor interactions.

Table 9.7. Screening experiment layout. Data matrix (randomized).

RUN	A	B	C	D	E	F	G	H	RESPONSE
1	+	−	−	−	−	+	+	+	65
2	+	−	+	+	−	+	−	−	85
3	+	+	−	−	+	+	−	−	58
4	−	+	−	−	+	−	+	+	57
5	−	−	−	−	−	−	−	−	63
6	+	+	+	+	+	+	+	+	75
7	−	+	−	+	−	+	+	−	77
8	−	+	+	−	−	+	−	+	60
9	+	−	+	−	+	−	−	+	67
10	+	+	+	−	−	−	+	−	56
11	−	−	+	−	+	+	+	−	63
12	−	−	−	+	+	+	−	+	81
13	+	+	−	+	−	−	−	+	73
14	+	−	−	+	+	−	+	−	87
15	−	+	+	+	+	−	−	−	75
16	−	−	+	+	−	−	+	+	84

In Table 9.7 the "−" indicates that the variable was run at its low level, while a "+" sign indicate that it was run at its high level. For example, the unit for run #16 was processed as follows:

✓ Pre-baking = No
✓ Pre-heat time = 10 seconds
✓ Pre-heat temperature = 200 degrees F
✓ Distance from preheat element to board surface = 50 cm
✓ Line speed = 3 fpm
✓ Solder temperature = 495 degrees F
✓ Circuit density = High
✓ Fixture used = Yes
✓ Defects per standard unit = 82

Experimental data were collected using the randomized run order recommended by the software. The "response" column are data that were recorded in terms of defective solder joints per "standard unit", where a standard unit represented a circuit board with a median number of solder joints.[*] The results are shown in Table 9.8.

Table 9.8. Results of experimental data analysis. Fractional factorial fit.

Estimated effects and coefficients for response (coded units)						
Term	*Effect*	*Coef*	*StDev coef*	*T*	*P*	
Constant		70.375	0.6597	106.67	0.000	
A	−0.750	−0.375	0.6597	−0.57	0.588	
B	8.000	4.000	0.6597	6.06	0.001	
C	−0.500	−0.250	0.6597	−0.38	0.716	
D	−18.500	−9.250	0.6597	−14.02	0.000	
E	0.000	0.000	0.6597	0.00	1.000	
F	−0.250	−0.125	0.6597	−0.19	0.855	
G	−0.250	−0.125	0.6597	−0.19	0.855	
H	0.250	0.125	0.6597	0.19	0.855	
ANOVA for defects (coded units)						
Source of variation	*df*	*Seq. SS*	*Adj. SS*	*Adj. MS*	*F*	*P-value*
Main effects	8	1629.00	1629.00	203.625	29.24	0.000
Residual error	7	48.75	48.75	6.964		
Total	15	1677.75				

---

[*]Technically, a Poisson model would be the correct choice here. However, use of a normal model, which the analysis assumes, is reasonably accurate for defect counts of this magnitude. The team also evaluated the variance, more specifically, the log of the variance. The variances at each factor combination did not differ significantly and are not shown here.

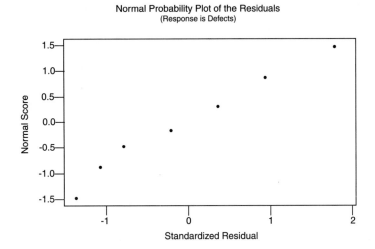

Figure 9.3. Residuals from experimental model.

A model that fit the data well would produce residuals that fall along a straight line. The black belt concluded that the fit of the model was adequate.

The analysis indicated that factors B (pre-heat time) and D (distance from pre-heat element to board surface) produced significant effects. Figure 9.3 shows a normal probability plot of the experimental effects. This figure shows the coefficients column from Table 9.8 plotted on a normal probability scale. If the factor's effect was due to chance variation it would plot close to the line representing normal variation. In Figure 9.4 the effects of B and D are shown to be further from the line than can be accounted for by random variation.

The effects of the significant factors are graphed in response units in Figure 9.4.

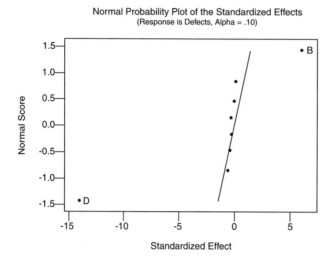

Figure 9.4. Significant factor effects.

Since the response is a defect count, the graph indicates that the low level of factor D gave better results, while the high level of factor B gave the better results. This can also be seen by examination of the coefficients for the variables. When D was low the average defect rate was 18.5 defects per unit better than when D was high; when B was high the average defect rate was 8 defects per unit better than when B was low.

The team met to discuss these results. They decided to set all factors that were not found to be statistically significant to the levels that cost the least to operate, and to set factors B and D at their midpoints. The process would be monitored at these settings for a while to determine that the results were similar to what the team expected based on the experimental analysis. While this was done, another series of experiments would be planned to further explore the significant effects uncovered by the screening experiment.

Phase II: Steepest ascent (descent)

"WHICH WAY IS UP?"

Based on the screening experiment, the linear model for estimating the defect rate was found from the coefficients in Table 9.8 to be

$$\text{Defect Rate} = 70.375 + 4B - 9.25D \qquad (9.2)$$

The team wanted to conduct a series of experiments to evaluate factors B and D. The Phase I experiment revealed the direction and ratio at which B and D should be changed to get the most rapid improvement in the defect rate, i.e., the direction of steepest ascent (where "ascent" means improvement in the measurement of interest). To calculate a series of points along the direction of steepest ascent, start at the center of the design and change the factors in proportion to the coefficients of the fitted equation; i.e., for every 4 unit increase in factor B, factor D is decreased 9.25 units. For the data at hand, the center of the experiment and unit sizes are shown in Table 9.9.

Table 9.9. Unit sizes and center of experiment.

FACTOR	UNIT SIZE	CENTER
B	5	15 seconds
D	12.5	37.5 cm

A test unit was produced at the center value of B and D. The team decided that they would reduce the pre-heat time (B) in increments of 5 seconds (1 unit), while lowering the distance from the heating element (D) by increments of $(9.25/4) \times 12.5\text{cm} = 28.75$ cm. This resulted in a single experiment where B = 20 seconds, D = 8.75 cm. The result was 52 defects per unit. However, despite the improved solder defect performance, the team noted that at the short distance the board was beginning to scorch. This necessitated that the team abandon the steepest ascent path. They conducted a series of experiments where board scorching was examined at different distances from the pre-heating element (factor D); they determined that a distance of at least 15cm was required to be confident that scorching would be avoided. To allow a margin of safety, the team set the distance D at 20cm. They then proceeded to increase pre-heat time in 5 second intervals, producing one board at each pre-heat setting. The results are shown in Table 9.10.

Table 9.10. Data for experiments on path of steepest descent.

RUN	B (sec.)	D (cm)	AVERAGE DEFECTS
1	15	37.5	70
2	20	8.75	52
3	25	20	51
4	30	20	31
5	35	20	18
6	40	20	12
7	45	20	10
8	50	20	13

These data are presented graphically in Figure 9.5.

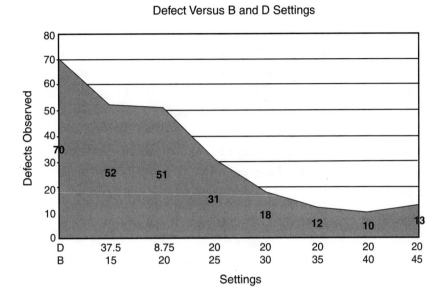

Figure 9.5. Steepest descent results.

With the distance fixed at 20 cm from the preheat element to the board surface, the best results were obtained with a pre-heat time of 40 seconds. Beyond that the defect rate was greater.

Phase III: The factorial experiment

The team decided to conduct a factorial experiment near the best settings to explore that experimental region more thoroughly. To do so, they decided to run a factorial experiment which would allow them to estimate the two-factor BD interaction as well as the main effects. They also wished to determine any "curvature" in the area. This required that more than two levels be explored (only linear estimates are possible with two-level designs). Finally, the team wanted to obtain an estimate of the experimental error in the region; this required replicating the experiment. The design selected is shown in Table 9.11.

Table 9.11. Replicated full-factorial design with center points.

RUN	B	D
1	40 (–1)	20.0 (–1)
2	45 (0)	22.5 (0)
3	50 (1)	25.0 (1)
4	40 (–1)	25.0 (1)
5	40 (–1)	20.0 (–1)
6	45 (0)	22.5 (0)
7	40 (–1)	25.0 (1)
8	40 (–1)	25.0 (1)
9	50 (1)	20.0 (–1)
10	50 (1)	25.0 (1)
11	40 (–1)	20.0 (–1)
12	40 (–1)	20.0 (–1)
13	50 (1)	25.0 (1)
14	50 (1)	20.0 (–1)
15	45 (0)	22.5 (0)

Code numbers used for the computer are shown in parentheses. The runs marked 0, 0 were center points. Note that each combination (i.e., set of plus and minus signs or zeros) was repeated three times. The team decided to center the design at the B value found in steepest B = 45 seconds. The interval for D was reduced to 2.5 cm and the experiment was centered one interval above D=20 (i.e., at D = 22.5).

Table 9.12. Results of full factorial experiment with center points and replicates.

RUN	B	D	RESULT
1	40 (-1)	20.0 (-1)	11
2	45 (0)	22.5 (0)	9
3	50 (1)	25.0 (1)	11
4	40 (-1)	25.0 (1)	15
5	50 (1)	20.0 (-1)	12
6	45 (0)	22.5 (0)	10
7	40 (-1)	25.0 (1)	17
8	40 (-1)	25.0 (1)	15
9	50 (1)	20.0 (-1)	11
10	50 (1)	25.0 (1)	11
11	40 (-1)	20.0 (-1)	13
12	40 (-1)	20.0 (-1)	13
13	50 (1)	25.0 (1)	11
14	50 (1)	20.0 (-1)	11
15	45 (0)	22.5 (0)	10

FRACTIONAL FACTORIAL FIT

Estimated effects and coefficients for defects (coded units)						
Term	Effect	Coef	StDev coef	T	P	
Constant		12.583	0.2357	53.39	0.000	
A	−2.833	−1.417	0.2357	−6.01	0.000	
B	1.500	0.750	0.2357	3.18	0.010	
A*B	−1.833	−0.917	0.2357	−3.89	0.003	
Ct Pt		−2.917	0.5270	−5.53	0.000	

Looking at the P column all terms in the model are significant (any P value below 0.05 indicates a significant effect.) This analysis is confirmed by the ANOVA table (Table 9.13).

Table 9.13. ANOVA for factorial experiment with center points.

ANOVA for defects (coded units)						
Source of variation	df	Seq. SS	Adj. SS	Adj. MS	F	P-value
Main effects	2	30.833	30.833	15.4167	23.13	0.000
2-way interactions	1	10.083	10.083	10.0833	15.13	0.003
Curvature	1	20.417	20.417	20.4167	30.63	0.000
Residual error	10	6.667	6.667	0.6667		
Pure error	10	6.667	6.667	0.6667		
Total	14	68.000				

Looking at the P column of the ANOVA table, it can be seen that main effects, the 2-way interaction, and "curvature" are all significant ($P < 0.05$). Curvature is measured by comparing the average response at the center points with the responses at the corner points of the design. The fact that curvature is significant means that we are no longer experimenting in a linear region of the responses. This means that the original coefficients, which were based on the linear model, are no longer adequate. Upon seeing these results, the black belt decided that it was necessary to proceed to Phase IV to better investigate the response region and to try to locate a stationary optimum.

Phase IV: The composite design

The black belt decided to try using a design known as a *composite design* or *central composite design* to obtain additional information on the region where the process was operating. This design involved augmenting the corner points and center point of the previous factorial experiment with additional points, as shown in Figure 9.6. The points extended the design beyond the levels previously designed by the high and low values for each factor. The team decided that they could allow the distance to be decreased somewhat below the 20cm "minimum" distance because they had added a 5cm margin of safety. They also noted that they were now taking relatively small experimental steps compared to the large jumps they took during steepest ascent.

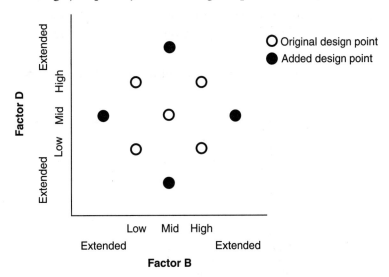

Figure 9.6. Central composite design for solder process.

DOE software finds the coefficients of the equation that describes a complex region for the responses. The equation being fitted is the following:

$$y = \beta_0 + \beta_1 x_1 + \beta_2 x_2 + \beta_{11} x_1^2 + \beta_{22} x_2^2 + \beta_{12} x_1 x_2 + \varepsilon \qquad (9.3)$$

The region described by this equation may contain a maximum, a minimum, or a "saddle point." At a maximum any movement away from the stationary point will cause the response to decrease. At the minimum any movement away from the stationary point will cause the response to increase. At a saddle point moving away from the stationary value of one variable will cause a decrease, while moving away from the stationary value of the other variable will cause an increase. Some DOE software will give the values of X and Y at the stationary point, and the nature of the stationary point (max, min, or saddle). Other DOE software display two and three dimensional drawings that graphically describe the region of experimentation. It is usually not difficult to interpret the response surface drawings.

The data collected by the team are shown in Table 9.14. Note that the data are shown in standard order, but the run order was random.

Table 9.14. Central composite design experiment and data.

B	D	DEFECTS
−1.41421	0.00000	16
1.00000	1.00000	11
0.00000	0.00000	9
0.00000	−1.41421	11
1.00000	−1.00000	9
1.41421	0.00000	4
0.00000	0.00000	10
0.00000	0.00000	10
0.00000	1.41421	15
0.00000	0.00000	9
0.00000	0.00000	10
−1.00000	1.00000	15
−1.00000	−1.00000	13

The computer analysis of these data is shown in Table 9.15.

Table 9.15. Analysis of central composite design.
Estimated regression coefficients for Y.

Estimated regression coefficients for defects					
Term	*Coef*	*StDev coef*	*T*	*P*	
Constant	9.600	0.5880	16.326	0.000	
B	−3.121	0.4649	−6.714	0.000	
D	1.207	0.4649	2.597	0.036	
B*B	0.325	0.4985	0.652	0.535	
D*D	1.825	0.4985	3.661	0.008	
B*D	0.000	0.6574	0.000	1.000	
S = 1.315		R–Sq = 90.3%		R–Sq(adj) = 83.4%	

The P-values indicate that all terms except the B^2 term and the interaction term are significant.

ANOVA for defects						
Source of variation	*df*	*Seq. SS*	*Adj. SS*	*Adj. MS*	*F*	*P*
Regression	5	112.821	112.8211	22.5642	13.05	0.002
Linear	2	89.598	89.5980	44.7990	25.91	0.001
Square	2	23.223	23.2231	11.6115	6.72	0.024
Interaction	1	0.000	0.0000	0.0000	0.00	1.000
Residual Error	7	12.102	12.1020	1.7289		
Lack-of-Fit	3	10.902	10.9020	3.6340	12.11	0.018
Pure Error	4	1.200	1.2000	0.3000		
Total	12	124.923				

Unusual observations for defects					
Observation	*Defects*	*Fit*	*StDev Fit*	*Residual*	*St Resid*
6	4.000	5.836	1.039	−1.836	−2.28R

R denotes an observation with a large standardized residual. The team confirmed the defect count for observation #6.

The ANOVA indicates that the lack-of-fit is not significant. It also indicates that the interaction term is not significant and could be removed from the model, gaining a degree of freedom for estimating the error.

The response surface 3D and contour plots are shown in Figure 9.7a and 9.7b.

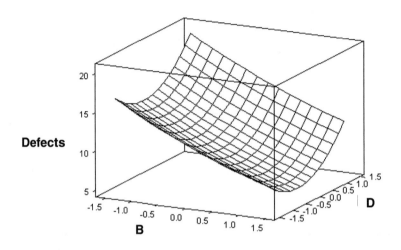

Figure 9.7a. Response surface plot for defect data.

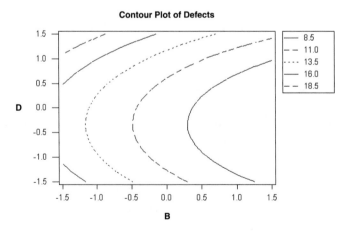

Figure 9.7b. Contour plot for defect data.

The analysis could become somewhat more advanced if the black belt chose to perform a *Canonical analysis* to investigate the nature of the response surface in greater detail. Canonical analysis involves finding a *stationary point S* and performing a coordinate system transformation to eliminate the cross-product and first order terms. The techniques for performing this analysis are described in a number of advanced texts (Box, G.E.P., and Draper 1987; Meyers and Montgomery, 1995). However, it is obvious from the contour plot and the 3D response surface plot that there may still be some room to improve by holding D constant and gradually increasing B.

At this point the team decided that they had reached a point of diminishing returns as far as the current process was concerned. The data indicated that the existing process for wave solder can, if properly controlled, manage to produce 10 or fewer defects per standard unit at the center of the last design. This was about 16 times better than the process was producing at the outset of the project and about 7 times better than the average result of the first experiment.

The team, guided by the black belt, decided to set the process at the center point of the last experiment (B=0, D=0) and to implement Evolutionary Operation (EVOP) to pursue further optimization. EVOP involves running a series of designed experiments on production units, with operating personnel making small changes (Box, G.E.P., and Draper, 1969). By restricting EVOP to small process changes the risk of producing scrap is reduced. Although the movements in process settings are small, the cumulative improvement in performance can be substantial. The apparent gradual slope of the defect rate in the +B direction also made it unlikely that the process would "fall off of a cliff" during EVOP.

The black belt helped set up EVOP on the process and train supervisory and hourly personnel in its use. She also agreed to provide ongoing support in the form of periodic visits and availability should questions arise. The team decided that after turning over process improvement to operating personnel, they would look at ways of maintaining their gains, while simultaneously investigating basic process and product design changes to obtain further improvement.

Phase V: Robust product and process design

Maintaining gains involves, among other things, creating processes and products that operate close to their optimum conditions even when changes occur. Robust design can begin with careful study of the contour plot. Note that if you start at B = D = 0 and move from along a line from left to right the response changes relatively slowly. However, if you move from the center along a line from lower to upper, the defect rate increases rapidly. Robust process control planning should take such non-linearity into account. If there is a need to change factor B or D, they should be changed in a way that avoids increasing the defect rate. This does *not* mean that all changes should be forbidden; after all, without change there can be no learning or improvement. However, changes should be monitored (as with EVOP) to provide a filter between the customer and the production of non-conforming product that may occur during the learning process.

More formally, robust design can be integrated into experimental design. The methods described by Genichi Taguchi are a well-known approach to integrating DOE and product and process design. While there has been much criticism of Taguchi's statistical approach, there is a broad consensus that his principles of robust parameter design are both valid and valuable contributions to engineering science.

TAGUCHI ROBUSTNESS CONCEPTS

This section will introduce some of the special concepts introduced by Dr. Genichi Taguchi of Japan. A complete discussion of Taguchi's approach to designed experiments is beyond the scope of this text. However, many of Taguchi's ideas are useful in that they present an alternative way of looking at quality in general.

Introduction

Quality is defined as the loss imparted to society from the time a product is shipped (Taguchi, 1986). Taguchi divides quality control efforts into two categories: on-line quality control and off-line quality control.

On-line quality control—involves diagnosis and adjusting of the process, forecasting and correction of problems, inspection and disposition of product, and follow-up on defectives shipped to the customer.

Off-line quality control—quality and cost control activities conducted at the product and the process design stages in the product development cycle. There are three major aspects to off-line quality control:

1. **System design**—is the process of applying scientific and engineering knowledge to produce a basic functional prototype design. The prototype model defines the initial settings of product or process design characteristics.

2. **Parameter design**—is an investigation conducted to identify settings that minimize (or at least reduce) the performance variation. A product or a process can perform its intended function at many settings of its design characteristics. However, variation in the performance characteristics may change with different settings. This variation increases both product manufacturing and lifetime costs. The term *parameter design* comes from an engineering tradition of referring to product characteristics as product parameters. An exercise to identify optimal parameter settings is therefore called *parameter design*.

3. **Tolerance design**—is a method for determining tolerances that minimize the sum of product manufacturing and lifetime costs. The final step in specifying product and process designs is to determine tolerances around the nominal settings identified by parameter design. It is still a common practice in industry to assign tolerances by convention rather than scientifically. Tolerances that are too narrow increase manufacturing costs, and tolerances that are too wide increase performance variation and the lifetime cost of the product.

Expected loss—the monetary losses an arbitrary user of the product is likely to suffer at an arbitrary time during the product's life span due to performance variation. Taguchi advocates modeling the loss function so the issue of parameter design can be made more concrete. The most often-used model of loss is the quadratic loss function illustrated in Figure 9.8. Note that the loss from operating the process is found by integrating the process pdf over the dollar-loss function. Under this model there is always a benefit to the following:

1. moving the process mean closer to the target value,
2. reducing variation in the process.

Of course, there is often a cost associated with these two activities. Weighing the cost/benefit ratio is possible when viewed from this perspective.

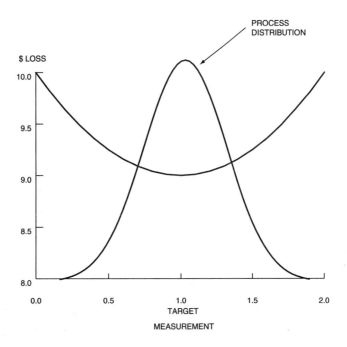

Figure 9.8. Taguchi's quadratic loss function.

Note the contrast between the quadratic loss function and the conceptual loss function implicit in the traditional management view. The traditional management approach to loss is illustrated in Figure 9.9.

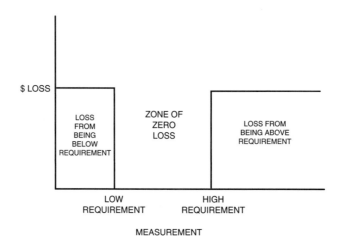

Figure 9.9. Traditional approach to loss.

Interpretation—there is no loss as long as a product or service meets requirements. There is no "target" or "optimum": just barely meeting requirements is as good as operating anywhere else within the zone of zero loss. Deviating a great deal from requirements incurs the same loss as being just barely outside the prescribed range. The process distribution is irrelevant as long as it meets the requirements.

Note that under this model of loss there is no incentive for improving a process that meets the requirements since there is no benefit; i.e., the loss is zero. Thus, cost exceeds benefit for any process that meets requirements. This effectively destroys the idea of continuous improvement and leads to the acceptance of an "acceptable quality level" as an operating standard.

Noise—the term used to describe all those variables, except design parameters, that cause performance variation during a product's life span and across different units of the product. Sources of noise are classified as either external sources or internal sources.

External sources of noise—variables external to a product that affect the product's performance.

Internal sources of noise—the deviations of the actual characteristics of a manufactured product from the corresponding nominal settings.

Performance statistics—estimate the effect of noise factors on the performance characteristics. Performance statistics are chosen so that maximizing the performance measure will minimize expected loss. Many performance statistics used by Taguchi use "signal to noise ratios" which account jointly for the levels of the parameters and the variation of the parameters.

Summary of the Taguchi method

The Taguchi method for identifying settings of design parameters that maximize a performance statistic is summarized by Kacker (1985):

- Identify initial and competing settings of the design parameters, and identify important noise factors and their ranges.
- Construct the design and noise matrices, and plan the parameter design experiment.
- Conduct the parameter design experiment and evaluate the performance statistic for each test run of the design matrix.
- Use the values of the performance statistic to predict new settings of the design parameters.
- Confirm that the new settings do indeed improve the performance statistic.

DATA MINING, ARTIFICIAL NEURAL NETWORKS AND VIRTUAL PROCESS MAPPING

As beneficial and productive as design of experiments can be, the process of conducting them has its drawbacks. The workplace, be it a factory, a retail establishment or an office, is designed around a routine. The routine is the "real work" that must be done to generate the sales which, in turn, produce the revenues that keep the enterprise in existence. By its very nature, experimenting means disrupting the routine. Important things are changed to determine what effect they have on various important metrics. Often, these effects are unpleasant; that's why they weren't changed in the first place! The routine was often established to steer a comfortable course that avoids the disruption and waste that results from making changes.

The problem is that without change things can never improve. Six Sigma generates as much improvement by changing things as it does by reducing variability. It's part of the Six Sigma paradox mentioned in the first chapter.

In this section a way of conducting "virtual" experiments using existing data and artificial neural network (neural net) software is presented. Neural nets are popular because they have a proven track record in many data mining and decision-support applications. Neural nets are a class of very powerful, general purpose tools readily applied to prediction, classification, and clustering. They have been applied across a broad range of industries from predicting financial series to diagnosing medical conditions, from identifying clusters of valuable customers to identifying fraudulent credit card transactions, from recognizing numbers written on checks to predicting failure rates of engines (Berry and Linoff, 1997). In this section only the application of neural nets to design of experiments for Six Sigma is explored; this merely scratches the surface of the potential applications of neural nets for quality and performance improvement.

Neural networks use a digital computer to model the neural connections in human brains. When used in well-defined domains, their ability to generalize and learn from data mimics our ability to learn from experience. However, there is a drawback. Unlike a well-planned and executed DOE, a neural network does not provide a mathematical model of the process.* For the most part, neural networks must be approached as black boxes with mysterious internal workings, much like the mystery of the human mind it is designed to imitate.

All companies record important data, some in well-designed data warehouses, some in file drawers. These data represent potential value to the Six Sigma team. They contain information that can be used to evaluate process performance. If the data include information on process settings, for example, they may be matched up to identify possible cause-and-effect relationships and point the direction for improvement. The activity of sifting through a database for useful information is known as *data mining*. The process works as follows:

1. Create a detailed inventory of data available throughout the organization.
2. Determine the variables which apply to the process being improved.
3. Using a subset of the data which includes the most extreme values, train the neural net to recognize relationships between patterns in the independent variables and patterns in the dependent variables.
4. Validate the neural net's predictive capacity with the remaining data.
5. Perform experimental designs as described in the section above entitled Empirical Model Building and Sequential Learning. However, instead of making changes to the actual process, make changes to the "virtual process" as modeled by the neural net.

---

*It is possible, however, to include various transformed variables to "help" the neural net if one has a model in mind. For example, in addition to feeding the neural net X1 and X2 raw, one could include higher-order polynomial and interaction terms as inputs to the neural network.

6. Once Phase IV has been completed, use the settings from the neural net as a starting point for conducting experiments on the actual process. In other words, begin experimenting at Phase I with a screening experiment.

It can be seen that the entire soft experimentation process is part of Phase 0 in the empirical model building process. It helps answer the question "Where are we?" It is important to recognize that neural net experiments are not the same as live experiments. However, the cost of doing them is minimal compared with live experiments and the process of identifying input and output variables, deciding at which levels to test these variable, etc. will bear fruit when the team moves on to the real thing. Also, soft experiments allow a great deal more "what if?" analysis, which may stimulate creative thinking from team members.

EXAMPLE

The data in Table 9.16 are from the solder process described above. Data were not gathered for a designed experiment, but were merely collected during the operation of the process. The data were used to train and validate a neural net.

Table 9.16. Solder process data for virtual process mapping.

PH Time	PH Distance	Defects
38	22.5	15
40	20	13
40	25	16
45	17.5	15
45	22.5	5
45	26	11
50	20	12
42	22.5	10
50	25	3
42	22	11
46	22	4
55	25	4
55	21	17
55	25	15
50	24	3
49	25	3
57	37	10

Continued at right . . .

PH Time	PH Distance	Defects
35	25	20
45	37.5	17
30	20	27
30	22.5	33
30	25	37
30	27.5	50
30	37.5	57
50	20	13
50	22.5	5
50	25	3
50	30	5
50	14	12
50	37.5	14
50	45	16
50	50	40
60	20	35
60	25	18
60	37.5	12

The neural net model is shown in Figure 9.10.

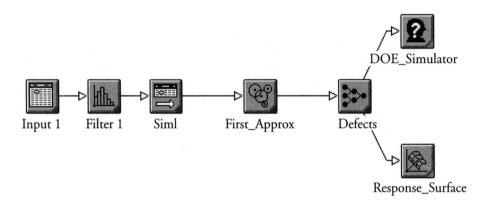

Figure 9.10. Neural net model for solder defects.

The model was trained using the above data, producing the process map shown in Figure 9.11.

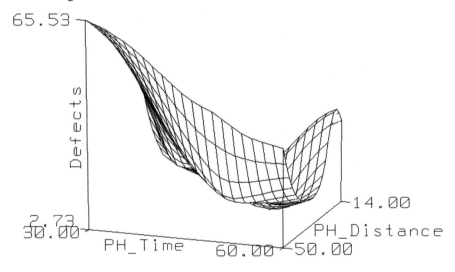

Figure 9.11. Neural net process map for solder defects.

It can be seen that the surface described by the neural net is similar to the one modeled earlier using DOE. Both models direct the B and D settings to similar levels and both make similar predictions for the defect rate.

The neural net software also allows "what if" analysis. Since these data are from the region where the team ran its last phase of experiments, they could be used to conduct virtual DOE. The neural net's What If? Contour plot dialog box is shown in Figure 9.12.

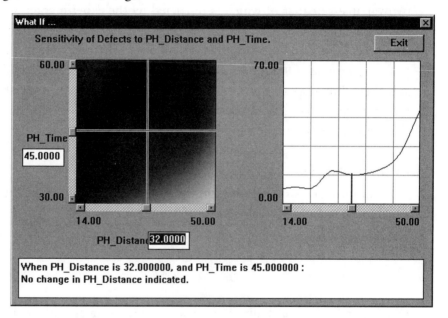

Figure 9.12. What If? contour plot dialog box.

The virtual DOE values are entered in the What If? Dialog box and the neural net's predictions are used in the experimental design just as if they had been obtained using data from a real experiment. If you have data covering the entire region of interest, the neural net may bring you very close to the optimum settings even before you do your first actual experiment.

REGRESSION AND CORRELATION ANALYSIS

Correlation analysis (the study of the strength of the linear relationships among variables) and regression analysis (modeling the relationship between one or more independent variables and a dependent variable) are activities of considerable importance in quality engineering. A regression problem considers the frequency distributions of one variable when another is held fixed at each of several levels. A correlation problem considers the joint variation of two variables, neither of which is restricted by the experimenter. Correlation and regression analyses are designed to assist the engineer in studying cause and effect. They may be employed in all stages of the problem-solving and planning process. Of course, statistics cannot by themselves establish cause and effect. Proving cause and effect requires sound scientific understanding of the situation at hand. The statistical methods described in this section assist the engineer in performing this task.

Linear models

A linear model is simply an expression of a type of association between two variables, x and y. A *linear relationship* simply means that a change of a given size in x produces a proportionate change in y. Linear models have the form:

$$y = a + bx \qquad (9.4)$$

where a and b are constants. The equation simply states that when x changes by one unit, y will change by b units. This relationship can be shown graphically.

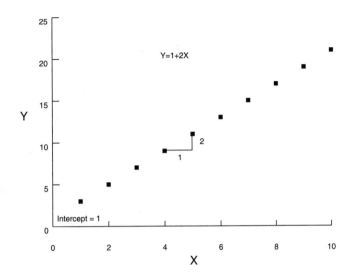

Figure 9.13. Scatter diagram of a linear relationship.

In Figure 9.13, a=1 and b=2. The term a is called the intercept and b is called the slope. When x=0, y is equal to the intercept. Figure 9.13 depicts a perfect linear fit; e.g., if x is known y can be determined exactly. Of course, perfect fits are virtually unknown when real data are used. In practice error must be dealt with in x and y. These issues are discussed below.

Many types of associations are non-linear. For example, over a given range of x values, y might increase, and for other x values, y might decrease. This *curvilinear relationship* is shown in Figure 9.14.

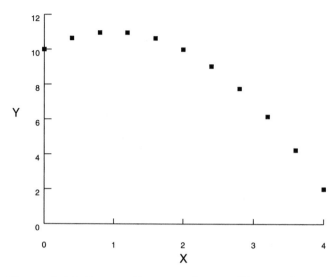

Figure 9.14. Scatter diagram of a curvilinear relationship.

Here we see that *y* increases when *x* increases and is less than 1, and decreases as *x* increases when *x* is greater than 1. Curvilinear relationships are valuable in the design of robust systems. A wide variety of processes produces such relationships.

It is often helpful to convert these non-linear forms to linear form for analysis using standard computer programs or scientific calculators. Several such transformations are shown in Table 9.17.

Table 9.17. Some linearizing transformations.

(Source: Experimental Statistics, NBS Handbook 51, p. 5–31)

IF THE RELATIONSHIP IS OF THE FORM:	PLOT THE TRANSFORMED VARIABLES		CONVERT STRAIGHT LINE CONSTANTS (B_0 AND B_1) TO ORIGINAL CONSTANTS	
	Y_T	X_T	b_0	b_1
$Y = a + \dfrac{b}{X}$	Y	$\dfrac{1}{X}$	a	b
$\dfrac{1}{Y} = a + bX$	$\dfrac{1}{Y}$	X	a	b
$Y = \dfrac{X}{a + bX}$	$\dfrac{X}{Y}$	X	a	b
$Y = a b^X$	$\log Y$	X	$\log a$	$\log b$
$Y = a e^{bx}$	$\log Y$	X	$\log a$	$b \log e$
$Y = a X^b$	$\log Y$	$\log X$	$\log a$	b
$Y = a + b X^n$ where n is known	Y	X^n	a	b

Fit the straight line $Y_T = b_0 + b_1 X_T$ using the usual linear regression procedures (see below). In all formulas, substitute Y_T for Y and X_T for X. A simple method for selecting a transformation is to simply program the transformation into a spreadsheet and run regressions using every transformation. Then select the transformation which gives the largest value for the statistic R^2.

There are other ways of analyzing non-linear responses. One common method is to break the response into segments that are piecewise linear, and then to analyze each piece separately. For example, in Figure 9.14 y is roughly linear and increasing over the range $0<x<1$ and linear and decreasing over the range $x>1$. Of course, if the engineer has access to powerful statistical software, non-linear forms can be analyzed directly.

When conducting regression and correlation analysis two main types of variables can be distinguished. One type is called *predictor variables* or *independent variables*; the other, *response variables* or *dependent variables*. Predictor or independent variables are usually variables that can either be set to a desired value (e.g., oven temperature) or else take values that can be measured but not controlled (e.g., outdoors ambient humidity). As a result of changes that are deliberately made, or simply take place in the predictor variables, an effect is transmitted to the response variables (e.g., the grain size of a composite material). We are usually interested in discovering how changes in the predictor variables affect the values of the response variables. Ideally, we hope that a small number of predictor variables will "explain" nearly all of the variation in the response variables.

In practice, it is sometimes difficult to draw a clear distinction between independent and dependent variables. In many cases it depends on the objective of the investigator. For example, a quality engineer may treat ambient temperature as a predictor variable in the study of paint quality, and as the response variable in a study of clean room particulates. However, the above definitions are useful in planning engineering studies.

Another idea important to studying cause and effect is that of the *data space* of the study. The data space of a study refers to the region bounded by the range of the independent variables under study. In general, predictions based on values outside the data space studied, called *extrapolations*, are little more than speculation and not advised. Figure 9.15 illustrates the concept of data space for two independent variables. Defining the data space can be quite tricky when large numbers of independent variables are involved.

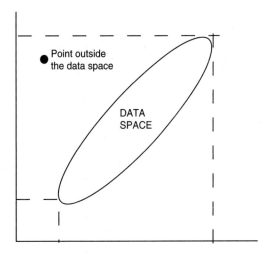

Figure 9.15. Data space.

While the numerical analysis of data provides valuable information, it should always be supplemented with graphical analysis as well. Scatter diagrams are one very useful supplement to regression and correlation analysis. The following illustrates the value of supplementing numerical analysis with scatter diagrams.

I		II		III		IV	
X	Y	X	Y	X	Y	X	Y
10	8.04	10	9.14	10	7.46	8	6.58
8	6.95	8	8.14	8	6.77	8	5.76
13	7.58	13	8.74	13	12.74	8	7.71
9	8.81	9	8.77	9	7.11	8	8.84
11	8.33	11	9.26	11	7.81	8	8.47
14	9.96	14	8.10	14	8.84	8	7.04
6	7.24	6	6.13	6	6.08	8	5.25
4	4.26	4	3.10	4	5.39	19	12.50
12	10.84	12	9.13	12	8.15	8	5.56
7	4.82	7	7.26	7	6.42	8	7.91
5	5.68	5	4.74	5	5.73	8	6.89

Statistics for Processes I-IV

$n = 11$

$\overline{X} = 9.0$

$\overline{Y} = 7.5$

best fit line: $Y = 3 + 0.5X$

standard error of slope: 0.118

$t = 4.24$

$\sum X - \overline{X} = 110.0$

regression SS = 27.50

residual SS = 13.75

$r = 0.82$

$r^2 = 0.67$

Figure 9.16. Illustration of the value of scatter diagrams.

(Source: *The Visual Display of Quantitative Information*, Edward R. Tufte, 13–14 pp.)

Continued on next page . . .

Figure 9.16—*Continued* . . .

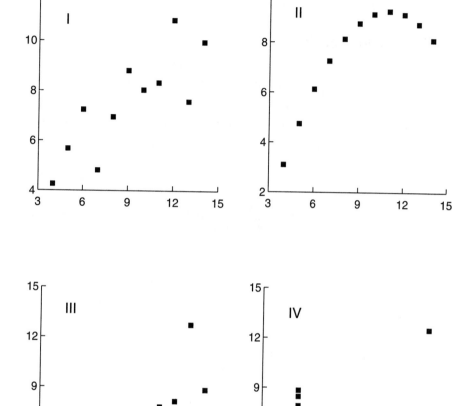

Figure 9.16. Illustration of the value of scatter diagrams.

(Source: *The Visual Display of Quantitative Information*, Edward R. Tufte, 13–14 pp.)

In other words, although the scatter diagrams clearly show four distinct processes, the statistical analysis does not. In quality engineering, numerical analysis alone is not enough.

Least-squares fit

If all data fell on a perfectly straight line it would be easy to compute the slope and intercept given any two points. However, the situation becomes more complicated when there is "scatter" around the line. That is, for a given value of x, more than one value of y appears. When this occurs, there is error in the model. Figure 9.17 illustrates the concept of error.

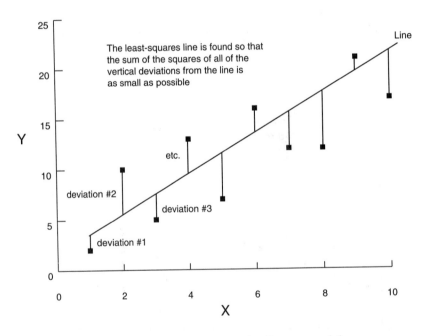

Figure 9.17. Error in the linear model.

The model for a simple linear regression with error is the following:

$$y = a + bx + \varepsilon \qquad (9.5)$$

where ε represents error. Generally, assuming the model adequately fits the data, errors are assumed to follow a normal distribution with a mean of 0 and a constant standard deviation. The standard deviation of the errors is known as the *standard error*. Ways of verifying assumptions are discussed below.

When error occurs, as it does in nearly all "real-world" situations, there are many possible lines which might be used to model the data. Some method must be found which provides, in some sense, a "best fit" equation in these everyday situations. Statisticians have developed a large number of such methods. The method most commonly used in quality engineering finds the straight line that minimizes the sum of the squares of the errors for all of the data points. This method is known as the "least-squares" best-fit line. In other words, the least-squares best-fit line equation is $y_i' = a + bx_i$ where a and b are found so that the sum of the squared deviations from the line is minimized. The best-fit equations for a and b are as follows:

$$b = \frac{\Sigma(X_i - \overline{X})(Y_i - \overline{Y})}{\Sigma(X_i - \overline{X})^2} \tag{9.6}$$

$$a = \overline{Y} - b\overline{X} \tag{9.7}$$

where the sum is taken over all n values. Most spreadsheets and scientific calculators have a built-in capability to compute a and b. As stated above, there are many other ways to compute the slope and intercept (e.g., minimize the sum of the absolute deviations, minimize the maximum deviation, etc.); in certain situations one of the alternatives may be preferred. The reader is advised to consult books devoted to regression analysis for additional information (see, for example, Draper and Smith, 1981).

The reader should note that the fit obtained by regressing x on y will not in general produce the same line as would be obtained by regressing y on x. This is illustrated in Figure 9.18.

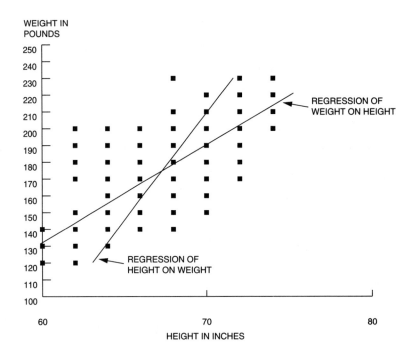

Figure 9.18. Least-squares lines of weight vs. height and height vs. weight.

When weight is regressed on height the equation indicates the average weight (in pounds) for a given height (in inches.) When height is regressed on weight the equation indicates the average height for a given weight. The two lines intersect at the average height and weight.

These examples show how a single independent variable is used to model the response of a dependent variable. This is known as *simple linear regression*. It is also possible to model the dependent variable in terms of two or more independent variables; this is known as *multiple linear regression*. The mathematical model for multiple linear regression has additional terms for the additional independent variables. Equation 9.8 shows a linear model when there are two independent variables.

$$\hat{y} = a + b_1 x_1 + b_2 x_2 + \varepsilon \qquad (9.8)$$

where $x_1 x_2$ are independent variables, b_1 is the coefficient for x_1 and b_2 is the coefficient for x_2.

EXAMPLE OF REGRESSION ANALYSIS

A restaurant conducted surveys of 42 customers, obtaining customer ratings on staff service, food quality, and overall satisfaction with their visit to the restaurant. Figure 9.19 shows the regression analysis output from a spreadsheet regression function (Microsoft Excel).

SUMMARY OUTPUT						
Regression statistics						
Multiple R	0.847					
R square	0.717					
Adjusted R square	0.703					
Standard error	0.541					
Observations	42					
ANOVA						
	df	*ss*	*ms*	*F*	*Significance F*	
Regression	2	28.97	14.49	49.43	0.00	
Residual	39	11.43	0.29			
Total	41	40.40				
	Coefficients	*Standard error*	*t Stat*	*P-value*	*Lower 95%*	*Upper 95%*
Intercept	-1.188	0.565	-2.102	0.042	-2.331	-0.045
Staff	0.902	0.144	6.283	0.000	0.611	1.192
Food	0.379	0.163	2.325	0.025	0.049	0.710

Figure 9.19. Regression analysis output.

The data consist of two independent variables, staff and food quality, and a single dependent variable, overall satisfaction. The basic idea is that the quality of staff service and the food are *causes* and the overall satisfaction score is an *effect*. The regression output is interpreted as follows:

Multiple R—the multiple correlation coefficient. It is the correlation between y and y'. For the example: multiple R=0.847, which indicates that y and y' are highly correlated, which implies that there is an association between overall satisfaction and the quality of the food and service.

R Square—the square of multiple R. It measures the proportion of total variation about the mean $\bar{Y}$ explained by the regression. For the example: R^2=0.717, which indicates that the fitted equation explains 71.7% of the total variation about the average satisfaction level.

Adjusted R Square—a measure of R^2 "adjusted for degrees of freedom." The equation is

$$Adjusted\ R^2 = 1 - \left(1 - R^2\right)\left(\frac{n-1}{n-p}\right) \qquad (9.9)$$

where p is the number of parameters (coefficients for the xs) estimated in the model. For the example: p=2, since there are two x terms. Some experimenters prefer the adjusted R^2 to the unadjusted R^2, while others see little advantage to it (e.g., Draper and Smith 1981, p. 92).

Standard error—the standard deviation of the residuals. The *residual* is the difference between the observed value of y and the predicted value based on the regression equation.

Observations—refer to the number of cases in the regression analysis, or n.

ANOVA, or ANalysis Of VAriance—a table examining the hypothesis that the variation explained by the regression is zero. If this is so, then the observed association could be explained by chance alone. The rows and columns are those of a standard one-factor ANOVA table (see earlier in this chapter). For this example, the important item is the column labeled "Significance F." The value shown, 0.00, indicated that the probability of getting these results due to chance alone was less than 0.01; i.e., the association is probably not due to chance alone. Note that the ANOVA applies to the entire *model*, not to the individual variables.

The next table in the output examines each of the terms in the linear model separately. The *intercept* is as described above, and corresponds to the term *a* in the linear equation. This model uses two independent variables. In this terminology staff=b_1, food=b_2. Thus, reading from the *coefficients* column, the linear model is: $\hat{y} = -1.88 + 0.902 \times staff\ score + 0.379 \times food\ score$. The remaining columns test the hypotheses that each coefficient in the model is actually zero.

Standard error column—gives the standard deviations of each term, i.e., the standard deviation of the intercept=0.565, etc.

t Stat column—the coefficient divided by the standard error, i.e., it shows how many standard deviations the observed coefficient is from zero.

P-value—shows the area in the tail of a *t* distribution beyond the computed *t* value. For most experimental work, a P-value less than 0.05 is accepted as an indication that the coefficient is significantly different than zero. All of the terms in this model have significant P-values.

Lower 95% and Upper 95% columns—a 95% confidence interval on the coefficient. If the confidence interval does not include zero, we will fail to reject the hypothesis that the coefficient is zero. None of the intervals in this example include zero.

Correlation analysis

As mentioned earlier, a correlation problem considers the joint variation of two variables, neither of which is restricted by the experimenter. Unlike regression analysis, which considers the effect of the independent variable(s) on a dependent variable, correlation analysis is concerned with the joint variation of one independent variable with another. In a correlation problem, the engineer has two measurements for each individual item in the sample. Unlike a regression study where the engineer controls the values of the *x* variables, correlation studies usually involve spontaneous variation in the variables being studied. Correlation methods for determining the strength of the linear relationship between two or more variables are among the most widely applied statistical techniques. More advanced methods exist for studying situations with more than two variables (e.g., canonical analysis, factor analysis, principal components analysis, etc.); however, with the exception of multiple regression, this discussion will focus on the linear association of two variables at a time.

In most cases, the measure of correlation used by engineers is the statistic r, sometimes referred to as *Pearson's product-moment correlation*. Usually x and y are assumed to have a bivariate normal distribution. Under this assumption r is a sample statistic which estimates the population correlation parameter ρ. One interpretation of r is based on the linear regression model described earlier, namely that r^2 is the proportion of the total variability in the y data which can be explained by the linear regression model. The equation for r is as follows:

$$r = \frac{s_{xy}}{s_x s_y} = \frac{n\sum xy - \sum x \sum y}{\sqrt{\left[n\sum x^2 - (\sum x)^2\right]\left[n\sum y^2 - (\sum y)^2\right]}} \qquad (9.10)$$

and, of course, r^2 is simply the square of r. r is bounded at -1 and +1. When the assumptions hold, the significance of r is tested by the regression ANOVA.

Interpreting r can become quite tricky, so scatter plots should always be used (see Chapter 7). When the relationship between x and y is non-linear, the "explanatory power" of r is difficult to interpret in precise terms and should be discussed with great care. While it is easy to see the value of very high correlations such as $r=0.99$, it is not so easy to draw conclusions from lower values of r, even when they are statistically significant (i.e., they are significantly different than 0.0). For example, $r=0.5$ does *not* mean the data show half as much clustering as a perfect straight-line fit. In fact, $r=0$ does *not* mean that there is no relationship between the x and y data, as Figure 9.20 shows. When $r>0$, y tends to increase when x increases. When $r<0$, y tends to decrease when x increases.

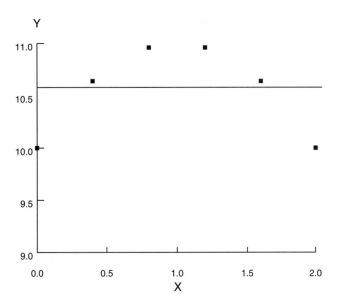

Figure 9.20. Interpreting $r=0$ for curvilinear data.

Although $r=0$, the relationship between x and y is perfect, albeit non-linear.

At the other extreme, $r=1$, a "perfect correlation," does not mean that there is a cause and effect relationship between x and y. For example, both x and y might be determined by a third variable, z. In such situations, z is described as a *lurking variable* which "hides" in the background, unknown to the experimenter. Lurking variables are behind some of the infamous silly associations, such as the association between teacher's pay and liquor sales (the lurking variable is general prosperity).*

Establishing causation requires solid scientific understanding. Causation cannot be "proven" by statistics alone. Some statistical techniques, such as path analysis, can help determine if the correlations between a number of variables are consistent with causal assumptions. However, these methods are beyond the scope of this book.

---

*It is possible to evaluate the association of x and y by removing the effect of the lurking variable. This can be done using regression analysis and computing partial correlation coefficients. This advanced procedure is described in most texts on regression analysis.

CHI-SQUARE CONTINGENCY TABLES

MAKING COMPARISONS USING CHI-SQUARE TESTS

In quality engineering, there are many instances when the engineer wants to compare the percentage of items distributed among several categories. The categories might include operators, methods, materials, or any other grouping of interest. From each of the groups a sample is taken, evaluated, and placed into one of several categories (e.g., high quality, marginal quality, reject quality). The results can be presented as a table with m rows representing the groups of interest and k columns representing the categories. Such tables can be analyzed to answer the question "Do the groups *differ* with regard to the proportion of items in the categories?" The chi-square statistic can be used for this purpose.

EXAMPLE OF CHI-SQUARE TEST

The following example is from Natrella (1963). Rejects of metal castings were classified by cause of rejection for three different weeks, as given in the following tabulation. The question to be answered is the following: Does the distribution of rejects differ from week to week?

	CAUSE OF REJECTION							
	Sand	Misrun	Shift	Drop	Core-break	Broken	Other	Total
Week 1	97	8	18	8	23	21	5	180
Week 2	120	15	12	13	21	17	15	213
Week 3	82	4	0	12	38	25	19	180
Total	299	27	30	33	82	63	39	573

Chi-square (χ^2) is computed by first finding the expected frequencies in each cell. This is done using the equation:

$$Frequency\ expected = f_e = \frac{Row\ sum * column\ sum}{overall\ sum}$$

For week 1, e.g., the frequency expected of sand rejects was (180*299)/573=93.93. The table below shows the frequency expected for the remainder of the cells.

	Sand	Misrun	Shift	Drop	Corebreak	Broken	Other
Week 1	93.93	8.48	9.42	10.37	25.76	19.79	12.25
Week 2	111.15	10.04	11.15	12.27	30.48	23.42	14.50
Week 3	93.93	8.48	9.42	10.37	25.76	19.79	12.25

The next step was to compute χ^2 as follows:

$$\chi^2 = \sum_{\text{over all cells}} \frac{\left(Frequency\ expected - Frequency\ observed\right)^2}{Frequency\ expected}$$

$$= \frac{(93.93-97)^2}{93.93} + \cdots + \frac{(12.25-19)^2}{12.25} = 45.60$$

Next, a value of $\alpha=0.10$ was used for this example. The degrees of freedom for the χ^2 test was $(k\text{-}1)(m\text{-}1) = 12$. Referring to Table 4 in the Appendix the critical value of $\chi^2 = 18.55$ was found for these values. Since the computed value of χ^2 exceeded the critical value, it was concluded that the weeks differed with regard to proportions of various types of defectives.

RELIABILITY ANALYSIS
Basic reliability terms and principles

Safety and reliability are specialties in their own right. The quality engineer is expected to have an understanding of certain key concepts in these subject areas. It is obvious that these two areas overlap the quality engineering body of knowledge to a considerable extent. Some concept areas are nearly identical (e.g., traceability) while others are merely complementary (e.g., reliability presumes conformance to design criteria, which quality engineering addresses directly). Modern ideas concerning safety share a common theoretical base with reliability.

While common usage of the term *reliability* varies, its technical meaning is quite clear: *reliability* is defined as the probability that a product or system will perform a specified function for a specified time without failure. For the reliability figure to be meaningful, the operating conditions must be carefully and completely defined. Although reliability analysis can be applied to just about any product or system, in practice it is normally applied only to complex products. Formal reliability analysis is routinely used for both commercial products, such as automobiles, as well as military products, like missiles.

RELIABILITY TERMS

MTBF—Mean time between failures, μ. When applied to repairable products, this is the average time a system will operate until the next failure.

Failure rate—The number of failures per unit of stress. The stress can be time (e.g., machine failures per shift), load cycles (e.g., wing fractures per 100,000 deflections of six inches), impacts (e.g., ceramic cracks per 1,000 shocks of 5 g's each), or a variety of other stresses. The failure rate $\Theta = 1 / \mu$.

MTTF or MTFF—The mean time to first failure. This is the measure applied to systems that can't be repaired during their mission. For example, the MTBF would be irrelevant to the *Voyager* spacecraft.

MTTR—Mean time to repair. The average elapsed time between a unit failing and its being repaired and returned to service.

Availability—The proportion of time a system is operable. This is only relevant for systems that can be repaired. Availability is given by the equation

$$Availability = \frac{MTBF}{MTBF + MTTR} \qquad (9.11)$$

b_{10} life*—The life value at which 10% of the population has failed.

---

*b_{10} life and b_{50} life are terms commonly applied to the reliability of ball bearings.

b_{50} **life**—The life value at which 50% of the population has failed. This is also called the median life.

Fault Tree Analysis (FTA)—Fault trees are diagrams used to trace symptoms to their root causes. *Fault tree analysis* is the term used to describe the process involved in constructing a fault tree. (See below for additional discussion.)

Derating—Assigning a product to an application that is at a stress level less than the rated stress level for the product. This is analogous to providing a safety factor.

Censored test—A life test where some units are removed before the end of the test period, even though they have not failed.

Maintainability—A measure of the ability to place a system that has failed back in service. Figures of merit for maintainability include availability and mean time to repair.

TYPES OF RELIABILITY SYSTEMS

The reliability of a given system is dependent on the reliability of its individual elements combined with how the elements are arranged. For example, a set of Christmas tree lights might be configured so that the entire set will fail if a single light goes out. Or it may be configured so that the failure of a single light will not effect any of the other lights (question: do we define such a set as having failed if only one light goes out? If all but one go out? Or some number in between?).

Mathematical models

The mathematics of reliability analysis is a subject unto itself. Most systems of practical size require the use of high speed computers for reliability evaluation. However, an introduction to the simpler reliability models is extremely helpful in understanding the concepts involved in reliability analysis.

One statistical distribution that is very useful in reliability analysis is the exponential distribution, which is given by Equation 9.12.

$$R = \exp\left[-\frac{t}{\mu}\right], \ t \geq 0 \qquad (9.12)$$

In Equation 9.12 R is the system reliability, given as a probability, t is the time the system is required to operate without failure, and μ is the mean time to failure for the system. The exponential distribution applies to systems operating in the constant failure rate region, which is where most systems are designed to operate.

Reliability apportionment

Since reliability analysis is commonly applied to complex systems, it is logical that most of these systems are composed of smaller subsystems. Apportionment is the process involved in allocating reliability objectives among separate elements of a system. The final system must meet the overall reliability goal. Apportionment is something of a hybrid of project management and engineering disciplines.

The process of apportionment can be simplified if we assume that the exponential distribution is a valid model. This is because the exponential distribution has a property that allows the system failure rate to be computed as the reciprocal of the sum of the failure rates of the individual subsystems. Table 9.18 shows the apportionment for a home entertainment center. The complete system is composed of a tape deck, television, compact disk unit, and a phonograph. Assume that the overall objective is a reliability of 95% at 500 hours of operation.

SUBSYSTEM	RELIABILITY	UNRELIABILITY	FAILURE RATE	OBJECTIVE
Tape deck	0.990	0.010	0.00002	49,750
Television	0.990	0.010	0.00002	49,750
Compact disk	0.985	0.015	0.00003	33,083
Phonograph	0.985	0.015	0.00003	33,083
	0.950	0.050		
TAPE DECK SUBSYSTEM				
SUBSYSTEM	RELIABILITY	UNRELIABILITY	FAILURE RATE	OBJECTIVE
Drive	0.993	0.007	0.000014	71,178
Electronics	0.997	0.003	0.000006	166,417
	0.990	0.010		

Table 9.18. Reliability apportionment for a home entertainment system.

The apportionment could continue even further; for example, we could apportion the drive reliability to pulley, engagement head, belt, capstan, etc. The process ends when it has reached a practical limit. The column labeled "objective" gives the minimum acceptable mean time between failures for each subsystem in hours. MTBFs below this will cause the entire system to fail its reliability objective. Note that the required MTBFs are huge compared to the overall objective of 500 hours for the system as a whole. This happens partly because of the fact that the reliability of the system as a whole is the *product* of the subsystem reliabilities which requires the subsystems to have much higher reliabilities than the complete system.

Reliability apportionment is very helpful in identifying design weaknesses. It is also an eye opener for management, vendors, customers, and others to see how the design of an entire system can be dramatically affected by one or two unreliable elements.

Series

A system is in series if all of the individual elements must function for the system to function. A series system block diagram is shown in Figure 9.21.

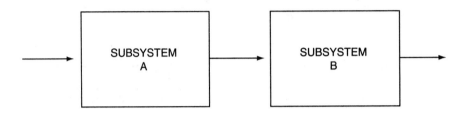

Figure 9.21. A series configuration.

In the above diagram, the system is composed of two subsystems, A and B. Both A and B must function correctly for the system to function correctly. The reliability of this system is equal to the product of the reliabilities of A and B, in other words:

$$R_S = R_A \times R_B \qquad (9.13)$$

For example, if the reliability of A is 0.99 and the reliability of B is 0.92, then $R_s = 0.99 \times 0.92 = 0.9108$. Note that with this configuration, R_s is always less than the *minimum* of R_A or R_B. This implies that the best way to improve the reliability of the system is to work on the system component that has the lowest reliability.

Parallel

A parallel system block diagram is illustrated in Figure 9.22. This system will function as long as A or B or C haven't failed. The reliability of this type of configuration is computed using Equation 9.14.

$$R_S = 1 - (1 - R_A)(1 - R_B)(1 - R_C) \qquad (9.14)$$

For example, if R_A = 0.90, R_B = 0.95, and R_C = 0.93 then R_s = 1 – (0.1 x 0.05 x 0.07) = 1 – 0.00035 = 0.99965.

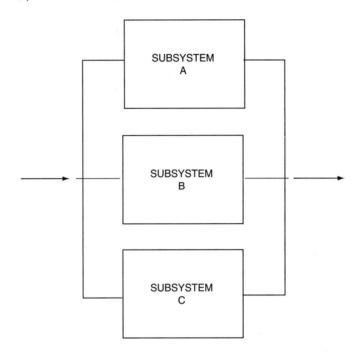

Figure 9.22. A parallel system.

With parallel configurations, the system reliability is always better than the best subsystem reliability. Thus, when trying to improve the reliability of a parallel system, first try to improve the reliability of the best component. This is precisely opposite of the approach taken to improve the reliability of series configurations.

Assessing design reliability
SEVEN STEPS IN PREDICTING DESIGN RELIABILITY

1. Define the product and its functional operation. Use functional block diagrams to describe the systems. Define failure and success in unambiguous terms.
2. Use reliability block diagrams to describe the relationships of the various system elements (e.g., series, parallel, etc.).
3. Develop a reliability model of the system.
4. Collect part and subsystem reliability data. Some of the information may be available from existing data sources. Special tests may be required to acquire other information.
5. Adjust data to fit the special operating conditions of your system. Use care to assure that your "adjustments" have a scientific basis and are not merely reflections of personal opinions.
6. Predict reliability using a mathematical model. Computer simulation may also be required.
7. Verify your prediction with field data. Modify your models and predictions accordingly.

SYSTEM EFFECTIVENESS

The effectiveness of a system is a broader measure of performance than simple reliability. There are three elements involved in system effectiveness:

1. Availability.
2. Reliability.
3. Design capability, i.e., assuming the design functions, does it also achieve the desired result?

System effectiveness can be measured with Equation 9.15.

$$P_{SEf} = P_A \times P_R \times P_C \qquad (9.15)$$

In this equation, P_{SEf} is the probability the system will be effective, P_A is the availability as computed with Equation 9.11, P_R is the system reliability, and P_C is the probability that the design will achieve its objective.

Monte Carlo simulation*

As seen in the previous sections, reliability modeling can be difficult mathematically. And in many cases, it is impossible to mathematically model the situation desired. Monte Carlo Simulation is a useful tool under these and many other circumstances, such as:

- Verifying analytical solutions
- Studying dynamic situations
- Gaining information about event sequences; often expected values and moments do not provide enough detail
- Determining the important components and variables in a complex system
- Determining the interaction among variables
- Studying the effects of changes without the risk, cost, and time constraints of experimenting on the real system
- Teaching

RANDOM NUMBER GENERATORS

The heart of any simulation is the generation of random numbers. If a programming language such as BASIC, C, or FORTRAN is used, random number generators will have to be created. If simulation languages such as Siman, Slam, Simscript, or GPSS are used, random number generators are part of the software.

Random numbers from specific distributions are generated by transforming random numbers from the unit, uniform distribution. Virtually all programming languages, as well as electronic spreadsheets, include a unit, uniform random number generator.** Technically, these unit, uniform random number generators are pseudo-random number generators, as the algorithms used to generate them take away a small portion of the randomness.

*The material in this section is taken from *The Complete Guide to the CRE* by Bryan Dodson and Dennis Nolan. ©1998 Quality Publishing LLC, Tucson, Arizona. Reprinted with permission of the publisher.

**A unit, uniform random variable can be generated using the "RND" function in the BASIC programming language (Visual Basic, Quick Basic, GWBasic, and BASICA), and the "@RAND" function in Lotus™ 123. Microsoft™ Excel includes a random generating tool that allows random numbers to be generated from several distributions.

Nevertheless, these algorithms are extremely efficient and for all practical purposes the result is a set of truly random numbers.

A simple way to generate distribution-specific random numbers is to set the
cumulative distribution function equal to a unit, random number and take
the inverse. Consider the exponential distribution

$$F(x) = 1 - e^{-\lambda x} \qquad (9.16)$$

By setting r (a random variable uniformly distributed from zero to one) equal
to F(x) and inverting the function, an exponentially distributed random variable, x, with a failure rate of λ is created.

$$r = 1 - e^{-\lambda x}$$
$$1 - r = e^{-\lambda x}$$
$$\ln(1 - r) = -\lambda x \qquad (9.17)$$
$$x = -\frac{\ln(1 - r)}{\lambda}$$

This expression can be further reduced; the term 1–r is also uniformly distributed from zero to one. The result is

$$x = -\frac{\ln r}{\lambda} \qquad (9.18)$$

Table 9.19 contains some common random number generators.

Table 9.19 Random number generators.

DISTRIBUTION	PROBABILITY DENSITY FUNCTION	RANDOM NUMBER GENERATOR
Uniform	$f(x) = \dfrac{1}{b-a}, a \leq x \leq b$	$x = a + (b-a)r$
Exponential	$f(x) = \lambda e^{-\lambda x}, 0 < x < \infty$	$x = -\dfrac{1}{\lambda}\ln r$
Normal	$f(x) = \dfrac{1}{\sigma\sqrt{2\Pi}}\exp\left[-\dfrac{1}{2}\left(\dfrac{x-\mu}{\sigma}\right)^2\right]$, $-\infty < x < \infty$	$x_1 = \left[\sqrt{-2\ln r_1}\,\cos(2\Pi r_2)\right]\sigma + \mu$ $x_2 = \left[\sqrt{-2\ln r_1}\,\sin(2\Pi r_2)\right]\sigma + \mu$ †
Lognormal	$f(x) = \dfrac{1}{\sigma x\sqrt{2\Pi}}\exp\left[-\dfrac{1}{2}\left(\dfrac{\ln x-\mu}{\sigma}\right)^2\right]$, $x > 0$	$x_1 = \exp\left[\sqrt{-2\ln r_1}\,\cos(2\Pi r_2)\right]\sigma + \mu$ $x_2 = \left[\sqrt{-2\ln r_1}\,\sin(2\Pi r_2)\right]\sigma + \mu$ †
Weibull	$f(x) = \dfrac{\beta x^{\beta-1}}{\theta^\beta}\exp\left(\dfrac{x}{\theta}\right)^\beta, x > 0$	$x = \theta(-\ln r)^{1/\beta}$
Poisson	$f(x) = \dfrac{e^{-\lambda t}(\lambda t)^x}{x!}, x = 0, 1, 2, ..., \infty$	$x = \begin{cases} 0, -\dfrac{1}{\lambda}\ln r > t & \ddagger \\ x, \displaystyle\sum_{i=1}^{x} -\dfrac{1}{\lambda}\ln r_i < t < \sum_{i=1}^{x+1} -\dfrac{1}{\lambda}\ln r_i \end{cases}$
Chi-square	$f(x) = \dfrac{1}{2^{v/2}\Gamma(v/2)}x^{(v/2-1)}e^{-x/2}, x > 0$	$x = \displaystyle\sum_{i=1}^{v} z_i^2$ z_i is a standard normal random deviate.
Beta	$f(x) = \dfrac{1}{B(p,q)}x^{p-1}(1-x)^{q-1}$, $0 \leq x \leq 1, p > 0, q > 0$	$x = \dfrac{r^{1/p}}{r^{1/p} + r^{1/q}}$

Continued on next page...

Table 9.19—*Continued...*

DISTRIBUTION	PROBABILITY DENSITY FUNCTION	RANDOM NUMBER GENERATOR
Gamma	$$f(x) = \frac{\lambda^{\eta}}{\Gamma(\eta)} x^{(\eta-1)} e^{-\lambda x},$$ $$x \geq 0, \quad \eta > 0, \quad \lambda > 0$$	1. η is a non-integer shape parameter. 2. Let η_1 = the truncated integer root of η. 3. Let $q = -\ln \prod_{j=1}^{\eta_1} r_j$ 4. Let $A = \eta - \eta_1$, and $B = 1 - A$. 5. Generate a random number and let $y_1 = r_j^{1/A}$ 6. Generate a random number and let $y_2 = r_{i+1}^{1/B}$ 7. If $y_1 + y_2 \leq 1$ go to 9. 8. Let $i = i+2$ and go to 5. 9. Let $z = y_1/(y_1+y_2)$. 10. Generate a random number, r_n. 11. Let $W = -\ln r_n$. 12. $x = (q+zW)\lambda$.
Binomial	$$p(x) = \binom{n}{x} p^x (1-p)^{n-x}, x = 0,1,...,n$$	$x = \sum_{i=1}^{n} y_i, \quad y_i = \begin{cases} 0, r_i > p \\ 1, r_i \leq p \end{cases}$
Geometric	$$p(x) = p(1-p)^{x-1}, \ x = 1, 2, 3, ...$$	$\dfrac{\ln(1-r)}{\ln(1-p)} \leq x \leq \dfrac{\ln(1-r)}{\ln(1-p)} + 1$ ‡
Student's t	$$f(x) = \frac{\Gamma[(\nu+1)/2]}{\Gamma(\nu/2)\sqrt{\Pi\nu}} \left(1 + \frac{x^2}{\nu}\right)^{-(\nu+1)/2},$$ $$-\infty < x < \infty$$	$x = \dfrac{z_1}{\left(\sum\limits_{i=2}^{\nu+1} \dfrac{z_i^2}{\nu}\right)^{1/2}}$ z_i is a standard normal random deviate.
F	$$f(x) = \left(\frac{\Gamma[(\nu_1+\nu_2)/2](\nu_1/\nu_2)^{\nu_1/2}}{\Gamma(\nu_1/2)\Gamma(\nu_2/2)}\right)$$ $$* \left(\frac{x^{\nu_1/2-1}}{(1+\nu_1 x/\nu_2)^{(\nu_1+\nu_2)/2}}\right), x > 0$$	$x = \dfrac{\nu_2 \sum\limits_{i=1}^{\nu_1} z_i^2}{\nu_1 \sum\limits_{i=\nu_1+1}^{\nu_1+\nu_2} z_i^2}$ z_i is a standard normal random deviate.

†Two uniform random numbers must be generated, with the result being two normally distributed random numbers.

‡Increase the value of x until the inequality is satisfied.

SIMULATION MODELING

After the construction of the desired random number generator(s), the next step is to mathematically model the situation under study. After completing the model, it is important to *validate* and *verify* the model. A valid model is a reasonable representation of the situation being studied. A model is verified by determining that the mathematical and computer model created represents the intended conceptual model.

Enough iterations should be included in the simulation to provide a *steady-state* solution, which is reached when the output of the simulation from one iteration to the next changes negligibly. When calculating means and variances, 1,000 iterations are usually sufficient. If calculating confidence limits, many more iterations are required; after all, for 99% confidence limits the sample size for the number of random deviates exceeding the confidence limit is 1/100th the number of iterations.

Simulation can be used to determine the result of transformations of random variables. Suppose the mean and variance of the product of two normally distributed variables are needed for design purposes. The following BASIC code will produce the desired result. A flowchart for this code is shown in Figure 9.23.

```
REM simulation for the product of two normally distributed variables
e1=100
v1=7
e2=120
v2=16
DEFINT I–L
FOR i = 1 TO 5000
a = RND
b = RND
REM x is normal with mean=e1 and standard deviation=v1
x = (((–2 * LOG(a)) ^ .5) * COS(2 * 3.141592654# * b)) * v1 + e1
REM y is normal with mean=e2 and standard deviation=v2
y = (((–2 * LOG(a)) ^ .5) * SIN(2 * 3.141592654# * b)) * v2 + e2
z = x * y
ztot# = ztot# + z
zsq# = zsq# + z ^ 2
PRINT i
NEXT i
PRINT "ztot zsq"; ztot#; zsq#
PRINT "mean="; ztot# / 5000
zvar# = (5000 * zsq# – ztot# ^ 2) / (5000 * 4999)
PRINT "variance="; zvar#
```

Note: "RND" generates uniform random deviates on the interval from zero to one. The "LOG" function in BASIC represents the natural logarithm.

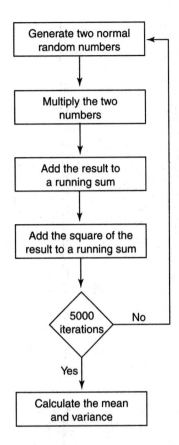

Figure 9.23. Flowchart for the simulation of two normally distributed normal variables.

In the above code two normal random numbers are generated with the desired parameters and multiplied. This is repeated 5,000 times; the mean and variance of these 5,000 random deviates are calculated. The result is a random variable with a mean of 12,009 and a variance of 3,307,380.

For the above example recall that the same result could have been obtained mathematically. A disadvantage of solving this problem mathematically is that there is no information regarding the shape of the resulting distribution.

With electronic spreadsheets simulations no longer require computer code. The previous example is simulated using Lotus 123™ with the following steps.*

1. In cell *A1* place the function @RAND
2. In cell *A2* place the function @RAND
3. In cell *A3* place the formula
   $$(((-2*@\ln(A1))^\wedge.5)*@\cos(2*@pi*A2))*7+100$$
4. In cell *A4* place the formula
   $$(((-2*@\ln(A1))^\wedge.5)*@\cos(2*@pi*A2))*7+100$$
5. In cell *A5* place the formula
   $$+A3*A4$$
6. Copy this row 5,000 times

In the above example, each row in the spreadsheet represents an iteration. The powerful @functions and graphics tools contained in the spreadsheet can then be used for analysis. Note that each change in the spreadsheet causes the random numbers to be changed. It may be helpful to convert the output from formulas to fixed numbers with the "Range Value" command.

Now consider a system consisting of four identical components which are exponentially distributed with a failure rate of 0.8. Three of the components are standby redundant with perfect switching. Information is needed regarding the shape of the resulting distribution. The following code produces four exponentially distributed random variables with a failure rate of 0.8, adds them, and writes the result to the file "c:\data."; this process is repeated 5,000 times. A flowchart for this problem is provided in Figure 9.24.

*Microsoft™ Excel can generate normal random variables directy.

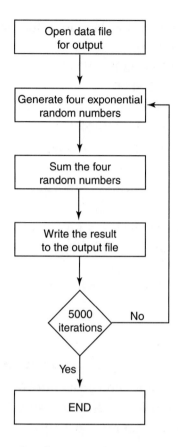

Figure 9.24. Simulation for the sum of exponential random variables.

```
REM simulation for the sum of four exponentially distributed variables
DEFINT I–L
OPEN "c:\data" FOR OUTPUT AS #1 LEN = 256
FOR i = 1 TO 5000
REM x1 is exponential with failure rate = 0.8
x1 = –(1 / .8) * LOG(RND)
REM x2 is exponential with failure rate = 0.8
x2 = –(1 / .8) * LOG(RND)
REM x3 is exponential with failure rate = 0.8
x3 = –(1 / .8) * LOG(RND)
REM x4 is exponential with failure rate = 0.8
x4 = –(1 / .8) * LOG(RND)
y = x1 + x2 + x3 + x4
PRINT #1, USING "##########.#####"; y
PRINT i
NEXT i
CLOSE
```

By importing the resulting data into an electronic spreadsheet or statistical program, a wide variety of analyses can be done on the data. A histogram of the data produced from the above code is shown in Figure 9.25.

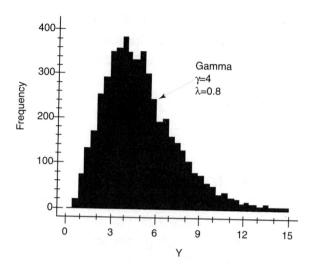

Figure 9.25. Histogram of the sum of four
exponentially distributed random variables.

As seen from Figure 9.25, the sum of n exponentially distributed random
variables with a failure rate of λ is a random variable that follows the gamma
distribution with parameters $\eta = n$ and λ.

This problem is also easily simulated using an electronic spreadsheet. The
steps required follow:

1. In cells *A1* through *A4*, place the formula

$$-(1/0.8)*@\ln(@rand)$$

2. In cell *A5* place the formula

$$@sum(A1..A4)$$

3. Copy the contents of row A 5000 times

Again, each row represents an iteration, and the spreadsheet can be used to
obtain the desired simulation output.

Now consider a system consisting of three components in series. The components are Weibully distributed with parameters $\beta = 2$, $\theta = 300$; $\beta = 4$, $\theta = 100$; and, $\beta = 0.5$, $\theta = 200$. The code below depicts this situation. Figure 9.26 shows a flowchart for this simulation.

```
REM simulation three Weibully distributed variables in series
DEFINT I–L
DIM x(99)
OPEN "c:\data" FOR OUTPUT AS #1 LEN = 256
FOR i = 1 TO 5000
REM x(1) is Weibull shape parameter=2 and scale parameter=300
x(1) = 300 * (–LOG(RND)) ^ (1 / 2)
REM x(2) is Weibull shape parameter=4 and scale parameter=100
x(2) = 100 * (–LOG(RND)) ^ (1 / 4)
REM x(3) is Weibull shape parameter=0.5 and scale parameter=200
x(3) = 200 * (–LOG(RND)) ^ (1 / .5)
min = 999999999
FOR j = 1 TO 3
IF x(j) < min THEN min = x(j)
NEXT j
y = min
PRINT #1, USING "##########.#####"; y
PRINT i
NEXT i
CLOSE
```

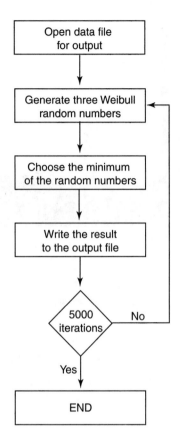

Figure 9.26. Simulation of a series system.

For a series system, the time to fail is the minimum of the times to fail of the components in series. A parallel system could be modeled by altering the above code to take the maximum time to fail of each of the components. Figure 9.27 is a histogram of the resulting data for the series system.

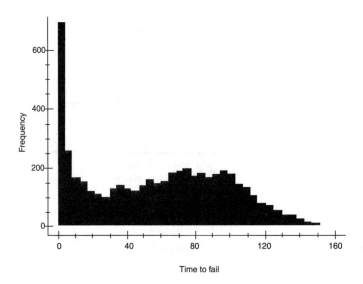

Figure 9.27. Histogram of a series system.

The large number of early failures can be attributed to the component with the high infant mortality rate ($\beta = 0.5$). The result is a distribution that does not appear to conform to any known distributions. However, with 5,000 points, a reliability function can be built empirically. The result is shown in Figure 9.28.

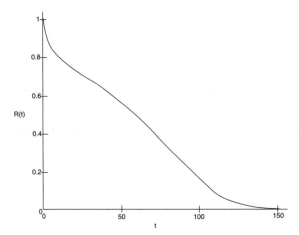

Figure 9.28. Reliability function for a series system.

The following steps are used to simulate the above problem using an electronic spreadsheet:

1. In cell *A1* place the formula
$$300*(-@ln(@rand))^\wedge(1/2)$$

2. In cell *A2* place the formula
$$100*(-@ln(@rand))^\wedge(1/4)$$

3. In cell *A3* place the formula
$$200*(-@ln(@rand))^\wedge(1/0.5)$$

4. In cell *A4* place the formula
$$@min(A1..A4)$$

5. Copy the contents of row A 5,000 times.

Now consider a system with two Weibully distributed components, A and B. Component B is standby redundant, and the switching mechanism has a reliability of 95%. The parameters of component A are $\beta = 3$, $\theta = 85$. The parameters of component B are $\beta = 4.4$, $\theta = 95$. The code below models this system; a flowchart is given in Figure 9.29.

```
REM simulation of a switch for two Weibully distributed variables
DEFINT I–L
OPEN "c:\data" FOR OUTPUT AS #1 LEN = 256
FOR i = 1 TO 5000
REM x is Weibull shape parameter=3 and scale parameter=85
x = 85 * (–LOG(RND)) ^ (1 / 3)
REM y is Weibull shape parameter=4.4 and scale parameter=97
y = 97 * (–LOG(RND)) ^ (1 / 4.4)
s = RND
IF s >= .05 THEN swr = 1 ELSE swr = 0
IF swr = 1 THEN z = x + y ELSE z = x
PRINT #1, USING "##########.#####"; y
PRINT i
NEXT i
CLOSE
```

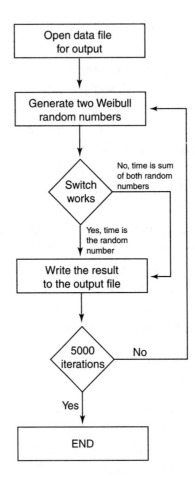

Figure 9.29. Simulation of a switching system.

A histogram of the 5,000 data points written to the data file is shown in Figure 9.30.

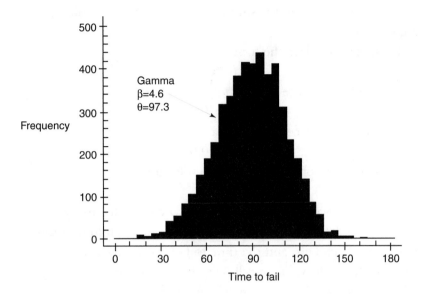

Figure 9.30. Histogram of a switching system.

The histogram shows the time to fail for the system following a Weibull distribution. The reliability function for this system, built from the 5,000 simulation points, is shown in Figure 9.31.

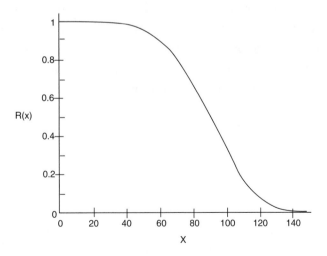

Figure 9.31. Reliability function for a switching system.

This situation can be simulated using an electronic spreadsheet. The required steps follow:

1. In cell *A1* place the formula
$$85*(@ln(@rand))^\wedge(1/3)$$
2. In cell A@ place the formula
$$97*(@ln(@rand))^\wedge(1/4.5)$$
3. In cell *A3* place the formula
$$@if(@rand<0.05,+A1,+A1+A2)$$
4. Copy the contents of row A 5,000 times.

In step 4 above the reliability of the switch is tested using the unit, uniform random number generator. If the unit, uniform random number is less than 0.05, the switch fails, and the time to fail for the system is the time to fail for component A (the value in cell A1). If the switch operates, the system time to fail is the sum of the values in cells A1 and A2.

In summary, simulation is a powerful analytical tool that can be used to model virtually any system. For the above examples, 5,000 iterations were used. The number of iterations used should be based on reaching a steady-state condition. Depending on the problem more or less iterations may be needed.

Once simulation is mastered, a danger is that it is overused because of the difficulty involved with mathematical models. Do not be tempted to use simulation before exploring other options. When manipulating models, mathematical models lend themselves to optimization whereas simulation models require trial and error for optimization.

RISK ASSESSMENT TOOLS

While reliability prediction is a valuable activity, it is even more important to design reliable systems in the first place. Proposed designs must be evaluated to detect potential failures prior to building the system. Some failures are more important than others, and the assessment should highlight those failures most deserving of attention and scarce resources. Once failures have been identified and prioritized, a system can be designed that is robust; i.e., it is insensitive to most conditions that might lead to problems.

DESIGN REVIEW

Design reviews are conducted by specialists, usually working on teams. Designs are, of course, reviewed on an ongoing basis as part of the routine work of a great number of people. However, the term as used here refers to the formal design review process. The purposes of formal design review are threefold:

1. Determine if the product will actually work as desired and meet the customer's requirements.
2. Determine if the new design is producible and inspectable.
3. Determine if the new design is maintainable and repairable.

Design review should be conducted at various points in the design and production process. Review should take place on preliminary design sketches, after prototypes have been designed, and after prototypes have been built and tested, as developmental designs are released, etc. Designs subject to review should include parts, subassemblies, and assemblies.

FAILURE MODE AND EFFECT ANALYSIS (FMEA)

Failure mode and effect analysis, or FMEA, is an attempt to delineate all possible failures and their effect on the system. The objective is to classify failures according to their effect. FMEA provides an excellent basis for classification of characteristics.

When engaged in FMEA, it is wise to bear in mind that the severity of failure is not the only important factor; one must also consider the probability of failure. As with Pareto analysis, one objective of FMEA is to direct the available resources toward the most promising opportunity. An extremely unlikely failure, even a failure with serious consequences, may not be the best place to concentrate reliability improvement efforts. Decision analysis methods may be helpful in dealing with this type of question.

FAILURE MODE, EFFECTS, AND CRITICALITY ANALYSIS (FMECA)

FMECA , like FMEA, is usually performed during the reliability apportionment phase. Also like FMEA, FMECA consists of considering every possible failure mode and its effect on the product. However, FMECA goes one step beyond FMEA in that it also considers the criticality of the effect and actions which must be taken to compensate for this effect. Typical criticality categories are similar to those discussed above under classification of defects: e.g., critical (loss of life or product), major (total product failure), minor (loss of function.) Preferably, FMECA will result in a design modified to eliminate unwanted seriously deleterious effects. A contingency plan will be prepared for dealing with those effects that cannot be removed from the design.

FAULT-TREE ANALYSIS (FTA)

While FMEA and FMECA are bottom-up approaches to reliability analysis, FTA is a top-down approach. FTA provides a graphical representation of the events that might lead to failure. Some of the symbols used in construction of fault trees are shown in Table 9.20.

Table 9.20. Fault-tree symbols.

Source: *Handbook of Reliability Engineering and Management*, McGraw-Hill, reprinted with permission of the publisher.

GATE SYMBOL	GATE NAME	CASUAL RELATIONS
	AND gate	Output event occurs if all the input events occur simultaneously
	OR gate	Output event occurs if any one of the input events occurs
	Inhibit gate	Input produces output when conditional event occurs
	Priority AND gate	Output event occurs if all input events occur in the order from left to right
	Exclusive OR gate	Output event occurs if one, but not both, of the input events occur
n inputs	m-out-of-n gate (voting or sample gate)	Output event occurs if m-out-of-n input events occur

Continued on next page . . .

Table 9.20—*Continued* . . .

EVENT SYMBOL	MEANING
rectangle	Event represented by a gate
circle	Basic event with sufficient data
diamond	Undeveloped event
switch or house	Either occurring or not occurring
oval	Conditional event used with inhibit gate
triangles	Transfer symbol

In general, FTA follows these steps:

1. Define the top event, sometimes called the *primary event*. This is the failure condition under study.
2. Establish the boundaries of the FTA.
3. Examine the system to understand how the various elements relate to one another and to the top event.
4. Construct the fault tree, starting at the top event and working downward.
5. Analyze the fault tree to identify ways of eliminating events that lead to failure.
6. Prepare a corrective action plan for preventing failures and a contingency plan for dealing with failures when they occur.

7. Implement the plans.
8. Return to step #1 for the new design.

Figure 9.32 illustrates an FTA for an electric motor.

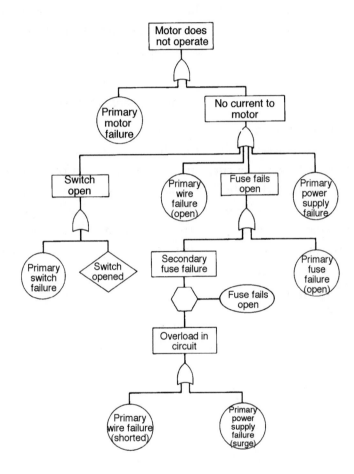

Figure 9.32. Fault tree for an electric motor.

Source: *Handbook of Reliability Engineering and Management*, McGraw-Hill,
reprinted with permission of the publisher.

SAFETY ANALYSIS

Safety and reliability are closely related. A safety problem is created when a critical failure occurs, which reliability theory addresses explicitly with such tools as FMECA and FTA. The modern evaluation of safety/reliability takes into account the probabilistic nature of failures. With the traditional approach a safety factor would be defined using Equation 9.19.

$$SF = \frac{average\ strength}{worst\ expected\ stress} \tag{9.19}$$

The problem with this approach is quite simple: it doesn't account for variation in either stress or strength. The fact of the matter is that both strength and stress will vary over time, and unless this variation is dealt with explicitly we have no idea what the "safety factor" really is. The modern view is that a safety factor is the difference between an improbably high stress (the maximum expected stress, or "reliability boundary") and an improbably low strength (the minimum expected strength). Figure 9.33 illustrates the modern view of safety factors. The figure shows two *distributions*, one for stress and one for strength.

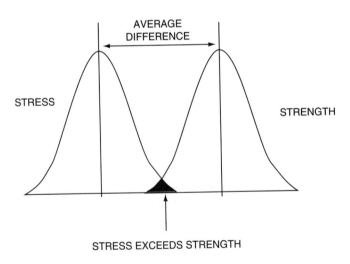

Figure 9.33. Modern view of safety factors.

Since any strength or stress is theoretically possible, the traditional concept of a safety factor becomes vague at best and misleading at worst. To deal intelligently with this situation, we must consider *probabilities* instead of *possibilities*. This is done by computing the probability that a stress/strength combination will occur such that the stress applied exceeds the strength. It is possible to do this since, if we have distributions of stress and strength, then the difference between the two distributions is also a distribution. In particular, if the distributions of stress and strength are normal, the distribution of the difference between stress and strength will also be normal. The average and standard distribution of the difference can be determined using statistical theory, and are shown in Equations 9.20 and 9.21.

$$\sigma^2_{SF} = \sigma^2_{STRENGTH} + \sigma^2_{STRESS} \tag{9.20}$$

$$\mu_{SF} = \mu_{STRENGTH} - \mu_{STRESS} \tag{9.21}$$

In Equations 9.20 and 9.21 the SF subscript refers to the safety factor.

EXAMPLE OF COMPUTING PROBABILITY OF FAILURE

Assume that strength and stress are normally distributed. Then the distribution of strength minus stress is also normally distributed with the mean and variance computed from Equations 9.20 and 9.21. Furthermore, the probability of a failure is the same as the probability that the difference of strength minus stress is less than zero. A negative difference implies that stress exceeds strength, thus leading to a critical failure.

Assume that the strength of a steel rod is normally distributed with $\mu = 50,000^{\#}$ and $\sigma = 5,000^{\#}$. The steel rod is to be used as an undertruss on a conveyor system. The stress observed in the actual application was measured by strain gages and it was found to have a normal distribution with $\mu = 30,000^{\#}$ and $\sigma = 3,000^{\#}$. What is the expected reliability of this system?

Solution

The mean variance and standard deviation of the difference are first computed using Equations 9.20 and 9.21, giving

$$\sigma^2_{DIFFERENCE} = \sigma^2_{STRENGTH} + \sigma^2_{STRESS} = 5{,}000^2 + 3{,}000^2 = 34{,}000{,}000$$

$$\sigma = \sqrt{34{,}000{,}000} = 5{,}831^{\#}$$

$$\mu_{DIFFERENCE} = \mu_{STRENGTH} - \mu_{STRESS} = 50{,}000^{\#} - 30{,}000^{\#} = 20{,}000^{\#}$$

We now compute Z which transforms this normal distribution to a standard normal distribution (see Chapter 8).

$$Z = \frac{0^{\#} - 20{,}000^{\#}}{5{,}831^{\#}} = -3.43$$

Using a normal table (Appendix Table 2), the probability associated with this Z value is found to be 0.0002. This is the probability of failure, about 1 chance in 5,000. The reliability is found by subtracting this probability from 1, giving 0.9998. Thus, the reliability of this system (and safety for this particular failure mode) is 99.98%. This example is summarized in Figure 9.34

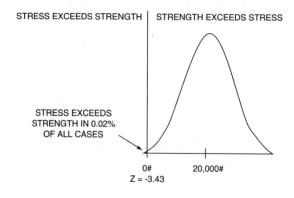

Figure 9.34. Distribution of strength minus stress.

PROCESS SIMULATION

Simulation is a means of experimenting with a detailed model of a real system to determine how the system will respond to changes in its structure, environment or underlying assumptions. A system is defined as a combination of elements that interact to accomplish a specific objective. A group of machines performing related manufacturing operations would constitute a system. These machines may be considered, as a group, an element in a larger production system. The production system may be an element in a larger system involving design, delivery, etc.

Simulations allow the system designer to solve problems. To the extent that the computer model behaves as the real world system it models, the simulation can help answer important questions. Care should be taken to prevent the model from becoming the focus of attention. If important questions can be answered more easily without the model, then the model should not be used.

The modeler must specify the scope of the model and the level of detail to include in the model. Only those factors which have a significant impact on the model's ability to serve its stated purpose should be included. The level of detail must be consistent with the purpose. The idea is to create, as economically as possible, a replica of the real world system that can provide answers to important questions. This is usually possible at a reasonable level of detail.

Well designed simulations provide data on a wide variety of systems metrics, such as throughput, resource utilization, queue times, and production requirements. While useful in modeling and understanding existing systems, they are even better suited to evaluating proposed process *changes*. In essence, simulation is a tool for rapidly generating and evaluating ideas for process improvement. By applying this technology to the creativity process, Six Sigma improvements can be greatly accelerated.

Simulation tools

Not long ago, computer simulation was the exclusive domain of highly trained systems engineers. These early simulations were written in some general purpose programming language, such as FORTRAN, Pascal, or C. However, modern computer software has greatly simplified the creation of simulation models. With graphical user interfaces and easy drawing-based model creation, it is now almost as easy to create a simulation as it is to draw a flow chart (see Figure 9.35).

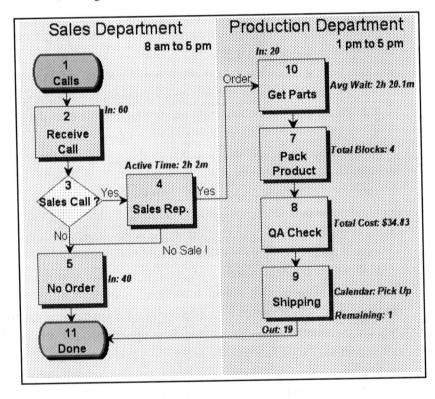

Figure 9.35. Simulation software interface.

While the user interface may *look* like an ordinary flowchart, it is much more powerful. A closer look at Figure 9.35 reveals that additional information is recorded on the chart. Next to box #2: Receive Call, In: 60 means that the simulation program looked at 60 simulated phone calls. Since 40 calls were not sales calls, 20 of these calls were sales calls that kept the simulated sales representatives active for 2 hours and 2 minutes. Other data is available from the diagram, including the fact that QA checking cost $34.83 and that one order remained to be shipped at the conclusion of the simulation. If the model is based on an existing system, these numbers will be compared to actual process numbers to validate the model. The first simulation should always model the past, otherwise how can the model's forecasts for the future be trusted?

The current system model is interesting and often educational. Many times managers and process operators will be surprised to see the model of the system. It is common to find that people focus on their particular task without ever really understanding their role in the larger scheme of things. The numbers are often a greater surprise. Good, clean data must be collected before the simulation model can be built and tested. The process of getting this data often reveals shortcomings with the existing management information systems. Once the confusion is cleared up and management gets their first good look at the process, they are often shocked at what they see. On more than one occasion, the author's clientele have asked him to place the project on hold until the obvious problems can be fixed.

As intriguing as models of existing systems can be, the real power and excitement begins when simulation models are applied to process changes. Refer to the simple model shown in Figure 9.35 above. There are many questions which might arise regarding this process, e.g.,

- A new promotion is expected to double the number of orders phoned in, what effect will that have on production?
- If the QA check was performed by production personnel, what effect would that have on QA cost? Total cost? Production throughput?

In general, the model helps determine what happens to Y if X is changed. Changes often create *unanticipated consequences* throughout a complex system due to their effects on inter-related processes. For example, changing the volume of calls might cause an increase in the idle time of the QA checker because it increases the delay time in the "Get Parts" bottleneck process. Once this fact has been revealed by the simulation, the manager can deal with it. Furthermore, the manager's proposed solution can also be tested by simulation before it's tried in the real world. For example, the manager might propose to cross-train the QA person to be able to help Get Parts. This would theoretically reduce the wait at the Get Times step while simultaneously increasing the utilization of the QA person. The simulation would allow this hypothesis to be tested before it's tried. Perhaps it will show that the result is merely to move the bottleneck from one process step to another, rather than eliminating it. Anyone who has spent any length of time in the working world is familiar with these "hydraulic models" where managers' attempts to fix one problem only results in the creation of new problems. By discovering this before trying it, money is saved and morale improved.

EXAMPLE: A SIMULATION OF RECEIVING INSPECTION[*]

This example describes a simulation model of a complex inspection operation at a factory of a large unionized defense contractor. The plant receives four types of parts: electrical, simple mechanical, complex mechanical, and parts or materials that require non-destructive testing (NDT). Union regulations required four different inspector grades. The plant experiences a growing backlog of orders awaiting inspection. The backlog has an adverse effect on production scheduling, including frequent missile assembly stoppages. A computer simulation will be conducted to answer the following questions:

---

[*]Pyzdek, 1991–92.

1. Is the backlog a chance event that will eventually correct itself without intervention, or is a permanent change of process required?
2. If additional personnel are hired, will they be adequately utilized?
3. Which type of job skills are required?
4. Will additional automated or semi-automated inspection equipment alleviate the problem?

Model development

The first phase of the project is to develop an accurate model of the Receiving Inspection process. One element to evaluate is the distribution of arrivals of the various parts. Figure 9.36 compares the empirical distribution of the electrical lots with the predictions of an exponential arrival time model (see Monte Carlo simulation above). Data were gathered from a recent work-month.

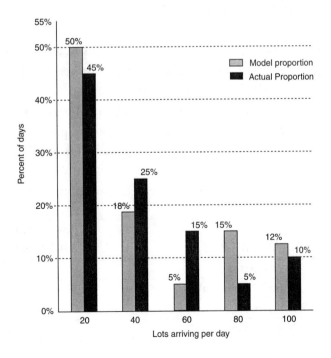

Figure 9.36. Electrical order arrivals predicted versus actual.

Similar "eyeball fits" were obtained from the arrival distributions of the other three part types. The exponential model seems to provide adequate representation of the data in each case (i.e., when we use the model parameters to simulate past performance, the results of the simulation are quite close to what actually happened). The parameter estimates (average arrival rates) used for the models are shown in Table 9.21.

Table 9.21. Average arrival rates.

ORDER TYPE	MEAN ARRIVAL RATE (ORDERS-PER-HOUR)
Electrical	4.292
Simple mechanical	6.849
Complex mechanical	1.541
Non-destructive test	0.630

Another aspect of the model development is to describe the distribution of inspection time per order. Recent time studies conducted in Receiving Inspection provide data of actual inspection times for the four different parts. The exponential model proved to be adequate, passing a Chi-square goodness-of-fit test as well as our "simulation of the past" check. The parameter estimates for the inspection times are given in Table 9.22.

Table 9.22. Average inspection times.

ORDER TYPE	AVERAGE INSPECTION TIME (ORDERS-PER-HOUR)
Electrical	1.681
Simple mechanical	2.500
Complex mechanical	0.597
Non-destructive test	0.570

Figure 9.37 shows the exponential curve, based on 228 orders, fitted to inspection times for electrical orders. Several studies showed that, on average, it took four times longer to check a complex mechanical order using a manual surface plate layout than it took on a coordinate measuring machine (CMM). (These interesting discoveries often result from simulation projects.)

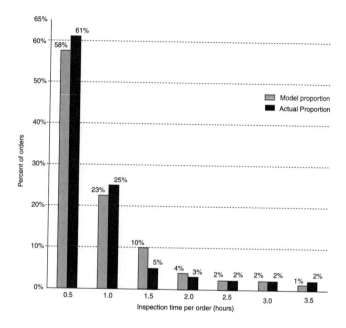

Figure 9.37. Electrical order inspection times.

Time studies indicated that rejected lots required additional time to fill out reject tags and to complete the return authorization paperwork. The distribution of this process time was uniform on the interval [0.1 h, 0.5 h]. The proportion of lots rejected, by order type, was evaluated using conventional statistical process control techniques. The charts indicated that, with few exceptions, the proportion of lots rejected was in statistical control and the binomial distribution can be used as the model. The resulting estimated reject rates are given in Table 9.23. The evaluated lots were produced over a relatively short period, so the data in Table 9.23 should be regarded as tentative.

Table 9.23. Average reject rates.

ORDER TYPE	% LOTS REJECTED	# LOTS EVALUATED
Electrical	2.2	762
Simple Mechanical	1.1	936
Complex Mechanical	25.0	188
Non-destructive Test	0.5	410

Management constraints

A very important input in the model development process is a statement of constraints by management. With this project, the constraints involved a description of permissible job assignments for each inspector classification, the overtime policy, the queue discipline and the priority discipline for assigning jobs to inspectors as well as to the CMM's. Table 9.24 summarizes the permissible job assignments. A "0" indicates that the assignment was not permitted, while a "1" indicates a permissible assignment.

Table 9.24. Permissible inspector assignments.

INSPECTOR TYPE	ORDER TYPE			
	Electrical	Simple mechanical	Complex mechanical	NDT
Electrical	1	0	0	0
Grade 11	0	1	0	0
Grade 19	0	1	1	0
NDT	0	0	0	1

The simulation would be run under the assumption that overtime was not permitted; 40 hours was considered a complete work week. Preference was given to the lower pay Grade 11 inspectors when a simple mechanical order was assigned. The CMM was to be used for complex mechanical parts when it was available. Inspection was conducted using a first-in first-out (FIFO) protocol.

Backlog

The backlog was a composite of all part types. Information on when the particular order entered the backlog was not available. At the time the simulation was proposed, the backlog stood at 662 orders with the composition shown in Table 9.25.

Table 9.25. Backlog composition.

ORDER TYPE	BACKLOG	PERCENT
Electrical	328	49
Simple mechanical	203	31
Complex mechanical	51	8
NDT	80	12

By the time the computer program was completed four weeks later, the backlog had dwindled to 200 orders. The assumption was made that the percentage of each order type remained constant and the simulation was run with a 200 order backlog.

The simulation

The first simulation mimicked the current system so the decision maker could determine if the backlog was just a chance event that would work itself out. The simulation began with the current staff, facilities, and backlog and ran 4 simulated regular weeks of 40 hours per week. This was done 6 times and the following statistics computed:

1. Average delay awaiting inspection.
2. Maximum delay awaiting inspection.
3. Average backlog.
4. Maximum backlog.
5. Utilization of the inspectors.
6. Utilization of the CMM.

Statistics 1 through 4 would be computed for each part type; statistic 5 would be computed for each inspector type.

MODIFIED SYSTEMS

Simulations provide an ideal way of evaluating the impact of proposed management changes. Such changes might include inspection labor and the number of CMMs; therefore, these were programmed as input variables. In discussions with management, the following heuristic rules were established:

$$\text{If } U_i < (n_i-1) \: / \: n_i, \, i = 1, 2, 3, 4, \text{ then let } n_i = n_i-1,$$

Where U_i = Utilization of inspector type i

n_i = Number of inspectors of type i.

For example, suppose there were three electrical inspectors (i.e., $n_i = 3$), and the utilization of electrical inspectors was 40% ($U_i = 0.4$). The heuristic rule would recommend eliminating an electrical inspector since $0.4 < (3-1)/3 = 0.67$.

A decision was made that the reductions would take place only if the backlog was under control for a given order type. The author interpreted this to mean that a two sigma interval about the average change in backlog should either contain zero backlog growth, or be entirely negative.

RESULTS OF SIMULATIONS

The first simulation was based on the existing system, coded 5–2–5–2–1, meaning

- 5 electrical inspectors
- 2 grade 11 inspectors
- 5 grade 19 inspectors
- 2 NDT inspectors
- 1 CMM

The results of this simulation are shown in Table 9.26.

Table 9.26. Current system 5–2–5–2–1 simulation results.

Type Inspection	Inspectors	Inspector Utilization	Backlog		CMM	
			Avg.	Max.	Number	Utilization
Run 1						
Electrical	5	0.577	8.5	98		
Mech-simple	2	0.704	1.6	61		
Mech-Complex	5	0.545	0.7	16	1	0.526
NDT	2	0.622	4.3	25		
Run 2						
Electrical	5	0.623	7.5	97		
Mech-simple	2	0.752	1.9	68.		
Mech-Complex	5	0.621	0.6	11	1	0.501
NDT	2	0.685	5.0	24		
Run 3						
Electrical	5	0.613	8.3	107		
Mech-simple	2	0.732	1.5	51		
Mech-Complex	5	0.596	2.0	30	1	0.495
NDT	2	0.541	3.5	23		
Run 4						
Electrical	5	0.608	4.9	93		
Mech-simple	2	0.726	1.5	67		
Mech-Complex	5	0.551	0.8	14	1	0.413
NDT	2	0.665	3.5	28		
Run 5						
Electrical	5	0.567	6.8	91		
Mech-simple	2	0.684	2.9	77		
Mech-Complex	5	0.554	0.6	13	1	0.506
NDT	2	0.592	2.1	21		
Run 6						
Electrical	5	0.598	6.6	96		
Mech-simple	2	0.755	2.4	65		
Mech-Complex	5	0.584	1.6	19	1	0.493
NDT	2	0.735	5.0	22		

After 6 simulated weeks:

JOB TYPE	AVERAGE UTILITY	AVERAGE CHANGE IN BACKLOG	STD. DEV. OF CHANGE IN BACKLOG
Electrical	0.598	−96.333	6.3140
Mech-simple	0.726	−64.000	8.4617
Mech-Complex	0.575	−14.500	3.5637
NDT	0.640	−22.500	3.7283

The heuristic rule describes the direction to go with staffing, but not how far. Based solely on the author's intuition, the following configuration was selected for the next simulation:

- 3 electrical inspectors
- 2 grade 11 inspectors
- 3 grade 19 inspectors
- 2 NDT inspectors
- 1 CMM

The results of simulating this 3–2–3–2–1 system are given in Table 9.27. All average utilization values passed the heuristic rule and the backlog growth was still, on the average, comfortably negative. However, the electrical order backlog reduction was considerably more erratic when the inspection staff was reduced.

Table 9.27. 3–2–3–2–1 System simulation results.

Type Inspection	Inspectors	Inspector Utilization	Backlog		CMM	
			Avg.	Max.	Number	Utilization
Run 1						
Electrical	3	0.935	49.4	101		
Mech-simple	2	0.847	7.5	61		
Mech-Complex	3	0.811	2.0	16	1	0.595
NDT	2	0.637	8.2	28		
Run 2						
Electrical	3	0.998	81.7	114		
Mech-simple	2	0.866	8.2	70		
Mech-Complex	3	0.863	2.5	16	1	0.629
NDT	2	0.631	3.5	22		
Run 3						
Electrical	3	0.994	74.3	109		
Mech-simple	2	0.889	12.0	73		
Mech-Complex	3	0.891	6.2	32	1	0.623
NDT	2	0.679	6.4	27		
Run 4						
Electrical	3	0.879	31.2	109		
Mech-simple	2	0.927	7.2	52		
Mech-Complex	3	0.924	5.6	26	1	0.632
NDT	2	0.715	3.8	25		
Run 5						
Electrical	3	0.992	45.6	117		
Mech-simple	2	0.791	3.7	43		
Mech-Complex	3	0.761	1.8	18	1	0.537
NDT	2	0.673	2.3	24		
Run 6						
Electrical	3	0.990	39.9	95		
Mech-simple	2	0.844	6.9	63		
Mech-Complex	3	0.800	1.7	18	1	0.606
NDT	2	0.716	4.2	24		

After 6 simulations:

JOB TYPE	AVERAGE UTILITY	AVERAGE CHANGE IN BACKLOG	STD. DEV. OF CHANGE IN BACKLOG
Electrical	0.965	−91.833	20.5856
Mech-simple	0.861	−54.667	8.7331
Mech-Complex	0.842	−15.833	1.3292
NDT	0.676	−23.500	1.3784

While this configuration was acceptable, the author believed that additional trials might allow replacement of one or more of the highly paid Grade 19 inspectors with the lower paid Grade 11 inspectors. A number of combinations were tried, resulting in the 3–3–1–2–1 system shown in Table 9.28.

Table 9.28. 3–3–1–2–1 System simulation results.

Type Inspection	Inspectors	Inspector Utilization	Backlog		CMM	
			Avg.	Max.	Number	Utilization
Run 1						
Electrical	3	0.937	37.0	110		
Mech-simple	3	0.885	13.1	61		
Mech-Complex	1	0.967	7.4	21	1	0.718
NDT	2	0.604	3.4	25		
Run 2						
Electrical	3	0.932	26.8	100		
Mech-simple	3	0.888	7.9	58		
Mech-Complex	1	0.925	17.8	49	1	0.722
NDT	2	0.607	4.0	27		
Run 3						
Electrical	3	0.997	74.1	119		
Mech-simple	3	0.915	14.6	58		
Mech-Complex	1	0.957	20.6	40	1	0.807
NDT	2	0.762	7.1	22		
Run 4						
Electrical	3	0.995	42.2	96		
Mech-simple	3	0.976	38.4	79		
Mech-Complex	1	0.997	23.8	56	1	0.865
NDT	2	0.758	4.8	30		
Run 5						
Electrical	3	0.996	61.3	121		
Mech-simple	3	0.913	7.7	50		
Mech-Complex	1	0.996	21.7	52	1	0.909
NDT	2	0.820	7.4	30		
Run 6						
Electrical	3	0.933	35.3	101		
Mech-simple	3	0.867	5.7	59		
Mech-Complex	1	0.938	17.8	49	1	0.736
NDT	2	0.674	8.8	33		

After 6 simulations:

JOB TYPE	AVERAGE UTILITY	AVERAGE CHANGE IN BACKLOG	STD. DEV. OF CHANGE IN BACKLOG
Electrical	0.965	−93.667	6.9762
Mech-simple	0.908	−57.500	5.8224
Mech-Complex	0.963	−5.500	18.1411
NDT	0.704	−25.500	2.7386

The 3–3–1–2–1 system complies with all management constraints relating to resource utilization and backlog control. It is recommended to management with the caution that the backlog of complex mechanical orders be carefully monitored. For this type of order, the simulation indicates negative backlog growth on average, but with periods of positive backlog growth being possible.

CONCLUSION

The simulation allowed the receiving inspection process to be "changed" without actually disrupting operations. In the computer, inspectors can be added, removed, or reassigned without the tremendous impact on morale and operations that would result from making these changes in the real world. It is a simple matter to add additional CMMs which would cost six figures in the real world. It is just as easy to evaluate any of the following: different job assignment protocols, the impact of a proposed new product line, new work area layouts, the effect of working overtime or hiring temporary workers, etc. The effect of such changes can be evaluated in a few days, rather than waiting several months to learn that the problem was not resolved.

STATISTICAL TOLERANCING

For the discussion of statistical tolerancing the definitions of limits proposed by Juran and Gryna (1993) will be used; these are shown in Table 9.29.

Table 9.29. Definitions of limits.

NAME OF LIMIT	MEANING
Tolerance	Set by the engineering design function to define the minimum and maximum values allowable for the product to work properly
Statistical tolerance	Calculated from process data to define the amount of variation that the process exhibits; these limits will contain a specified proportion of the total population
Prediction	Calculated from process data to define the limits which will contain all of k future observations
Confidence	Calculated from data to define an interval within which a population parameter lies
Control	Calculated from process data to define the limits of chance (random) variation around some central value

In manufacturing it is common that parts interact with one another: a pin fits through a hole, an assembly consists of several parts bonded together, etc. Figure 9.38 illustrates one example of interacting parts.

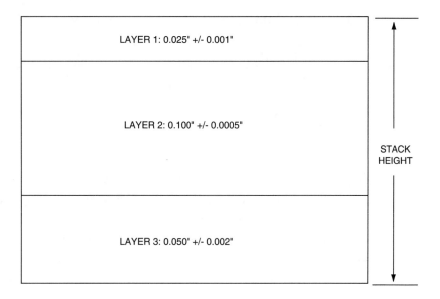

Figure 9.38. A multilevel circuit board assembly.

Suppose that all three layers of this assembly were manufactured to the specifications indicated in Figure 9.38. A logical specification on the overall stack height would be found by adding the nominal dimensions and tolerances for each layer, e.g., 0.175" ± 0.0035", giving limits of 0.1715" and 0.1785". The lower specification is equivalent to a stack where all three layers are at their minimums; the upper specification is equivalent to a stack where all three layers are at their maximums, as shown in Table 9.30.

Table 9.30. Minimum and maximum multilayer assemblies.

MINIMUM	MAXIMUM
0.0240	0.0260
0.0995	0.1005
0.0480	0.0520
0.1715	0.1785

Adding part tolerances is the usual way of arriving at assembly tolerances, but it is usually too conservative, especially when manufacturing processes are both capable and in a state of statistical control. For example, assume that the probability of getting any particular layer below its low specification was 1 in 100 (which is a conservative estimate for a controlled, capable process). Then the probability that a particular stack would be below the lower limit of

0.1715" is $\frac{1}{100} \times \frac{1}{100} \times \frac{1}{100} = \frac{1}{1,000,000}$. Similarly, the probability of get-

ting a stack that is too thick would be 1 in a million. Thus, setting component and assembly tolerances by simple addition is extremely conservative, and often costly.

The statistical approach to tolerancing is based on the relationship between the variances of a number of independent causes and the variance of the dependent or overall result. The equation is the following:

$$\sigma_{result} = \sqrt{\sigma^2_{cause\ A} + \sigma^2_{cause\ B} + \sigma^2_{cause\ C} + \cdots}$$
(9.22)

For this example, the equation is

$$\sigma_{stack} = \sqrt{\sigma^2_{layer\ 1} + \sigma^2_{layer\ 2} + \sigma^2_{layer\ 3}}$$
(9.23)

Of course, engineering tolerances are usually set without knowing which manufacturing process will be used to manufacture the part, so the actual variances are not known. However, a worst-case scenario would be where the process was just barely able to meet the engineering requirement. In Chapter 8 (process capability) we learned that this situation occurs when the engineering tolerance is 6 standard deviations wide (±3 standard deviations). Thus, Equation 9.24 can be rewritten.

$$\frac{T}{3} = \sqrt{\left(\frac{T_A}{3}\right)^2 + \left(\frac{T_B}{3}\right)^2 + \left(\frac{T_C}{3}\right)^2}$$

or (9.24)

$$T_{stack} = \sqrt{T_{layer\,1}^2 + T_{layer\,2}^2 + T_{layer\,3}^2}$$

In other words, instead of simple addition of tolerances, the squares of the tolerances are added to determine the square of the tolerance for the overall result.

The result of the statistical approach is a dramatic *increase* in the allowable tolerances for the individual piece-parts. For this example, allowing each layer a tolerance of ±0.002" would result in the same stack tolerance of ±0.0035". This amounts to doubling the tolerance for layer 1 and quadrupling the tolerance for layer 3, without changing the tolerance for the overall stack assembly. There are many other combinations of layer tolerances that would yield the same stack assembly result, which allows a great deal of flexibility for considering such factors as process capability and costs.

The penalty associated with this approach is a slight probability of an out-of-tolerance assembly. However, this probability can be set to as small a number as needed by adjusting the 3 sigma rule to a larger number. Another alternative is to measure the subassemblies prior to assembly and selecting different components in those rare instances where an out-of-tolerance combination results.

It is also possible to use this approach for internal dimensions of assemblies. For example, assume an assembly had a shaft assembled with a bearing as shown in Figure 9.39.

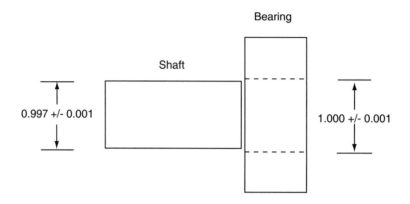

Figure 9.39. A bearing and shaft assembly.

The clearance between the bearing and the shaft can be computed as

Clearance = Bearing inside diameter – Shaft outside diameter

The minimum clearance will exist when the bearing inside diameter is at its smallest allowed and the shaft outside diameter is at its largest allowed. Thus,

Minimum clearance = 0.999" – 0.998" = 0.001"

The maximum clearance will exist when the bearing inside diameter is at its largest allowed and the shaft outside diameter is at its smallest allowed,

Maximum clearance = 1.001" – 0.996" = 0.005"

Thus, the assembly tolerance can be computed as

$$T_{assembly} = 0.005" - 0.001" = 0.004"$$

The statistical tolerancing approach was used here in the same way as it was used above. Namely,

$$\frac{T}{3} = \sqrt{\left(\frac{T_A}{3}\right)^2 + \left(\frac{T_B}{3}\right)^2}$$

or   (9.25)

$$T_{assembly} = \sqrt{T_{bearing}^2 + T_{shaft}^2}$$

For this example

$$T_{assembly} = 0.004'' = \sqrt{T_{bearing}^2 + T_{shaft}^2} \tag{9.26}$$

If we assume equal tolerances for the bearing and the shaft the tolerance for each becomes

$$(0.004)^2 = T_{bearing}^2 + T_{shaft}^2 = 2T^2$$

$$T = \sqrt{\frac{(0.004)^2}{2}} = \pm 0.0028 \tag{9.27}$$

Which nearly triples the tolerance for each part.

ASSUMPTIONS OF FORMULA

The formula is based on several assumptions:

- The component dimensions are independent and the components are assembled randomly. This assumption is usually met in practice.
- Each component dimension should be approximately normally distributed.
- The actual average for each component is equal to the nominal value stated in the specification. For the multi-layer circuit board assembly example, the averages for layers 1, 2, and 3 must be 0.025", 0.100", and 0.050" respectively. This condition can be met by applying SPC to the manufacturing processes.

Reasonable departures from these assumptions are acceptable. The author's experience suggests that few problems will appear as long as the subassembly manufacturing processes are kept in a state of statistical control.

1

Glossary of Basic Statistical Terms*

Acceptable quality level—The maximum percentage or proportion of variant units in a lot or batch that, for the purposes of acceptance sampling, can be considered satisfactory as a process average.

Analysis of Variance (ANOVA)—A technique which subdivides the total variation of a set of data into meaningful component parts associated with specific sources of variation for the purpose of testing some hypothesis on the parameters of the model or estimating variance components.

Assignable cause—A factor which contributes to variation and which is feasible to detect and identify.

Average Outgoing Quality (AOQ)—The expected quality of outgoing product following the use of an acceptance sampling plan for a given value of incoming product quality.

Average Outgoing Quality Limit (AOQL)—For a given acceptance sampling plan, the maximum AOQ over all possible levels of incoming quality.

---

*From *Glossary & Tables for Statistical Quality Control*, prepared by the ASQ Statistics Division. Copyright © 1983, ASQ Quality Press (800) 248–1946. Reprinted by permission of the publisher.

Chance causes—Factors, generally numerous and individually of relatively small importance, which contribute to variation, but which are not feasible to detect or identify.

Coefficient of determination—A measure of the part of the variance for one variable that can be explained by its linear relationship with a second variable. Designated by ρ^2 or r^2.

Coefficient of multiple correlation—A number between 0 and 1 that indicates the degree of the combined linear relationship of several predictor variables X_1, X_2,...,X_p to the response variable Y. It is the simple correlation coefficient between predicted and observed values of the response variable.

Coefficient of variation—A measure of relative dispersion that is the standard deviation divided by the mean and multiplied by 100 to give a percentage value. This measure cannot be used when the data take both negative and positive values or when it has been coded in such a way that the value X = 0 does not coincide with the origin.

Confidence limits—The end points of the interval about the sample statistic that is believed, with a specified confidence coefficient, to include the population parameter.

Consumer's risk (β)—For a given sampling plan, the probability of acceptance of a lot, the quality of which has a designated numerical value representing a level which it is seldom desired to accept. Usually the designated value will be the **Limiting Quality Level (LQL)**.

Correlation coefficient—A number between –1 and 1 that indicates the degree of linear relationship between two sets of numbers:

$$r_{xy} = \frac{s_{xy}}{s_x s_y} = \frac{n\sum XY - \sum X \sum Y}{\sqrt{\left[n\sum X^2 - (\sum X)^2\right]\left[n\sum Y^2 - (\sum Y)^2\right]}}$$

Defect—A departure of a quality characteristic from its intended level or state that occurs with a severity sufficient to cause an associated product or service not to satisfy intended normal, or reasonably foreseeable, usage requirements.

Defective—A unit of product or service containing at least one defect, or having several imperfections that in combination cause the unit not to satisfy intended normal, or reasonably foreseeable, usage requirements. The word *defective* is appropriate for use when a unit of product or service is evaluated in terms of usage (as contrasted to conformance to specifications).

Double sampling—Sampling inspection in which the inspection of the first sample of size n_1, leads to a decision to accept a lot; not to accept it; or to take a second sample of size n_2, and the inspection of the second sample then leads to a decision to accept or not to accept the lot.

Experiment design—The arrangement in which an experimental program is to be conducted, and the selection of the versions (levels) of one or more factors or factor combinations to be included in the experiment.

Factor—An assignable cause which may affect the responses (test results) and of which different versions (levels) are included in the experiment.

Factorial experiments—Experiments in which all possible treatment combinations formed from two or more factors, each being studied at two or more versions (levels), are examined so that interactions (differential effects) as well as main effects can be estimated.

Frequency distribution—A set of all the various values that individual observations may have and the frequency of their occurrence in the sample or population.

Histogram—A plot of the frequency distribution in the form of rectangles whose bases are equal to the cell interval and whose areas are proportional to the frequencies.

Hypothesis, alternative—The hypothesis that is accepted if the null hypothesis is disproved. The choice of alternative hypothesis will determine whether "one-tail" or "two-tail" tests are appropriate.

Hypothesis, null—The hypothesis tested in tests of significance is that there is no difference (null) between the population of the sample and specified population (or between the populations associated with each sample). The null hypothesis can never be proved true. It can, however, be shown, with specified risks of error, to be untrue; that is, a difference can be shown to exist between the populations. If it is not disproved, one usually acts on the assumption that there is no adequate reason to doubt that it is true. (It may be that there is insufficient power to prove the existence of a difference rather than that there is no difference; that is, the sample size may be too small. By specifying the minimum difference that one wants to detect and β, the risk of failing to detect a difference of this size, the actual sample size required, however, can be determined.)

In-control process—A process in which the statistical measure(s) being evaluated are in a "state of statistical control."

Kurtosis—A measure of the shape of a distribution. A positive value indicates that the distribution has longer tails than the normal distribution (platykurtosis); while a negative value indicates that the distribution has shorter tails (leptokurtosis). For the normal distribution, the kurtosis is 0.

Mean, standard error of—The standard deviation of the average of a sample of size n.

$$s_{\bar{X}} = \frac{s_X}{\sqrt{n}}$$

Mean—A measure of the location of a distribution. The centroid.

Median—The middle measurement when an odd number of units are arranged in order of size; for an ordered set $X_1, X_2, \ldots, X_{2k-1}$

$$\text{Med} = X_k$$

When an even number are so arranged, the median is the average of the two middle units; for an ordered set $X_1, X_2, \ldots, X_{2k}$

$$\text{Med} = \frac{X_k + X_{k+1}}{2}$$

Mode—The most frequent value of the variable.

Multiple sampling—Sampling inspection in which, after each sample is inspected, the decision is made to accept a lot; not to accepts it; or to take another sample to reach the decision. There may be a prescribed maximum number of samples, after which a decision to accept or not to accept must be reached.

Operating Characteristics Curve (OC Curve)—

1. For isolated or unique lots or a lot from an isolated sequence: a curve showing, for a given sampling plan, the probability of accepting a lot as a function of the lot quality. (Type A)

2. For a continuous stream of lots: a curve showing, for a given sampling plan, the probability of accepting a lot as a function of the process average. (Type B)

3. For continuous sampling plans: a curve showing the proportion of submitted product over the long run accepted during the sampling phases of the plan as a function of the product quality.

4. For special plans: a curve showing, for a given sampling plan, the probability of continuing to permit the process to continue without adjustment as a function of the process quality.

Parameter—A constant or coefficient that describes some characteristic of a population (e.g., standard deviation, average, regression coefficient).

Population—The totality of items or units of material under consideration.

NOTE: The items may be units or measurements, and the population may be real or conceptual. Thus *population* may refer to all the items actually produced in a given day or all that might be produced if the process were to continue *in-control*.

Power curve—The curve showing the relation between the probability $(1-\beta)$ of rejecting the hypothesis that a sample belongs to a given population with a given characteristic(s) and the actual population value of that characteristic(s). NOTE: if β is used instead of $(1-\beta)$, the curve is called an operating characteristic curve (OC curve) (used mainly in sampling plans for quality control).

Process capability—The limits within which a tool or process operate based upon minimum variability as governed by the prevailing circumstances.

NOTE: The phrase "by the prevailing circumstances" indicates that the definition of inherent variability of a process involving only one operator, one source of raw material, etc., differs from one involving multiple operators, and many sources of raw material, etc. If the measure of inherent variability is made within very restricted circumstances, it is necessary to add components for frequently occurring assignable sources of variation that cannot economically be eliminated.

Producer's risk (α)—For a given sampling plan, the probability of not accepting a lot, the quality of which has a designated numerical value representing a level which is generally desired to accept. Usually the designated value will be the **Acceptable Quality Level (AQL)**.

Quality—The totality of features and characteristics of a product or service that bear on its ability to satisfy given needs.

Quality assurance—All those planned or systematic actions necessary to provide adequate confidence that a product or service will satisfy given needs.

Quality control—The operational techniques and the activities which sustain a quality of product or service that will satisfy given needs; also the use of such techniques and activities.

Random sampling—The process of selecting units for a sample of size n in such a manner that all combinations of n units under consideration have an equal or ascertainable chance of being selected as the sample.

R (range)—A measure of dispersion which is the difference between the largest observed value and the smallest observed value in a given sample. While the range is a measure of dispersion in its own right, it is sometimes used to estimate the population standard deviation, but is a biased estimator unless multiplied by the factor $(1/d_2)$ appropriate to the sample size.

Replication—The repetition of the set of all the treatment combinations to be compared in an experiment. Each of the repetitions is called a *replicate*.

Sample—A group of units, portion of material, or observations taken from a larger collection of units, quantity of material, or observations that serves to provide information that may be used as a basis for making a decision concerning the larger quantity.

Single sampling—Sampling inspection in which the decision to accept or not to accept a lot is based on the inspection of a single sample of size *n*.

Skewness—A measure of the symmetry of a distribution. A positive value indicates that the distribution has a greater tendency to tail to the right (positively skewed or skewed to the right), and a negative value indicates a greater tendency of the distribution to tail to the left (negatively skewed or skewed to the left). Skewness is 0 for a normal distribution.

Standard deviation—

1. σ—population standard deviation. A measure of variability (dispersion) of observations that is the positive square root of the population variance.

2. s—sample standard deviation. A Measure of variability (dispersion) that is the positive square root of the sample variance.

$$\sqrt{\frac{1}{n}\Sigma\left(X_i - \overline{X}\right)^2}$$

Statistic—A quantity calculated from a sample of observations, most often to form an estimate of some population parameter.

Type I error (acceptance control sense)—The incorrect decision that a process is unacceptable when, in fact, perfect information would reveal that it is located within the "zone of acceptable processes."

Type II error (acceptance control sense)—The incorrect decision that a process is acceptable when, in fact, perfect information would reveal that it is located within the "zone of rejectable processes."

Variance—

1. σ^2—population variance. A measure of variability (dispersion) of observations based upon the mean of the squared deviation from the arithmetic mean.

2. s^2—sample variance. A measure of variability (dispersion) of observations in a sample based upon the squared deviations from the arithmetic average divided by the degrees of freedom.

2

Area Under the Standard Normal Curve

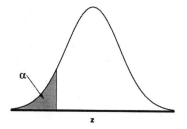

z	0.00	0.01	0.02	0.03	0.04	0.05	0.06	0.07	0.08	0.09
−3.4	0.0003	0.0003	0.0003	0.0003	0.0003	0.0003	0.0003	0.0003	0.0003	0.0002
−3.3	0.0005	0.0005	0.0005	0.0004	0.0004	0.0004	0.0004	0.0004	0.0004	0.0003
−3.2	0.0007	0.0007	0.0006	0.0006	0.0006	0.0006	0.0006	0.0005	0.0005	0.0005
−3.1	0.0010	0.0009	0.0009	0.0009	0.0008	0.0008	0.0008	0.0008	0.0007	0.0007
−3.0	0.0013	0.0013	0.0013	0.0012	0.0012	0.0011	0.0011	0.0011	0.0010	0.0010
−2.9	0.0019	0.0018	0.0018	0.0017	0.0016	0.0016	0.0015	0.0015	0.0014	0.0014
−2.8	0.0026	0.0025	0.0024	0.0023	0.0023	0.0022	0.0021	0.0021	0.0020	0.0019
−2.7	0.0035	0.0034	0.0033	0.0032	0.0031	0.0030	0.0029	0.0028	0.0027	0.0026
−2.6	0.0047	0.0045	0.0044	0.0043	0.0041	0.0040	0.0039	0.0038	0.0037	0.0036
−2.5	0.0062	0.0060	0.0059	0.0057	0.0055	0.0054	0.0052	0.0051	0.0049	0.0048

Continued on next page . . .

Continued . . .

z	0.00	0.01	0.02	0.03	0.04	0.05	0.06	0.07	0.08	0.09
-2.4	0.0082	0.0080	0.0078	0.0075	0.0073	0.0071	0.0069	0.0068	0.0066	0.0064
-2.3	0.0107	0.0104	0.0102	0.0099	0.0096	0.0094	0.0091	0.0089	0.0087	0.0084
-2.2	0.0139	0.0136	0.0132	0.0129	0.0125	0.0122	0.0119	0.0116	0.0113	0.0110
-2.1	0.0179	0.0174	0.0170	0.0166	0.0162	0.0158	0.0154	0.0150	0.0146	0.0143
-2.0	0.0228	0.0222	0.0217	0.0212	0.0207	0.0202	0.0197	0.0192	0.0188	0.0183
-1.9	0.0287	0.0281	0.0274	0.0268	0.0262	0.0256	0.0250	0.0244	0.0239	0.0233
-1.8	0.0359	0.0351	0.0344	0.0336	0.0329	0.0322	0.0314	0.0307	0.0301	0.0294
-1.7	0.0446	0.0436	0.0427	0.0418	0.0409	0.0401	0.0392	0.0384	0.0375	0.0367
-1.6	0.0548	0.0537	0.0526	0.0516	0.0505	0.0495	0.0485	0.0475	0.0465	0.0455
-1.5	0.0668	0.0655	0.0643	0.0630	0.0618	0.0606	0.0594	0.0582	0.0571	0.0559
-1.4	0.0808	0.0793	0.0778	0.0764	0.0749	0.0735	0.0721	0.0708	0.0694	0.0681
-1.3	0.0968	0.0951	0.0934	0.0918	0.0901	0.0885	0.0869	0.0853	0.0838	0.0823
-1.2	0.1151	0.1131	0.1112	0.1093	0.1075	0.1056	0.1038	0.1020	0.1003	0.0985
-1.1	0.1357	0.1335	0.1314	0.1292	0.1271	0.1251	0.1230	0.1210	0.1190	0.1170
-1.0	0.1587	0.1562	0.1539	0.1515	0.1492	0.1469	0.1446	0.1423	0.1401	0.1379
-0.9	0.1841	0.1814	0.1788	0.1762	0.1736	0.1711	0.1685	0.1660	0.1635	0.1611
-0.8	0.2119	0.2090	0.2061	0.2033	0.2005	0.1977	0.1949	0.1922	0.1894	0.1867
-0.7	0.2420	0.2389	0.2358	0.2327	0.2296	0.2266	0.2236	0.2206	0.2177	0.2148
-0.6	0.2743	0.2709	0.2676	0.2643	0.2611	0.2578	0.2546	0.2514	0.2483	0.2451
-0.5	0.3085	0.3050	0.3015	0.2981	0.2946	0.2912	0.2877	0.2843	0.2810	0.2776
-0.4	0.3446	0.3409	0.3372	0.3336	0.3300	0.3264	0.3228	0.3192	0.3156	0.3121
-0.3	0.3821	0.3783	0.3745	0.3707	0.3669	0.3632	0.3594	0.3557	0.3520	0.3483
-0.2	0.4207	0.4168	0.4129	0.4090	0.4052	0.4013	0.3974	0.3936	0.3897	0.3859
-0.1	0.4602	0.4562	0.4522	0.4483	0.4443	0.4404	0.4364	0.4325	0.4286	0.4247
-0.0	0.5000	0.4960	0.4920	0.4880	0.4840	0.4801	0.4761	0.4721	0.4681	0.4641
0.0	0.5000	0.5040	0.5080	0.5120	0.5160	0.5199	0.5239	0.5279	0.5319	0.5359
0.1	0.5398	0.5438	0.5478	0.5517	0.5557	0.5596	0.5636	0.5675	0.5714	0.5753
0.2	0.5793	0.5832	0.5871	0.5910	0.5948	0.5987	0.6026	0.6064	0.6103	0.6141
0.3	0.6179	0.6217	0.6255	0.6293	0.6331	0.6368	0.6406	0.6443	0.6480	0.6517
0.4	0.6554	0.6591	0.6628	0.6664	0.6700	0.6736	0.6772	0.6808	0.6844	0.6879

Continued on next page . . .

Continued . . .

z	0.00	0.01	0.02	0.03	0.04	0.05	0.06	0.07	0.08	0.09
0.5	0.6915	0.6950	0.6985	0.7019	0.7054	0.7088	0.7123	0.7157	0.7190	0.7224
0.6	0.7257	0.7291	0.7324	0.7357	0.7389	0.7422	0.7454	0.7486	0.7517	0.7549
0.7	0.7580	0.7611	0.7642	0.7673	0.7704	0.7734	0.7764	0.7794	0.7823	0.7852
0.8	0.7881	0.7910	0.7939	0.7967	0.7995	0.8023	0.8051	0.8078	0.8106	0.8133
0.9	0.8159	0.8186	0.8212	0.8238	0.8264	0.8289	0.8315	0.8340	0.8365	0.8389
1.0	0.8413	0.8438	0.8461	0.8485	0.8508	0.8531	0.8554	0.8577	0.8599	0.8621
1.1	0.8643	0.8665	0.8686	0.8708	0.8729	0.8749	0.8770	0.8790	0.8810	0.8830
1.2	0.8849	0.8869	0.8888	0.8907	0.8925	0.8944	0.8962	0.8980	0.8997	0.9015
1.3	0.9032	0.9049	0.9066	0.9082	0.9099	0.9115	0.9131	0.9147	0.9162	0.9177
1.4	0.9192	0.9207	0.9222	0.9236	0.9251	0.9265	0.9279	0.9292	0.9306	0.9319
1.5	0.9332	0.9345	0.9357	0.9370	0.9382	0.9394	0.9406	0.9418	0.9429	0.9441
1.6	0.9452	0.9463	0.9474	0.9484	0.9495	0.9505	0.9515	0.9525	0.9535	0.9545
1.7	0.9554	0.9564	0.9573	0.9582	0.9591	0.9599	0.9608	0.9616	0.9625	0.9633
1.8	0.9641	0.9649	0.9656	0.9664	0.9671	0.9678	0.9686	0.9693	0.9699	0.9706
1.9	0.9713	0.9719	0.9726	0.9732	0.9738	0.9744	0.9750	0.9756	0.9761	0.9767
2.0	0.9772	0.9778	0.9783	0.9788	0.9793	0.9798	0.9803	0.9808	0.9812	0.9817
2.1	0.9821	0.9826	0.9830	0.9834	0.9838	0.9842	0.9846	0.9850	0.9854	0.9857
2.2	0.9861	0.9864	0.9868	0.9871	0.9875	0.9878	0.9881	0.9884	0.9887	0.9890
2.3	0.9893	0.9896	0.9898	0.9901	0.9904	0.9906	0.9909	0.9911	0.9913	0.9916
2.4	0.9918	0.9920	0.9922	0.9925	0.9927	0.9929	0.9931	0.9932	0.9934	0.9936
2.5	0.9938	0.9940	0.9941	0.9943	0.9945	0.9946	0.9948	0.9949	0.9951	0.9952
2.6	0.9953	0.9955	0.9956	0.9957	0.9959	0.9960	0.9961	0.9962	0.9963	0.9964
2.7	0.9965	0.9966	0.9967	0.9968	0.9969	0.9970	0.9971	0.9972	0.9973	0.9974
2.8	0.9974	0.9975	0.9976	0.9977	0.9977	0.9978	0.9979	0.9979	0.9980	0.9981
2.9	0.9981	0.9982	0.9982	0.9983	0.9984	0.9984	0.9985	0.9985	0.9986	0.9986
3.0	0.9987	0.9987	0.9987	0.9988	0.9988	0.9989	0.9989	0.9989	0.9990	0.9990
3.1	0.9990	0.9991	0.9991	0.9991	0.9992	0.9992	0.9992	0.9992	0.9993	0.9993
3.2	0.9993	0.9993	0.9994	0.9994	0.9994	0.9994	0.9994	0.9995	0.9995	0.9995
3.3	0.9995	0.9995	0.9995	0.9996	0.9996	0.9996	0.9996	0.9996	0.9996	0.9997
3.4	0.9997	0.9997	0.9997	0.9997	0.9997	0.9997	0.9997	0.9997	0.9997	0.9998

3

Critical values of the *t*-Distribution

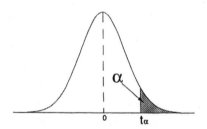

df	α				
	0.1	0.05	0.025	0.01	0.005
1	3.078	6.314	12.706	31.821	63.657
2	1.886	2.920	4.303	6.965	9.925
3	1.638	2.353	3.182	4.541	5.841
4	1.533	2.132	2.776	3.747	4.604
5	1.476	2.015	2.571	3.365	4.032

Continued on next page . . .

Continued . . .

df	α				
	0.1	0.05	0.025	0.01	0.005
6	1.440	1.943	2.447	3.143	3.707
7	1.415	1.895	2.365	2.998	3.499
8	1.397	1.860	2.306	2.896	3.355
9	1.383	1.833	2.262	2.821	3.250
10	1.372	1.812	2.228	2.764	3.169
11	1.363	1.796	2.201	2.718	3.106
12	1.356	1.782	2.179	2.681	3.055
13	1.350	1.771	2.160	2.650	3.012
14	1.345	1.761	2.145	2.624	2.977
15	1.341	1.753	2.131	2.602	2.947
16	1.337	1.746	2.120	2.583	2.921
17	1.333	1.740	2.110	2.567	2.898
18	1.330	1.734	2.101	2.552	2.878
19	1.328	1.729	2.093	2.539	2.861
20	1.325	1.725	2.086	2.528	2.845
21	1.323	1.721	2.080	2.518	2.831
22	1.321	1.717	2.074	2.508	2.819
23	1.319	1.714	2.069	2.500	2.807
24	1.318	1.711	2.064	2.492	2.797
25	1.316	1.708	2.060	2.485	2.787
26	1.315	1.706	2.056	2.479	2.779
27	1.314	1.703	2.052	2.473	2.771
28	1.313	1.701	2.048	2.467	2.763
29	1.311	1.699	2.045	2.462	2.756
∞	1.282	1.645	1.960	2.326	2.576

4

Chi-Square Distribution

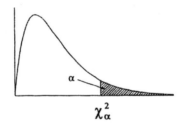

$$\chi^2_\alpha$$

		α									
γ	0.995	0.99	0.98	0.975	0.95	0.90	0.80	0.75	0.70	0.50
	0.00004	0.000	0.001	0.001	0.004	0.016	0.064	0.102	0.148	0.455
2	0.0100	0.020	0.040	0.051	0.103	0.211	0.446	0.575	0.713	1.386
3	0.0717	0.115	0.185	0.216	0.352	0.584	1.005	1.213	1.424	2.366
4	0.207	0.297	0.429	0.484	0.711	1.064	1.649	1.923	2.195	3.357
5	0.412	0.554	0.752	0.831	1.145	1.610	2.343	2.675	3.000	4.351
6	0.676	0.872	1.134	1.237	1.635	2.204	3.070	3.455	3.828	5.348
7	0.989	1.239	1.564	1.690	2.167	2.833	3.822	4.255	4.671	6.346
8	1.344	1.646	2.032	2.180	2.733	3.490	4.594	5.071	5.527	7.344
9	1.735	2.088	2.532	2.700	3.325	4.168	5.380	5.899	6.393	8.343
10	2.156	2.558	3.059	3.247	3.940	4.865	6.179	6.737	7.267	9.342

Continued on next page . . .

Continued . . .

γ	α									
	0.995	0.99	0.98	0.975	0.95	0.90	0.80	0.75	0.70	0.50
11	2.603	3.053	3.609	3.816	4.575	5.578	6.989	7.584	8.148	10.341
12	3.074	3.571	4.178	4.404	5.226	6.304	7.807	8.438	9.034	11.340
13	3.565	4.107	4.765	5.009	5.892	7.042	8.634	9.299	9.926	12.340
14	4.075	4.660	5.368	5.629	6.571	7.790	9.467	10.165	10.821	13.339
15	4.601	5.229	5.985	6.262	7.261	8.547	10.307	11.037	11.721	14.339
16	5.142	5.812	6.614	6.908	7.962	9.312	11.152	11.912	12.624	15.338
17	5.697	6.408	7.255	7.564	8.672	10.085	12.002	12.792	13.531	16.338
18	6.265	7.015	7.906	8.231	9.390	10.865	12.857	13.675	14.440	17.338
19	6.844	7.633	8.567	8.907	10.117	11.651	13.716	14.562	15.352	18.338
20	7.434	8.260	9.237	9.591	10.851	12.443	14.578	15.452	16.266	19.337
21	8.034	8.897	9.915	10.283	11.591	13.240	15.445	16.344	17.182	20.337
22	8.643	9.542	10.600	10.982	12.338	14.041	16.314	17.240	18.101	21.337
23	9.260	10.196	11.293	11.689	13.091	14.848	17.187	18.137	19.021	22.337
24	9.886	10.856	11.992	12.401	13.848	15.659	18.062	19.037	19.943	23.337
25	10.520	11.524	12.697	13.120	14.611	16.473	18.940	19.939	20.867	24.337
26	11.160	12.198	13.409	13.844	15.379	17.292	19.820	20.843	21.792	25.336
27	11.808	12.879	14.125	14.573	16.151	18.114	20.703	21.749	22.719	26.336
28	12.461	13.565	14.847	15.308	16.928	18.939	21.588	22.657	23.647	27.336
29	13.121	14.256	15.574	16.047	17.708	19.768	22.475	23.567	24.577	28.336
30	13.787	14.953	16.306	16.791	18.493	20.599	23.364	24.478	25.508	29.336

Continued on next page . . .

Continued . . .

γ	α									
	0.30	0.25	0.20	0.10	0.05	0.025	0.02	0.01	0.005	0.001
1	1.074	1.323	1.642	2.706	3.841	5.024	5.412	6.635	7.879	10.828
2	2.408	2.773	3.219	4.605	5.991	7.378	7.824	9.210	10.597	13.816
3	3.665	4.108	4.642	6.251	7.815	9.348	9.837	11.345	12.838	16.266
4	4.878	5.385	5.989	7.779	9.488	11.143	11.668	13.277	14.860	18.467
5	6.064	6.626	7.289	9.236	11.070	12.833	13.388	15.086	16.750	20.515
6	7.231	7.841	8.558	10.645	12.592	14.449	15.033	16.812	18.548	22.458
7	8.383	9.037	9.803	12.017	14.067	16.013	16.622	18.475	20.278	24.322
8	9.524	10.219	11.030	13.362	15.507	17.535	18.168	20.090	21.955	26.124
9	10.656	11.389	12.242	14.684	16.919	19.023	19.679	21.666	23.589	27.877
10	11.781	12.549	13.442	15.987	18.307	20.483	21.161	23.209	25.188	29.588
11	12.899	13.701	14.631	17.275	19.675	21.920	22.618	24.725	26.757	31.264
12	14.011	14.845	15.812	18.549	21.026	23.337	24.054	26.217	28.300	32.909
13	15.119	15.984	16.985	19.812	22.362	24.736	25.472	27.688	29.819	34.528
14	16.222	17.117	18.151	21.064	23.685	26.119	26.873	29.141	31.319	36.123
15	17.322	18.245	19.311	22.307	24.996	27.488	28.259	30.578	32.801	37.697
16	18.418	19.369	20.465	23.542	26.296	28.845	29.633	32.000	34.267	39.252
17	19.511	20.489	21.615	24.769	27.587	30.191	30.995	33.409	35.718	40.790
18	20.601	21.605	22.760	25.989	28.869	31.526	32.346	34.805	37.156	42.312
19	21.689	22.718	23.900	27.204	30.144	32.852	33.687	36.191	38.582	43.820
20	22.775	23.828	25.038	28.412	31.410	34.170	35.020	37.566	39.997	45.315
21	23.858	24.935	26.171	29.615	32.671	35.479	36.343	38.932	41.401	46.797
22	24.939	26.039	27.301	30.813	33.924	36.781	37.659	40.289	42.796	48.268
23	26.018	27.141	28.429	32.007	35.172	38.076	38.968	41.638	44.181	49.728
24	27.096	28.241	29.553	33.196	36.415	39.364	40.270	42.980	45.559	51.179
25	28.172	29.339	30.675	34.382	37.652	40.646	41.566	44.314	46.928	52.620
26	29.246	30.435	31.795	35.563	38.885	41.923	42.856	45.642	48.290	54.052
27	30.319	31.528	32.912	36.741	40.113	43.195	44.140	46.963	49.645	55.476
28	31.391	32.620	34.027	37.916	41.337	44.461	45.419	48.278	50.993	56.892
29	32.461	33.711	35.139	39.087	42.557	45.722	46.693	49.588	52.336	58.301
30	33.530	34.800	36.250	40.256	43.773	46.979	47.962	50.892	53.672	59.703

5

F Distribution ($\alpha=1\%$)

$F_{.99}\ (n_1,\ n_2)$

n_1 = degrees of freedom for numerator

n_2 \ n_1	1	2	3	4	5	6	7	8	9	10
1	4052	4999.5	5403	5625	5764	5859	5928	5982	6022	6056
2	98.50	99.00	99.17	99.25	99.30	99.33	99.36	99.37	99.39	99.40
3	34.12	30.82	29.46	28.71	28.24	27.91	27.67	27.49	27.35	27.23
4	21.20	18.00	16.69	15.98	15.52	15.21	14.98	14.80	14.66	14.55
5	16.26	13.27	12.06	11.39	10.97	10.67	10.46	10.29	10.16	10.05
6	13.75	10.92	9.78	9.15	8.75	8.47	8.26	8.10	7.98	7.87
7	12.25	9.55	8.45	7.85	7.46	7.19	6.99	6.84	6.72	6.62
8	11.26	8.65	7.59	7.01	6.63	6.37	6.18	6.03	5.91	5.81
9	10.56	8.02	6.99	6.42	6.06	5.80	5.61	5.47	5.35	5.26
10	10.04	7.56	6.55	5.99	5.64	5.39	5.20	5.06	4.94	4.85
11	9.65	7.21	6.22	5.67	5.32	5.07	4.89	4.74	4.63	4.54
12	9.33	6.93	5.95	5.41	5.06	4.82	4.64	4.50	4.39	4.30
13	9.07	6.70	5.74	5.21	4.86	4.62	4.44	4.30	4.19	4.10
14	8.86	6.51	5.56	5.04	4.69	4.46	4.28	4.14	4.03	3.94
15	8.68	6.36	5.42	4.89	4.56	4.32	4.14	4.00	3.89	3.80
16	8.53	6.23	5.29	4.77	4.44	4.20	4.03	3.89	3.78	3.69
17	8.40	6.11	5.18	4.67	4.34	4.10	3.93	3.79	3.68	3.59
18	8.29	6.01	5.09	4.58	4.25	4.01	3.84	3.71	3.60	3.51
19	8.18	5.93	5.01	4.50	4.17	3.94	3.77	3.63	3.52	3.43
20	8.10	5.85	4.94	4.43	4.10	3.87	3.70	3.56	3.46	3.37
21	8.02	5.78	4.87	4.37	4.04	3.81	3.64	3.51	3.40	3.31
22	7.95	5.72	4.82	4.31	3.99	3.76	3.59	3.45	3.35	3.26
23	7.88	5.66	4.76	4.26	3.94	3.71	3.54	3.41	3.30	3.21
24	7.82	5.61	4.72	4.22	3.90	3.67	3.50	3.36	3.26	3.17
25	7.77	5.57	4.68	4.18	3.85	3.63	3.46	3.32	3.22	3.13
26	7.72	5.53	4.64	4.14	3.82	3.59	3.42	3.29	3.18	3.09
27	7.68	5.49	4.60	4.11	3.78	3.56	3.39	3.26	3.15	3.06
28	7.64	5.45	4.57	4.07	3.75	3.53	3.36	3.23	3.12	3.03
29	7.60	5.42	4.54	4.04	3.73	3.50	3.33	3.20	3.09	3.00
30	7.56	5.39	4.51	4.02	3.70	3.47	3.30	3.17	3.07	2.98
40	7.31	5.18	4.31	3.83	3.51	3.29	3.12	2.99	2.89	2.80
60	7.08	4.98	4.13	3.65	3.34	3.12	2.95	2.82	2.72	2.63
120	6.85	4.79	3.95	3.48	3.17	2.96	2.79	2.66	2.56	2.47
∞	6.63	4.61	3.78	3.32	3.02	2.80	2.64	2.51	2.41	2.32

n_2 = degrees of freedom for denominator

Continued on next page . . .

Continued . . .

n_1 = degrees of freedom for numerator

n_2 \ n_1	12	15	20	24	30	40	60	120	∞
1	6106	6157	6209	6235	6261	6287	6313	6339	6366
2	99.42	99.43	99.45	99.46	99.47	99.47	99.48	99.49	99.50
3	27.05	26.87	26.69	26.60	26.50	26.41	26.32	26.22	26.13
4	14.37	14.20	14.02	13.93	13.84	13.75	13.65	13.56	13.46
5	9.89	9.72	9.55	9.47	9.38	9.29	9.20	9.11	9.02
6	7.72	7.56	7.40	7.31	7.23	7.14	7.06	6.97	6.88
7	6.47	6.31	6.16	6.07	5.99	5.91	5.82	5.74	5.65
8	5.67	5.52	5.36	5.28	5.20	5.12	5.03	4.95	4.86
9	5.11	4.96	4.81	4.73	4.65	4.57	4.48	4.40	4.31
10	4.71	4.56	4.41	4.33	4.25	4.17	4.08	4.00	3.91
11	4.40	4.25	4.10	4.02	3.94	3.86	3.78	3.69	3.60
12	4.16	4.01	3.86	3.78	3.70	3.62	3.54	3.45	3.36
13	3.96	3.82	3.66	3.59	3.51	3.43	3.34	3.25	3.17
14	3.80	3.66	3.51	3.43	3.35	3.27	3.18	3.09	3.00
15	3.67	3.52	3.37	3.29	3.21	3.13	3.05	2.96	2.87
16	3.55	3.41	3.26	3.18	3.10	3.02	2.93	2.84	2.75
17	3.46	3.31	3.16	3.08	3.00	2.92	2.83	2.75	2.65
18	3.37	3.23	3.08	3.00	2.92	2.84	2.75	2.66	2.57
19	3.30	3.15	3.00	2.92	2.84	2.76	2.67	2.58	2.49
20	3.23	3.09	2.94	2.86	2.78	2.69	2.61	2.52	2.42
21	3.17	3.03	2.88	2.80	2.72	2.64	2.55	2.46	2.36
22	3.12	2.98	2.83	2.75	2.67	2.58	2.50	2.40	2.31
23	3.07	2.93	2.78	2.70	2.62	2.54	2.45	2.35	2.26
24	3.03	2.89	2.74	2.66	2.58	2.49	2.40	2.31	2.21
25	2.99	2.85	2.70	2.62	2.54	2.45	2.36	2.27	2.17
26	2.96	2.81	2.66	2.58	2.50	2.42	2.33	2.23	2.13
27	2.93	2.78	2.63	2.55	2.47	2.38	2.29	2.20	2.10
28	2.90	2.75	2.60	2.52	2.44	2.35	2.26	2.17	2.06
29	2.87	2.73	2.57	2.49	2.41	2.33	2.23	2.14	2.03
30	2.84	2.70	2.55	2.47	2.39	2.30	2.21	2.11	2.01
40	2.66	2.52	2.37	2.29	2.20	2.11	2.02	1.92	1.80
60	2.50	2.35	2.20	2.12	2.03	1.94	1.84	1.73	1.60
120	2.34	2.19	2.03	1.95	1.86	1.76	1.66	1.53	1.38
∞	2.18	2.04	1.88	1.79	1.70	1.59	1.47	1.32	1.00

n_2 = degrees of freedom for denominator

6

F Distribution (α=5%)

$$F_{.95}\,(n_1,\,n_2)$$

n₁ = degrees of freedom for numerator

n_2 \ n_1	1	2	3	4	5	6	7	8	9	10
1	161.4	199.5	215.7	224.6	230.2	234.0	236.8	238.9	240.5	241.9
2	18.51	19.00	19.16	19.25	19.30	19.33	19.35	19.37	19.38	19.40
3	10.13	9.55	9.28	9.12	9.01	8.94	8.89	8.85	8.81	8.79
4	7.71	6.94	6.59	6.39	6.26	6.16	6.09	6.04	6.00	5.96
5	6.61	5.79	5.41	5.19	5.05	4.95	4.88	4.82	4.77	4.74
6	5.99	5.14	4.76	4.53	4.39	4.28	4.21	4.15	4.10	4.06
7	5.59	4.74	4.35	4.12	3.97	3.87	3.79	3.73	3.68	3.64
8	5.32	4.46	4.07	3.84	3.69	3.58	3.50	3.44	3.39	3.35
9	5.12	4.26	3.86	3.63	3.48	3.37	3.29	3.23	3.18	3.14
10	4.96	4.10	3.71	3.48	3.33	3.22	3.14	3.07	3.02	2.98
11	4.84	3.98	3.59	3.36	3.20	3.09	3.01	2.95	2.90	2.85
12	4.75	3.89	3.49	3.26	3.11	3.00	2.91	2.85	2.80	2.75
13	4.67	3.81	3.41	3.18	3.03	2.92	2.83	2.77	2.71	2.67
14	4.60	3.74	3.34	3.11	2.96	2.85	2.76	2.70	2.65	2.60
15	4.54	3.68	3.29	3.06	2.90	2.79	2.71	2.64	2.59	2.54
16	4.49	3.63	3.24	3.01	2.85	2.74	2.66	2.59	2.54	2.49
17	4.45	3.59	3.20	2.96	2.81	2.70	2.61	2.55	2.49	2.45
18	4.41	3.55	3.16	2.93	2.77	2.66	2.58	2.51	2.46	2.41
19	4.38	3.52	3.13	2.90	2.74	2.63	2.54	2.48	2.42	2.38
20	4.35	3.49	3.10	2.87	2.71	2.60	2.51	2.45	2.39	2.35
21	4.32	3.47	3.07	2.84	2.68	2.57	2.49	2.42	2.37	2.32
22	4.30	3.44	3.05	2.82	2.66	2.55	2.46	2.40	2.34	2.30
23	4.28	3.42	3.03	2.80	2.64	2.53	2.44	2.37	2.32	2.27
24	4.26	3.40	3.01	2.78	2.62	2.51	2.42	2.36	2.30	2.25
25	4.24	3.39	2.99	2.76	2.60	2.49	2.40	2.34	2.28	2.24
26	4.23	3.37	2.98	2.74	2.59	2.47	2.39	2.32	2.27	2.22
27	4.21	3.35	2.96	2.73	2.57	2.46	2.37	2.31	2.25	2.20
28	4.20	3.34	2.95	2.71	2.56	2.45	2.36	2.29	2.24	2.19
29	4.18	3.33	2.93	2.70	2.55	2.43	2.35	2.28	2.22	2.18
30	4.17	3.32	2.92	2.69	2.53	2.42	2.33	2.27	2.21	2.16
40	4.08	3.23	2.84	2.61	2.45	2.34	2.25	2.18	2.12	2.08
60	4.00	3.15	2.76	2.53	2.37	2.25	2.17	2.10	2.04	1.99
120	3.92	3.07	2.68	2.45	2.29	2.17	2.09	2.02	1.96	1.91
∞	3.84	3.00	2.60	2.37	2.21	2.10	2.01	1.94	1.88	1.83

n₂ = degrees of freedom for denominator

Continued on next page . . .

Continued . . .

n_1 = degrees of freedom for numerator

n_2 = degrees of freedom for denominator

n_2 \ n_1	12	15	20	24	30	40	60	120	∞
1	243.9	245.9	248.0	249.1	250.1	251.1	252.2	253.3	254.3
2	19.41	19.43	19.45	19.45	19.46	19.47	19.48	19.49	19.50
3	8.74	8.70	8.66	8.64	8.62	8.59	8.57	8.55	8.53
4	5.91	5.86	5.80	5.77	5.75	5.72	5.69	5.66	5.63
5	4.68	4.62	4.56	4.53	4.50	4.46	4.43	4.40	4.36
6	4.00	3.94	3.87	3.84	3.81	3.77	3.74	3.70	3.67
7	3.57	3.51	3.44	3.41	3.38	3.34	3.30	3.27	3.23
8	3.28	3.22	3.15	3.12	3.08	3.04	3.01	2.97	2.93
9	3.07	3.01	2.94	2.90	2.86	2.83	2.79	2.75	2.71
10	2.91	2.85	2.77	2.74	2.70	2.66	2.62	2.58	2.54
11	2.79	2.72	2.65	2.61	2.57	2.53	2.49	2.45	2.40
12	2.69	2.62	2.54	2.51	2.47	2.43	2.38	2.34	2.30
13	2.60	2.53	2.46	2.42	2.38	2.34	2.30	2.25	2.21
14	2.53	2.46	2.39	2.35	2.31	2.27	2.22	2.18	2.13
15	2.48	2.40	2.33	2.29	2.25	2.20	2.16	2.11	2.07
16	2.42	2.35	2.28	2.24	2.19	2.15	2.11	2.06	2.01
17	2.38	2.31	2.23	2.19	2.15	2.10	2.06	2.01	1.96
18	2.34	2.27	2.19	2.15	2.11	2.06	2.02	1.97	1.92
19	2.31	2.23	2.16	2.11	2.07	2.03	1.98	1.93	1.88
20	2.28	2.20	2.12	2.08	2.04	1.99	1.95	1.90	1.84
21	2.25	2.18	2.10	2.05	2.01	1.96	1.92	1.87	1.81
22	2.23	2.15	2.07	2.03	1.98	1.94	1.89	1.84	1.78
23	2.20	2.13	2.05	2.01	1.96	1.91	1.86	1.81	1.76
24	2.18	2.11	2.03	1.98	1.94	1.89	1.84	1.79	1.73
25	2.16	2.09	2.01	1.96	1.92	1.87	1.82	1.77	1.71
26	2.15	2.07	1.99	1.95	1.90	1.85	1.80	1.75	1.69
27	2.13	2.06	1.97	1.93	1.88	1.84	1.79	1.73	1.67
28	2.12	2.04	1.96	1.91	1.87	1.82	1.77	1.71	1.65
29	2.10	2.03	1.94	1.90	1.85	1.81	1.75	1.70	1.64
30	2.09	2.01	1.93	1.89	1.84	1.79	1.74	1.68	1.62
40	2.00	1.92	1.84	1.79	1.74	1.69	1.64	1.58	1.51
60	1.92	1.84	1.75	1.70	1.65	1.59	1.53	1.47	1.39
120	1.83	1.75	1.66	1.61	1.55	1.50	1.43	1.35	1.25
∞	1.75	1.67	1.57	1.52	1.46	1.39	1.32	1.22	1.00

Poisson Probability Sums

$$\sum_{x=o}^{r} p(x;\mu)$$

r	μ								
	0.1	**0.2**	**0.3**	**0.4**	**0.5**	**0.6**	**0.7**	**0.8**	**0.9**
0	0.9048	0.8187	0.7408	0.6703	0.6065	0.5488	0.4966	0.4493	0.4066
1	0.9953	0.9825	0.9631	0.9384	0.9098	0.8781	0.8442	0.8088	0.7725
2	0.9998	0.9989	0.9964	0.9921	0.9856	0.9769	0.9659	0.9526	0.9371
3	1.0000	0.9999	0.9997	0.9992	0.9982	0.9966	0.9942	0.9909	0.9865
4	1.0000	1.0000	1.0000	0.9999	0.9998	0.9996	0.9992	0.9986	0.9977
5	1.0000	1.0000	1.0000	1.0000	1.0000	1.0000	0.9999	0.9998	0.9997
6	1.0000	1.0000	1.0000	1.0000	1.0000	1.0000	1.0000	1.0000	1.0000

Continued on next page . . .

Continued . . .

r	μ								
	1.0	1.5	2.0	2.5	3.0	3.5	4.0	4.5	5.0
0	0.3679	0.2231	0.1353	0.0821	0.0498	0.0302	0.0183	0.0111	0.0067
1	0.7358	0.5578	0.4060	0.2873	0.1991	0.1359	0.0916	0.0611	0.0404
2	0.9197	0.8088	0.6767	0.5438	0.4232	0.3208	0.2381	0.1736	0.1247
3	0.9810	0.9344	0.8571	0.7576	0.6472	0.5366	0.4335	0.3423	0.2650
4	0.9963	0.9814	0.9473	0.8912	0.8153	0.7254	0.6288	0.5321	0.4405
5	0.9994	0.9955	0.9834	0.9580	0.9161	0.8576	0.7851	0.7029	0.6160
6	0.9999	0.9991	0.9955	0.9858	0.9665	0.9347	0.8893	0.8311	0.7622
7	1.0000	0.9998	0.9989	0.9958	0.9881	0.9733	0.9489	0.9134	0.8666
8	1.0000	1.0000	0.9998	0.9989	0.9962	0.9901	0.9786	0.9597	0.9319
9	1.0000	1.0000	1.0000	0.9997	0.9989	0.9967	0.9919	0.9829	0.9682
10	1.0000	1.0000	1.0000	0.9999	0.9997	0.9990	0.9972	0.9933	0.9863
11	1.0000	1.0000	1.0000	1.0000	0.9999	0.9997	0.9991	0.9976	0.9945
12	1.0000	1.0000	1.0000	1.0000	1.0000	0.9999	0.9997	0.9992	0.9980
13	1.0000	1.0000	1.0000	1.0000	1.0000	1.0000	0.9999	0.9997	0.9993
14	1.0000	1.0000	1.0000	1.0000	1.0000	1.0000	1.0000	0.9999	0.9998
15	1.0000	1.0000	1.0000	1.0000	1.0000	1.0000	1.0000	1.0000	0.9999
16	1.0000	1.0000	1.0000	1.0000	1.0000	1.0000	1.0000	1.0000	1.0000

r	μ								
	5.5	6.0	6.5	7.0	7.5	8.0	8.5	9.0	9.5
0	0.0041	0.0025	0.0015	0.0009	0.0006	0.0003	0.0002	0.0001	0.0001
1	0.0266	0.0174	0.0113	0.0073	0.0047	0.0030	0.0019	0.0012	0.0008
2	0.0884	0.0620	0.0430	0.0296	0.0203	0.0138	0.0093	0.0062	0.0042
3	0.2017	0.1512	0.1118	0.0818	0.0591	0.0424	0.0301	0.0212	0.0149
4	0.3575	0.2851	0.2237	0.1730	0.1321	0.0996	0.0744	0.0550	0.0403
5	0.5289	0.4457	0.3690	0.3007	0.2414	0.1912	0.1496	0.1157	0.0885
6	0.6860	0.6063	0.5265	0.4497	0.3782	0.3134	0.2562	0.2068	0.1649
7	0.8095	0.7440	0.6728	0.5987	0.5246	0.4530	0.3856	0.3239	0.2687
8	0.8944	0.8472	0.7916	0.7291	0.6620	0.5925	0.5231	0.4557	0.3918
9	0.9462	0.9161	0.8774	0.8305	0.7764	0.7166	0.6530	0.5874	0.5218
10	0.9747	0.9574	0.9332	0.9015	0.8622	0.8159	0.7634	0.7060	0.6453
11	0.9890	0.9799	0.9661	0.9467	0.9208	0.8881	0.8487	0.8030	0.7520
12	0.9955	0.9912	0.9840	0.9730	0.9573	0.9362	0.9091	0.8758	0.8364
13	0.9983	0.9964	0.9929	0.9872	0.9784	0.9658	0.9486	0.9261	0.8981
14	0.9994	0.9986	0.9970	0.9943	0.9897	0.9827	0.9726	0.9585	0.9400

Continued on next page . . .

Continued . . .

r	μ 5.5	6.0	6.5	7.0	7.5	8.0	8.5	9.0	9.5
15	0.9998	0.9995	0.9988	0.9976	0.9954	0.9918	0.9862	0.9780	0.9665
16	0.9999	0.9998	0.9996	0.9990	0.9980	0.9963	0.9934	0.9889	0.9823
17	1.0000	0.9999	0.9998	0.9996	0.9992	0.9984	0.9970	0.9947	0.9911
18	1.0000	1.0000	0.9999	0.9999	0.9997	0.9993	0.9987	0.9976	0.9957
19	1.0000	1.0000	1.0000	1.0000	0.9999	0.9997	0.9995	0.9989	0.9980
20	1.0000	1.0000	1.0000	1.0000	1.0000	0.9999	0.9998	0.9996	0.9991
21	1.0000	1.0000	1.0000	1.0000	1.0000	1.0000	0.9999	0.9998	0.9996
22	1.0000	1.0000	1.0000	1.0000	1.0000	1.0000	1.0000	0.9999	0.9999
23	1.0000	1.0000	1.0000	1.0000	1.0000	1.0000	1.0000	1.0000	0.9999
24	1.0000	1.0000	1.0000	1.0000	1.0000	1.0000	1.0000	1.0000	1.0000

r	μ 10.0	11.0	12.0	13.0	14.0	15.0	16.0	17.0	18.0
0	0.0000	0.0000	0.0000	0.0000	0.0000	0.0000	0.0000	0.0000	0.0000
1	0.0005	0.0002	0.0001	0.0000	0.0000	0.0000	0.0000	0.0000	0.0000
2	0.0028	0.0012	0.0005	0.0002	0.0001	0.0000	0.0000	0.0000	0.0000
3	0.0103	0.0049	0.0023	0.0011	0.0005	0.0002	0.0001	0.0000	0.0000
4	0.0293	0.0151	0.0076	0.0037	0.0018	0.0009	0.0004	0.0002	0.0001
5	0.0671	0.0375	0.0203	0.0107	0.0055	0.0028	0.0014	0.0007	0.0003
6	0.1301	0.0786	0.0458	0.0259	0.0142	0.0076	0.0040	0.0021	0.0010
7	0.2202	0.1432	0.0895	0.0540	0.0316	0.0180	0.0100	0.0054	0.0029
8	0.3328	0.2320	0.1550	0.0998	0.0621	0.0374	0.0220	0.0126	0.0071
9	0.4579	0.3405	0.2424	0.1658	0.1094	0.0699	0.0433	0.0261	0.0154
10	0.5830	0.4599	0.3472	0.2517	0.1757	0.1185	0.0774	0.0491	0.0304
11	0.6968	0.5793	0.4616	0.3532	0.2600	0.1848	0.1270	0.0847	0.0549
12	0.7916	0.6887	0.5760	0.4631	0.3585	0.2676	0.1931	0.1350	0.0917
13	0.8645	0.7813	0.6815	0.5730	0.4644	0.3632	0.2745	0.2009	0.1426
14	0.9165	0.8540	0.7720	0.6751	0.5704	0.4657	0.3675	0.2808	0.2081
15	0.9513	0.9074	0.8444	0.7636	0.6694	0.5681	0.4667	0.3715	0.2867
16	0.9730	0.9441	0.8987	0.8355	0.7559	0.6641	0.5660	0.4677	0.3751
17	0.9857	0.9678	0.9370	0.8905	0.8272	0.7489	0.6593	0.5640	0.4686
18	0.9928	0.9823	0.9626	0.9302	0.8826	0.8195	0.7423	0.6550	0.5622
19	0.9965	0.9907	0.9787	0.9573	0.9235	0.8752	0.8122	0.7363	0.6509
20	0.9984	0.9953	0.9884	0.9750	0.9521	0.9170	0.8682	0.8055	0.7307

Continued on next page . . .

Continued . . .

r	μ								
	10.0	11.0	12.0	13.0	14.0	15.0	16.0	17.0	18.0
21	0.9993	0.9977	0.9939	0.9859	0.9712	0.9469	0.9108	0.8615	0.7991
22	0.9997	0.9990	0.9970	0.9924	0.9833	0.9673	0.9418	0.9047	0.8551
23	0.9999	0.9995	0.9985	0.9960	0.9907	0.9805	0.9633	0.9367	0.8989
24	1.0000	0.9998	0.9993	0.9980	0.9950	0.9888	0.9777	0.9594	0.9317
25	1.0000	0.9999	0.9997	0.9990	0.9974	0.9938	0.9869	0.9748	0.9554
26	1.0000	1.0000	0.9999	0.9995	0.9987	0.9967	0.9925	0.9848	0.9718
27	1.0000	1.0000	0.9999	0.9998	0.9994	0.9983	0.9959	0.9912	0.9827
28	1.0000	1.0000	1.0000	0.9999	0.9997	0.9991	0.9978	0.9950	0.9897
29	1.0000	1.0000	1.0000	1.0000	0.9999	0.9996	0.9989	0.9973	0.9941
30	1.0000	1.0000	1.0000	1.0000	0.9999	0.9998	0.9994	0.9986	0.9967
31	1.0000	1.0000	1.0000	1.0000	1.0000	0.9999	0.9997	0.9993	0.9982
32	1.0000	1.0000	1.0000	1.0000	1.0000	1.0000	0.9999	0.9996	0.9990
33	1.0000	1.0000	1.0000	1.0000	1.0000	1.0000	0.9999	0.9998	0.9995
34	1.0000	1.0000	1.0000	1.0000	1.0000	1.0000	1.0000	0.9999	0.9998
35	1.0000	1.0000	1.0000	1.0000	1.0000	1.0000	1.0000	1.0000	0.9999
36	1.0000	1.0000	1.0000	1.0000	1.0000	1.0000	1.0000	1.0000	0.9999
37	1.0000	1.0000	1.0000	1.0000	1.0000	1.0000	1.0000	1.0000	1.0000

Tolerance Interval Factors

Table 8.1a. Values of *k* for two-sided limits.

n	γ=0.90				γ=0.95				γ=0.99			
	P=0.90	P=0.95	P=0.99	P=0.999	P=0.90	P=0.95	P=0.99	P=0.999	P=0.90	P=0.95	P=0.99	P=0.999
2	15.978	18.800	24.167	30.227	32.019	37.674	48.430	60.573	160.193	188.491	242.300	303.054
3	5.847	6.919	8.974	11.309	8.380	9.916	12.861	16.208	18.930	22.401	29.055	36.616
4	4.166	4.943	6.440	8.149	5.369	6.370	8.299	10.502	9.398	11.150	14.527	18.383
5	3.494	4.152	5.423	6.879	4.275	5.079	6.634	8.415	6.612	7.855	10.260	13.015
6	3.131	3.723	4.870	6.188	3.712	4.414	5.775	7.337	5.337	6.345	8.301	10.548
7	2.902	3.452	4.521	5.750	3.369	4.007	5.248	6.676	4.613	5.488	7.187	9.142
8	2.743	3.264	4.278	5.446	3.316	3.732	4.891	6.226	4.147	4.936	6.468	8.234
9	2.626	3.125	4.098	5.220	2.967	3.532	4.631	5.899	3.822	4.550	5.966	7.600
10	2.535	3.018	3.959	5.046	2.839	3.379	4.433	5.649	3.582	4.265	5.594	7.129
11	2.463	2.933	3.849	4.906	2.737	3.259	4.277	5.452	3.397	4.045	5.308	6.766
12	2.404	2.863	3.758	4.792	2.655	3.162	4.150	5.291	3.250	3.870	5.079	6.477
13	2.355	2.805	3.682	4.697	2.587	3.081	4.044	5.158	3.130	3.727	4.893	6.240
14	2.314	2.756	3.618	4.615	2.529	3.012	3.955	5.045	3.029	3.608	4.737	6.043
15	2.278	2.713	3.562	4.545	2.480	2.954	3.878	4.949	2.945	3.507	4.605	5.876

Continued on next page . . .

Table 8.1a—*Continued* . . .

n	γ=0.90				γ=0.95				γ=0.99			
	P=0.90	P=0.95	P=0.99	P=0.999	P=0.90	P=0.95	P=0.99	P=0.999	P=0.90	P=0.95	P=0.99	P=0.999
16	2.246	2.676	3.514	4.484	2.437	2.903	3.812	4.865	2.872	3.421	4.492	5.732
17	2.219	2.643	3.471	4.430	2.400	2.858	3.754	4.791	2.808	3.345	4.393	5.607
18	2.194	2.614	3.433	4.382	2.366	2.819	3.702	4.725	2.753	3.279	4.307	5.497
19	2.172	2.588	3.399	4.339	2.337	2.784	3.656	4.667	2.703	3.221	4.230	5.399
20	2.152	2.564	3.368	4.300	2.310	2.752	3.615	4.614	2.659	3.168	4.161	5.312
21	2.135	2.543	3.340	4.264	2.286	2.723	3.577	4.567	2.620	3.121	4.100	5.234
22	2.118	2.524	3.315	4.232	2.264	2.697	3.543	4.523	2.584	3.078	4.044	5.163
23	2.103	2.506	3.292	4.203	2.244	2.673	3.512	4.484	2.551	3.040	3.993	5.098
24	2.089	2.480	3.270	4.176	2.225	2.651	3.483	4.447	2.522	3.004	3.947	5.039
25	2.077	2.474	3.251	4.151	2.208	2.631	3.457	4.413	2.494	2.972	3.904	4.985
30	2.025	2.413	3.170	4.049	2.140	2.549	3.350	4.278	2.385	2.841	3.733	4.768
35	1.988	2.368	3.112	3.974	2.090	2.490	3.272	4.179	2.306	2.748	3.611	4.611
40	1.959	2.334	3.066	3.917	2.052	2.445	3.213	4.104	2.247	2.677	3.518	4.493
45	1.935	2.306	3.030	3.871	2.021	2.408	3.165	4.042	2.200	2.621	3.444	4.399
50	1.916	2.284	3.001	3.833	1.996	2.379	3.126	3.993	2.162	2.576	3.385	4.323

Table 8.1b. Values of *k* for one-sided limits.

n	γ=0.90				γ=0.95				γ=0.99			
	P=0.90	P=0.95	P=0.99	P=0.999	P=0.90	P=0.95	P=0.99	P=0.999	P=0.90	P=0.95	P=0.99	P=0.999
3	4.258	5.310	7.340	9.651	6.158	7.655	10.552	13.857	-	-	-	-
4	3.187	3.957	5.437	7.128	4.163	5.145	7.042	9.215	-	-	-	-
5	2.742	3.400	4.666	6.112	3.407	4.202	5.741	7.501	-	-	-	-
6	2.494	3.091	4.242	5.556	3.006	3.707	50.62	6.612	4.408	5.409	7.334	9.540
7	2.333	2.894	3.972	5.201	2.755	3.399	4.641	6.061	3.856	4.730	6.411	8.348
8	2.219	2.755	3.783	4.955	2.582	3.188	4.353	5.686	3.496	4.287	5.811	7.566
9	2.133	2.649	3.641	4.772	2.454	3.031	4.143	5.414	3.242	3.971	5.389	7.014
10	2.065	2.568	3.532	4.629	2.355	2.911	3.981	5.203	3.048	3.739	5.075	6.603

Continued on next page . . .

Table 8.1b—*Continued . . .*

n	γ=0.90				γ=0.95				γ=0.99			
	P=0.90	P=0.95	P=0.99	P=0.999	P=0.90	P=0.95	P=0.99	P=0.999	P=0.90	P=0.95	P=0.99	P=0.999
11	2.012	2.503	3.444	4.515	2.275	2.815	3.852	5.036	2.897	3.557	4.828	6.284
12	1.966	2.448	3.371	4.420	2.210	2.736	3.747	4.900	2.773	3.410	4.633	6.032
13	1.928	2.403	3.310	4.341	2.155	2.670	3.659	4.787	2.677	3.290	4.472	5.826
14	1.895	2.363	3.257	4.274	2.108	2.614	3.585	4.690	2.592	3.189	4.336	5.651
15	1.866	2.329	3.212	4.215	2.068	2.566	3.520	4.607	2.521	3.102	4.224	5.507
16	1.842	2.299	3.172	4.146	2.032	2.523	3.463	4.534	2.458	3.028	4.124	5.374
17	1.820	2.272	3.136	4.118	2.001	2.468	3.415	4.471	2.405	2.962	4.038	5.268
18	1.800	2.249	3.106	4.078	1.974	2.453	3.370	4.415	2.357	2.906	3.961	5.167
19	1.781	2.228	3.078	4.041	1.949	2.423	3.331	4.364	2.315	2.855	3.893	5.078
20	1.765	2.208	3.052	4.009	1.926	2.396	3.295	4.319	2.275	2.807	3.832	5.003
21	1.750	2.190	3.028	3.979	1.905	2.371	3.262	4.276	2.241	2.768	3.776	4.932
22	1.736	2.174	3.007	3.952	1.887	2.350	3.233	4.238	2.208	2.729	3.727	4.866
23	1.724	2.159	2.987	3.927	1.869	2.329	3.206	4.204	2.179	2.693	3.680	4.806
24	1.712	2.145	2.969	3.904	1.853	2.309	3.181	4.171	2.154	2.663	3.638	4.755
25	1.702	2.132	2.952	3.882	1.838	2.292	3.158	4.143	2.129	2.632	3.601	4.706
30	1.657	2.080	2.884	3.794	1.778	2.220	3.064	4.022	2.029	2.516	3.446	4.508
35	1.623	2.041	2.833	3.730	1.732	2.166	2.994	3.934	1.957	2.431	3.334	4.364
40	1.598	2.010	2.793	3.679	1.697	2.126	2.941	3.866	1.902	2.365	3.250	4.255
45	1.577	1.986	2.762	3.638	1.669	2.092	2.897	3.811	1.857	2.313	3.181	4.168
50	1.560	1.965	2.735	3.604	1.646	2.065	2.963	3.766	1.821	2.296	3.124	4.096

Table 8.2. Proportion of population covered with γ%
confidence and sample size *n*.

n	γ=0.90	γ=0.95	γ=0.99	γ=0.995
2	0.052	0.026	0.006	0.003
4	0.321	0.249	0.141	0.111
6	0.490	0.419	0.295	0.254
10	0.664	0.606	0.496	0.456
20	0.820	0.784	0.712	0.683
40	0.907	0.887	0.846	0.829
60	0.937	0.924	0.895	0.883
80	0.953	0.943	0.920	0.911
100	0.962	0.954	0.936	0.929
150	0.975	0.969	0.957	0.952
200	0.981	0.977	0.968	0.961
500	0.993	0.991	0.987	0.986
1000	0.997	0.996	0.994	0.993

Table 8.3. Sample size required to cover (1-α)% of the population
with γ% confidence.

α	γ=0.90	γ=0.95	γ=0.99	γ=0.995
0.005	777	947	1325	1483
0.01	388	473	662	740
0.05	77	93	130	146
0.01	38	46	64	72
0.15	25	30	42	47
0.20	18	22	31	34
0.25	15	18	24	27
0.30	12	14	20	22
0.40	6	10	14	16
0.50	7	8	11	12

9

Durbin-Watson Test Bounds

Table 9.1. Level of significance $\alpha=.05$

n	$p-1=1$		$p-1=2$		$p-1=3$		$p-1=4$		$p-1=5$	
	d_L	d_U	d_L	d_U	d_L	d_U	d_L	d_U	d_L	d_U
15	1.08	1.36	0.95	1.54	0.82	1.75	0.69	1.97	0.56	2.21
16	1.10	1.37	0.98	1.54	0.86	1.73	0.74	1.93	0.62	2.15
17	1.13	1.38	1.02	1.54	0.90	1.71	0.78	1.90	0.67	2.10
18	1.16	1.39	1.05	1.53	0.93	1.69	0.82	1.87	0.71	2.06
19	1.18	1.40	1.08	1.53	0.97	1.68	0.86	1.85	0.75	2.02
20	1.20	1.41	1.10	1.54	1.00	1.68	0.90	1.83	0.79	1.99
21	1.22	1.42	1.13	1.54	1.03	1.67	0.93	1.81	0.83	1.96
22	1.24	1.43	1.15	1.54	1.05	1.66	0.96	1.80	0.86	1.94
23	1.26	1.44	1.17	1.54	1.08	1.66	0.99	1.79	0.90	1.92
24	1.27	1.45	1.19	1.55	1.10	1.66	1.01	1.78	0.93	1.90
25	1.29	1.45	1.21	1.55	1.12	1.66	1.04	1.77	0.95	1.89
26	1.30	1.46	1.22	1.55	1.14	1.65	1.06	1.76	0.98	1.88
27	1.32	1.47	1.24	1.56	1.16	1.65	1.08	1.76	1.01	1.86
28	1.33	1.48	1.26	1.56	1.18	1.65	1.10	1.75	1.03	1.85
29	1.34	1.48	1.27	1.56	1.20	1.65	1.12	1.74	1.05	1.84

Continued on next page . . .

Table 9.1—*Continued . . .*

n	p-1=1		p-1=2		p-1=3		p-1=4		p-1=5	
	d_L	d_U	d_L	d_U	d_L	d_U	d_L	d_U	d_L	d_U
30	1.35	1.49	1.28	1.57	1.21	1.65	1.14	1.74	1.07	1.83
31	1.36	1.50	1.30	1.57	1.23	1.65	1.16	1.74	1.09	1.83
32	1.37	1.50	1.31	1.57	1.24	1.65	1.18	1.73	1.11	1.82
33	1.38	1.51	1.32	1.58	1.26	1.65	1.19	1.73	1.13	1.81
34	1.39	1.51	1.33	1.58	1.27	1.65	1.21	1.73	1.15	1.81
35	1.40	1.52	1.34	1.58	1.28	1.65	1.22	1.73	1.16	1.80
36	1.41	1.52	1.35	1.59	1.29	1.65	1.24	1.73	1.18	1.80
37	1.42	1.53	1.36	1.59	1.31	1.66	1.25	1.72	1.19	1.80
38	1.43	1.54	1.37	1.59	1.32	1.66	1.26	1.72	1.21	1.79
39	1.43	1.54	1.38	1.60	1.33	1.66	1.27	1.72	1.22	1.79
40	1.44	1.54	1.39	1.60	1.34	1.66	1.29	1.72	1.23	1.79
45	1.48	1.57	1.43	1.62	1.38	1.67	1.34	1.72	1.29	1.78
50	1.50	1.59	1.46	1.63	1.42	1.67	1.38	1.72	1.34	1.77
55	1.53	1.60	1.49	1.64	1.45	1.68	1.41	1.72	1.38	1.77
60	1.55	1.62	1.51	1.65	1.48	1.69	1.44	1.73	1.41	1.77
65	1.57	1.63	1.54	1.66	1.50	1.70	1.47	1.73	1.44	1.77
70	1.58	1.64	1.55	1.67	1.52	1.70	1.49	1.74	1.46	1.77
75	1.60	1.65	1.57	1.68	1.54	1.71	1.51	1.74	1.49	1.77
80	1.61	1.66	1.59	1.69	1.56	1.72	1.53	1.74	1.51	1.77
85	1.62	1.67	1.60	1.70	1.57	1.72	1.55	1.75	1.52	1.77
90	1.63	1.68	1.61	1.70	1.59	1.73	1.57	1.75	1.54	1.78
95	1.64	1.69	1.62	1.71	1.60	1.73	1.58	1.75	1.56	1.78
100	1.65	1.69	1.63	1.72	1.61	1.74	1.59	1.76	1.57	1.78

Table 9.2. Level of significance $\alpha=.01$.

n	$p-1=1$ d_L	d_U	$p-1=2$ d_L	d_U	$p-1=3$ d_L	d_U	$p-1=4$ d_L	d_U	$p-1=5$ d_L	d_U
15	0.81	1.07	0.70	1.25	0.59	1.46	0.49	1.70	0.39	1.96
16	0.84	1.09	0.74	1.25	0.63	1.44	0.53	1.66	0.44	1.90
17	0.87	1.10	0.77	1.25	0.67	1.43	0.57	1.63	0.48	1.85
18	0.90	1.12	0.80	1.26	0.71	1.42	0.61	1.60	0.52	1.80
19	0.93	1.13	0.83	1.26	0.74	1.41	0.65	1.58	0.56	1.77
20	0.95	1.15	0.86	1.27	0.77	1.41	0.68	1.57	0.60	1.74
21	0.97	1.16	0.89	1.27	0.80	1.41	0.72	1.55	0.63	1.71
22	1.00	1.17	0.91	1.28	0.83	1.40	0.75	1.54	0.66	1.69
23	1.02	1.19	0.94	1.29	0.86	1.40	0.77	1.53	0.70	1.67
24	1.04	1.20	0.96	1.30	0.88	1.41	0.80	1.53	0.72	1.66
25	1.05	1.21	0.98	1.30	0.90	1.41	0.83	1.52	0.75	1.65
26	1.07	1.22	1.00	1.31	0.93	1.41	0.85	1.52	0.78	1.64
27	1.09	1.23	1.02	1.32	0.95	1.41	0.88	1.51	0.81	1.63
28	1.10	1.24	1.04	1.32	0.97	1.41	0.90	1.51	0.83	1.62
29	1.12	1.25	1.05	1.33	0.99	1.42	0.92	1.51	0.85	1.61
30	1.13	1.26	1.07	1.34	1.01	1.42	0.94	1.51	0.88	1.61
31	1.15	1.27	1.08	1.34	1.02	1.42	0.96	1.51	0.90	1.60
32	1.16	1.28	1.10	1.35	1.04	1.43	0.98	1.51	0.92	1.60
33	1.17	1.29	1.11	1.36	1.05	1.43	1.00	1.51	0.94	1.59
34	1.18	1.30	1.13	1.36	1.07	1.43	1.01	1.51	0.95	1.59
35	1.19	1.31	1.14	1.37	1.08	1.44	1.03	1.51	0.97	1.59
36	1.21	1.32	1.15	1.38	1.10	1.44	1.04	1.51	0.99	1.59
37	1.22	1.32	1.16	1.38	1.11	1.45	1.06	1.51	1.00	1.59
38	1.23	1.33	1.18	1.39	1.12	1.45	1.07	1.52	1.02	1.58
39	1.24	1.34	1.19	1.39	1.14	1.45	1.09	1.52	1.03	1.58

Continued on next page . . .

Table 9.2—*Continued* . . .

n	p-1=1 d_L	d_U	p-1=2 d_L	d_U	p-1=3 d_L	d_U	p-1=4 d_L	d_U	p-1=5 d_L	d_U
40	1.25	1.34	1.20	1.40	1.15	1.46	1.10	1.52	1.05	1.58
45	1.29	1.38	1.24	1.42	1.20	1.48	1.16	1.53	1.11	1.58
50	1.32	1.40	1.28	1.45	1.24	1.49	1.20	1.54	1.16	1.59
55	1.36	1.43	1.32	1.47	1.28	1.51	1.25	1.55	1.21	1.59
60	1.38	1.45	1.35	1.48	1.32	1.52	1.28	1.56	1.25	1.60
65	1.41	1.47	1.38	1.50	1.35	1.53	1.31	1.57	1.28	1.61
70	1.43	1.49	1.40	1.52	1.37	1.55	1.34	1.58	1.31	1.61
75	1.45	1.50	1.42	1.53	1.39	1.56	1.37	1.59	1.34	1.62
80	1.47	1.52	1.44	1.54	1.42	1.57	1.39	1.60	1.36	1.62
85	1.48	1.53	1.46	1.55	1.43	1.58	1.41	1.60	1.39	1.63
90	1.50	1.54	1.47	1.56	1.45	1.59	1.43	1.61	1.41	1.64
95	1.51	1.55	1.49	1.57	1.47	1.60	1.45	1.62	1.42	1.64
100	1.52	1.56	1.50	1.58	1.48	1.60	1.46	1.63	1.44	1.65

10

y Factors for Computing AOQL

c	0	1	2
y	0.368	0.841	1.372

c	3	4	5
y	1.946	2.544	3.172

c	6	7	8
y	3.810	4.465	5.150

c	9	10	11
y	5.836	6.535	7.234

11

Control Chart Constants

Observations in Sample, n	CHART FOR AVERAGES — Factors for Control Limits			CHART FOR STANDARD DEVIATIONS — Factors for Central Line		Factors for Control Limits			
	A	A_2	A_3	c_4	$1/c_4$	B_3	B_4	B_5	B_6
2	2.121	1.880	2.659	0.7979	1.2533	0	3.267	0	2.606
3	1.732	1.023	1.954	0.8862	1.1284	0	2.568	0	2.276
4	1.500	0.729	1.628	0.9213	1.0854	0	2.266	0	2.088
5	1.342	0.577	1.427	0.9400	1.0638	0	2.089	0	1.964
6	1.225	0.483	1.287	0.9515	1.0510	0.030	1.970	0.029	1.874
7	1.134	0.419	1.182	0.9594	1.0423	0.118	1.882	0.113	1.806
8	1.061	0.373	1.099	0.9650	1.0363	0.185	1.815	0.179	1.751
9	1.000	0.337	1.032	0.9693	1.0317	0.239	1.761	0.232	1.707
10	0.949	0.308	0.975	0.9727	1.0281	0.284	1.716	0.276	1.669
11	0.905	0.285	0.927	0.9754	1.0252	0.321	1.679	0.313	1.637
12	0.866	0.266	0.886	0.9776	1.0229	0.354	1.646	0.346	1.610
13	0.832	0.249	0.850	0.9794	1.0210	0.382	1.618	0.374	1.585
14	0.802	0.235	0.817	0.9810	1.0194	0.406	1.594	0.399	1.563
15	0.775	0.223	0.789	0.9823	1.0180	0.428	1.572	0.421	1.544
16	0.750	0.212	0.763	0.9835	1.0168	0.448	1.552	0.440	1.526
17	0.728	0.203	0.739	0.9845	1.0157	0.466	1.534	0.458	1.511
18	0.707	0.194	0.718	0.9854	1.0148	0.482	1.518	0.475	1.496
19	0.688	0.187	0.698	0.9862	1.0140	0.497	1.503	0.490	1.483
20	0.671	0.180	0.680	0.9869	1.0133	0.510	1.490	0.504	1.470
21	0.655	0.173	0.663	0.9876	1.0126	0.523	1.477	0.516	1.459
22	0.640	0.167	0.647	0.9882	1.0119	0.534	1.466	0.528	1.448
23	0.626	0.162	0.633	0.9887	1.0114	0.545	1.455	0.539	1.438
24	0.612	0.157	0.619	0.9892	1.0109	0.555	1.445	0.549	1.429
25	0.600	0.153	0.606	0.9896	1.0105	0.565	1.435	0.559	1.420

Continued on next page . . .

Continued . . .

CHART FOR RANGES

Observations in Sample, n	Factors for Central Line			Factors for Control Limits			
	d_2	$1/d_2$	d_3	D_1	D_2	D_3	D_4
2	1.128	0.8865	0.853	0	3.686	0	3.267
3	1.693	0.5907	0.888	0	4.358	0	2.574
4	2.059	0.4857	0.880	0	4.698	0	2.282
5	2.326	0.4299	0.864	0	4.918	0	2.114
6	2.534	0.3946	0.848	0	5.078	0	2.004
7	2.704	0.3698	0.833	0.204	5.204	0.076	1.924
8	2.847	0.3512	0.820	0.388	5.306	0.136	1.864
9	2.970	0.3367	0.808	0.547	5.393	0.184	1.816
10	3.078	0.3249	0.797	0.687	5.469	0.223	1.777
11	3.173	0.3152	0.787	0.811	5.535	0.256	1.744
12	3.258	0.3069	0.778	0.922	5.594	0.283	1.717
13	3.336	0.2998	0.770	1.025	5.647	0.307	1.693
14	3.407	0.2935	0.763	1.118	5.696	0.328	1.672
15	3.472	0.2880	0.756	1.203	5.741	0.347	1.653
16	3.532	0.2831	0.750	1.282	5.782	0.363	1.637
17	3.588	0.2787	0.744	1.356	5.820	0.378	1.622
18	3.640	0.2747	0.739	1.424	5.856	0.391	1.608
19	3.689	0.2711	0.734	1.487	5.891	0.403	1.597
20	3.735	0.2677	0.729	1.549	5.921	0.415	1.585
21	3.778	0.2647	0.724	1.605	5.951	0.425	1.575
22	3.819	0.2618	0.720	1.659	5.979	0.434	1.566
23	3.858	0.2592	0.716	1.710	6.006	0.443	1.557
24	3.895	0.2567	0.712	1.759	6.031	0.451	1.548
25	3.931	0.2544	0.708	1.806	6.056	0.459	1.541

Control Chart Equations

	np CHART	p CHART
LCL	$LCL = n\bar{p} - 3\sqrt{n\bar{p}\left(1 - \dfrac{n\bar{p}}{n}\right)}$ or 0 if LCL is negative	$LCL = \bar{p} - 3\sqrt{\dfrac{\bar{p}(1 - \bar{p})}{n}}$ or 0 if LCL is negative
Center Line	$n\bar{p} = \dfrac{\text{Sum of items with problems}}{\text{Number of subgroups}}$	$\bar{p} = \dfrac{\text{Sum of items with problems}}{\text{Number of items in all subgroups}}$
UCL	$UCL = n\bar{p} + 3\sqrt{n\bar{p}\left(1 - \dfrac{n\bar{p}}{n}\right)}$ or n if UCL is greater than n	$UCL = \bar{p} + 3\sqrt{\dfrac{\bar{p}(1 - \bar{p})}{n}}$ or 1 if UCL is greater than 1

Continued on next page . . .

Continued . . .

		c CHART	u CHART
LCL		$LCL = \bar{c} - 3\sqrt{\bar{c}}$ or 0 if LCL is negative	$LCL = \bar{u} - 3\sqrt{\dfrac{\bar{u}}{n}}$ or 0 if LCL is negative
Center Line		$\bar{c} = \dfrac{\text{Sum of problems}}{\text{Number of subgroups}}$	$\bar{u} = \dfrac{\text{Sum of problems}}{\text{Number of units in all subgroups}}$
UCL		$UCL = \bar{c} + 3\sqrt{\bar{c}}$	$UCL = \bar{u} + 3\sqrt{\dfrac{\bar{u}}{n}}$
		X CHART	**$\bar{X}$ CHART**
LCL		$LCL = \bar{X} - 2.66(M\bar{R})$	$LCL = \bar{\bar{X}} - A_2\bar{R}$
Center Line		$\bar{X} = \dfrac{\text{Sum of measurements}}{\text{Number of measurements}}$	$\bar{\bar{X}} = \dfrac{\text{Sum of subgroup averages}}{\text{Number of averages}}$
UCL		$UCL = \bar{X} + 2.66(M\bar{R})$	$UCL = \bar{\bar{X}} + A_2\bar{R}$
		R CHART	
LCL		$LCL = D_3\bar{R}$	
Center Line		$\bar{R} = \dfrac{\text{Sum of ranges}}{\text{Number of ranges}}$	
UCL		$UCL = D_4\bar{R}$	

13

Table of d_2^* Values

		m = repeat readings taken						
		2	3	4	5	6	7	8
g = # parts x # inspectors	1	1.41	1.91	2.24	2.48	2.67	2.83	2.96
	2	1.28	1.81	2.15	2.40	2.60	2.77	2.91
	3	1.23	1.77	2.12	2.38	2.58	2.75	2.89
	4	1.21	1.75	2.11	2.37	2.57	2.74	2.88
	5	1.19	1.74	2.10	2.36	2.56	2.73	2.87
	6	1.18	1.73	2.09	2.35	2.56	2.73	2.87
	7	1.17	1.73	2.09	2.35	2.55	2.72	2.87
	8	1.17	1.72	2.08	2.35	2.55	2.72	2.87
	9	1.16	1.72	2.08	2.34	2.55	5.72	2.86
	10	1.16	1.72	2.08	2.34	2.55	2.72	2.86
	11	1.16	1.71	2.08	2.34	2.55	2.72	2.86
	12	1.15	1.71	2.07	2.34	2.55	2.72	2.85
	13	1.15	1.71	2.07	2.34	2.55	2.71	2.85
	14	1.15	1.71	2.07	2.34	2.54	2.71	2.85
	15	1.15	1.71	2.07	2.34	2.54	2.71	2.85
	> 15	1.128		2.059		2.534		2.847
			1.693		2.326		2.704	

Continued on next page . . .

Continued

		m = repeat readings taken						
		9	10	11	12	13	14	15
	1	3.08	3.18	3.27	3.35	3.42	3.49	3.55
	2	3.02	3.13	3.22	3.30	3.38	3.45	3.51
	3	3.01	3.11	3.21	3.29	3.37	3.43	3.50
	4	3.00	3.10	3.20	3.28	3.36	3.43	3.49
	5	2.99	3.10	3.19	3.28	3.35	3.42	3.49
g = # parts x # inspectors	6	2.99	3.10	3.19	3.27	3.35	3.42	3.49
	7	2.99	3.10	3.19	3.27	3.35	3.42	3.48
	8	2.98	3.09	3.19	3.27	3.35	3.42	3.48
	9	2.98	3.09	3.18	3.27	3.35	3.42	3.48
	10	2.98	3.09	3.18	3.27	3.34	3.42	3.48
	11	2.98	3.09	3.18	3.27	3.34	3.41	3.48
	12	2.98	3.09	3.18	3.27	3.34	3.41	3.48
	13	2.98	3.09	3.18	3.27	3.34	3.41	3.48
	14	2.98	3.08	3.18	3.27	3.34	3.41	3.48
	15	2.98	3.08	3.18	3.26	3.34	3.41	3.48
	> 15		3.078		3.258		3.407	
		2.970		3.173		3.336		3.472

Power Functions for ANOVA

(Graphs on the pages to follow.)

Table 14.1. $v_1 = 1$.

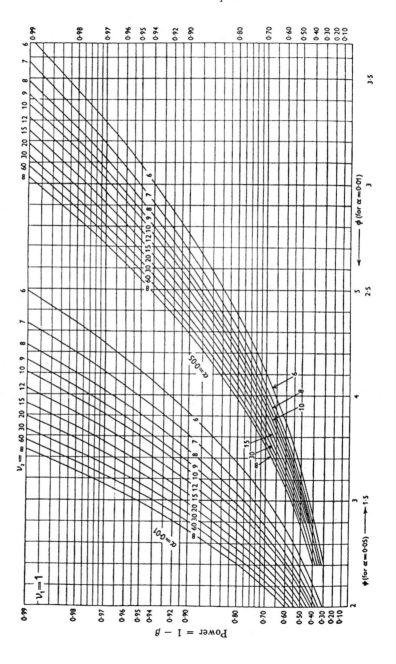

Table 14.2. $v_1 = 2$.

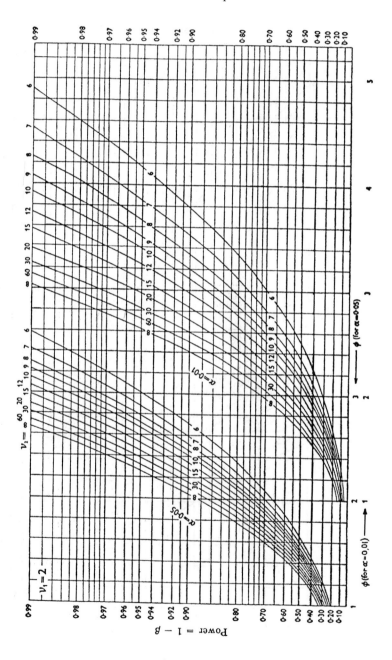

Table 14.3. v_1=3.

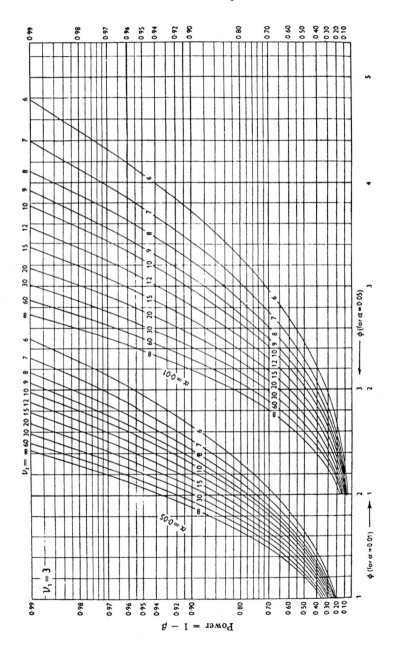

Table 14.4. $v_1=4$.

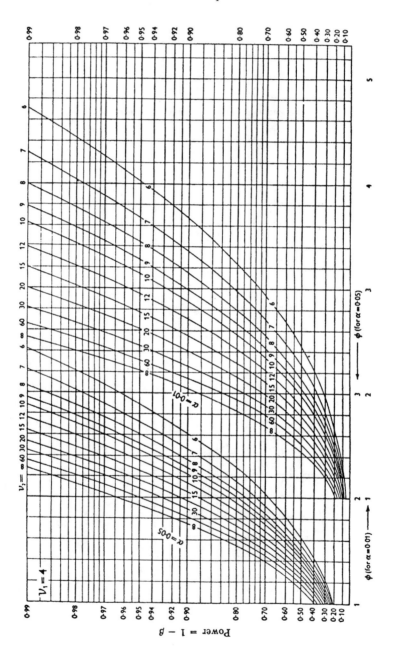

Table 14.5. $v_1=5$.

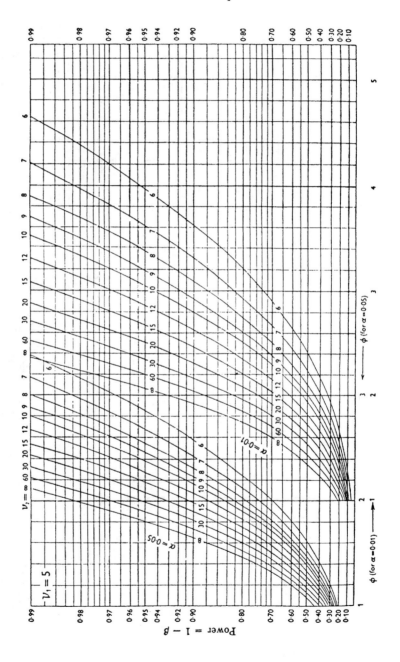

Table 14.6. $v_1=6$.

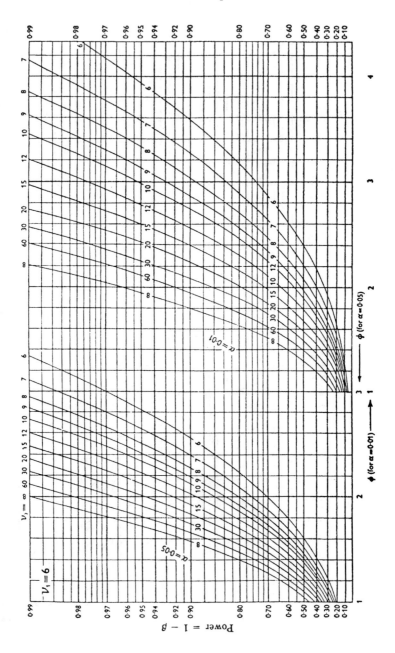

Table 14.7. $v_1 = 7$.

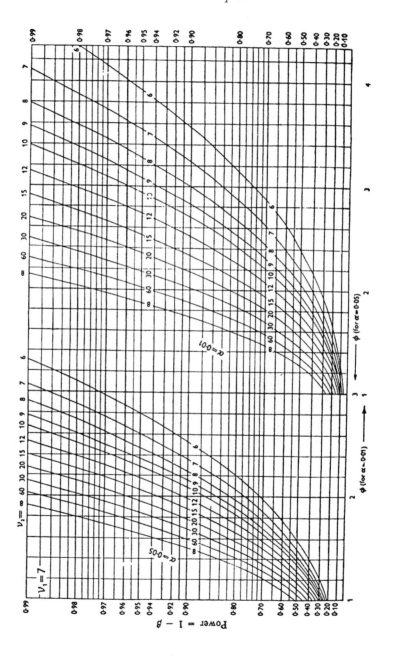

Table 14.8. $v_1=8$.

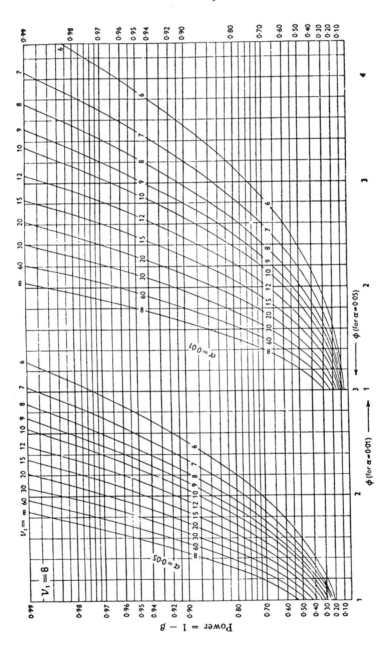

Factors for Short Run Control Charts for Individuals, X-bar, and R Charts

g	SUBGROUP SIZE											
	1 (R based on moving range of 2)				2				3			
	A_{2F}	D_{4F}	A_{2S}	D_{4S}	A_{2F}	D_{4F}	A_{2S}	D_{4S}	A_{2F}	D_{4F}	A_{2S}	D_{4S}
1	NA	NA	236.5	128	NA	NA	167	128	NA	NA	8.21	14
2	12.0	2.0	20.8	16.0	8.49	2.0	15.70	15.6	1.57	1.9	2.72	7.1
3	6.8	2.7	9.6	15.0	4.78	2.7	6.76	14.7	1.35	2.3	1.90	4.5
4	5.1	3.3	6.6	8.1	3.62	3.3	4.68	8.1	1.26	2.4	1.62	3.7
5	4.4	3.3	5.4	6.3	3.12	3.3	3.82	6.3	1.20	2.4	1.47	3.4
6	4.0	3.3	4.7	5.4	2.83	3.3	3.34	5.4	1.17	2.5	1.39	3.3
7	3.7	3.3	4.3	5.0	2.65	3.3	3.06	5.0	1.14	2.5	1.32	3.2
8	3.6	3.3	4.1	4.7	2.53	3.3	2.87	4.7	1.13	2.5	1.28	3.1
9	3.5	3.3	3.9	4.5	2.45	3.3	2.74	4.5	1.12	2.5	1.25	3.0
10	3.3	3.3	3.7	4.5	2.37	3.3	2.62	4.5	1.10	2.5	1.22	3.0
15	3.1	3.5	3.3	4.1	2.18	3.5	2.33	4.1	1.08	2.5	1.15	2.9
20	3.0	3.5	3.1	4.0	2.11	3.5	2.21	4.0	1.07	2.6	1.12	2.8
25	2.9	3.5	3.0	3.8	2.05	3.5	2.14	3.8	1.06	2.6	1.10	2.7

Numbers enclosed in bold boxes represent the recommended minimum number of subgroups for starting a control chart.

Continued on next page . . .

Continued . . .

g	SUBGROUP SIZE							
	4				5			
	A_{2F}	D_{4F}	A_{2S}	D_{4S}	A_{2F}	D_{4F}	A_{2S}	D_{4S}
1	NA	NA	3.05	13	NA	NA	1.8	5.1
2	0.83	1.9	1.44	3.5	0.58	1.7	1.0	3.2
3	0.81	1.9	1.14	3.2	0.59	1.8	0.83	2.8
4	0.79	2.1	1.01	2.9	0.59	1.9	0.76	2.6
5	0.78	2.1	0.95	2.8	0.59	2.0	0.72	2.5
6	0.77	2.2	0.91	2.7	0.59	2.0	0.70	2.4
7	0.76	2.2	0.88	2.6	0.59	2.0	0.68	2.4
8	0.76	2.2	0.86	2.6	0.59	2.0	0.66	2.3
9	0.76	2.2	0.85	2.5	0.59	2.0	0.65	2.3
10	0.75	2.2	0.83	2.5	0.58	2.0	0.65	2.3
15	0.75	2.3	0.80	2.4	0.58	2.1	0.62	2.2
20	0.74	2.3	0.78	2.4	0.58	2.1	0.61	2.2
25	0.74	2.3	0.77	2.4	0.58	2.1	0.60	2.2

Numbers enclosed in bold boxes represent the recommended minimum number of subgroups for starting a control chart.

16

Significant Number of Consecutive Highest or Lowest Values from One Stream of a Multiple-Stream Process

On average a run of the length shown would appear no more than 1 time in 100.

# streams, k	2	3	4	5	6	7	8	9	10	11	12
Significant run, r	7	5	5	4	4	4	4	4	3	3	3

17

Sample Customer Survey

Taken from *How did <u>we</u> do?*, a patient satisfaction survey for the XXX Community Hospital. (3/15/94)

For each of the following statements, please check the appropriate box. Mark the NA box if you had no opportunity to judge that aspect of care during your stay at XXX Community Hospital.	Strongly agree	Agree	Neither agree nor disagree	Disagree	Strongly disagree	NA
I received my medication on time	☐	☐	☐	☐	☐	☐
The menu offered foods I liked	☐	☐	☐	☐	☐	☐
My doctor kept me informed	☐	☐	☐	☐	☐	☐
My room was clean	☐	☐	☐	☐	☐	☐
The discharge process was smooth	☐	☐	☐	☐	☐	☐
My doctor was available	☐	☐	☐	☐	☐	☐

Continued on next page . . .

Continued . . .

	Strongly agree	Agree	Neither agree nor disagree	Disagree	Strongly disagree	NA
The hospital was well supplied	☐	☐	☐	☐	☐	☐
I received the foods I selected from the menu	☐	☐	☐	☐	☐	☐
The staff answered my call light quickly	☐	☐	☐	☐	☐	☐
The food looked good	☐	☐	☐	☐	☐	☐
I was informed of what I should do after discharge	☐	☐	☐	☐	☐	☐
My bed was comfortable	☐	☐	☐	☐	☐	☐
The hospital staff took good care of me	☐	☐	☐	☐	☐	☐
I knew my doctor's name	☐	☐	☐	☐	☐	☐
The staff treated one another with respect	☐	☐	☐	☐	☐	☐
The hospital was well maintained	☐	☐	☐	☐	☐	☐
The food tasted good	☐	☐	☐	☐	☐	☐
My medications were ready when I was ready to go	☐	☐	☐	☐	☐	☐
The billing procedures were explained to me	☐	☐	☐	☐	☐	☐
I was served the right amount of food	☐	☐	☐	☐	☐	☐
The nurse checked on me frequently	☐	☐	☐	☐	☐	☐
I had assistance making plans to leave the hospital	☐	☐	☐	☐	☐	☐
My doctor told me when I was going home	☐	☐	☐	☐	☐	☐
The food servers were pleasant	☐	☐	☐	☐	☐	☐

Continued on next page . . .

Continued . . .

	Strongly agree	Agree	Neither agree nor disagree	Disagree	Strongly disagree	NA
The hospital was clean	☐	☐	☐	☐	☐	☐
Overall, the hospital staff treated me with respect	☐	☐	☐	☐	☐	☐
My room was quiet	☐	☐	☐	☐	☐	☐
The staff met my special needs	☐	☐	☐	☐	☐	☐
The attitude of the staff was nice	☐	☐	☐	☐	☐	☐
I was escorted out of the hospital at discharge	☐	☐	☐	☐	☐	☐
My room was comfortable	☐	☐	☐	☐	☐	☐
My diet was what the doctor ordered	☐	☐	☐	☐	☐	☐
The staff kept me informed about my care	☐	☐	☐	☐	☐	☐
I was satisfied with my doctor(s)	☐	☐	☐	☐	☐	☐
Meals were served on time	☐	☐	☐	☐	☐	☐
The staff were helpful	☐	☐	☐	☐	☐	☐
The discharge process was speedy	☐	☐	☐	☐	☐	☐
My doctor knew who I was	☐	☐	☐	☐	☐	☐
My medications/wound care/equipment were explained to me	☐	☐	☐	☐	☐	☐
I was treated well	☐	☐	☐	☐	☐	☐
I was prepared to go home	☐	☐	☐	☐	☐	☐
The staff was attentive to my needs	☐	☐	☐	☐	☐	☐

Continued on next page . . .

Continued . . .

	Strongly agree	Agree	Neither agree nor disagree	Disagree	Strongly disagree	NA
I had the same doctor(s) throughout my hospitalization	☐	☐	☐	☐	☐	☐
The nurses acted in a professional manner	☐	☐	☐	☐	☐	☐
The staff knew what care I needed	☐	☐	☐	☐	☐	☐
I would refer a family member to XXX Community Hospital	☐	☐	☐	☐	☐	☐
I would choose to come back to XXX Community Hospital	☐	☐	☐	☐	☐	☐

Were there any incidents you remember from your stay that were especially PLEASANT?

Were there any incidents you remember from your stay that were especially UNPLEASANT?

We welcome any other suggestions you have to offer.

Thank you for your assistance!

18

Process σ Levels and Equivalent PPM Quality Levels

Based on the assumption that in the long term the process could drift by plus or minus 1.5σ.

Process σ Level	Process PPM	Process σ Level	Process PPM	Process σ Level	Process PPM
6.27	1	5.27	80	3.96	7,000
6.12	2	5.25	90	3.91	8,000
6.0	3.4	5.22	100	3.87	9,000
5.97	4	5.04	200	3.83	10,000
5.91	5	4.93	300	3.55	20,000
5.88	6	4.85	400	3.38	30,000
5.84	7	4.79	500	3.25	40,000
5.82	8	4.74	600	3.14	50,000
5.78	9	4.69	700	3.05	60,000
5.77	10	4.66	800	2.98	70,000
5.61	20	4.62	900	2.91	80,000
5.51	30	4.59	1,000	2.84	90,000
5.44	40	4.38	2,000	2.78	100,000
5.39	50	4.25	3,000	2.34	200,000
5.35	60	4.15	4,000	2.02	300,000
5.31	70	4.08	5,000	1.75	400,000
		4.01	6,000	1.50	500,000

Continued . . .

Continued . . .

References

Abraham, B. and Whitney, J.B. (1990). "Applications of EWMA Charts to Data from Continuous Processess," *Annual Quality Congress Transactions*, Milwaukee, WI: ASQ.

Akao, Y., Editor (1990). *Quality Function Deployment: Integrating Customer Requirements into Product Design*, Cambridge, MA: Productivity Press.

Alden, J. and Kirkhorn, J. (1996). "Case Studies," in *The ASTD Training and Development Handbook: A Guide to Human Resources Development*, Craig, R.L., Editor-in-chief, New York: McGraw-Hill, pp. 497–516.

Alloway, J.A., Jr. (1994). "The Card Drop Shop," *Quality Progress*, July.

Alwan, L.C. and Roberts, H.V. (1989). "Time Series Modeling for Statistical Process Control," in *Statistical Process Control in Automated Manufacturing*, Keats, J.B. and Hubel, N.F., Editors, New York: Marcel Dekker.

ASQ Statistics Division. (1983). *Glossary and Tables for Statistical Quality Control*, Milwaukee, WI: ASQ Quality Press.

Aubrey, C.A. and Felkins, P.K. (1988). *Teamwork: Involving People in Quality and Productivity Improvement*, Milwaukee, WI: ASQ Quality Press.

Benneyan, J.C. (1994). "The Merits of Merit Review...?: Bibliography of Recommended Study and Summary of Arguments Against Annual Merit Review," Amherst, MA: University of Massachusetts, Industrial Engineering/Operations Research, benneyan@ecs.umass.edu.

Berry, Michael J.A. and Linoff, Gordon. (1997). *Data Mining Techniques: for Marketing, Sales, and Customer Support*, New York: John Wiley & Sons, pp. 369–370.

Boardman, T.J. and Boardman, E.C. (1990). "Don't Touch That Funnel!" *Quality Progress*, December.

Box, G.E.P. and Draper, N.R. (1987). *Empirical Model-Building and Response Surfaces*, New York: John Wiley & Sons.

Box, Hunter and Hunter. (1978). *Statistics for Experimenters*, New York: John Wiley & Sons.

Brassard, M. (1989). *The Memory Jogger Plus+*, Methuen, MA: GOAL/QPC.

Brookfield, D. (1986). *Understanding and Facilitating Adult Learning*, San Francisco, CA: Jossey-Bass.

Burr, I.W. (1976). *Statistical Quality Control Methods, Statistics: Textbooks and Monographs*, Vol. 16, New York: Marcel-Dekker, Inc.

Byrne, John A. "Jack: A Close-up Look at How America's #1 Manager Runs GE," *Business Week*, June 8, 1998, p. 99.

Camp, R.C. (1989). *Benchmarking: The Search for Industry Best Practices That Lead to Superior Performance*, Milwaukee, WI: ASQ Quality Press and White Plains, NY: Quality Resources.

Campanella, J., Editor. (1990), *Principles of Quality Costs*, 2nd Edition, Milwaukee, WI: ASQ Quality Press.

Campanella, J., Editor. (1999), *Principles of Quality Costs*, 3rd Edition, Milwaukee, WI: ASQ Quality Press.

Carder, B. and Clark, J.D. (1992). "The Theory and Practice of Employee Recognition," *Quality Progress*, December.

Daltas, A.J. (1977). "Protecting Service Markets with Consumer Feedback," *Cornell Hotel and Resaurant Administration Quaterly*, May, pp. 73–77.

Daugherty, Ray; Lowe, Victor, Jr.; Down, Michael H.; and Gruska, Gregory. (1995). *Measurement Systems Analysis Reference Manual*, Detroit, MI: Automotive Industry Action Group.

Deming, W.E. (1975). "On Probability as a Basis for Action," *The American Statistician*, 29(4), pp. 146–152.

Deming, W.E. (1986). *Out of the Crisis*, Cambridge, MA: MIT Center for Advanced Engineering Study.

Deming, W.E. (1993). *The New Economics for Industry, Government, Education*, Cambridge, MA: MIT Center for Advanced Engineering Study.

DeToro, I. (1995). "The 10 Pitfalls of Benchmarking," *Quality Progress*, January, pp. 61–63.

Dillman, D.A. (1983). "Mail and Other Self-Administered Questionnaires," in *Handbook of Survey Research*, Rossi, P., Wright, J., and Anderson, A., Editors, New York: Academic Press, Inc., pp. 359–377.

Dodson, Bryan and Nolan, Dennis. (1998). *The Complete Guide to the CRE*, Tucson, Arizona: Quality Publishing, LLC.

Draper, N. and Smith, H. (1981). *Applied Regression Analysis*, 2nd Edition, New York: John Wiley & Sons.

Dudewicz, E.J. (1988). "Basic Statistical Methods," in *Juran's Quality Control Handbook*, 3rd Edition, Juran, J.M., New York: McGraw-Hill, 23.29.

Duncan, A.J. (1974). *Quality Control and Industrial Statistics*, 4th Edition, Homewood, IL, Irwin.

Edosomwan, J.A. (1993). *Customer and Market-Driven Quality Management*, Milwaukee, WI: ASQ Quality Press.

Efron, B. (1982). *The Jackknife, the Bootstrap, and Other Resampling Plans*, Philadelphia, PA: Society for Industrial and Applied Mathematics.

Finnerty, M.F. (1996). "Coaching for Growth and Development," in *The ASTD Training and Development Handbook: A Guide to Human Resources Development*, Craig, R.L., Editor-in-chief, New York: McGraw-Hill, pp. 415–436.

Fivars, G. (1980). "The Critical Incident Technique: a Bibliography," Research and Publication Service, American Institutes for Research ED 195 681.

Flanagan, J.C. (1954). "The Critical Incident Technique," *Psychological Bulletin*, 51(4), July, pp. 327–358.

Galloway, D. (1994). *Mapping Work Processes*, Milwaukee, WI: ASQ Quality Press.

GAO (1986). "Developing and Using Questionnaires—Transfer Paper 7," Washington, D.C.: United States General Accounting Office.

Gould, Stephen Jay. (1993). "An Earful of Jaw," *Eight Little Piggies*, New York: W. W. Norton and Company.

Hammer, M. and Champy, J. (1993). *Reengineering the Corporation: A Manifesto for Business Revolution*, New York: HarperCollins Publishers.

Harrington, H.J. (1992). "Probability and Statistics," in *Quality Engineering Handbook*, Pyzdek, T. and R.W. Berger, Editors, Milwaukee, WI: ASQ Quality Press, pp. 513–577.

Hayes, Bob E. (1992). *Measuring Customer Satisfaction: Development and Use of Questionnaires*, Milwaukee, WI: ASQ Quality Press.

Hicks, Charles R. (1973). *Fundamental Concepts in the Design of Experiments*, 2nd Edition, New York: Holt, Rinehart, Winston, pp. 31–38.

Hicks, Charles R., (1993). *Fundamental Concepts in the Design of Experiments*, New York: Holt, Rinehart, Winston.

Hillier, F.S. (1969). "X-bar and R-chart Control Limits Based on a Small Number of Subgroups," *Journal of Quality Technology*, Vol. 1, No. 1, January, pp. 17–26.

Hillier, F.S. and Lieberman, G.J. (1980). *Introduction to Operations Research*, 3rd Edition, San Francisco, CA: Holden-Day, Inc.

Holland, John H. (1996). *Hidden Order: How Adaptation Builds Complexity*, Reading, MA: Perseus Books, p.56.

Howell, J.J. and Silvey, L.O. (1996). "Interactive Multimedia Training Systems," in *The ASTD Training and Development Handbook: A Guide to Human Resources Development*, Craig, R.L., Editor-in-chief, New York: McGraw-Hill, pp. 534–553.

Hunter, J.S. (1986). "The Exponentially Weighted Moving Average," *Journal of Quality Technology*, 18, pp. 203–210.

Hunter, J.S. (1989). "A One Point Plot Equivalent to the Shewhart Chart with Western Electric Rules," *Quality Engineering*, 2, pp. 13–19.

Hurley, H. and Loew, C. (1996). "A Quality Change for New Product Development," *Quality Observer*, January, pp. 10–13.

Hutton, D.W. (1994). *The Change Agent's Handbook: A Survival Guide for Quality Improvement Champions*, Milwaukee, WI: ASQ Quality Press.

Imai, M. (1986). *Kaizen*, New York: Random House.

Ishikawa, K. (1985). *What is Total Quality Control the Japanese Way?* Englewood Cliffs, NJ: Prentice-Hall, Inc.

Iverson, Ken. (1998). *Plain Talk: Lessons from a Business Maverick*, New York: John Wiley & Sons, p. 149.

Johnson, D.W. and Johnson, F.P. (1999). *Joining Together: Group Theory and Group Skills*, Englewood Cliffs, NJ: Prentice-Hall.

Johnson, R.S. (1993a). *TQM: Management Processes for Quality Operations*, Milwaukee, WI: ASQ Quality Press.

Johnson, R.S. (1993b). *TQM: The Mechanics of Quality Processes*, Milwaukee, WI: ASQ Quality Press.

Joiner, B.L. (1994). *Fourth Generation Management: The New Business Consciousness*, New York: McGraw-Hill, Inc.

Juran, J.M. and Gryna, F.M. (1988). *Juran's Quality Control Handbook*, 4th Edition, New York: McGraw-Hill.

Juran, J.M. and Gryna, F.M. (1993). *Quality Planning and Analysis*, 3rd Edition, New York: McGraw-Hill.

Kano, N. (1993). "A Perspective on Quality Activities in American Firms," *California Management Review*, 35(3), Spring, pp. 12–31.

King, B. (1987). *Better Designs in Half the Time: Implementing QFD in America*, Methuen, MA: Goal/QPC.

Kirkpatrick, D.L. (1996). "Evaluation," in *The ASTD Training and Development Handbook: A Guide to Human Resources Development*, Craig, R.L., Editor-in-chief, New York: McGraw-Hill, pp. 294–312.

Kirkpatrick, J. (1992–1993). "Pragmatism and the Harvard Case Method of Business Education," *The Intellectual Activist*, 6(6) pp. 9–18, and 7(1) pp. 11–15.

Koch, G.G. and Gillings, D.B. (1983). "Statistical Inference, Part I," in *Encyclopedia of Statistical Sciences*, vol. 4, 84–88, Kotz, Samuel and Johnson, Normal L., Editors-in-chief, New York: John Wiley & Sons.

Kohn, A. (1993). *Punished by Rewards: The Trouble with Gold Stars, Incentive Plans, A's, Praise and Other Bribes*, New York: Houghton Mifflin Company.

Kotler, P. (1991). *Marketing Management: Analysis, Planning, Implementation, and Control,* 7th Edition, Englewood Cliffs, NJ: Prentice-Hall.

Krishnamoorthi, K.S. (1991). "On Assignable Causes that Cannot be Eliminated—an Example from a Foundry," *Quality Engineering,* 3, pp. 41–47.

Lewis, C.I. (1929), *Mind and the World Order,* New York: Scribners.

Main, Jeremy (1994). *Quality Wars: The Triumphs and Defeats of American Business,* The Free Press, p. 173.

Meyers, Raymond H. and Montgomery, Douglas C. (1995). *Response Surface Methodology: Process and Product Optimization Using Designed Experiments,* New York: John Wiley & Sons.

Mizuno, S., Editor. (1988). *Management for Quality Improvement: The 7 New QC Tools,* Cambridge, MA: Productivity Press.

Montgomery, D.C. (1984). *Design and Analysis of Experiments,* 2nd Edition. New York: John Wiley & Sons.

Montgomery, Douglas C., (1996). *Design and Analysis of Experiments,* New York: John Wiley & Sons.

Natrella, M.G. (1963). *Experimental Statistics: NBS Handbook 91,* Washington, DC: US Government Printing Office.

Nolan, M. (1996). "Job Training," in *The ASTD Training and Development Handbook: A Guide to Human Resources Development,* Craig, R.L., Editor-in-chief, New York: McGraw-Hill, pp. 747–775.

Palm, A.C. (1990). "SPC Versus Automatic Process Control," *Annual Quality Congress Transactions*, Milwaukee, WI: ASQ.

Phillips, J.J. (1996). "Measuring the Results of Training," in *The ASTD Training and Development Handbook: A Guide to Human Resources Development*, Craig, R.L. Editor-in-chief, New York: McGraw-Hill, pp. 313–341.

Piskurich, G.M. (1996). "Self-directed Learning," in *The ASTD Training and Development Handbook: A Guide to Human Resources Development*, Craig, R.L. Editor-in-chief, New York: McGraw-Hill, pp. 453–472.

Proschan, F. and Savage, I.R. (1960). "Starting a Control Chart," *Industrial Quality Control*, Vol. 17, No. 3, September, pp. 12–13.

Provost, L.P. (1988). "Interpretation of Results of Analytic Studies," paper presented at 1989 NYU Deming Seminar for Statisticians, March 13, New York: New York University.

Pyzdek, T. (1976). "The Impact of Quality Cost Reduction on Profits," *Quality Progress*, May.

Pyzdek, T. (1985). "A Ten-step Plan for Statistical Process Control Studies," *Quality Progress*, April, 77–81.

Pyzdek, T. (1989), *What Every Engineer Should Know About Quality Control*, New York: Marcel-Dekker, Inc.

Pyzdek, T. (1990). *SPC-PC: Statistical Process Control for Personal Computers*, Tucson, Arizona: Quality America.

Pyzdek, T. (1991), *What Every Manager Should Know About Quality*, New York: Marcel-Dekker, Inc.

Pyzdek, T. (1991–92). "A Simulation of Receiving Inspection," *Quality Engineering*, 4(1), 9–19.

Pyzdek, T. (1992). *Pyzdek's Guide to SPC Volume Two—Applications and Special Topics*, Tucson, AZ: Quality Publishing, Inc.

Pyzdek, T. (1994). *Pocket Guide to Quality Tools*, Tucson, AZ: Quality Publishing, Inc.

Pyzdek, T. (1996a). *The Complete Guide to the CQE*, Tucson, AZ: Quality Publishing, Inc.

Pyzdek, T. (1996b). *The Complete Guide to the CQM*, Tucson, AZ: Quality Publishing, Inc.

Pyzdek, T. (1997). *The Complete Guide to the CQT*, Tucson, AZ: Quality Publishing, Inc.

Pyzdek, T. (1999). *The End of Management*, Tucson, AZ: Atlantis Publishing.

Reichheld, F.F. (1996). *The Loyalty Effect: The Hidden Force Behind Growth, Profits, and Lasting Value*, New York: McGraw-Hill.

Roberts, L. (1994). *Process Reengineering: The Key to Achieving Breakthrough Success*, Milwaukee, WI: ASQ Quality Press.

Rose, K.H. (1995). "A Performance Measurement Model," *Quality Progress*, February, pp. 63–66.

Ruskin, A.M. and Estes, W.E. (1995). *What Every Engineer Should Know About Project Management*, 2nd Edition. New York: Marcel-Dekker, p. 193.

Saaty, T.L. (1988). *Decision Making for Leaders: The Analytic Hierarch Process for Decisions in a Complex World*, Pittsburgh, PA: RWS Publications.

Scholtes, P.R. (1988). *The Team Handbook: How to Use Teams to Improve Quality*, Madison, WI: Joiner Associates, Inc.

Schuman, S.P. (1996). "What to Look for in a Group Facilitator," *Quality Progress*, June, pp. 69–72.

Senge, P.M. (1990), *The Fifth Discipline–The Art and Practice Of The Learning Organization*, New York: Doubleday.

Shainin, D. and Shainin, P.D. (1988). "Statistical Process Control," in *Juran's Quality Control Handbook*, 3rd Edition, New York: McGraw-Hill, p. 24.34.

Shainin, Dorian (1984). "Better than Good Old X-Bar and R-charts Asked by Vendees," *ASQ Quality Congress Transactions*, Milwaukee, pp. 302–307.

Sheridan, B.M. (1993). *Policy Deployment: The TQM Approach to Long-Range Planning*, Milwaukee, WI: ASQ Quality Press.

Shewhart (1939, 1986). *Statistical Method from the Viewpoint of Quality Control*, New York: Dover Publications.

Shewhart, W.A. (1930, 1980). *Economic Control of Quality of Manufactured Product*, Milwaukee, WI: ASQ Quality Press.

Shewhart, W.A. (1931, 1980). *Economic Control of Quality of Manufacturing*, Milwaukee, WI: ASQ Quality Press.

Simon, J.L. (1992). *Resampling: the New Statistics*, Arlington, VA: Resampling Stats, Inc.

Simon, J.L. and Bruce, P. (1992). "Using Computer Simulation in Quality Control," *Quality Progress*, Statistics Corner Column.

Stewart, T.A. (1995). "After All You've Done for Your Customers, Why are They Still NOT HAPPY?" *Fortune*, December 11, 1995.

Suminski, L.T., Jr. (1994). "Measuring the Cost of Quality," *Quality Digest*, March, pp. 26–32.

Taguchi, G. (1986). *Introduction to Quality Engineering: Designing Quality into Products and Processes*, White Plains, NY: Quality Resources.

Taha, H. (1976). *Operations Research: An Introduction*, 2nd Edition. New York: Macmillian Publishing Co., Inc.

Thiagarajan, S. (1996). "Instructional Games, Simulations, and Role-plays," in *The ASTD Training and Development Handbook: A Guide to Human Resources Development*, Craig, R.L., Editor-in-chief, New York: McGraw-Hill, pp. 517–533.

Tuckman, B.W. (1965). "Development Sequence in Small Groups," *Psychological Bulletin*.

Tukey, J.W. (1977). *Exploratory Data Analysis*, Reading, MA: Addison-Wesley.

Vaziri, H.K. (1992). "Using Competitive Benchmarking to Set Goals," *Quality Progress*, November.

Wearring, C. and Karl, D.P. (1995). "The Importance of Following GD&T Specifications," *Quality Progress*, February.

Wheeler, D.J. (1991). "Shewhart's Charts: Myths, Facts, and Competitors," *Annual Quality Congress Transactions*, Milwaukee, WI: ASQ.

Index

7M tools, 62, 290, 297
@Rand, 577, 584, 587, 591, 594

—A—

Abraham, B.,440, 683
acceptable quality level (AQL), 544, 627, 632
acceptance sampling, 627
activity network diagram(s), 300
actual size, 630
adjusted R square, 267, 563–564
advocate, 51, 69
affinity diagram(s), 290–292
aggregation, 29, 178, 192, 233
aggressor, 76
AHP, 297
AIAG, 246, 248, 260, 266
Akao, Y., 150, 683
Alden, J., 118–119, 683
Alloway, J.A., Jr., 126, 683

alpha (α) error, 373
alpha (α) risk, 19, 91, 182
alternate hypothesis, 336, 374, 509
Alwan, L.C., 439–440, 683
Analysis of Variance (ANOVA), 225, 334, 507, 511, 513, 564, 627
analytic hierarchy process (AHP), 297
analytic study, 333–334
analytic, 33, 369, 691, 693
ANOVA procedure, 509
ANOVA, 225, 267, 346, 503, 507–516, 520, 534, 538, 564, 566, 627, 666
ANSI, 272
AOQ, 627
AOQL, 627, 659
appraisal costs, 164, 170, 172–173, 175
arrow diagram(s), 188, 197, 199, 201–202, 300
artificial neural networks, 546
as-is map, 270–271

ASQ Quality Press, 165, 171, 176, 232, 244, 379, 383, 385, 627, 683–689, 692–693

ASQ Statistics Division, 627, 683

ASQ, 22–23, 96, 135, 149, 248, 691–694

assessment, 31, 47, 53, 63, 88, 97–98, 116, 178, 218, 595

assignable causes, 382, 448, 690

AT&T, 449

attribute charts, 400, 455, 457, 484, 490–491

Aubrey, C.A., 78, 684

audit, 58, 97, 356–357, 417, 468

auditor, 37

autocorrelation, 305

availability, 570–571, 576

average charts, 386

average outgoing quality (AOQ), 627

average outgoing quality limit (AOQL), 627

average sample size, 404

average, calulation, 360

—B—

b_{10} life, 570

b_{50} life, 570–571

background variables, 501

Baldrige, 1, 88, 134, 219

barriers, 59–60, 93, 145, 194, 230, 232, 270

basic quality, 143–144

batch, 396, 514, 627

bell curve, 359

benchmarking, 3, 77, 216, 685, 694

benchmarks, 218, 222

benefit-cost analysis, 155, 157, 226

Benneyan, J.C., 82, 684

Berry, M., 25–26, 546, 684

Bersbach, P.L., 149

best-fit line, 561

best-fit, 561

beta (β)risk, 628, 630

bias, 64, 247, 251–252, 254–256, 259, 265–268, 349, 504

biased estimator, 349, 632

binomial, 245, 336, 355–357, 580, 609

block diagram(s), 574, 576

block, 443, 500, 505

blocker, 76

blocking factor, 505

blueprint, 20, 124

Boardman, 126, 684

bootstrapping, 376

bottlenecks, 197

Box, 511, 539, 684

boxplot, 327–329

brainstorming, 62, 280, 283, 290, 296, 303, 427

Brassard, M., 297, 684

break-even, 155–157

breakthrough, 17, 22, 146, 186, 692

Brookfield, D., 111, 684

Bruce, P., 127, 694

budget reports, 194, 224–225

budget, 187, 194, 209, 214, 223

Burr, I.W., 387, 496, 684

Byrne, J., 5, 684

—C—

c charts, 412–414, 490

calibration system, 433

caliper, 255

Camp, R.C., 217, 520–521, 685

Campanella, J., 165, 170–171, 175–176, 179, 685

capability indexes, 458–459, 461

Carder, B., 80, 685

cash flow, 15, 159–160, 162, 180

cause and effect diagrams, 277, 280, 291, 427

CDFs, 351–352, 354

CEDAC, 283

censored test, 571

central limit theorem, 378–379

central tendency, 312, 316, 328, 333, 386, 396, 400, 407, 412, 443, 460–461

centroid, 312, 345, 630

certification, 229, 417

Champy, J., 228, 270, 687

chance cause, 382

change agents, 49, 52–53, 56–58, 88

change leader, 51

change management, 50

characteristic, 46, 65, 248–250, 434, 438, 467, 628, 631

chartering, 68, 190, 228

check sheets, 108, 274–277

checklists, 274, 472

chi-square test, 568, 608

chi-square, 244, 355, 364, 375, 568–569, 579, 608, 640–641

CIT, 35, 39–41, 686

Clark, J.D., 80, 685

classification of characteristics, 596

classification of defects, 596

client, 58, 107

coaching, 22, 88, 92, 110–114, 686

coalitions, 66

coefficient of determination, 628

coefficient of multiple correlation, 628

coefficient of variation, 628

coefficient, 563–565, 628, 631

combinations, 341–342, 358, 501, 629

common cause, 382, 440–441, 444, 449, 451, 455

communication and presentation skills, 62

communication(s), 3, 51, 90

competition, 49, 92

competitive analysis, 147, 150, 223

complaint handling, 182

complement, 30, 338

complementary, 30, 71, 134, 221, 569

completely randomized design, 505

composite design, 521, 535

compounding, 158–159

compromiser, 75

concurrent engineering, 89

confessor, 76

confidence interval, 331–332, 369–373, 375–376, 565

confidence limits, 371–372, 581, 628

conflict resolution, 70, 89, 91, 93, 110

conflict, 56, 89, 125

conflicts, 67, 112, 210, 237

conformance quality, 166

conformance, 141, 164, 166, 172, 569, 629

consensus criteria method, 297, 299–300

consensus decision rule, 70, 299
consumer's risk, 359, 628
contingency tables, 245, 568–569
continuous data, 311, 340, 352, 354,
    386, 452, 473
continuous improvement, 13, 17, 78, 89,
    167, 222, 239, 301, 380–381, 456,
    544
continuous process improvement, 88,
    136, 456
contract, 171
control chart equations, 662–663
control chart patterns, 421–428
control chart selection, 419
control limit equations for average and
    range charts, 387
control limit equations for c charts, 413
control limit equations for np charts, 405
control limit equations for sigma charts,
    392
control limit equations for u charts, 408
control plan, 209, 416, 418, 454, 466,
    472, 487
coordinator, 74
corrective action, 170, 173, 175, 220,
    276, 428, 598
correlation analysis, 552, 556–557, 565
correlation coefficient, 564, 628
correlation, 146, 244, 288, 416–417,
    427, 564–567
cost of poor quality, 151, 163
cost of quality examples, 171
cost of quality, 89, 163, 694
counter-productive group, 75

C_p, 459–461, 463
C_{pk}, 376, 459–461, 463–464, 466–467,
    480
CPM, 197, 300
C_{pm}, 461, 463
C_R, 458, 460, 462–463
Craig, 101–102, 683, 686, 688–691,
    694
crash schedule, 210–212, 234
critical defects, 596
Critical Incident Technique (CIT), 35,
    39–41, 686
critical path method (CPM), 197, 300
critical path, 203, 207–209, 211–212,
    271
cross-functional management, 60, 169
culture, 31–32, 56, 113, 115, 185, 222,
    234
curvilinear relationship, 553–554
customer audits, 194
customer expectations, 19, 88, 143–145,
    150
customer feedback, 48
customer relationship management, 88
customer retention, 89, 182
customer satisfaction, 28, 32–33, 87–88,
    99–100, 134–136, 143–144, 151,
    165, 179, 181, 227, 239
customer service, 88, 91, 219, 239
customer value, 169, 180
cusum chart, 443
cycle-time, 2, 88
cycles, 423, 444

—D—

Daltas, 48, 685
data collection, 33, 94, 150, 178, 217, 274, 297
data mining, 24, 28–30, 546, 684
data space, 556–557
Daugherty, R., 246, 685
decision tree, 419
decomposition, project, 189
defect, 171, 275–276, 291, 497, 529, 531, 628–629
defective, 36, 400, 407, 490–491, 629
demerits, 496
Deming Prize, 219
Deming, W.E., 8, 10, 12, 14–15, 82, 93–94, 126–127, 219, 333–334, 382, 418, 432, 439, 456, 685, 691
dependent variable, 284, 289, 501, 552, 562–563, 565
derating, 571
descriptive statistics, 29, 312, 315
design change, 529
design of experiments, 17, 23, 377, 500, 509, 520, 546, 687, 690
design process, 522, 540, 595
design review, 595
design-based inferences, 335
designed experiment, 100, 499–501, 548
destructive testing, 396
detailed plan WBS, 193
DeToro, I., 220, 685
development process, 270–271, 292, 610
diameter, 323, 348, 438, 624
Dillman, D.A., 44–46, 685
direct costs, 212–213
discovery, 28–30, 171, 217, 304, 520

discrete data, 340, 351, 425
discrimination, 252–253, 263
distributions, 312, 315, 329, 342, 347, 377–378, 590, 600–601, 608
documentation, 145, 187, 230, 240
Dodson, B., 577, 686
DOE, 499, 511, 535–536, 540, 547, 551
dominator, 76
Down, M., 685
Draper, N., 539, 561, 564, 684, 686
drift, 422, 440–441, 443–444, 448, 459–461, 480
Dudewicz, E.J., 357, 686
dummy activity, 198
Duncan, A.J., 484, 686
Durbin-Watson, 655
dysfunctional process, 228

—E—

earliest time event, 204
earliest time, 203–204, 206
Economic Control of Quality of Manufactured Product, 379, 383, 385, 693
EDA, 323–324
Edosomwan, J.A., 135, 686
education, 53, 56–57, 63, 80, 83, 164, 172, 685, 689
effective group, 66, 70–71
effectiveness, 67, 78, 93, 99, 119, 127, 576
Efron, B., 377, 686
elaborator, 74
empirical distribution, 349, 607

empirical model building, 520–521, 547–548

employee attitudes, 78, 98

employee involvement, 81

employee selection, 124

empty set, 338

encourager, 75

energizer, 74

enumeration, 283, 340

enumerative study, 333–334

enumerative, 33, 331, 340, 348, 369, 420

Estes, W.E., 188, 191–192, 214, 223, 237–238, 692

European Foundation for Quality Management (EFQM), 219

European Quality Award, 219

evaluator, 74

EWMA charts, 305, 438, 683

Excel, Microsoft™, 71, 160–162, 444, 507, 511–516, 563, 577, 584

exciting quality, 144

expectation, 342–345

expected loss, 542, 545

expected value, 342–343, 345

experiment design, 629

experimental design, 500, 505, 540, 551

experimental error, 499–501, 504, 532

experimental plan, 501, 503, 505, 522

exploratory data analysis, 323, 346, 694

exponential distribution, 355, 363–364, 571–572, 578

external customer, 28

external failure costs, 164, 170, 174–175

external validity, 336

extrapolations, 556

—F—

F distribution, 355, 367–368, 502, 643

facilitation techniques, 64, 117

facilitator training, 95

facilitator, 64–65, 68–70, 95, 190, 693

factorial experiments, 500, 516–517, 629

failure costs, 164, 166, 170, 173–175

Failure Mode, Effects, and Criticality Analysis (FMECA), 187, 294, 596–597, 600

failure rate, 570, 572, 578

Failure, Mode and Effects Analysis (FMEA), 596

fault-tree analysis (FTA), 187, 571, 597–600

fault-tree symbols, 597–598

FDA, 231

feasibility analysis, 186, 188

feature of size, 433

feedback loops, 15, 17, 193

feedback system, 380

feedforward, 214

Felkins, P.K., 78, 684

FFA, 303

fill-in-the-blank questions, 36

final inspection and test, 164

financial analysis of benefit and cost, 155

financial analysis, 155, 161

finished goods, 175

Finnerty, M.F., 111, 113, 686

fishbone diagram, 280

Fivars, G., 40, 686

fixed costs, 155–156

fixed-effects model, 504

Flanagan, J.C., 39–41, 686

flow chart symbols, 272

flow chart(s), 8, 272, 280, 334, 604
FMEA, 596–597
FMECA, 187, 294, 596–597, 600
focus group, 32, 39, 46–47, 216
follower, 75
fool-proofing, 417
force field analysis (FFA), 301, 303
Ford Motor Company, 94, 377, 453
forecasting, 15, 225, 541
forming stage, 71–72
Forsha, H.I., 232
fractional factorial, 516, 526, 534
freak, 421, 452
frequency distribution, 29, 274, 347, 629
FTA, 187, 571, 597–600
full factorial experiment, 516, 533
funnel rules, 432, 439

—G—

G.E.P., 539, 684
Galloway, D., 269, 687
game(s), 59, 125, 694
Gantt chart, 186, 195
GAO, 34, 687
garbage-in, garbage-out (GIGO), 170
gate-keeper, 73, 75
Gaussian distribution, 359
General Electric, 3, 5
General Motors, 20
geometric dimensioning and tolerancing, 127
GIGO, 170
Gillings, D.B., 335, 689
goal setting, 223
Gould, S., 6–7, 687

great care, 566
group development, 71
group maintenance process, 69
group maintenance roles, 56, 74–75
group roles, 74–76
group task process, 68
Gruska, G., 685
Gryna, F.M., 31, 163, 166, 185, 229, 464, 620, 689
Gugliamino, 115
Guttman format, 37

—H—

Hammer, M., 228, 270, 687
happenstance data, 289
harmonizer, 75
Harrington, H.J., 163, 244, 687
Hayes, B., 41, 43, 687
help-seeker, 76
Hicks, C., 511, 513, 687
hidden pain signals, 227
Hillier, 201–202, 474, 478, 484, 687
histogram, 274, 316, 586–587, 589–590, 592–593, 629
Holland, J., 14, 687
honesty, 92
House of Quality, 145–147, 416–417
Howell, J.J., 129–130, 688
human resource management, 89
Hunter, J.S., 449, 451, 511, 684, 688
Hurley, H., 270–271, 688
Hutton, D.W., 51–52, 58, 688
hygiene theory, 82, 111
hypergeometric distribution, 355, 358
hypothesis test of a standard deviation, 375

hypothesis test of sample mean, 373
hypothesis test of two sample variances, 375
hypothesis testing, 336, 370, 373, 375–376
hypothesis, 9, 37–38, 312, 502, 509, 564–565, 606, 629
hypothesis, alternative, 629
hypothesis, null, 629

—I—

IBM, 20
Imai, M., 81, 688
in process inspection, 164
in-control process, 630
inadvertent errors, 455
incentive pay, 82
independent variable, 284, 286, 288–289, 501, 556, 562, 565
indirect costs, 210, 213
inductive thinking, 334
industry standards, 164
infant mortality, 590
inference, 335–336, 369, 689
inferential statistics, 335, 369
informal change agent, 52
information giver, 74
information seeker, 74
initiator, 74
inspection and test, 172
integration WBS, 193
integrity, 92, 472
interactions, 500, 506, 629
intercept, 560–561, 565
interdepartmental teams, 60
internal audits, 228

internal customer, 416
internal failure costs, 164, 173–175
internal rate of return, 161–162
Internet, 104, 128, 218
interrelationship digraph(s), 291, 296, 334
intersection, 338
interval scale(s), 245–246
interview, 39, 41, 114
Ishikawa Diagram, 280
Ishikawa, K., 274, 280, 688
ISO 14000, 230
ISO 9000, 230
Iverson, K., 8, 688

—J—

JIT, 103, 464
job analysis, 124
job training, 122, 690
Johnson, 50, 66, 84, 105, 135, 688–689
Joiner, B.L., 151, 689, 693
Journal of Quality Technology, 431, 687–688
Juran's Spiral of Progress in Quality, 13
Juran's Trilogy, 465
Juran, J.M., 13, 31, 163, 166–167, 185, 187, 229, 357, 464–465, 620, 686, 689, 693
just-in-time (JIT), 103–104, 116, 464

—K—

Kacker, 545
Kaizen, 60, 167, 271, 688
Kano model, 143–144
Kano, N., 143–144, 689
Karl, D.P., 127, 694

King, B., 145, 148, 689
Kirkhorn, J., 118, 120, 683
Kirkpatrick, 100, 120, 689
Koch, G.C., 335, 689
Kohn, A., 81–82, 139, 689
Kotler, P., 133–134, 690
Krishnamoorthi, K.S., 443, 690
KSAs, 97–98
kurtosis, 314, 316, 630

—L—

latest time, 203–206
Latin square, 506–507
leadership support activities, 56
leadership training, 90
least-squares fit, 560
length, 153, 159, 306, 311, 677
lesson plans, 84, 99, 105–106
level of confidence, 334, 369, 371, 373
Lewis, C.I., 10, 690
liability, 174, 231
Lieberman, G.J., 201–202, 687
Likert, 37
limiting quality, 628
linear models, 552
linear relationship, 552–553, 565, 628
linearity, 251–252, 265
linearizing transformations, 555
Linoff, G., 25–26, 546, 684
LL Bean, 217
Loew, C., 270–271, 688
loss function, 109, 542–543
Lowe, V., 685
loyalty-based management, 182
lurking variable, 567

—M—

Macabe approach, 148
Main, J., 1, 690
maintainability, 571
Malcolm Baldrige National Quality
    Award, 1, 134
management training, 87
mapping, 53, 243, 270, 687
Maslow, 81, 111
material plans, 189
mathematical expectation, 342–343
matrix chart, 187, 297
matrix diagram, 295
McGregor, 111
mean time between failures (MTBF),
    364, 570, 573
mean time to first failure (MTFF,
    MTTF), 570
mean time to repair (MTTR), 570–571
mean, standard error of, 630
measurement error, 252, 261, 264, 472,
    480
measurement scales, 243–244
measurement system linearity, 251–252,
    266
measurement system repeatability, 257
measurement system reproducibility,
    253, 259–260
measurement system stability, 254
measurement systems, 246, 266, 685
median, 313, 315, 327–328, 347, 571,
    630
meeting management, 69, 95
meetings, 54, 68–70, 185, 194, 214, 270
mentoring, 22, 93, 113, 235
Meyers, R., 539, 690

micrometer, 488
midpoint, 476
Miles, 522
milestone charts, 186, 196–197
mission, 55, 88, 152, 179, 189–191, 194, 222, 228, 236, 523, 570
mixture, 225, 312, 428
Mizuno, S., 290, 690
mode, 83, 127, 136, 313, 315, 602, 630
model-based inferences, 336
Monte Carlo simulation, 577, 607
Montgomery, D.C., 509, 511, 539, 690
motivation, 79, 82, 111–112, 115
Motorola, 1–3, 141, 144, 270
moving range charts, 396
moving ranges, 396–399, 472
MTBF, 364, 570
MTFF, 570
MTTF, 570
MTTR, 570
multimedia, 110, 128–131, 688
multiple correlation coefficient, 564
multiple customers, 237
multiple linear regression, 562
multiple R, 564
multiplication principle, 340–341
mutually exclusive, 35, 336, 338, 340
mystery shoppers, 48

—N—

National Institute of Standards and Technology (NIST), 219
Natrella, M.G., 500, 503, 506, 568, 690
natural tolerance, 459–460, 463
NDT, 606
negotiation, 93, 110

net present value, 159–161, 181
network diagram, 198–199, 202–203, 300
network, 57, 188, 218, 546–547
NGT, 301–303
NIST, 255
noise, 501, 544–545
Nolan, D., 122, 125, 577, 686, 690
nominal group technique (NGT), 300–303
nominal scale, 245
non-destructive testing (NDT), 606
non-linear responses, 556
non-parametric, 305
nonconformance, 179
Nordstrom, 91, 138
normal distribution, 141–142, 353, 355, 359, 361, 367, 370, 378–379, 429, 630, 633
norming stage, 72
np chart(s), 404–407, 412–413, 419, 490–491, 662
null hypothesis, 336, 374, 509, 629
null, 338

—O—

observer/commentator, 75
OC curve, 631
off-line quality control, 541
official change agent, 51–52
ogive, 348
on-line quality control, 541
on-the-job training (OJT), 122–125
one-way ANOVA, 507, 520
open-ended questions, 31, 35, 44

operating characteristics curve (OC curve), 373, 631
operations research, 300, 684, 687, 694
opinion giver, 74
opinion seeker, 74
ordinal, 108, 244–245
organization chart, 20, 133, 233, 235
organization culture, 31, 185
organizational assessment, 88
organizational hierarchy, 52, 113, 238
organizational structures, 88, 237
orientor, 74
outliers, 323, 327, 346–347
overspending, 225–226

—P—

p charts, 400–401, 404, 484, 490
p-value, 565
Palm, A.C., 450, 691
parallel activities, 200
parallel system, 574–575, 589
parameter design, 540–542, 545
Pareto analysis, 170, 187, 198, 227, 274, 277–279, 290, 453, 596
Pareto Priority Index (PPI), 229
Pareto, 170–171, 280, 523
part deployment matrix, 148
PDCA, 8, 10, 12, 49, 94, 194, 215, 233
PDFs, 351–353
PDPC, 187, 209, 236–237, 294
PDSA, 8, 10–11, 13–18
Pearson correlation, 245
Pearson's product-moment correlation, 566
Pearson, 245, 566
performance evaluation, 77, 92, 173

permutation, 341
PERT, 197, 201–202, 300–301
Phillips, J.J., 100–102, 691
Piskurich, G.M., 114, 116, 691
Plan-Do-Check-Act (PDCA), 8
Plan-Do-Study-Act (PDSA), 10
planning process, 46, 86, 135, 145, 209, 552
playboy, 76
point estimators, 369
Poisson distribution, 355–357
policy deployment, 145, 693
polynomial, 547
population mean, 312, 344, 360, 372–373
population standard deviation, 346, 360, 632–633
population variance, 313, 349, 360, 633–634
position descriptions, 89
power and sample size, 502
power curve, 631
power of the test, 502
Pre-Control, 434
precedence relationship, 201–202
precision, 87, 161, 248
predictor variables, 556, 628
preliminary requirements WBS, 193
present value, 157–161, 181
presentation skills, 62, 95
prevention cost, 166, 170–171
prevention versus detection, 380
primary variables, 501
prioritization matrix, 297–298
probability concepts, 337, 339, 341

probability density functions, 351,
    579–580
problem-solving, 62, 65, 67, 94, 119,
    126, 129, 274, 552
procedure technician, 74
process audit, 97, 468, 523
process capability analysis, 273, 305,
    434, 452
process capability indexes, 458–459
process capability studies, 391, 454, 460,
    466, 472, 480, 485
process control plan, 416, 466, 472, 487
process control system, 50, 380
process control, 17, 172, 228, 265, 396,
    416, 438–439, 441, 450, 453, 468,
    523, 540
process decision program chart (PDPC),
    187, 209, 236, 294
process design, 522, 540
process improvement teams, 7, 60–61
process improvement, 7–8, 36, 89, 94,
    219, 221, 239, 269, 280, 380, 451,
    453, 523, 540, 603
process mapping, 89, 269–271, 546
process planning matrix, 148
process validation, 172
producer's risk, 632
product planning matrix, 148
production planning matrix, 148
profound knowledge, 93
program evaluation and review
    technique, 197, 300
project budget, 209, 214
project charter, 190, 194, 215–216
project decomposition, 189

project management tools, 186–187,
    271, 300
project management, 21, 89, 186, 191,
    197, 215–216, 223, 230, 239, 300,
    454, 572, 692
project plan, 186, 193, 195, 198, 214,
    216, 223, 236, 238–239
project scheduling, 197, 210, 234
proportion defective, 400, 457
Proschan, F., 474, 691
prototype, 154, 270, 541
Provost, L.P., 333, 691
Pyzdek, T., 6, 107–109, 169, 253,
    285–288, 292, 303–304, 318–322,
    453, 466, 472–473, 498, 606, 687,
    691–692

—Q—
QFD, 145, 187, 218, 295, 416–417,
    689
quadratic loss function, 542–543
quality assurance, 150, 632
Quality Award, 88
quality circles, 61–62
quality control tools, 33, 94, 215
quality cost bases, 174
quality cost model, 167
quality cost trend analysis, 177
quality cost, 60, 163, 193, 219, 691
Quality Council, 216
Quality Digest, 128, 694
quality engineering, 355, 372, 466, 480,
    560, 569, 687–688, 690, 692, 694
quality function deployment (QFD),
    145, 150, 187, 295, 683

quality functions within the organization, 88

quality goals, 2

quality management tools, 93–94, 221

quality management, 13, 46, 87, 179, 216, 221, 239, 245, 686

quality organization, 31, 50, 230, 292

quality plan, 88, 99, 145, 150, 214

quality planning, 164, 171–172, 689

quality policy, 55

Quality Progress, 154, 171, 683–685, 691–694

quality standards, 88, 163–164

quality system, 166, 168, 170, 178

quality tools, 130, 170, 304, 692

quincunxes, 127

—R—

R (range), 319, 632

R square, 267, 563–564

random samples, 367, 370, 509

random sampling, 420, 632

random variables, 337, 343, 353, 581, 584–585, 587

random-effects model, 504

randomization, 102, 502, 504

range charts, 254, 386–387, 396, 425

ranking questions, 36

rating questions, 36

ratio scale, 244, 246

rational subgroups, 386, 420, 428

re-expression, 323

readiness evaluation, 31

reasonable care, 274–275

receiving inspection, 417, 606–608, 619, 692

recognition and reward, 79, 81

recorder, 74

redundancy, 6–7, 19, 145, 228

reengineering, 60, 167, 221, 228, 271, 687, 692

reference group, 233

regression analysis, 265, 267, 552, 561, 563–565, 567, 686

Reichheld, F.F., 180, 182, 692

reliability analysis, 569, 597

reliability apportionment, 572–573, 596

reliability engineering, 187, 294, 597, 599

repeatability, 248, 252

repeating patterns, 424

replication, 504, 512, 515, 632

reporting plans, 189, 193

reports, 68, 174, 193–194, 214, 224–225, 238–242

reproducibility, 249, 252

requirement matrix, 146

resampling, 376–377, 686, 693

residual(s), 267, 323, 526–527, 534, 537, 563–564

resistance, 20, 50, 210, 233, 323, 346, 450, 485–486, 488

resolution, 70, 93, 110, 183, 252, 468, 524

resource allocation, 195, 210, 214

resource conflicts, 210

response variable, 501, 556, 628

responsibility accounting, 168

revolution, 128, 144, 687

reward systems, 81–82

rework, 163–164, 173–174, 228, 272

risk assessment, 595

Roberts, 439–440, 683, 692
robust product, 522, 540
robustness, 346, 541
role-plays, 125, 127, 694
root cause, 98, 276
Rose, K., 151–152, 154, 692
run charts, 175, 305, 334
run tests, 312, 429–430, 442, 449
Ruskin, A.M., 188, 191–192, 214, 223, 237–238, 692

—S—

Saaty, T.L., 297, 692
sabotage, 139, 215–216
safety analysis, 600–601
safety factors, 600
safety, 67, 231, 569, 571
sample mean, 312, 349, 367, 369–370, 373, 441
sample space, 337–340
sample standard deviation, 346, 349, 369, 375, 633
sample variance, 313, 349, 366, 369, 633–634
sampling distributions, 348
sampling plan, 356, 359, 627–628, 631–632
Savage, I.R., 474, 691
scatter diagram(s), 284, 439, 553–554, 557–560
scatter plot, 284–285
scheduling, 57, 68, 104, 454
Scholtes, P.R., 72, 190, 302, 693
Schuman, S.P., 64–65, 693
scientific management, 63
screening experiment, 521, 548

selecting projects, 227
self-control, 17, 58, 95
self-directed learning readiness scale (SDLRS), 115
self-directed learning, 111, 114, 691
self-directed teams, 114
self-managed teams, 62–63
semantic differential format, 38
Senge, P.M., 126, 693
sequential learning, 520–521, 547
series system, 574, 589–590
service quality, 32, 38, 40, 144, 163, 172
sets, 336–338
Shainin, 434, 438, 693
shape, 312, 314, 316, 347, 377–378, 583–584, 630
Sheridan, B.M., 145, 693
Shewhart, W.A., 8–10, 12, 16, 49, 290, 378–379, 381–382, 431, 442–443, 688, 693–694
short runs, 464, 474, 487–489, 491, 495, 498
should-be map, 270–271
sigma charts, 391–392
significance level, 370, 372, 509
Silvey, L.O., 129–130, 688
Simon, J.L., 127, 377, 693–694
simple linear regression, 560, 562
simulation, 126–127, 130, 188, 576, 603, 612, 692, 694
skewness, 314–315, 633
skill-based pay, 102
slack time, 206
small runs, 464
Smith, H., 561, 564, 686
special cause, 382–386, 391

specifications, 9, 145, 437, 459, 629, 694

sponsor, 51, 112, 178, 220, 224

sponsorship, 52, 220

SPSS, 324–326

stability, 62, 130, 234, 250, 254, 434

stable system, 254

staff functions, 57–59

staffing plans, 189, 193

stakeholder(s), 139–140, 190, 194, 215–216, 238

standard deviation control charts, 391, 393

standard error, 267, 350, 561, 563–565, 630

standard operating procedures, 230

standard setter, 75

standards, 25, 53, 123, 247, 272, 433

statistical association, 427

statistical control, 16, 347, 369, 391, 429, 438, 452, 474, 486, 504, 609, 626, 630

statistical distributions, 368

statistical inference, 335–336, 369, 689

statistical process control (SPC), 377, 379, 382, 464, 472, 609, 683, 691, 693

statistical quality control, 373, 449, 627, 683–684

statistical stability, 254

statistical tolerancing, 620

status reports, 68, 193, 238–240

steepest ascent (descent), 529

stem-and-leaf, 324–327, 347–348

Stewart, T.A., 180, 694

storming stage, 71

strategic plan, 88, 98–99, 137, 139, 179, 303

strategic planning for quality training, 86, 89

strategic planning, 17, 46, 135, 179

strategic quality management, 86, 179

strategic quality plan, 99, 145

strength, 14, 298–299, 304, 552, 565, 600–602

stress, 570–571, 600–602

student's t distribution, 355, 366, 371

subproject, 189

subset, 338, 353, 361

suggestion systems, 47–48

Suminski, L.T., 179, 694

supplier management, 88, 239

surveys, 32, 89, 100, 164, 171

system effectiveness, 576

—T—

t distribution, 355, 366–367, 371, 565

tactical quality planning, 145

Taguchi loss function, 109, 542–543

Taguchi method, 545

Taguchi, G., 433, 499, 540–543, 545, 694

Taha, H., 199, 694

tampering, 108, 126, 194, 216, 432, 457

TDM, 44–45, 70

Team Dynamics Management (TDM), 40–45, 70

tests for out of control patterns on control charts, 431

theoretical expected value, 342

theory X, 111

theory Y, 111

Thiagarajan, S., 125, 694
time series analysis, 305
time value of money, 155
tolerance design, 542
tolerance intervals, 372
tolerance limits, 372
tolerance, 256–257, 266–267, 434–437,
    459, 480, 623–625, 651
total design method, 44
Total Quality Management (TQM), 88,
    221
total quality, 165–166, 170, 175, 221,
    688
TQM, 50, 54, 88, 94, 134–135, 149,
    179, 191, 301, 688–689, 693
traceability, 569
train-the-trainer, 94, 433
training budgets, 87
training evaluation and reinforcement,
    99
training needs assessment, 97, 130
training plan, 84, 86–87, 97–99, 124
training, 22, 24, 47, 50, 53, 83, 164,
    433, 494, 683, 686, 688–691, 694
treatment, 336, 500–501
tree diagram(s), 236, 293, 297–298
trend analysis, 89, 170, 177
trend(s), 310, 441, 472
Tuckman, B.W., 71, 694
Tufte, E., 558–559
Tukey, J.W., 323–324, 327, 694
type I error (acceptance control sense),
    633
type I error, 334, 373–374, 513, 516,
    633

type II error (acceptance control sense),
    633
type II error, 373, 633
typical subsystem WBS, 193

—U—
u charts, 407–409, 490
unbalanced designs, 506
underspending, 226
union, 139, 338
union(s), 139, 215, 230, 233, 606
universal set, 337

—V—
validation WBS, 193
validity, 30, 32, 47, 246, 335–336
value engineering, 237
variable charts, 386
variable costs, 155–156
variable selection, 416
variance reporting, 224
variation, common cause, 451
variation, special cause, 194, 224, 307,
    310, 386, 391, 429–430, 455–457
Vaziri, H.K., 220, 694
Venn diagram, 338–339
virtual process mapping, 546
vision, 57, 90–91, 94, 137–138
visual aid, 96
visual display of quantitative
    information, 558–559
visual display, 323
visual language, 577

—W—

Wahl, P.R., 149
WBS, 191, 236
Wearring, C., 127, 694
Wheeler, D.J., 439, 694
Whitney, J.B., 440, 683
work breakdown structures (WBS), 191,
    236
work elements, 189
work groups, 61–62
workmanship standards, 36
World War II, 39, 123
written communication, 69, 127

—XYZ—

X charts, 396, 400, 420, 661
Xerox, 217
Yates, 517, 519
yes/no questions, 36
Z transformation, 361, 460
zero defects, 144, 167, 495
zero sum game, 59
Z_L, 460–461, 463
Z_{MIN}, 461–463
zones on a control chart, 430
Z_U, 460–461, 463

About the Author

Thomas Pyzdek is a quality consultant, entrepreneur, author, educator, software developer, and speaker. He conducts seminars on Six Sigma for the American Society for Quality—of which he is a Fellow—and has received that organization's "Edwards" award. Pyzdek's clients and employers include Intuit, Hughes, McDonald's, and Tucson Medical Center.